SOCIAL CONFLICT

SOCIAL CONFLICT

READINGS IN RULE STRUCTURES
AND CONFLICT RELATIONSHIPS

Philip Brickman

Northwestern University

D. C. HEATH AND COMPANY

Lexington, Massachusetts   Toronto   London

HM
136
.B734

Preface

Every social science deals with social conflict as an important theoretical issue. Psychologists study violence and aggression; sociologists study conformity and deviance; economists study buying, selling, and bargaining; political scientists and historians study war and revolution; anthropologists study cross-cultural misunderstandings and ethnocentrism.

The implication of all this for a book of readings on social conflict should be clear. Such a book cannot hope to build a general understanding of social conflict unless it draws upon the contributions of the different disciplines. This book is interdisciplinary in that it draws upon work in many fields, especially psychology and sociology, but also anthropology, economics, political science, and history. It is not, however, interdisciplinary in its perspective. Its perspective is social psychological, both because I am a social psychologist and because I think that social psychology provides a useful framework for drawing together work in different disciplines. Indeed, social psychology may for certain purposes be defined as the study of the interrelationships among the different behavioral sciences, such as psychology, sociology, and anthropology. Thus we will not try to trace social conflict back to root causes at one level of analysis (the individual, the group, or the culture), but rather try to see how each level of analysis is relevant to an understanding of what happens in social conflict and how social conflicts are organized.

Just as this book of readings aims to be interdisciplinary without using discipline as a basis of organization, so also it hopes to be "relevant" without using relevance as a basis of organization. The major issues of our times, like the major issues of social science theories, involve social conflict: race relations, school administration, religious conflict, guerrilla warfare, women's liberation, and nuclear confrontation, to name a few. Teachers and students alike are often moved to reject our narrow, rigorous, laboratory research studies as unsatisfactory fragments which seem unrelated to these broader social problems. But to abandon laboratory research entirely in favor of broad, relevant, real-world studies may be to substitute one set of fragments for another.

Though it might be easier not to seek both theoretical relevance and real-world relevance, I would suggest that both are needed if we have any hope of building a general understanding of conflict. The real challenge, the real fun, is to seek some kind of framework that enables us to move back and forth between the theoretical and the applied, the laboratory and the field, the abstract and the relevant, searching for commonalities without losing sight of the tension that separates them.

v

In this book we will move from laboratory experiments to family struggles to international warfare, as the issues warrant. My hope is that these juxtapositions will add the intellectual excitement of seeing analytical similarities in different conflict areas without detracting from the excitement of relevance in certain areas. Intellectual excitement may come from seeing, for example, that Berkowitz's work on aggressive stimuli, Deutsch's work on bargaining, Milgram's studies of obedience, and Kenniston's investigations of alienation and activism all bear on the study of social conflict in a coherent manner. I enjoyed doing this book (most of the time) because I enjoyed trying to put together these different bodies of literature, each rigorous in its own way. The way in which I have tried to put them together cuts across the distinctions between the different disciplines, between different research traditions, and between "laboratory" and "relevant" research. Instead, the readings are organized around a set of analytical distinctions among various kinds of conflict relationships and by substantive themes within these relationships.

But in good measure the integrative contribution of this book consists of merely laying out side by side some of the major traditions of research on social conflict. The further organization should be understood as one person's effort to illuminate the interconnections between these vastly diverse traditions of research. The task is one begun, not completed; one hopefully to be shared by the reader, not dismissed by him or taken by him as a given.

Since a full explanation of the conceptual framework of this book is the topic of the introductory essay, "Rule structures and conflict relationships," its detailed presentation will be postponed until then. Here I would like to introduce the conceptual scheme of the book very briefly in order to discuss how the book is organized. The analytical framework of this book emphasizes the way in which conflicts are organized or structured by social rules. We will distinguish four kinds of conflict, the first three by the degree of structure or constraint placed upon the actors by the rules of their situation, and the fourth as a special kind of conflict in which the struggle is over the nature of the rules themselves. These conflict situations will also be distinguished by whether they draw upon impulsive, rational, moral, or revolutionary orientations of actors. The book is divided into four major sections corresponding to these four kinds of conflict.

Within each of the major sections of this book, readings are organized around general themes or issues that have been the focus of important theory and research. Since the literature in one area (such as the study of established bargaining relationships and rational factors of conflict strategy) has focused on quite different issues than the literature in other areas (such as the study of normative conflict relationships and moral factors in obedience), the themes used to organize readings within each major section are quite different. Thus while the major headings or major divisions of this book rest upon logical distinctions among different kinds of conflict, the subheadings within these divisions are not parallel across sections and are less designed to highlight logical distinctions than important themes and common issues (such as the role of frustration in producing aggression, or problems of communication in conflict situations).

The short introductions to each individual section describe the problem addressed, and the suggested interrelationship of the readings. A real effort was made to juxtapose readings that would interrelate, or that could be used to raise further questions about each other. However, the elucidation of these multiple areas of overlap, extension, or disagreement among the readings is only begun by the section introductions. That is by and large the task of the student, the teacher, and the course. If this book merely succeeds in challenging the reader to seek such integrations for himself, and in providing both the appropriate raw materials and a helpful general map for this effort, it will have succeeded in its pedagogical aim.

The vastness of the terrain involved in the study of social conflict makes it inevitable that no organizational framework will encompass all the material without strain, or be equally congenial to persons who approach the field from different vantage points. The individual readings in this book, however, should be of value even to readers who find the organizational framework uncongenial or inappropriate to their needs. In no case has the quality of an individual reading been sacrificed to the goal of organization. Illuminating "bad examples" or even "best available examples" have been avoided, since past teaching has convinced me that such negative instances are never appreciated as much as positive ones no matter how diligently the instructor may labor to show their potential. Besides, there were too many excellent readings that could not be included for lack of space to permit the inclusion of any pieces not worthy on their own merits. The individual readings were chosen for both readability and importance, either theoretical or practical, and I would recommend each of them separately almost as highly as I recommend the whole together. I have not shied away from reproducing familiar classics from various areas. Indeed the reader familiar primarily with his own area may not realize to what extent the book consists of generally well-known pieces.

Apart from the ability to read journal articles and similar material, no formal background is required for this book. Teachers of introductory courses in psychology, social psychology, or sociology who wish to make social conflict an important subtheme for their courses may find this book useful. This book could also serve as the basic text material for a course in social conflict, of which there are at present relatively few. Stimulating the growth of the study of social conflict, and in particular the more widespread teaching of this area, would be the ultimate possible success for this book.

Finally, a word about value biases. Is this book radical or conservative? Whose side is it on? I don't think the value biases of this work are obtrusive, or such as to interfere with the use of this book by those who do not share its value orientation, any more than the logical organization of the readings should impede their use by those who do not wish to draw on the organization. However, the values are there, and they do not try to masquerade as something else. Nor is this cause for apology, for we have come to understand that the study of human behavior cannot be free of values. The distinguishing feature of science is that in science it is not opinions themselves which are persuasive, but the facts on which the opinions are based. If asked explicitly whose side I am on, I would like to draw on the reply made by Ross MacDonald's fictional detective Lew Archer: "I'm on the side of justice when I can find it; on the side of the underdog when I can't."

I do think that an understanding of conflict is essential to efforts to make the world a better place, and especially to efforts by the disadvantaged and oppressed. To liberate themselves people must be able to recognize the often obscure social and psychological forces that are the sources of their oppression.

The oppressed must be able to analyze objective conflicts of interest and to appreciate how such conflicts may be exaggerated or concealed by impulses, by calculations, or by various social norms. The powerful already know these things, since knowledge, like other sources of power, flows more readily into their hands. The readings in this book deal explicitly with conflict, but implicitly they deal with justice. They have much to say about why justice is so hard to achieve, and even something to say about how it might be sought.

Apart from the question of one's political orientations toward particular social movements, there is also the somewhat more subtle value bias involved in one's general orientation toward social conflict. Is social conflict generally a "bad" thing that disrupts the harmony and organization of society, that brings injury and grief to participants, that we should study mainly to find ways of resolving? This theme is implicit in the work of many writers, including the sociologist Talcott Parsons and the psychologist B. F. Skinner. Or is conflict a "good" thing, or at least something necessary to other good things, such as social change, group solidarity, and individual freedom? This theme too is implicit in the work of many writers, such as the sociologist Georg Simmel and the psychologist A. S. Neill. I think social conflict is both of these things, as the readings in this book will make clear.

I would like to thank Elizabeth Brickman, Thomas Cook, William Gamson, Miriam Keiffer, Louise Kidder, Andre Modigliani, and Marc Pilisuk for helpful comments at various points, and Patricia Meyer for skillful assistance in preparing the manuscript.

Philip Brickman

Contents

II   Conflict in Partially Structured Relationships: Strategic Factors in Conflict

III Conflict in Fully Structured Relationships: Moral Factors in Conflict

IV   Conflict Over the Rules of Conflict: Revolutionary Conflict

ELEMENTS OF CONFLICT SITUATIONS

OBJECTIVE AND SUBJECTIVE PERSPECTIVES ON CONFLICT

ACTORS: PARTIES TO CONFLICT

PAYOFFS: DEGREE AND BASIS OF CONFLICT

ALTERNATIVES: STRUCTURE OF CONFLICT

A STRUCTURAL ANALYSIS OF CONFLICT RELATIONSHIPS

UNSTRUCTURED CONFLICT RELATIONSHIPS:
STIMULUS FACTORS IN CONFLICT

PARTIALLY STRUCTURED CONFLICT RELATIONSHIPS:
STRATEGIC FACTORS IN CONFLICT

FULLY STRUCTURED CONFLICT RELATIONSHIPS:
MORAL FACTORS IN CONFLICT

REVOLUTIONARY CONFLICT: CONFLICT OVER
THE RULES OF CONFLICT

AN INTEGRATED APPROACH TO THE STUDY OF CONFLICT

SOCIAL SYSTEMS AND CONFLICT RELATIONSHIPS

THIRD PARTIES AND COALITIONS

FUNCTIONS OF CONFLICT

CONFLICT RESOLUTION

RULE STRUCTURES AND SOCIAL RELATIONSHIPS

RULE STRUCTURES AND CONFLICT RELATIONSHIPS

What is and what is not "social conflict"? The very question has generated much conflict among scholars. Some authors define social conflict as behavior by one party that injures or damages the interests of another party, regardless of whether either party is aware of the conflict or has any hostile feelings toward the other; others maintain that conflict exists when two parties feel hostile or antagonistic toward each other, regardless of whether either one engages in any overt behavior that injures the other. Some authors define social conflict as a special case of competition in which the rules that ordinarily govern and restrain the competition have broken down; others argue that competition is itself a special case of social conflict in which the aims of the antagonists are mutually exclusive. Fink (1969), after an exhaustive review of the many proposed definitions of conflict, calls for a moratorium on the dispute over definitions. The effort to build a general theory of conflict can only be retarded by definitions that restrict study to one situation while excluding other relevant cases.

In this spirit, the definition of conflict and the distinctions drawn among kinds of conflict in this paper are not intended to be restrictive or exhaustive, but only to provide a heuristic basis for inquiry. For present purposes we will adopt a situational definition of conflict, saying that conflict exists in situations in which parties must divide or share resources so that, to some degree, the more one party gets, the less others can have. This situational definition seems to ignore other factors, such as whether or not the parties feel hostile toward each other. But the passing over of these questions in our definition is not to say they are unimportant questions, or even that they would not constitute an adequate alternative basis for defining conflict. It is simply to say that we do not choose to make them part of our definition of conflict, but rather to treat them as empirical or substantive questions. Indeed, I can think of no more important area of inquiry than the study of what kinds of conflict situations lead people to be accurately and acutely aware of their conflicts of interest, versus distorting these conflicts either in the direction of underestimating them or overestimating them. I can think of no more fascinating topic than the study of what kinds of conflict situations generate hostile feelings in persons, versus leaving them well-disposed or indifferent to each other. But, as will be further indicated, these seem to me best left as empirical rather than definitional concerns.

ELEMENTS OF CONFLICT SITUATIONS

As a general analytical language for the description of conflict relationships we propose to draw upon the language of game theory. This does not mean that we share the special concerns of mathematical game theory (von Neumann and Morgenstern, 1944; Luce and Raiffa, 1957), but rather that, like Thibaut and Kelley (1959), we find the language of game theory a convenient one for designating important parameters in social situations. Basically, this language calls for us to specify as precisely as we can in a given situation who the actors are, what their alternatives are or what choices are available to each of them, and what the payoffs in the situation are or what the consequences are for each actor of having various choices made. It might be noted that other widely-used languages in the behavioral sciences define terms that may be coordinated to the actors, alternatives, and payoffs of game theory. Learning theory specifies organisms, responses, and reinforcements, generally in non-social situations. Field theory specifies identities, locomotions, and valences. Other writers might well choose one of these vocabularies to talk about what we will discuss using a game theory vocabulary.

We intend to focus our concern on how conflict situations are organized, or how implicit and explicit rule structures limit actors' choices from among a theoretically infinite number of alternatives. Previous writers on social conflict, however, have drawn their primary distinctions among types of conflict on the basis of either the actors or the payoffs in the conflict situations, and it is to a consideration of these factors that we turn first.

OBJECTIVE AND SUBJECTIVE PERSPECTIVES ON CONFLICT

"Conflict" in popular usage may refer to things other than a divergence of interest between two parties. One may talk about the conflict a person experiences in trying to decide whether to dress neatly or in a usual sloppy manner before proceeding through customs, or even the conflict a person experiences in deciding whether or not to try to smuggle something through customs. Neither of these experiences specifies a social conflict in our sense. We could specify such a conflict by introducing the customs agent as an additional actor, who stands to gain or lose as a joint function of the first person's decision of whether to smuggle or not and his own decision of whether or not to inspect the traveler's luggage (but not, ordinarily, by whether the traveler chooses to dress neatly or sloppily, at least not in any objective sense of gain or loss such as that demanded for legal redress).

On the other hand, conflict defined as tension or antagonism may imply there is no conflict in cases where we would in fact specify an objective conflict of interest. Two people amicably sitting next to one another on a train or a plane trip might not seem to be in a conflict situation. Yet in fact we can specify the actors, we can specify a scarce resource (the time during the trip) whose use is dependent upon the choices that both parties make, and we can specify a set of alternatives available to each party (to talk or to remain silent, to smoke or not to smoke). Unless the parties begin with identical preferences, or unless they coordinate their choices in a reasonably satisfactory exchange, or unless the rules prescribe a particular set of choices that they must adhere to, the potential conflict in the objective situation may well result in some actual conflict behavior and mutual antagonistic feeling. We wish to call attention to the potential conflict in such social situations, the objective conflict, regardless of its subjective manifestation. The most famous instances of objective conflict of interest that may go unrecognized concern oppressed classes and ruling classes who agree on a mutual fable that there is no conflict, thus perpetuating myths about happy slaves, happy workers, and happy housewives that may have some social or psychological function for both classes.

The foregoing examples should make clear that objective situational conflict and subjective motivational conflict are not necessarily identical. We might take either one as our starting point, provided that we do not presume its relationship to the other but make this relationship a matter of empirical investigation. We must not do what Gestalt psychologists and field theorists sometimes did and presume that subjective representations are isomorphic with actual situations or stimuli; nor should we do what psychoanalysts have sometimes done and presume that subjective representations need have no relationship to objective reality. If our perceptions did not provide reasonably accurate and valid representations of reality it is doubtful that we could have survived evolutionary selection processes (Campbell, 1970). Thus as an initial guess we might venture that people's perceptions of social conflict will be generally but not always valid, and may sometimes be serious overestimates or underestimates due to inadequate training in conflict sensitivity. As usual in psychology, people's subjective impressions of a situation may prove to be better predictors of their behavior than the objective parameters of the situation (see Edwards, 1954, 1961). But we still feel it the best strategy to begin our inquiry with the best possible specification of these objective parameters.

ACTORS: PARTIES TO CONFLICT

One distinction often made in the study of conflict concerns the nature of the parties to the conflict. Conflict between individuals is distinguished from conflict between groups, organizations, or nations, and all of these are distinguished from conflicts that take place within an indvidual. This last form of conflict would seem somewhat different in kind from all the others, and would appear to be excluded from consideration by our definition of social conflict as involving divergent interests of different parties. (One might reintroduce subjective conflict into our analysis by specifying that a single person contained within himself competing "actors," referring to different motive systems or subidentities that were in some sense making independent choices for the person. But, although not uninteresting, the effort to consider one person as two or more actors seems a little too bizarre and novel for inclusion in a general scheme of social conflict.)

The effort to organize the study of social conflict around the nature of parties to the conflict suffers from the fact that the list of different parties, such as families, tribes, corporations, nations, classes, teams, may be endless. That conflict between individuals might differ from conflict between groups seems a reasonable proposition, though we must always remember that individuals are usually members of groups and groups usually consist of particular individuals. The question of how the nature of the parties to conflict affects the conflict calls for empirical study of a sort that this question has not yet received. One particularly interesting question is whether conflict behavior is continuous or discontinuous across group and individual levels. Are individuals who experience a lot of conflict on an individual level likely to be members of groups that also experience a lot of conflict, and to favor a vigorous conflict policy for these groups? Or does conflict at the group level tend to damp, replace, and gratify conflict needs on other levels? Some conflicting evidence on this point is reviewed by LeVine and Campbell (1972).

PAYOFFS: DEGREE AND BASIS OF CONFLICT

The pattern of rewards and punishments that can accrue to each party from their various possible joint decisions defines the extent to which conflict exists in the relationship. To make this clear, let us consider the simplest possible case in which two parties must each choose between two alternatives. Initially, let the alternatives themselves be neutral, like the alternatives of going to one of two equally satisfactory railroad stations. The only question is whether both parties wind up at the same railroad station (both make the same choice), or whether they wind up at different stations (one makes one choice, the other makes the opposite choice).

Conflict in this relationship is minimal, indeed zero, if the rewards to the two parties are always identical, or are at least perfectly correlated, so that in situations where one party gets more, the other party also gets more. Two people whose only interest is in trying to meet each other, like a visitor and a host who hope to arrive at the same station, are playing a cooperative game. Either they both win, by choosing the same station, or they both lose, by choosing opposite stations. Two people whose only interest is in trying to avoid each other, like two ex-lovers who are going their separate ways, are in this case also playing a cooperative game. Either they both win, by choosing different stations, or they both lose, by choosing the same station. These relationships do not involve any conflict of interest at all, and are sometimes called "pure cooperation" or "pure coordination" games. If the parties in such situations recognize their identity of interests and are able to communicate with one another about their choices, they are usually able to "solve" these situations without much trouble by making appropriate arrangements in advance, although this might be easier in the more common case of a mutual desire to meet versus the case of a mutual desire to avoid meeting. If the parties are unaware of their common interest, or are unable to communicate about their choices even if they are aware of their common interest, then this simple coordination game is no longer trivial.

Schelling (1960) has shown that in this last case the parties are well-advised to look for irrelevant features of the alternatives that would make one of them more salient than the other, and to choose that one as a meeting place. Thus people should know that the number "one" is more common and more likely to be chosen than the number "two." In a game where both will win if both choose the same number without communicating about their choices, people should be inclined to choose the number "one," and they are. Note, however, that this process does not provide as simple a solution to cases of mutual avoidance, where to win the parties must choose opposite choices. In this case, besides trying to differentiate the alternatives, the parties would also have to try to find irrelevant clues about themselves that would lead to a general, implicit understanding that one party would choose the more salient alternative and the other, the less salient one.

Conflict in our simple relationship is maximal if the rewards for one party always come at the expense of costs to the other, or if their rewards are perfectly negatively correlated, so that in situations where one party gets more, the other party always gets less. If one person is only interested in trying to meet the other, while the other person is interested only in trying to avoid meeting the first, they are playing a competitive game. Either the first party wins, if they both choose the same station, or the second party wins, if they choose opposite stations. An example would be a murderer who is seeking a victim, or a policeman who is seeking a criminal. Only one of the parties can win; the other must lose.

These relationships are sometimes called "pure competition" games or "zero-sum" games. The phrase "zero-sum" refers to the fact that the total possible payoff in the situation is constant, as when two people begin to gamble with additions for one person always being perfectly balanced by subtractions from the stake of the other person. In pure competition situations it is of no particular help for parties to recognize their antagonistic interests or to be able to communicate with one another, for these should only lead to more sophisticated efforts to deceive and mislead each other.

Finally, our simple relationship may contain an intermediate degree of conflict, or a mixture of common interests and antagonistic interests. Both parties may be interested in meeting, for example, but they may not be indifferent as to which station they meet at. One station may be a more convenient meeting place for one party, and the other station more convenient for the other party. Both parties suffer substantial costs if they choose different stations and fail to meet. Similarly, both parties are rewarded if they choose the same station. But the rewards or costs are not quite the same for each person in each meeting place, since one of the parties is better off by having to travel less far to get there. Relationships like this are sometimes called "mixed-motive situations," since each party may be partly motivated by a desire to cooperate around the common interests in the relationship and partly motivated by a desire to compete for the more favorable share of those resources which must be divided up.

Most real-world situations are mixed-motive situations rather than pure competition or pure cooperation. Two football players on opposing teams might seem at first glance to be playing a game of pure competition, but in fact they also have certain common interests in seeing that various rules of the game are enforced to make the game itself enjoyable, or at least playable. Two players on the same team might seem at first glance to be playing a game of pure cooperation, but in fact they also have certain competitive interests in dividing up the glory that may come from winning or the blame that may come from losing. Likewise, two drivers who meet at an intersection have both common interests (in avoiding a crash) and competitive ones (in deciding who goes first). The bulk of our concern here will be with mixed-motive situations and how the conflicts in them, of whatever degree, are structured.

We have defined degree of conflict as determined by the relationship between the rewards one party can get and the rewards another party can get, regardless of exactly what these rewards are. The nature of the rewards, or what is at stake in the relationship, may also influence the degree of conflict (or perhaps we should say the quantity of conflict involved in a given degree of conflict). Higher stakes may make people more willing to compromise where a solution of mutual benefit is possible (Druckman, 1971), but more vigorous in pursuing their antagonistic aims where such a solution is not possible. Distinctions may also be drawn among conflicts according to the nature of the stakes, apart from their magnitude, so that conflicts over power are distinguished from conflicts over money or love.

Perhaps the most important distinction among types of conflict according to their payoffs is the distinction between conflicts over means or procedures, or conflicts over differing beliefs about what course of action is most likely to achieve a given goal, and conflicts over ends or values, or conflicts over which of several goals would in fact be most desirable to achieve. Our broad definition of conflict as conflict of interest limits our focus to conflict over values or valued goods rather than conflicts over means or beliefs. It might be noted, however, that disagreements about means can often be considered either disguised instances of pure cooperation situations under conditions of uncertainty, or disguised instances of conflict of interest or value conflict.

Suppose, for example, that two people disagree about which remedy should be applied to their son, who has a certain ailment. (This example is taken from Deutsch, 1969; but see also Hammond, 1965; Kuhn, 1962). If in fact the only interest of either party is in seeing the son get well, and each party is indifferent as to whether the son gets well by means of his own suggestion or the other party's suggestion, then the situation is in fact one of pure cooperation. There is no conflict of interest between the parties, and thus, so long as the problem remains one of pure problem-solving by individuals who are otherwise positively disposed to one another, the problem falls outside our domain of social conflict. As soon as other issues are introduced, however, such as an ego-investment by each party in his own suggestion, or the mentioning of some related dispute in which interests are not identical, then the situation is no longer simply one of belief conflict or conflict over means, but becomes one of conflict of interest or value conflict as well, and hence within our province. The belief conflict over best means to achieve a common goal may also be seen as a value conflict if different means in fact inflict different costs on the parties pursuing the goal, as in the case of deciding how taxes may best be raised to support a war effort.

ALTERNATIVES: STRUCTURE OF CONFLICT

Most analyses of social conflict have taken as their point of departure the previously discussed elements, the nature of the parties to the conflict or the nature and structure of the payoffs in the conflict. The present analysis is likewise set within this general framework, but focuses primarily on the nature of the alternatives available to each party in the conflict relationship: how many there are, which are considered legitimate, and what are the general orientations of the parties to these alternatives. This is the subject of the next section, which we will not attempt to anticipate now. Here let us merely note that the number and nature of conflict alternatives are independent of who is fighting or what is the degree of conflict. Knowing the parties to the conflict and knowing the degree of conflict does not tell us much about the nature of the struggle (if any) that will ensue until we inquire also into what resources, options, or alternatives are available to each party, and what constraints may exist on the use of those resources, options, or alternatives. For a fixed degree of conflict there are still wide variations in how this conflict may be organized or structured by the rules characterizing the general relationship between the parties to the conflict. This is the topic of our inquiry.

A STRUCTURAL ANALYSIS OF CONFLICT RELATIONSHIPS

The present analysis of social conflict distinguishes among conflict relationships according to their degree of structure. In particular, we will distinguish unstructured conflict relationships, partially structured conflict relationships, and fully structured conflict relationships. In unstructured conflicts the parties are not bound by any rules, in fully structured conflicts the parties are fully bound by rules, while in partially structured conflicts rules constrain certain behaviors but leave others to the free choice of the parties. In fact, the distinctions among these ideal types of relationships are complex and not strictly a matter of specifying how many alternatives are allowed by the rule structure of the situation. This is our starting point, however, and our primary dimension of concern.

Before elaborating our formal definitions of these types of conflict, it may be useful to give a quick overview of the scheme together with some examples. First of all, unstructured, partially structured, and fully structured relationships must be understood as points along a continuum, rather than discrete cases that have nothing in common. Relative to each other, it should be easy to see that the encounter of two anonymous strangers in a dark alley is an unstructured conflict relationship, the encounter of a salesman with a client is a partially structured conflict relationship, and the encounter of an army private with a sergeant is a fully structured conflict relationship.

In the first case each party can make virtually no assumptions about what the other might do. Friendly gestures, hostile gestures, violence, exchange, persuasion are all in theory possible, and there is no situational understanding that would allow parties to count on certain of these responses as being normative in these circumstances. In the salesman-client example, many possible conflict alternatives have ordinarily been ruled out both by general cultural understandings that pervade such relationships and also by the specific history of the sales relationship and the anticipation by both parties that a continuing relationship between them would be profitable. In the last case, the private-sergeant example, still more alternatives have been ruled out on each side, and indeed the institutional setting in general specifies both what sergeants should do in most situations and what privates should do in response—obey.

The sense that these three relationships represent important differences in their degree of structuredness, and in the structurally appropriate conflict possibilities as well, should be clear. Yet this clarity should not in turn disguise the fact that even in relationships involving strangers, at least strangers who share a common culture, there are some conventions and expectations that each may expect the other to understand. At the other extreme, even in the most highly structured authority systems, subordinates will have legitimate choices as to how they will carry out orders, and superiors will have choices about which orders are appropriate in particular situations.

Subsidiary to our primary concern for the number of legitimate alternatives that are available to the parties, our three types of relationships may also be distinguished by a secondary, related set of distinctions that concern the kind of orientation typically adopted by parties to such relationships. We will suggest that parties in an unstructured conflict relationship are typically oriented to each other merely as sources of noxious stimulation that must be eliminated, escaped, or avoided. Parties in a partially structured conflict relationship are typically oriented to each other as rational actors each pursuing their own selfish interests, who need to be outwitted or outmaneuvered. Parties in a fully structured conflict relationship are typically oriented to each other as moral actors who need to be disciplined or obeyed.

Thus, although the terms unstructured, partially structured, and fully structured are elegant and convey the primary dimension of concern to our analysis of conflict relationships, these labels may on occasion be inadequate to remind us of the complex differences that characterize these different conflict relationships. To this end, it will be convenient to have other terms that can be used in turn to refer to unstructured, partially structured, and fully structured conflict relationships as the occasion warrants. Unstructured relationships may also be called anomic or anarchic conflict relationships, referring in the main to their absence of rules and to the non-social orientation of their actors. Partially structured relationships may also be called established bargaining relationships, not so much because they always involve bargaining in the narrow economic sense, but because they regularly involve a contest between actors with a rational orientation toward maximizing their respective shares of the common resources. The word "established" refers to the fact that conflict in these instances is both organized (in contrast to unstructured conflict relationships) and visible as conflict (in contrast to many fully structured relationships). Finally, fully structured relationships will also be called normative conflict relationships, because the conflict behavior of the parties in these relationships is specified by social norms.

UNSTRUCTURED CONFLICT RELATIONSHIPS:
STIMULUS FACTORS IN CONFLICTS

By an unstructured conflict relationship we mean a relationship in which there are no social constraints on either party. The options, the moves, or the means available to a party are limited only by his own capacity and disposition. Even the resources at stake in the conflict may be unspecified. Parties in an unstructured conflict relationship will typically recognize their conflict, but this is not necessary, as for instance in certain ecological struggles in which two animal species exploit the same environment at completely different times.

Considering now the orientation of the parties to one another and to the conflict, we may specify that each party in an unstructured conflict relationship sees the other primarily as a source of threatening or painful stimulation that needs to be escaped, avoided, or destroyed. Parties in these relationships are likely to use coercive means on one another, but this is not necessary in the definition. Impulsive or emotional aggression, activated by stimulus factors that operate independently of the structure of the relationship or even in the absence of any relationship, is an important element of unstructured conflict. The reactions of the parties are often immediate responses to internal drives or external shocks rather than results of rational calculations of the nature and purpose of the other party.

It may be helpful to illustrate our typology of conflict relationships by taking a single concrete instance and watching this instance take on greater degrees of structure. For a first example let us take a traffic situation at a crossroads, in which the limited resource at stake is the right-of-way, or who shall go first. Anarchic conflict is characteristic of situations in which there is no clear right of way and indeed no clear structuring of alternatives. Suppose two vehicles meet on a street that is only wide enough for one, without immediate space for one to pull off the road for the other to pass. (This is the very situation used in the 1960 Deutsch and Krauss trucking game experiment, although these authors in fact sharply limited what the actors could do in response to the conflict.)

In the general case, the parties must not only decide whether to stop, go forward, or go backward, but must also consider a variety of other behaviors they might engage in—talking, offering money, or fighting. (One can compromise or back up in this situation and still win a related battle of wits. Driver A says: "I never back up for a fool." Driver B, throwing his car into reverse: "I always do.") Although the drivers may share certain cultural predispositions, if they come from the same culture and the same area (Shor, 1972) that may help them arrive at a solution, rules that govern this encounter are minimal relative to other traffic conflicts we shall consider shortly.

It should be noted that anarchic conflict in our traffic situation does not require a narrow arena, or a road wide enough for only one car. Anarchic conflict may also be observed in wide arenas such as unmarked parking lots, where cars may encounter one another from any direction and may veer in any direction. There are many ways to avoid collision, but the multiplicity of ways and the uncertainty about other drivers' responses counteract this advantage and allow us to recognize this as an anarchic conflict situation. Indeed the chances for collision are so great that this situation is used as the basis for a popular amusement park game called bumper cars (in which the cars are sufficiently small, slow, and cushioned to minimize the impact of collisions). The parking-lot game is made more complex by the fact that it is usually played by many cars at once, rather than just two. It is only a short jump from this situation to the escape panic situation (Mintz, 1951; Kelley, Condry, Dahlke, and Hill, 1965), a classic form of anomic conflict in which many parties traverse competing paths to a limited number of exits.

A second example that lends itself to many possible conflict structures is the case in which one party has goods or services that another party wishes to obtain. This is the prototypical situation for economic exchange. But we cannot yet talk about economic exchange or a market system, because to do so we must specify rules that limit the means one party may use to obtain the goods or services from the other, or the means that the second party may use to obtain recompense from the first. In unstructured conflict situations, for instance between warring groups, there are no such limits. Theft of goods from the other party may actually be more highly valued than purchase or gift. Even within a market system, however, we may follow the economists in characterizing the relationships between buyer and seller as structured to the extent that one or both has a monopoly over the market. In the theoretical situation of "perfect competition," an infinite number of buyers can choose from an infinite number of sellers, and vice versa. In these circumstances prices are fixed solely by the play of supply and demand, and unregulated or ecological elements may be regarded as the most important determinants of which price shall prevail (Boulding, 1962).

PARTIALLY STRUCTURED CONFLICT RELATIONSHIPS: STRATEGIC FACTORS IN CONFLICT

A partially structured conflict relationship is a relationship in which certain social constraints are imposed upon the conflict behavior of each party, but a definite area of conflict remains, an acknowledged area of dispute within a larger context of agreement and rules. The options, the moves, or the means available to a party are limited by these rules as well as by his own capacities and predispositions. Certain possible alternatives are declared illegitimate in the situation and can be employed by a party only if this party can disguise their use or is willing to violate these rules. In partially structured conflicts the resources at stake are generally specified and limited, with the conflict being over the as yet unspecified allocation of these resources. Since partially structured conflict relationships contain an acknowledged area of conflict within a domain of agreement, the fact of conflict is almost always recognized and discussed.

With regard to the orientation of the parties in partially structured conflict relationships, we may specify that each party sees the other primarily as a competitive actor rationally pursuing his own self-interest. Parties in partially structured conflicts are likely to use inducements or reinforcements to influence one another, but this is not necessary in our definition. Intentional or selfish aggression, activated by calculation that this aggression will be rewarded by more favorable outcomes, is an important part of partially structured conflict. The reactions of the parties are often the result of their strategic or tactical calculations, and assume similar maneuverings on the part of the other, rather than results of reflex, emotion, or moral consideration.

Our traffic example becomes a partially structured conflict situation when we consider the case of two cars arriving simultaneously at an intersection which is either unmarked or has stop signs facing in all directions. There are implicit norms or "rules of the road" that are designed to help manage such situations such as the rule that the party on the right has the right of way. But these rules are imperfect, not uniformly known, nor easy to enforce, so the situation in most instances is a bargaining relationship—a polite form of the game of chicken—in which the parties exchange implicit offers to wait or proceed. Flashing red or yellow lights may also be used to alert drivers to relative priorities at intersections while still leaving the ultimate burden of a stop-or-go decision on the shoulders of sometimes foolish individual drivers.

While our traffic example does not contain explicit offers of rewards by one party to another for certain behavior, or threats of fines or sanctions for other behavior, these important elements of partially structured conflict relationships are clearly visible in our market example. Consider the case in which one person is negotiating to buy a house from another person. The parties to the sale have a wide range of means they may employ to influence one another, including of course varying the inducements for buying or selling. Certain means of completing the transaction, such as theft, violence, or blackmail, are ordinarily ruled out. This does not mean that these alternatives no longer exist, but only that a party who chooses to employ one of them must risk whatever the costs are of engaging in an illegitimate act.

FULLY STRUCTURED CONFLICT RELATIONSHIPS:
MORAL FACTORS IN CONFLICT

A fully structured conflict relationship is a relationship in which the behavior of each party is completely specified or prescribed by social norms.

The only option, move, or means available to a party is the one specified as his right or his obligation. In fully structured relationships not only are the resources at stake specified, but the allocation of these resources among participants is also specified. The fact of conflict in such relationships is often not recognized and not discussed, since the actual resolution of the conflict, or at least a commitment toward a resolution by each party, is explicitly indicated by the social norms of the situation. Thus in many fully structured relationships overt conflict may appear only if one party violates or challenges the rules, and in the process creates what we will call a revolutionary conflict situation.

The orientation of parties in fully structured conflict relationships is a moral orientation, involving a concern with the other primarily as a moral agent whose actions are either right or wrong. Parties in fully structured relationships will often use persuasion on one another, but this is by no means necessary. Obedient or altruistic aggression, activated by a sense that this aggression is the only morally appropriate response in the situation, is an important part of fully structured conflict. The reactions of the parties are often the result of their concerns to guide, respect, or obey the other party, and assume similar moral orientations on the part of the other, rather than personal calculations of advantage or self-interest.

In our traffic example, normative control of conflict over the right-of-way takes the familiar form of traffic lights. If traffic lights exist at an intersection, the behavior of the various parties may be so well coordinated that no conflict is evident. The behavior of each party is under the normative control of the traffic signal, and the signal is so programmed that traffic along one street is allowed to move only while traffic along the other is stopped. The fact that the traffic light successfully regulates conflict behavior and allocates the resource of the right-of-way equitably should not be taken to mean that no conflict exists, but only that the conflict relationship has been fully structured by means of the normative controls in the situation. It should be noted that the normative solution need not be equitable. The lights could be "unfairly" programmed so that parties on one street were given priority over parties on the other. Other rules could be established that would give priority to certain kinds of vehicles, say cars, over other kinds, like buses and trucks.

Many normative structurings of conflict situations take the form of role allocations that specify various rights and duties for particular actors. The example in which cars are favored over trucks is one instance. The allocation of various family responsibilities such as doing the dishes or doing the shopping is a general set of conflict situations that are typically subject to normative solution by role allocation. Again, the fact that a perfectly harmonious arrangement may be worked out should not obscure our understanding of the fact that the more one party is freed from the cost of doing this work, the greater the cost borne by the other parties.

Our exchange example may be transformed into a fully structured relationship by removing the legitimate degrees of freedom the parties to the exchange may have to consider various prices and various means to influence the other's consideration of these prices. When a person walks into an American supermarket and buys a loaf of bread, the fact that no bargaining takes place over the price of the bread obtains because the price is normatively regulated by general pricing policies of food chains. The individual grocer may have no legitimate options, and the customer only the option of buying or not buying. In many other countries prices are not so standardized, and bargaining or haggling between merchant and customer is expected. Although Americans may become uncomfortable when commercial transactions take on a bargaining character (for larger, non-standard purchases like cars or houses), persons from other cultures may become upset when commercial transactions do not involve bargaining (even when the merchant profits because the foolish American tourist pays the asking price). Of course, exchange conflicts may be turned into fully structured conflict relationships by governmental as well as non-governmental authorities. In many countries, especially during wartime, an official body specifies that transactions for particular goods and services may be carried out only in particular quantities or at particular prices. Other alternatives may still be employed by the parties (they may sell at higher than official prices, as in a black market in wartime), but these alternatives are now understood as violations.

REVOLUTIONARY CONFLICT: CONFLICT

OVER THE RULES OF CONFLICT

If conflict relationships are distinguished by their degree of structure, how can we characterize conflict that occurs over what this structure should be? I would like to suggest that we reserve the term "revolutionary conflict" for conflicts over the rules that govern the relationships themselves. Revolutionary conflict in this sense is always conflict over fundamental issues in a conflict relationship, which is an appropriate connotation for the idea of revolution. However, as we shall discuss more fully, revolutionary conflict in the present sense does not completely coincide with popular notions that require all revolutions to be violent and dramatic.

The simplest case of revolutionary conflict in the present sense occurs when the parties in a relationship differ over whether particular options, moves, or means should be considered legitimate or not. Revolutionary conflict necessarily involves some sort of challenge to an existing rule structure by a party who regards this structure as in some way unfair. In this sense revolutionary conflict relationships, like normative relationships, involve a moral orientation on the part of actors. Unlike normative conflicts, however, revolutionary conflicts are almost always recognized as conflict, because the conflict involves a challenge to the rule structure of the previous relationship. It should be noted, however, that not all challenges to existing rule structures may be considered revolutionary. Defiance of rules may also be termed aberrant or criminal as well as revolutionary, depending upon whether the defiance is perceived as having no comprehensible justification, a justification only in the form of an exception or an excuse that nonetheless accepts the basic rules, or a justification in the form of a challenge to the rules themselves.

It is thus revolutionary conflict which transforms normative relationships into bargaining ones (for example by recognizing the right of a subordinate party to organize for its own protection), or bargaining relationships into normative ones (for example by agreement or legislation prohibiting the occurrence of certain conflict tactics; see Thibaut and Faucheux, 1965). It is also revolutionary conflict which alters the balance of power in a bargaining relationship (by adding or taking away conflict alternatives available to the parties, as distinct from affecting the choices the parties may make from existing alternatives) or the balance of privilege in a normative relationship (by reassigning prerogatives or resource allocation in the relationship). Apart from challenges to the legitimacy or illegitimacy of various options, revolutionary conflict may also arise from historical change in the options that are physically available to parties in a relationship. The invention of new means of conflict requires that these new techniques be classified and assigned a degree of legitimacy or illegitimacy in particular situations. Not only may the new techniques (such as guns) themselves have revolutionary consequences for a balance of power, but defining their appropriate use may provoke revolutionary conflict. Similarly, change that removes a historic option from a particular person or class may stimulate this party to reassess the entire range of options available in a relationship.

In our traffic example, revolutionary conflict would involve a questioning by partisans of one street or one type of vehicle as to whether they had been given appropriate priority at the intersection. In our market or exchange example, revolutionary conflict would occur if there were a struggle between the parties over what the appropriate price level should be, given that only one price would be declared legitimate, or a struggle between the parties over what means should be employed in fixing a price. If the commodity whose price were to be fixed was of sufficient importance to enough people (like grain), it is not hard to imagine a struggle between interest groups of buyers and sellers that would undermine or transcend their relationship. The struggle might take place in a national legislature, and the failure of settlement to the satisfaction of one or the other party might result in a movement against the national government that all would recognize as revolutionary. It is important to understand, however, that in our sense, on the level of the buyer-seller relationship, the struggle over a legitimate price is itself revolutionary because it involves a disagreement between parties to a relationship over what the appropriate rules of that relationship should be. That these two parties should then wage a struggle in the appropriate political arena established for the management of such struggles would of course not be revolutionary at the level of the political system. The struggle would become revolutionary at that level as well only if one of the parties raised questions about his relationship with the political or judicial authority in question.

There is no contradiction to our analysis in accepting the fact that a given relationship between two parties may be embedded in a larger system of relationships and that certain conflicts may be appealed to representatives of this larger collectivity. This does not make the conflict over rules in the given relationship any the less revolutionary in its consequences for that relationship. It is only when there is no larger system to which a disagreement over rules can be appealed that such revolutionary conflicts are likely to result in general system breakdowns ordinarily associated with "revolution." This, however, refers to the consequences of a particular revolutionary conflict, or the means available for handling the conflict, rather than its inherent revolutionary nature. In our system, transitions between different rule structures, of the sort to transform the nature of the relationship or to alter the powers, privileges or alternatives available to the parties, are all revolutionary changes. The means by which they are carried out, and the momentousness of their consequences, depend upon the location of the conflict relationship undergoing revolutionary change in the larger system.

Some of this confusion surrounding the concept of revolution may be traced to an inadvertent shifting between the questions of revolutionary conflict and revolutionary change. In our sense, revolutionary change is change in the rules of a relationship, and revolutionary conflict is disagreement over whether or not such change should take place. It is clear that one can have revolutionary change without revolutionary conflict: a change in the rules may be consensual on the part of everyone involved. It is also clear that one can have revolutionary conflict without revolutionary change: one party's desire to have the rules changed may never surface in the form of an overt challenge, or the challenge may be repulsed and the previously established rules retained without change. In this sense, neither revolutionary conflict nor revolutionary change need be dramatic, violent, or "revolutionary" in a more popular sense, though they can be. Our approach differs from others in making a dispute over appropriate rules or legitimate norms a sufficient element for revolutionary conflict, rather than merely a necessary element.

Although it does not coincide with previous definitions, the present notion of revolution can nonetheless be reconciled with the spirit of previous definitions. For example, Smelser (1963) defines revolutionary movements as those concerned with changing the fundamental values of a society. The spirit of this definition comes through in the present conception of revolutionary conflict as conflict oriented toward changing the fundamental rules of relationships. On the other hand, Stinchcombe (1965) defines revolutionary conflicts as those in which all restraints on the means of conflict have been removed, which is reminiscent of the present conception of unstructured conflict relationships. Now in fact conflicts over the structure of rules are generally less likely to be bound by these rules, and once outside these rules the means of conflict may rapidly escalate. Thus revolutionary conflicts are likely to become unstructured conflicts in some ways, but this should not obscure the differences between the two. Unstructured conflicts are not in general oriented to changing system rules, and conflicts about rules need not reach unlimited violence. Whether they do so or not is in the present framework an empirical question rather than a matter of definition.

AN INTEGRATED APPROACH TO THE STUDY OF CONFLICT

Our analysis of conflict relationships permits the natural juxtaposition of work on conflict done in very different areas by researchers using very different approaches. In the domain of unstructured conflict falls much of the research on violence and aggression that either ignores rule structures, like many laboratory studies of frustration and aggression, or assumes that such rules are largely absent, as in studies of mob behavior, or irrelevant, as in studies of personality influences on aggression. In the domain of partially structured conflict falls much of the research on bargaining, threat, and exchange in mixed-motive situations, including work on the escalation and de-escalation of conflict and the role that communication and communication difficulties may play in conflict relationships. In the domain of fully structured conflict falls much of the research on obedience, conformity, equity, and socialization, with its focus on how actors learn rules of right and wrong, how these rules are enforced, and how these rules manage conflict in situations that may not even appear to involve conflict. Finally, in the domain of revolutionary conflict falls much of the research on the historical, economic, and psychological dynamics of revolution.

It is interesting to note that our distinctions among types of conflict relationships correspond in part to theoretical and methodological divisions in the social sciences. Biologists and psychologists are the scientists most likely to deal with stimulus factors in conflict while social psychologists and economists are the ones most likely to deal with strategic factors in conflict. With the exception of economists (but see Siegel and Fouraker, 1960) all of the foregoing are sciences that often employ laboratory studies in their pursuit of knowledge about conflict. Sociologists and anthropologists are the scientists most likely to deal with normative factors in conflict, while historians and political scientists are the ones most likely to deal with revolutionary conflict. The latter disciplines are all ones that do not typically employ laboratory experiments. The reason these different aspects of social conflict have so rarely been treated as a whole may well lie in the fact of their disciplinary separation. Though the present analysis of conflict relationships may be only a modest beginning toward an integrated theory of social conflict, it has the important virtue of forcing us to think about the interrelationships of these many different forms of social conflict and forms of study of social conflict.

The present scheme offers a general language that not only encompasses but may perhaps also help rationalize the differences in approach of the various social sciences. In a rough and ready way, our scheme combines the basic distinction of psychologists between rational and non-rational behavior, and the basic distinction of sociologists between normative and non-normative behavior. Rational and non-rational elements are distinguished in the difference between impulsive aggression, the predominant element of unstructured situations, and intentional or selfish aggression, the predominant element of partially structured conflict relationships. Normative and non-normative elements are distinguished in the differences between the foregoing, all of which are non-normative, and obedient, moral, or altruistic aggression, the predominant element of fully structured conflict relationships. (Following Freud, a psychoanalytically inclined reader might be tempted to label these categories as id-based aggression, ego-based aggression, and superego-based aggression, respectively. This is not our preferred language, but it never hurts to acknowledge one of the intellectual founders of our era. These categories also correspond in some ways, it may be noted, to Plato's still more venerable distinctions among appetite, reason, and spirit as the three bases of human action.) Previously psychology and sociology have each tended to ignore the importance of the distinction considered fundamental by the other. It would seem clear, however, that for an integrated approach to the study of social conflict (or, for that matter, to the study of any form of social behavior), we need to consider both distinctions.

The present analysis of conflict relationships has antecedents in other analyses of social conflict or social influence by a number of writers, as indeed it should to have any hope of representing the diverse elements in the field of social conflict. It is informative in two ways to compare this analysis to other schemes: the similarities suggest a recurrent set of basic issues, while the differences help to refine and sharpen our understanding of the present structural analysis. The analyses of Gamson (1968), Etzioni (1961), Boulding (1964), and Rapoport (1960) are all similar to the present one in describing three basic kinds of social relationships. Gamson (1968) distinguishes between constraints, inducements, and persuasion as three bases of influence relationships. Etzioni (1961) distinguishes between coercive, utilitarian, and normative sanctions as different bases of compliance relationships. Boulding (1964) contrasts threat systems, exchange systems, and integrative systems as three bases of social order, while Rapoport (1960) describes fights, games, and debates as three basic kinds of conflict.

All of these previous authors tend to see their distinctions as primarily a matter of the means that parties are willing and able to use on others, although they also consider the aims and orientations of the parties, while the present analysis would prefer to see identical means (for example force) as potentially available for use in any of our types of conflict relationship. Furthermore, none of the previous typologies has a conception of revolutionary conflict relationships that would distinguish revolutionary relationships from others using similar means. Despite these differences, however, there is a certain similarity to the spirit of these analyses that should give us some confidence that the questions being discussed are viable ones.

It may be useful to take one of these previous analyses and compare it in more detail with the present scheme. Rapoport's (1960) analysis of fights, games, and debates is in some ways closest to ours. For Rapoport, fights are conflicts in which each party has the aim of eliminating the antagonist entirely. Games are conflicts in which each party has the aim of winning as much as possible from the other. Debates are conflicts in which each party has the aim of persuading the other to agree with the first party's views.

In the present perspective, unstructured conflicts are most likely to be concerned with eliminating the antagonist entirely and established bargaining relationships are most likely to be concerned with winning or allocating resources. Normative conflict and revolutionary conflict relationships seem most clearly related to debates, but differ first in that Rapoport's category of debates does not distinguish between these two types of conflict and second in that these two types of conflict are not limited to persuasion as a means.

No analytical scheme can be pushed too hard or stretched too far without breaking down into contradiction or ambiguity. In organizing the field of social conflict, the present scheme has been pushed very hard, and it is not immune to breakdown. Unstructured conflict, bargaining conflict, normative conflict, and revolutionary conflict are only ideal types whose distinctions are only clear-cut in theory, if at all. In actual practice it will soon be recognized that each type of relationship may also contain elements of the other types. In descriptions of why men fight in military combat situations, for example (see Marshall, 1947; Moskos, 1969), a preponderance of normative elements (obedience to orders, loyalty to peers, underlying patriotism) is mixed with elements of strategic calculation (minimizing personal danger) and elements of almost reflex reaction to stimuli (anger at shocks administered by the enemy). Nonetheless, although actual situations may represent a mixture of elements, the point remains that these situations can be characterized and differentiated by the dominant rule structures that affect participants. Furthermore, embedded secondary elements are by no means identical to the same elements when they constitute the primary factors in the relationship: thus strategic bargaining embedded in a normative conflict relationship like that between husband and wife may be quite different from strategic bargaining at work in an established bargaining relationship like that of salesman and client. In any event, if this analysis serves simply as a useful heuristic base for beginning an integrated study of social conflict, it will have been amply successful.

We may hope that future work will deal more extensively with the interrelationships among these different forms and elements of social conflict, and study the structure of conflict relationships as both an independent variable (whose consequences for both actors and third parties need to be understood) and as a dependent variable (whose antecedents or determinants need to be explored). The author is involved in one such research project applying the structural analysis of conflict relationships to the study of Prisoner's Dilemma. In Prisoner's Dilemma situations, each of two parties must decide either to trust the other and make a friendly move, such as disarming, or to distrust the other and make a hostile move, such as arming. In fact, if a person knows that the other party is making a trusting move, it is rational to make a distrustful one, since this will give the first person a great advantage in the situation. Also, if a person knows that the other party is making a distrustful move, it is again rational to make a distrustful one, since this will enable the first person to protect himself. Thus in either event it is "rational" for each party to distrust the other. Yet both players are worse off if they distrust each other than if they would be if both could trust each other—thus the dilemma. (See Gallo and McClintock, 1965, for an overview of some studies in this area.)

Although the stakes and the exact nature of the dilemma situations have been varied, most past research has implied that the dilemma is a strategic one and structured the situation as a partially structured conflict relationship. In these circumstances distrustful choices are more frequent than trusting ones, and women are typically more distrustful than men (see Kahn, Hottes, and Davis, 1971). It was hypothesized that these differences would reverse if the dilemma were set in situations that made normative elements in the relationship between the parties salient (such as choosing whether or not to reveal information about another student versus choosing whether or not to compete against another businessman). Preliminary results from two studies support this reasoning.

SOCIAL SYSTEMS AND CONFLICT RELATIONSHIPS

Conflict relationships, like all social relationships, are typically subsystems of a larger social system. Each party to the conflict in turn has relationships with many others who may turn out to be witnesses, allies, enemies, or judges. So far, however, we have been looking at conflict relationships in isolation and focusing only on the two parties directly involved in the conflict. Furthermore, conflict, again like other social relationships, has consequences that may be either positive or negative, good or bad, functional or dysfunctional, both for the parties directly involved and for the larger social system. So far we have not addressed the issue of the functional or dysfunctional consequences of conflict, an issue of prime concern to many writers on the subject. Finally, in cases where the consequences of conflict are judged to be dysfunctional or destructive, the pressing question of how to resolve or reduce the conflict arises, another question that has preoccupied many writers on conflict. What are the implications of our structural analysis of conflict relationships for these system-oriented questions about third parties, functions of conflict, and conflict resolution? These are the concerns that will be addressed in this section.

THIRD PARTIES AND COALITIONS

A minimum of three parties is necessary for the study of coalition behavior (see Caplow, 1968), in which two (or more) parties join forces against one (or more) others. Our primary focus so far has been on relationships between two parties. Our distinctions might be fruitfully applied to coalitions, for example, a distinction between strategically based coalitions and normatively based coalitions. In other ways, however, the addition of a third party adds considerable complexity to our structural analysis. For example, we might have to consider situations in which certain parties were in fully structured conflict relationships, while others simultaneously stood in partially structured relationships to each other.

In general, for the present, our scheme would suggest handling the multi-party situation by taking the parties in that situation two at a time, and looking at the relationship between those two, treating decisions to enter a coalition with a third or fourth party as possible conflict options available to one or both of the parties in the focal relationship. Thus Caplow (1968) defines a "revolutionary coalition" as one in which two weaker members of a triad combine to dominate the superior member, a definition of revolution quite different from, though not incompatible with, the present one. The present approach would suggest analyzing this situation by taking a particular dyadic relationship (say the one between the strongest and the next strongest member), and considering the conditions under which each of these would choose the option of accepting a coalition with the weakest member. Whether such a coalition was revolutionary in our sense would depend upon whether its formation challenged previously existing situational norms.

If it seems unduly arbitrary to limit our analysis of conflict to dyadic or two-party relationships, it should be remembered that in our view a person has as many potential conflict relationships as he has relationships with other people. Since this number of relationships is ordinarily very great, the restriction that we consider them one at a time, in dyadic units, is not in fact much more stringent or arbitrary than a restriction that we consider them two at a time or in triads. Thus we may recognize that a guard in a prison has conflict-relevant relationships with many different prisoners, with fellow guards, with his superiors, with his family, and with many others, and we may focus upon all of these in turn. I do not think we are yet in a position to focus on all of them simultaneously. Nor does this seem to me an embarrassing deficiency. The mathematics of N-person games or N-dimension situations are much more complex than the mathematics of two-person games or two-dimension situations, and in physics the two-body problem was solved a long time ago while the three-body problem is still incompletely understood.

The question of third parties and coalitions also has another, somewhat more subtle relationship to our analysis of conflict relationships. Apart from their relevance as potential coalition partners, third parties often enter into our consideration of conflict relationships as factors which establish the nature of what is legitimate and what is illegitimate in a relationship. This is not always true. The parties directly involved in a conflict relationship may themselves evolve agreements that regulate and structure their conflict behavior, as for example in the classic study by Thibaut and Faucheux (1965), and this basis of legitimacy is easily handled by our conceptualization. In many instances, however, legitimacy is established by what an authoritative third party thinks, or what conforms to the rules established, sanctioned, and enforced by an authoritative third party. The legitimacy of various possible actions by two automobile drivers at an intersection, or a buyer and a seller in a market, is in large part a function of whether these actions coincide with views held by policemen, judges, legislators, or other observers of the relationship. When subjects in the well-known experiment by Milgram (1965) administered powerful shocks to the slow "learner" in the other room, or when respondents in the survey by Kelman and Lawrence (1972) indicated that they would in certain circumstances shoot to kill innocent civilians in Vietnam, they both sought to establish the legitimacy of these actions by appeal to the views of a responsible authority figure (the experimenter, the officers) who stood outside their immediate relationship with the victims. If we reverse our focus so we take the relationship between the subject and the authority figure as the primary one, then we likewise find that the subject's willingness to come in conflict with this figure, by protecting the victim, is justified by reference to the legitimacy of claims by the third party, the victim (Milgram, 1965; Stouffer, 1949). Thus in studying legitimacy in dyadic conflict relationships we are already in some measure widening our focus, indirectly, to include the study of the relationship of this dyad to third parties.

The relevance of third parties to questions of legitimacy is perhaps clearest when we consider transactions which are desired by both parties to them, both a buyer and a seller, yet are illegal. Abortion, gambling, prostitution, and marijuana sales are well-known examples of what are sometimes called "crimes without victims." A more recent example is the transaction which can be entered into by students with professional term paper agencies who for a fee will supply the student with a term paper. In previous discussions of legitimacy we have always been talking about particular actions that may be illegitimate. Although we can retain this basic understanding, these examples make us notice that relationships as well as particular actions may be illegitimate. The illegitimacy here cannot come from the violation of views held by either party, but rather from views held by society. In each case it can be argued whether the disapproval of society stems from concern with the implications of the act for third parties who will be directly or indirectly affected but have not given consent (the unborn baby in an abortion, or the people who will suffer in the future from one party's drug addiction), or a dislike of the act itself (prostitution, gambling, drunkenness). Interestingly, although most public concern is focused on the "simpler" criminal actions which have clear first-party victims (robbery, murder, rape, arson), most police and judicial activity deals with the second category of criminal transactions discussed above. This fact has led several authors to suggest that one priority in law and order should be a radical reorienting of police priorities (Morris and Hawkins, 1970).

As all of these points make clear, third parties may on occasion intervene in a dyadic relationship. Indeed the study of when third parties feel they can or should intervene in dyadic conflict relationships, or when parties to such a relationship feel that third parties can or should intervene (cf. Slater, 1963; Pruitt, 1971), is an important problem area. The study of third party interventions can serve as a means of detecting when norms have been violated in a dyadic relationship, as an approach to understanding the strength or cohesiveness of dyadic relationships, and as an important beginning on the study of how particular conflict relationships are embedded in larger social systems. The study of the two party relationship is not itself complete without a study of its limits.

FUNCTIONS OF CONFLICT

On a very general level, much of the writing about social conflict may be divided into two parts: one concerned with conflict resolution and one concerned with the functions of conflict. Writers who focus on conflict resolution are concerned with the destructive potential of social conflict, especially war, and regard the most pressing task of study to be the discovery of reasonable means for ameliorating or removing the causes of conflict. Examples include Sherif, 1958; Osgood, 1962; Rapoport, 1962; Fisher, 1964; Frank, 1968; and Pruitt, 1972. Writers who focus on the functions of conflict emphasize both the inevitability of conflict and the positive or constructive potential that conflict may release. Examples include Coser, 1956, 1957; Murphy, 1957; Dahrendorf, 1958; Julian, Bishop, and Fiedler, 1966; and Lorenz, 1963.

There have of course been authors who were equally concerned with both the systemic functions of conflict and with the destructive potential of conflict, such as Boulding, 1964; Gamson, 1968; or Campbell, 1972. On the whole, however, the division between the functions-of-conflict and the conflict-resolution traditions has been rather sharp. The present structural analysis might conceivably help to bridge these different traditions by encouraging each to supplement its existing focus with a new dimension, the structuring of conflict relationships, that the other tradition might respect. As each perspective contributes to the development of understanding as to how conflict relationships are structured, and what are the consequences of this structuring, each may come to see more of value in the other perspective and in a unified approach to the study of social conflict.

It does not seem possible to categorize existing work on the functions of social conflict as dealing primarily with unstructured, partially structured, or fully structured conflict relationships. Nonetheless, one can think of some ways in which the most frequently mentioned functions of conflict might be enhanced by their consideration in the present framework. Functional theorists (Coser) make a number of general arguments for the virtues of social conflict, of which we may select three as central. The first is that conflict is a useful, if not a necessary, ingredient in producing loyalty, solidarity, and cohesiveness in social groups that unite in the face of an antagonist. The second argument is that conflict is a crucial impetus for innovation, change, and progress in groups that are driven to seek a competitive advantage in the conflict. A third argument, perhaps less central, is that conflict is a useful condition for particular individuals to enjoy freedom to choose their own courses of action, the freedom deriving from the inability of either side in the conflict (Protestant versus Catholic Church) to enforce its value system in its entirety. We might only speculate here that these different functions of conflict might very well be best served by rather different conflict structures. The solidarity function seems most clearly related to normative or fully structured conflict relationships. The innovation function seems most clearly related to rational, strategic, or partially structured conflict relationships. Finally, drawing on the literature on anarchy (Shatz, 1971), the freedom function seems most salient as an aspect of unstructured conflict.

On the question of tactics for maximizing the functional value of different conflict situations, some of the material in the following section on conflict resolution will also be relevant.

CONFLICT RESOLUTION

In considering means of conflict resolution it is certainly relevant to understand the nature of conflict relationships. If one believes that social conflict is largely a function of man's responding to deep-seated internal stimulation (as do most instinctive theories of aggression), one's efforts at conflict resolution must be aimed at finding alternative outlets for these instinctual energies. If one believes that social conflict is largely a function of man's rational calculation of what behaviors or what strategies will yield the maximum gain, then one's efforts at conflict resolution must be to make conflict behaviors less promising than various non-conflict alternatives. If one believes that social conflict is largely a function of man's obeying orders or following prescribed conflict norms, then one's efforts at conflict resolution must be aimed at changing the orders and the norms that legitimate destructive conflicts.

These approaches are not necessarily mutually exclusive. Nonetheless, which view we hold and which approach we decide to emphasize is not a trivial decision, for it specifies how we should invest our scarce resources for ameliorating the consequences of conflict.

In a preliminary way, we might regard different proposals in the existing literature on conflict resolution as contributing primarily to unstructured, partially structured, and fully structured conflict relationships. The following authors seem most concerned with fully structured relationships and offer proposals whose success rests upon introducing normative elements into the relationship between antagonists:

1) Sherif (1958) emphasizes the introduction of superordinate or shared goals into a conflict relationship. Once the antagonists have been induced to work together to achieve a common goal (which may of course also have rational elements), their respect for each other and their view of the relationship that is right or appropriate between them will change in a positive direction. Sherif demonstrated these views in an experiment using rival gangs of boys in a summer camp. It is not so easy to see how a common goal of sufficient importance could be imposed on the interests of all mankind, though an extra-terrestrial danger has been a popular solution among science fiction writers (Wells, 1898; Sturgeon, 1955).

2) Rapoport (1962) suggests that parties to conflict take turns role-playing each other's point of view as a means of increasing their mutual understanding and empathy. This strategy is also of relevance to partially structured conflict situations in which the parties may be distorting the true intentions or capacities of their opponents, although here evidence has been collected by Johnson (1967) to indicate that role-reversal exercises will reduce conflict

only if the true or objective interests of the parties are not incompatible. The normative contribution of the role-play experience may again be to increase each party's respect for the other and the other's point of view and to shift the views of both parties as to what is right or appropriate in their relationship. Here there is interesting evidence that under certain conditions, where the role-play is meaningful and involves some degree of commitment, the exercise may change the attitudes of the role-players toward the position they were made to argue for but did not initially believe in (see Elms, 1969).

3) James (1910) in a classic essay argued that mankind should search for "the moral equivalent of war," by which he meant an activity considered as manly, vital, exciting, and valuable as war in defense of one's people, but without the destructiveness involved in actual warfare. One possibility, suggested James, was sport. This proposal is also relevant to conflict viewed as unstructured or instinctual in origin, since the assumption that the urge to fight is instinctual in man also leads to an emphasis on finding an acceptable outlet for these aggressive energies. But the normative emphasis of James' suggestion is evident in his view that men engage in particular conflict behaviors because these behaviors are widely admired and believed to embody moral virtues. To reduce these behaviors, we must thus reduce the degree of respect and virtue they are given by our social norms, and reinvest this normative respect in less destructive forms of behavior.

We might regard the following authors as most concerned with partially structured conflict relationships. The success of their proposals rests upon tactics designed to allow the parties involved to maximize their long-run self-interest without undue fear that the other party will take advantage of them.

1) Osgood (1962) has presented an ingenious and elaborate proposal to reverse the typical spiral of escalation in conflict situations into a spiral of de-escalation. His proposal is a plan for what he calls "graduated reciprocated unilateral initiatives for peace." The essence of the plan is that one party be willing to make a small initial sacrifice in the interests of peace, such as a minor reduction in a weapons system. To make the purpose of the move clear, it is to be unilateral and announced in advance. To preserve the basic security of the party taking the initiative, the move is to be relatively minor and the party making it is to wait for some gesture of reciprocation before taking a further step. Etzioni (1967) has argued that something like this did indeed take place between Kennedy and Khrushchev following the Cuban missile crisis. The aim of the Osgood proposal is to allow a party to conflict to act in a rational manner to pursue its long-term interests in peace without at the same time endangering its short-term interests in armed security. In its emphasis on the rational pursuit of self-interest within the broad guidelines of an enduring relationship, the Osgood proposal is clearly in the domain of partially structured conflict, though its by-product (the building up of trust between parties) could lead to the introduction of normative elements as well.

2) Fisher (1964) has argued that particular conflict situations are often hard to resolve not because they are so difficult or because each party cannot

stand defeat, but rather because each party fears the implications of even a local or temporary defeat. The stakes in the particular conflict may be trivial, but if the procedure, the outcome, or the solution of the conflict is seen as setting a precedent for procedures or outcomes in the future, the loss may be momentous. Thus, each party may be led to invest far more in the contest than is justified by the actual stakes. The so-called "domino theory" of conflict represents one version of this view, in which one victory for the other side is seen as setting off a chain reaction of victories for the enemy all over the globe. As with many theories that are based on a mixture of rational and irrational fear, the domino theory is difficult to refute with evidence. The fact that the fall of China to Communism in 1949 or the fall of Cuba in 1959 did not in either case set off a round of dominoes was not taken as negative evidence for the domino theory in Vietnam in 1969.

At any rate, Fisher suggests that a great effort be made by parties to conflict to define particular conflict situations wherever possible as "special cases" that will not be treated as precedents by either side or their presumed allies. Fisher calls this "fractionating conflict," or dividing up a major conflict between parties into a series of fractional or little conflicts. Each little conflict can then presumably be settled on its own rational merits without involving the larger, emotional, and possibly insoluble issues of the general conflict between the parties. Again the emphasis of this proposal is on the rational pursuit of self-interest by parties within the context of an enduring relationship, and on how this might best be done.

In passing, incidentally, it might be noted that several other authors (Kopytoff, 1961; Schattschneider, 1960) have dealt with conflict management strategies that involve enlarging, rather than restricting, the domain of a particular conflict. However, these strategies involve enlarging the conflict by bringing in an additional party or parties to the situation, and not merely bringing in additional issues or consequences (which would of course be a direct contradiction of Fisher; but see Sawyer and Guetzkow (1965) on the advantages of more room for bargaining when multiple issues are considered simultaneously). The idea of these authors is that conflicts that have become impossible to resolve between two parties, or possible to resolve only in a manner totally unacceptable to one of the parties, may be resolved by introducing the opinion and the resources of a third party. The third party may have no interest in the initial struggle but only an interest in calming a feud before it gets out of hand (Kopytoff, 1961), or the third parties may have considerable interest in the initial struggle and sufficient resources to resolve it in favor of one side or the other (Schattschneider, 1961). Note that the third party in these instances is not an impartial judge or mediator, which would involve us in normative conflict, but rather a potential actor. Thus the decision to involve a third party in either of these cases is presented as a strategic calculation by one of the parties to the initial conflict.

It is harder to think of conflict resolution proposals that are relevant to unstructured conflict situations, although the previously mentioned work of James fits well with the view of theorists like Lorenz (1963) who see the basic source of conflict as an instinctual aggressive energy that must find some means of expression. Perhaps the work of Frank (1968), outlining the possibilities of non-violence in the manner of Gandhi and King as a general approach to conflict situations, may also be taken as an application of thinking about conflict resolution in unstructured relationships. Frank argues that non-violence is not merely a second-best conflict tactic where violent means seem doomed to failure, but an alternative with powerful advantages in its own right. The advantages of accepting this degree of self-restraint in an unstructured situation which itself imposes no restraints, says Frank, lie primarily in enabling the non-violent party to preserve its own respect for human integrity in a manner that cannot be taken away by an antagonist, who should ultimately be led to the same respect. Some animal species appear to have an instinctual respect for non-violent gestures by con-specifics (see Lorenz, 1963), but there is no evidence for such an instinct among humans.

Perhaps more important than attempting to organize previous work on conflict resolution from a structural perspective is a consideration of how the present structural perspective might generate new ideas on conflict resolution. As a general principle, we might consider the notion that if undesirable or destructive conflict occurs in a particular relationship, efforts to resolve or manage that conflict should consider means of transforming that conflict relationship into one with either a greater or lesser degree of structure. It is important to note that either a greater or a lesser degree of structure may be appropriate, because much of our previous discussion may have implied that adding structure to a conflict relationship is the best way to minimize conflict. As we have already noted, however, normative conflict relationships, in which the parties pursue goals regarded as the only right or legitimate ones, may be the most dangerous form of conflict of all. An extensive literature on anarchy (see Shatz, 1971) argues that rules and governments are the basic source of exploitation and destructive conflicts. Whether anarchy, or a doing away with all rules and governments, is a "natural" or a possible state, it must be acknowledged that a theoretical situation in which actors pursued their own interests both without constraint and without damage to others would be a most admirable one. In this sense, depending upon the behavior actually exhibited by the parties, unstructured or anarchic situations might represent both the best and the worst, the most mature and the least mature form of relationships.

Let us consider a case in which an unstructured conflict relationship is improved by the introduction of structure, and then a case in which a fully structured relationship is improved by a decrease in structure. One of the best known examples of an unstructured conflict situation is the so-called panic situation in which many people simultaneously rush to escape a common danger, or to obtain a scarce resource, often to the great disadvantage of all. There are no rules in the situation guiding each party's progress toward the exits, and thus each party responds to whatever emotional or rational elements catch his attention. Mintz (1951) performed a classic experiment involving an analogue to an escape panic. Subjects all had cones on strings which they had to remove from a bottle before that bottle filled with water. Where subjects had a stake in getting their own cone out of the bottle before it got wet, the typical result of the experiment was a jam-up at the bottleneck preventing anyone from getting out, even though everyone could have done so if progress toward the exit had been orderly. Now how might we add structure to this situation, and what might the consequences be? We could transform the situation into a partially structured conflict by emphasizing rational calculation and strategic bargaining by parties on the best means of exit. A prerequisite for this transformation is of course the ability of the parties in the situation to communicate with one another about their various alternatives and intentions. Communication and bargaining might result in some limited form of contest (such as drawing lots) to decide who goes first, or even a decision to take turns going first, if the situation is a recurring one. It will of course help if certain individuals take the lead in communicating these possibilities, as Kelley, Condry, Dahlke, and Hill (1965) found in their elaboration and extension of the Mintz experiment.

The rational bargaining solution to the Mintz situation is not, however, the preferred structural transformation of this conflict situation. Society in general employs a normative solution in potential panic situations, a solution in which each individual is taught that an orderly movement toward the exit is the only course of action that is right. Thus schoolchildren and other groups are given fire drills in which they are trained to file out in a disciplined manner.

Unstructured situations often involve a degree of anonymity and isolation for participants, conditions which in turn are conducive to certain antisocial acts, like robbery and rape. Consider the not uncommon problem of making a particular office or dormitory building safe for off-hours use. Ironically, certain common mechanical solutions to the problem (issuing warnings, installing locks and distributing keys), while valuable, may actually increase the sense of isolation and insecurity and decrease people's willingness to build and extend their contacts with others in such a situation. The present analysis would suggest, however, that danger from attacks can be decreased by building or rebuilding these human contacts, establishing what can be established of a territorial community, and decreasing the sense of anonymity and isolation. The bases of individual security are norms of community, formal or informal understandings of who other people in the area are, where they habitually stay, and when they stay there. With these understandings, people can adapt their own habits to maximize their security of work and travel. With these understandings, people can identify strangers more easily, and, if necessary, respond to them more effectively. With these understandings, a person in an emergency can call on people or to people rather than merely calling out, and thus probably increase both the chances of getting help and the chances of scaring off an attacker.

Fully structured relationships, even ones in which the norms specify friendly and cooperative behavior from all parties, may sometimes be improved by an alteration of structure. Riecken (1952) found that normative suppression of antagonistic behavior in a pacifist-oriented community led to persistent frustration over relatively minor issues. Bach (Bach and Wyden, 1968) has recently developed an elaborate therapy designed to teach married couples how to express disagreement and to fight with each other without undoing their basic relationship. The general point in such cases is to loosen the structure of the relationship and thus facilitate the understanding of conflict and the communication about conflict issues, or to transform the relationship into a partially structured one in which more options are legitimately available to both parties.

Another and still more general problem with structural solutions is that any rule adopted to cope with certain problems will inevitably produce new problems. The most a pragmatic legislator should hope for is that the problems created by a rule will be less serious than the problems solved by the rule. Thus suppose that after a disastrous fire a law is passed requiring all new buildings in a city to adhere to a new fire safety code. The law may achieve its primary purpose of ensuring safer buildings. Eventually, however, we may find that the law is being used to force certain parties out of business, or that the law has opened new possibilities for corruption by agents authorized to enforce it, or that the law discourages valuable do-it-yourself initiative by homeowners, or that the law impedes the adoption of new and more efficient building materials. Only a periodic review of the law and its effects can ascertain whether the changing balance of gains and costs justifies retaining the original law, a fact which most legislative systems have been very slow to recognize.

RULE STRUCTURES AND SOCIAL RELATIONSHIPS

As might be evident by now, the analysis of conflict relationships in this essay is really only a special case of what is in fact a general analysis of rule structures and social relationships. This is as it should be. A theory of conflict should be an application of a general theory of social relationships. Conflict always takes place in a context of social relationships, and social relationships always involve the objective potential of conflict.

This may be clearer if we take our analysis of conflict and apply it to the understanding of other relationships. Consider helping relationships and altruistic behavior, in many ways the mirror image of conflict relationships and aggressive behavior (Macaulay and Berkowitz, 1970). We might distinguish as a relatively unstructured helping relationship one in which a broad or unspecified range of responses is available to both the giver and the receiver, as is typically the case in the sidewalk emergencies or the anonymous appeals for charity that are often studied by psychologists interested in the phenomenon of helping. A partially structured helping relationship would be one in which certain forms of helping are specified but the precise nature and degree of help remain to be determined by the negotiations in the particular case, as for example when a student seeks a tutor. A fully structured helping relationship would be one in which particular forms of helping are obligatory for one party and particular responses are obligatory for the other, as for instance when a priest delivers confession to a penitent. A revolutionary helping relationship would be one in which the parties disagreed over the appropriateness of various helpful or non-helpful alternatives, or various grateful or non-grateful responses, as for example when one party wished to charge a fee for a service that the other regarded as his by right or custom, or where one party attempted to give away what others had been accustomed to pay for. Considering the orientation of the actor, we might distinguish an impulsive generosity, in which the actor responds primarily to an immediate stimulus of need on the part of another or surplus on his own part; versus a calculated generosity, in which the actor gives with a rational expectation that giving will best serve his own general self-interest; or a normative generosity, in which the actor gives to another in deference to a moral or religious norm of charity. It is interesting to note that certain apparent contradictions in the helping literature (being exposed to a warm and nurturant model increases children's tendencies to do something to rescue another but decreases their tendencies to share or donate to another) may depend on the fact that the first kind of helping (rescue behavior) typically involves violating rules while the second kind of helping (donation behavior) typically involves adhering to situational norms (Weissbrod, 1973).

We could apply the same analysis to sexual relationships. Briefly, so as not to belabor the point, we might distinguish unstructured sexual encounters in which a broad and unpredictable range of responses are possible and parties are responding purely to erotic stimuli in their near or distant pasts, of which rape is a possible example; partially structured sexual relationships, in which a few responses are all considered relatively legitimate and parties calculate their own self-interest in choosing whether to seek, refuse, or yield, as perhaps in explicit or implicit prostitution; and fully structured sexual relationships in which only one general response is considered legitimate, which may be either participation or abstinence depending upon the circumstances, such as before or after marriage. Challenges to these definitions would lead to revolutionary relationships.

A consideration of sexual relationships and other general social relationships brings our analysis to another important general issue, how the structure of relationships typically changes or evolves over time. In one sense, relationships typically acquire increasing structure as a function of the length of time they are established. Relatively speaking, a first date, especially a blind date, might be considered an unstructured relationship, while a regular but not exclusive dating relationship might be considered partially structured, and a marriage relationship, fully structured. In part, the continuation of the relationship over time permits vague and unsatisfactory role expectations for the other party to be superseded by more precise and differentiated individual understandings. In a somewhat different sense, however, the blind date relationship may be taken as the most highly structured and the marriage relationship as the least highly structured. This is true if we restrict our understanding of structure to conventions or norms prescribed by the larger society for handling the various eventualities of a situation. Formal rules, conventions, and proprieties are more likely to govern an arranged and limited encounter between strangers, or an encounter in which the performance of one of the parties is suspect (Rushing, 1966), than an ongoing and multifaceted living arrangement between intimates. The confusion arises from the important fact that to some extent structure in a relationship may derive from the witnessing and supervising of the relationship by the larger society, and to some extent from the evolution of understandings on the part of the people immediately involved. As time goes by, the former, exterior source of structural control in a relationship is typically superseded by the latter, interior source.

Thus we see that all social relationships may be characterized by rule structures and the orientations that these rule structures elicit in participants. Our understanding of these rule structures may be rudimentary, as are the descriptions in this essay, but it seems clear that this perspective brings an extraordinary range of social phenomena under the power of a single form of analysis. Furthermore, the focus on rules is a focus compatible with already existing theoretical emphases in psychology, sociology, and the other social sciences, as is the methodology for studying perception of rules, adherence to rules, maneuver within rules, and challenge to rules. Recognizing that the different disciplines share this highly general task and are indeed already embarked on their partial solutions may be a first step toward building a general social science.

References

Bach, G., and Wyden, P. *The Intimate Enemy.* New York: Morrow, 1968.

Boulding, K. E. *Conflict and Defense: A General Theory.* New York: Harper, 1962.

————. Toward a Theory of Peace. In R. Fisher (Ed.), *International Conflict and Behavioral Science.* New York: Basic Books, 1964.

Campbell, D. T. Natural Selection as an Epistemological Model. In R. Naroll and R. Cohen (Eds.), *A Handbook of Method in Cultural Anthropology.* New York: Natural History Press, 1970.

————. On the Genetics of Altruism and the Counter-hedonic Components in Human Culture. *Journal of Social Issues,* 1972, **28,** 21–37.

Caplow, T. *Two Against One: Coalitions in Triads.* Englewood Cliffs, New Jersey: Prentice-Hall, 1968.

Coser, L. *The Functions of Social Conflict.* New York: Free Press, 1956.

————. Social Conflict and the Theory of Social Change. *British Journal of Sociology,* 1957, **8,** 197–207.

Dahrendorf, R. Toward a Theory of Social Conflict. *Journal of Conflict Resolution,* 1958, **2,** 170–183.

Deutsch, M. Conflicts: Productive and Destructive. *Journal of Social Issues,* 1969, **25,** 7–41.

————, Krauss, R. M. The Effect of Threat upon Interpersonal Bargaining. *Journal of Abnormal and Social Psychology,* 1960, **61,** 181–189.

Druckman, D.   The Influence of the Situation in Interparty Conflict.   *Journal of Conflict Resolution*, 1971, **15**, 523–554.

Edwards, W.   The Theory of Decision Making.   *Psychological Bulletin*, 1954, **51**, 380–417.

———.   Behavioral Decision Theory.   *Annual Review of Psychology*, 1961, **12**, 473–498.

Elms, A. C. (Ed.), *Role Playing, Reward, and Attitude Change*.   New York: Van Nostrand Reinhold, 1969.

Etzioni, A.   *A Comparative Analysis of Complex Organizations*.   New York: Free Press, 1961.

———.   The Kennedy Experiment.   *Western Political Quarterly*, 1967, **20**, 361–380.

Fink, C. F.   Difficulties in the Theory of Conflict.   *Journal of Conflict Resolution*, 1968, **12**, 412–460.

Fisher, R.   Fractionating Conflict.   In R. Fisher (Ed.), *International Conflict and Behavioral Science*.   New York: Basic Books, 1964.

Frank, J. D.   *Sanity and Survival: Psychological Aspects of War and Peace*.   New York: Random House (Vintage), 1968.

Gallo, P. S., Jr., & McClintock, C. G.   Cooperative and Competitive Behavior in Mixed-motive Games.   *Journal of Conflict Resolution*, 1965, **9**, 68–78.

Gamson, W. A.   *Power and Discontent*.   Homewood, Illinois: Dorsey Press, 1968.

Hammond, K. R.   New Directions in Research on Conflict Resolution.   *Journal of Social Issues*, 1965, **21**, 44–66.

James, W.   The Moral Equivalent of War.   *McClure's Magazine*, August, 1910. Reprinted in L. Bramson, and G. W. Goethals (Eds.), *War: Studies from Psychology, Sociology, and Anthropology*. (Rev. ed.) New York: Basic Books, 1968.

Johnson, D. W.   Use of Role Reversal in Intergroup Competition.   *Journal of Personality and Social Psychology*, 1967, **7**, 135–141.

Julian, J. W., Bishop, D. W., & Fiedler, F. E.   Quasi-therapeutic Effects of Intergroup Competition.   *Journal of Personality and Social Psychology*, 1966, **3**, 321–327.

Kahn, A., Hottes, J., & Davis, W. L.   Cooperation and Optimal Responding in the Prisoner's Dilemma Game: Effects of Sex and Physical Attractiveness. *Journal of Personality and Social Psychology*, 1971, **17**, 267–279.

Kelley, H. H., Condry, J. C., Dahlke, & Hill, A. H.   Collective Behavior in a Simulated Panic Situation.   *Journal of Experimental Social Psychology*, 1965, **1**, 20–54.

Kelman, H. C., & Lawrence, L. H.   Assignment of Responsibility in the Case of Lt. Calley: Preliminary Report on a National Survey.   *Journal of Social Issues*, 1972, **28**, 177–212.

Kopytoff, I.   Extension of Conflict as a Method of Conflict Resolution Among the Suku of the Congo.   *Journal of Conflict Resolution*, 1961, **5**, 61–69.

Kuhn, T.   *The Structure of Scientific Revolutions*.   Chicago: University of Chicago Press, 1962.

Levine, R. A., & Campbell, D. T.   *Ethnocentrism: Theories of Conflict, Ethnic Attitudes and Group Behavior*.   New York: Wiley, 1972.

Lorenz, K. *On Aggression.* (1963) New York: Harcourt, Brace and World, 1966.

Luce, R. D., & Raiffa, H. *Games and Decisions.* New York: Wiley, 1957.

Macaulay, J. R., & Berkowitz, L., (Eds.), *Altruism and Helping Behavior: Social Psychological Studies of Some Antecedents and Consequences.* New York: Academic Press, 1970.

Marshall, S. L. A. *Men Against Fire.* (1947) New York: William Morrow, 1961.

Milgram, S. Some Conditions of Obedience and Disobedience to Authority. *Human Relations,* 1965, **18,** 57–76.

Mintz, A. Non-adaptive Group Behavior. *Journal of Abnormal and Social Psychology,* 1951, **46,** 150–159.

Morris, N., & Hawkins, G. *The Honest Politician's Guide to Crime Control.* Chicago: University of Chicago Press, 1970.

Moskos, C. C., Jr. Why Men Fight. *Trans-action,* 1969, **7,** 13–23.

Murphy, R. F. Intergroup Hostility and Social Cohesion. *American Anthropologist,* 1957, **59,** 1018–1035.

Osgood, C. E. *An Alternative to War or Surrender.* Urbana, Illinois: University of Illinois Press, 1962.

Pruitt, D. G. Indirect Communication and the Search for Agreement in Negotiation. *Journal of Applied Social Psychology,* 1971, **1,** 205–239.

———. Methods for Resolving Differences of Interest: A Theoretical Analysis. *Journal of Social Issues,* 1972, **28,** 133–154.

Rapoport, A. *Fights, Games and Debates.* Ann Arbor: University of Michigan Press, 1960.

———. Rules for Debate. In Q. Wright, W. M. Evan, and M. Deutsch (Eds.), *Preventing World War III: Some Proposals.* New York: Simon and Schuster, 1962.

Riecken, H. Some Problems of Consensus Development. *Rural Sociology,* 1952, **17,** 245–252.

Rushing, W. A. Organizational Rules and Surveillance: Propositions in Comparative Organizational Analysis. *Administrative Science Quarterly,* 1966, **10,** 423–443.

Sawyer, J. and Guetzkow, H. Bargaining and Negotiation in International Relations. In H. Kelman (Ed.), *International Behavior: A Social-Psychological Analysis.* New York: Holt, Rinehart, and Winston, 1965.

Schattschneider, E. E. *The Semisovereign People: A Realist's View of Democracy in America.* New York: Holt, Rinehart and Winston, 1960.

Schelling, T. C. *The Strategy of Conflict.* Cambridge, Massachusetts: Harvard University Press, 1960.

Shatz, M. S. (Ed.), *The Essential Works of Anarchism.* New York: Bantam, 1971.

Sherif, M. Superordinate Goals in the Reduction of Intergroup Conflict. *American Journal of Sociology,* 1958, **63,** 349–356.

Shor, R. E. Shared Patterns of Nonverbal Normative Expectations in Automobile Driving. *Journal of Social Psychology,* 1964, **62,** 155–163.

Siegel, S., and Fouraker, L. E. *Bargaining and Group Decision Making: Experiments in Bilateral Monopoly.* New York: McGraw-Hill, 1960.

Slater, P. E.   On Social Regression. *American Sociological Review,* 1963, **28,** 339–364.

Smelser, N. J. *Theory of Collective Behavior.* Glencoe, Illinois: Free Press, 1963.

Stinchcombe, A. L.   Social Structure and Organizations.   In J. G. March (Ed.), *Handbook of Organizations.* Chicago, Illinois: Rand McNally, 1965.

Stouffer, S.   On Analysis of Conflicting Social Norms. *American Sociological Review,* 1949, **14,** 107–117.

Sturgeon, T.   (Real name: E. H. Waldo) Unite and Conquer.   In T. Sturgeon, *A Way Home: Stories of Science Fiction and Fantasy.* New York: Funk and Wagnalls, 1955.

Thibaut, J. W., & Faucheux, C.   The Development of Contractual Norms under Two Types of Stress. *Journal of Experimental Social Psychology,* 1965, **1,** 89–102.

———, & Kelley, H. H.   *The Social Psychology of Groups.* New York: Wiley, 1959.

von Neumann, J., & Morgenstern, O. *Theory of Games and Economic Behavior.* Princeton, New Jersey: Princeton University Press, 1944.

Weissbrod, C. S.   The Effect of Adult Warmth on Reflective and Impulsive Children's Donation and Rescue Behavior.   Unpublished Doctoral Dissertation, Northwestern University, 1973.

Wells, H. G. *War of the Worlds.* (1898) London: Heinemann, 1965.

I Conflict in Unstructured Relationships: Stimulus Factors in Conflict

Chapter   1
CONFLICTS WITHOUT RULES

The readings in this section are all instances of social conflict in which there is minimal regulation of the conflict by rules. None of the examples is perfect, for it is hard to find a conflict situation in which the parties have no shared understandings at all, but in all of the examples the ordinary relationships that limit the destructiveness of conflict are largely absent or have broken down.

First Calhoun describes what happens when a population of laboratory rats is crowded together in a confined space. Paradoxically, even more crowding develops as normal behavior sequences break down, leading to what Calhoun calls "a behavioral sink." The continual intense social stimulation disrupts such basic social relationships as mating, care of the young, and contests between males, introducing serious conflicts into all of them with severe consequences for population mortality rates.

Next Mintz describes a somewhat less destructive but perhaps equally important experiment with humans, a laboratory analogue of a panic during a fire, in which each individual's unrestrained pursuit of his own selfish interest results in a disaster for everyone. While Mintz emphasizes that this "panic" may in fact be quite rational, Zimbardo in the next selection focuses on emotional release and temporary loss of identity (deindividuation) as factors leading to apparently random orgies of destructiveness. The objective condition of anonymity is perhaps a special characteristic of unstructured conflict relationships.

Finally, Zawodny discusses what he calls unconventional warfare, in which any form of treachery or violence is acceptable in dealing with an enemy who has been defined as less than human. Conflict in this last instance is an organized form of conflict, unlike those of the earlier readings, and thus is also relevant to our later treatment of normative relationships. But such warfare may still serve as a clear example of conflict in which there are no restraints on the ends or means employed by the antagonists.

A "BEHAVIORAL SINK"

John B. Calhoun

Unexpected results frequently prove of more interest than anticipated ones. Such has proved to be the case in a study I have pursued during the past two years of social behavior of domesticated Norway rats. In this study rats were reared in slightly different environments. In one, the artificial "burrows" provided (Figure 1) consisted of five nesting boxes connected by a system of tunnels in which alternate routes between any pair of boxes were possible. In the other, the five nesting boxes were lined up in a row along a single straight tunnel. It was my original hypothesis that these two different communication systems would alter the social organization of populations developing under their influence. Actually differences were so slight as to be of little importance.

However, certain similar characteristics of these two slightly different types of environments did produce common effects of profound influence upon the lives of the inhabitants. I shall attempt to show how certain characteristics of the environment led to the development of a pathological aggregation or a pathological togetherness of the inhabitants.

Development of such pathological aggregations led to the formulation of the concept of "behavioral sinks." A brief definition of a "behavioral sink" will facilitate the gradual unfolding of the evolution of this concept in the account presented below.

Stationary places whose characteristics are such as to lead to securing a reward by the individual who responds there may be designated as *positive response situations* (PRS). One or more PRS may be distrib-

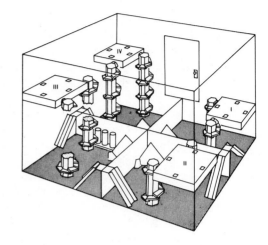

Figure 1. The environment

uted through the environment in such a way that when more than one is present each is sufficiently removed from the others for an animal responding to it to be unable to detect the others. If sufficient animals are present it will frequently happen that one animal will be close to another when they simultaneously respond. Each then serves as a secondary reinforcer for the response executed by the other. In time, each animal redefines the PRS as requiring the presence of another individual. By chance, or under the influence of factors biasing the way the animals move through the environment, some one PRS will have a higher probability of animals arriving at it than will others. The animals will gradually learn that at this particular PRS they will most likely realize their developing redefinition of a PRS which requires the presence of another individual. Thus, more and more animals will gradually increase their frequency of visiting this particular PRS, which may now be designated as the alpha PRS, until very few responses are engaged in at any other PRS. These conditions and processes which culminate in a greater-than-

Source: J. B. Calhoun, "A 'Behavioral Sink,'" from *Roots of Behavior* ed. by E. L. Bliss (New York: Paul Hoeber, 1962), pp. 294–306, 314–315. Reprinted with the permission of the author, E. L. Bliss and The Hafner Publishing Company. Copyright 1968 Hafner Publishing Company.

chance reoccurrence of accentuated aggregations of individuals in the vicinity of the
alpha PRS comprise a behavioral sink.

THE ENVIRONMENT

Each of the four populations included in
this study inhabited a room 10 × 14 × 9
feet (Figure 1). Two-foot high partitions
surmounted by a single-strand cattle fence
electric guard divided each room into four
subareas. Starting from the door into the
room these subareas were designated as Pens
I, II, III, and IV. V-shaped ramps adjacent
to the walls connected Pens I and II, II and
III, III and IV, but not Pens I and IV.
Thus, insofar as locomotor communication
was concerned, the environment was essentially one of four pens in a row. Mounted
on the wall in the corner of each pen was an
artificial "burrow" designed from a study of
many burrows excavated by the author in the
Norway rat's natural habitat. Each had a
9-square-foot surface through which four
openings gave access to a trough or "tunnel"
underneath. Along this tunnel the rats had
access to five 8-inch-square nesting boxes.
Two spiral ramps provided communication
between the floor and each burrow. Three
inches of sawdust covered the floor. A hopper
containing 25 pounds of Purina Chow was
located in the center corner of each pen. An
8-inch high mesh surface provided access to
food around the entire circumference. In
Figure 1 the food hopper may be identified
by its cone-shaped dorsal aspect. Water was
available in each pen from a series of two-
quart chicken water hoppers placed in a row
against one wall. During the winter months,
air temperature was maintained at near 65°F.
During the summer months the forced air
circulating through each room made the
temperature closely parallel that outside the
laboratory. Each room was lighted from
1000 to 2200 o'clock by four 100-watt bulbs
and from 2200 to 1000 o'clock by four additional 100-watt bulbs. A 3 × 5 foot window
on the roof of the room enabled observation.

Strips of paper, which the rats could use
for building nests, were placed periodically
on the floor in the center of each pen.

Burrows in Pens I and II stood at an elevation of 3 feet from the floor while in Pens
III and IV, they were at a 6-foot elevation.
This introduced an "income" factor in the
environment since rats living in Pens I and II
had to expend only half the effort in going to
the floor to secure food and water as did rats
in Pens III and IV.

These environments formed two types,
A and B, which differed only slightly. On
one (the A type), the burrow was as shown
in Figure 1. Its tunnel ran around the underneath side of the 3 × 3 foot surface. In
addition, a tunnel cut across from one side to
the opposite one. In the B type the surface
was 1 foot wide and 9 feet long. Four openings, equally distributed along this surface
gave access to a single straight tunnel underneath, along which there was access to five
nesting boxes. We shall not be concerned
here with the slight differences in behavior
induced by these two types of burrows.

Rooms 1A and 2A contained the A-type
burrows. Rooms 1B and 2B contained the
B-type burrows.

In all other details the attempt was
made to make the environment ideal for the
support of a population of not more than
80 rats. The criteria were based upon a
three-year study of the ecology and social behavior of wild Norway rats.

SUBJECTS

Osborne-Mendel strain domesticated albino rats from the National Institutes of
Health random-bred closed colony formed
the original stock. In each room a pregnant female was confined to each pen by
removing the ramps connecting pens. At 10
days of age litters were mixed so that in a
room each female reared one male and a
female progeny from each of the four litters
in that room. All 32 young in each room
survived to weaning. These 16 males and
16 females in each room were designated as
the *1st tier* of rats. These 1st-tier rats were
born February 10–20, 1958.

At 45 days of age the mothers were removed, and communication between pens

was permitted by placing in the ramps as described above. From the litters born to 1st-tier parents during the latter part of May and the first of June, 1958, four males and four females born in each pen were permitted to survive. These 16 males and 16 females in each room formed the *2nd tier*.

Similarly, a *3rd tier* in each room was formed from young born during the middle of August, 1958. Their parents were either 1st-tier or 2nd-tier rats. Up to the time of weaning of 3rd-tier rats, few deaths of weaned rats had occurred other than those relating to removal of excess young by the investigator.

All rats were individually marked by either metal ear tags or by coded removal of one to three toes. In addition, each rat was marked with two colored dye markings of the pelage which permitted identification from the overhead window.

OBSERVATIONAL PROCEDURES

Each four to eight weeks, or occasionally at shorter intervals, all animals were captured. Each was weighed and measured, and additional data were recorded for each individual: pregnancy, lactation, condition of pelage, number and location of wounds, and various other signs of health. At this time, size, age, and health of litters were noted. Records were kept of complexity of nests and extent of fouling with urine or feces.

Periodically, three to six hours of observation of each room was made through the overhead window. Dictated records, later transcribed for analyses, supplemented tallied records of more frequent and easily categorized behaviors. Emphasis was placed on sexual, aggressive, feeding, drinking, and nest-building behavior as well as movements and place of activity.

A record was maintained of the total amount of water and food consumed in each pen through each consecutive two-week period.

DIFFERENTIAL RESIDENCE

Place of capture during the 12 hours of minimum activity and amount of water consumed both reflect residence. Water con-

Table 1. Frequency of Residence According to Pen of Residence 1st- and 2nd-tier Rats, May–September 1958

	Pen				Total
	I	II	III	IV	
Observed	343	467	331	245	1386
Expected (3:4:3:2 ratio)	347	462	347	232	1388

Contingency $X^2 = 1.57$. p of X^2 between .7 and .5.

sumption as a residence index derives from the typical observed behavior that a rat usually drank just after emerging from a period of inactivity and just prior to reinitiating a period of inactivity. Such drinking usually took place in the pen where the rat slept.

Surveys of all rooms from May through September, 1958, provided 735 capture locations for 1st-tier rats and 651 for 2nd-tier rats (Table 1). Figure 2 shows the mean relative water consumption for a somewhat longer period.

Both sets of data reflect a greater usage of Pen II for residence-related behavior. Pens I and III exhibited nearly equal usage, while Pen IV consistently fell below all the other three pens.

I recognized from the beginning one factor which might contribute to such a differential usage. Use of burrows should be inversely proportional to their distance from the floor. Thus the operation of this factor alone would result in a 2:2:1:1 ratio of usage for Pens I:II:III:IV.

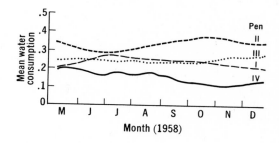

Figure 2. Mean water consumption by pen across Rooms 1A, 2A, 1B, 2B. For each room, every two weeks, the consumption in each pen was converted to the proportion it formed of the total in that room

During the first few months, frequent movement between pens was the rule. In fact, from watching the activity going on as I sat at the window above the room, I developed a fairly strong impression that there was some interval of time after which if a rat continued to be active it just had to get out of the pen it was then in and go elsewhere. The operation of this process leads to a condition where in time there will be only half as many rats in the two end pens as in the two center ones. A rat in an end pen (I and IV) can only go to a center pen (II or III), whereas a rat in a center pen can go to either the adjoining end pen or the other center pen. Thus more rats will leave the end pens than will be compensated by rats entering from center pens. In time this will lead to a 1:2:2:1 ratio of usage of Pens I:II:III:IV.

· · ·

If these two factors which might affect the probability of a rat's selecting a particular pen as a place of residence were of equal importance, their values for each pen might be summated. This produces a 3:4:3:2 ratio of expected usage of Pens I:II:III:IV. In other words the expected probabilities respectively will be: 0.250, 0.333, 0.250, and 0.167.

As may be seen from Table 1 the observed and expected number of rats from each place of capture closely approximate each other. Similarly, water-consumption levels for the four pens vary rather closely about the expected levels. Thus the effort required to reach the burrow from the floor and the departure from one pen to another following the lapse of some average period of time form the most logical, as well as the minimum, assumptions to account for the differential usage of pens as places of residence. For the purpose of considering the development of a behavioral sink, attention must be focused on Pen II with its higher probability of residence.

THE FOOD HOPPERS AS A POSITIVE RESPONSE SITUATION (PRS)

Three types of PRS existed in each pen of each room. They were the water hoppers,

the nesting boxes, and the food hoppers. The former two may be summarily dispensed with as potentially being involved in the development of a behavioral sink on the following grounds. The act of drinking required only a few seconds to complete. Thus the chance of two rats drinking side by side was low. Furthermore, the probability of drinking in a pen being visited, but not the rat's pen of residence, was low. Whereas sleeping was a prolonged response, its major duration involved reduced perceptual awareness. Furthermore, the presence of five nesting boxes in each burrow reduced the opportunity of contact with another rat at the time of initiation of sleep.

Eating typically occurred intermittently during most phases of the rat's travels from one pen to another. Securing sufficient food to satiate the rat's hunger required a continuous effort of up to several minutes. The necessity of gnawing through the wire mesh of the hopper called for this greater effort. Thus when one rat was eating there was a fair chance that another rat might join it with an ensuing period of eating side by side.

With this background we may now turn our attention to the detailed history of food consumption (Fig. 3) in Room 2B. The history of the four rooms was somewhat different, but 2B closely reflected the typical changes which occurred in all the rooms.

Initially, in marked contrast to the more uniform distribution of sleeping and drinking, eating was almost entirely concentrated in Pen II. Through the next three

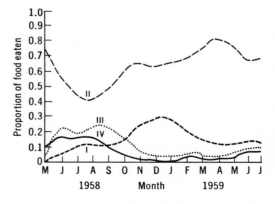

Figure 3. Food consumption, Room 2B. Roman numerals refer to pens

months, eating in Pen II declined but never quite reached the level of 0.333 anticipated on the basis of the forces governing probability of determining residence.

Initial concentration of eating in one of the four pens has been interpreted as resulting from a "litter-association factor." During nursing each rat gains contact with one or more of its litter mates. Presumably by the time of weaning each rat has defined the food acquisition behavior as requiring the presence of another individual. Behavior of recently weaned rats supports this notion. Most frequently several young rats feed simultaneously, and furthermore, they crowd their mouths together as if attempting to gnaw at the same piece of food—this despite the fact that most of the extensive feeding surface remains bare of any rats eating.

Nearly immediately following insertion of the ramps between pens the young rats concentrated all of their feeding in the one pen where, by the operation of factors previously discussed, they were most likely to find their conditioned definition of a feeding PRS. The pens thus selected were 1AIII, 2AII, 2BII, and 1BII. That Pen III might occasionally be selected is not surprising in view of the indeterminancy of the system. However, the probability of Pen IV's ever becoming a major pen of feeding is rather remote. For the rats to maintain their concentrated eating in one pen each rat must experience frequent reinforcements in the form of proximity with another while eating. Obviously such frequency was not sufficient for there ensued a period of continuous decline in amount of eating in the pen originally selected by the weanling 1st-tier rats.

By the end of June, 1958, the 32 2nd-tier rats were weaned, and by mid-September the 32 3rd-tier rats joined the others in free-feeding acts. The same forces affecting residence of the 1st tier also applied to those two younger tiers. On the average, one-third of the rats lived in Pen II. However, the pen where young rats were most likely to find other rats eating was the one where their elders were still concentrating their eating. Thus, sometime between June and September sufficient numbers of rats were present to re-

initiate the social definition of the feeding PRS among the older rats and retard its loss among the younger rats. Gradually more rats came to 2BII to feed and simultaneously reduced their eating elsewhere. A common observation was that a rat resident in Pen IV would go down to the floor, perhaps drink, and then cross over and through Pen III to Pen II before engaging in eating.

This latter phenomenon facilitated the development of territoriality. In each pen there were usually one or more very aggressive males who became active later than their subordinates. By the time the dominant male in Pen IV became active he would likely find himself alone. As a subordinate rat living in Pen IV started back over the ramp connecting Pens III and IV after a period of eating in Pen II, he was likely to run into the dominant Pen-IV male as he was starting on his trip to Pen II to eat. These circumstances were ideal for the subordinate rat's associating departure from Pen IV with escape from the dominant male there. Without himself being completely responsible, the dominant male in Pen IV also became territorial. In time the process extended to Pen III so that he was left with a harem of 20 females.

This forms a circular series of events in which the development of the food hopper in Pen II as an alpha PRS facilitated development of a territorial male. In turn, the territoriality of this male increased the effectiveness of the food hopper in Pen II as an alpha PRS. All this time Pen II and, in particular, the immediate environs of its food hopper had developed all the attributes of what I now term a "behavioral sink."

An important facet of this sink is the relative numbers of individuals so involved in comparison with the group size typical of the species. In an unpublished extensive study of wild Norway rats the average group size was 11 individuals. Yet here in proximity to the alpha feeding PRS the size commonly exceeded this figure. Further discussion of this topic will be presented further on in this paper.

Before turning to consequences of the behavioral sink, a brief comment regarding the other three rooms is in order. In Rooms 1A and 2A, territorial males with associated harems developed in Pen I. As was the case for the pens dominated by the territorial males in Room 2B, these pens could also be designated as "brood pens" since here the females were markedly successful in rearing young in comparison to females residing elsewhere. Room 1B exhibited a very odd history. Following the accidental death by suffocation of seven 1st-tier male residents in Pen II in June, 1958, the major pen of feeding shifted from Pen II to Pen III. But Pen III never gained real ascendency. In fact during the last few months there developed a marked oscillation in relative amount of feeding in each of the four pens. All abnormal behaviors developing in the other rooms became even more accentuated here.

NORMAL BEHAVIOR

Abnormal behavior associated with the development of a behavioral sink must be viewed against the normal. I use the term *behavior* in the following sense. It includes both a perceptual and a motor phase. Sustained attention to one stimulus characterizes the perceptual phase. Similarly, a sustained period of repeating a specific response characterizes the motor phase. Higher levels of behavior require sustained attention toward an object or situation whose identification involves integration of several distinct cues or stimuli. In the motor phase there must be expressed an orderly sequence of discrete but different acts.

The following normal behavior characterized most 1st- and 2nd-tier rats of reproductive age through September, 1958. They exemplify my definition of normal behavior.

NEST BUILDING

Rats of both sexes build nests, but this behavior becomes intensified by females just preceding and just following parturition. If a rat picks up a strip of paper from the floor and carries it up into a nesting box, it will most likely make several such trips in close succession before engaging in an unrelated behavior. Completion of a nest may require several nest-building behaviors such as the one described. The end product forms a fluffy intermeshed mass of paper strips surrounding a deep cuplike depression, and frequently the mesh work extends dorsally over the cup to form a hood.

TRANSPORT OF YOUNG

This behavior characterizes females having young under 15 days of age. When such a female, while with her young, is disturbed by either the experimenter or by an invading strange rat, she customarily transports the entire litter from one place to another. Such a transport is not interrupted by any other behavior until the entire litter has been moved to the same place.

EATING

As described previously the behavior of eating involves quite a long series of gnawings at the surface of the hopper.

SEXUAL BEHAVIOR

For the present discussion, emphasis will be placed upon the male's behavior. Its culmination involves mounting an appropriate receptive female. However, it includes a passive perceptual phase and an active pursuit phase. In the latter, following the withdrawal of a receptive female into a burrow, the male follows her to the burrow opening but does not pursue her into the burrow. He waits there quietly or with intermittent movements back and forth with his head protruding into the burrow opening. The full sexual dance characteristics of wild Norway rats in their natural habitat did not develop fully on the artificial burrows in the absence of the conical mound of dirt. Eventually the fully receptive female emerges and is pursued by the male until he overtakes her. The chase culminates in intromission as the male mounts the receptive female while holding her with his teeth so gently by the scruff of her neck as not to cut the skin. Simultaneously he exhibits pelvic thrusting as she exhibits lordosis.

The passive sexual behavior is perceptual, involving the integration of a graded set of cues. The male must perceive that the sexual object is an adult, that it is a female, and that it is a receptive female. This formulation of a passive perceptual sexual behavior is an inference derived from the development of inability to select appropriate sex partners as discussed below.

AGGRESSIVE BEHAVIOR

Males more frequently than females inflict wounds on other rats, usually other adult males. I shall not attempt here to describe the full sequence of related acts which culminates in one rat's biting another. Suffice it to say that there arises a stage in the conflict when one rat turns and flees. At this moment the dominant member frequently bites the fleeing rat on its posterior dorsal aspect. Wounds rarely were noted on other parts of the body preceding development of the behavioral sink. Wounds typically do not exceed 5 mm. in length and rarely extend through the skin.

ABNORMAL BEHAVIOR

Beginning in September, 1958, and continuing to a climax by April, 1959, these behaviors markedly changed in character. The change was gradual both in terms of degree of change characterizing any one individual and with reference to the number of individuals exhibiting more marked abnormality of behavior. This period started with the weaning of the 3rd tier and continued to their full adulthood at 8 to 9 months of age. The average number of 1st-to 3rd-tier adults per room in February, 1959, was 77.

NEST BUILDING

Failure to organize paper strips taken into the nesting boxes formed the first indicator of disruption of this behavior. Although many strips were transported they were just left in a pile and trampled into a flat pad with little sign of cup formation. Then fewer and fewer strips reached the nesting box. Frequently a rat would take a single strip, and somewhere along the way it would drop the strip and then engage in some other behavior. In the extreme state of disruption, characterizing at least all major pens of feeding, the nesting material would remain in the center of the room for days. Even when females delivered litters in the burrow in the major pen of eating, no nest was formed; the young were merely left on the bare sawdust periodically placed in every box by the experimenter.

TRANSPORT OF YOUNG

In the normal condition when females had litters in separate boxes, the litters were maintained intact with no mixing. As the behavioral sink developed, litters became more and more mixed. When only one litter was present in a burrow the young frequently became scattered among several boxes. This resulted from the female's interrupting the transport behavior by some other behavior. The consequence of a reinitiation of transport resulted in even greater scattering because the second terminus of transport was likely to be some nesting box other than the first. In the extreme state of disruption the terminus of transport was undirected. The mothers would take a pup out of the burrow and start toward the floor with it. Anywhere along the way or any place on the floor the mother would drop the pup. Such pups were rarely ever retrieved. They eventually died where dropped and then were eaten by other rats.

EATING

Unfortunately, no measures of disruption of this behavior were made. I say unfortunate because, as discussed below, alteration of the duration of this behavior—that is, shortening it—should be the first behavior disrupted. See the discussion for elaboration of this point.

SEXUAL BEHAVIOR

The first sign of disruption involved more frequent attention to and attempts at mounting females who indicated no sign of being receptive. Later, males mounted other males, and a few of these, particularly 3rd-tier males, seemed to prefer other males as sexual partners. In the final phase, young rats, even recently weaned ones of both sexes, were mounted. Such abnormality may best be termed *pansexuality*. In essence, the perceptual behavioral phase of recognition of a sexual partner became so disrupted that fewer and fewer elements of the perceptual pattern were requisite for shifting from the perceptual phase of recognition of sex partners to the active behavioral phase of pursuit, mounting, and pelvic thrusting. Pursuit also became altered. With increasing frequency males who followed a receptive female to the burrow also followed her into and through the burrow. Such intrusion produced further disturbance to lactating females and thus aggravated the already disturbed transport behavior. Another element of disruption of normal sexual behavior involved the scruff-of-the-neck biting act during mounting. As the behavioral sink became accentuated in its influence, many females following their period of receptivity were characterized by literally dozens of nicks about the dorsal aspect of the neck. Males subjected to homosexual advances exhibited similar wounds, but fewer in number.

AGGRESSIVE BEHAVIOR

Three abnormal aggressive acts developed as the behavioral sink became established. The first of these was tail biting. A peculiarity of this behavior was that males alone exhibited tail biting insofar as I could determine. Furthermore, the population became divided into tail biters and those who were bitten on the tail. The latter category included both sexes. At times it was impossible to enter a room without observing fresh blood splattered about the room from tail wounds. A rat exhibiting tail biting would frequently just walk up to another and clamp down on its tail. The biting rat would not loosen its grasp until the bitten rat had pulled loose. This frequently resulted in major breaks or actual severance of the tail.

The population in each room passed through this phase of tail biting of adults by other adults. Its duration varied from one to three months following the peak development of the behavioral sink. Young weaned during this period received similar treatment from adult biters, although in earlier, more normal states no tail wounds were inflicted on young rats and only rarely were body wounds received until well after sexual maturity. The population in Room 1A was allowed to survive beyond July, 1959, when rats living in the other three rooms were autopsied. A sixth tier was allowed to survive to Room 1A until many of them had reached sexual maturity. And yet from weaning to sexual maturity most of these 6th-tier young received several tail bites despite the fact that adults were rarely any longer receiving such wounds. It is difficult to escape the conclusion that the behavior of bitten rats in some way influences the probability of attack by biters. In some way the rats who are subject to being bitten on the tail alter their behavior in such a way as to avoid elicitation of attack by biters. That the biters do not alter their behavior is evinced by the fact that young rats which have not had the opportunity to learn the appropriate alteration to their behavior are attacked by the biters.

The basis of this behavior has so far eluded me. From several very incomplete lines of evidence presently available I can only say that I suspect that tail biting derives from a displacement of eating behavior rather than stemming from modification of aggressive behavior.

Inflicting small nicks about the shoulders during sexual mounts becomes an aggressive behavior insofar as the recipient is concerned. The third aberration takes the form of slashing attacks. Gashes ranging from 10 to 30 mm. may be received by either sex on any portion of the body. The depth of such wounds frequently extend down into the muscles or through the abdominal wall.

CHANGES IN REPRODUCTIVE PHENOMENA

A general survey of all the records supports the conclusion that there was a reduction in conception or at least a reduction in pregnancies continued to the age when embryos could be detected by palpation. However, as yet no detailed analysis has been prepared. Also, pregnant females exhibited difficulty in continuing pregnancy to term or in delivering full-term young. Both phenomena were noted only after the behavioral sink began developing. Several females were found near term lying on the floor with dark bloody fluid exuding from the vagina. I never found any evidence that these females delivered. One died while I watched her from the overhead observation window. She was immediately autopsied. Extensive dark hemorrhagic areas in the uterus suggested that the fetuses died before the mother. Another apparently full-term female was autopsied shortly after death and found to contain several partially resorbed full-term embryos. Some of these had been released into the abdominal cavity following rupture of the uterus.

Upon palpation for pregnancy, more and more females were recorded as containing large hard masses in the abdomen. These sometimes reached a diameter of 90 mm. Usually death occurred before attainment of such size. A group of females with these abdominal masses were autopsied. The enlargements proved to be thick-walled dilatations of the uterus. Usually these dilatations contained a purulent mass. Partially decom-posed fetuses were found in some of the rats in which these dilatations were still relatively small.

Eleven females with these masses, some from each of the three tiers, were autopsied by Dr. Katherine C. Snell of the National Cancer Institute. The general picture of the uterus was one of severe chronic suppurative endometritis, myometritis, and peritonitis with extension of the process to the fallopian tubule and ovary on one or both sides. Areas of focal inflammation of slight to moderate degree occurred in all kidneys.

The adrenal glands were normal in rats from the 3rd tier. Among 1st-tier rats all showed some degree of congestion of the adrenal glands with dilated vascular spaces in the cortex filled with red blood cells or fibrin or both. The adrenal of one 2nd-tier rat was normal. The other four 2nd-tier rats showed marked congestion of the reticular and fasicular zones of the cortex with dilated vessels filled with red blood cells, precipitated fibrin, or both.

Some of these 11 rats, as well as 4 others autopsied because of obvious mammary tumors, showed the following pathologic lesions in one or more females: (1) fibromyoma of a uterine horn; (2) fibrosarcoma of the mammary gland; (3) fibroadenoma of the mammary gland; (4) angiomatous adenoma of the adrenal cortex; (5) granulomas of the liver; (6) papillary cyst of the thyroid.

One 2nd-tier female was autopsied because a few days previously she was noted to be apparently near term, but she had considerable dark blood about the vagina. Upon autopsy the uterus was found to contain five healthy-appearing fetuses, four in the right horn and one in the left. The myometrium of the corpus and the cervix of this rat were inflamed, and the lumen of the horn near the cervix contained clotted blood that may have been associated with premature separation of the placenta.

From my own observations and the brief synopsis of Dr. Snell's findings, it appears that concomitant with the development of the behavioral sink females experienced difficulty in carrying young to term or if they carried to term they were sometimes unable to deliver.

The extent to which the uterine infections preceded or followed failure to deliver is unknown.

Presence of tumors was from a highly selected sample. No conclusion is warranted concerning the influence of behavior upon incidence of the tumors. Dr. Snell pointed out another complicating factor. First-tier rats were marked with a black hair dye. Second-tier rats were marked with a red stamp-pad ink, and third-tier rats were marked with a combination of picric acid and a green oscillograph pen ink. Known or suspected constituents of these dyes are known to be absorbed through the skin, to be toxic, and some possibly carcinogenic. That these dyes might have had some effect upon reproductive success and even upon behavior cannot be ruled out on the basis of present data. Evidence will be cited below why I suspect they were unimportant in producing abnormal behavior or in altering reproductive success.

MORTALITY IN FEMALES

By June, 1959, the populations in Rooms 1A, 2A and 2B had become predominately male in composition. Many females were known to have died following symptoms indicating complications with pregnancy or delivery. Others were too far decomposed when found dead to warrant autopsy. Comparative mortality for males and females to June, 1959 is shown in Table 2. Comparisons are based upon an original N of 48 rats in each of the six tier and sex categories.

Second-tier females despite their younger age experienced a much higher risk of death than did their older 1st-tier associates. Apparently attainment of sexual maturity under conditions of a developing behavioral sink predisposes rats to complications of pregnancy more acutely than among rats who matured in a more placid environment.

The population in Room 1A was allowed to survive for several months beyond the termination of the populations in the other three rooms during July, 1959. Between June and September, 1959, only 0.140 of the

Table 2. Mortality

Tier	Months of Age, June, 1959	Proportion Dead by June, 1959 Males	Females	Females Dying for Each Male Dying
1st	15.5	.187	.582	3.1
2nd	12.0	.104	.562	5.4
3rd	9.5	.061	.125	2.1

43 males alive in June died. In contrast 0.375 of the 32 females alive in June died.

* * *

SUMMARY

Populations of domesticated albino rats were allowed to develop in rooms such that each population had access to four similar pens, each 5 × 7 feet. Ramps over adjacent pens formed a linear communication system such that there were two end pens and two center pens. In one end pen and its adjoining center pen artificial "burrows" were placed on the wall 3 feet above the floor. In the other two pens these burrows were 6 feet above the floor.

The endedness of the row of four pens tended to make twice as many rats select the two central pens as places of living as selected the two end pens. On the other hand, the lower elevation of the burrows tended to make twice as many rats select the two pens on one end of the series as places of habitation as selected the two pens on the other end of the series. Operating together, these two biasing factors formed a theoretical biasing residence ratio of 3:4:3:2 along the series of four pens. Observed residence closely approximated the theoretical.

A large food hopper was located on the floor of each pen. Such spatially restricted structures are defined as *positive response situations*. Since more rats lived in one pen than in any of the other three, the chances were greatest there that when one rat was eating another would come and eat beside it. Once the number of rats in a room increased above a certain level, this frequency of contact while eating increased sufficiently that the rats developed a new definition of the feeding situation to include the presence of another rat. Gradually eating in the other three pens declined until 60–80 per cent of all food consumption was in this one of the four pens.

The development of this atypical aggregation under the influence of the several conditions and processes involved forms what I have termed a *behavioral sink*.

Concomitant with its development many abnormal behaviors and disturbances of reproduction began to appear. Females experienced difficulty in carrying fetuses to term, and if they carried to term they were sometimes unable to deliver young. Death frequently occurred at this time. If they survived, one region of the uterus enlarged until it was sometimes as large as the former size of the rat. Such affected rats always died. Females developed a mortality rate 3.5 times that for males.

On the behavioral side, males developed a pansexuality in which they would mount other rats regardless of their age, sex, or receptivity. Infliction of wounds during mounting developed. An abnormal response of biting the tails of other rats also developed. Nest-building behavior became completely disrupted. Transport of young by lactating rats became so disorganized that young became so scattered that they were no longer nursed.

A theoretical model for the origin of these abnormal behaviors is proposed. Briefly it points to reasons why the duration of each feeding behavior should become shortened. This change in rhythm of eating causes other behaviors to shorten with the end result that the behavior becomes inappropriate or incomplete. Thus the development of a behavioral sink leads to a state of sustained inordinate aggregation which may be called "pathological togetherness."

NON-ADAPTIVE GROUP BEHAVIOR

Alexander Mintz

THEORETICAL CONSIDERATIONS

It is common knowledge that groups of people frequently behave in a way which leads to disastrous consequences not desired or anticipated by the members of the group. At theater fires, people often block the exits by pushing, so that individuals are burned or

trampled. Since it normally takes only a few minutes for a theater to be emptied the strikingly non-adaptive character of this behavior is obvious.

In the explanations for the occurrence of such behavior offered by social psychologists, intense emotional excitement resulting from mutual facilitation (or "contagion" or "suggestion") and leading to interference with thinking, adaptive behavior, and the operation of moral codes, has tended to be viewed as the decisive factor. Explanations of this general type can be found in numerous textbooks on social psychology, from that by Ross (21) to those by Britt (3), Vaughn

Source: A. Mintz, "Non-Adaptive Group Behavior," *Journal of Abnormal and Social Psychology*, Vol. 46, 1951, pp. 150–159. Copyright 1951 by The American Psychological Association and reprinted by permission.

(27), and Young (31). Ultimately they stem from the theories of the nature of crowd behavior of Le Bon (12), who has been an extremely influential figure in the thinking on social issues of the past fifty years. He has been an important ideological ancestor of fascism[1] and nazism; thus Hitler's ideas on social psychology as expressed in *Mein Kampf* closely resemble those of Le Bon. Le Bon's theories embodied features which were severely criticized by a number of psychologists. In speaking of emotional interaction between members of a group leading to personality alterations, he postulated the emergence of a group mind based on collective racial unconscious tendencies. These notions of a group mind and racial unconscious were rejected by most psychologists. Nevertheless, his critics often accepted the more essential features of his theory, and crowd membership is often viewed as having an essentially brutalizing effect on people as a result of allegedly regressive, non-adaptive consequences of intense emotion generated by social facilitation.

The explanations of the non-adaptive behavior in panics in terms of emotional excitement are related to a tendency still prevalent in modern psychology to view all emotion as essentially superfluous and even harmful. For a number of years, many textbooks defined emotion as "disorganized response" and the like. In some textbooks, emotion was treated mainly as something to be controlled. Until quite recently, many books of child rearing contained advice designed to weaken the emotional intimacy between parent and child (28). Actually, a distrust of emotion has been endemic in Western thought ever since the days of Stoic philosophy. In recent years, however, another point of view has tended to emerge. The desirable features of emotional spontaneity have been emphasized by many psychotherapists for a number of years and there are psychoanalysts who characterize the cure in

psychotherapy as a process of emotional liberation. More recently, the notion that emotion is essentially non-adaptive has been severely criticized in theoretical psychology (14), and a lively controversy about the question appears to be in progress.

Material will be presented in this paper suggesting that violent emotional excitement is not the decisive factor[2] in the non-adaptive behavior of people in panics and related situations. Instead, it appears to be possible to explain the non-adaptive character of such behavior in terms of their perception of the situation and their expectation of what is likely to happen. In recent times, a number of psychologists have tended to interpret features of human behavior in terms of the phenomenal properties of the situation in which it occurs. Thus Katona reported several studies of the role of the economic situation as experienced by consumers and of their expectations in their economic behavior (7, 8). S. Asch and others explained the effects on value judgment, commonly attributed to prestige suggestion, in terms of the additional cognitive background of the material to be judged provided by the supposedly prestige-loaded items (1, 2). G. Murphy (19) attempted to make the behavior of a foreign government understandable in terms of the political situation as it must be perceived by its members. Wertheimer (29) and his collaborator, E. Levy (15), discussed a number of cases of mental disorder as understandable in terms of the phenomenal properties of their phenomenal environment. As a general postulate, the congruence between the organization of our perception, thought, and expectation on one hand, and our motivation, valuation, and action on the other hand, has been discussed extensively by Koffka (10), Tolman (26), Rogers, Snygg and Combs (25), Cantril (4), Lewin (17), Krech and Crutchfield (11), and others. The theoretical approaches just mentioned are by no means entirely identical; in some of them the role of ego factors and action potentialities is stressed more than in others (e.g., by Cantril

---

[1] In his last book, Le Bon (13) quotes an interview with Mussolini in which the latter stated that he read *The Crowd* many times and that he often refers to it.

---

[2] Its existence is not denied.

as contrasted with the Gestalt group), but in all of them behavior is viewed as understandable in terms of the phenomenal world.

What are the reasonable expectations of people at a theater fire or in similar circumstances in which a panic is apt to develop? Situations of this type tend to have a characteristically unstable reward structure, which has been generally overlooked by social scientists as a factor in panics. Cooperative behavior is required for the common good but has very different consequences for the individual depending on the behavior of others. Thus at a theater fire, if everyone leaves in an orderly manner, everybody is safe, and an individual waiting for his turn is not sacrificing his interests. But, if the cooperative pattern of behavior is disturbed, the usual advice, "Keep your head, don't push, wait for your turn, and you will be safe," ceases to be valid. If the exits are blocked, the person following this advice is likely to be burned to death. In other words, if everybody cooperates, there is no conflict between the needs of the individual and those of the group. However, the situation changes completely as soon as a minority of people cease to cooperate. A conflict between the needs of the group and the selfish needs of the individual then arises. An individual who recognizes this state of things and who wants to benefit the group must sacrifice his own selfish needs.

It is suggested here that it is chiefly the reward structure of the situations which is responsible for non-adaptive behavior of groups at theater fires and similar situations. People are likely to recognize the threats to themselves, as they appear, and behave accordingly. These situations may be compared to states of unstable equilibrium in mechanics; a cone balanced on its tip is not likely to remain in this position a long time because a slight initial displacement of its center of gravity allows the force of gravity to make it fall all the way. Similarly, cooperative behavior at a theater fire is likely to deteriorate progressively as soon as an initial disturbance occurs. If a few individuals begin to push, the others are apt to recognize that their interests are threatened; they can expect to win through to their individual rewards only by pressing their personal advantages at the group's expense. Many of them react accordingly, a vicious circle is set up, and the disturbance spreads. Competitive behavior (pushing and fighting) may result, as at theater fires, or the group may disperse as in military panics. There is another factor which makes for further disintegration. As the behavior of the group becomes increasingly disorderly, the amount of noise is apt to increase, and communication may then become so difficult that no plan for restoring order can emerge.

This interpretation is almost the reverse of the conventional ones which ascribe non-adaptive group behavior to emotional facilitation and to the supposed alterations of personality in group situations.

The existence of mutual emotional facilitation is not denied; its operation can be readily observed, for example, in college students during final examinations, or in audiences at sports events etc. However, it is not believed that emotional excitement as such is responsible for non-adaptive group behavior. There are many situations in which intense emotional excitement is the rule, and yet no non-adaptive group behavior appears. Thus it has been reported that intense fear is practically universally present in soldiers about to go into battle and yet no panic need develop. Similarly, participants in an athletic contest are apt to be so emotionally excited that vomiting is common; no markedly non-adaptive group behavior appears to develop as a result of this kind of intense excitement.

The assumption of personality alterations of people due to crowd membership appears to be entirely unsubstantiated in the case of panics. On the contrary, the competitive behavior or dispersal occurring in panics suggests that group cohesion disappears and that people begin to behave purely as individuals in accordance with their selfish needs.[3] Rather similarly Freud has explained certain types of panics in terms of the disappearance

---

[3] The writer is indebted to Dr. M. Scheerer for pointing out this inference from the suggested theory.

of the libidinal ties between individuals (5, pp. 45–48).

As a first step towards the verification of the proposed theory, a set of laboratory experiments was devised. It was thought that if the theory is correct it should be possible to illustrate its functioning in the laboratory. If not substantiated by laboratory findings, the theory would have to be discarded.

EXPERIMENTAL DESIGN

The experiments were conducted with groups of people, 15 to 21 subjects in each group. The subjects had the task of pulling cones out of a glass bottle; each subject was given a piece of string to which a cone was attached. Cooperation on the part of the subjects was required if the cones were to come out; the physical setup made it easy for "traffic jams" of cones to appear at the bottle neck. Only one cone could come out at a time; even a near-tie between two cones at the bottle neck prevented both from coming out because the narrow apex of the second cone, wedged into the bottle neck, blocked the path for the wide base of the cone ahead of it. The cones had to arrive at the bottle neck in order, one at a time.

EXPERIMENTAL SITUATIONS

1. One of the experimental setups was designed to show that it was possible to produce disorganized, uncooperative, non-adaptive group behavior resulting in "traffic jams" by duplicating the essential features of panic-producing situations, as explained in the theoretical section of this paper. The experimental situation was represented to the subjects as a game in which each participant could win or lose money. A subject could win or lose depending on how successful he was in pulling out his cone. Success was defined in terms of arbitrary time limits in some experiments. In other experiments water was made to flow into the bottle through a spout near the bottom and the subject was success-

ful if his cone came out of the bottle untouched by the water. Inasmuch as the rewards and fines were offered to individuals, depending on what would happen to their particular cones, it was thought that the cooperative pattern of behavior, required for group success, would be easily disrupted; a momentary "traffic jam" at the bottleneck would be perceived by some of the subjects as threatening them with loss in the game as a result of the anticipated failure of cooperative behavior. These subjects would be tempted to save themselves from the loss by pulling out of turn. Some of them would probably do so, and thus the situation could be expected rapidly to deteriorate after an initial disturbance occurred.

In order that subjects who recognized that full success was out of their reach should not stop trying, intermediate steps between full success and full failure were announced. The details and the amounts of rewards and fines are summarized in the table of results.[4] The monetary rewards and fines were very small, the rewards for full success ranging from 10 to 25 cents, the fines for full failure from 1 to 10 cents. The very small fines were decided upon because it was intended to show that the characteristically inefficient, non-adaptive features of group behavior such as occurs in panics can be reproduced in a situation in which there was no opportunity for fear. It was not thought that the small rewards and fines were likely to constitute real financial incentives for college students. They were introduced so as to emphasize the nature of the experimental situation as a game in which individuals could win or lose.

2. In the contrasting experimental setups there were no individual rewards or fines, and there was no flow of water except for a

---

[4] The appendix, including a detailed table of the data from each experiment, has been deposited with the American Documentation Institute to reduce printing costs. For the six pages of the appendix, order Document 2815 from American Documentation Institute, 1719 N Street, N.W., Washington 6, D.C., remitting $0.50 for microfilm (images 1 inch high on standard 35 mm. motion picture film) or $0.60 for photocopies (6 x 8 inches) readable without optical aid.

few control experiments. The experiments were described as attempts to measure the ability of groups of people to behave cooperatively. Good performances of other groups were quoted. It was expected that under these conditions no "traffic jams" would develop. Subjects had no motivation to disregard any plan that might be devised by the group; the only incentive offered was membership in a group of people who were going to show their ability to cooperate effectively with each other.[5] Thus the reward structure was the principal experimental variable studied in these two experimental situations.

3. Another variable investigated was the excitement built up by mutual facilitation. In a number of "no-reward" experiments several subjects were asked to act as accomplices. They were secretly instructed before the experiment began to scream, behave excitedly, swear, and make as much noise as possible. To limit their influence to emotional facilitation they were asked not to give specific bad advice nor to disturb the workings of any plan the group might decide upon. It was expected that the added emotional excitement, which is the major factor in Le Bon's and similar theories of panics, would not have much effect on the results.

4. In certain of the reward-and-fine experiments an attempt was made to minimize the opportunities for mutual emotional facilitation by largely preventing the subjects from seeing each other. This was accomplished by a circular screen with holes for eyes and arms and with vertical partitions on the outside, placed around the glass bottle. Each subject stood in an individual "stall" hiding him from his neighbors; he saw the bottle standing on the floor through the eye hole; only his arm and eyes could be seen by the other subjects, and the eyes were not likely to be seen because the subjects were mainly looking at the bottle tied to the floor. In order to pre-

vent excited screams, the subjects were asked to remain silent after the experiment began, which request was largely complied with. It was expected that the results would be essentially the same as those in the other reward-and-fine experiments.

5. A third variable which was introduced in a few of the experiments was interference with the opportunity to arrive at a plan of action. In most of the experiments the subjects were not prevented from conducting preliminary discussions; in almost all instances either they started such a discussion immediately or asked for permission to do so, which was given. Only twice did a group fail to discuss and agree upon a plan when discussion was not explicitly forbidden. On the other hand, in two of the reward-and-fine experiments conducted early in the study the subjects were forbidden to talk to each other both before and during the experiment; in one reward-and-fine experiment conducted immediately after three no-reward experiments with the same group, the subjects were prevented from having a preliminary discussion so that no plan could be agreed upon beforehand, but were allowed to talk during the experiment.

APPARATUS AND PROCEDURE

Figure 1 gives the shapes and dimensions of the cones and of the bottle and shows where the pieces of string were attached. The cones were made of wood in the early experiments. Later, aluminum cones were substituted because the wooden one tended to become tightly forced into the bottle neck and had to be loosened by hand (which was done promptly by the experimenter). In the experiments with the aluminum cones the glass bottle had too large an opening, which was remedied by the insertion of a cylinder with a 1-inch hole bored through it. This cylinder, made of aluminum, had rubber tape wound on the outside. It was forced tightly into the bottle neck and was tied down with wire. In addition to cutting down the opening of the bottle to the desired diameter, it also protected the glass from the impact of

---

[5] The need to belong has been particularly emphasized as an important motive, among others, by E. Fromm and M. Sherif. The important role which group membership plays in industry has been investigated particularly in the Hawthorne studies.

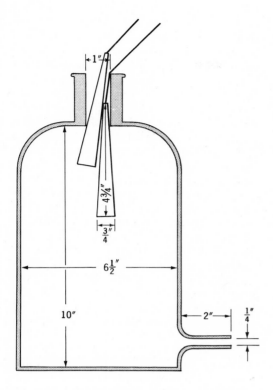

Figure 1. Cross-section of the glass bottle with two cones shown blocking the bottle neck (Main dimensions of the equipment are given.)

the aluminum cones. A sponge rubber pad was cemented to the bottom of the glass bottle. A rubber tube could be attached to the spout and lead either to a water faucet or to another similar bottle placed high up.

The screen was made of corrugated cardboard. Two strips 23.5 feet in length were cut off a 3-foot-wide roll and glued together, so that a strip 6 feet wide resulted. The ends of the strip could be brought together and the strip could be made to stand on edge in the shape of a cylinder around the bottle. Pieces of corrugated cardboard, 3 feet by 1 foot, were attached to the screen at intervals of 1 foot 3 inches, subdividing the space immediately around the screen into individual stalls. The rectangular eye holes cut in each stall were 1.5 inches high, 5 inches wide; their bottom was 4 feet 8 inches above the ground; the roughly circular arm holes were about 5 inches in diameter and 3 feet 1.5 inches from

the ground, near the right hand edges of the stalls. There were 18 stalls altogether.

In putting the cones into the bottle, care was taken to prevent the tangling of strings; as an added precaution, the fishing line used as string was waxed in later experiments. In the early experiments the bottle was tied to the legs of a table on which it was placed. In the later experiments it was placed on the floor and tied to nails driven into the floor like tent stakes.

The instructions were not rigidly standardized. The rewards were always larger than the fines, ranging from 10 to 25 cents in different experiments. The fines ranged from 1 to 10 cents. Examples of the two main types of instructions and other details of the experimental procedures follow:

1. A *Reward-and-Fine Experiment.* "I need volunteers for an experiment which is set up as a game in which you can win up to a quarter or lose up to 2 cents [or 5 or 10 cents as the case may have been]." Then, after the volunteers (sometimes after some urging) assembled: "As I said, this is going to be like a game. Each of you will receive a cone with an attached piece of string. All cones will be placed into the bottle. The object of the game is to get your cone out before it gets wet. You may start pulling when I give the signal, 'ready-go!' but only one cone can come out at a time. If two get into the bottle neck, neither comes out (demonstration). Simultaneously, I shall start water flowing into the bottle. If your cone comes out dry you get a quarter. If less than a third of it is wet, you get nothing; if more than a third but less than two-thirds of it gets wet, you pay a penny fine. If the cone is more than two-thirds wet, you pay a two-cent fine. The fines will be contributed to the Student Council." Then the students were asked to put their cones in the bottle. While they were doing it, a discussion of a plan for action generally started and was not interfered with by the experimenter.

The signal to begin was given after an agreement was reached by the subjects.

When in doubt, the experimenter asked the group whether they were ready.

2. *A No-Reward Experiment.* "This is going to be an experiment in which your ability to cooperate with each other will be measured. I need volunteers." Then, after the subjects assembled around the bottle, the procedure continued exactly as in the reward-and-fine experiments except that no rewards were offered, the rubber tube was not attached, and no reference to water was made. Instead, after the possibility of "traffic jams" was demonstrated, the experimenter said: "In spite of the smallness of the opening, a group of students from the University of Nevada succeeded in cooperating with each other so well that they got all their cones out in 10.5 seconds. See if you can do as well as the Westerners!"

RESULTS

The conditions and results of all of the experiments conducted so far are indicated in a table in an appendix.[6] Forty-two experiments with 26 groups of subjects were performed altogether, including some preliminary and control experiments conducted to investigate potential sources of error. In the table each experiment is identified by a code symbol consisting of letters and a number.

One experiment (R1) was conducted before the procedure was fully developed; there were no fines and only one reward level was announced. No "traffic jam" resulted.

There were 16 experiments with rewards and fines. In three of them (RF1 to RF3) discussion was interfered with before the experiment, so that the subjects had no opportunity to devise a plan of action. In all three experiments "traffic jams" developed. In only one of them did the subjects succeed in pulling *any* cones out of the bottle—two cones out of 19 in 40 seconds; these same subjects had successfully pulled out *all* cones

in 18.6 seconds and 23 seconds in two immediately preceding trials in which there had been no rewards and in which they had had the opportunity to agree upon a plan of action.

In the other 13 reward-and-fine experiments (RF4 to RF16) discussion was not interfered with. In eight of these experiments (RF4 to RF6, RF9, RF10, RF12, RF13, and RF16) there were serious "traffic-jams," the large majority of the cones failing to be pulled out of the bottle within times ranging from one to approximately two minutes. In another experiment almost half of the cones were in the bottle after 1 minute (RF15). In two of these experiments (RF15 and RF16) the factor of mutual emotional facilitation was minimized by the use of the screen. The results were much the same as in most of the other reward-and-fine experiments, suggesting that this factor was not primarily responsible for the results.

In four of the reward-and-fine experiments (RF7, RF8, RF11, RF14) there were no serious "traffic jams"; all or almost all of the cones came out of the bottle in less than a minute. In three of these experiments the experimenter was unable to persuade the winners to take the rewards; apparently the subjects had failed to accept the situation as a game with winners and losers. In one of these experiments there was an additional factor which probably interfered with "traffic jams"; immediately before this experiment (RF14) these subjects had participated in another (NR5) in which no rewards had been offered and in which the fastest time of any group was achieved (10 seconds). The subjects knew the time of this trial; the time allowance for winning exceeded it by 5 seconds, so that the chances of losing must have been recognized as slight by the subjects.

In the remaining 25 experiments there were no rewards or fines. Twenty of these experiments were described to the subjects as measures of cooperation. These experiments fell into three groups. Experiments NR1 to NR5 were conducted with groups of subjects who had not been previously exposed to similar experiments, and under "natural" conditions, i.e., without the experimenter

---

[6] See footnote 4.

entering into a conspiracy with accomplices. Experiments NR6 to NR12 were similar but were conducted immediately after experiments with accomplices. Experiments ANR1 to ANR8 were the experiments with accomplices who had been instructed to make noise and to stir up excitement in the group.

No serious "traffic jam" developed in any of these experiments, not in those with new subjects, nor in those with accomplices, nor in those preceded by experiments with accomplices. The times for taking *all* cones out of the bottle ranged in these three groups of experiments from 10 to 22 seconds, from 10.5 to 30 seconds and from 13.4 to 59 seconds.

The experimenter's accomplices were generally able to stir up excitement but this excitement failed to disrupt the cooperative behavior of the group to an extent comparable to that of the effect of the individual rewards and fines. In most of the reward-and-fine experiments the majority of the cones were still in the bottle after a minute or longer had elapsed.

Did the accomplices have any effect? The mean times of the two groups of the no-reward, no-accomplice experiments were 16.8 seconds (NR1 to NR5) and 19.6 seconds (NR6 to NR12); the mean time of the accomplice experiments was 34.4 seconds. The difference between the times of the two groups of experiments without accomplices is very small and not statistically significant. In the accomplice experiments the mean time was longer, significantly so at the .01 level of confidence, suggesting that the accomplices did have some disrupting effect. However, a closer examination of the data shows that the two longest times in the accomplice experiments were obtained when some of the accomplices had misunderstood the instructions and gave bad advice to the group. If the results of these two experiments (ANR1 and ANR8) are eliminated, the mean time drops to 26.4 seconds, and the critical ratio (Fisher's *t* for small, uncorrelated samples) indicates that the difference between this time and that of the no-accomplice experiments is too small to reach the conventional standards of statistical significance ($t = 1.82$, $d.f. = 16$, $P > .05$). Thus it was not estab-

lished with certainty that the accomplices who made noise and stirred up excitement without giving bad advice had a disrupting effect on group cooperation. They may have had; the evidence was inconclusive. More experiments would have been needed to establish this point. The experiments with accomplices were designed merely to discover whether an additional opportunity for mutual emotional facilitation would seriously disrupt group cooperation. They served their purpose in showing that it did not; and since the question whether it had a minor disrupting effect was not directly related to the main problem of this study in any case, the matter was not further investigated.

There were several additional no-reward experiments (PC1 to PC5). One of these was described to the subjects as a preliminary trial conducted in order to determine the proper conditions for the next experiment in which rewards were to be offered. This was the only no-reward experiment in which a serious "traffic jam" developed; there was no organized plan for action in this group, probably because the subjects were not sufficiently motivated to devise one before the experiment began. The remaining four experiments were described to the subjects, who had previously participated in reward-and-fine experiments, as control experiments conducted in order to demonstrate to the group what were the effects of the rewards. In view of the common claim of the subjects that the flow of water was primarily responsible for the "traffic jams" water was made to flow in three of them. No serious "traffic jam" developed in any of the control experiments. On the other hand, three out of the four times were distinctly slow ones as compared to those in the other no-reward experiments. It is not clear whether this finding was due to fluctuations of random sampling ("chance"), whether the subjects were inadequately motivated in these "control" experiments, or whether the earlier reward-and-fine experiments had continued bad effects on the cooperative behavior of the subjects. The matter was not investigated at this time.

After each experiment or group of experiments the subjects were told by the experimenter about the true nature of the experiments and about the results obtained so far. The explanations were followed by discussions. In the groups which had failed to pull out the cones from the bottle, marked tendencies towards rationalization appeared during these discussions. Subjects tended to explain the bad results of their group in terms of supposedly tangled strings, effects of the water, or insufficient time for the formulation of a plan, disregarding the fact that these factors failed to produce "traffic jams" in no-reward experiments.

DISCUSSION

The theory presented at the beginning of this paper is opposed to the common tendency to view emotion as a predominantly disruptive factor in behavior. It developed out of an attempt to reconstruct the phenomenal situation in circumstances leading to a panic. The present writer views this approach as a fruitful one and finds it congenial. On the other hand, it is not considered to be the only fruitful approach to psychology and the experiments reported in this paper do not constitute a crucial test of this type of approach. One can treat the same situation and behavior occurring in it in phenomenal terms (25), or in terms of psychological "genotypical" constructs (17), or in physiological terms, or in terms of stimuli, responses, and operants which are not defined physiologically (24). In other words, one can operate within any one of several possible universes of discourse. One such universe of discourse may be more convenient and more suggestive of fruitful hypotheses to a particular investigator, than another, and one universe of discourse may have philosophical advantages compared to another one. Generally speaking, the choice of the universe of discourse cannot be definitely settled by any experiments. Personal preferences of investigators vary, and facts tend to be equally compatible with virtually all philosophical systems except possibly in very advanced sciences.

The experiments provide laboratory demonstrations for our hypothesis and partially verify the hypothesis. The behavior of the subjects did not tend towards inefficiency unless the reward structure of the situation provided them with incentives to behave uncooperatively after the cooperative pattern of group behavior was disturbed. There were no "traffic jams" in the no-reward experiments. Emotional excitement produced by the experimenter's accomplices interfered with the efficiency of group behavior only to a minor extent, if at all, compared to the effects of individual rewards and fines. On the other hand, there were inefficient behavior and "traffic jams" in more than half of the reward-and-fine experiments, in which the subjects were confronted with the probability of individual failure, as soon as the bottle neck was temporarily blocked. This result was obtained without any more serious threat to the individuals than the loss of ten cents at most and probably a mild feeling of failure in a game. Thus intense fear was not found to be an essential condition of chaotic, non-adaptive group behavior analogous to that occurring in panics.

"Traffic jams" did not occur in all of the reward-and-fine experiments and were not expected to. In an experiment with 15 to 20 subjects one cannot be certain that one or a few subjects will create a disturbance within the short time available. With larger groups the percentage of "traffic jams" should be larger; the more people there are, the more likely it becomes that one uncooperative individual will create the initial disturbance which leads to deterioration of the situation.

The theory presented here, if correct, appears to apply to many situations and to contribute to the understanding of a number of social and economic phenomena. Situations with reward structures resembling that of panics and the reward-and-fine experiments reported here seem to be numerous. Tendencies towards non-adaptive group behavior are clearly present in many such situations, regardless of the presence or absence of face-to-face contacts between people and opportunities for mutual emotional facilitation. Runs on banks resulting in bank failures, violations of price-fixing agreements among business men resulting in cut-throat competition, hoarding behavior of consumers during periods of scarcity of goods resulting in shortages are all forms of ultimately non-adaptive behavior which can be interpreted in terms of unstable reward structures of the situations. On the other hand, there are situations in which the appearance of danger does not provide incentives for anti-social behavior. In such situations no chaotic non-adaptive behavior of groups seems to occur in spite of the catastrophic nature of the danger and ample opportunity for face-to-face contacts. There seem to be no panics when people are trapped so that there can be no struggle for an exit, e.g., at submarine and mine disasters (32).

It is intended to deal in future publications with social and economic data pertaining to both group behavior which tends to deteriorate and group behavior which tends to remain adaptive in nature. Full verification of the theory cannot be accomplished in terms of laboratory experiments; it requires investigation of real life situations. An examination of one set of relevant data, viz., gasoline consumption figures during the period of developing gasoline shortages in 1941, is in progress at present.

The experiments reported here belong also in a second theoretical context. In these experiments a system of individual rewards resulted in strikingly inefficient behavior, while the goal of demonstrating the ability of the group to cooperate produced much more orderly action. These findings may be compared with those of the type reported by Maller (18) and Sims (23), who found that individual competition led to greater efficiency than group competition. It should be noted that the structure of the tasks in these earlier experiments and those reported here differed. In the former experiments the subjects worked separately and could not interfere with each other as readily as in our experiments. Thus the experiments provide an additional illustration for the caution that any generalization pertaining to the effect of competition on behavior is limited not only by the prevalent social norms and personality characteristics, but also by the nature of the

task, as was pointed out, for example, by Klineberg (9, p. 338).

SUMMARY

A theory is suggested, explaining the non-adaptive features of behavior occurring in panics in terms of the reward structure of the situations rather than in terms of mutual facilitation of emotion. In panic-producing situations cooperative behavior is needed for success and is rewarding to individuals as long as everybody cooperates. However, once the cooperative pattern of behavior is disturbed, cooperation ceases to be rewarding to the individuals; then a competitive situation is apt to develop which may lead to disaster. Thus at a theater fire it pays not to push if everybody cooperates, but if a few uncooperative individuals block the exits by pushing, then any individual who does not push can expect that he will be burned. Pushing becomes the advantageous (or least disadvantageous) form of behavior for individuals, and disorder leading to disastrous consequences spreads rapidly.

Laboratory experiments with miniature social situations are reported in which the effects of the reward structure on group behavior in situations in which cooperation was required for success was studied. In these experiments the subjects had to take cones out of a bottle; only one cone could be taken out at a time and the bottle neck was easily blocked by too many cones arriving simultaneously, so that the cones came out only if the subjects cooperated with each other. The situation was represented to some of the groups of subjects as a game in which one could win or lose small sums of money; to other groups the experiment was described as a measure of their ability to cooperate. The opportunities for mutual emotional facilitation were also varied in some experiments.

In the majority of cases, serious "traffic jams" resulted when individual rewards and fines were offered, preventing the taking out of any or most of the cones. No similar disturbances were observed in the "measure of cooperativeness" experiments. In the reward-and-fine experiments, the introduction of a screen hiding the subjects from each other, so as to minimize opportunities for mutual emotional facilitation, did not prevent "traffic jams" from occurring. In the experiments without individual rewards, excited screaming in the group (arranged by the experimenter) had little if any effect on the results.

The experiments gave the expected results, thus contributing to a partial verification of the theory; full verification would require examination of real life data, which is planned. The theory appears to apply to other social phenomena in addition to panic.

References

1. Asch, S. E. Understanding vs. Suggestion in the Social Field. *Psychol. Bull.*, 1940, **39**, 466–467.

2. ———. The Doctrines of Suggestion, Prestige and Imitation in Social Psychology. *Psychol. Rev.*, 1948, **55**, 250–276.

3. Britt, S. H. *Social Psychology of Modern Life.* New York: Farrar and Rinehart, 1941.

4. Cantril, H. *Understanding Man's Social Behavior, Preliminary Notes.* Princeton: Office of Public Opinion Research, 1947.

5. Freud, S. *Group Psychology and Analysis of the Ego.* London: Hogarth Press, 1910.

6. Fromm, E. *Escape from Freedom.* New York: Farrar and Rinehart, 1941.

7. Katona, G. *War Without Inflation.* New York: Columbia Univ. Press, 1942.

8. ———. Expectations and Buying Intentions of Consumers. *Amer. Psychologist*, 1948, **3**, 273.

9. Klineberg, O. *Social Psychology.* New York: Holt, 1940.

10. Koffka, K. *Principles of Gestalt Psychology.* New York: Harcourt, Brace, 1935.

11. Krech, D., and Crutchfield, R. C. *Theory and Problems of Social Psychology.* New York: McGraw-Hill, 1948.

12. Le Bon, G. *The Crowd.* London: Unwin, 1916.

13. ———. *Bases Scientifiques d'une Philosophie de l'Histoire.* Paris: Flammarion, 1931.

14. Leeper, R. W. A Motivational Theory of Emotion to Replace "Emotion as Disorganized Response." *Psychol. Rev.*, 1948, **55**, 5–21.

15. Levy, E. A Case of Mania with Its Social Implications. *J. Soc. Research*, 1936, **3**, 488–493.

16. Lewin, K. Vorsatz, Wille und Bedürfnis. *Psychol. Forsch.*, 1926, 7, 330–385.

17. ———. *Principles of Topological Psychology.* New York and London: McGraw-Hill, 1936.

18. Maller, J. B. Cooperation and Competition. *Teach. Coll. Contr. Educ.*, 1929, No. 384.

19. Murphy, G. Address at Symposium: The Role of the Psychologist in the Establishment of Better Human Relations. Meeting of Amer. Psychol. Assn., Boston, Sept. 7, 1948.

20. Reichenbach, H. *Relativitätstheoriz und Erkenntnis a Priori.* Berlin: Springer, 1920.

21. Ross, E. A. *Social Psychology.* New York: Macmillan, 1908.

22. Sherif, M. *An Outline of Social Psychology.* New York: Harper, 1948.

23. Sims, V. M. The Relative Influence of Two Types of Motivation on Improvement. *J. Educ. Psychol.*, 1928, **19**, 480–484.

24. Skinner, B. F. *The Behavior of Organisms.* New York: Appleton-Century-Crofts, 1938.

25. Snygg, D., and Combs, A. W. *Individual Behavior.* New York: Harper, 1949.

26. Tolman, E. C. Cognitive Maps in Rats and Men. *Psychol. Rev.*, 1948, **55**, 189–208.

27. Vaughn, W. F. *Social Psychology.* New York: Odyssey Press, 1948.

28. Watson, J. B. *Psychological Care of Infant and Child.* New York: Norton, 1928.

29. Wertheimer, M. Unpublished lectures.

30. Whitehead, T. N. *The Industrial Worker.* Cambridge, Mass.: Harvard Univ. Press, 1938. Vol. 1.

31. Young, K. *Social Psychology.* New York: Crofts, 1944.

32. Dying Miners Wrote Notes to Their Families as Deadly Gas Crept on Them in Illinois Pit (Anon.). *New York Times*, March 31, 1947, p. 8.

ANONYMITY AND DESTRUCTION IN THE REAL WORLD

Philip G. Zimbardo

Now we must return to our starting point in the real world to demonstrate that the aggression observed under our contrived laboratory conditions of anonymity or unidentifiability is really a genuine phenomenon of the human condition. It should follow, from what we have described thus far, that where social conditions of life destroy individual identity by making people feel anonymous, then what will follow is the deindividuated types of behaviors outlined previously. Assaultive aggression, senseless acts of destruction, motiveless murders, great expenditure of energy and effort directed toward shattering traditional forms and institutionalized structures become our dependent variables. Vandalism is the prototype of this behavior and represents a social problem

Source: Reprinted from *The Human Choice: Individuation, Reason and Order versus Deindividuation, Impulse and Chaos* by Philip G. Zimbardo, pp. 282–293 in William J. Arnold and David Levine, *Nebraska Symposium on Motivation, 1969,* by permission of University of Nebraska Press. Copyright 1970 University of Nebraska Press.

which will soon reach epidemic proportions. How serious is the problem now? Can it be understood in terms of our analysis of de-individuation?

VANDALISM

The extent and intensity of the mindless, wanton destruction of property and the expenditure of effort on the part of vandals may be extracted from the following sampling of individual cases and summary statistics. Following a Halloween celebration (October 31, 1967), a mob of teenagers began overturning gravestones in Montefiore Cemetery in Queens, New York, and throwing rocks at passing cars. Public School 26 in Brooklyn was broken into 15 times and 700 panels of glass broken in a two-month period (April to June, 1968). The principal reported that vandals threw library books and catalog cards all over the floor and covered them with glue. Vandalism was also a major problem at the recent New York World's Fair. The Ford Company's cars, which conveyed visitors into a Disney-designed "past" and "future," were also reminders of the reality of the present. The exhibit supervisor remarked that vandals "tear things apart. They carve up the upholstery and pull some of the components out of the dash board. One Thunderbird came back with every wire ripped out."

"God is dead" may be a provocative intellectual issue of debate for theologians, but for kids in the Southeast Bronx (my primal neighborhood), its truth is reflected much more concretely; within a recent six-month period, 47 Christian churches and 20 synagogues were vandalized. One of them was the Netzach Israel Synagogue, where children broke the Torah scrolls, ripped curtains and prayer books, splashed paint on the walls, threw rocks through the stained-glass window, and finally tore the Star of David down from the roof. Anti-Semitism? That assumes motivation and purpose. The rector of the famed St. Mark's in the Bowery Episcopalian Church has threatened to close it down unless similar acts of theft and vandalism in his church are halted. During the past year the church has been broken into about a dozen

times and graves in the adjoining churchyard have been desecrated.

While major cities provide a conducive setting for the appearance of vandalism, it is by no means solely an urban phenomenon. In Union Township, New Jersey, roving vandals damaged more than 250 autos parked on streets (March 21, 1968) by ramming them and breaking their windows. Across the country in Richmond, California, a small city near San Francisco, vandals stormed through six schools one weekend (February 25, 1969) causing $30,000 worth of damage. Equipment and furniture were overturned, windows were smashed, food was thrown on the floor and ink squirted on the walls and on library books. Vandals recently destroyed an irreplaceable arbor of beautiful trees in San Francisco's Golden Gate Park, to the puzzlement of all who couldn't understand why anyone would commit such a senseless act.

The incidence of vandalism can be appreciated by reference to the following statistics obtained from the relevant public and private agencies in a single city—New York City.

Schools. In 1967 there were 202,712 window panes broken (replacement cost over $1 million); there were 2,359 unlawful entries (causing $787,000 damage); there were 199 fires (costing $154,000 in destruction, but not including the loss of one entire school, P.S. 5 in Queens). The January, 1968, bulletin of the Board of Education's Division of Maintenance, noting that these figures do not include costs from defaced desks, walls, fixtures, etc., concludes, "It is almost impossible to estimate the costs of these items, but it is a huge amount." Even without a complete accounting of the havoc wrought on the free public education system in New York City, the bulletin indicates that the nearly $2 million cost of repairs in 1967 was up 21 percent from 1966, and preliminary 1969 reports reveal that the vandalism has continued its spiraling rise.

Public Transportation. Well over $100,000 was spent in 1967 to repair the damage caused by vandals to buses and subways.

Public Parks. The $650,000 damage to benches, rest rooms, playgrounds, lights, trees, and fences in 1967 represented an increase of more than 11 percent from the previous year, and it, too, continues to climb. In Brooklyn alone, there were 35 fires set in park buildings, mostly comfort stations.

Public Telephones. The convenience provided by the city's 100,000 pay phones is rapidly being undermined by hordes of vandals who wreck an average of 35,000 of them *monthly.* At least 25 percent of the sidewalk phones are out of service all the time, and it is a rarity to find a subway station phone in operation. Recently I tried 15 phone booths in the Times Square Station before I could find one whose metal-encased wires were not severed, dial ripped off, mouthpiece dismantled, change slots clogged, or money containers ripped out. The New York Telephone Company estimates that last year it lost nearly $1 million in stolen coins and spent another $4 million to repair vandalized phones.

Automobiles. The Sanitation Department reports that over 31,500 abandoned cars had to be removed from New York's streets last year (an increase of 5,000 from the previous year). These are cars which either had been stolen or were abandoned by their owners because they were no longer in good running condition. What is interesting is that most of them are stripped of usable parts and then battered and smashed almost beyond recognition. During the past several years I have been systematically observing this new phenomenon of ritual destruction of the automobile—the symbol of America's affluence, technology, and mobility, as well as the symbol of its owner's independence, status, and (according to motivation researchers) sexual fantasies. In a single day, on a 20-mile route from my home in Brooklyn to the campus of New York University in the Bronx, I recorded 218 such vandalized cars.

Repeated observations of the transformation of a typical car lead me to conclude that there are six distinct stages involved. First, the car must provide some "releaser" stimuli to call attention to itself, such as lack of license plates, hood or trunk open, or a tire removed. However, there are also less ob-

vious cues, such as a flat tire not repaired within a day or two, or simply a car which has not been moved from one place for several days. In a city that is always on the go, anything static must be dead, and it becomes public domain if no one calls for the body. Older boys and men are attracted by the lure of usable or salable parts, and so the car is stripped of all items of possible value. Either late in this stage or after it is completed (depending on implicit neighborhood norms), younger children begin to smash the front and rear windows. Then all easily broken, ripped, or bent parts are attacked. Next, the remainder of the car is smashed with rocks, pipes, and hammers. Sometimes it is set on fire, and sometimes even the body metal is torn off. Finally, and most ignominiously, the last stage in the metamorphosis occurs when people in the neighborhood (and even Sanitation Department clean-up men) use it as a big garbage can, dumping their refuse into it.

A FIELD EXPERIMENT ON "AUTO-SHAPING"

In order to observe in a more systematic fashion who are the vandals and what are the conditions associated with their acts of vandalism, Scott Fraser and I bought a car and left it on a street across from the Bronx campus of New York University, where it was observed continuously for 64 hours. At the same time, we repeated this procedure in Palo Alto, California, on a street near the Stanford University campus. The license plates of both cars were removed and the hoods opened to provide the necessary releaser signals.

What happened in New York was unbelievable! Within ten minutes the 1959 Oldsmobile received its first auto strippers—a father, mother, and eight-year-old son. The mother appeared to be a lookout, while the son aided the father's search of the trunk, glove compartment, and motor. He handed his father the tools necessary to remove the battery and radiator. Total time of destructive contact: seven minutes.

By the end of the first 26 hours, a steady parade of vandals had removed the battery, radiator, air cleaner, radio antenna, wind-shield wipers, right-hand-side chrome strip, hubcaps, a set of jumper cables, a gas can, a can of car wax, and the left rear tire (the other tires were too worn to be interesting). Nine hours later, random destruction began when two laughing teenagers tore off the rearview mirror and began throwing it at the headlights and front windshield. Eventually, five eight-year-olds claimed the car as their private playground, crawling in and out of it and smashing the windows. One of the last visitors was a middle-aged man in a camel's hair coat and matching hat, pushing a baby in a carriage. He stopped, rummaged through the trunk, took out an unidentifiable part, put it in the baby carriage and wheeled off. [As reported in Time *magazine, February 28, 1969]*

In less than three days what remained was a battered, useless hulk of metal, the result of 23 incidents of destructive contact. The vandalism was almost always observed by one or more other passersby, who occasionally stopped to chat with the looters. Most of the destruction was done in the daylight hours and not at night (as we had anticipated), and the adults' stealing clearly preceded the window-breaking, tire-slashing fun of the youngsters. The adults were all well-dressed, clean-cut whites who would under other circumstances be mistaken for mature, responsible citizens demanding more law and order. The one optimistic note to emerge from this study is that the number of people who came into contact with the car but did not steal or damage it was twice as large as the number of actual vandals.

In startling contrast, the Palo Alto car not only emerged untouched, but when it began to rain, one passerby lowered the hood so that the motor would not get wet!

VANDALISM IS ALIVE, THOUGH SLEEPING, IN STANFORD

Next, this car was abandoned on the Stanford University campus for over a week without incident. It was obvious that the releaser cues which were sufficient in New York were not adequate here. I expected that vandalism needed to be primed where it did not occur with a higher "natural" frequency. To do so, two of my graduate students (Mike Bond and Ebbe Ebbesen) and I decided to provide a better model for destruction by taking a sledge hammer to the car ourselves and then seeing if others would follow suit.

Several observations are noteworthy. First of all, there is considerable reluctance to take that first blow, to smash through the windshields and initiate the destruction of a form. But it feels so good after the first smack that the next one comes more easily, with more force, and feels even better. Although everyone knew the sequence was being filmed, the students got carried away temporarily. Once one person had begun to wield the sledge hammer, it was difficult to get him to stop and pass it to the next pair of eager hands. Finally they all attacked simultaneously. One student jumped on the roof and began stomping it in, two were pulling the door from its hinges, another hammered away at the hood and motor, while the last one broke all the glass he could find. They later reported that feeling the metal or glass give way under the force of their blows was stimulating and pleasurable. Observers of this action, who were shouting out to hit it harder and to smash it, finally joined in and turned the car completely over on its back, whacking at the underside. There seemed little hope to expect spontaneous vandalism of this car since it was already wrecked so badly. However, that night at 12:30 A.M. three young men with pipes and bars began pounding away at the carcass so intensely that dormitory residents (a block away) shouted out for them to stop.

We might conclude from these preliminary studies that to *initiate* such acts of destructive vandalism, the necessary ingredients are the acquired feelings of anonymity provided by the life in a city like New York, along with some minimal releaser cues. Where social anonymity is not a "given" of one's everyday life, it is necessary to have more extreme releaser cues, more explicit models for destruction and aggression, and physical anonymity—a large crowd or the darkness of the night. A heightened state of preparatory general arousal would serve to make the action go, with less direct priming. To maintain and intensify the action, the ideal conditions occur where the physical act is a gross one involving a great deal of energy, thus producing considerable noncognitive feedback. It is pleasurable to behave at a purely sensual, physical, unthinking level—regardless of whether the act is making love or making war.

It is only proper to conclude this section with two final, recently gathered anecdotes. 1) A tank, which was part of an army convoy traveling through the Bronx, developed trouble and had to be left in the street while a mechanic was dispatched. He arrived a few hours later to find it totally stripped of all removable parts (which earned it the *Esquire* Dubious Prize of the Year, 1968). 2) A motorist pulled his car off a highway in Queens, New York, to fix a flat tire. He jacked his car up and, while removing the flat tire, was startled to see his hood being opened and a stranger starting to pull out the battery. The stranger tried to mollify his assumed car-stripping colleague by telling him, "Take it easy, buddy, you can have the tires; all I want is the battery!"

What is being destroyed here is not simply a car, but the basic fabric of social norms which must regulate all communal life. The horrible scene from *Zorba the Greek* in which the old townswomen begin to strip the home of the dying Bubbalina before she is yet dead is symbolically enacted many times every day in cities like New York where young and old, poor and affluent strip, steal, and vandalize cars, schools, churches, and almost all symbols of social order.

It is for the sociologist to discover the specific roots of this induced anonymity,[1] but Hall (1966)[2] sees the type of behaviors we have discussed as one consequence of squeezing man into too small a space and limiting his personal distance (the study of proxemics).

The animal studies also teach us that crowding per se is neither good nor bad, but rather that overstimulation and disruptions of social relationships as a consequence of overlapping personal distances lead to population collapse.

* * *

---

[1] One social indicator of urban anonymity is the failure of people living in tenement houses to display their name on their mailbox, at their downstairs doorbell, or on their door. In a survey I conducted of 100 tenements, the apartments of only 24 percent of the occupants could be located from their name plates on the ground-floor bells or mailboxes.

[2] Hall, E. T. *Hidden Dimensions.* New York: Doubleday, 1966, p. 175.

UNCONVENTIONAL WARFARE

J. K. Zawodny

In the third century B.C. in the city of Argos, Pyrrhus of Epirus, known as the Red King, was killed by a chamber pot thrown from a roof top by an elderly lady. The basic elements of what is today known as "unconventional warfare" were embodied in her action: there was surprise, and an unusual—if not extraordinary—weapon; the object of attack was strategically important; the attack was successful; and it was performed by a nonprofessional warrior. The performer, not the technique, is the significant element of this episode.

The outstanding feature of unconventional warfare is that it is carried out by people of all ages and backgrounds and of both sexes. It is a "People's Warfare." A warfare of masses who have lost patience, it is an unremittingly violent way of saying to the enemy by all possible means: "We hate you; we are everywhere; we will destroy you!" Unconventional warfare is the effective weapon of the weaker adversary; and, strange as it may sound, the United States is as vulnerable to this sort of warfare as Cuba. It is, furthermore, an extremely cheap weapon—at least, monetarily. . . .

Unconventional warfare is that part of "Special Warfare" that employs violence. It can be broadly classified as offensive and defensive. It is offensive when one government promotes the overthrow of a foreign government or a change of its political elite. In these circumstances, organization, manipulation and assistance are carried into another territory; the recent affair with Cuba is an example. It is defensive when a frustrated political group structures itself into a disciplined organization to apply violence against the government of its own nation or when a people fight the occupational forces of an invading army. This classification does not preclude both types from being (and they usually are) *strategically and tactically* offensive.

There seem to be three prerequisites for initiating unconventional warfare. First, an organization must be created to support those who will carry the violence directly to the enemy. Leadership, supplies and money are indispensable for the inception and survival of the underground. Guerrilla and saboteur units are only a small part of the structure; also included are Headquarters, Intelligence, Communications, Propaganda, Cadres in Reserve and Training, and Logistics.

The second ingredient essential for the initiation of unconventional warfare is a culture that allows or promotes violence, and the effectiveness of the organization usually depends on the degree to which the cultural values and traditions of a people condition them to use violence. . . .

The third prerequisite for unconventional warfare is the volunteer, the guerrilla and saboteur, who carries violence to the enemy. Any movement aimed at using violence gathers to its ranks those who are threatened and/or dissatisfied. In the Polish underground movement between 1939 and 1945, the resentment against the cruelty and oppression of the German and Soviet occupation, the absence of formal channels for voicing grievances and the lack of opportunities to change conditions caused the people to band together. Such at least were the usual explanations. Many men were unable to articulate the reasons why they fought. But they did believe that it was the only way they could "do something" about their problems. The messenger of a company in the Uprising of Warsaw (1944) was eight years old. No one knew why he was there; but the boy wanted to fight and was depend-

Source: J. K. Zawodny, "Unconventional Warfare," *The American Scholar*, Vol. 31, No. 3, 1962, pp. 384–394. Copyright by J. K. Zawodny and reprinted by permission.

able. In one of the actions a sergeant who had been a university professor was fighting because it was "his moral duty to uphold justice."

Women, following precedents in Polish history, were splendid unconventional fighters and did men's jobs, including manning street barricades and shooting. In fact it appeared to this writer that when prolonged and steady physical effort was necessary, women, particularly peasant women, had more stamina and resilience than men. Like the men, they were of all ages and from all social classes. Women with high levels of intelligence worked themselves up into the policy-making levels of the underground (and of the enemy). Nor were they lacking in heroism. A beautiful Polish girl, who was a superb linguist in the movement's Intelligence, was captured and tortured by the Gestapo in a most sadistic fashion. When she could no longer stand it, she asked for poison through a bribed guard. She revealed no information.

It should be emphasized, however, that not only the noblest are attracted by this kind of fighting. Because its participants spring from a very broad cross-section of the population, unconventional forces are also a cesspool of killers and people with aberrations looking for a formalized excuse to use violence. There was many a man ready and willing to kill a prisoner to get "even" for some real or imaginary reason known only to himself. Many kinds of men can be found, particularly among guerrillas. To idealize them is self-destructive.

Guerrillas and saboteurs are the true "unconventional fighters" for they carry violence directly to the enemy. It seems that, irrespective of culture and country, the people who are close to the soil and nature are the main stock of guerrilla units. These are not, on the whole, rich peasants; the well-to-do tend to stay out of the fighting. The guerrillas' pattern of living requires stamina, physical endurance and a rather philosophical acceptance of hardship. The greatest hardship, other than physical, is the lack of women. Pleasures are scarce. . . . Mobility is one of the guerrilla's greatest assets: yet, the men tend to get overequipped, particu-

larly with heavy weapons when they are available. Such weapons provide them with some feeling of security. Another painful problem is the lack of identity. In many societies it appears that men would rather fight in uniforms and be identified as a military unit rather than a guerrilla band.

Their lives are largely regulated by the degree of support given by the indigenous population, and also by the climatic conditions and the terrain. While valleys are avoided because they might become deadly traps, guerrillas can operate in literally any terrain so long as the distance between their hideouts and the targets is relatively short. When in danger of being encircled by the enemy, the guerrilla units will try to "evaporate" by disbanding and reassembling at a predetermined point. This is not a difficult task if the climate and terrain are favorable.

When possible, the members of the group try to live within communities among the peasants, and to assemble only when necessary for action. The Chinese Communist guerrillas during the revolutionary war tried to be self-sustaining and in some instances even operated cooperatives helping peasants produce food and the necessities of daily life; at the same time they carried on very intense political indoctrination. This kind of approach has two direct gains: first, it conserves energy which can be utilized at the time of action; second, it cements the relationship between the guerrillas and the local population.

Guerrilla fighting has no rules. For security reasons it might be necessary to shoot one's own wounded—an act practically unheard-of in conventional forces. Participants usually do not wear uniforms; thus captives in many instances are treated as "bandits" and shot. Tactics are basically offensive in spirit. Hit-and-run fighting is practiced. Mobility, surprise and dispersions are necessary. Ideally guerrillas follow the principle of "Move while attacking; attack while moving." (Han Wu-ti, 140 B.C.) It would be this writer's axiom that if the enemy has a chance to reload his weapon, the guerrilla action was poorly planned or executed and should be abandoned.

The smaller the groups, the more active they seem to be in searching out and hitting the enemy. The greater the imagination of the leader, the more enterprising and unusual are the actions of the group. In July 1950, four Koreans in a jeep rode into an American post and wanted their gas tank filled. After this was done they rode away, spraying the Americans with automatic fire. Successful action to some extent seems to depend upon determination and a cool head.

Guerrillas are not after territorial gains. Their effectiveness lies rather in binding the enemy forces, killing and spreading terror, destroying elements that are of strategic and tactical importance. Furthermore, they preserve and protect to a considerable degree the economic wealth and structure of a community.

In regard to the destruction of tactically and militarily important objectives, one can point to the techniques of French guerrillas dealing with German transportation. The range of their activities was broad: faking, changing and turning the directional signs; felling roadside trees; spreading spikes on the roads; burning wooden bridges; mining roads; attacking telephone lines; blocking inland waterways.

Needless to say, picking off a high-ranking officer or a member of the political elite is considered a coup by any guerrilla. Soviet partisans poisoned at least one German general and carried another out of his own headquarters wrapped in a carpet.

In many instances guerrillas in Italy and the Soviet Union acted as protectors of the local industry, at the last moment preventing the German dismantling effort. One of the techniques by which guerrillas may preserve the integrity of the plants is to synchronize with their activities public riots and general strikes. Both of these weapons were used in China, Italy and the Soviet Union.

One final facet of guerrilla activities worth mentioning here is the organization of evasion. This term may encompass attempt to evacuate allied prisoners, airmen shot down, or sympathizers. It can also refer to the establishment of an underground railroad facilitating the escape of ablebodied men or specialists to join guerrillas or their supporters

abroad. As many as two thousand French volunteers to the Free French forces were entering England monthly in the late summer of 1940, in spite of the fact that the Vichy Government and the Germans were trying to stop them.

Troublesome as they may be to the enemy, guerrillas at certain times become as troublesome to their own political leadership. This happens when the country is liberated or when the political leadership feels obliged to set forth a concrete political program. Political leaders try to avoid specific pronouncements at the inception of the organization. By remaining vague they are able to accommodate individual aspirations and thus increase their ranks. When the elite feels strong enough to seize power officially, however, or when, for one reason or another, they are compelled to state their political objectives, they prefer to do so when the guerrillas have been disarmed. Hence a gentle, and sometimes not so gentle, tug-of-war arises between the political leadership and the guerrillas. "Give us the weapons and we will give you the political program." "Give us the political program and we will give you the weapons." If the leaders have a label of legality and have the territory under control, the usual practice is to incorporate the guerrillas into the conventional military forces. Thus the guerrillas retain the weapons but they have little to say about the direction and content of political programs. Any successful guerrilla movement, however, carries within it the seeds of violent opposition to its own political leadership.

If guerrilla fighters are the artisans in violence, those who are engaged in sabotage are the artists. They are the "surgeons of violence" by profession: they deal with the nerves, heart and brain of the enemy. They hit power stations, transformers, high tension lines and all possible centers of communication. They work themselves into the industrial network of the enemy, causing stoppages, faulty production, delays and physical destruction of anything that might be of value.

The ingenuity with which sabotage men choose and attack their targets is boundless. There was one instance when even condoms produced for the Germany army were punctured. (How this was supposed to contribute to Allied victory is not clear.) They might put sugar in gas tanks, cause faulty execution of aircraft engine parts, spike oil wells and change the labels on freight cars. This latter procedure was used by the Polish underground in diverting precious metals used in the production of high-grade steel from Berlin to a small town in southern Greece. It took three months for this transport to reach Berlin, part of it having been blown up by Greek saboteurs.

If these groups really want to get a man, there is practically no chance for him to survive. The German general who commanded the security police in Warsaw rode to and from his office by different routes every day with an escort of armored cars. Nonetheless he was ambushed and killed.

There is no logistics problem with the members of sabotage units as there is in the case of guerrillas. They live "ordinary" lives and maintain themselves. The Polish experience showed that to pass information to the members of the group took about ten hours in a large city; to get them ready and assembled at the point of action took an additional six to ten hours. Outside of their time in action, they are responsible for their own maintenance and their own lives.

It must be emphasized that as effective as is the guerrilla and sabotage units' tactical and strategic contribution to defeating the enemy, this does not adequately explain their value in the struggle for political power. Here, *the greatest contribution of guerrillas and saboteurs lies in catalyzing and intensifying counterterror which further alienates the enemy from the local population.* The enemy as a rule will relegate the responsibility for dealing with unconventional fighters to military forces or security agencies. These groups deal with the fighters by using the only methods available to them—those involving force. Because the guerrillas are elusive and the saboteurs even more so, the frustration of the pursuers results in counterviolence, which falls on the lifeline and source of manpower of these units—the local population. Reprisals begin.

This is what sophisticated political leaders of guerrillas may expect. There is no better way to alienate a regime in power from the population than to incite it to apply nonselective terror. Guerrillas and saboteurs serve this purpose eminently. The ebb and flow of membership in these units is not related to the number of tactical victories, to their losses or even to their prospects for success. The rate of recruitment is directly related to the intensity of terror applied by the enemy in suppressing the movement. Any counterterror by the enemy brings to the ranks of the unconventional fighters new recruits who are escaping from the reprisals or who wish revenge. In this way the movement perpetuates itself. Unless the guerrillas are also using terror against the population, the more terror the enemy applies, the more fighters he produces, provided, of course, that the cultural values permit violence. (Certainly Quakers would react to counterterror differently from Catholic Poles.)

The existence of an underground and its result—unconventional warfare—is evidence of the breakdown of social order. When this occurs, there is a considerable alteration of the operational values and social mores of the society. What was a crime before the struggle can become exemplary behavior during strife. Killing, destroying property that may be of use to the enemy and slowing production become not only respectable, but also moral obligations. This modification of values affects the process of socialization of the generation growing up while the underground activities are in progress. Violence becomes an acceptable means and part of solving problems for that generation. Polish underground authorities were aware of this and established a special "Pedagogical Council" to see that the boys would not become one-track killers, but would continue with the acquisition of education and the development of moral values necessary for existence in a normal democratic society. A man who grows up in the Judaic-Christian tradition of compassion and love has to go through intellectual calisthenics to rationalize his participation in the ruthless operation of unconventional warfare. This is not the case with the Communists, where all activities of this kind can be explained and justified in terms of class struggle.

In terms of American cultural values, it seems that to engage in unconventional warfare we would have to abandon two rules in our code of manly conduct—waiting for the enemy to reach for his gun first and face-to-face combat. These two ideals are the very antithesis of unconventional fighting.

Mass movements using unconventional warfare exist at this time in at least eleven countries: Algeria, South Africa, Angola, Burma, China, Vietnam, South Korea, Kenya, Laos, Venezuela and Guatemala. There are also "dormant" underground movements in at least ten countries in East Central Europe now within the sphere of Soviet influence. In the years since the end of World War II, the political elites and forms of governments in six countries have been changed through the application or with the assistance of the techniques of unconventional warfare: China, Israel, Vietnam, Iraq, Cuba and Laos. Such techniques for gaining political power will be used frequently by technologically backward people because they are cheap and effective.

Our political leadership ought to face this question squarely: Is unconventional warfare an instrument of foreign policy to be applied in international relations as an element of power and pressure, or is it merely an infantry combat technique to be used in wartime? If the latter is what we have in mind, then we are really using "unconventional warfare" in the most "conventional" fashion. On the other hand, *if* we intend to enter the game of systematically initiating, manipulating and fostering political mass movements in order to help peoples realize their political objectives through violence, then we must understand and clearly distin-guish between the prerequisites, the techniques and the objectives of unconventional warfare.

If such a definition takes place, then the aspirations and expectations of the indigenous people with whom we plan to work ought to be given paramount attention and faced squarely and honestly! Otherwise we shall fail as we did in Cuba.

This is even more important when we try to fight guerrillas, as we are doing now in Southeast Asia. True, in some situations it is necessary to deal with guerrillas in the most stern and unyielding manner. (Seek them out and put such pressure on them that the guerrilla will not have a chance to stop behind a bush to relieve himself. . . .) But this is a short-term tactical answer; the final solution should not rest at this. For a long-range consideration, it is necessary that a basic question be asked: "Why did guerrillas emerge and what are their values, goals and grievances?"

You cannot expect a starved peasant in an underdeveloped country to fight on behalf of "free enterprise"—he has experienced it already from his landlord. Neither does the word "freedom" mean much to him—freedom to do what? Behind a guerrilla's gun is a man; that man shoots in the direction from which there is no hope. He shoots because he does not believe that for him justice and satisfaction can be achieved in any other way. In the long run, therefore, he should be met on the level of his expectations and hopes, and not with a rifle. "For a partisan may be completely wrong on what he is fighting *for*, but is not likely to be nearly so wrong on what he is fighting *against*."

Chapter 2

EXTERNAL STIMULUS FACTORS IN CONFLICT

The important point in this section is not so much the degree of structure of the relationships involved, though most of them (involving strangers placed together in an experiment) are again only very weakly structured. The focus of this section is on external stimulus events that can dramatically influence the degree of conflict, regardless of whether there exists any prior relationship between the potential parties to the conflict.

In the first study, Ulrich and Azrin demonstrate that merely delivering an electric shock to two rats placed together in a cage is a sufficient stimulus for the rats to begin fighting. In the next selection, Rabbie and Horwitz demonstrate that a mere flip of a coin may be sufficient to produce negative attitudes toward an outgroup, if differential reward for the ingroup and the outgroup is the result of that coin flip. Frustration is not a necessary condition for this outgroup rejection, since the group receiving the reward shows the effect quite as much as the group not receiving the reward.

Finally, Berkowitz reviews much of the recent laboratory research on aggression to emphasize the general importance of stimulus factors in aggression, or the general role that external cues play in producing aggressive behavior. Observing someone else aggress, observing oneself aggress, or observing the results of aggression may each serve to stimulate further aggression.

REFLEXIVE FIGHTING IN RESPONSE TO AVERSIVE STIMULATION

R. E. Ulrich and N. H. Azrin

ABSTRACT

Reflexive fighting was elicited between paired rats as a reflex reaction to electric shock prior to any specific conditioning. Such fighting was fairly stereotyped and easily differentiated from the rats' usual behavior. The strength of this reflex was not attributable to any apparent operant reinforcement. Elicitation of fighting was a direct function of the enclosed floor area and a nonmonotonic function of the shock intensity.

Failure to scramble the polarity of the electrified grid produced inconsistent fighting. Under optimal conditions fighting was consistently elicited by shock regardless of the rat's sex, strain, previous familiarity with each other, or the number present during shock. Repeated shock presentations did not produce an appreciable decrease in fighting until signs of physical debility appeared. Although shock did not cause a rat to attack inanimate objects, it did produce attack movements toward other small animals. Failure of guinea pigs to defend themselves revealed that the elicitation of fighting from the rat does not require reciprocal attack. Paired hamsters showed fighting reactions similar to those of the rats, whereas guinea pigs failed to fight. Electrode shock and a heated floor elicited fighting between the rats, but intense noise and a cooled floor did not.

Source: R. E. Ulrich and N. H. Azrin, "Reflexive Fighting in Response to Aversive Stimulation," *Journal of the Experimental Analysis of Behavior,* Vol. 5, 1962, pp. 511–520. Reprinted with the permission of the authors and The Society for the Experimental Analysis of Behavior, Inc. Copyright 1962 by The Society for the Experimental Analysis of Behavior, Inc.

When electric foot-shock is delivered to paired rats, a stereotyped fighting reaction results (O'Kelly & Steckle, 1939; Daniel, 1943; Richter, 1950). The present investigation studies several possible determinants of this fighting reaction.

METHOD

SUBJECTS

Male Sprague-Dawley rats of the Holtzman strain were used because rats of this strain were found to be very docile and non-aggressive in the absence of electric shock. At the beginning of the experiment the subjects were approximately 100 days old and weighed between 295–335 g. None of the rats had prior experience with the apparatus.

APPARATUS

The experimental compartment measured 12 in. by 9 in. by 8 in., two sides of which were constructed of sheet metal and the other two of clear plastic. The floor consisted of steel rods, 3/32 in. in diameter and spaced 0.5 in. apart. An open chest contained the experimental chamber, thereby permitting a clear view through the transparent door of the chamber. A shielded, 10-watt bulb at the top provided illumination, and a speaker produced a "white" masking noise. An exhaust fan provided additional masking noise as well as ventilation. The temperature was maintained at about 75° F. The various stimulus conditions used were programmed by electrical apparatus located in a room separate from the experimental chamber. A cumulative recorder, counters, and timers provided a record of the responses. Shock was delivered to the subjects through the grid floor for 0.5 sec. duration from an Applegate constant current stimulator. A shock scrambler provided a changing pattern of polarities so that any two of the floor grids would be opposite polarity during a major part of each presentation of shock.

PROCEDURE AND RESULTS

DEFINITION OF THE

FIGHTING RESPONSE

When two Sprague-Dawley rats were first placed in the experimental chamber, they moved about slowly, sniffing the walls, the grid, and occasionally each other. At no time did any fighting behavior appear in the absence of shock. Soon after shock was delivered, a drastic change in the rats' behavior took place. They would suddenly face each other in an upright position, and with the head thrust forward and the mouth open they would strike vigorously at each other assuming the stereotyped posture shown in Figure 1.

This behavior has typically been referred to as fighting (Scott & Fredericson, 1951), and it was found to be readily identifiable provided that the topography of the response was well specified. For this experiment, a fighting response was recorded by an observer who depressed a microswitch for any striking or biting movement of either or both animals toward the other while in the stereotyped fighting posture. Once a shock was delivered, the subjects would typically assume and maintain this posture for brief periods during which several striking movements might be made. A new response was recorded only for those striking movements which were separated from previous striking movements by approximately 1 sec. Typically, rats struck at each other for only a brief duration (less than 1 sec.) following a delivery of shock; therefore, the number of

Figure 1. Example of the stereotyped fighting posture

fighting episodes was more easily recorded than the duration of fighting. The duration for which the rats maintained the stereotyped fighting posture could not be reliably measured since this posture often blended imperceptibly in time into a more normal posture.

A measure of the reliability of recording was obtained by having two observers simultaneously score the fighting behavior. Figure 2 shows the cumulative records of the fighting responses which occurred during a 10-min. period in which shock was presented at a frequency of 20 shocks per min. The number of fighting responses recorded by each observer agreed within 5%. The parallel slopes of the two lines indicate that there was close agreement between the two observers on both the total number of responses and also on the momentary changes in the rate of fighting.

FREQUENCY OF SHOCK

PRESENTATION

Six rats were divided into three pairs, and each pair was exposed to electric foot-

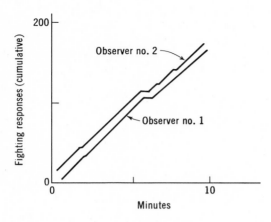

Figure 2. Agreement between observers in the simultaneous recording of fighting responses

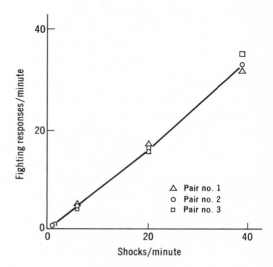

Figure 3. The elicitation of fighting responses as a function of the frequency of presentation of foot-shock for each of three pairs of rats

shock (2 ma) delivered at frequencies of 0.1, 0.6, 2, 20, and 38 shocks per min. Each of these frequencies was administered during each of three different sessions (10 min. per session) with a 24-hr. interval usually allowed after each session. The order of presentation of frequencies was irregular. Figure 3 is the rate of fighting for each of the three pairs of subjects as a function of the frequency of shock presentation. The frequency of fighting for each pair of subjects increased from zero responses in the absence of shock to 33 fighting responses per min. at a frequency of 38 shocks per min. Individual differences between the pairs of rats were largely absent; the frequency of fighting of the different pairs of subjects was almost identical at each of the shock frequencies.

If each delivery of shock produced a fighting response, the rate of fighting would be directly known from the frequency of shock presentation. Indeed, the higher frequencies of shock presentation did result in a relationship of this sort. Shock frequencies in excess of 6 per min. produced fighting in response to 82–93% of the shocks (Table 1). Lower frequencies of shock (less than 1 per min.) produced fighting in response to no more than 66% of the shocks. Visual observation of the rats revealed that shortly after a shock was presented, the subjects slipped out of the fighting posture and assumed other positions. It was also apparent

that fighting in response to shock was more likely if the animals were facing each other at the moment of shock-delivery. Thus, the probability of fighting appeared to be lower at the lower frequencies of shock presentation because of the likelihood that the rats were at some distance from each other. This direct relationship between rate of shock presentation and rate of fighting reversed at very high frequencies. In an additional study with two pairs of rats, the shock was made so frequent as to be continuous. Although occasional

Table 1. Examples of the consistency of fighting elicited by shock from three pairs of subjects during two sessions at each of the different shock frequencies. The consistency of the fighting reflex is expressed as the percentage of shocks that resulted in a fighting response.

Frequency of Shocks (Shocks/Min.)	Consistency of Fighting Reflex (Responses) (Shocks)		
	Pair No. 1	Pair No. 2	Pair No. 3
0.1	0.33	0.66	0.66
0.6	0.61	0.55	0.61
2.0	0.83	0.58	0.58
6.0	0.83	0.94	0.77
20.0	0.92	0.91	0.82
38.0	0.85	0.89	0.93

fighting responses occurred, much of the behavior of the rats appeared directed toward
escape from the experimental chamber. This
"escape" behavior appeared to interfere somewhat with the usual reflexive fighting. Such
behavior was also noted during the early part
of the initial session when the subjects were
first presented with shock. However, in this
case the escape behavior did not persist.

Intrasession changes in fighting behavior
were conspicuously absent (Figure 4). The
bottom curve is the cumulative record of the
fighting for a 10-min. session in which only
one shock was delivered at the middle of the
session. This single shock produced an immediate fighting response. At a shock frequency of 0.6 shocks per min. (second curve
from bottom) the rats did not fight after all
of the six shock deliveries, but observation revealed that the four fighting responses which
did occur were immediately preceded by the
presentation of a shock. At no time did
fighting occur during the interval between
shock presentations although the stereotyped

fighting posture was often maintained during
that time. No warm-up period appeared at
the beginning of the session; nor did the frequency of fighting decrease toward the end of
the session.

SEQUENTIAL EFFECTS

Elicitation of the fighting reflex on a
given day was virtually independent of the
shock frequency used on preceding days or
even on the same day. As a rule, the number
of fighting responses at a given shock frequency varied less than 10%, irrespective of
the preceding shock frequency. On several
occasions, the sessions followed within 10
min. of each other in order to determine the
effects of a shorter interval between sessions.
At a frequency of 2 shocks per min., 68% of
the shocks were effective when 24 hr. were
allowed between sessions; 63% of the shocks
were effective when only 10 min. were allowed between sessions. This small difference in responding as a function of the interval between sessions was typical. The
strength of the fighting reflex appears to be
fairly independent of its history of elicitation.

REFLEX FATIGUE

Figure 2 revealed little change in the
consistency with which the fighting reflex was
elicited, even after 300 elicitations at the
higher rates of shock presentation. In order
to evaluate reflex fatigue, frequent shocks
(every 1.5 sec.) were delivered to a pair of
rats for an uninterrupted period of 7½ hr.
The fighting reflex proved extremely resistant
to fatigue (Figure 5). During the first 2,400
presentations (1 hr.) of the shock, fighting
was elicited after 82% of the shocks. After
7,200 presentations of shock (third hour),
fighting still occurred after 70% of the
shocks. Only during the last 1.5 hr., after 6
hr. and nearly 15,000 shocks, did the consistency of elicitation drop below 40%. By
this time the rats were damp with perspira-
tion and appeared to be weakened physically.
By the end of the 7.5 hr., approximately
10,000 fighting responses had been elicited.

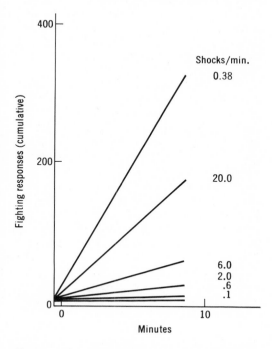

Figure 4. Typical curves for one pair of rats
of the fighting responses at various frequencies
of presentation of shock

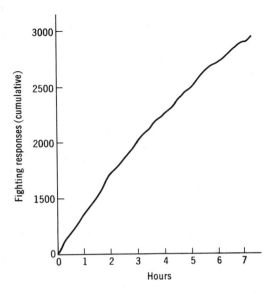

Figure 5. Cumulative record of the fighting responses that were elicited from a pair of rats during a long period (7.5 hr) of frequent (every 1.5 sec) shock presentation

Several observers were required because of the extended observation period.

INTENSITY OF SHOCK PRESENTATION

Three pairs of rats were exposed to various intensities of shock at a fixed frequency of 20 shocks per min. Each intensity was presented for at least 10 min. The sequence of intensities was varied and several 10-min. periods were given at each intensity. The cumulative-response curves of Figure 6 for one pair of rats were typical of those obtained with all three pairs of rats. Increasing the shock intensity from 0–2 ma produced an increased frequency of fighting; at still higher intensities (3–5 ma), the rate of fighting was somewhat reduced. Visual observations indicated that lower intensities produced a fighting response of less vigor and longer latency. Also, at the lower intensities, chance factors, such as the orientation of the rats relative to each other and to the grid floor, appeared to influence greatly the likelihood of a fighting response. If the rats were making good contact across several of the floor grids,

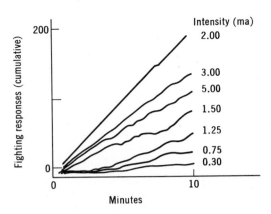

Figure 6. Typical cumulative records of the fighting responses that were elicited from one pair of rats at various intensities of foot-shock

and were also oriented toward each other, a fighting response was likely to result. Even so, this response was relatively short in duration, slow in onset, less vigorous, and less likely to result in a maintained fighting posture than the responses elicited by the higher current intensities. At these lower intensities, the definition of a movement as a fighting response often became arbitrary. At the higher intensities, the attack movement was unmistakable.

The slight decrease in fighting behavior at the highest intensity (5 ma) appeared to be partly a consequence of the debilitating effects of the shock. Prolonged exposure to this intensity often resulted in a complete loss of fighting because of the paralysis of one or both of the subjects. Even during the initial exposure to this very high intensity, fighting behavior appeared to be reduced by the strong tendency of the rats to engage in other shock-induced behavior, such as biting the grids, jumping, running, or pushing on the walls.

Thus, the optimal current intensity for eliciting fighting was approximately 2 ma. At lower intensities, the shock did not appear to be sufficiently aversive, while at higher intensities, the shock appeared to be debilitating and generated competing behavior. Tedeschi (1959) also found that 2 to 3-ma intensity is optimal for producing fighting between mice.

UNIFORMITY OF SHOCK PRESENTATION

All previous investigations of shock-pro-duced fighting appear to have used the same type of shock circuit. Alternate bars of the floor grid have been wired in parallel so that adjacent bars were of opposite polarity, but many nonadjacent bars were of the same polarity. Such a design permits the rat to avoid the scheduled shocks by standing on bars of the same polarity. Skinner and Campbell (1947) found that this unau-thorized avoidance could be eliminated by a scrambling circuit which insured that any two bars would be of opposite polarity during a major part of each shock delivery. A scram-bling circuit of this sort was used throughout the present investigation. Three pairs of rats were now studied to determine the effects of omitting this scrambling circuit. An hour-long period of shock (2-ma intensity at a rate of 20 per min.) was given to each pair of rats on each of three successive days. On one or two of these days, the scrambler was omitted. For all three pairs of rats, the omis-sion of the scrambler produced less than half as many fighting responses as were obtained with the scrambler. The curves in Figure 7 for one pair of rats reveal great variability in the frequency of fighting; periods of frequent

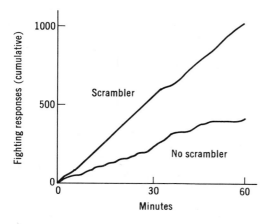

Figure 7. The elicitation of fighting responses by foot-shocks that were delivered with or without a polarity scrambler for the floor grids

fighting alternate with periods of little or no fighting. Visual observation revealed that one or both rats often avoided shocks by standing on bars of like-polarity. This safe posture was often maintained for several min-utes during which no fighting was produced. When a part of the rat happened to contact a bar of different polarity, the resulting shock usually jolted the rat out of this safe posture. For the next few minutes, the rat was likely to receive the scheduled shocks and fighting resumed until once again a safe position was discovered. When the scrambler was in use, no safe position was possible and the rats typi-cally fought immediately following each scheduled shock. The omission of a polarity scrambler in past studies may account for the frequent failure of shock to elicit fighting behavior (Miller, 1948; Richter, 1950).

PREVIOUS EXPERIENCE

In this study, each rat had been housed individually and had no prior contact with his fighting-mate. This general unfamiliarity of the rats with each other might have been a factor in obtaining the fighting response to shock. This possibility was evaluated by housing two rats together in a single cage for several weeks. Subsequent exposure to foot-shock in the experimental chamber produced the same degree of fighting that had been obtained when the same rats had been housed separately. These results were replicated with 24 other animals. It appears, therefore, that previous familiarity of rats with each other does not appreciably effect the elicitation of fighting through foot-shock. On the other hand, nonreflexive fighting behavior has been found to be affected by previous familiarity (Seward, 1945).

SEX

Male rats are known to fight more often than female rats in a natural (no-shock) situa-tion (Beeman, 1947; Scott & Fredericson, 1951). The relevance of sex for the elicitation of fighting by foot-shock was investigated by pairing a female rat with a second female, and a male rat with a female. Several such pairings revealed the same type of fighting in response to foot-shock (2 ma, 20 deliveries per min.) as had been obtained between the two male rats. Indeed, the sexual behavior between the male-female pair was completely displaced by the elicitation of fighting soon after the first few shocks were delivered. Unlike "natural" fighting behavior, reflexive fighting behavior does not appear to be appreciably affected by sexual differences.

NUMBER OF RATS

Reflexive fighting also resulted when more than two rats were shocked. When 2, 3, 4, 6, or 8 rats were simultaneously given foot-shock, the same stereotyped fighting reaction occurred, two or more rats often aggressing against a single rat.

SIZE OF CHAMBER

Throughout the present study the size of the experimental chamber was 12- by 9- by 8 in. In this phase a pair of rats was given shock (2 ma) for 10 min. (20 shocks per min.) in a square chamber having an adjustable floor area. The height was held constant at 17 in. Figure 8 shows the number of fighting responses as a function of the floor area at each of the different floor sizes. With only a very small amount of floor space (6 by 6 in.) the fighting response was elicited by approximately 90% of the shocks. At the larger floor areas, the number of fighting responses decreased; with the largest floor space (24 by 24 in.), only 2% of the shocks elicited fighting. The amount of fighting between rats in response to shock appears to depend critically upon the amount of floor space in the fighting chamber. When the rats were only a few inches apart, the shock was likely to cause them to turn and lunge at each other. At the larger distances, the rats largely ignored each other.

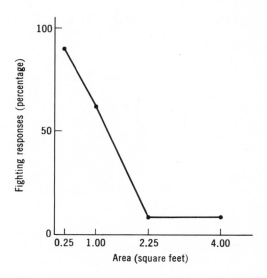

Figure 8. Elicitation of fighting responses from two rats by foot-shock in a square chamber of constant height and variable floor area

STRAIN

As mentioned above, the Holtzman Sprague-Dawley rats are unusually docile in the absence of shock. Additional study revealed that other less docile strains of rats also exhibited this shock-elicited fighting. Two pairs of mature male rats from four other strains (Long-Evans hooded, Wistar, General Biological hooded, Charles River Sprague-Dawley)[1] were exposed to the optimal shock conditions (2 ma at 20 shocks per min.) in the same experimental chamber (12 by 9 by 8 in.) as had been used for the Holtzman strain. In all of the strains the same stereotyped fighting reaction occurred

[1] The different strains of rats were obtained from the following suppliers:
Long-Evans hooded: Small Animal Industry, Chamberland, Indiana;
Wistar: Albino Farms, Redbank, New Jersey;
General Biological hooded: General Biological Supply House, Inc., Chicago, Illinois;
Charles River Sprague-Dawley: Charles River Laboratories, Inc., Brookline, Massachusetts;
Holtzman Sprague-Dawley: Holtzman Company, Madison, Wisconsin.

following the presentations of shock. However, less than 50% of the shocks produced fighting between rats of the Wistar strain, whereas over 70% of the shocks produced fighting between rats in each of the other strains. The Wistar rats appeared to be more sensitive to the shock since much competing behavior was generated by shocks of 2-ma intensity, and two out of the four Wistar rats died after exposure to these shocks. Apart from this seemingly greater sensitivity of the Wistar-strain rats, all of the strains showed the same stereotyped fighting response to foot-shock.

SPECIES

Mature guinea pigs and hamsters were studied under the same conditions of shock presentation and in the same experimental chamber to ascertain the existence of reflexive fighting in other species. Delivery of shock to a pair of hamsters produced a similar type of stereotyped fighting posture and attack as was seen with rats. These fighting responses could be consistently elicited at lower intensities of shock (0.75 ma) than was required with the rats. Also, the hamsters persisted longer in their fighting, often biting and rolling over each other. Tedeschi (1959) found that paired mice also fought vigorously in response to foot-shock. In contrast, the paired guinea pigs never showed the fighting posture or any attack movements in response to shock. Variations in the intensity and frequency of shock presentation, as well as food deprivation up to 72 hr., did not alter this failure to fight.

INTERSPECIES FIGHTING

When a Sprague-Dawley rat was paired with a hamster, shock produced the same fighting reaction by both animals. However, when a rat was paired with a guinea pig, all of the attacking was done by the rat. The guinea pig reacted only by withdrawing from the rat's biting attacks following the shock delivery. The rat attacked only the head of the guinea pig. During this attack, the rat assumed a semi-crouching position with the forepaws raised only slightly off the floor, a posture which differed from the upright position assumed by rats in fighting each other. Since the guinea pig never stood upright, the crouching position of the rat brought its head to the level of the guinea pig's head. The otherwise inflexible and stereotyped fighting posture of the rat appeared to be modified by the position of the guinea pig. No fighting occurred in the absence of shock.

INANIMATE OBJECTS

When an insulated doll was placed into the experimental chamber while a rat was being shocked, no attack was attempted. Similarly, no attack movements were made toward either a conducting doll or a recently deceased rat. Dolls moved rapidly about the cage also failed to produce fighting. Fighting responses were elicited only when the dead rat was moved about the cage on a stick.

ELECTRODE SHOCK

In using foot-shock, both rats are shocked simultaneously since they are standing on the same grid floor. Does the elicitation of fighting require that both rats be shocked? This question might be investigated by electrifying only that section of the grid under one of the rats. However, the rat quickly learns to stand on a nonelectrified section. A second solution is to shock the rats through implanted electrodes. The two rats were placed in an experimental chamber, and electrodes were implanted beneath a fold of skin on the back of one rat. A harness and swivel arrangement allowed the rat complete freedom in moving about. When a 0.5 sec. shock was delivered at an intensity of 2 ma, only a spasmodic movement of the rat resulted if no other rat were present. When the shock was delivered in the presence of a second rat, the stimulated rat usually assumed the stereotyped fighting posture and attacked the unstimulated rat. Upon being attacked, the unstimulated rat in turn often assumed the stereotyped posture and returned the attack. Once the attack was initiated by the shock, the continuance of the fighting appeared to be partly under social control. Fighting was elicited, then, even when only one member of the pair of rats was stimulated. Somewhat the same result was seen above when foot-shock elicited fighting in a rat paired with a guinea pig, in spite of the failure of the guinea pig to reciprocate. Similarly, in the course of delivering foot-shock to a pair of rats, occasionally a rat would learn to eliminate the shock by lying motionless on its back, thereby producing a situation in which only one rat was being stimulated. Under these circumstances, the rat stimulated by foot-shock often attacked the supine rat in the same way that the rat stimulated by electrode shock attacked the unstimulated rat. It should be noted that in each of these situations where only one rat was being stimulated, the full-blown fighting response was elicited less frequently than when both rats were stimulated. Stimulation of a second rat is not a necessary condition for producing the fighting reaction but does, nevertheless, increase the likelihood of its occurrence.

INTENSE HEAT

The elicitation of the fighting reflex through electrode-shock as well as foot-shock suggested that other aversive stimulation also might elicit fighting. A pair of rats was placed in an experimental chamber with a thin metal floor that could be heated from below by a heating coil. After the heating coil was energized, the metal floor became progressively hotter and the two rats began jumping about and licking their feet. No fighting was produced in spite of the agitated movements of both rats. However, when the same pair later was placed on a preheated floor, fighting consistently resulted. The same results were obtained with additional rats. The rats scrambled about the chamber, interrupting their movements frequently to assume a fixed position and attack each other

before resuming their running about. It is very likely that the rats received more painful heat stimulation during the fighting episodes than they would have received if they had jumped about. No more than 2 min. of exposure to the heated floor was given because of the possibility of tissue damage. Nevertheless, the heated floor appeared to elicit fighting in much the same manner as a continuously electrified floor grid. It is probable that the gradual heating of the floor grid allowed the reinforcement of competing behavior, especially licking of the forepaws. This wetting the paws appeared to be effective in cooling the animal at the initially lower temperature of the gradually heated floor but not at the high temperature of the preheated floor. Once fighting was elicited by a preheated floor, subsequent exposure to a gradually heated floor did elicit some fighting, and the competing licking behaviors were reduced.

COLD AND INTENSE NOISE

In spite of the effectiveness of intense heat in eliciting fighting behavior, no fighting was elicited by placing rats on a sheet metal floor pre-cooled by dry ice. It is possible that the temperature induced by the dry ice was not sufficiently aversive; no pain was felt by a human observer upon touching the cooled floor for periods less than 2 sec. Since the rats were consistently moving about, it is quite likely that they did not allow a given paw to remain in contact with the cold floor for a sufficient period of time. Since the cool floor did not produce pain upon immediate contact, unlike electric shock and heat, the rat probably could eliminate pain completely in much the same manner as the rat lying upon its insulated back can completely eliminate painful foot-shock.

Intense noise was similarly ineffective in producing fighting behavior between paired rats. The noise was at an intensity of 135 db (re 0.0002 dyne/cm^2) and enclosed a band from 200–1500 cps. The delivery of noise was varied from brief bursts of less than 1 sec. to periods of more than 1 min. No fighting resulted. A pair of guinea pigs was subjected to the same treatment in the expectation that guinea pigs might be more reactive to intense noise. No fighting resulted.

Fighting appears to be elicited by foot-shock, electrode shock, and intense heat, but not by intense noise or moderate cold.

DISCUSSION

The present investigation found that fighting behavior could be elicited from several paired species by several different types of aversive stimulation. The elicitation of this fighting occurred in almost a one-to-one relationship to the aversive stimulus when the optimal value of the aversive stimulus was used. When a response, such as salivation, is consistently made to a stimulus, such as meat powder, with no previous training, that response is referred to as an unconditioned response (Pavlov, 1927; Sherrington, 1947) or as a respondent (Skinner, 1938). Physiologists have supplied us with the term reflex to designate such specific stimulus-response relationships and in fact have extended the term to denote responses for which related stimuli are not always clearly observable (Keller & Schoenfeld, 1950). The consistent elicitation of the fighting response by aversive stimulation without prior conditioning appears to be best defined as an unconditional reflex. Miller (1948), however, has taken a different approach in the study of fighting behavior. He reports that he trained his subjects to fight by removing the shock each time the animals approximated the fighting position. In this case fighting is presumed to be an escape reaction that is reinforced by the termination of electric shock. In spite of the virtual one-to-one relationship between shock and fighting observed in the present study, it is possible that this apparently reflexive fighting was maintained by some unsuspected and perhaps subtle operant reinforcement. Several possible sources of operant reinforcement seem apparent. First, it is possible that the rats were simply attempting to stand on each other in order to eliminate the aversive stimu-

lation. Several observations made during the course of these experiments bear upon this interpretation: (1) When one of a pair of rats was lying on its back and effectively avoiding all shock, the shocked rat, rather than attempting to climb upon the other rat, often directed an attack specifically at the other rat's head. (2) Fighting was maintained by electrode shock even though no escape was available to the rat stimulated through the electrodes. (3) Leaning against the other rat eliminated the shock no more than simply leaning against one of the insulating plastic walls of the experimental chamber. (4) On the heated floor, the fighting behavior served to increase rather than decrease the amount of aversive stimulation. (5) When an insulated doll was placed in the experimental chamber while a rat was given foot-shock, no attempt was made by the rat to jump upon the doll until several minutes of stimulation had elapsed.

A second possible source of operant reinforcement of fighting is that the fixed-duration shock delivery happened to terminate at the moment that the rats moved toward each other; thus, superstitious reinforcement of these movements would have resulted (Skinner, 1948). Again, several observations indicated that reinforcement of this sort was not operative in producing fighting: (1) Fighting often occurred with the onset of the first shock delivery when prior reinforcement through shock reduction was necessarily impossible. (2) Continuous and uninterrupted delivery of either foot-shock or severe heat produced fighting. Of course, no reinforcement through the termination of the stimulus can result if the stimulus is not terminated

A plausible interpretation of the fighting reflex is that a rat will attack any nearby object or organism upon being aversively stimulated. However, rats did not attack a nearby doll, either insulating or conducting, upon being shocked. Nor was the movement of an inanimate object in the presence of a shocked rat a sufficient condition for eliciting fighting. No fighting resulted when the dolls were moved about the cage at the end of a stick during and between shock presentations. Additional experiments revealed that even a recently deceased rat would not be attacked by a second rat that was given foot-shock, unless the dead rat was moved about the cage on a stick. It would seem, therefore, that a second moving animal either rat, guinea pig or hamster is a necessary condition for eliciting the fighting response from a rat stimulated by foot-shock.

References

Beeman, E. A.   The Effect of Male Hormone on Aggressive Behavior in Mice. *Physiol. Zool.*, 1947, **20**, 373–405.

Daniel, W. J.   An Experimental Note on the O'Kelly-Steckle Reaction.   *J. Comp. Psychol.*, 1943, **35**, 267–268.

Keller, F. S., and Schoenfeld, W. N.   *Principles of Psychology*.   New York: Appleton-Century-Crofts, Inc., 1950.

Miller, N. E.   Theory & Experiment Relating Psychoanalytic Displacement to Stimulus-response Generalization.   *J. Abn. & Soc. Psychol.*, 1948, **43**, No. 2, 155–178.

O'Kelly, L. E. and Steckle, L. C.   A Note on Long-enduring Emotional Responses in the Rat.   *J. Psychol.*, 1939, **8**, 125–31.

Pavlov, I. P.   Conditioned Reflexes: *An Investigation of the Physiological Activity of the Cerebral Cortex*.   London: Oxford University Press, 1927.

Richter, C. P.   Domestication of the Norway Rat and Its Implications for the Problem of Stress.   *Assoc. Res. in Nerv. and Ment. Dis. Proc.*, 1950, **29**, 19.

Scott, J. P., and Fredericson, E.   The Causes of Fighting in Mice and Rats. *Physiol. Zool.*, 1951, **24**, No. 4, 273–300.

Seward, J. P.   Aggressive Behavior in the Rat.   I. General Characteristics: Age and Sex Differences; II. An Attempt to Establish a Dominance Hierarchy; III. The Role of Frustration; IV. Submission as Determined by Conditioning, Extinction, and Disuse. *J. Comp. Psychol.*, 1945, **38**: 175–97, 213–24, 225–38; **39**: 51–76.

Sherrington, C.   *The Integrative Action of the Nervous System*.   New Haven: Yale University Press, 1947.

Skinner, B. F.   *The Behavior of Organisms*.   New York: D. Appleton Century Co., 1938.

————.   "Superstition" in the Pigeon.   *J. Exp. Psychol.*, 1948, **33**, 168–72.

————, and Campbell, S. L.   An Automatic Shocking Grid Apparatus for Continuous Use.   *J. Comp. Physiol. Psychol.*, 1947, **40**, 305–307.

Tedeschi, R. E.   Effects of Various Centrally Acting Drugs on Fighting Behavior of Mice.   *J. Pharmacol. Exp. Therap.*, 1959, **125**, 28.

AROUSAL OF INGROUP-OUTGROUP BIAS BY A CHANCE WIN OR LOSS

Jacob M. Rabbie and Murray Horwitz

ABSTRACT

An experiment, conducted with 112 Dutch teenagers formed into pairs of groups, investigated the minimal conditions that produce a more favorable evaluation of the ingroup than the outgroup. Members of each pair of groups, all of whom were strangers, rated first impressions of each other and of the two groups under one of a graded series of experimental treatments. Simply classifying subjects into two distinct groups yielded no difference between the evaluations of ingroups and outgroups. However, flipping a coin to decide which of the two groups would receive a gift produced a significant bias in favor of the ingroup and its members. A proposed interpretation is that the chance win-loss created intergroup bias by leading subjects to anticipate better outcomes from interpersonal encounters with ingroup members than outgroup members.

Since the work of Sumner (1906), who coined the term "ethnocentrism," social scientists have speculated about the conditions that lead ingroups to devaluate outgroups. The extent to which this devaluative tendency occurs among natural groups is uncertain. Merton (1957) believed that attitudes toward an outgroup may be positive or neutral as well as negative. Schmidt (1960), on the other hand, contended that the very growth of group consciousness entails rejective attitudes toward outsiders.

Whatever its extent in everyday life, invidiousness between groups is surprisingly easy to evoke in experiments. Sherif, Harvey, White, Hood, and Sherif (1961) worked with children's groups that had developed interdependent roles, a hierarchical status structure, and common norms. By simply placing these groups in competition, they produced severe intergroup antagonism. The same effect was readily obtained with groups of adults competing in a training exercise (Blake & Mouton, 1961). According to Sherif, intergroup hostility will arise where well-developed groups operate in a competitive or reciprocally frustrating situation.

It is doubtful that the two conditions proposed by Sherif et al. are necessary to evoke the effect. In pilot experiments, the present authors found that even a newly formed group composed of strangers becomes sharply antagonistic to another group during the course of competition. More surprisingly, we found that well-developed groups working face-to-face on a *cooperative* task also become antagonistic.[1] In the latter experiment, members of each group tended to be suspicious of the other group's intentions, for example viewing offers of assistance as acts of condescension. They also tended to distort the other's communications, for example interpreting proposals for joint action as ultimata. In addition, they tended to attribute hostile motives to the other's ambiguous behavior, for example viewing silence as malevolence. The sheer fact of interaction between groups seemed to produce unstable conditions.

Source: J. M. Rabbie and M. Horwitz, "Arousal of Ingroup-Outgroup Bias by a Chance Win or Loss," *Journal of Personality and Social Psychology*, Vol. 13, 1969, pp. 269–277. Copyright 1969 by The American Psychological Association and reprinted by permission.

[1] A training exercise in 1963 at the National Training Laboratory conducted in collaboration with Marvin Kaplan, Seymour Levy, Henry Riecken, Leonard Solomon, Robert Tannenbaum, and Eric Trist.

that erupted into hostility, even on a cooperative task. The question remains an open one as to the source of the antagonism.

The present research aims to isolate the minimal conditions that are sufficient to generate discriminatory ingroup-outgroup attitudes. Our point of departure is that expressed by Lewin (1948). Addressing himself to Jewish adolescents, he wrote,

regardless of whether the Jewish group is a racial, religious, national or cultural one, the fact that it is classified by the majority as a distinct group is what counts . . . the main criterion of belongingness is interdependence of fate [p. 184].

In the present experiment, we attempted to separate some of the components of Lewin's formulation and to ascertain their effects.

The experiment was designed to answer the following questions concerning "interdependence of fate." First, will merely classifying persons into two groups lead to discriminatory ingroup-outgroup evaluations? If not, will adding the experience of one group's being rewarded by chance while the other is deprived lead to discriminatory intergroup evaluations? Third, if reward-deprivation by chance is insufficient, will reward-deprivation due to the partiality of some external agent produce the effect? Finally, if neither of these forms of reward-deprivation is sufficient, will reward-deprivation due to action by the ingroup or outgroup suffice for the effect? The questions move from the most rudimentary, concerning the impact of group classification per se, to those which progressively add other possible components of interdependence of group fate.

Corresponding to these questions, the experiment included four conditions, in each of which subjects were classified into two groups. In one condition, the groups were neither rewarded nor deprived. In three others the groups were either rewarded or deprived by chance alone, by the arbitrary choice of the experimenter, or by the choice of one of the groups. In order to test for possible sex differences in ingroup-outgroup attitudes, we employed male and female groups within each condition.

METHOD

SUBJECTS

Fifty-six girls and 56 boys, average age about 15 years, were recruited as volunteers from junior high schools in or near Utrecht. Eight subjects of the same sex, all from different schools, participated in each experimental session. All subjects present in a given session were strangers.

CLASSIFYING SUBJECTS INTO GROUPS

The experimenter and an assistant, both Dutch-speaking, introduced the experiment as a study of first impressions. Subjects were divided at random into two groups of four and seated at either side of a screen to prevent their seeing each other. The experimenter publicly designated one group as the blue group and the other as the green. Members of each group wore green or blue identification cards, wrote with green or blue ballpoint pens, used green or blue forms, and were repeatedly addressed by the experimenter and his assistant as "greens" or "blues." In order to diminish any expectation that subjects would interact with one another, the experimenter stated that he had divided them into groups for "administrative reasons only" and that subjects would not work together in any way. The experimenter asked the subjects not to talk with one another "since this would interfere with your task later on— to give unbiased impressions of the personality characteristics of other subjects in this room."

ACTIVITIES PRIOR TO THE
FIRST-IMPRESSION RATINGS

(*a*) To accustom subjects to working in each other's presence in the laboratory, the experimenter administered a Dutch version of the Hidden Patterns Test (Educational Testing Service, 1962). This brief, 5-minute test was explained as measuring how "you perceive things and figures, rather than people." (*b*) Each subject then filled out a short Personal Background Form on which he entered his name, address, size of family, and ordinal position. Subjects were told they would use this information in introducing themselves to each other. (*c*) Subjects next rated two photographs depicting persons of their age and sex. These ratings aimed to give subjects experience with the scales they would later apply to each other. The ratings also provided a base line of subjects' impressions of persons with whom they had no relationship whatsoever.

EXPERIMENTAL MANIPULATIONS

The experimenter introduced each of the experimental variations of reward and deprivation with the following common statement:

We very much appreciate your willingness to cooperate with us and we would like to give you a reward for participating in this research. We have a few transistor radios available and would like to give these to you. Unfortunately, we have only a limited number of these radios. In fact, we have only four available in this session. We are very sorry, but only four of you can get one.

During the statement, the experimenter displayed one of the radios, a pocket transistor model worth about 25 guilders (approximately $7). The procedures then varied according to each experimental treatment as follows:

In the *chance* condition, the experimenter stated:

Perhaps the best thing we can do is to flip a coin to decide which group gets the radios and which does not. O.K.? Do you want heads or tails? The group whose side is up gets the radios.

The experimenter tossed a coin, announced the winning group, and expressed regrets to the losing group about not having more radios. He proceeded to test the radios, wrap

them up, and deliver them to the winning subjects requesting signed receipts.

In the *experimenter* condition, the experimenter arbitrarily designated one of the groups to receive radios, saying, "Let's see— I'll give the radios to this group." Following his decision, the experimenter proceeded to deliver the radios as described above.

In the *group* condition, the experimenter contrived to make the rewarded group appear responsible for the decision. He stated:

Perhaps the easiest way of deciding who gets the radios is for me to give them to one group rather than the other. However, I feel it would be more fair to give you some voice in the decision. It would take too long and be too much trouble to have all of you vote on this. It would be better if only one group takes the vote. Which group wants to make this decision? . . . Oh, you want to vote. O.K., I'll distribute the ballots to you then.

The experimenter distributed voting forms to one of the groups selected at random in advance of the experiment. As the groups could not see each other, each group could assume that the other had been either faster or slower than itself in attracting the experimenter's attention. Regardless of the actual vote, the experimenter announced after collecting the ballots that the voting group decided "they themselves will receive the radios." The delivery of the radios then proceeded as above.

Finally, the *control* condition dispensed with the prize. Between the steps of rating photographs and rating fellow subjects, the control subjects had no intervening experience of reward or deprivation.

RATINGS OF FIRST IMPRESSIONS

Removing the screen so that all subjects could see one another, the experimenter continued:

You are now ready to give your first impressions of each other. Let's start with introducing yourselves. I would like each of you to stand up in turn and read aloud the personal background information you pre-

*pared before—you remember, the form on
which you put your name, address, etc. After
a person finishes reading this material, you
will rate him on the rating scales that I will
give you. Don't think too long about your
answer. We realize you can't give a considered judgment. It's your first impression
that counts.*

The experimenter distributed an eight-
page booklet of rating scales, one page for
each subject. Subjects rated themselves and
the others on eight characteristics: responsibility, consideration, fearfulness, cordiality,
openness, familiarity, soundness of judgment,
and desirability as a friend. The items contained 7-point scales ordered along a favor-
able-unfavorable dimension. To counteract
possible response-set tendencies, some scales
ran from favorable to unfavorable while
others ran in the reverse direction. Subjects
introduced themselves in a random order.
[Ratings of the other group as a group were
also collected. The description of these scales
appears to have been omitted from the method
section of the original.]

ADDITIONAL DATA COLLECTION

(a) After collecting the group ratings,
the experimenter announced that he had "forgotten to pass out some of the photographs"
and obtained subjects' ratings of two additional ones. (b) In order to measure possible
treatment effects on action as well as on attitude, the experimenter obtained subjects'
sociometric choices under the following instructions:

*We said earlier that you would not work
together, but we have changed our minds
about that. You see, we now have your first
impressions about each other. It would be
very interesting to know to what extent these
impressions change as a result of your getting
to know each other a little better. That is
why we would like you to work on a group
task which I will describe in a moment. But
it is important for this task that you like the
people you have to work with. Would you
please rank in order the three people here*

with whom you would most *like to work and
the two with whom you would* least *like to
work? We need this information to form
the new groups in which you'll be working.
In this way, we can take account of your
preferences.*

(c) A final questionnaire, tapping subjects'
feelings of belongingness to own and other
groups, followed the sociometric measure.
The questionnaire checked, too, on various
aspects of subjects' experience during the experiment: to whom subjects attributed responsibility for the reward-deprivation, how
they felt about the experimenter, his conduct, and the value of the prize,[2] and whether
they were acquainted with any other subjects.

After the questionnaire, the experimenter divulged the true purpose of the experiment and stated in the group condition
that the announced vote did not necessarily
correspond with the actual vote. The experimenter urged subjects not to talk about the
experimental procedures with future subjects.
We found no subsequent evidence that they
did.

In summary, the experimental treatments comprised two overlapping variations.
In one variation, half the subjects experienced
a reward and half a deprivation. In the
second variation, subjects experienced the
source of reward or deprivation as chance,
the experimenter, or a group, respectively.
The term "experimental condition" refers to
each of the six cells defined by these twofold
variations. Each experimental condition contained equal numbers of males and females
and each subject rated both own and other
groups. We obtained in consequence a
$3 \times 2 \times 2 \times 2$ repeated-measurements design
as illustrated in Tables 1 and 2 below. Fi-
nally, the control comprised eight girls and
eight boys who were neither rewarded nor
deprived. In what follows, we examine the
effects of the control and experimental con-

---

[2] The mean rating of the value of the radio was
6.02 on a 7-point scale. The rating shows an interesting "sour grapes effect" in that deprived subjects rated the radio much lower than rewarded
subjects ($p < .025$), suggesting the great potency
the prize must have had.

ditions separately, and then compare the data from each.

RESULTS

CONTROL CONDITION

Subjects evaluated own and other groups by rating the personal attributes of members, the attributes of each group as a whole, and by sociometric choice, in that order. In this section, we examine whether classifying subjects in the control condition into two groups differentially affected subjects' ingroup and outgroup evaluations.

Excluding self-ratings, each subject rated the personal attributes of three ingroup and four outgroup members. We converted the ratings where necessary so that the more favorable the rating the higher the score, and computed the mean ratings for ingroup and for outgroup members. As we were uncertain whether two of the scales, "wanting to be friends with" and "familiar-unfamiliar," referred directly to personal attributes of the ratee, we excluded these from the computation of means in advance of the analysis. The means of the six remaining scales were 4.37 for ingroup members and 4.41 for outgroup members. Subjects in the control condition appeared to evidence no bias in rating the attributes of own and other members.

A subject's attitude toward each group as a whole is indicated by the mean of his ratings on the eight scales of positive and negative group attributes. For the 16 subjects in the control condition the mean ratings were 4.28 for own group and 4.41 for the other group. No reliable difference appeared between the ratings of ingroup and outgroup attributes.

Finally, each subject ranked the three persons with whom he most liked and the two with whom he least liked to work. By placing each of the two unchosen persons at rank 4½, we obtain a subject's ranking of his seven fellow subjects. An index of the tendency to choose within own group is the sum of ranks for ingroup members. Including

ties, this index has 16 possible values whose own rank order has a midrank of 8.5. If subjects discriminated in favor of ingroup members, significantly more of the indexes should be above the midrank than below. Nine indexes in the control condition were above and seven were below, indicating no significant partiality toward working with own members.

In the control condition the experimenter classified subjects into distinct groups whose remaining experiences were identical. With regard to member attributes, group attributes, and sociometric choice, subjects did not differentiate own from other groups. Group classification per se appears to be insufficient to produce discriminatory evaluations.

EXPERIMENTAL CONDITIONS

In the experimental conditions, subjects were not only classified into groups, but were rewarded or deprived by virtue of their membership. Whether the groups were rewarded or deprived depended, according to treatment, on the toss of a coin, the experimenter's decision, or the decision of one of the groups. To check on subjects' awareness of these variations, we obtained ratings on three 7-point scales of the degree to which subjects viewed the outcome as determined by chance, the experimenter, or one of the groups, respectively. Subjects' respective mean ratings were 5.96, 2.11, 1.88 in the chance treatment, 4.46, 6.14, 1.81 in the experimenter treatment, and 2.27, 2.85, 4.70 in the group treatment. All of the expected within and between differences are significant beyond the .01 level. Clearly, subjects differed as intended in their perceptions of the source of reward or deprivation in each treatment.

RATINGS OF GROUP ATTRIBUTES

The experience of reward and deprivation markedly affected subjects' combined ratings on the eight scales of positive and negative group attributes. Across treatments, the

Table 1. Mean ratings of group attributes

Treatment	Chance		Experimenter		Group	
	Own group	Other group	Own group	Other group	Own group	Other group
Reward						
Boys	5.19	4.71	4.41	4.28	4.20	4.34
Girls	4.84	3.64	4.72	4.21	4.30	3.81
Deprivation						
Boys	4.65	4.58	4.90	4.09	4.84	4.21
Girls	4.71	4.12	4.22	4.40	4.81	4.05
Overall *M*	4.85	4.26	4.56	4.24	4.54	4.10

Note.—Own group versus other group, $F = 25.76$, $df = 1/84$, $p < .001$. All other main effects and interactions are not significant.

mean rating of own groups ($M = 4.65$) is significantly more favorable than that of other groups ($M = 4.20$) beyond the .001 level. On individual scales, subjects do not significantly distinguish between the two groups with regard to ratings of goodness-badness, future cohesion, and future performance. However, they view their own group relative to the other as less likely to be hostile ($p < .001$), more desirable to belong to ($p < .001$), more familiar ($p < .005$). None of these perceived differences in group attributes could have been based on the experience of actual differences in group behavior.

RATINGS OF PERSONAL ATTRIBUTES

Subjects display the same ingroup-outgroup bias in their ratings of individuals. Table 2 shows the mean ratings of ingroup and outgroup members on the six scales of personal attributes. Across treatments, subjects' mean rating of ingroup members ($M = 4.68$) is significantly more favorable than that of outgroup members ($M = 4.47$) beyond the .001 level. Relative to outgroup members, subjects rate ingroup members as more open ($p < .001$), more responsible ($p < .05$), but no different in fearfulness. On the two personal attribute scales not included in Table 2, subjects rated ingroup members as more familiar ($p < .01$) and more desirable as friends ($p < .001$) than outgroup members.

The ratings of personal attributes are based on a greater number of scores than those of group attributes. Perhaps because of the increased reliability of the personal ratings, three significant effects appear in Table 2 that are not evident in Table 1.

Two of these effects, each significant at the .025 level (Table 3), appear in the analysis of *combined* ingroup-outgroup ratings. These ratings progressively decline from the chance ($M = 4.74$), to experimenter ($M = 4.51$), to group treatments ($M = 4.45$), and they decline primarily among rewarded rather than deprived subjects. The probable explanation is suggested by a surprising fact. When the experimenter delegated the responsibility for awarding the prize to one of the groups in the group treatment, 10 of these 16 subjects unexpectedly voted for the *other* group. The experimenter's subsequent false announcement that the group had voted for itself must have led these "altruistic" subjects to downgrade severely their fellow members ($M = 4.35$). It would seem likely that subjects viewed their winning in the group treatment as "selfish," in the experimenter treatment as "arbitrary," but in the chance treatment as "fair." In the chance treatment, rewarded subjects produced the highest ingroup ratings ($M = 5.07$), probably reflecting their uncontaminated good fortune. These elevated ratings in the chance treatment and the depressed ones in the group treatment largely account for the two significant effects found among the combined ingroup-outgroup ratings.

The third significant effect ($p < .005$, Table 3) is that among rewarded subjects girls show a stronger ingroup-outgroup bias than boys, but among deprived subjects boys

Table 2. Mean ratings of personal attributes

Treatment	Chance		Experimenter		Group	
	Own members	Other members	Own members	Other members	Own members	Other members
Reward						
Boys	5.04	4.93	4.41	4.40	4.31	4.37
Girls	5.10	4.35	4.66	4.71	4.40	4.06
Deprivation						
Boys	4.84	4.57	4.87	4.31	4.76	4.20
Girls	4.63	4.50	4.25	4.55	4.86	4.68
Overall M	4.90	4.58	4.55	4.50	4.58	4.32

show a stronger bias than girls. A proposed explanation of this finding is presented in the Discussion section.

SOCIOMETRIC CHOICES

The final measure of intergroup attitudes is that based on subjects' choices of work partners. The index of choice, described above, is the sum of the ranks that each sub-

Table 3. Analysis of variance of ratings of member attributes

Source	df	MS	F
Between Ss	95		
Chance/Experimenter/ Group (B)	2	148.58	4.44*
Reward/ Deprivation (C)	1	.33	<1
Sex (D)	1	4.08	<1
B × C	1	132.52	3.96*
B × D	2	36.58	1.09
C × D	1	.00	<1
B × C × D	2	87.06	2.60
Error between	84	33.48	
Within Ss	96		
Difference own/other group (A)	1	229.69	13.36***
A × B	2	21.94	1.28
A × C	1	6.02	<1
A × D	1	2.52	<1
A × B × C	2	28.58	1.66
A × C × D	1	165.02	9.60**
A × B × D	2	43.27	2.51
A × B × C × D	2	.33	<1
Error within	84	17.20	
Total	191		

* $p < .025$.
** $p < .005$.
*** $p < .001$.

ject assigned to members of his group. Table 4 shows the distribution of these indexes above and below their midrank. The relative frequencies of indexes that are above the midrank for both reward (72%) and deprivation (71%) significantly exceed those that are below ($p < .01$). Since the indexes of ingroup choice cluster above their midrank, the reverse must be true of outgroup choices. The evidence is clear-cut that on measures of sociometric choice, as well as of group and personal attributes, subjects markedly favor the ingroup over the outgroup.

COMPARISON OF CONTROL AND EXPERIMENTAL CONDITIONS

While the experimental conditions show a significant bias in favor of ingroups, the control condition shows none. We ask next whether the tendency to favor own groups is reliably greater in the experimental than in the control conditions.

On the combined ratings of group attributes, the mean ingroup-outgroup differentiation is −.12 in control and .48 in the experimental conditions. The difference is significant ($p < .025$).[3] Considering sepa-

---

[3] Two-tailed tests would assess probabilities where subjects either favor own or other groups and where either type of bias is greater or less in the experimental than in the control conditions. Since we already know that the experimental conditions showed a significant favoring of ingroups over outgroups and that the control did not, we assess the significance of differences in one direction only by using one-tailed tests in this and the following comparisons.

Table 4. Frequency distribution of indexes of ingroup choice

Treatments	Number	Chance	Experimenter	Group	Total
Reward	Above midrank	11	8	12	31
	Below midrank	3	6	3	12
Deprivation	Above midrank	11	8	13	32
	Below midrank	4	6	3	13

Note.—By the sign test the distributions of the separate total frequencies for reward, deprivation, chance, and group, respectively, are significant beyond the .01 level. The frequencies for reward and for deprivation within chance and group, respectively, are each significant beyond the .05 level.

rate treatments, only the chance treatment significantly exceeds ($p < .025$) control; the experimenter and group treatments do not.

The ratings of personal attributes of members display a similar pattern of results. The mean ingroup-outgroup differentiation for combined personal ratings is $-.04$ in control and .21 in the experimental conditions, although the difference is only nearly significant ($p < .06$). With regard to separate treatments, again it is only the chance treatment that significantly exceeds ($p < .025$) control.

Finally, we compare the extent to which subjects in the control and experimental treatments differ in sociometrically choosing ingroup rather than outgroup members. By the Mann-Whitney U test, the ranks of indexes of ingroup choice are significantly higher ($p < .03$) in the experimental conditions than in the control, due mainly to the joint effects of the chance and group treatments, although neither considered separately differs significantly from the control.

The consistent differences between experimental conditions and control are due mainly to the chance condition. In the experimenter treatment, ingroup-outgroup differentiation was reduced by the losing girls who favored the outgroup (Tables 1 and 2), which probably reflects their experience that the male experimenter had discriminated against their group. In the group treatment, as noted above, differentiation was again reduced by subjects giving low ratings to fellow members who had been falsely described as "selfishly" voting to reward themselves. The chance treatment alone is uncontaminated by possible perceptions of experimenter discrimination or ingroup unfairness, which probably accounts for the clear-cut difference between chance and control.

DISCUSSION

The experiment has yielded two statistically reliable facts. First, the act of flipping a coin to award a prize to one of two collections of strangers produces a significant ingroup preference. Second, the strength of this preference is greater among winning girls than winning boys, but greater among losing boys than losing girls.

When the experimenter made the chance award, he changed several components of the subjects' social field. Prior to the flip of the coin, each subject confronted an experimenter, two relatively indistinguishable groups, and several relatively indistinguishable persons within the groups. The flip of the coin changed the subjects' view of each of these units except the experimenter, whose action they saw as dictated by chance. The two groups became distinguishable as winner or loser, and the several persons in these groups became at least distinguishable as satisfied or dissatisfied with their outcomes. We consider next to which of these changes subjects reacted when they developed a bias in favor of their ingroups.

The bias could have been produced if subjects simply reacted with satisfaction or dissatisfaction to their group's winning or losing. According to the theory of group cohesiveness (Cartwright & Zander, 1960), winners should rate their ingroup positively where it mediates a reward. According to the theory of frustration-aggression (Rosenblatt, 1964), losers should rate an outgroup negatively where it mediates a deprivation. The joint occurrence of these processes could account for both winners and losers rating ingroups higher than outgroups. There is evidence, however, that neither process operated in the present experiment. The self-ratings by winning groups were not higher than those by losing groups, the respective means being 4.61 versus 4.69 for own-group attributes, 4.65 versus 4.70 for own-member attributes, and 72% versus 71% for percentages above the midrank of ingroup sociometric choice. Nor were the outgroup ratings by losing groups lower than those by winning groups, the respective means being 4.24 versus 4.17 for outgroup attributes and 4.47 in each case for outgroup-member attributes. It is thus unlikely that subjects' ingroup preference stemmed from their satisfaction or dissatisfaction with the changed state of each group.

It is also conceivable that subjects reacted not to the state of each group separately, but to the difference between the groups. According to the theory of cognitive balance, subjects who view themselves as having a common experience with ingroup members should generate positive sentiments toward the ingroup, since "p similar to o induces p likes o [Heider, 1958, p. 184]." Correspondingly, subjects who view themselves as having a contrasting experience with outgroup members should generate negative sentiments toward the outgroup, since a disjunctive relation carries a negative sign. As regards the prize, subjects had contrasting experiences with outgroup members in the experimental conditions, but identical experiences with outgroup members in the control condition. Nevertheless, subjects' ratings of outgroup members were *not* lower in the experimental conditions ($M = 4.47$) than in the control ($M = 4.41$). On this evidence, subjects do not appear to have downgraded groups whose fate differed from that of their own group.

Finally, we consider the possibility that subjects were reacting to the changed emotional states of the persons in the room rather than to the changed states of the groups. After one group won at the other's expense, subjects could readily perceive themselves and others as feeling gratified or disappointed, thereby changing the ease or difficulty of face-to-face encounters. Winners who interacted with losers would need to suppress any display of satisfaction with winning, lest they communicate that they were pleased with the

others' loss. Losers who interacted with winners would need to suppress their feelings of dissatisfaction with losing, lest they communicate that they were displeased with the others' gain. By contrast, interaction with members of the subjects' own group would be devoid of conflict and, indeed, offer subjects social support for freely expressing their feelings about winning or losing. Subjects were in visual and sometimes oral communication with each other during the experiment and could anticipate later encounters in the hallway or elevator. A demand characteristic of this, or any psychological experiment, is that subjects respond to their face-to-face encounters. If they perceive that interaction with ingroup members will be easy, but interaction with outgroup members will be difficult, subjects should tend to approach the one and avoid the other, manifesting these approach-avoidance tendencies in their discriminatory ratings of the two groups.

The case for this interpretation is strengthened by its capacity to explain the paradoxical difference between the responses of girls and boys to winning or losing (Table 3). Girls usually show greater compassion than boys (Terman & Miles, 1936) and strive more than boys for fair outcomes rather than to win at another's expense (Bond & Vinacke, 1961, Uesigi & Vinacke, 1963). Yet, where girls and boys were winners in the present study, the supposedly compassionate girls discriminated more strongly than boys against losers; where girls and boys were losers, the supposedly competitive boys favored more strongly than girls their fellow losers. The paradox can be resolved by noting the special conflicts that compassion or competitiveness engenders in encounters between winners and losers. A compassionate winner should desire to express sympathy to a loser although constrained by the method of allocating rewards to be pleased about winning at the other's expense. A competitive loser should desire to avoid the ignominy of facing his conqueror. Thus, winning girls may strongly discriminate against losers because sympathy leads them to avoid those whom they have beaten, while losing boys may strongly discriminate against winners because pride leads them to avoid those who have beaten them.

A testable implication is that under non-competitive conditions, winning girls will show little ingroup-outgroup bias. By tossing two separate coins instead of a single one, the experimenter could cause one group to win and the other to lose, each independently of the other. Winners should then experience no conflict in interacting with losers since their satisfaction with the prize does not imply satisfaction with the others' loss. If winning girls especially desired to express their sympathy to losers, they might under this non-competitive condition even prefer to interact with the losing outgroup rather than the winning ingroup.[4]

What is striking in the present experiment is how little it evidently takes to move two randomly formed groups of strangers into mutual antipathy. Flipping a coin to decide the allocation of a scarce resource is commonly used in everyday social life in the effort to be fair. Yet this simple act triggered processes within the two groups of strangers that were farreaching enough to affect the perception of personal traits. Although subjects had no prior experience with anyone in the room, the flip of the coin was sufficient to shape their views of outgroup members as less friendly, less familiar, less considerate, and less desirable as associates than ingroup members.

However, the act of awarding a prize by chance is only apparently simple. Viewed as an intervention in the social system of the experiment, this single act ramifies widely into changes in the states of the two groups, of the persons within the groups, and of the interrelations among each of these units. In evincing ingroup-outgroup bias, subjects could have been reacting to any or all of these changes. Our reading of the present evidence is that they were reacting to the perceived emotional changes in themselves and others and to the consequent change in ease or difficulty of face-to-face interaction. Intergroup prejudice can obviously cause difficulties in interpersonal encounters. It is perhaps less obvious that the perceived difficulties of interpersonal encounters can cause intergroup prejudice.

Methodologically, the present experiment was not designed to test a theory, but to determine which, if any, of several experimental interventions suffice to produce a given effect. If the experimental situation is conceived as a social system, the experimental interventions correspond to actions designed to produce social change. There is thus a natural transition from laboratory methodology to the methodology of social action. The present study says to those who intervene in real-life systems that they can use the equitable method of allocating rewards by chance to produce group cohesiveness, on the one hand, and intergroup divisiveness, on the other. To reduce divisiveness, we suggest, social practitioners should work to ease the difficulties of here-and-now interaction between the members of two groups. A parallel task for experimental inquiry is to find methods of distributing group rewards that will lessen rather than heighten the difficulties of interpersonal encounters across group lines.

---

[4] This experiment has since been run with positive results.

References

Blake, R. R., & Mouton, J. S. Reactions to Intergroup Competition Under Win-lose Conditions. *Management Science*, 1961, 7, 420–435.

Bond, J. R., & Vinacke, W. E. Coalitions in Mixed-sex Triads. *Sociometry*, 1961, **24**, 61–75.

Cartwright, D., & Zander, A. (Eds.). *Group Dynamics: Research and Theory.* Evanston, Ill.: Row, Peterson, 1960.

Educational Testing Service. *The Hidden Patterns Test.* Princeton, N.J.: Author, 1962.

Heider, R. *The Psychology of Interpersonal Relations.* New York: Wiley, 1958.

Lewin, K. *Resolving Social Conflicts.* New York: Harper, 1948.

Merton, R. K. *Social Theory and Social Structure.* Glencoe, Ill.: Free Press, 1957.

Rosenblatt, P. C. Origins and Effects of Group Ethnocentrism and Nationalism. *Journal of Conflict Resolution,* 1964, 8, 131–164.

Schmidt, H. D. Bigotry in School Children. *Commentary,* 1960, 29, 253–257.

Sherif, M., Harvey, O. J., White, J., Hood, W. R., & Sherif, C. W. *Intergroup Conflict and Cooperation: The Robbers Cave Experiment.* Norman, Okla.: University Book Exchange, 1961.

Sumner, W. G. *Folkways.* Boston: Ginn, 1906.

Terman, L. M., & Miles, C. C. *Sex and Personality.* New York: McGraw-Hill, 1936.

Uesigi, T. K., & Vinacke, W. E. Strategy in a Feminine Game. *Sociometry,* 1963, 26, 75–88.

EXPERIMENTAL INVESTIGATIONS OF HOSTILITY CATHARSIS

Leonard Berkowitz

ABSTRACT

Discussions of hostility catharsis often maintain that the instigation to aggression is lowered by aggressive actions, whether directed against animate or inanimate objects, and may even be reduced by a variety of other behaviors such as competition and fantasy. The energy model of motivation on which this reasoning generally rests is coming under increasing attack, while there is growing support for standard, experimentally based analyses. Tests of the catharsis hypothesis indicate that observers do not lower their aggressive tendencies by watching other persons fight. Witnessed aggression provides stimuli that can elicit aggressive responses in these observers who are ready to attack someone, and even one's own aggressive responses may produce stimuli evoking further aggression, although several processes may contribute to this self-stimulating effect. Evidence presumably indicative of hostility catharsis is reinterpreted. It is proposed that the sight of people being injured aggressively (to an appropriate degree) is a reinforcement for those observers who are angry or who

Source: L. Berkowitz, "Experimental Investigations of Hostility Catharsis," *Journal of Consulting and Clinical Psychology,* Vol. 35, 1970, pp. 1–7. Copyright 1970 by The American Psychological Association and reprinted by permission.

have been frequently rewarded for aggression. As a reinforcement, this stimulus might be gratifying, but it is also capable of eliciting further aggression. The catharsis hypothesis blinds us to the important social principle that aggression is all too likely to lead to still more aggression.

Several years ago the movie "The Tenth Victim" proposed a straightforward and dramatic method for controlling violence and lessening wars: The most aggressive people in society should try to kill each other in a socially sanctioned hunt, with the winner gaining a fortune. The hunters would drain their pent-up aggressive urges by killing or trying to kill others—or by dying. Onlookers, participating vicariously in the hunt, would also discharge their hostile energy as they watched the goings-on. With all of this energy drainage taking place in the hunt, there would not be any aggression left for extracurricular violence or for wars.

Essentially similar proposals based on theoretically comparable analyses have been advanced by other writers. In his book, *On Aggression*, Konrad Lorenz (1966) tells us that members of socially isolated groups must inevitably experience a build-up of aggressive drive; outsiders are not available to be attacked and thus provide an outlet for the accumulating aggressive energy. The wise person in these circumstances, Lorenz says, would smash a vase with as loud and resounding a crash as possible. We do not have to destroy other people in order to lessen our aggressive urges; it is enough merely to destroy inanimate objects.

Of course, it may be expensive to go around breaking vases, and some people have argued for a much cheaper solution to the problem of violence. All that need be done is to show lots of aggression on the TV and movie screens. If this violates our aesthetic sensibilities, or if we grow tired of Westerns and war movies, there is always competitive sports, or maybe canal digging. And what about the race to the moon? Cannot these competitive and hazardous activities provide a "moral equivalent to war"—socially acceptable and even constructive ways of reducing aggressive drive?

In one form or another, these ideas date back at least as far as Aristotle, although many contemporary discussions along these lines have been influenced by early psychoanalytic theorizing. While Freud later discarded his original belief that the display or experience of emotion could, by itself, bring about therapeutic improvement, this catharsis doctrine—maintaining that pent-up emotions can be "purged" or "discharged" by expressing one's feelings—is still inherent in such psychoanalytic concepts as displacement and sublimation.

With classical psychoanalysis and Lorenzian ethology, proponents of the energy-discharge formulation often maintain that the human body is constantly generating some mysterious substance or excitation which automatically goads man to aggression. This unmeasured and unidentified chemical or force presumably must be released in action or else the accumulating drive will burst outward, causing an impulsive explosion of violence. While many laymen seem to believe this line of thought has a sound scientific basis—largely because they mistakenly regard Lorenz's popular writings as representative of the general field of animal behavior—technically qualified authorities have severely criticized this analysis on both logical and empirical grounds (cf. Berkowitz, 1969; Montagu, 1968). Other advocates of the catharsis doctrine assume that the trials and tribulations of life result in a build-up of anger which ordinarily does not subside unless the emotion can be discharged in aggressive action, or displaced, sublimated, or transformed. Here, too, evidence is lacking.

Nevertheless, the widespread popularity of the idea of hostility catharsis is easily understood. The energy model of motivation on which this doctrine is based is a familiar one and seems to make sense. This kind of motivational analysis is probably accepted more because of its readily grasped, metaphorical nature, however, than because of its essential validity. Although those people who confine their reading to the traditional psychoanalytic literature and to the popular writings of Konrad Lorenz might not know this, the energy model of motivation is falling into increasing disrepute among experimental biologists and psychologists. The model is much too simple and even hinders the search for important behavioral determinants.[1] In the case of aggression, the energy model usually maintains that a wide variety of activities (including fantasy, competitive sports, and indirect as well as direct aggression), involving many different types of people, can lower the person's inclination to attack others. However, a rapidly growing body of carefully controlled research raises serious questions about this overly simple formulation and even casts considerable doubt on its validity. Rather than producing a lowered probability of further violence, aggression in the absence of guilt or anxiety is all too likely to stimulate still more aggression. If policymakers were to follow the classic catharsis doctrine or accept the similar ideas of Konrad Lorenz as a guide for social actions, the results could well be unfortunate indeed.

There are alternatives to the energy analyses: explanatory schemes based on ideas of stimulus-response relationships and learning. I will argue here that these alternative conceptions are better able, by far, to account for the available evidence.

But first, what is this evidence? Let me summarize some of these studies briefly.

EFFECTS OF OBSERVING AGGRESSIVE ACTIONS BY OTHERS

A decade of laboratory research has virtually demolished the contention that people will lessen their aggressive tendencies by watching other persons beat each other up. Experiments with young children, high school and college students, and even older adults,

have shown again and again that under certain circumstances, witnessed aggression can[2] heighten the chances that the observer will act aggressively himself (cf. Bandura, 1965; Berkowitz, 1965a; Geen & Berkowitz, 1967; Walters & Thomas, 1963). Several different processes seem to contribute to this increased probability of aggression (cf. Bandura & Walters, 1963): (a) the observer learns something—he can acquire new aggressive action patterns imitatively through seeing how the aggressor behaves on the screen; (b) the film violence may lower restraints against aggression in audience members, either by showing that aggression pays off or by seeming to legitimize violence. Several experiments conducted in my own laboratory illustrate this legitimizing phenomenon (Berkowitz, 1965b; Berkowitz, Corwin, & Heironimus, 1963; Berkowitz & Geen, 1967; Berkowitz & Rawlings, 1963). Deliberately provoked college students saw a filmed prize fight in which the protagonist, played by Kirk Douglas, received a bad beating. In some cases, the film introduction led the audience to regard the beating as "bad" and ethically unjustified; Kirk Douglas was said to be a "good guy." By contrast, for other Ss, Kirk Douglas was portrayed in a much less sympathetic manner so that his beating was viewed as proper and justified. Later, when all of the men were given an opportunity to attack the person who had angered them, the Ss shown the "justified" film violence generally exhibited the strongest aggression. It is as if the justified aggression on the screen made their own aggression seem morally proper, thereby temporarily lessening their inhibitions against aggression. (There is also the other side of the coin, I might add. Film

---

[1] See Hinde (1959) for a discussion of various energy conceptions of motivation, such as that found in Lorenz's and psychoanalytic theories. Hinde argued that these concepts have impeded the development of a more adequate motivational formulation.

[2] I use the word "can" instead of "will" advisedly, since a good many situational and personal factors influence the relationship between witnessed violence and the likelihood of aggressive actions by observers, including the observers' attitudes toward the violent event, the extent to which they are set to act aggressively, the strength of their aggressiveness habits, etc. People concerned with the effects of movie and TV violence should ask not what are the consequences of media violence, but under what conditions do particular effects arise?

violence that is regarded as "bad," unjustified, or horrible serves to restrain the observers' later aggression.[3])

But also note that the "legitimate" movie violence did not lead to a fantasy catharsis. There was no purge of anger or discharge of hostile impulses through watching the screen villain getting the beating he deserved. A recently completed experiment (Turner & Berkowitz[4]) adds further corroboration to this point. All of the Ss were angered by E's confederate, and again, all saw the fight scene. This time, however, before the movie went on, one-third of the men were asked to imagine themselves as one of the film characters (the person who would beat up Kirk Douglas), while another group was instructed to take the role of a watching judge, and a control group did not do any role taking. The people told to imagine themselves as the fight winner subsequently made stronger attacks on E's accomplice than did either of the other groups. The make-believe as the winning aggressor led to more, not less, open aggression following the film.

ELICITATION OF AGGRESSIVE RESPONSES

At least one other process may also be at work in witnessed violence in addition to imitative learning and the lowering of restraints: The aggressive movie can stimulate transient aggressive ideas and feelings and even overt aggressive responses. There is nothing mysterious about this principle; it can be regarded as a special case of a much more general stimulus-response relationship. Simply put, stimuli that have frequently been associated with a certain type of action are capable of evoking that response on later occasions. If a certain stimulus has been repeatedly connected with aggressive behavior, it will be able to elicit aggressive responses from people who are ready to act aggressively.

One such stimulus, obviously, is a weapon, and several experiments have demonstrated that the mere presence of guns can heighten aggressive behavior. In at least two studies involving children playing with toy weapons (Feshbach, 1956; Mallick & McCandless, 1966), the aggressive gun play led to an increase in aggressive encounters with other youngsters. Many of these encounters were much more aggressive than just a continuation of make-believe shooting at each other. Here too, then, fantasy aggression did not increase peacefulness. An experiment with college men also shows how weapons can stimulate aggressive reactions merely by being present (Berkowitz & LePage, 1967). Although nonangered Ss were not affected to any detectable extent, insulted men gave more electric shocks to their tormentor if weapons were nearby than if neutral objects or no other objects were present with the shock machine. The weapons had evidently served as aggressive stimuli, eliciting stronger attacks from those Ss who, because they were angry, were ready to act aggressively.

Aggressive behavior, even aggressive words, can also furnish aggression-evoking stimuli. The sight of people fighting, and perhaps especially seeing someone receive deserved or proper injury, can also provide these stimuli. Several experiments indicate that emotion arousal facilitates the occurrence of aggressive responses to the stimulus of a witnessed fight. While most of these studies were carried out in my own laboratory, two interesting investigations were conducted elsewhere. In one of these, Geen and O'Neal (1969) recently found that men who heard a loud but not painful sound after seeing the prize fight attacked their partner more strongly than did other Ss who had not

---

[3] Richard Goranson (1969) found that angry college men restrained their attacks on their tormentor after learning that the loser in the filmed prize fight had died later because of the beating he had received in the fight. Interestingly, he also found that the reporting of a death unrelated to the witnessed fight (the character played by Kirk Douglas supposedly died in an auto accident) also served to inhibit S's later aggression.

[4] C. Turner and L. Berkowitz. Unpublished manuscript, 1970.

watched the fight or who had not heard the sound. The excitation resulting from the loud sound had strengthened the aggressive reactions stimulated by the aggressive movie. As this experiment suggests, anger is not the only arousal state that can facilitate aggressive stimuli. Similarly, when Tannenbaum and Zillman[5] showed a brief sex film to one group of men who had just been provoked by a partner, these sexually aroused Ss then gave him stronger electric shock punishment than did similarly angered but nonsexually aroused men in the control group. The sexual arousal had evidently strengthened the aggressive responses elicited by the provocation and the opportunity to attack the partner. In a later variation on this study, these investigators obtained results consistent with the previously cited Berkowitz and LePage (1967) experiment. The strongest electric attacks on the peer tormentor were given by men who watched the sex film, and at the same time heard a tape recording of the woman character's thoughts about killing her lover. In this case, the sex arousal apparently also "energized" the aggressive responses elicited by the aggressive tape recording. This kind of phenomenon, in which sexual arousal functions like other arousal sources to facilitate aggressive responses to aggressive stimuli, could contribute to the apparent connection between sexual and aggressive motivation postulated by some writers.

Sometimes the aggressive stimuli can come from our own behavior. Under some conditions at least, an attack on an available target person leads to still stronger aggression, as if the first attack had introduced additional aggression-evoking stimuli. Some such process may be involved in the finding typically obtained with the Buss "aggression-machine" procedure; the electric shocks inflicted by experimentally provoked or thwarted men generally increase in intensity over the series of opportunities given them to punish their partner (e.g., Buss, 1963; Geen, 1968). Rather than producing a purge of all hostile

inclinations, the first shocks seem to stimulate still stronger aggressive reactions. Hostile words might also have an aggression-eliciting effect. According to an experiment by Loew (1967), college students trained to speak aggressive words aloud in a learning task subsequently administered stronger electric shocks to a peer whenever he made a mistake than did a control group of Ss trained to speak only nonaggressive words. The Ss' aggressive language could have stimulated aggressive responses in them which then strengthened their electric attacks on the other person.

More obviously has to be learned about the conditions governing this kind of effect and the mechanisms producing it. Sometimes the result can be understood in terms of response generalization; thus, in the Loew (1967) study, the reinforcement given the aggressive words generalized to intensify the physical attacks. In other instances, self-justification, or dissonance reduction, may be at work; people who voluntarily attack or derogate someone else often seek to justify their initial hostility by expressing further criticism of their victim, presumably when the initial hostility is inconsistent with the values they hold for themselves and they cannot compensate the victim (cf. Brock & Pallak, 1969). Whatever the processes involved in this apparent self-stimulation to further aggression, it is clear that aggressive behavior at times leads to more, not less, aggression by the attacker. We are often told that people should express their hostile ideas and feelings; telling someone we hate him supposedly will purge pent-up aggressive inclinations and will "clear the air"—whatever this last cliche means. Quite frequently, however, when we tell someone off, we stimulate ourselves to continued or even stronger aggression.

REINTERPRETING SUPPOSED EVIDENCE FOR HOSTILITY CATHARSIS

I probably should stop now and address myself to a common criticism of the argu-

---

[5] P. H. Tannenbaum and D. Zillman. Unpublished study, 1969.

ment I have been spelling out. The objection might take this form: The traditional catharsis doctrine surely would not have gained such wide popularity if it did not have some basis in reality. Why do so many persons enjoy watching aggressive events or say that they feel better after seeing an aggressive game or movie? And further, How do I account for the pleasure that people often feel after telling someone off or hurting him?

These are important questions, clearly, and deserve careful answers. While space limitations do not permit me to give these matters as much attention as they deserve, I will say something about these problems and will try to show that there are several different mechanisms at work rather than a single energy discharge.

There is little doubt that many people find pleasure in watching others fight. What I do doubt is that this pleasure necessarily signifies a long-term reduction in some aggressive drive. Sometimes the pleasure stems from the ebb and flow of excitement; the game or match is simply an exciting event which is pleasant through the build-up and decline of internal tension. Angry people, or persons with a history of aggressive behavior, are apparently particularly inclined to seek out such aggressive scenes (Eron, 1963). But again, this seems to be due to the reinforcing quality of such scenes for them rather than being due to a discharge of aggressive energy. Suggesting this, Hartmann (1969) found that deliberately provoked juvenile delinquents exhibited a greater volume of aggression toward a peer (in the form of electric shocks) after watching a movie showing a boy receiving a painful beating in a fight than after seeing a film focusing on the aggressor's actions. The sight of the movie victim's suffering was presumably gratifying in some way, but enhanced their subsequent attacks on their own tormentor. Let me point out another reason why people say that they feel better after watching aggressive events: they were so carried away by the interesting scene before them that they forgot their troubles, at least momentarily, and stopped brooding or stirring themselves up.

SIGHT OF HURT AS REINFORCEMENT FOR AGGRESSION

Now let me return to this matter of seeing someone injured. I have suggested here, on the basis of several different experiments, that the sight of someone being hurt is a reinforcement for angry people. As a reinforcement, this perception can lead to increased aggression, but may also produce a pleasant tension reduction, especially if the injured person is the frustrater.

A series of experiments by Hokanson and his students provides pertinent physiological evidence (Hokanson & Burgess, 1962; Hokanson, Burgess, & Cohen, 1963; Hokanson & Edelman, 1966). The college students in these investigations displayed a marked increase in systolic blood pressure after being insulted by E, and then showed a quick reduction in systolic pressure after they had an opportunity to give their tormentor electric shocks. The researcher found that there was a much slower decline in physiological tension (in systolic pressure) when the angered S attacked someone other than his frustrater. According to this research, displacing hostility is no more effective than no aggression at all in reducing physiological tension. The Hokanson studies also demonstrated that physical activity, in and of itself, does not lead to the rapid decline in systolic pressure, even when the motor responses are the same as those involved in the attacks on the frustrater. The Ss had to believe that they had attacked, and presumably hurt, their tormentor if the rapid decline in systolic pressure was to occur. More recent experiments in this program (for example, Stone & Hokanson, 1969) suggest the cause of the decline in vascular response. Rather than being indicative of an energy discharge, the physiological tension reduction stems from prior rewarding experiences. That is, the rapid drop in blood pressure following aggression comes about to the extent that the person had previously learned that injuring his frustraters is rewarding or gratifying. Thus, when one group of Ss was rewarded for reacting *non*aggressively to attacks made on them, they later displayed the "cathartic-like," quick decrease in vascular response only after behaving in a friendly, rather than hostile, fashion.

Whatever the explanation, we evidently feel better when we see that the person who had angered us has been hurt. (Of course, the extent of the injury probably must be in keeping with our level of anger toward that person and our judgment of what he deserves.) We do not have to hurt the frustrater ourselves in order to experience this pleasure. In one of our Wisconsin studies (Berkowitz, Green, & Macaulay, 1962), for example, angered Ss reported feeling better after hearing that their insulter had performed poorly on an assigned task. Similarly, in another study (Bramel, Taub, & Blum, 1968) deliberately provoked college students were relatively more interested in listening to a tape recording in which their tormentor said he was suffering than in hearing him say that he was happy—even though the Ss were told that the tape recording had been made six to nine months earlier. In comparison to a nonangered group, the recording of the frustrater's earlier suffering also led to a greater expressed liking for that person than did a control recording in which the obnoxious person said he was in a neutral mood. If we are angry with someone, the knowledge that he has been hurt or has suffered is evidently gratifying.[6]

This information, to repeat myself, is a reinforcement and, as such, can influence the probability of further aggression. We may

stop or refrain from attacking our frustrater when we learn that he has been injured sufficiently, and we may feel much better than before. Retribution has been achieved. But this could well be only a temporary effect. Our aggressiveness habit has also been reinforced, so that, consequently, over the long run there actually is a greater likelihood that we will attack someone again in the future. There is empirical as well as theoretical support for this possibility. One research team (Patterson, Littman, & Bricker, 1967) observed the encounters among nursery school children over a nine-month period, taking particular note of aggressive and assertive actions. According to their data, the frequency of aggression by any one child after he had fought with another youngster was influenced by the victim's reactions to the initial attack. If the victim had reinforced the aggressor's behavior by showing defeat and submission, and perhaps some injury as well, there was an increased chance that the aggressor would again attack someone, particularly the first victim, later on.

CONCLUSION

The traditional energy model of aggression is clearly inadequate to account for many of the findings I have reported here. Not only is this conventional analysis much too simple, but it has also impeded recognition of the important role played by environmental stimuli and learning in aggressive behavior. Above all, this energy model and the associated catharsis doctrine have helped to justify the expression of aggression and have delayed our recognition of an important social principle: Aggression is all too likely to lead us to still more aggression.

---

[6] Very much in the same vein, Feshbach, Stiles, and Bitter (1967) have demonstrated that the sight of an anger instigator being hurt (not seriously) facilitates learning by Ss this person had provoked.

References

Bandura, A.   Vicarious Processes: A Case of No-trial Learning.   In L. Berkowitz (Ed.), *Advances in Experimental Social Psychology*. Vol. 2.   New York: Academic Press, 1965.

————., & Walters, R. H.   *Social Learning and Personality Development*.   New York: Holt, Rinehart & Winston, 1963.

Berkowitz, L.   The Concept of Aggressive Drive: Some Additional Considerations. In L. Berkowitz (Ed.), *Advances in Experimental Social Psychology*. Vol. 2. New York: Academic Press, 1965.   (a)

————.   Some Aspects of Observed Aggression. *Journal of Personality and Social Psychology*, 1965, **2**, 359–369.   (b)

————.   Simple Views of Aggression: Review of Five Recent Books on Aggression. *American Scientist*, 1969, **57**, 372–383.

————., Corwin, R., & Heironimus, M.   Film Violence and Subsequent Aggressive Tendencies. *Public Opinion Quarterly*, 1963, **27**, 217–219.

————., & Geen, R. G.   Stimulus Qualities of the Target of Aggression: A Further Study. *Journal of Personality and Social Psychology*, 1967, **5**, 364–368.

————., Green, J. A., & Macaulay, J. R.   Hostility Catharsis as the Reduction of Emotional Tension. *Psychiatry*, 1962, **25**, 23–31.

————., & LePage, A.   Weapons as Aggression-eliciting Stimuli. *Journal of Personality and Social Psychology*, 1967, **7**, 202–207.

————., & Rawlings, E.   Effects of Film Violence on Inhibitions Against Subsequent Aggression. *Journal of Abnormal and Social Psychology*, 1963, **66**, 405–412.

Bramel, D., Taub, B., & Blum, B.   An Observer's Reaction to the Suffering of His Enemy. *Journal of Personality and Social Psychology*, 1968, **8**, 384–392.

Brock, T. C., & Pallak, M. S.   The Consequences of Choosing to Be Aggressive. In P. G. Zimbardo (Ed.), *The Cognitive Control of Motivation*.   Glenview, Ill.: Scott, Foresman, 1969.

Buss, A. H.   Physical Aggression in Relation to Different Frustrations. *Journal of Abnormal and Social Psychology*, 1963, **67**, 1–7.

Eron, L.   Relationship of TV Viewing Habits and Aggressive Behavior in Children. *Journal of Abnormal and Social Psychology*, 1963, **67**, 195–196.

Feshbach, S.   The Catharsis Hypothesis and Some Consequences of Interaction With Aggressive and Neutral Play Objects. *Journal of Personality*, 1956, **24**, 449–462.

————., Stiles, W. B., & Bitter, E.   The Reinforcing Effect of Witnessing Aggression. *Journal of Experimental Research in Personality*, 1967, **2**, 133–139.

Geen, R. G.   Effects of Frustration, Attack, and Prior Training in Aggressiveness upon Aggressive Behavior. *Journal of Personality and Social Psychology*, 1968, **9**, 316–321.

————., & Berkowitz, L.   Some Conditions Facilitating the Occurrence of Aggression After the Observation of Violence. *Journal of Personality*, 1967, **35**, 666–676.

————., & O'Neal, E. C. Activation of Cue-elicited Aggression by General Arousal. *Journal of Personality and Social Psychology*, 1969, **11**, 289–292.

Goranson, R. Observed Violence and Aggressive Behavior: The Effects of Negative Outcomes to the Observed Violence. Unpublished Doctoral Dissertation, University of Wisconsin, 1969.

Hartmann, D. P. Influence of Symbolically Modeled Instrumental Aggression and Pain Cues on Aggressive Behavior. *Journal of Personality and Social Psychology*, 1969, **11**, 280–288.

Hinde, R. A. Unitary Drives. *Animal Behavior*, 1959, **7**, 130–141.

Hokanson, J. E., & Burgess, M. The Effects of Three Types of Aggression on Vascular Processes. *Journal of Abnormal and Social Psychology*, 1962, **64**, 446–449.

————., Burgess, M., & Cohen, M. F. Effects of Displaced Aggression on Systolic Blood Pressure. *Journal of Abnormal and Social Psychology*, 1963, **67**, 214–218.

————., & Edelman, R. Effects of Three Social Responses on Vascular Processes. *Journal of Personality and Social Psychology*, 1966, **3**, 442–447.

Loew, C. A. Acquisition of a Hostile Attitude and Its Relation to Aggressive Behavior. *Journal of Personality and Social Psychology*, 1967, **5**, 335–341.

Lorenz, K. *On Aggression*. New York: Harcourt, Brace & World, 1966.

Mallick, S. K., & McCandless, B. R. A Study of Catharsis of Aggression. *Journal of Personality and Social Psychology*, 1966, **4**, 591–596.

Montagu, M. F. A. (Ed.). *Man and Aggression*. New York: Oxford Press, 1968.

Patterson, G. R., Littman, R. A., & Bricker, W. Assertive Behavior in Children: A Step Toward a Theory of Aggression. *Monographs of the Society for Research in Child Development*, 1967, **32**, No. 5, 1–43.

Stone, L. J., & Hokanson, J. E. Arousal Reduction Via Self-punitive Behavior. *Journal of Personality and Social Psychology*, 1969, **12**, 72–99.

Walters, R. H., & Thomas, E. L. Enhancement of Punitiveness by Visual and Audiovisual Displays. *Canadian Journal of Psychology*, 1963, **17**, 244–255.

Chapter 3
INTERNAL STIMULUS FACTORS IN CONFLICT

Individuals may be predisposed by internal factors either to engage in or to avoid conflict behavior relative to other individuals in the same unstructured or structured situations. These internal predispositions are at least in part genetically determined or hereditary, and in the first paper Campbell presents the implications for social conflict of the basic, awesome fact of evolution, namely, genetic competition through natural selection. It appears that animals must be reproductively selfish, or must engage only in behaviors that give them and their kin every possible competitive advantage in the genetic competition of life, or else be displaced by others who do engage in optimal reproductive behavior. Thus whatever constitutes man's hereditary nature, it must predispose him to compete effectively for progeny in the game of evolution.

Note, however, that unavoidable genetic competition does not imply (as some popularizers would have it) that animals must inherit aggressive drives or engage in violent behavior. Violent aggression could be detrimental to evolutionary survival in many circumstances (if directed against kin, or against opponents who could fully retaliate, or at the cost of neglecting other vital behaviors such as care of the young). On the other hand, there are a great many inherited capacities and behaviors besides aggression that would give their possessors reproductive advantages, including those that involve cooperation with others and those that involve conformity designed to secure group support and approval, without which reproduction in many species is all but impossible.

The evidence that man's internal programming does indeed involve an aggressive "drive" (or more precisely, built-in circuits whose activation triggers aggressive behavior) is next reviewed by Moyer, who concludes that it does, but that such aggressive circuitry (like similar internal mechanisms for eating or mating) is only activated under certain circumstances. Moyer notes recent evidence that the violent behavior of certain individuals may result from excessive firing of these aggressive circuits as well as from possible hormone imbalances, and reviews evidence that these reactions may be controlled by developing techniques of brain surgery, brain stimulation, and drug therapy. Not all internal predispositions need of course be a matter of biological inheritance. Personality may be regarded as a kind of internal stimulation that is in large measure produced by socialization, and Christiansen in the next selection presents some classic evidence that a particular personality structure known as the authoritarian personality may predispose people to perceive conflict and hostility in the world and to prefer aggressive policies.

ON THE GENETICS OF ALTRUISM AND THE COUNTER-HEDONIC COMPONENTS IN HUMAN CULTURE

Donald T. Campbell

Civilization is a process in the service of Eros whose purpose is to combine single human individuals, and after that, families, then races, peoples, nations, into one great unity, the unity of mankind. . . . But man's natural aggressive instinct, the hostility of each against all and of all against each, opposes this program of civilization. . . . The struggle between Eros and Death, between the instinct of life and the instinct of destruction . . . is what all life essentially consists of, and the evolution of civilization may therefore be simply described as the struggle for life of the human species [Freud, 1930, p. 122].

Why do our relatives the animals not exhibit any such cultural struggle? We do not know. [Oh, wir wissen es nicht.] Very probably some of them—the bees, the ants, the termites—strove for thousands of years before they arrived at the state institutions, the distribution of functions, and the restrictions upon individuals, for which we admire them today. It is indicative of our present state that we should not think ourselves happy in any of these animal states, nor in any of the roles assigned by them to the individual [Freud, 1930, p. 123].

These verses of scripture from Freud set the problem for this essay. I believe Freud right in identifying the social insects as our most similar relatives insofar as complex social interdependence, *Kultur*, and self-sacrificial

altruism are concerned. I believe he was also right in noting in man a profound ambivalence toward his social role, an ambivalence absent in the bees, the ants, and the termites. Current technical discussions in evolutionary genetics regarding the possibility of selecting traits which are good for the group but are costly for the procreational opportunities of the individual offer an explanation of that difference. It is a difference which mere evolutionary time will not cure, being a by-product of the fact that among humans, unlike the social insects, there is genetic competition among the cooperators. (Among vertebrates each member produces offspring, potentially in different numbers. Among the social insects all of the cooperators are sterile and are thus not in genetic competition.) The major disagreement with Freud is as to the nature of the ambivalence. Rather than a death instinct, modern evolutionary genetics points to something closer to Freudian narcissism: self-serving aggressiveness in competition with coworkers for food, space, and mates; self-serving cowardice in war; self-serving dishonesty to fellow ingroup members; cheating, greed, disobedience, etc. Freud's view of the pervasively counter-hedonic content of culture is accepted and given a functional interpretation: The survival value of complex social coordination, with full division of labor, professional soldiers, and apartment-house living, has been achieved in man as a *social*-evolutionary product which has had to inculcate behavioral dispositions directly counter to the selfish tendencies being produced by genetic selection.

The occasion for this essay is not any special competence in these matters, but rather a wish to correct certain misstatements made at a time when I was still less competent. That we psychologists as a whole

Source: D. T. Campbell, "On the Genetics of Altruism and the Counterhedonic Components in Human Culture," *Journal of Social Issues*, 1972, Vol. 28, No. 3. Copyright by The Society for the Psychological Study of Social Issues and reprinted by permission.

need to be more informed on these matters is illustrated by the fact that our other major discussions of the genetics of altruism (e.g., Krebs, 1970, 1971; Hebb, 1971; Hebb & Thompson, 1954; Wright, 1971) have also been unaware of it—Aronfreed (1970) is a partial exception.

ETHNOCENTRIC ALTRUISM

The article I wish now to revise was entitled "Ethnocentric and Other Altruistic Motives" (Campbell, 1965b). In relation to this issue's theme, it derived altruistic individual behavior from the superior survival value of group-organized complex social interdependence, as compared with individualistic modes of adaption. Individual motivations, it was argued, are what they are in substantial part because they make group functioning possible. Most such motives are correctly classified as "altruistic." But although altruistic, not all are "positive," "wise," or "good." The willingness to die for group causes and related motives make possible tribalism, nationalism, and war, and are thus suicidal for modern man. While the essay recognized that man's achievement of a termite-like degree of division of labor and social interdependence (far exceeding that of the chimpanzee or wolf) is preponderantly a matter of cultural cumulation or social evolution (Cohen, 1962; Campbell, 1965a), it nonetheless also argued that genetic tendencies would be accumulated around these social functions. It is on this point that I now judge the essay in need of revising.

The "realistic group conflict" theory there reviewed and propositionalized (see also LeVine & Campbell, 1972) is one of the most impressive convergences in social science theory, with extensive documentation and independent invention in political science, sociology, psychology, and economics. Opposing psychological theories which interpret intergroup conflicts as projective displacements or byproducts of intragroup or intraindividual conflicts, realistic group conflict theory assumes that intergroup conflicts

are rational in that groups do have incompatible goals and are in competition for scarce resources. But while the theory is stated at the level of group function and process, six of the ten propositions emerging posit individual-dispositional laws. These are laws of "altruism," of individual commitment to group survival. This group functionality of individual altruistic dispositions is still strongly recommended to the attention of psychologists. What I now wish to revise is the source of these dispositions. In greater continuity with the mainstream of social psychological thought, I now believe that these self-sacrificial dispositions, including especially the willingness to risk death in warfare, are in man a product of a social indoctrination, which is counter to rather than supported by genetically transmitted behavioral dispositions.

The line of thought in both the 1965 paper and the present amendments must be sharply distinguished from the currently popular biological-evolutionary explanation of war. The concept of territoriality has added much to our understanding of aggression at the level of the individual fighting fish and gander (Lorenz, 1966). Realistic group conflict theory may be thought of as a theory of social group territoriality and social group aggression. But the relationship between these two levels of territoriality should be kept clear. Vertebrate territoriality as studied by the ethologists represents the behavioral syndrome of an individual male protecting a single female or harem and his offspring. Realistic group conflict theory is not the same theory and does not explain intergroup conflict as an expression of this territorial instinct in individual males. Rather, it is an analogous theory at a different level of organization. Realistic group conflict theory refers to organized groups involving many males and many families. In terms of the behavioral dispositions of individuals involved, the two levels of territoriality are in opposition rather than coterminous. Even though efforts to mobilize human ethnocentrism often make reference to protecting home and family, group-level territoriality has always required that the soldier abandon for extensive periods the protecting of his own wife, children, and home. Individual territoriality and aggression mean *intra*group conflict, and is regularly suppressed in the service of *inter*group conflict. Proposition 4 of realistic group conflict theory (1965b, p. 288) states that *real threat causes ingroup solidarity*. In an early statement, Sumner says: "The exigencies of war with outsiders are what make peace inside, lest internal discord should weaken the we-group for war. These exigencies also make government and law in the ingroup, in order to prevent quarrels and enforce discipline [1906, p. 12]." It is the "internal discord" and the "quarrels within" that are the aggressive manifestations of instinctive territoriality, if any. This is the most recurrent proposition in the many sources of realistic group conflict theory. The Sherifs (1953) make a major point of it. And with the help of reviewers such as Coser (1956), Berkowitz (1962), and Rosenblatt (1964) one can readily assemble several dozen citations affirming it. It is also a major theme of the anthropological description of pyramidal-segmental societies (LeVine & Campbell, 1972). Thus it is not mammalian or primate territoriality which explains war in this theory. It is instead an analogous function at a larger organizational level, and one which requires the inhibition of the lower-level individual mammalian territoriality. It is this discontinuity which makes the social insects rather than the higher apes the closest functional analogue for complex human social organization.

GENETICS OF ALTRUISM

Wynne-Edwards's book, *Animal Dispersion in Relation to Social Behavior* (1962; see also Wynne-Edwards 1963, 1965), has assembled the evidence and made the case for the natural selection of traits leading to the survival of breeding groups and whole species, even at the expense of individual procreational success. While mechanisms for the restriction of population are the preponderant illustration, his viewpoint supports the genetic speculations regarding altruism of my 1965

paper, and certainly should have been cited, although that would not have altered my conclusions.

George Williams, in *Adaptation and Natural Selection* (1966), challenges Wynne-Edwards's major conclusions, arguing that mechanisms which inhibit the effective fertility of the individual are incompatible with the theory of natural selection in its most developed statistical form. In so doing, he applies an argument on the problem of "altruistic" genes first presented by J. B. S. Haldane (1932) in a special appendix to his pioneering book on the statistical theory of evolution. The prohibition is not against all altruistic tendencies, but rather against those which are altruistic at some risk to the individual and which thus impair to some degree the individual's chances at procreation, effectively diminishing the frequency of his genes in later generations.

While the argument takes a mathematical form in Haldane, and briefly so in Williams's very readable book, its core concept can be stated simply. Let us suppose that mutations have produced a heterogeneity within a social group so that there are some individuals with genes predisposing a self-sacrificial bravery which furthers group survival, and others with genes predisposing a self-saving cowardice. Let us suppose that due to the presence of the bravery genes in some individuals, the group as a whole survives better. This increases the average reproductive opportunity of both the brave and the cowardly among the group members. The net gain for the brave is reduced to some degree because of the costs of risks they incur. The net gain for the cowardly has no such subtraction. Thus while all gain, the cowardly gain more, and their genes will gradually become more frequent as a result. There is no way in which the altruistic genetic tendencies could increase relative to the cowardly, to say nothing of becoming predominant, if there is a self-sacrificial component to the bravery.

Wynne-Edwards and others argue for a group-versus-group selection process that could, if strong enough, counter the individual-versus-individual selection processes within each group. Thus if competing social groups of the same species varied greatly in the frequency of the altruistic bravery gene and if there were a strong group selection favoring altruistic bravery, this could counteract the selection against altruistic bravery within each group. Williams argues that such a process is virtually impossible. For breeding groups of expected sizes, the only way group-to-group differences in gene frequency can be achieved is by systematic selection on an individual-to-individual level within each group. Thus the only way the groups with high frequency of the altruistic gene could have developed would be if they had migrated into an ecology where the trait was *not* self-sacrificial, and then migrated back into a common ecology. Even if this unlikely set of coincidences were to occur, if the brave group were to any extent heterozygous or if there were mutants back to the cowardly gene, the individual-versus-individual selection processes would erode the prevalence of the bravery gene in favor of the cowardly.

The one qualification to this argument follows Sewell Wright in pointing out that if the breeding groups were very small and highly inbred, then by chance alone some groups would end up being homozygous on the gene for altruistic bravery. Williams plausibly argues that such genetic isolation of small groups could not persist, and that in becoming heterozygous the individual-versus-individual selection would take over. When Wright's argument is extended to trait-complexes involving many genes, it becomes less likely to the *n*th power of the number of such genes.

While reviewers have found Williams's book too extreme and one sided (e.g., Lewontin, 1966), and while the issues it raises are far from settled within biology, I am tentatively persuaded to regard it as correct, and to accept the fact that for us vertebrates and others for whom there is genetic competition among the cooperators there are stringent restraints against genetic selection for self-sacrificial altruism.

The kind of "selfishness" selected needs to be spelled out in more detail. Self-sacrificial altruism in the defense of offspring is selected, as it is only through these offspring that the increase in gene frequency can be achieved. Sibling mutual defense is selected since they share 50 percent of the same genes. But tendencies to sacrifice for the protection of more remote relatives such as cousins or nephews are rarely if ever advantageous. Williams accents this point by noting that parental defense of offspring only occurs in species in which parents can distinguish between their own and their neighbors' offspring. Thus familial solidarity is selected for, but group solidarity on larger than family lines that involves much risk or sacrifice on the part of the cooperator is in general selected against. Much cooperative behavior involves a direct gain rather than risk or loss, and such cooperative behavior is positively selected. Williams uses the hunting of elks by groups of wolves as one of many examples. In other instances, the gains to the individual outweigh the losses, as Trivers (1971) argues for warning cries in birds. The degree of vertebrate sociality thus produced probably reaches its limit in that found within packs of wolves and chimpanzees which include several families, that is, a very limited degree of social interdependence.

The case of the social insects—the termites, ants, and bees—is fundamentally different. Among them, there is little or no "genetic competition" between the cooperators. A cowardly soldier within one nest will not have more offspring than a self-sacrificially brave one, for both are sterile. It is only the queen and the drones that have offspring— and their chances of offspring increase with the frequency of effectively brave soldiers. Likewise, the soldier termite that stands, fights, and dies is not in genetic competition with the also sterile worker whose conscience calls him to flee back into the nest when enemies are near. As a result, the social insects have achieved extreme degrees of complex social interdependence involving dramatic degrees of self-sacrificial bravery and other extreme division-of-labor adaptations (Allee, Emerson, Park, Park, & Schmidt, 1949; Brian, 1965; Krishna & Weesner, 1969; Wilson, 1971b). Undoubtedly the first prerequisite to this evolution was the development of a sterile caste. After that invention the further evolution of a complex division of labor could take place. For the ants, wasps, and bees, this development was furthered by the fact that male drones are haploid, having only one set of chromosomes rather than pairs. They thus give all of their offspring an identical set of genes, with the result that females share 3/4 of their genes with full sisters and only 1/2 of their genes with daughters. There is thus a selective advantage to furthering the life chances of younger eggs from the same mother over their own offspring. As judged by the more primitively social forms, this furthers a first stage of social life lacking morphological differences between queen and worker except for inhibited fertility. Wilson (1971b), building upon Hamilton (1964), presents the details. (He also provides evidence of some forms of genetic competition within the nest, using this to predict drone selfishness and other anomalies. These qualifications do not affect the arguments and illustrations which I have used above.) The achievement of the first sterile castes in termites is less well understood. It no doubt first involved a survival value for immature sibling assistance with brood care, upon which was superimposed a prolongation of the period of infantile infertility. Again, once an infertile worker caste was achieved, the subsequent development of complex multi-caste differentiation of structure and function was possible. The key step was elimination of genetic competition among the cooperators (Williams, 1966).

Parenthetically, it should be noted that Williams is worth reading by psychologists on many other grounds. His discussion of the genetic competition between males and females is fascinating and includes both the specification of how that competition leads to 50–50 sex ratios at the age of sexual maturity and a discussion of the genetics of coyness versus aggressive promiscuity. (It is the sexual partner who incurs the greater risks in child bearing who will be the coy and selective one. Usually this is the female, but not so among the pipefish-seahorse family in which the eggs are incubated in a brood pouch in the male.) It should also be noted

that Williams's main approach in attacking Wynne-Edwards's claims on group-selected population-restrictive mechanisms (postponement of fertility when food is short or conditions are crowded, decrease in brood size, postponement of age of fertility, territorial spacing, etc.) is to demonstrate how these mechanisms actually increase the effective fertility of the animals showing them and are thus achievable by individual selection. But some of Wynne-Edwards's facts he finds necessary to doubt or deny.

While Williams (1966, 1971) has influenced me the most, it is only fair to note that an impressive group of evolutionary geneticists take a more moderate position, allowing a larger role to group selection and for more selection for altruism even among us vertebrates. Adoption of their point of view would, however, modify only slightly the contrast between the genetics of altruism in man and in the social insects which I have presented. Lewontin (1965, 1970) accepts the existence under some conditions of group selection, but the examples he provides are unusual exceptions and not at all typical of Wynne-Edwards's illustrations: By and large Lewontin endorses Williams's criticisms of Wynne-Edwards (Lewontin, 1966, 1970).

Hamilton (1964) has provided basic analyses and mathematical formulations upon which Williams has built his arguments. Hamilton's own conclusions, however, are more moderate. He emphasizes that the extremes of selfishness and spitefulness are also selected against, just as is extreme self-sacrificial altruism. He uses the Prisoner's Dilemma analysis to present the evolutionary predicament (Hamilton, 1971). If the preponderant tendency is to choose the cooperative alternative, then it is genetically advantageous to cheat; but if most choose the opportunistic selfish alternative, it is dysgenic. The more there are repeated interactions with the same other individuals and the closer the genetic relation between those interacting, the stronger the selection pressure for cooperative dispositions. But once cooperation is well established, there is genetic selection in favor of cheating. Under transient and random contracts, selfishness is favored.

Hamilton (1971) makes one statement that is more in keeping with my 1965 paper than the present one:

With still further increase in intelligence, with increase in ability to communicate (and hence also to organize), with invention of new weapons (primarily for hunting) and ability to transmit culturally the techniques acquired, and with increase in possessions that could be carried off or usurped and used in situ, I find no difficulty in imagining that it could become advantageous for groups to make organized forcible incursions into the territory of weaker neighbors. In other words, I suggest that warfare was a natural development from the evolutionary trends taking part in the hominid stock. . . . If we accept that the elaborate instinctive patterns involved in the "war," "slavery," and "robbery" of the social insects are evolved by natural selection, can we consider it unlikely that in man also the corresponding phenomena have a natural basis? [pp. 78–79].

With this final statement I must disagree. It is an off-hand conclusion to which he has not yet applied his own careful mathematics and computer simulations. When he does, I am sure he will find that there is a selection pressure favoring cowardly soldiers in man which has no counterpart in the social insects just because they have no genetic competition among the soldiers or between soldiers and workers. I am sure my conclusions are more loyal to Hamilton's overall analysis of the genetics of altruism than is this comment. I of course agree with the first two sentences quoted, if a social evolution rather than a purely genetic one is included. I feel sure my conclusion on this point is one Williams would agree with, as well as Wilson (1971a, 1971b), Lewontin, and Trivers. Probably Hamilton on second thought would also.

Trivers's recent paper (1971) is one that psychologists should find of particular interest because he relates the psychological literature on altruism to the controversy in genetics. Following Hamilton (1971), he also uses the Prisoner's Dilemma paradigm. Still more than Hamilton, he emphasizes selection pressures for disguised cheating and sham cooperation.

He posits a selection pressure for a contingent cooperation with cooperators, made possible by long interaction with the same specific others. His paper is full of valuable subtle considerations that cannot be treated here but should eventually be incorporated into psychology's literature on this topic. But his paper will not be the final word, and may be internally inconsistent. For example, his two animal examples fail to illustrate his principle. Symbiotic cleaning relations involve no genetic competitions of the type under consideration, because the two cooperators are of different species. Further, it is to the direct survival advantage of the cleaned fish not to eat the cleaner; it is selfishly motivated, as Trivers makes clear. Similarly, he persuasively argues that while the bird that utters a warning cry increases his risks, his own chances of survival are more than compensated for by the advantages of keeping the predator from being sustained by a meal and learning to eat his type in his locale. In Trivers's discussion of human reciprocal altruism, he makes use of learned individual tendencies as well as genetic ones, but he fails to give explicit consideration to the social evolution of reward and punishment customs and tends to consider all personality and behavioral dispositions as genetically inherited. While he uses the mathematical models of evolutionary genetics, these are not developed for many of his most crucial speculations on human altruism.

One of Trivers's major conceptual contributions is to raise the issue of genetic selection for *moralistic aggression* against cheaters. Genes favoring such tendencies are unambivalently selected for. Insofar as such action changes the cheater's behavior in a more altruistic direction, or eliminates his genes through ostracism and death, it benefits equally those holding the genes and those not. Trivers focuses unnecessarily on the effects of such action (and sham moralistic aggression) as a two-party interaction initiated by the one cheated and producing specific restitution to him by the cheater. Most important would seem the "altruistic" eagerness to see cheaters punished even when one has not been directly harmed or will not directly benefit from their punishment. Svend Ranulf (1938) has portrayed such tendencies, although mistakenly identifying them with middle class psychology rather than with complex division of labor society. Such tendencies can be selected by group selection, because they benefit the whole group without the special costs to the individuals holding the genes. Similarly for tendencies to applaud and reinforce altruists.

In my 1965 paper, there is a section on "ambivalence as optimal compromise." In it, with ample quotes from William James on the ambivalent balance of curiosity and fear of new objects, I argued that natural selection could produce opposed genetic tendencies, and that ambivalence was a better resolution of opposed utilities than was an averaged indifference to novel objects. I argued that in man (but not in the social insects) genetically determined altruism or bravery were in a similar ambivalent balance with genetically determined selfishness or cowardice. Trivers's analysis and Hamilton's support this view. What I argue for in the present paper is an ambivalence between socially induced altruistic bravery and a genetically induced selfish cowardice. While I will stick to this position in the present paper both for reasons of conviction and clarity, a mixture of both sources of ambivalence is of course possible.

ON THE CONFLICT BETWEEN SOCIAL AND BIOLOGICAL EVOLUTION IN MAN

Human complex social interdependence greatly exceeds that of wolves and chimpanzees. If animal counterparts are to be found at all, it is among the social insects. And while the ambivalence Freud noted is present, plus uneven execution of the self-sacrificial roles in the social machine, in many ways civilized man even exceeds the social insects in his complex social interdependency.

Man and the social insects demonstrate the great survival value of extreme social interdependence. The case of the social insects shows that some complex forms of it can be achieved on a genetic base. That wolves and chimpanzees have never achieved it is due to the evolutionary trap or conflict produced by genetic competition among the cooperators. Man is in the same genetic predicament. The conclusion seems to me inevitable that man can have achieved his social-insect-like degree of complex social interdependence only through his social and cultural evolution, through the historical selection and cumulation of educational systems, intragroup sanctions, supernatural (superpersonal, superfamilial) purposes, etc. A detailed discussion of the selective-retention evolution of social customs and artifacts has been provided elsewhere (Campbell, 1965a; Cohen, 1962).

Not only must man's complex social interdependence be a product of social evolution, the evolved socially induced dispositions must also have directly opposed the selfish dispositional tendencies continually selected for by the concurrent biological evolution. It is this opposition between the dispositional products of biological and social evolution that explains Freud's observations on man's ambivalence toward his social roles, and his contrast with the unambivalent insects. But Freud was wrong in believing that length of *time* in evolutionary history is the problem, it is rather the more fundamental fact of the evolutionary *route* toward social complexity.

This suggestion goes far beyond Williams in its emphasis on the role of social evolution (note, however, Auger, 1952, pp. 122–123). But the conclusion provides for me, as a social scientist interested in the puzzles of his own cultural background, a strong reason for accepting Williams's point of view. For it makes an evolutionary sense out of the otherwise anomalous or incomprehensible preoccupation with sin and temptation in the folk morality that our religious traditions provide. The commandments, the proverbs, the religious "law" represent social evolutionary products directed at inculcating tendencies that are in direct opposition to the "temptations" representing for the most part the dispositional tendencies produced by biological evolution. For every commandment we may reasonably hypothesize a tendency to do otherwise which runs counter to some social-systemic optimum.

This hypothesis predicts certain uniformities in the popular moralizings of all complex societies, a scholarly investigation which I have not yet undertaken. All should have preachments against cowardice in battle. (Inspection of fragments of the anthropological literature leads me to expect this to be nearly universal even among societies without a full-time division of labor or storable food stuffs. The very ubiquity of this morality may account for its being assumed rather than preached anew in the written ethics of the more complex societies.) All should preach against lying for personal gain (if not lying for group advantage), ingroup theft, greed, murderous rage, and arrogant self-pride. Industry, abstemiousness, doing one's unique duty, group loyalty—all should be praised. A detailed study of this aspect of the moralizings of the presumably independently developed complex societies is called for: ancient China, the valleys of the Indus and the Ganges, the Aztecs, Mayas, and Incas. For these purposes, shame cultures and guilt cultures (if such differences exist) share a functional equivalence.

CAVEAT

This is a shallow overview for which even detailed and disciplined speculation is lacking, to say nothing of research. If these issues are important, meticulous examination of both the genetic and the social selection processes is required. For example, it must be made clearer than I have done how a social transmission could avoid the restrictions that genetic transmission encounters. Attention has recently been focused on the fact that in social exchange processes the optimizing of individual well-being is often or even usually destructive of collective good (Olson, 1968; Hardin, 1968; Crowe, 1969; Frohlich & Oppenheimer, 1970; Schelling, 1971). These cross interests are directly analogous to those involved in the genetics of altruism. How can a social evolution not

only have avoided them but gone further and also counteracted their genetic product? If the socialization process were predominantly from parent to child, social evolution could not produce self-sacrificial altruism. The predicament would be the same as for genetic inheritance. Childe (1951), Ginsberg (1961), and Waddington (1961) are among the astute commentators on social evolution who have noted the important disanalogy between biological and social evolution in that social evolution permits crosslineage borrowing. While their focus was on group-to-group borrowing, this liberation applies also to lineage-to-lineage borrowing within a group. Thus effective group indoctrination to self-sacrificial bravery, which resulted in group success, would perhaps avoid the differential propagation that genetic transmission runs into. But if there were genetic differences in indoctrinability, potentiality for identification with group purposes, etc., and if warfare were the main selective system operating, then there would be genetic selection against indoctrinability and capacity for identification.

No doubt there is positive genetic selection for gregariousness and fear of ostracism. Indoctrinability makes possible cultural cumulation and hence is probably in general positively selected for at the individual level, as Waddington in his remarkable *The Ethical Animal* (1960) argues. Probably the overall adaptive advantage for indoctrinability, group identification, and fear of ostracism is strong enough to overweigh the negative selection produced when the most indoctrinable incur greater fatality rates in wartime. Looking at the individual's role as an indoctrinator and enforcer of group-adaptive altruistic behavior on the part of others, such tendencies would be selected for at both social and genetic levels as long as these others were not in one's own family. There could be a *social* selection for customs granting extra procreational opportunities to surviving heroes, but a *genetic* tendency for women to be most attracted to the altruistically brave would be weeded out through the diminished survival rate of these women's sons. There is probably positive selection for heroic bluff that persists as long as successful but turns into cowardly retreat when the odds become overwhelming; such a pattern is not technically altruistic in Haldane's usage.

Expanding the perspective only slightly reveals still more problems. The moralizings in the Old Testament against onanism, homosexuality, and the temptation to sacrifice one's firstborn son (Bakan, 1966; Wellisch, 1954) must be directed against socially produced dispositions, since these tendencies would be genetically self-eliminating. How can one account for effective individual commitment to ideals and future social arrangements when these run counter to the survival of both one's own genes and one's own current social system? To label such positive self-sacrificial altruism "masochism" or "ethnophobia" merely provides a disparaging description, not an explanation, unless one can specify a plausible genetic or social selective system that would provide it. Etc., etc. If we are to take this problem area seriously, we should make the issues and alternatives explicit and test out their joint effects in the disciplined speculation of mathematical and computer simulation.

IMPLICATIONS FOR PEACE

Skipping the doubts of the last paragraph, and accepting the conclusion that man's termite- and ant-like capacity for military heroism is in culturally transmitted dispositions, not genetic ones, makes me more optimistic about the possibilities of social inventions eliminating war, for such developments will have the temptations of biological selfishness on their side. However resistant culture is to change, it is probably less so than the gene pool. In the 1965 paper I argued that intransigent public leaders in the United States had a popular advantage over peacemakers, as exemplified in the competition between Nixon and Kennedy for the most bellicose stand in the 1960 campaign, the public pillorying after the Cuba crisis of 1962 of

Kennedy's more conciliatory advisors rather than the more warlike, etc. Perhaps the Johnson-Goldwater campaign, Johnson's decision not to run in 1968, the public acceptance of conscientious objection and draft resistance show a shift in public preference so that the apparent peacemaker now has the popular advantage. These optimistic observations do not of course imply optimism about the organizational future of those societies which are first to lose the archaic capacity to fight wars, for until all nations have achieved this state of intelligent cultural decay, those that achieve it first will be at a decided disadvantage in international competition. We should note too that our great cities and large populations are also manifestations of our termite-like capacity for complex social interdependence; they are thus also in jeopardy as we tear down the belief systems of the past and the altruistic purposes and dispositions they provided. What are grounds for optimism with regard to the problem of war may also be grounds for pessimism about our capacity to maintain the still functional aspects of complex social interdependence.

SUMMARY

Man is more similar to the social insects than to the wolf and the chimpanzee in complex social coordination, division of labor, and self-sacrificial altruism. In the social insects the behavioral dispositions involved are genetically determined, an evolution made possible by the absence of genetic competition among the cooperators. In man genetic competition precludes the evolution of such genetic altruism. The behavioral dispositions which produce complex social interdependence and self-sacrificial altruism must instead be products of culturally evolved indoctrination, which has had to counter self-serving genetic tendencies. Thus, unlike the social insect, man is profoundly ambivalent in his social role—as Freud noted.

References

Allee, W. C., Emerson, A. E., Park, O., Park, T., & Schmidt, K. P. *Principles of Animal Ecology.* Philadelphia: Saunders, 1949.

Aronfreed, J. The Socialization of Altruistic and Sympathetic Behavior: Some Theoretical and Experimental Analyses. In J. Macaulay & L. Berkowitz, (Eds.), *Altruism and Helping Behavior.* New York: Academic Press, 1970.

Auger, P. *L'homme Microscopique: Essai de Monodologie.* Paris: Flammarion, 1952.

Bakan, D. *The Duality of Human Existence.* Chicago: Rand McNally, 1966.

Berkowitz, L. *Aggression: A Social Psychological Analysis.* New York: McGraw-Hill, 1962.

Brian, M. V. *Social Insect Populations.* New York: Academic Press, 1965.

Campbell, D. T. Variation and Selective Retention in Sociocultural Evolution. In R. W. Mack, G. I. Blanksten, & H. R. Barringer (Eds.), *Social Change in Under-developed Areas: A Reinterpretation of Evolutionary Theory.* Cambridge, Mass.: Schenkman, 1965. (a)

Campbell, D. T. Ethnocentric and Other Altruistic Motives. In D. Levine (Ed.), *Nebraska Symposium on Motivation: 1965.* Lincoln: University of Nebraska Press, 1965. (b)

Childe, V. G. *Social Evolution.* London: Watts, 1951.

Cohen, R. The Strategy of Social Evolution. *Anthropologica,* 1962, **4,** 321–348.

Coser, L. A. *The Functions of Social Conflict.* Glencoe, Ill.: Free Press, 1956.

Crowe, B. L. The Tragedy of the Commons Revisited. *Science,* 1969, **166,** 1103–1107.

Freud, S. *Civilization and Its Discontents.* London: Hogarth, 1930. (Standard ed., Vol. **21,** 1961.)

Frohlich, N., & Oppenheimer, J. A. I Get By with a Little Help from My Friends: The "Free-rider" Problem. *World Politics,* 1970, **23,** 104–120.

Ginsberg, M. Social Evolution. In M. Banton (Ed.), *Darwinism and the Study of Society.* Chicago: Quadrangle Books, 1961.

Haldane, J. B. S. *The Causes of Evolution.* London: Longmans, 1932.

Hamilton, W. D. The Genetical Evolution of Social Behavior. *Journal of Theoretical Biology,* 1964, **7,** 1–51.

Hamilton, W. D. Selection of Selfish and Altruistic Behavior in Some Extreme Models. In J. F. Eisenberg & W. S. Dillon (Eds.), *Man and Beast: Comparative Social Behavior.* Washington, D.C.: Smithsonian Institution Press, 1971.

Hardin, G. The Tragedy of the Commons. *Science,* 1968, **162,** 1243–1248.

Hebb, D. O. Comment on Altruism: The Comparative Evidence. *Psychological Bulletin,* 1971, **76,** 409–410.

Hebb, D. O., & Thompson, W. R. The Social Significance of Animal Studies. In G. Lindzey (Ed.), *Handbook of Social Psychology.* Vol. 1. Cambridge, Mass.: Addison Wesley, 1954. Reprinted in G. Lindzey & E. Aronson (Eds.), *Handbook of Social Psychology.* (2nd ed.) Vol. **2,** 1968.

Krebs, D. L. Altruism: An Examination of the Concept and a Review of the Literature. *Psychological Bulletin*, 1970, **73**, 258–302.

Krebs, D. L. Infrahuman Altruism. *Psychological Bulletin*, 1971, **76**, 411–414.

Krishna, K., & Weesner, F. M. (Eds.). *Biology of Termites*. New York: Academic Press, 1969.

LeVine, R. A., & Campbell, D. T. *Ethnocentrism: Theories of Conflict, Ethnic Attitudes and Group Behavior*. New York: Wiley & Sons, 1972.

Lewontin, R. C. Selection in and of Populations. In J. A. Moore (Ed.), *Ideas in Modern Biology*. Garden City, N.Y.: Natural History Press, 1965.

Lewontin, R. C. Review of G. C. Williams, *Adaptation and Natural Selection*. *Science*, 1966, **152**, 338–339.

Lewontin, R. C. The Units of Selection. *Annual Review of Ecology and Systematics*, 1970, **1**, 1–18.

Lorenz, K. *On Aggression*. New York: Harcourt, Brace and World, 1966.

Olson, M. *The Logic of Collective Action*. New York: Schocken, 1968.

Ranulf, S. *Moral Indignation and Middle Class Psychology*. Copenhagen: Levin & Munksgaard, 1938.

Rosenblatt, P. C. Origins and Effects of Group Ethnocentrism and Nationalism. *Journal of Conflict Resolution*, 1964, 8, 131–146.

Schelling, T. C. On the Ecology of Micromotives. *The Public Interest*, 1971, **25**, 61–98.

Sherif, M., & Sherif, C. W. *Groups in Harmony and Tension*. New York: Harper, 1953.

Sumner, W. G. *Folkways*. New York: Ginn, 1906.

Trivers, R. L. The Evolution of Reciprocal Altruism. *Quarterly Review of Biology*, 1971, **46**, 35–37.

Waddington, C. H. *The Ethical Animal*. London: Allen & Unwin, 1960.

————. The Human Evolutionary System. In M. Banton (Ed.), *Darwinism and the Study of Society*. Chicago: Quadrangle Books, 1961.

Wellisch, E. *Isaac and Oedipus: A Study in Biblical Psychology of the Sacrifice of Isaac, the Akedah*. London: Routledge and Kegan Paul, 1954.

Williams, G. C. *Adaptation and Natural Selection*. Princeton, New Jersey: Princeton University Press, 1966.

Williams, G. C. (Ed.) *Group Selection*. Chicago: Aldine-Atherton, 1971.

Wilson, E. O. The Prospects for a Unified Sociobiology. *American Scientist*, 1971, **59**, 400–403. (a)

Wilson, E. O. *The Insect Societies*. Cambridge, Mass.: Belknap Press, 1971. (b)

Wright, D. *The Psychology of Moral Behaviour*. Harmondsworth, England: Penguin, 1971.

Wynne-Edwards, V. C. *Animal Dispersion in Relation to Social Behavior*. Edinburgh: Oliver & Boyd, 1962.

————. Intergroup Selection in the Evolution of Social Systems. *Nature*, 1963, 200, 623–626.

————. Self-regulating Systems in Populations of Animals. *Science*, 1965, **147**, 1543–1547.

INTERNAL IMPULSES TO AGGRESSION

K. E. Moyer

This paper will consider the internal impulses to aggressive behavior and the implications this information has for aggression control. A discussion of the *internal* impulses to aggression necessitates a consideration of the current controversy over whether or not there is an aggressive drive.

Some investigators maintain that there is no drive for aggressive behavior in the same sense that there is a drive for eating, drinking, or sex behavior (2, 23, 37). J. P. Scott, who has done excellent and extensive research on the problem of aggression, is an enthusiastic proponent of this position (58, 59, 61–63). In 1965 he said,

All that we know (and this comprises a considerable body of information in certain species) indicates that the physiological mechanisms associated with fighting are very different from those underlying sexual behavior and eating. There is no known physiological mechanism by which spontaneous internal stimulation for fighting arises. (Ref. 61, p. 820).

Another group of individuals studying this problem has arrived at exactly the opposite conclusion. Lorenz (36) on the basis of ethological studies, Lagerspetz (29) on the basis of behavioral studies with mice, and Feshbach (16) on the basis of experiments with humans, have all concluded that there is indeed a drive for aggressive behavior.

Much of this controversy results from the looseness of the various definitions of drive. The concept means very different things to different people. Drive is frequently given the status of an intervening variable which is essentially an expression of ignorance or lack of concern with what is going on inside the organism. However, Dr. Ethel Tobach and others have expressed the view that the term drive, to be useful, must be given a sound physiological basis (60). However, the more I investigate the physiological basis of behavior, the less need I find for the concept of drive. The difficulties with this construct have been considered elsewhere (5, 6, 8) so I need not detail them here. In addition to the criticism offered in those sources, it appears to me that there are certain philosophical problems with the term drive as it is sometimes used. I find the implied mind-body interaction neither necessary nor useful in making predictions about behavior. Further, the drive concept frequently implies a hedonistic interpretation of behavior (the pleasure principle of psychoanalytic thinking and the affective arousal of Young are examples) which is also neither necessary nor useful.

It appears to me that the time has come to reject the term drive in order to avoid further confusion. There are certain basic circuits in the nervous system. When they are active, certain complex behaviors occur. The problem for the student of behavior is to determine the variables, both internal and external, which activate and deactivate these circuits. There are certainly differences in the mechanisms for turning the basic neuronal circuits on and off. There are also remarkable similarities. The evidence seems to indicate that there are basic (in a sense, built in) circuits for aggressive behavior just as there are for consummatory and sex behavior. Some of these similarities will now be considered.

Much of the discussion about the similarity of aggressive behavior to other basic behaviors seems to revolve around whether aggression is endogenously or exogenously determined (73). Scott and Fredericson (64,

Source: K. E. Moyer, "Internal Impulses to Aggression," *Transactions of the New York Academy of Sciences*, Series II, Vol. 31, 1969, pp. 104–114. Copyright 1969 by The New York Academy of Sciences and reprinted by permission.

p. 820) have suggested that, "There is no evidence for any sort of spontaneous internally arising stimulation which would cause a need for fighting per se. Instead, we have a mechanism which will produce fighting in response to predictable external stimulation." However, the same statement can be made about all basic behavior patterns. Behavior does not occur in a vacuum. A deprived animal does not make random chewing movements nor does it attempt to eat all available objects. Regardless of the intensity of the internal state produced by deprivation, the animal responds to a very limited set of stimuli with an eating response. It eats only food objects. In the same manner, the aggressive subject behaves aggressively only toward a very limited number of stimulus objects. The converse is also true. An animal will not engage in eating behavior or in aggressive behavior to an appropriate stimulus object unless a certain characteristic physiological state is present. Some of these physiological mechanisms will now be examined.

FACILITATION OF CONSUMMATORY AND AGGRESSIVE BEHAVIOR BY BRAIN STIMULATION

It has been demonstrated repeatedly that when certain areas of the brain are activated an animal will become restless and engage in exploratory behavior. If that behavior brings it into contact with food, the animal, even though satiated, will begin to eat (1). An extensive series of experiments by N. E. Miller and his colleagues (40, 41) has shown that the eating behavior resulting from brain stimulation has many of the characteristics of normal deprivation-induced behavior. A rat stimulated in the lateral hypothalamus will eat lab chow or lap milk, but it will not drink pure water. Thus, the response is stimulus bound.

In a similar manner, an animal can be induced to display aggressive behavior by the stimulation of specific brain areas. Cats which normally do not attack rats will do so during electrical stimulation of the hypothalamus (81). If the lateral hypothalamus is stimulated, the cat ignores the experimenter and quietly and efficiently stalks and kills the rat, usually by biting in the neck region as is characteristic of this species. In my own laboratory, Richard Bandler has been able to induce a similar predatory mouse killing in rats by carbochol stimulation of the lateral hypothalamus. If there is no stimulus object available, the animal may explore in a restless manner, but it does not behave aggressively. The cat stimulated in the lateral hypothalamus shows distinct and evidently unlearned preferences in the types of stimulus objects it will attack. An anesthetized rat will be attacked more quickly and persistently than a stuffed rat, and there is little tendency for the cat to attack a foam rubber block about the size of a rat (33).

Stimulation of the medial hypothalamus produces a very different kind of aggression. The cat shows pronounced sympathetic arousal and attacks with a high-pitched scream, tearing at the stimulus object with unsheathed claws. It may ignore an available rat but viciously attack a person (13).

Just as food is reinforcing to the animal whose "feeding system" is activated, the opportunity to attack is reinforcing to an animal whose "predator system" is activated. Cats which will attack rats during hypothalamic stimulation will learn a Y maze "to obtain a rat they could attack." (Ref. 49, p. 187.)

One must, of course, be careful about generalizing data obtained from animal research to humans. For obvious reasons, there is a limited amount of data on the effects of brain stimulation in man. Nothing is known about the effects of brain stimulation of humans on eating behavior. However, somewhat more is known about aggression. King (27) describes a patient with an electrode implanted in the amygdaloid region who became angry, verbally hostile, and threatened to strike the experimenter when stimulated with a current of 5 milliamperes. When the current was reduced or turned off, she again became mild mannered and apologetic for her aggressive behavior.

There is also indirect evidence that spontaneous activity of the neurones in the temporal lobe, as well as other areas of the brain, results in aggressive behavior. In some individuals, spontaneous firing of the cells in the temporal lobe and in the thalamus leads to subjective feelings of rage and the execution of incredibly violent behavior (17, 76). A number of studies have shown that aggressive behavior, such as fire setting, aggressive sex behavior, and murder, and other acts of violence are associated with 14/second and 6/second positive spikes in the EEG record (70, 71, 86). This assaultive aggressive behavior may or may not be associated with epileptic motor seizures. Even when it is, there is reason to believe that the neurohumoral substrates underlying the two behaviors are different in that they are differentially affected by brain lesions and drugs (F. R. Ervin, 1968, personal communication).

It might be suggested that "spontaneous neurological rage reactions" are abnormal and that they have little to do with the bulk of human behavior. However, "abnormal" is a statistical concept, not a neurological one. There seems to be good evidence that some individuals are born with a tendency for certain neurones to fire spontaneously and that the amount of spontaneous firing is on a continuum, occurring more in some individuals than in others. The most relevant question is not whether aggressive behavior *can* occur spontaneously as a result of the internal activation of certain brain areas, but how common it is. A mechanism for internally activated aggressive behavior appears to exist. Perhaps it occurs in many people, but less frequently in most. (See Ref. 24 for a further discussion of this point and an excellent review of the literature.)

REDUCTION OF CONSUMMATORY AND AGGRESSIVE BEHAVIOR BY BRAIN LESIONS

The above evidence indicates that there exist in the brain of man and of animals well-integrated mechanisms which, when activated, result in complex, well-organized, well-directed behavior. Whether it is consummatory behavior or aggressive behavior depends on the particular circuit involved. Both types of behavior are directed toward particular stimuli. As one might suspect, when these brain mechanisms are damaged, the individual is unable to respond appropriately to the relevant stimuli.

Damage to the lateral nucleus of the hypothalamus produces an animal which does not show the slightest interest in food. It will, if left alone, starve to death in the midst of plenty. If tube fed (in some cases for several months), it may begin to respond to only the most preferred taste stimulation (42, 72).

The brain mechanisms for aggression can also be damaged with dramatic reductions in aggressive behavior. It has been shown that bilateral lesions in the amygdala will surgically tame the untameable wildcat (*Lynx rufus*) (57), the fierce, wild Norway rat (85), and a variety of other innately hostile animals including the agouti, cat, monkey, hamster, and cotton rat (see Ref. 45 for details). These normally vicious animals can be handled without gloves immediately after the operation. Lesions in a number of other brain areas will also reduce aggressive tendencies (45).

In man the data are limited, but do exist. Ursin (79) summarizes several cases of hostility control through brain surgery. He refers to one of Sawa's patients (55) who reported that after the operation he could not get angry even if he wanted to. Lesions in the temporal lobe (47), dorsomedial thalamus (67), posterior hypothalamus (53, 54), and the anterior cingulum (75) have all been used successfully to reduce uncontrollable hostility in man. Le Beau (30, p. 315) suggests, "Cingulectomy is specially indicated in intractable cases of anger, violence, aggressiveness, and permanent agitation."

FACILITATION OF CONSUMMATORY AND AGGRESSIVE BEHAVIOR BY BRAIN LESIONS

There are neurological mechanisms in the brain which prevent the manifestation of both excessive eating behavior and excessive aggressive behavior. When these mechanisms, located in well-defined areas of the brain, are destroyed, the individual's reaction to particular kinds of stimuli becomes excessive. Lesions in the ventromedial nucleus of the hypothalamus, for example, frequently result in the well-known syndrome of hypothalamic hyperphagia (14). Soon after recovery from surgery the animal begins to eat voraciously, doubling or tripling its food intake with a resulting weight increase of similar magnitude. However, the animal is "finicky" (19) and its excessive eating response is elicited only by certain preferred taste stimuli.

Bilateral destruction of either the basal or central nucleus of the amygdala will convert a friendly, affectionate, domestic cat into one which will attack without provocation (84). Wheatley (82) has produced extremely vicious cats by lesioning the ventromedial hypothalamus. Increased aggressive behavior has also been produced by destruction of the septal region, frontal lobes, cingulum, and portions of the hippocampus. These aggressive responses are well directed, stimulus oriented, and are not comparable to the sham rage produced by decerebration (see Ref. 45 for specific studies).

Specific brain lesions in man will also increase hostile tendencies (80, 82).

INHIBITION OF CONSUMMATORY AND AGGRESSIVE BEHAVIOR BY BRAIN STIMULATION

The evidence from lesion experiments is sometimes difficult to interpret because of the possibility of resulting irritative scars. However, further evidence on the role of inhibitory mechanisms in the control of both eating behavior and aggressive behavior comes from brain stimulation experiments. Again, there is considerable evidence that the types of physiological mechanisms underlying eating behavior are similar in kind to those underlying aggressive behavior.

Eating can be inhibited by stimulation

of the "satiety" center in the ventromedial hypothalamus (88). Septal stimulation can block eating behavior in the deprived monkey (10).

Brain stimulation can also block aggression without interfering with normal motor responses. Amygdaloid stimulation can block normal mousing in cats as well as predation induced by hypothalamic stimulation (13). Stimulation of the caudate nucleus will inhibit continuing aggressive behavior in a dominant male monkey (11). In humans, Heath (22) has reported the immediate reduction of agitated, violent, psychotic behavior by stimulation in the septal region. The patient's behavior changes almost instantly from disorganized rage to happiness and mild euphoria. Heath indicates further that this phenomenon has been repeated in a large number of patients.

INFLUENCE OF BLOOD CHEMISTRY CHANGES ON CONSUMMATORY AND AGGRESSIVE BEHAVIOR

There is a generally held theoretical conviction that eating behavior is regulated by the action of certain components in the blood which in turn act to produce increases in sensitivity in particular brain circuits. Glucose changes have been suggested as important in the short-run control of eating (39) and lipids in long-run control (26).

In light of the available evidence, it is not unreasonable to postulate a similar mechanism in the regulation of aggressive behavior. However, as there may well be various kinds of aggression, there must also be a variety of contributing regulators. Androgens in the blood stream are undoubtedly critical to the development of inter-male aggression (3, 34, 65, 66, 78). There is recent evidence that these androgenic effects may be masked or inhibited by estrogens, at least in isolated male mice (69). Female irritability is cyclical and increases during estrus in the shrew (46), and in the guinea pig (28). Further, aggressiveness in the ovariectomized female guinea pig can be inhibited by a series of estrogen injections followed by an injection of progesterone (28).

Changes in the hormone balance in the blood stream can also inhibit maternal aggression. The domesticated mother rat will attack and kill a frog that is put into her cage only during the period of lactation. This maternal aggressiveness can be completely abolished without interfering with the care of the young if the rat is given a few days of oestrone therapy (15). Some of the test rats which did not show the frog-killing response did so when they were administered hydrocortisone. Hydrocortisone injections also overcame the killing inhibition produced by oestrone.

Clinical endocrinology offers further support for the importance of blood components in the regulation of aggressive tendencies. Care must be exercised in the interpretation of these data because they are not from controlled laboratory studies. Certainly, however, the data are suggestive and can result in hypotheses which should be followed up in the laboratory.

Irritability is a frequent component of the premenstrual tension syndrome in the human female and is successfully treated by the administration of progesterone (9, 20). It has also been shown that crimes of violence committed by women are related to the menstrual cycle. In a study of 249 women prison inmates, it was shown that 62 percent of the crimes of violence were committed during the premenstrual week and only 2 percent at the end of the period (43). Diandrone (dehydroisoandrosterone) increases confidence in adolescents with feelings of inferiority and promotes aggressive responses (52). In patients with a history of aggressiveness, diandrone is likely to produce excessive irritability and outbursts of rage (51, 68). On the other hand, castration reduces the asocial acts of individuals convicted of sex crimes (21, 31), and the administration of stilboestrol, in some cases, provides dramatic control of both hypersexuality and irritable aggression (12, 51).

It is generally recognized that frustration and stress, particularly if prolonged, are likely to result in increased irritability and aggressive behavior. It may well be that the frustration-induced irritability results from the sensitization of certain brain areas by the particular hormone balance which characterizes the stress syndrome. Both the adrenal cortex and the thyroid are intimately involved in the stress syndrome, and dysfunctions of either gland result in increased irritability (7, 18).

INFLUENCE OF LEARNING ON CONSUMMATORY AND AGGRESSIVE BEHAVIOR

The influence of learning on aggressive responding has received considerable emphasis (58, 59, 64). Scott and Fredericson (64) suggest that training can overcome hereditary predispositions and conclude that, "Training includes by far the most important group of factors which affect agonistic behavior" (p. 306). The implication of these discussions is that aggressive behavior is in some way set apart from other basic behaviors because learning has a strong influence on it. It is obvious, however, that learning has a strong influence on all basic behavior patterns. Psychiatrists' couches are filled with individuals who have learned hypo, hyper, or deviate sexual behavior. Learning also has a potent influence on consummatory behavior (87). Eating behavior reinforced by shock termination results in excessive food consumption with marked obesity (83).

It is possible through training to inhibit all consummatory behavior (35, 38). In one study, negative reinforcement in the form of sublethal doses of poison produced a complete inhibition of eating behavior with the result that the subjects (rats) starved to death (48). Since training can completely inhibit consummatory behavior, leading to the death of the organism, one might conclude, as Scott and Fredericson (64) did about aggression, that training can overcome hereditary predispositions and that training includes by far the most important group of factors which affect consummatory behavior.

Further, while there is good evidence that all eating behavior can be completely inhibited by training, there is some doubt that the same thing is true for all aggressive behavior. Swade and Geiger (70) conclude that the aggressive behavior which is correlated with the 6 and 14 per second positive spiking on the EEG can no more be controlled by the individual than a grand mal seizure can be controlled by an epileptic. After a study of over 1000 cases, these authors (Ref. 71, p. 616) characterize that form of aggressive behavior as follows:

The control by rage is so absolute that parents fear for their lives and those of others. Typical complaints are extreme rage outbursts, larceny, arson, violent acts without motivation, sexual acts (aggressive), threats to stab, shoot, mutilate or beat, poor social adjustment (not schizophrenic), rage reactions, mutilation of animals, and total inability to accept correction or responsibility for the act.

AGGRESSION CONTROL

Once the facts are sorted out, it can be seen that, as Tinbergen (73) suggests, the argument of whether or not aggression is a drive is very much a matter of emphasis and the two theoretical positions are not as far apart as it seems. The entire argument might be purely academic and of little consequence, except for the implications for further research and for the control of aggression. One certainly need not conclude with Scott (62) that the instinctual analysis of behavior is a complete explanation of behavior and so offers no new leads for research. The term instinct has a confused history and may not be the best term. However, most authors who postulate instinctive aggression agree that it has a physiological basis. Therefore, there are innumerable leads for research which emanate from this point of view. If there is an "instinctual urge to aggression," there must be a physiological basis for it, and that basis can be delineated experimentally.

Further, there are many hypotheses to be tested to determine the specific neural and endocrine mechanisms underlying various kinds of aggressive behavior.

The theoretical position that one takes on the determinants of aggressive behavior strongly influences the kinds of control measures considered. The manipulation of the internal environment is not mentioned by either Scott (53) or Hinde (23) when they deal with the problem of aggression control. Lorenz (36) certainly accepts the idea of internal impulses to aggression, but he conceives of them in terms of the rather vaguely defined energy concept. Since he also considers that "aggressive energy" is closely linked with the energy of ambitions, love, and other socially acceptable attributes, he confines his recommendations for aggression control to suggestions for the redirection of "aggressive energy" and does not consider reducing aggressive tendencies per se.

As indicated in the analysis above, aggressive behavior is determined by both external and internal variables, and aggressive response tendencies can be modified by learning. This should provide us with at least three approaches to the most important problem of aggression control. The external environment can be manipulated to reduce the number of stimuli which instigate aggression; the individual can be taught to inhibit aggressive responses; and finally, the internal environment can be manipulated directly. Although the last approach will be dealt with here, there is no intention to imply that the first two approaches are unimportant.

The physiological control of aggressive tendencies may be accomplished by brain stimulation, brain lesions, hormone administration, and the administration of drugs. As indicated above, continuing aggressive behavior in the monkey can be blocked immediately by direct stimulation of the caudate nucleus (11). In man, a violent, profane, destructive individual is transformed into one who is calm, friendly, and sociable by direct septal stimulation. At the moment, very little is known about this method of control, but there seems little doubt that it is possible. How practical it will become is a matter of conjecture. Two developments could make it eminently practical: one is the development of a method of pinpoint brain stimulation without opening the skull (74); the second is the discovery of a drug which selectively stimulates these nuclei. Both of these developments are well within the realm of possibility.

As already mentioned, selective brain lesions may reduce or eliminate aggressive behavior. The reader will recall Sawa's patient (55) who, after the operation, felt that he could not become angry if he wanted to. Brain surgery is currently being used effectively for the control of extremely assaultive individuals.

Control of aggressive tendencies can also be achieved through the adjustment of hormone balances. Progesterone is frequently used to reduce the irritability associated with premenstrual tension (20). Maternal aggression in the rat has been controlled by the administration of oestrone (15). Stilboestrol has been used clinically to diminish irritable aggression in the male (12, 51). Further understanding of the role of hormones in aggressive behavior should lead to a rational endocrine therapy for certain kinds of aggressive behavior. Lerner's work with androgen antagonists may be particularly important here (32).

Finally, drugs are a currently useful and practical means of altering the internal environment so that aggressive tendencies are reduced. There are a number of chemical agents that appear to be specific inhibitors of hostility, which reduce aggression without appreciably affecting the individual's alertness or motor coordination. The vast literature on this topic cannot be renewed here, but a few examples will illustrate the point. The use of Dilantin®* for the control of aggressive tendencies has recently received national publicity (50). Turner (77) has presented numerous case studies demonstrating the effectiveness of this drug for that purpose and has presented a theoretical statement which may guide research on this problem. Scheckel and Boff (56) have shown that chlordiazepoxide and diazepam reduce aggressiveness in squirrel monkeys at doses that do not interfere with other behaviors. Diazepam has been used with "remarkable success" in eliminating the destructive rampages of psychotic criminals (25).

Research on drugs to control behavior is in its infancy and yet there is good reason to believe that the judicious use of the fruits of this research can help to control the minor, but uncomfortable, irritability of such dysfunctions as premenstrual tension as well as the major assaultive crimes of individuals afflicted with discontrol syndrome.

In summary, we must conclude that aggressive behavior is determined by an interwoven complex of internal, external, and experiential factors. The solution to the multifaceted and critical problem of the control of destructive, aggressive tendencies will only be approached when all of these factors are given adequate consideration.

---

* Registered trademark for diphenylhydantoin, Parke, Davis & Co., Detroit, Mich.

References

1. Akert, K. 1961. Diencephalon. *In* Electrical Stimulation of the Brain. D. E. Sheer, ed. Hogg Foundation, Austin, Tex.

2. Altman, J. 1966. Organic Foundations of Animal Behavior. Holt, Rinehart & Winston, Inc., New York, N.Y.

3. Beeman, E. A. 1947. The Effect of Male Hormone on Aggressive Behavior in Mice. Physiol. Zool. **20**: 373–405.

4. Berkowitz, L. 1962. Aggression, A Social Psychological Analysis. Mc-Graw-Hill Book Co., New York, N.Y.

5. ———. 1965. The Concept of Aggressive Drive: Some Additional Considerations. *In* Advances in Experimental Social Psychology. Vol. 2. L. Berkowitz, ed. Academic Press, Inc., New York, N.Y.

6. Bolles, R. C. 1958. The Usefulness of the Drive Concept. *In* Nebraska Symposium on Motivation. M. R. Jones, ed. University of Nebraska Press, Lincoln, Neb.

7. Cleghorn, R. A. 1957. Steroid Hormones in Relation to Neuropsychiatric Disorder. *In* Hormones, Brain Function and Behavior. H. Hoagland, ed. Academic Press, Inc., New York, N.Y.

8. Cofer, C. N., and Appley, M. H. 1964. Motivation: Theory and Research. John Wiley & Sons, Inc., New York, N.Y.

9. Dalton, K. 1964. The Premenstrual Syndrome. Charles C Thomas, Publisher, Springfield, Ill.

10. Delgado, J. M. R. 1960. Emotional Behavior in Animals and Humans. Psychiat. Res. Rep. **12:** 259–271.

11. Delgado, J. M. R. 1963. Cerebral Heterostimulation in a Monkey Colony. Science **141:** 161–163.

12. Dunn, G. W. 1941. Stilbestrol Induced Testicular Degeneration in Hypersexual Males. J. Clin. Endocr. **1:** 643–648.

13. Egger, M. D., and Flynn, J. P. 1963. Effect of Electrical Stimulation of the Amygdala on Hypothalamically Elicited Attack Behavior in Cats. J. Neurophysiol. **26:** 705–720.

14. Ehrlich, A. 1964. Neural Control of Feeding Behavior. Psychol. Bull. **61:** 100–114.

15. Endroczi, E., Lissak, K., and Telegdy, G. 1958. Influence of Sexual and Adrenocortical Hormones on the Maternal Aggressivity. Acta Physiol. Acad. Sci. Hung. **14:** 353–357.

16. Feshbach, S. 1964. The Function of Aggression and the Regulation of Aggressive Drive. Psychol. Rev. **71:** 257–272.

17. Gibbs, F. A. 1951. Ictal and Non-ictal Psychiatric Disorders in Temporal Lobe Epilepsy. J. Nerv. Ment. Dis. **113:** 522–528.

18. Gibson, J. G. 1962. Emotions and the Thyroid Gland. J. Psychosom. Res. **6:** 91–116.

19. Graff, H., and Stellar, E. 1962. Hyperphagia, Obesity and Finickiness. J. Comp. Physiol. Psychol. **55:** 418–424.

20. Greene, R., and Dalton, K. 1953. The Premenstrual Syndrome. Brit. Med. J. 1007–1014.

21. Hawke, C. C. 1950. Castration and Sex Crimes. Am. J. Ment. Defic. **55:** 220–226.

22. Heath, R. G. 1963. Electrical Self Stimulation of the Brain in Man. Am. J. Psychiat. **120:** 571–577.

23. Hinde, R. A. 1967. The Nature of Aggression. New Society **9:** 302–304.

24. Jonas, A. D. 1965. Ictal and Subictal Neurosis, Diagnosis and Treatment. Charles C. Thomas, Publisher, Springfield, Ill.

25. Kalina, R. K. 1962. Use of Diazepam in the Violent Psychotic Patient: A Preliminary Report. Colorado GP **4:** 11–14.

26. Kennedy, G. C. 1953. The Role of Depot Fat in the Hypothalamic Control of Food Intake in the Rat. Proc. Roy. Soc. (Biol.) **140:** 578–592.

27. King, H. E. 1961. Psychological Effects of Excitation in the Limbic System. *In* Electrical Stimulation of the Brain. D. E. Sheer, ed.: 477–486. University of Texas Press, Austin, Tex.

28. Kislak, J. W., and Beach, F. A. 1955. Inhibition of Aggressiveness by Ovarian Hormones. Endocrinology **56:** 684–692.

29. Lagerspetz, K. 1964. Studies on the Aggressive Behaviour of Mice. Ann. Acad. Sci. Fenn.: 1–131.

30. Le Beau, J. 1952. The Cingular and Precingular Areas in Psychosurgery (Agitated Behavior, Obsessive Compulsive States, Epilepsy). Acta Psychiat. Scand. **27:** 305–316.

31. Le Maire, L. 1956. Danish Experiences Regarding the Castration of Sexual Offenders. J. Criminal Law Criminol. **47:** 294–310.

32. Lerner, L. J. 1964. Hormone Antagonists: Inhibitors of Specific Activities of Estrogen and Androgen. Recent Prog. Hormone Res. **20:** 435–490.

33. Levison, P. K., and Flynn, J. P. 1965. The Objects Attacked by Cats During Stimulation of the Hypothalamus. Animal Behaviour **13:** 217–220.

34. Levy, J. V., and King, J. A. 1953. The Effects of Testosterone Priopionate on Fighting Behavior in Young Male C57 BL/10 Mice. Anat. Rec. **117:** 562–653.

35. Lichenstein, P. E. 1950. Studies of Anxiety: II. The Effects of Lobotomy on a Feeding Inhibition in Dogs. J. Comp. Physiol. Psychol. **43:** 419–427.

36. Lorenz, K. 1966. On Aggression. Methuen, London, England.

37. Marler, P., and Hamilton, W. J. 1966. Mechanisms of Animal Behavior. John Wiley & Sons, Inc., New York, N.Y.

38. Masserman, J. H. 1943. Behavior and Neuroses. University of Chicago Press, Chicago, Ill.

39. Mayer, J. 1953. Glucostatic Mechanism of Regulation of Food Intake. New Engl. J. Med. **249:** 13–16.

40. Miller, N. E. 1957. Experiments on Motivation. Science **126:** 1271–1278.

41. ———. 1961. Implications for Theories of Reinforcement. *In* Electrical Stimulation of the Brain. D. E. Sheer, ed.: 515–581. Hogg Foundation, Austin, Tex.

42. Morrison, S. D., and Mayer, J. 1957. Adipsia and Aphagia in Rats After Lateral Subthalamic Lesions. Am. J. Physiol. **191:** 248–254.

43. Morton, J. H., Additon, H., Addison, R. G., Hunt, L., and Sullivan, J. J. 1953. A Clinical Study of Premenstrual Tension. Am. J. Obstet. Gynec. **65:** 1182–1191.

44. Moyer, K. E. 1967. Kinds of Aggression and Their Physiological Basis. Carnegie-Mellon University, Pittsburgh, Pa., Report No. 67–12.

45. Moyer, K. E. 1968. Kinds of Aggression and Their Physiological Basis. Commun. Behavioral Biol. **2:** 65–87.

46. Pearson, O. P. 1944. Reproduction in the Shrew (Blarina Brevicauda Say). Am. J. Anat. **75:** 39–93.

47. Pool, J. L. 1954. The Visceral Brain of Man. J. Neurosurg. **11**: 45–63.

48. Richter, C. P. 1950. Psychotic Behavior Produced in Wild Norway and Alexandrine Rats Apparently by Fear of Food Poisoning. *In* Feelings and Emotions. M. L. Reymert, ed.: 189–202. McGraw-Hill Book Co., New York, N.Y.

49. Roberts, W. W., and Kiess, H. W. 1964. Motivational Properties of Hypothalamic Aggression in Cats. J. Comp. Physiol. Psychol. **58**: 187–193.

50. Rosenfeld, A. 1967. 10,000-to-1 Payoff. Life Magazine **63**(13): 121–128.

51. Sands, D. E. 1954. Further Studies on Endocrine Treatment in Adolescence and Early Adult Life. J. Ment. Sci. **100**: 211–219.

52. ———, and Chamberlain, G. H. A. 1952. Treatment of Inadequate Personality in Juveniles by Dehydroisoandrosterone. Brit. Med. J.: 66–68.

53. Sano, K. 1962. Sedative Neurosurgery: With Special Reference to Posteromedial Hypothalamotomy. Neurol. Medicochir. **4**: 112–142.

54. Sano, K., Yoshioka, M., Ogashiwa, M., Ishijima, B., and Ohye, C. 1966. Posteromedial Hypothalamotomy in the Treatment of Aggressive Behaviors. Second Intern. Symp. Stereoencephalotomy, Confin. Neurol. **27**: 164–167.

55. Sawa, M., Ueki, Y., Arita, M., and Harada, T. 1958. Preliminary Report on the Amygdaloidectomy on the Psychotic Patient, with Interpretation of Oral-Emotional Manifestation in Schizophrenics. Folia Psychiat. Neurol. Jap. **7**: 309–329.

56. Scheckel, C. L., and Boff, E. 1966. Effects of Drugs on Aggressive Behavior in Monkeys. Excerpta Med. Intern. Congr. Ser. 129, Proc. Fifth Intern. Congr. Collegium Intern. Neuropsychopharmacologicum: 789–795.

57. Schreiner, I., and Kling, A. 1956. Rhinencephalon and Behavior. Am. J. Physiol. **184**: 486–490.

58. Scott, J. P. 1958. Aggression. University of Chicago Press, Chicago, Ill.

59. ———. 1962. Hostility and Aggression in Animals. *In* Roots of Behavior. E. L. Bliss, ed. Harper & Row, Publishers, New York, N. Y.

60. ———. 1967. The Development of Social Motivation. *In* Nebraska Symposium on Motivation. D. Levine, ed. University of Nebraska Press, Lincoln, Neb.

61. Scott, J. P. 1965. Review of J. D. Carthy and F. J. Ebling. The Natural History of Aggression. Science **148**: 820–821.

62. Scott, J. P. 1966. Review of K. Lorenz, On Aggression. Science **154**: 636–637.

63. ———. 1966. Agonistic Behavior of Mice and Rats: A Review. Am. Zool. **6**: 683–701.

64. Scott. J. P., and Fredericson, E. 1951. The Causes of Fighting in Mice and Rats. Physiol. Zool. **24**: 273–309.

65. Seward, J. P. 1945. Aggressive Behavior in the Rat: I. General Characteristics; Age and Sex Differences. J. Comp. Psychol. **38**: 175–197.

66. Sigg, E. B. 1968. Relationship of Aggressive Behavior to Adrenal and Gonadal Function of Male Mice. Paper Presented at First Intern. Symp. Aggression. Milan, Italy.

67. Speigel, E. A., Wycis, H. T., Freed, H., and Orchinik, C. 1951. The Central Mechanism of the Emotions. Am. J. Psychiat. **108**: 426–532.

68. Strauss, E. B., Sands, D. E., Robinson, A. M., Tindall, W. J., and Stevenson, W. A. H. 1952. Use of Dehydroisoandrosterone in Psychiatric Treatment. Brit. Med. J.: 64–66.

69. Suchowski, G. K. 1968. Sexual Hormones and Aggressive Behavior. Paper Presented at First Intern. Symp. Aggressive Behavior. May 2–4, 1968. Milan, Italy.

70. Swade, E. D., and Geiger, S. C. 1956. Abnormal EEG Findings in Severe Behavior Disorder. Dis. Nerv. Sys. **17**: 307–317.

71. Swade, E. D., and Geiger, S. C. 1960. Severe Behavior Disorders with Abnormal Electroencephalograms. Dis. Nerv. Sys. **21**: 616–620.

72. Teitelbaum, P. and Epstein, A. N. 1962. The Lateral Hypothalamic Syndrome. Psychol. Rev. **69**: 74–90.

73. Tinbergen, N. 1968. On War and Peace in Animals and Man. Science **160**: 1411–1418.

74. Tobias, C. A. 1962. The Use of Accelerated Heavy Particles for Production of Radiolesions and Stimulation in the Central Nervous System. *In* Responses of the Nervous System to Ionizing Radiation. Haley, T. J. and Snider, R. S., eds. Academic Press, Inc., New York, N.Y.

75. Tow, P. M., and Whitty, C. W. M. 1953. Personality Changes After Operations on the Cingulate Gyrus in Man. J. Neurol. Neurosurg. Psychiat. **16**: 186–193.

76. Treffert, D. A. 1964. The Psychiatric Patient with an EEG Temporal Lobe Focus. Am. J. Psychiat. **120**: 765–771.

77. Turner, W. J. 1967. The Usefulness of Diphenylhydantoin in Treatment of Nonepileptic Emotional Disorders. Intern. J. Neuropsychiat. **3**(Suppl. 2): S8–S20.

78. Urich, J. 1938. The Social Hierarchy in Albino Mice. J. Comp. Psychol. **25**: 373–413.

79. Ursin, H. 1960. The Temporal Lobe Substrate of Fear and Anger. Acta Psychiat. Neurol. Scand. **35**: 278–396.

80. Vonderahe, A. R. 1944. The Anatomic Substratum of Emotion. The New Scholasticism **18**: 76–95.

81. Wasman, M. and Flynn, J. P. 1962. Directed Attack Elicited from Hypothalamus. Arch. Neurol. **6**: 220–227.

82. Wheatley, M. D. 1944. The Hypothalamus and Affective Behavior in Cats. Arch. Neurol. Psychiat. **52**: 296–316.

83. Williams, D. R., and Teitelbaum, P. 1956. Control of Drinking Behavior by Means of an Operant-Conditioning Technique. Science **124**: 1294–1296.

84. Wood, C. D. 1958. Behavioral Changes Following Discrete Lesions of Temporal Lobe Structures. Neurology **8**(Suppl. 1): 215–220.

85. Woods, J. W. 1956. "Taming" of the Wild Norway Rat by Rhinencephalic Lesions. Nature (London) **178**: 869.

86. Woods, S. M. 1961. Adolescent Violence and Homicide: Ego Disruption and the 6 and 14 Dysrhythmia. Arch. Gen. Psychiat. **5**: 528–534.

87. Wright, J. H. 1965. Test for a Learned Drive Based on the Hunger Drive. J. Exp. Psychol. **70**: 580–584.

88. Wyrwicka, W., and Dobrzecka, C. 1960. Relationship Between Feeding and Satiation Centers of the Hypothalamus. Science **123**: 805–806.

ATTITUDES TOWARDS FOREIGN AFFAIRS AS A FUNCTION OF PERSONALITY

Bjorn Christiansen

THE CHANNELIZATION HYPOTHESIS:

A PRELIMINARY ANALYSIS

The Channelization Hypothesis contends that various psychological conditions are of decisive importance for the degree to which deeper personality layers will influence a person's attitudes towards foreign affairs. We have previously discussed three such conditions: nationalism, international knowledge, and manifest reaction tendencies in everyday situations.

In what follows we shall take as our point of departure our previous demonstration of a positive correlation between psychodynamic conflicts and aggressive attitudes towards foreign affairs. We shall consider this correlation as supporting the fact that latent, character-conditioned aggression has a tendency to become displaced on to the sphere of foreign affairs, and investigate the degrees

to which such displacement is related to nationalism (patriotism), international knowledge, and aggressive everyday ways of reacting.

Next we shall start out with our earlier demonstration of a positive correlation between aggressive everyday and international reaction patterns, and investigate the degree to which this correlation is related to psychodynamic conflicts (latent aggression), nationalism (patriotism), and international knowledge respectively.

The latter proposition perhaps falls outside what should strictly be described as the Channelization Hypothesis. However, it can at any rate be said to complement it, since it often seems to be assumed that a lack of displacement of aggression implies an independent and rational stand in foreign affairs. In our opinion a lack of displacement will provide a basis for increased generalization of aggression unless tendencies in this direction are counterbalanced by other psychological conditions.

Source: B. Christiansen, *Attitudes Towards Foreign Affairs as a Function of Personality* (Oslo, Norway: Universitetsforlaget, 1959), chs. 5 and 12. The condensed version here is from H. Proshansky and B. Seidenberg (eds.), *Basic Studies in Social Psychology* (New York: Holt, Rinehart and Winston, 1965), pp. 706-716. Copyright 1959 by Universitetsforlaget and reprinted with their permission.

PROCEDURE

SUBJECTS

Applicants to and students of the Military Academy and the Naval Academy in

Oslo were used as subjects. The empirical data were collected in two stages: in August and the beginning of September, 1952, and at the end of January, 1954. In the first session which lasted approximately three hours for each subject, various attitude-scales and questionnaires as well as projective methods were administered. In the second session, which lasted approximately one hour for each subject, two projective techniques and a sociometric scale were given.

In the first stage a total of 103 applicants to the Military Academy and 64 students at the Naval Academy were used. The subjects were divided into groups, with 15–20 persons in each group. The students of the Naval Academy worked under completely anonymous conditions. The applicants to the Military Academy were given repeated assurances that all answers would be strictly confidential, that no names would be mentioned, and that their responses would have no bearing on their admission to the Academy —which they had the opportunity to verify through their own representatives.

The samples of Military Academy applicants had an average age of 23 years. The majority, 84 or 82%, were between 21 and 24 years of age, and the total ranged from 20 to 30 years. We have no complete specification of the age-distribution for the students of the Naval Academy. However there are many indications that there is no great difference between them and the Military Academy applicants.

The second stage of our data collection occurred exactly a year and a half after the first. This time we used 70 students of the Military Academy in Oslo as subjects. The sample represented a part of our original sample of subjects, specifically, those of the previous applicants who had been accepted by the Academy. The sample included practically all of the students in the second year of training, and the investigation was again based on groups. We worked with three groups in all—three classes—consisting of 21, 24, and 25 students respectively. These three classes were studied successively, and we have every reason to assume that none of the subjects had any prior knowledge of the tests and instruments applied.

In other words, our sample of subjects consists exclusively of men in their twenties. They come from all over the country. They have a similar educational background, all having completed gymnasium.[1] Unquestionably the most striking characteristic is the subjects' specific occupational position.

The fact that they all wanted military training and had roughly the same previous educational background undoubtedly limits considerably the possible variation in group membership. Our subjects represent a very homogeneous sample in many ways; but at the same time—psychologically speaking—a less homogeneous sample than one might be inclined to assume. In informal interviews with some of the subjects, for example, it was clearly evident that their occupational motivations were highly varied. In certain cases distinct signs of "authoritarian" traits could be discerned, the wish to defend King and Fatherland, conventionalism, authoritarian submission and identification with strong leaders. In other cases these motives did not seem to occur at all. The desire for a relatively well-paid and diversified occupation, one offering unique opportunities for exercise and outdoor living, was usually in evidence.

We will not deny the fact that a certain homogeneity exists. Our sample of respondents is by no means representative of the Norwegian population, nor of Norwegian men, nor of Norwegian men of the same age-group and the same general educational background.

VARIABLES AND MEASURING INSTRUMENTS

1. Aggressive Reactions in Foreign Affairs (E Score of the IR Scale). Types of reactions to international incidents which threaten Norwegian interests were measured by the forty-item IR scale. Each item described a conflict for Norway created by either the United States or the Soviet Union or nations

---

[1] Secondary school to university entrance standard.

oriented to either side of the East-West controversy, or nations or events which were neutral to this controversy. Choosing from among six alternatives, the subject indicated his strongest preference and his next strongest preference in the action he would prefer Norway to take in the conflict. Each alternative could be classified in terms of the direction of the reaction (inward, outward, or passive) and its form (threat-oriented or problem-oriented), thereby providing six types of possible reaction patterns to international conflict. Scores were obtained for each of these patterns based on an appropriate weighting of the subject's first and second choices from the six alternatives for each of the forty items. Of concern in the present study is the E score which measures the degree to which the subject's reactions to international conflict are threat-oriented in an outward direction, that is, they indicate aggressive reactions toward other nations. A reliability coefficient of .86 was obtained for this measure.

2. Aggressive Reactions in Everyday Situations (E Score of the ER Scale). Measures of reaction patterns to conflict situations in everyday life were obtained by means of the ER scale, which, except for its item content, was identical in design and approach to the IR scale. The everyday situations involved incidents which could happen to anyone in an ordinary day's activity, for example, splattered by dirty water by a passing car. The items covered relationships between the subject and the conflict-producing object which were either impersonal, intimate, formal, or involved the subject in conflict with a child. Here again the subject made two choices from the six alternatives provided for each item, indicating what he would be most likely to do and next most likely to do in the situation. His choices reflected particular directions and forms of response as noted above for the IR scale. The E score of the ER scale therefore provided a measure of aggressive reaction tendencies in everyday situations which corresponded to the measure of aggression in international situations, i.e., the E score of the IR scale. A reliability measure of .86 was obtained for the E score of the ER scale.

3. Latent Aggression as a Function of Psychodynamic Conflicts (Blacky Test). The extent of conflict in connection with psychosexual impulses was measured by means of a modified form of the Blacky Test (Blum, 1949; 1950), a projective technique in which a family of dogs consisting of a puppy Blacky, Blacky's parents, and a sibling is depicted cartoon style in a variety of situations. The eleven pictures (slides) in the test were designed to detect conflict with respect to various psychosexual dimensions (oral eroticism, sibling jealousy), based on the spontaneous stories told by the subject about each picture as well as his responses to a series of questions (the inquiry) presented immediately following his story about the picture. In order to adapt the test to both the Norwegian setting and the requirements of the immediate research problem, appropriate translations from English to Norwegian were made, only the four pictures focused on early psychosexual development were used, the test was group administered rather than given on an individual basis, as well as other minor changes in the details of administering the test being made. The scoring of the test was also modified with greatest emphasis placed on the spontaneous stories which were scored for the extent to which they reflected conflict-free or conflict-charged manifestations in the handling of basic psychosexual impulses. Scoring reliabilities in assessing the presence or absence of such conflict in the stories told for each of the four pictures were in the order of 86 to 99 per cent rater agreement involving two reliability studies.

4. National Patriotism (NP Scale). National patriotism is defined as a general tendency to see one's own nation as superior to the rest of mankind. A prominent trait would be a superordinate loyalty to one's own nation in relation to other reference and membership groups. Loyalty to one's own nation will take priority over loyalty to (a) national sub-groups, (b) supra-national organizations, (c) national outgroups, and (d) humanity as a whole. To measure patriotism of this kind a nine-item scale was constructed reflecting the "loyalty dimensions" listed above. The subjects were asked to give their opinions about each of the statements by indicating the extent to which they agreed or disagreed with it on a five-point evaluation scale extending from "strong agreement" to "strong disagreement." Each statement was numerically scored for the degree of patriotism indicated by the subject's extent of agreement or disagreement with it, and on this basis a total patriotism score for the nine-item scale was obtained.

5. *International Knowledge (IK Scale)*. International knowledge refers to the degree of accuracy in the subject's perceptions of how Norway compares with "most other nations" with respect to a series of twenty national attributes, such as "General Education," "Artistic Standards," "Educational Facilities." The subject judged each attribute on a five-point scale extending from the view that Norway had this trait to a considerably greater degree than other nations, to the view that it had this trait to a considerably lesser degree than these other nations. These judgements were then compared with the average corresponding judgments made by a panel of three experts. In establishing the judgements of the latter as criteria for accuracy, it was found that the judgements of the experts never involved more than one expert disagreeing with the others concerning a trait, and except for one case the deviation was never more than one scale interval in the five-point scale. The sum of the differences in intervals between the subject's judgements and the average judgements of the panel for the twenty national traits provided a total deviation score. The lower the score the less the deviation from the accuracy criteria and therefore the greater the international knowledge.

METHOD OF ANALYSIS

To obtain a survey of the effect of various factors on tendencies towards generalization and displacement of aggression, we proceeded in the following manner: first we examined the score distribution on the factor whose effect we wished to study, and isolated the approximately highest, middle, and lowest third of the distribution. On the basis of this delimitation we undertook a division of the subjects into three sub-samples and calculated the trend towards generalization (or displacement) in each of the sub-samples. Finally we compared the sub-samples and examined the differences among them.

RESULTS

There follows a statistical analysis of the connection of various factors with tendencies towards displacement of aggression, after which we shall present a parallel analysis of the connection of various factors with tendencies towards generalization of aggression. In both cases the analyses will be based on a comparison of fairly small groups since our total sample included a comparatively small number of subjects. On the whole the results will serve rather as a basis for elaborating hypotheses than providing material for final conclusions.

DISPLACEMENT OF AGGRESSION IN RELATION TO NATIONALISM

For our total sample we found a significant positive correlation between "number of conflict scores" on the Blacky test and the E category of the IR scale ($r = .33$). We have interpreted this as indicating that there is a connection between latent aggression and aggressive international reaction patterns.

To investigate the degree to which nationalism (patriotism) influences the connection between these two factors, we isolated the subjects who had answered both the IR scale and the Blacky Pictures, and divided the sample approximately into three groups according to the individual scores on the NP scale. We delimited three sub-samples: those who had achieved a score in the highest, middle, and lowest third of the score distribution on the NP scale. We then calculated for each sub-sample the correlation between "number of conflict scores" on the Blacky test and the E category of the IR scale.

Table 1. Correlation (*r*) between the *E* category of the IR scale and conflict scores on the Blacky test in samples with different scores on the NP scale

Score Intervals on NP Scale	N	r	p
19–26 (Least Nationalistic)	20	.18	.45
27–29 (Moderately Nationalistic)	21	.26	.26
30–38 (Most Nationalistic)	21	.56	.01

Table 1 presents the correlation coefficients in these three cases, showing that there are respectively highest and lowest correlations in the sub-sample with the highest and lowest scores on the NP scale. A comparison between the samples with the highest and lowest scores shows a difference between correlations of .38. Because of the small samples, however, the difference does not achieve statistical significance ($p = .18$).[2] In spite of this fact our data suggest that displacement tendencies might be associated with the degree of nationalism in the sense of patriotism. The correlation only achieves a satisfactory statistical significance in the sub-sample with the highest scores on the NP scale ($p = .007$).[3] In other words a certain degree of nationalism seems to be a prerequisite for the displacement of aggression on to the international sphere. Our data thus tend to support Durbin and Bowlby's view of nationalism as a channelizing factor (1939).

DISPLACEMENT OF AGGRESSION IN RELATION TO EVERYDAY AGGRESSION

To investigate the degree to which manifest aggressive reaction tendencies in everyday situations influence the connection between latent aggression and aggressive international reaction patterns, we proceeded in the same way as above and undertook a triple division of the total sample according to the scores of the individual subjects on the *E* category of the ER scale.

Table 2 surveys the correlation coefficients in these three instances.

The table shows highest correlation in the sub-sample with medium scores on the ER scale, and lowest correlation in the sub-sample with the highest scores. Only in the sub-sample with medium scores does the correlation achieve statistical significance ($p < .05$).

In spite of the fact that the difference between correlations in the sub-samples does not achieve statistical significance it is interesting to note that high scores on the ER scale's *E* category are associated with a comparatively smaller displacement tendency than low and medium scores. This is exactly what we might expect from the point of view of the "drainage theory": that aggressive tendencies in everyday situations function as a draining of latent aggression, so that less remains for international situations. An argument against such a view is the higher correlation in the sub-sample with medium scores than in the sub-sample with the lowest scores on the ER scale's *E* category. This does not necessarily mean that the "drainage theory" is untenable, but that it must be complemented by other considerations. A view which is opposite in the present connection is that inhibitions of everyday aggression—if sufficiently strong—may be transferred or generalized to affect aggressive international tendencies. If this were the case we should in fact expect greatest displacement to occur when more moderate inhibition of aggression is present. In those

---

[2] If a one-tail criterion is applied, the difference obtains an approximate statistical significance ($p < .10$).

[3] In testing the significance of an obtained correlation in sub-samples where *N* is less than 30, the *r* to *z* transformation has consistently been used.

Table 2. Correlation (*r*) between the *E* category of the IR scale and conflict scores on the Blacky test in samples with different scores on the *E* category of the ER scale

Score Intervals on the ER Scale	N	r	p
0–10 (Least Aggressive)	23	.32	.14
12–22 (Moderately Aggressive)	23	.43	.04
24–45 (Most Aggressive)	20	.22	.36

cases where we are dealing with a generalized inhibition of aggression we should further expect, from a depth psychological point of view, a comparatively greater tendency towards hypochondria and somatization. No examination was undertaken on this point. Some support for such a view is found in the fact that the frequency of certain heart and circulatory diseases (and also of certain mental diseases) was considerably reduced in Norway during the occupation period from 1940–45, compared with pre- and post-war periods.[4] An intense positive sanctioning and encouragement of aggressive social attitudes may possibly under certain circumstances be positively stimulating and "health bringing" for strongly affect-inhibited persons. Here we are faced with an extremely interesting hypothesis which invites further exploration.[5]

DISPLACEMENT OF AGGRESSION IN RELATION TO INTERNATIONAL KNOWLEDGE

In investigating the effect of international knowledge on the connection between latent aggression and international attitudes we proceeded in the same way as above, dividing the total sample into three sub-samples according to the individual subjects' scores on the IK scale.

Table 3 surveys the correlation coefficients in this case. The table shows that there is comparatively little difference between the sub-samples. The highest correlation turns out to be in the sub-sample with medium scores on the IK scale, the lowest correlation in the sub-sample with the highest scores. The fact that we find the least displacement of aggression to occur in the sub-sample characterized by least international knowledge is in accordance with a point of view previously referred to, that the influence of latent personality layers presupposes an orientation towards international relations. The very slight trend which exists in the direction of a lower displacement tendency in the case of most as compared to moderate knowledge, or the mere fact that here we do not find a corresponding higher displacement tendency in the case of most knowledge, fits in with the viewpoint that international knowledge may contribute in keeping character-conditioned aggression under control.

The differences found between the three sub-samples are much too small to verify these hypotheses. The differences achieve no statistical significance and the reason for the above comments is therefore mainly to indicate some lines for future research on more heterogeneous samples of subjects.

GENERALIZATION OF AGGRESSION IN RELATION TO LATENT AGGRESSION

As we have previously stated we found a significant positive correlation ($r = .42$) between the E categories of the ER and IR scales. We interpreted this as indicating

---

[4] A personal communication from H. J. Ustvedt.
[5] An observation relevant in the present context is that aggressive persons by and large seem to be in a much better state of physical health than people of similar age taken from the general population. In an American investigation of paranoid patients, nearly all diagnosed as dementia praecox, paranoid type, it was found that the manifestation of arteriosclerosis, including cerebral arteriosclerosis, was less frequent than in the general population. (See H. S. Alpert, et al., "Central arteriosclerosis in the paranoid state," *Psychiat. Quart.*, 1947, 21, 305–313.) Since the paranoid is a personality type who continually acts out his hostilities, the data indirectly support the hypothesis that repressed hostility often is a causal factor of hypertension and somatization.

Table 3. Correlation (*r*) between the *E* category of the IR scale and conflict scores on the Blacky test in samples with different scores on the IK scale

Score Intervals on IK Scale	N	r	p
14–21 (Least Knowledge)	24	.26	.22
11–13 (Moderate Knowledge)	15	.39	.15
4–10 (Most Knowledge)	26	.37	.06

that a generalization of aggressive reaction tendencies takes place from everyday to international situations.

In order to investigate the degree to which latent aggression (psychodynamic conflicts) affects tendencies towards the generalization of aggression, we delineated the subjects who had given complete responses on both the ER and IR scales, and divided the sample into approximately three groups according to the individuals' "number of conflict scores" on the Blacky test.

Table 4 surveys the correlation between the E categories in the sub-samples with 2 or less, 3, and 4 conflict scores on the Blacky test. The table shows that the highest and lowest correlations occur in the sub-sample having the lowest and highest "number of conflict scores" respectively on the Blacky test.

While the correlation in the sub-sample with most conflict scores achieves a very limited statistical significance ($p = .13$), the correlation in the sub-sample with least conflict scores shows a significance well below the 1% level ($p \approx .001$). The difference between correlations in these two samples is .40 and statistically significant at the 6% level.[6] The frequency of conflicts in connection with basic impulse patterns thus seems to be approximately significantly associated with a lack of generalization of aggression. The less the amount of latent aggression the greater the generalization tendency which seems to be present.[7]

Our empirical material thus supports the view we previously put forward, that lack of repression of aggression does not necessarily

---

[6] If a one-tail criterion is used the difference reaches a statistical significance at the 3% level.

[7] In concluding our empirical investigation of the Generalization Hypothesis it was pointed out that the hypothesis cannot explain why aggressive reactions do not show highest generalization despite the fact that this reaction type seems to be more consistent than others both in everyday and international situations. It is not inconceivable that this discrepancy might be abolished were we to concentrate on subjects who were unburdened by latent aggression.

Table 4. Correlation (r) between the E categories of the IR and ER scales in samples with different scores on the Blacky test

Score Intervals on the Blacky Test	N	r	p
0–2 (Least Conflict Charged)	23	.69	.001
3 (Moderately Conflict Charged)	14	.56	.04
4 (Most Conflict Charged)	29	.29	.13

lead to attitudes towards foreign affairs independent of personality factors, but to an increased generalization, unless tendencies in this direction are counteracted by other factors.

GENERALIZATION OF AGGRESSION IN RELATION TO NATIONALISM

We proceeded in the same fashion as above in investigating the degree to which nationalism (patriotism) affects the correlation between aggressive everyday and international reaction patterns, by making a triple division of the total sample according to the individual scores on the NP scale.

Table 5 shows the correlation between the E categories in the three sub-samples.

The table shows that the highest and lowest correlations occur in the sub-sample with the highest and lowest scores respectively on the NP scale. The difference between correlations in these two sub-samples is .39 and statistically significant below the 5% level ($p = .02$). We may therefore conclude that the score values on the NP scale are significantly associated with a tendency towards generalization of aggression. The more the patriotism present, the greater appears to be the tendency towards generalization.

Our data indicate on the whole that nationalism (patriotism) co-varies with tendencies towards displacement as well as towards generalization; in other words, it probably facilitates the influence of various personality factors on international attitudes.

GENERALIZATION OF AGGRESSION IN RELATION TO INTERNATIONAL KNOWLEDGE

In examining the degree to which international knowledge affects the connection between aggressive everyday and international reaction patterns we proceeded in the same manner as above, dividing the total sample according to the individuals' scores on the IK scale.

Table 6 surveys the correlation between the E categories of the ER and IR scales in the three sub-samples. The table shows highest correlation in the sub-sample with the highest scores on the IK scale, and least correlation in the sub-sample with medium scores. The difference between correlations in these two samples is .16, but it achieves no statistical significance ($p = .36$).

Our data give no basis for any definite conclusion, but there is a certain tendency for the greatest generalization to occur in the case of most and least international knowledge. In the two latter sub-samples only we find correlation coefficients obtaining a statistical significance below the 1% level. However, the difference between correlations in these two samples and the sample with moderate scores on the IK scale does not achieve statistical significance ($p = .33$).

In spite of the obvious shortcomings of the IK scale it nevertheless may be worth while to venture some speculations concerning our results: the relatively higher correlation coefficient in the sub-sample with the lowest scores on the IK scale (those with most knowledge), than in the sub-sample with medium scores, is in accordance with the aforementioned hypothesis: that the effect of personal values (*in casu* such values as are

Table 6. Correlation (*r*) between the *E* categories of the IR and ER scales in samples with different scores on the IK scale

Score Intervals on the IK Scale	N	r	p
15–23 (Least Knowledge)	56	.46	.001
11–14 (Moderate Knowledge)	45	.30	.05
2–10 (Most Knowledge)	59	.43	.001

reflected in everyday reaction patterns) on a person's attitudes towards foreign affairs will be the greater, the greater the international knowledge present. The same hypothesis is, however, weakened by our findings of a relatively higher correlation coefficient in the sub-sample with the highest scores on the IK scale, than in the sub-sample with medium scores. The latter relationship supports the hypothesis that little international knowledge implies small ability to differentiate between everyday and international situations, and that tendencies towards generalization are greater the less a person differentiates between different situations.

On the whole our data do not weaken the hypothesis that a curvilinear correlation exists between international knowledge and tendencies towards generalization. Furthermore, a comparison between Tables 3 and 6 suggests an inverse relationship between the influence of international knowledge on tendencies towards generalization and displacement respectively. Among the subjects characterized by least knowledge, the correlation between the R scales ("generalization") is somewhat higher than the correlation between the Blacky test and the IR scale ("displacement"), while the opposite is true in the rest of the sample. Here again interesting prospects open up for later empirical research on more heterogeneous samples of subjects based upon a more adequate method for registering international knowledge.

SUMMARY AND CONCLUSION

The intention of our investigation was the clarification of the influence of various psychological factors on tendencies towards generalization and displacement of aggres-

Table 5. Correlation (*r*) between the *E* categories of the IR and ER scales in samples with different scores on the NP scale

Score Intervals on NP Scale	N	r	p
16–25 (Least Nationalistic)	50	.23	.11
26–29 (Moderately Nationalistic)	56	.55	.001
30–40 (Most Nationalistic)	47	.62	.001

sion. We have previously shown that both these psychological mechanisms seem to have a certain validity as regards the explanation of aggressive reaction patterns towards foreign affairs.

By *generalization* we refer to the fact that a person reacts similarly to everyday and international situations, in other words, that a person's preference with regard to his nation's ways of reacting in international conflict situations are connected with his own reaction patterns in everyday conflict situations. The greater the correlation present in this area, the greater the generalization.

For the registration of ways of reacting to everyday and international situations we made use of two parallel attitude scales, the ER and IR scales. In the present investigation we concentrated entirely on the generalization of aggressive ways of reacting, that is, on the E categories of these two scales.

By *displacement* we refer to the fact that reaction tendencies which are repressed in relation to certain objects or situations find an outlet towards other objects or in other situations. In the present thesis we have concentrated exclusively on displacement of latent reaction tendencies on to international matters. We have said that greater displacement occurs the higher the correlation between a person's way of reacting to international conflict situations and his latent tendencies. In this chapter we have dealt with displacement of aggression only. To register the latter factor we made use of a shortened version of Blum's Blacky Pictures, and presumed that the frequency of conflicts in connection with basic psychosexual impulse patterns gives an approximate measure of the degree of latent aggression present.

As well as investigating how far latent aggression (or psychodynamic conflicts) influence tendencies towards generalization of aggression, and how far aggressive ways of reacting in everyday situations influence tendencies towards displacement of aggression, we concentrated on the influence of nationalism in the sense of patriotism and international knowledge respectively. For registering these last two factors we made use of two scales called the NP and IK scales.

The results of our investigation give support to the following statements:

A *certain degree of nationalism (patriotism) is generally a necessary precondition for the displacement of aggression towards foreign affairs.* In spite of the fact that our data do not give any conclusive evidence, on the whole there seems to be a closer connection between latent aggression and aggressive attitudes towards foreign affairs the more a person identifies himself with his own nation. Nationalism therefore seems to represent a mediating factor of importance for the degree to which latent personality layers are likely to colour a person's international attitudes.

There is no direct (linear) connection between aggressive ways of reacting in everyday situations and tendencies towards the displacements of aggression. Our data give no basis for concluding that tendencies towards aggressive ways of reacting to everyday situations represent a mediating factor of importance for the degree to which latent personality layers are likely to colour a person's attitudes towards foreign affairs; they nevertheless indicate hypothetically that extremely strong as well as extremely weak tendencies towards everyday aggression are associated with less pronounced displacement than moderate everyday aggression.

There is no direct (linear) connection between international knowledge and tendencies towards the displacement of latent aggression. Due to the inadequacy of our research instrument this statement must be considered with great cautiousness. As a hypothesis for later studies we may propose that displacement of aggression increases with increased knowledge up to a certain point, after which it decreases or remains approximately constant.

There exists an inverse connection between latent aggression (psychodynamic conflicts) and generalization of everyday aggressive reaction patterns. Our data indicate that there is a closer connection between aggressive ways of reacting to everyday and international conflict situations the more basic psychosexual impulse patterns are conflict-free and assimilated. Latent aggression seems to represent a mediating factor of importance for the degree to which everyday reaction patterns are likely to colour a person's attitudes towards foreign affairs.

A *direct connection exists between nationalism (patriotism) and generalization of everyday aggressive reaction patterns.* Our data indicate that there is a closer connection between aggressive reaction patterns towards everyday and international conflict situations the more a person is characterized by patriotic attitudes. Nationalism in the sense of patriotism therefore seems to represent a mediating factor of importance for the degree to which everyday aggression is likely to colour a person's attitudes towards foreign affairs.

No direct (linear) connection exists between international knowledge and generalization of everyday aggressive reaction patterns.

Here too we wish to stress the shortcomings of our measurement of international knowledge. As a hypothesis for further investigations we wish to point to the possibility that extremely great as well as extremely little international knowledge may be associated with greater generalization than moderate international knowledge.

We can summarize the above conclusions by stressing that the following three factors at least should be considered in attempting a psychological explanation of aggressive reaction patterns towards foreign affairs: 1) tendencies towards everyday aggressive ways of reacting, 2) scope of latent aggression or degree of psychodynamic conflicts; and 3) degree of nationalism or patriotism.

References

Blum, G. S. A Study of the Psychoanalytic Theory of Psycho-sexual Development. *Genet. Psychol. Monogr.*, 1949, **3**, 3–99.

————. *The Blacky Pictures: A Technique for the Exploration of Personality Dynamics.* New York: Psychological Corp., 1950.

Durbin, E. F. M., and Bowlby, J. *Personal Aggressiveness and War.* New York: Columbia Univer. Press, 1939.

II Conflict in Partially Structured Relationships: Strategic Factors in Conflict

Chapter 4

ESTABLISHED BARGAINING RELATIONSHIPS

In this section we are concerned with studies of conflict in which the participants perceive a definite structuring of their conflict options, and at least recognize their mutual interest in accepting various limitations on their conflict regardless of whether or not they succeed in doing so in the long run. The parties to these conflicts are bound together in an enduring relationship which they wish to maintain despite the fact that within this relationship they must bargain and contend for their own individual interests.

In the first selection, Boulding discusses economic exchanges (including gift-giving) as a general class of relationships involving both cooperative and competitive elements. Next Sawyer and Guetzkow use the general tools of what is called the theory of games to analyze the negotiation of a conflict of interest, and discuss some of the strategic elements that enable a given party to make a successful bargain for himself in a limited market.

Deutsch and Krauss then report on what happens in potential bargaining relationships when one or both parties is equipped with the means to threaten the other, and find that threat can disrupt the success of the bargaining for both the person who has the threat power and the one who does not. But how can parties be persuaded to give up their threatening power, if they also perceive this power as the basis of their own security against the power of the other? This is perhaps the crucial problem of our nuclear age, and is the problem addressed by Pilisuk and Skolnick in their experimental simulation of a disarmament dilemma. They see some grounds for hope in their finding that several flexible strategies (gradual initiatives toward disarmament, and a matching of either friendly or hostile moves by the other) led to an improvement in relationships.

ECONOMIC CONFLICT

Kenneth E. Boulding

Up to this point in the argument, we have been trying to formulate general principles of conflict and conflict processes that are common to all or to most conflict situations; that is, we have been developing an abstract model of a conflict situation or a conflict process that applies no matter what the setting, who the parties, or what the issues. . . . we have moved from the most general analysis to some more specific discussion of types of parties and the conflicts that are appropriate to each type. We still, however, have left the matter at a very general level: the processes that we have described hitherto are applicable equally, with some modifications, to industrial conflict and strikes, international conflict and war, family conflict and divorce, legal conflict and a judgment, race conflict and a riot, and political conflict and an election. Now we want to take a closer look at the differences between different kinds of conflict situations. It is a major argument of this work that all conflicts have common elements and general patterns and that it is in the search for these common elements that we are most likely to understand the phenomenon in any of its manifestations. A major corollary, however, is that all conflicts are not alike; there are important differences between, say, industrial and international conflict or between intrafamilial and interracial conflict. For a complete understanding of the phenomenon, we must understand these differences as well as the similarities. Otherwise, we shall be misled by analogy and will try to find elements in international conflict, for instance, that are really peculiar to industrial conflict. A strike is not a war, a divorce is

not a riot, and so on. We may note that these differences appear most striking in what might be described as the *boundary process*. The processes by which relations go from bad to worse are rather similar in all cases; these are the familiar Richardson processes. It is the crisis, or the overt breakdown of relationship into combat, that differs most from situation to situation.

In our drive toward the specific cases, let us first look at the peculiar characteristics of economic conflict. At first sight, economic conflict looks like a fairly simple example of field conflict in which two or more parties are trying to occupy a limited field and in which the field is not large enough to satisfy the preferred amount of occupancy of all the competing organizations or persons. The field, in this case, is commodities—goods and services. Whether these are thought of as a stock or a flow, as capital or an income, the same principle of scarcity holds; there is not enough of these things to satisfy all demands for them, which is what the economist means by saying that these things are scarce. Out of the fact of scarcity arises both exchange value, or the price system, and economic conflict. The conflict arises because of a famous law that I have sometimes called the Duchess's law, from one of the morals of the Duchess in *Alice in Wonderland*—"The more there is of yours, the less there is of mine." If there is only so much pie to go around and if demands cannot be satisfied by any distribution of pie among the claimants, economic conflict inevitably arises, in the sense that, if one gets more, everybody else taken together must get less and that the "more" and the "less" are significant to the parties. If everyone could be satisfied with existing supplies, of course, there would be no conflict, but this happy state of affairs is still far off in spite of economic development and technical progress.

The poorer the society and the scarcer commodities are in general, the more intense

Source: "Economic Conflict" (pp. 189–207) in *Conflict and Defense: A General Theory* by K. E. Boulding. Copyright 1962 by K. E. Boulding. By permission of Harper & Row, Publishers, Inc.

will be this conflict. The intensity of economic conflict in this general sense can be measured hypothetically by the marginal utility of income, that is, by the significance to the individual of a unit increase or decrease in real income. There are difficulties of measurement here that we shall ignore, as they do not destroy the general validity of the concept. In a very poor society, a little more income may be a matter of life and death; here, the conflict is acute, for my life may perhaps be bought, in extreme conditions, only by your death. In a famine, for instance, the richest and most powerful part of the population survives literally by depriving the rest of the means of life. As society gets richer, the significance to the individual of additions to income presumably grows less and less: this is the famous principle of the diminishing marginal utility of income. Galbraith has argued that, in the affluent society, economic conflict virtually disappears, for who can get excited about another square foot of chrome on the tail fin when all major needs are satisfied? In most of the world, of course, we are still a very long way from affluence, and even the United States is not as affluent as Galbraith seems to imply; but the general point is well taken.

Economic conflict of the kind discussed above may be called the *personal distribution conflict*, as it is concerned primarily with the distribution of the total economic product of society among persons. It takes on a very different appearance in a progressive society, that is, a society in which per capita real income is rising, from what it does in a stationary society, where per capita real income is not changing. In a stationary society, the conflict is perceived as an acute one. If one gets more, then, automatically, the rest of the people together must get less. The luxuries of the rich are literally paid for by the destitution of the poor. It is little wonder that such societies tend to generate acute class conflicts that occasionally burst forth into violent revolution. In a stagnant society, the only road to relieve the poverty of the poor seems to be to expropriate the rich and divide up the proceeds. The popularity of killing landlords remains unaffected by the economist's

timid reminder that, in a poor society, people would still be very poor even if all incomes were equal.

In a progressing society, the situation takes a very different turn, especially under conditions of rapid progress. Here, the rich can get richer without the poor getting poorer; indeed, anybody can get richer, up to a point, without anybody else getting poorer. There is still economic conflict, in the sense that some get richer faster than others. This is very different, however, from the conflict in a stationary society, where one only rises by pushing another down. This is the difference, of course, between the positive-sum game of the progressive society and the zero-sum game of a stationary society. In the negative-sum game of a declining society, the conflict is even more acute: here, one can only succeed in staying where one is by pushing someone else down. The negative or zero-sum game, as we have seen, is pure conflict, the positive-sum game is a mixture of conflict and cooperation, especially if cooperation can increase the positive sum. There is cooperation in increasing the pie and competition in sharing it, but if each man gets the increase for which he is cooperatively responsible, the conflictual element is reduced to the vanishing point.

An interesting example of the mixture of conflict and cooperation that is found in a positive-sum game is observed in the very phenomenon of free exchange itself, which is the core of economic life and organization. In a free exchange, both parties must benefit by the fact of the exchange; otherwise, the exchange will not take place. Some economists, especially Marx, have worried about how this could be so, especially as, in pure exchange, nothing seems to be created, for there is only a reshuffling of the ownership of commodities or exchangeables among the exchangers. The marginal-utility school cleared up this problem and showed how exchange could increase the total utility of each party, in spite of the fact that it represented only a redistribution of exchangeables, because each party gave up something that was less significant to him in return for something that was more significant. This could take place partly because of differences in tastes (some people like nuts more than apples, and some like apples more than nuts, even if everybody has the same quantity) but mainly because of differences in specialization and in distribution of stocks of goods before exchange; everybody gives up what he has too much of in return for what he has too little of. Specialization, however, increases the total product, at least up to a point, according to the famous principle that the jack-of-all-trades is master of none. Exchange, therefore, up to a point, is a positive-sum game even in commodities as well as in utilities.

This is not to say, of course, that specialization cannot be taken too far. Even Adam Smith himself has a much neglected passage in which he denounces the division of labor as a creator of stupidity and torpor of mind.[1] Overspecialization can put a limited horizon on economic development both for an individual or for a region, and it exposes the specialist to the winds of changing taste and techniques in a way that the less specialized person or society avoids. There may be, therefore, a case for the restraint of specialization, and many of the economic arguments for protection, for regulation, and for discriminatory taxation rest on the fear of too great specialization. The point of optimum specialization is not easy to find; up to this point, however, specialization is clearly a positive-sum game.

In exchange, the peculiar combination of cooperation and competition that is characteristic of the positive-sum game takes the form of cooperation in the fact of organization of exchange and competition in regard to the *terms* of the exchange, that is, the ratio of exchange. For any act of exchange, there will normally be a range of exchange ratios within which both parties benefit and a free exchange will take place. Within this range, however, the distribution of the benefit depends on where the actual exchange ratio lies. At one extreme, all the benefit goes to one party, and, at the other extreme, all goes to the other party. Thus, in an exchange of

wheat for money, there is a price of wheat that is so low that the seller receives no advantage, and all the gains of the exchange go to the buyer. There is another price that is so high that the buyer receives no advantage, and all the gain goes to the seller. Within this range, exchange benefits both parties, but the higher the price, the more of this gain goes to the seller, and the lower the price, the more of this gain goes to the buyer. Here, there is clearly a conflict that has to be resolved by a bargain, and the settlement of the conflict depends on a mysterious magnitude known as bargaining power. We shall return to this concept later.

In the model of perfect competition, where there are large numbers of buyers and sellers in contact and no loyalties to divert individuals from the serious business of maximizing individual gains, it should be observed that the conflict element in the act of exchange tends to disappear. This is because, with large numbers of buyers and sellers, the range of prices at which any particular pair of exchangers can trade with mutual advantage shrinks, simply because of the alternative buyers or sellers who are available. Thus, if we have only a single buyer and a single seller in the wheat market, the buyer might be willing to pay as much as $4 a bushel rather than go without, and the seller might be willing to get as little as $1 a bushel rather than not sell. There is a wide range of mutual advantage and much scope for conflict in bargaining about the price. Suppose now, however, that there are a considerable number of other buyers and sellers and that some sellers are selling at $2.51 while some buyers are buying at $2.49. This automatically reduces the range of mutual advantage of our original pair of exchangers to $2.49 to $2.51, for our original buyer will not buy from the original seller at any price above $2.51, for he can buy in the market at that price, and our original seller will not sell to the original buyer at any price below $2.49 for he can sell in the market at that price. The range of bargaining, then, is only 2 cents, and the conflict between the original pair is very small. In the absolutely perfect market of the economist's imagination, the range shrinks to zero, and there is no conflict between any

[1] Adam Smith, *The Wealth of Nations.* New York: Modern Library, 1937, V, ch. 1, p. 734.

particular pair of bargainers at all, simply because there is no range of bargaining.

Even in perfect competition, a change in price will make some people better off and some people worse off. Even though, therefore, there is no conflict in the bargain in perfect competition, there is competition, in the sense that circumstances over which no individual has any control may make one group of people gain and another group of people lose. In general any change in the structure of prices will cause extensive redistributions of wealth and of income among the persons of a society. If one price rises relative to others, the people who hold this commodity, security, or whatever the exchangeable happens to be will gain in the relative distribution of the total market value of assets, relative to those who do not hold it: people who hold much of it will gain more than those who hold little. Because of the vast interconnectedness of the price system, however, and the fact that it is almost impossible to change one price without setting off a vast reverberation among other prices, the ultimate effects of the change of a single price may be very different from its immediate effects. This means that the nature of economic competition, that is, the actual effects on the distribution of wealth and income of any particular change, is very obscure, and as long as this is the case, the lines of real economic conflict remain even more obscure.

Generally speaking, the short-run effects are more apparent; the long-run effects are more obscure because of the difficulties of tracing the dynamic consequences of any particular change. Some examples will illustrate the problem. Consider, for instance, the effect of an increase in the import duty on a particular commodity, say, watches. The immediate result is that foreign producers who have previously been exporting are probably harmed and that domestic producers are benefited, as they can sell their watches dearer or can sell more of them. Domestic purchasers of watches are probably harmed, as they have a narrower choice and may have to pay more for their watches, and as people were purchasing the imported watches before the raise in duty, the inference is that these were preferred by some people to the domestic

product. Foreign purchasers of watches may be benefited, as watches that previously went to the original market are now diverted to others, where they will probably be sold cheaper than before. If we confine ourselves to these short-run effects and to the comparison of an equilibrium position before the change with an equilibrium after it, it is not difficult to show that, on fairly plausible assumptions, the net benefit to all concerned is likely to be negative, though there may be important exceptions to this rule.

Though, in the short run, it is fairly easy to allocate gains and losses, at least qualitatively, in the long run the position is much more obscure. Suppose, for instance, that there is no monopoly and that there is complete freedom of entry into the domestic watch industry. The benefits that are the result of the increased duties attract new producers, and it will not be long before the profits in the industry are down to normal; the net long-run result is that there is a larger domestic watch industry than before, but the industry will be no more profitable than before. If the unusual profitability of the industry attracts an excessive number of new producers, as is not impossible, there may be a middle period in which the industry is actually abnormally unprofitable before the final adjustments are made. In the long run, therefore, the net gain to a competitive protected industry is dubious and may even be negative. The long-run impact on purchasers of watches depends on the consequences of expansion of the domestic industry. If there are what the economist calls external economies, so that the expansion of the industry makes it more efficient as a whole and reduces its costs per unit, prices to the purchasers of watches may actually be reduced, and the purchasers will be better off. If, however, the expansion of the industry means that less suitable resources have to be drawn into it, its costs per unit will rise, and purchasers will ultimately be somewhat worse off. The long-run effects on the foreign industry are equally obscure, depending on the nature of the long-run-cost curve.

The above analysis is merely one example of a large class of problems that illustrates the great difficulty of assessing the long-run effects on the distribution of wealth and income of any particular policy. We shall see later that wage policy involves exactly the same difficulties; it is very difficult to assess the long-run effects, for instance, of a given increase in wages. Similarly, it is by no means clear who is benefited and who is injured in the long run by subsidies to particular industries, such as agriculture. Indeed, one almost is forced to the cynical conclusion sometimes that an almost sure way to harm people is to try to help them. Subsidies to farmers, for instance, by encouraging them to remain in a low-income, declining industry when, otherwise, they would have got out into an advancing sector of society, may actually harm them as persons. Technical assistance, like the introduction of the potato in Ireland in the eighteenth century or the rapid spread of malaria control in the tropics since 1945, may set off a population explosion that makes the final condition of the assisted people worse than before. Aid to dependent children may create a subculture within the larger society in which children are raised to perpetual dependence. Pension plans for workers may tie them to their jobs and weaken their bargaining power. Conversion to a higher faith may disorganize the life of a primitive people, so that they can follow neither the old ways nor the new. Independence and self-government may cut a small country off from the world centers and leave it eventually to fester in misery and disorganization. These deplorable consequences are not, of course, necessary, and one does not want to abandon the desire to do good merely because its practice is difficult. Nevertheless, the social scientist has a certain duty to point out that it is hard to do good and hard to establish justice and that, the more we know about the intricate processes of social dynamics, the better chance we shall have of doing those things which will, in fact, promote human welfare and social justice.

In spite of the complexity of the problem of economic conflict, there are one or two fairly simple things that can be said about it. One is that the impact of any given change on an individual depends on his adaptibility and mobility. Suppose, for instance, that we have a fall in the price of a single commodity, say, coffee. This will lower the income of almost all those engaged in the coffee industry. The first impact will be on the owners of coffee estates, whose profits will be reduced; the impact will soon be transmitted, however, to workers on these estates, through either lower wages or unemployment, and to small coffee growers. If there is absolutely nothing else for coffee growers to do but to grow coffee, their lot is hard indeed; there is no way that they can escape from this reduction in income, and if it is severe enough, they may be driven to destitution. If, however, they are adaptable, if the coffee growers can easily turn to some more profitable crop, and if displaced coffee workers can easily find opportunities for employment elsewhere, the injury done to them is slight, and the conflict implied in a shift in relative prices is small.

A second proposition is that the impact of any given change on a group depends on the mobility of people into it or out of it and that, hence, the severity of economic conflict among groups depends on the mobility of their individual members. Where it is very hard for an individual to leave the occupational or cultural group to which he belongs or to join another, a reduction of the price of the group's product, or, as an economist would say, the worsening of its terms of trade, is likely to be long-lasting and unresponsive to any attempt at corrective behavior on the part of the group itself. Conversely, favorable movements, likewise, may have lasting effects if the group can prevent entry of new members. Where groups are mobile and shifting, so that individuals can easily shift from one to another, a disadvantaged group soon loses members to more advantaged groups, and this shift of membership normally tends to equalize the advantages of the two groups. Under these circumstances, group competition is ephemeral, strong group loyalties and identifications are not likely to develop, and group conflict will be slight. When, however, there is no mobility between groups, group identification and loyalty are likely to be strong, and conflict, therefore, is likely to be acute. There is a curious problem here in the dynamics of development of immobility and group loyalties, for the immobility that generates group loyalties is intensified by these loyalties themselves. A group may begin by being quite open to ingress and egress, but if mobility is low enough to begin to generate group self-consciousness and group loyalties, this fact in itself makes ingress and egress harder, and this, in turn, intensifies the group loyalties. One suspects that the development of nationality obeys a dynamics of this kind; similarly, the development of strong class consciousness, say, among factory workers, tends to prevent upward mobility into the managerial or professional group, and so the class consciousness may be increased by the very immobility that it generates.

A good example of a potential group conflict that is constantly being undermined by mobility is the conflict among age groups. The competition among age groups, especially in unstable times, can be very severe. It is reflected at a particular moment of time in the competition of the young, the middle-aged, and the aged for the product of society. By and large, it is those in the middle-aged groups between adolescence and senility who produce the product of society. They have to share it, however, with the young, who must be fed, clothed, sheltered, and educated in the nonproductive years, and also with the aged, who must also be supported when they are not producing anything. The conflict is a very real one; the more of the product goes to one group, the less is currently available for the others. Fine schools and generous old-age pensions mean smaller current real incomes for those in middle life. The conflict occasionally breaks out into the open in the form, for instance, of a struggle about school appropriations, refusals to pass school bonds, debates about old-age pensions, old-age political movements like the Townsend Plan, and revolutions of young insurgents against the (presumably) corrupt old men in positions of power. In spite of the very real nature of the competition, however, age-group conflicts tend to be sporadic, disorganized, and unstable, and they soon peter out. Age-group organizations, in which the common interests of a given age group are the only bond, likewise, are sporadic and have difficulty in maintaining themselves. Youth organizations are generally maintained by the middle-aged in a framework of some larger organization: it is not the young, after all, who run schools, universities, boy scouts, or even youth movements, and where students, for instance, do take over the administration of a university, the results are not always too happy. Organizations of the old, likewise, are likely to peter out as they find it difficult to replace leadership as it dies off.

The reason for the instability of age-group organizations is, of course, that this is the one group that has perfect one-way mobility through the mere passage of time. The young get middle-aged, the middle-aged get old, and the old die. Consequently, the young always have at least one eye on the group to which they are soon going to join, and likewise with the middle-aged. By the time a youth group has succeeded in winning something from the middle-aged, its members are likely to be middle-aged themselves and suffering from their own earlier success. The middle-aged are willing to support the old, as a matter of principle, because they will soon be old themselves, and supporting the old eventually pays off for anybody who does not die first; and if he does die first, he presumably does not have to worry anyway.

The conflict between the age groups is a very interesting example of an economic institution which is only partially in the exchange system and which involves gifts or support. If we look at the economic system in strictly current terms, it is clear that a good deal of income is, in fact, derived not from production but from support (transfers). The consumption of the young, of the old, of the sick, and of the indigent is received as a kind of gift from the productive sectors of the population, in the sense that the recipients of this real income do not give anything currently for it in return. There is, therefore, an interesting economic conflict between the supporters and the supported that is not a conflict about terms of trade or the price system but is a conflict about how much should be given in support of the currently nonproductive. The tax system is a particularly important arena of this conflict, because a major function of the tax system is precisely that of financing support—taking money away from those who derive income from the production and sale of goods and services and giving it to those who currently produce nothing.

When we take a longer time perspective, a good deal of income that looks like support in a short time period is seen as long-term exchange. Thus, when the young and the middle-aged save for their old age, they are purchasing future consumption by sacrificing present consumption. Their sacrifice of present consumption may, in fact, represent a transfer to the current group of aged, but it can be represented as in a sense a bargain with the future. In a large and rather vague way, we can regard the support that the middle-aged give to the young and to the old as a bargain across the generations: the middle-aged support the young now in return for an implicit bargain that in twenty-five or thirty years the young, who will then be middle-aged, will support the middle-aged, who will then be old. The support that the middle-aged give to both the old and the young can then be thought of as two bargains: the support given to the young is the first part of a bargain that will be fulfilled one generation hence, and the support given to the old is the second part of a bargain made one generation ago. Thus we have moved away from support conflict into bargain conflict; there is, then, as we have seen, community of interest in the fact of the bargain but conflict about its terms.

The rate of interest in one of its many functions is an expression of the terms of the bargain between the generations. If the rate of interest is high, the middle-aged will support the old generously, and if the young have borrowed for their support and education, the middle-aged will likewise be supporting the young generously. The savings of the middle-aged will accumulate at a high rate of interest, and when this generation is old, it will be able to live better than if the rate of interest had been low. Similarly, if the middle-aged

have borrowed when young, they will have to pay a high interest on these borrowings.

The problem of age-group conflict is greatly complicated by the introduction of fluctuations and dynamic disequilibriums. The rise and fall of birth and death rates, for instance, may substantially change the proportion of the population in different age groups. In the 1930s, for instance, the number of people of working age in most developed countries was unusually large; birth rates had been declining, so that the middle-aged came from a larger cohort than the children, and the rise in the expectation of life had not fully worked out its influence on the number of old people. In a rising population, in any case, the old come from a smaller cohort than the young or the middle-aged. In the 1960s on the other hand, the proportion of people of working age is much smaller; the birth rate has been rising sharply in most countries, so that there is a large cohort of children and young people, and the rise in the expectation of life is now being felt in an increasing number of old people. The burden of current support of the young and old, therefore, is much greater than it was a generation ago, and the burden is likely to increase.

Another aspect of the same problem concerns the age-specific character of the labor market and the size of the cohorts coming onto it. Normally, there is a rough distribution of jobs available by the age of the worker, and when there is a sharp distortion in the size of the cohorts coming onto the market, labor shortages or surpluses may result. Thus, in Britain, there was an acute youth problem in 1935, as the large generation of 1919, when the end of the first World War raised the birth rate nearly 50 percent, left school at 14 and came onto the labor market. Conversely, in the United States in the 1950s, the unusually small cohorts of the 1930s were coming onto the labor market, and it was very easy for them to get jobs. In the 1960s, the much larger cohorts of the 1940s (almost twice the size) will be coming onto the labor market; and it may, therefore, be quite difficult to place them, and a sharp rise of unemployment among the young may be expected. Similarly, in many tropical countries, there was a large reduction in infant mortality following the health revolution of the late 1940s, and an acute youth problem may be expected very soon as a result.

The business cycle and the war cycle, likewise, cause acute disparities in the experience of different generations. The generations, for instance, that came to maturity during the two world wars or during the Great Depression, had a much harder time of it than generations that came to maturity in times of peace and of prosperity. The generation that graduated in 1933, for instance, never really recovered from the experience of coming onto the labor market at the depth of the Great Depression. Similarly, the generation that was in its 20s in 1914 or in 1939 suffered not only war casualties but missed economic opportunities in a way that veterans legislation only partly compensates. The young farmer who bought a farm in 1919 at the peak of prices was almost doomed to fail no matter how great his abilities; even if he survived the agricultural depression of the 1920s, he was almost sure to lose his farm in the Great Depression of the 1930s. A young man, by contrast, who bought a farm, a business, or a house or who went into debt for almost any purpose in 1934 was likely to succeed no matter how inefficient he might be.

These conflicts among the generations are perhaps the most acute sources of real economic competition in the sense of group benefits and misfortunes. Nevertheless, they do not result in a strong sense of conflict, and only rarely do they develop organization for conflict. No greater demonstration could be made of the proposition that it is not mere homogeneity or similarity of fortune that makes an economic group or that sets the lines of organized economic conflict. A group may be very heterogeneous from the point of view of economic conflict, in the sense that, whatever happens or whatever the organized group does, some of its members will benefit and some will be harmed; and

yet the group may have a strong sense of identity, and some of its members may support policies as members of the group that, in fact, injures them as individuals. Group consciousness is more important in setting the lines of conscious conflict than group interest. We shall run across the same phenomenon in the discussion of international conflict.

The two main types of self-conscious economic groups are the commodity or service groups—occupational, industrial, or professional—on the one hand and the class or cultural groups on the other. The occupational and industrial groups have perhaps the clearest common interest; almost all people in agriculture, for example, are interested in a high price for agricultural products, and all people in the steel industry are interested in a high price for steel. These commodity groups, therefore, tend to form political pressure groups to extract laws and regulations from the state with the object of making their product scarcer. Tariffs are one aspect of this conflict, and we have seen how dubious a benefit this is likely to be. Subsidies are another aspect. Restriction of entry and licensing is a third important aspect. Of these, only those legal restrictions which give the commodity or service groups the right to exclude would-be members—which is the essence of monopoly power—give much hope of benefiting the group in the long run. Nevertheless, the pulling and hauling of commodity groups is perhaps the largest business of any legislative assembly.

Agriculture presents such an important special case and has so many peculiarities that it deserves special mention. In most societies, agriculture is in trouble; agriculturalists have a strong group consciousness, wield a political power frequently out of proportion to their numbers, and have usually succeeded in getting the state to intervene in the price system and in the system of support gifts and transfers, ostensibly with a view to shifting income toward agriculture and away from other sectors. The reasons for this pattern are complex, though they operate in nearly all modern societies. Agriculture does tend to have lower per capita incomes than other occupations, especially in a rapidly developing society. This is mainly because of technical improvement in agriculture itself, paradoxical as this may seem. Technical improvement in agriculture in the sense of greater output of food and fibers per man inevitably means a relative decline in the agricultural labor force, because of the inelastic demand for most agricultural products. With medieval techniques, it took about 80 percent of the people to feed the population; with modern techniques, we can grow all we need with less than 10 percent of the people. In the course of this transition, there must be a constant decline in the proportion of people engaged in agriculture, and this can be achieved only by making agriculture less attractive than other occupations. How much the differential must be depends on the mobility of resources out of agriculture and into other vocations. If agricultural resources are very immobile, large differentials in income must develop before resources will move out of it. If resources are mobile, the transition can be achieved relatively painlessly.

Unfortunately, the problem has usually been conceived in terms of a static justice rather than in terms of dynamic adjustment. Hence, the remedy has been sought not in facilitating the adjustment and in speeding the movement from agriculture into industry but in trying to raise agricultural incomes by creating artificial scarcities of agricultural products or by giving direct subsidies. These measures, however, tend to prevent the inevitable adjustment and so frequently prolong the agony. Price supports have led to unwanted accumulations of surplus products, subsidies tend to feed on themselves and require constant increase until they become unmanageably burdensome, output restrictions either have defeated themselves, as acreage restrictions usually do through the increase in yield per acre, or where they are effective as in the case of marketing quotas, they tend to be capitalized in the rents of quota-bearing land or in the market value of the quota itself where this is salable and, hence, benefit only the generation that happens to be in the saddle when the quotas are

imposed, thus leading to further injustice between the generations. The basic fallacy behind much agricultural policy is the attempt to do justice to a commodity rather than to people. Thus, agricultural policy is frequently sold, politically, even in countries with predominantly urban populations, by an appeal to social justice; farmers are poor, the argument goes, and should, therefore, be helped. What actually gets helped, however, is wheat or corn, and when this is done, only some farmers get helped, and these are usually the richer farmers. The paradox of trying to cure agricultural poverty by raising agricultural prices is that poverty in agriculture is mainly due to small farmers and subsistence farmers having so little to sell. When we raise prices, we do little for the man who has little to sell; we do much for the man who has much to sell.

The other type of economic conflict that has received attention is the class conflict. This is, of course, particularly associated with the Marxist ideology. Here the classification of society is not by commodity groups but by income groups; the class conflict, roughly speaking, is the conflict of the poor and the rich, of the privileged and the unprivileged, or of the dominant and the dominated. Like all other group conflicts, this conflict is likely to be more acute, the less mobility there is between the groups and the more self-conscious of their identity and distinctiveness the groups become. The most acute case of class conflict is where the rich and the poor have totally different cultures, perhaps even different languages, and where there is no mobility from one group to the other. In rich and fluid societies, where there is a continuum from the rich to the poor through the middle class, where there are no sharp breaks in the income distribution and there is a good deal of mobility between income groups, with some individuals or families getting richer and some poorer, and where there is a common language and a widely diffused common culture in spite of income differences, class consciousness will be low and class conflict unimportant.

Underlying the whole problem of class conflict is the problem of what really determines the distribution of wealth and income. This is a problem of such complexity that one despairs of reducing it to simple terms. The distribution of wealth is the result of a long historic process of inheritance, saving, capital gain and loss, marriage, taxation, expropriation and redistribution, and so on. We can point to certain institutions that will make for a movement toward greater equality in distribution, such as inheritance taxes, equal distribution of estates among children, public education, and so on. Similarly, we can point to institutions that make for inequality, such as primogeniture, regressive taxation, caste, and so on. Inflation and deflation are great redistributors of wealth: inflation tends to discriminate against settled and customary payments, fixed money incomes, bond-holders, and so on; deflation discriminates against profit makers, farmers, the unemployed, and so on. The very complexity of these processes, however, makes it hard to draw clear lines of conflict. The decisions that affect the dynamic process of distribution are not usually taken with any clear notion of consequences in mind; they are taken or are often not taken as a result of events, pressures, and images that have nothing to do with their ultimate or even their immediate consequences. Both deflation and inflation occur as a result of a failure to do things rather than as a result of doing things; they are seldom planned deliberately. Tax structures, likewise, which may have a profound effect on distribution, are often thrown together out of the exigencies of a period of war or crisis finance and remain to have profound but unsuspected repercussions on subsequent decades.

This is not to deny the existence of class conflict; the class struggle has been and still is a powerful symbol, and a good deal of history can be interpreted in terms of the rise and fall of classes. What must be emphasized, however, is that the class struggle is a much more complex phenomenon than the simple struggle of the poor to take from the rich and of the rich to defend themselves against the poor and more complex also than the struggle of the workers against the capitalists, . . . This is because the struggle is not a static conflict about a fixed aggregation of wealth or income but a conflict about an immensely complex dynamic process in which it is very hard to trace causes and effects. The class conflict is not like two dogs struggling for a bone in which, if one gets more, the other gets less. It is much more like the evolutionary conflict of species, in which temporary advantages often lead to ultimate defeat. . . .

THE PROCESS OF NEGOTIATION

Jack Sawyer and Harold Guetzkow

The prospect of achieving their interdependent goals through negotiation leads nations to the process itself. The process of negotiation includes all actions or communications, by any party to the negotiation, either made within the negotiating situation or intended to influence its outcome. Steps in this process, as treated in the following sections, include (a) preliminary negotiation concerning procedure and agenda, (b) formulation of alternatives and preferences of each party into a joint decision matrix, (c) communication and persuasion intended to alter the other party's perception of the situation, and (d) threats and promises, *faits accomplis*, and creative problem-solving activity intended to narrow or widen the range of available outcomes and alternatives.

PREPARATION FOR NEGOTIATION

Specific motivations to seek negotiation include impending expiration of a previous agreement (such as a lease of a foreign location for a defense base), the development (often through technological advance) of a previously inconsequential or nonexistent area (such as production of fissionable materials), and specific political acts of another nation (such as violation of an existing agreement). Changing circumstances such as these may initiate a sequence of procedural negotiation, agenda development, and finally, a decision to enter upon substantive negotiation.

Source: From "Bargaining and Negotiation in International Relations" by Jack Sawyer and Harold Guetzkow, in *International Behavior: An Social-Psychological Analysis*, edited by Herbert E. Kelman. Copyright 1965, Holt, Rinehart and Winston, Inc. Reprinted by permission of Holt, Rinehart and Winston, Inc.

PROCEDURAL NEGOTIATION

At the Peace of Westphalia in 1648, it took six months for delegates to decide in what order they should enter and be seated in the negotiating chamber (Durant & Durant, 1960). Three centuries later, at the Potsdam Conference of 1945, Churchill, Stalin, and Truman were able to agree upon a mode of entering the conference room only by arranging to emerge simultaneously from three separate doors (Morgenthau, 1960). Such continuing concern illustrates and attests to the importance of procedural matters in negotiation. If granting precedence in entering a room is an acknowledgment of general superiority, then it will be resisted as prejudicial to ensuing negotiation. To obviate such questions by arbitrary procedures (like alphabetical seating) is a major end of formal diplomatic protocol, such as represented in Satow's *Guide to Diplomatic Practice* (1957).

Other questions of procedure include the number and rank of participants to represent a party, the length and frequency of sessions, the languages to be employed (treated separately later), and the rules by which discussion is to proceed. Any of these arrangements may have an influence upon later negotiation, and consequently, particularly if the stakes in the eventual substantive negotiation are large, much time may be consumed in this stage. When problems of *how* negotiation is to be conducted are settled, however, attention may be concentrated upon the question of specifically *what* is to be negotiated.

AGENDA DEVELOPMENT

Starting with proposals from each party for issues to be negotiated, the parties must jointly decide which issues shall constitute the agenda. The choice is critical, as it influences the outcome of negotiation itself; Schatt-schneider (1957), referring to domestic politics, asserts that, "The definition of alternatives is the supreme instrument of power . . . [it] is the choice of conflicts, and the choice of conflict allocates power" (p. 937). For this reason, many higher-level officials will enter negotiation only after the agenda has been specified.

Agenda vary markedly in the number of issues they contain, and advantages can be cited for both the long and the short. Narrow agenda may confine negotiation to that area that has best promise of resolution and prevent jeopardizing it by unduly contentious items. However, upon any single issue, parties are likely to reach alternatives in which their interests are strictly opposed, and relative gain by one implies relative loss by the other. As Rusk (1955, p. 129) observed of debate in the United Nations, the tendency to isolate issues makes them more difficult to adjust. Through widening the agenda to include unrelated items, it may be possible to effect trading, in which, for each party, losses in one area are balanced by gains in another. The large number of contract clauses considered simultaneously in labor-management negotiation serves this function. A wider agenda may also provide room for placing less controversial issues at the beginning, as suggested by Sharp (1953), to permit group procedure to develop more fully before critical matters are treated.

THE DECISION TO ENTER
NEGOTIATION

Given the prospective agenda, the parties make a decision (perhaps implicit) to go ahead with substantive negotiation at that time, to postpone negotiation, or to call it off altogether. To enter negotiation implies expectation of a better result from participating than from refraining, whether based upon the motivations for delay or propaganda characterized earlier or upon the expected out-come of the negotiation itself. To evaluate the expected benefit from negotiation involves assessment of possible outcomes in relation to original national goals, a task commonly reserved for higher policy officials, though the creation of alternatives is often a function of staff persons at lower levels. The highlighting of alternatives is emphasized by Black (1960) in discussing the role of the World Bank; the prime task, he asserts, of diplomats involved in economic development is ". . . to illuminate the choices . . . and to provide evidence on which the decision-makers can weigh the benefits and costs of alternative courses of action" (pp. 24–25). If the evaluation of prospective outcomes is favorable, negotiation will generally ensue, though even then the rules of procedure, the agenda, and the specific alternatives may continue to evolve.

INTERSECTION OF ALTERNATIVES
AND UTILITIES

At the onset of negotiation, the situation may be conceptualized in terms of four main elements: (a) the negotiating parties, (b) the alternative actions that might be taken by each party, (c) the various outcomes expected to result from their combined actions, and (d) the utility each party ascribes to each of the various outcomes. Such a formulation, derived from the theory of games, has proven highly stimulating of both theory and empirical research dealing with interaction situations, not only in the field of economics (Shubik, 1959), which originally motivated game theory (Von Neumann & Morgenstern, 1944), but in other social sciences as well, including both social psychology (Rapoport, 1960; Thibaut & Kelley, 1959) and international relations (Kaplan, 1957; Schelling, 1960). In the following two sections, game theoretic models are articulated with international negotiation; then empirical evidence of actual choice in such game situations is presented.

THE DECISION MATRIX

The four elements of parties, alternatives, outcomes, and utilities may profitably be placed in matrix form, of which Figure 1 provides a highly simplified example. Consider two nations, A and B, negotiating over possible reduction in tariffs. For purposes of illustration, let Nation A have but two alternative actions that it might eventually take (though game theory can accommodate any number of alternatives): to reduce its tariff on the commodity in question to a lower "compromise" level, or to "hold out" at the present higher level. These two alternatives are represented by the first and second rows of the matrix. Nation B has two corresponding alternatives, represented by the two columns.

Designation of the alternatives as "compromise" and "hold out" is intended to suggest that such a matrix formulation as here illustrated with tariffs may also be applied to a much wider range of interaction situations. The alternatives at stake could just as well involve the number of inspections of suspected nuclear explosions, the terms of a development loan, or the size and extent of cultural exchanges.

In the illustration involving tariffs, if each nation can take either action, independently of the other, there are four possible outcomes, as indicated in the four cells of the matrix: both tariffs may be lowered, only A's may be lowered, only B's may be lowered, or both may remain high. Let each of these four outcomes have a certain utility for each party, as shown by the numbers in Figure 1.

Alternatives for Nation B Alternatives for Nation A	HOLD OUT for present high tariff	Lower tariff to a COMPROMISE level
HOLD OUT for present high tariff	*Outcome* Status quo: both tariffs remain high *Utility* 0 for A 0 for B	*Outcome* A's tariff remains high B's tariff lowered *Utility* +10 for A −5 for B
Lower tariff to a COMPROMISE level	*Outcome* A's tariff lowered B's tariff remains high *Utility* −5 for A +10 for B	*Outcome* Both tariffs are lowered *Utility* +5 for A +5 for B

Figure 1. Illustrative matrix of outcomes and utilities when each of two nations may alternatively lower its tariff to a "compromise" level or "hold out" at the present high level

The status quo of the existing higher tariffs is taken as a reference point, so that this outcome has zero utility for each party. The utilities of the other outcomes are shown as incremental amounts over the utility of the status quo; the negative utility for a nation when it alone lowers its tariff represents a worsening over the status quo for that nation.

It is important to note that the sum of the utilities to the two parties is higher for some outcomes than for others; in other words, this matrix belongs to the class referred to as non-constant-sum (or non-zero-sum). These are to be distinguished from zero-sum situations, in which one party gains only at the direct expense of the other; in such situations, negotiation is pointless. When some outcomes are better for both parties, however, and some worse, negotiation offers promise; it is these situations with which the present analysis is concerned.

The utilities in a decision matrix represent the over-all value placed upon the particular outcomes. In some cases, it is possible to translate this directly into monetary terms; for example, the values given in Figure 1 might represent millions of dollars. More commonly, political and other values for which, unlike money, there is no standard metric, do not permit such ready translation between objective and subjective utility measures. In practice, then, utility of outcomes is generally assessed by the judgmental evaluation of policy officials, as described earlier. In any event, utility is taken, both operationally and conceptually, to correspond directly to preference; outcomes of higher utility are those that are more highly preferred, and vice versa. The correspondence, though, is strictly definitional: Higher utilities do not "cause" higher preferences.

It is the resulting matrix of utility values that makes explicit the "intersecting alternatives and utilities" with which the present section is concerned. This matrix specifies the way in which the utility experienced by each party depends upon the choices of both, thus promoting the ability of a party to understand how it may achieve as good an outcome as possible, given that the other party is trying to do the same.

In the present example, the best outcome for either nation occurs when it retains high tariffs while the other nation reduces its tariffs. Regardless of whether the other nation retains or lowers its tariffs, however, it is better for a nation to retain its own at the high level. (For example, if B retains its tariffs, A prefers 0 to −5; if B has lowered its tariffs, A prefers 10 to 5.) Yet if each nation adopts this orientation and independently chooses to retain its current high tariffs, the result is the status quo, which both prefer less than a mutual reduction. Thus, such a choice situation presents a dilemma, in that two parties, each choosing independently to its own advantage, together produce an outcome neither prefers.[1] The way out of such a dilemma, of course, is for the choices to be not independent, but rather the result of mutual agreement. For analyzing this more complex but more realistic case of non-independent choices, a graphical representation is particularly illuminating.

---

[1] Some economists argue that unilateral tariff reduction benefits a nation, regardless of the actions of other nations—which says that the utilities in the illustrative matrix misrepresent the actual value that would be derived. Nonetheless, the reluctance of nations to reduce tariffs implies they do not perceive such unconditional gain—and it is their *perception*, right or wrong, that determines their decisions.

When perceived utilities *are* as in Figure 1, the situation, given another context, is the "Prisoner's Dilemma" (Luce & Raiffa, 1957), whose peculiarly self-defeating characteristics have stimulated much theoretical and empirical investigation, some of which is later analyzed. The context of the original formulation involves two prisoners, whom the district attorney knows to be guilty, though he lacks the evidence to convict. He holds the two prisoners separately and tells each that if he confesses and the other does not, he will be given but a very light sentence for turning state's evidence whereas the other will receive a maximum sentence. If both confess, each will receive heavy sentences, though less than maximum. If neither confesses, the district attorney will press other minor but provable charges which would result in moderately light sentences for each. Thus, choosing independently, each prisoner finds it better to confess, regardless of whether he expects the other to confess or not.

THE NEGOTIATION GRAPH

When choices are made jointly rather than independently, it is useful to regard them as being made among outcomes (four, in the tariff example) rather than between the (two) alternative actions. Thus a *decision matrix* of independently chosen alternatives may be contrasted with a *negotiation graph* of jointly selected outcomes. The four outcomes of our example are plotted in the negotiation graph of Figure 2 according to the utility each outcome possesses for A and for B. In this formulation the special character of "both holding out" is readily apparent; for this outcome alone, the utility of *both* parties could be increased by choosing another outcome. Among the other three outcomes, however, an increase in the utility for one party necessarily means a decrease in the utility for the other; thus these three points are Pareto optima, and the parties might be expected to restrict their bargaining to them. Each point represents the best outcome a party can achieve given a particular level of outcome for the other; together they define the "utility frontier" (Bishop, 1963),

"social optima" (Pareto, 1909), or "contract curve" (Edgeworth, 1881).

For any point that is not Pareto-optimal, another point can be found providing greater utility for one party without decreasing the utility for the other. Hence, bargaining "solutions" widely assume that parties will settle upon one of these Pareto optima. A further restriction to the outcomes among which negotiation takes place is furnished by the minimum guarantee to each party by acting unilaterally. In the example of Figures 1 and 2 either party can, by holding out, guarantee himself an outcome no worse than the status quo (whereas if he compromises unilaterally, he may lose 5).

Consequently, it is reasonable to assume that negotiation is further restricted to those outcomes whose utility at least equals that of the status quo resulting from no agreement; such outcomes compose the "negotiation set" (Luce & Raiffa, 1957). In Figure 2, the negotiation set includes only the mutual compromise. However, formulation of alternatives in the form of a graph makes obvious the possibility for intermediate actions and outcomes; tariffs could be cut by varying amounts, creating a nearly continuous set of outcomes falling in the area of the line connecting the three points in Figure 2. The utility frontier would then probably take the form of a curve, concave toward the origin.

On this essentially continuous utility frontier, the negotiation set would comprise that portion (encompassed by the dotted lines in Figure 2) where neither party's outcome is worse than the status quo. Within the negotiation set, however, many outcomes are possible and among these neither practicing negotiators nor game theorists are presently able to specify universally accepted principles of choice, though game theory has developed one more or less plausible solution, presented later in the section on outcome. In the absence of a definitive theoretical solution to negotiation, it is profitable to ascertain empirically what outcomes result in practice. A number of experiments using a game-theory formulation have been conducted, most of them employing the procedure of subjects independently selecting alternative actions in

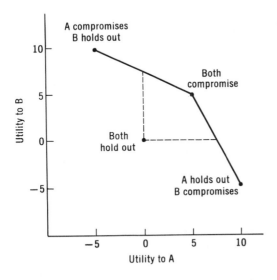

Figure 2. Graph of illustrative utilities for the four possible outcomes when each of two interacting parties has the alternatives of "compromising" and of "holding out"

a matrix rather than that of jointly negotiating over outcomes.

ACTUAL CHOICE IN

CONFLICT SITUATIONS

Using a Prisoner's Dilemma game matrix where the preferences for outcomes were similar to those in Figure 1, Deutsch (1958) found that his subjects, in line with the rationale presented above, tended to hold out: 64 percent of subjects, instructed simply to maximize their own reward, chose this strategy. Similarly competitive results have been found by Scodel, Minas, Ratoosh, and Lipetz (1959), Minas, Scodel, Marlowe, and Rawson (1960), and others.

When choice in conflict situations is repeated over a number of occasions, even though each choice is made in ignorance of the other's immediate choice at that time, it is no longer clearly best to adopt the "hold out" strategy. Even in the absence of formal communication, tacit communication may permit concerting upon the joint compromise that each prefers to lack of agreement. Such a process may take some time. In from ten to fifty repetitions, Scodel *et al.* (1959), Deutsch (1958), Minas *et al.* (1960), and Rapoport (1963) each found stable or declining probabilities of choosing the compromise response; but when Rapoport continued his observations for another 250 to 650 trials, he found the compromise response to rise to substantially above the initial level.

Like repeated sessions, communality of goals also promotes choice of the compromise alternative. Pilisuk and Rapoport (1964) employed seven different Prisoner's Dilemma matrices that varied in the relative utilities resulting from joint compromise, from lack of agreement, and from one party holding out while the other compromised. They found the proportion of persons choosing the compromise solution to increase consistently as the conflict in goals became less pronounced.

Even where there is some communality of goals, however, if there is sufficient negative feeling between the parties, they may redefine the matrix of outcomes as a zero-sum situation by looking, in effect, at the difference in utilities to each, rather than at their absolute level. The prime concern of each party, then, is simply to obtain an outcome relatively better than that of the other, even if neither outcome is particularly desirable. This has frequently been the case at the termination of a war, when the absolute welfare of the winning as well as of the losing party was less than it would have been in the absence of a war, or sometimes even less than in the prewar state.

An increase in a zero-sum or competitive orientation can also arise when the absolute level of the utilities is small. It seems quite possible that "winning"—getting more than the other by trying to force him to compromise while holding out oneself—might be valued more when there is little or no absolute reward. To get 100 points in a parlor game is good or bad only in relation to what others receive. But to get $100 is good, regardless of what others receive.

The relatively high level of noncompromising choice in the preceding experiments has in every case been in a situation in which the monetary reward was nil or negligible. The few experiments using larger rewards find substantially more cooperative results. Using a Prisoner's Dilemma matrix similar to the preceding (though employing many alternatives rather than only two), Messé and Sawyer (1964) found an unexpectedly high degree of cooperation, which they attributed in part to rewards that, particularly to subjects of ages thirteen and seventeen, appeared rather large: from 0 to 75 cents for each of ten trials. Siegel and Fouraker (1960), in an experiment on bilateral monopoly also employing sizeable rewards, likewise found subjects concerting upon the alternatives that maximized their joint reward. Subjects could agree to exchange any number of units between one and thirty; but when each subject knew both his own and the other's reward structure, the average discrepancy from the Pareto-optimal solution of exchanging exactly nine units was less than one-fifth of a unit. Even when neither subject knew the reward structure for the other, the discrepancy from the Pareto optimum was only one and one-quarter units.

Though the findings just referred to all derive from experimental research, at least one large-scale test of a game theory model in actual political decisions has been conducted. In the three-member districts of the Illinois House of Representatives, committees from each party decide to run either one, two, or three candidates, thus creating a situation that can be modeled by a 3×3 matrix, in which the rows and columns indicate the number of candidates nominated by each party, and the cell entries indicate the number elected, presumably representing the utility of that outcome. The model specifying the number of candidates a party should run, given the expected distribution of the vote, predicted the actual decisions in 69 percent of the more than 1300 elections between 1902 and 1954 (Sawyer & MacRae, 1962).

At the level of international relations, Zinnes, North, and Koch (1961) record how "hold-out" strategies were employed during the negotiation of July 1914 between the Allies and the Central Powers in which the world situation was defined essentially as a Prisoner's Dilemma. Feeling grievously ". . . trapped, by a 'hated, lying, conscienceless nation of shopkeepers,' Germany would go down fighting nevertheless. For the Kaiser asserted [in a note jotted in the margin of a diplomatic report of July 30th] '. . . if we are bled to death, England shall at least lose India.' "

DYNAMIC ALTERNATIVES

AND UTILITIES

In virtually all the analyses of interacting alternatives and utilities just considered—theoretical and empirical alike—both alternatives and utilities for outcomes have been assumed, explicitly or implicitly, to be completely static. In an experiment, for example, this assumption may be reflected by a fixed matrix in which there is no opportunity over the course of interaction for change either in

the utilities in the cells of the matrix or in the alternatives repesented by the rows and columns. Yet such a static situation, while providing a basic formulation for negotiation, is rare in practice.

Two modifications of the basic situation, more common in practice, are (a) those in which utilities for outcomes may change during the course of negotiation, though alternatives remain fixed, and (b) those in which alternatives themselves may also be added, modified, or eliminated. Thus change results either in the utility entries in the matrix, or in the defining rows and columns themselves, producing in either case a new matrix. These two important cases provide the foci for the remaining two sections dealing with process; they are, indeed, the core of what is generally taken as the central process of negotiation—reciprocal argument and counterargument, proposal and counterproposal, in an attempt to agree upon actions and outcomes mutually perceived as beneficial. We shall first examine communication and persuasion—processes fundamental to changing utilities, and then turn to processes of a creative or problem-solving nature leading to modified alternatives. . . .

MODIFICATION OF UTILITIES:

COMMUNICATION AND PERSUASION

To change the utilities certain outcomes hold for the other party is frequently a major interim goal for a negotiator, for if the other party can be made to value more highly the outcomes one prefers himself, the probability of obtaining these is increased. Communication and persuasion, major agents in the process of modifying utilities, concern the way in which the arguments and proposals of each party are understood by the other.

COMMUNICATION

Communication between parties to an international negotiation is complicated first of all by language. Shades of connotative differences and culturally specific meanings hinder effective translation. The critical concept, "to compromise," is illustrative: Both in English and in French, it has two principal meanings, yet their priority is reversed. Hence an American's request "to adjust and settle a difference by mutual agreement" might be interpreted by a Frenchman as a suggestion "to expose, to endanger, to embarrass (one's character, reputation, and so on)." If the Russian phrase whose literal translation is "We will bury you" and which connotes "We will outlive you" is instead interpreted "We will destroy you," quite different implications are perceived (Klineberg, 1964, p. 153).

The history of diplomatic practice suggests that as the fullness of communication increases, negotiation becomes easier. For example, of diplomatic communication in the nineteenth century, Prime Minister Gladstone observed that, "Personal and domestic relations with the ruling families abroad give openings, in delicate cases, for saying more, and saying it at once more gently and more efficaciously than could be ventured in the more formal correspondence and under contacts of governments" (Nicolson, 1939, p. 67). At the other extreme, Schelling and Halperin (1961) point out how confusing it may be to employ silence as "a mode of communication." They note that, ". . . failure to deny rumors, refusal to answer questions, attempts to take emphasis away from certain issues, all tend to communicate something . . ." (p. 81) which may variously be revealing, deceptive, or confusing.

In laboratory experimentation, the Prisoner's Dilemma matrix has been employed to assess the effects of communication. Deutsch (1958) finds that among pairs of college students motivated to maximize their own reward, the opportunity to communicate is associated with an increase in the proportion choosing cooperatively from 13 to 59 percent. Using a similar situation, Loomis (1959) finds that students having more opportunity for communication not only behave more cooperatively but also express more trust in each other.

But the very conflict that negotiation might resolve may itself make communication more difficult to commence. As the result of another experiment, Deutsch and Krauss (1962) suggest that, "Where barriers to communication exist, a situation in which the parties are compelled to communicate will be more effective than one in which the choice to talk or not is put on a voluntary basis" (p. 75). The increasing activity of international organizations, such as the United Nations, provides considerable opportunity for communication, much of it of an informal nature where specific issues are not at stake or in public view and hence wider exploration of alternatives may be conducted.

PERSUASION

The aim of much communication in negotiation is to persuade the other party that his self-interest is not what he thought, by providing information, interpretation, or implications that cause him to reassess the utility of various outcomes. This purported misevaluation may stem from three sources—the effect of the act itself upon its maker, the effect of consequent behavior by the other, and the effect of consequent behavior by third parties—thus furnishing a persuader three somewhat distinct appeals:

1. Intrinsic interest: You should want to do this, for its direct benefit, which possibly you do not fully perceive. "Lower tariffs will permit your people to buy imported goods more cheaply."

2. Second party effects (for example, threat of force): If you don't do it, I may do something you won't like. "If you do not lower your tariffs, we may raise ours."

3. Third party effects (for example, norms): Others want you to do so, and will give their approval. "Other countries will approve if you lower your tariffs." (This and the preceding case are most applicable in "variable-threat" bargaining [Bishop, 1963] in which, if no agreement results, parties may take unilateral actions; if nonagreement simply preserves

the status quo, persuasion may only appeal, as in case 1, to intrinsic interest.)

Each of these appeals, if successful, would result in the reappraisal of the values of certain outcomes, so that a party's self-interest might dictate different choices than before.

Self-interest, in diplomacy and elsewhere, has been a durable concept. In 1716, Callieres enjoined diplomats to "make each proposition which you put forward appear as a statement of the interests of those with whom you are negotiating, for since diplomacy is the attempt to find a basis for common action or agreement, it is obvious that the more the opposing party can be brought to see your designs in their own light and to accept them thus, the more surely will their cooperation for any action be fruitful alike to themselves and to you" (1919, pp. 122–123).

The modification of utilities by the most skillful diplomatic persuasion, however, will seldom result in situations in which the most favored outcome of one party is also the most favored outcome of the other. Rather there will usually remain, not a single Pareto point, but several, and in choosing among these one party gains only at the loss of the other. At this point, bargaining often becomes a matter of trying to establish what is the least the other will take and convincing him that that is the most one will give.

The least favorable terms a party will accept in preference to lack of agreement is thus a crucial concept; it enters into analysis of competition between firms as the "threat point" (Bishop, 1963), of labor-management relations as the "resistance points" (Walton & McKersie, 1965), and of political negotiation as the "minimum disposition" (Iklé & Leites, 1962). A lower limit to the minimum disposition is often formed by the value of the status quo. In Figure 1, for example, the minimum disposition for each might be the value of 0 from mutual holding out; each of the unilateral compromises then falls below the minimum disposition of one or the other party.

Thus it is important that each party estimate not only its own "minimum disposition," but also that of the other party. Yet the minimum dispositions of the two parties are clearly related; how much one will take depends in part upon how much the other will give. Consequently, knowing that the other party is making a similar estimate, I may try to modify his minimum disposition ". . . to make him believe or feel that he would prefer an agreement to no agreement on terms more favorable to me than he originally thought. . . . (1) By altering the actual situation on which his Minimum Disposition is based. . . . (2) By pointing out the advantages and minimizing the disadvantages of my proposed terms. . . . (3) By conveying to my opponent (actual or faked) estimates of his Minimum Disposition, and (4) By portraying to my opponent a certain intrinsic development of the negotiations and convincing him that the *Negotiation Mores* require that he follow this development" (Iklé & Leites, 1962, p. 23).

I may also attempt to modify the other's estimate of my own minimum disposition "(1) By altering the actual situation on which my opponent's estimate of my Minimum Disposition is based. . . . (2) By convincing my opponent that it would be disastrous or impossible for me to agree to less than my proposed terms. . . . (3) By exhibiting attitudes consistent with a Minimum Disposition more favorable than my opponent's estimates" (Iklé & Leites, 1962, p. 24).

A related question is whether one should advance a "sham bargaining position" which one thinks the other considers less favorable than his minimum disposition (as with "blue sky" proposals in labor-management negotiation). Advantage may accrue if the other's minimum disposition is initially lower than thought or if simply forwarding the sham position lowers the other's minimum disposition; further, a sham position leaves more room for expected "concessions" and also makes it more difficult for the other to estimate one's own minimum disposition. On the other hand, it may be difficult to obtain public support for extreme positions, and if such support is obtained the other may think agreement is impossible and discontinue negotiation; in any event agreement may be delayed and concessions from a sham position may set precedent for future real concessions. The abundant rationale both for and against sham positions strongly suggests need for systematic empirical test.

Psychological experimentation has explored the related concept of "level of aspiration," which may be a factor in determining initial minimum disposition and rates of concession from the initial position. Siegel and Fouraker (1960) operationalized this concept by telling one member of a bargaining pair that if he achieved $6.10, he could participate in the second part, in which he would have a chance to double his winnings; the other subject was told the same, but the amount specified was $2.10. In an otherwise symmetrical situation, the former group averaged $6.25, the latter $3.25. On the basis of empirical and rational analyses, Siegel and Fouraker suggest that ". . . the bargainer who (1) opens negotiations with a high request, (2) has a small rate of concession, (3) has a high minimum level of expectation, and (4) is very perceptive and quite unyielding, will fare better than his opponent who provides the base upon which these relative evaluations were made" (p. 93). Some of the same principles are applied to international negotiation by Kissinger (1960), who argues that ". . . effectiveness at the conference table depends on overstating one's demands" and on the other hand, "If we make proposals in which we really believe, we must inevitably be somewhat rigid about them" (p. 205).

A party's communications are more likely to be effective in modifying the utilities of the other if the party is regarded as a credible source (Hovland, Janis, & Kelley, 1953); this can vary both among nations and among various offices and individuals within a nation. In addition, Aronson, Turner, and Carlsmith (1963) found that for persons reading a communication attributed to a highly credible source, the more discrepant the communication from their own opinion, the more they changed (consonant with Kissinger's assertion). For persons exposed to the same communication attributed, however, to a source of only moderate credibility, increasing discrepancy led to increased change

only to a point; as discrepancy became extreme, opinion change decreased.

Thus it appears that the effectiveness of sham bargaining positions, and possibly of other tactics of communication and persuasion, may depend markedly upon the circumstances under which they are employed. One of the most important of these circumstances concerns just what alternatives are available to each party; the following section explores how alternatives themselves may be changed.

MODIFICATION OF ALTERNATIVES

If modifications are considered to be of two kinds—those that only subtract from the available set of alternatives, and those that add as well as possibly subtract—successful threats, promises, and *faits accomplis* are of the first kind, and creative problem-solving approaches are of the second kind. Which may be called for depends, as we shall see, on the initial state of the decision matrix of alternatives and preferences.

THREATS AND PROMISES

A threat is a representation that if another party acts in a way one disfavors, one will take an action detrimental to the other. It is important, however, that the other party be convinced that the detrimental action will not also be taken even if he complies. For this reason, as pointed out by Schelling (1960), a threatened action must be detrimental not only to the recipient, but to the initiator as well. The threat of massive retaliation furnishes an example: Its purpose (as that of threats generally) is to deter; but whether it succeeds or fails in deterring, the initiator has no immediate motivation to carry out the threat, since it harms him as well as the other.

The logical structure of promises is essentially similar to that of threats. Promises are representations that if the other behaves in a way one favors, one will then take an action beneficial to the other, even though one would then prefer not to do so. In the Prisoner's Dilemma matrix of Figure 1, B, if he is choosing after A, may induce a cooperative solution of 5 to each by making an enforceable promise that he will choose his compromise alternative if A has chosen his, though in fact B would then prefer to choose to hold out, gaining 10.

Thus, in either threats or promises, one represents that given certain action by the other, meant to be deterred or induced, he will choose against his own immediate welfare. For such a representation to be credible, a party must have a way of demonstrating to the other that he would in fact be bound (by honor, public opinion, or other restraints) to carry out the otherwise undesired action; it will be most convincing, indeed, if he can show the other how the carrying out is an automatic consequence of the other's action, in which no intervention is possible.

Liska (1960) emphasizes, in the area of foreign aid, the importance of the credibility of threatened withdrawal of aid, pointing out that, "The policy of aid and its results will suffer as long as any existing alliance or strategic facility is treated as indispensable"; he concludes that, "To demonstrate American nondependence and alternatives repeatedly, even at great economic and political cost in the individual instance, is the greatest single requirement of an effective policy . . ." (p. 33).

If a threat or promise is sufficiently credible for the party who is its target to believe that it would actually be carried out, then it should have the primary effect intended: effectively to reduce the possibilities with which the party is confronted. (The reduction actually occurs directly in outcomes: The target party knows that if he chooses a certain alternative, only an undesired outcome is possible; then effectively that entire alternative is eliminated.) Thus the result is a reduced matrix of alternatives and preferences defining a different interaction situation.

Deutsch and Krauss (1960, 1962) have examined experimentally the effect of threat upon interpersonal bargaining, using the "trucking game" where the optimal solution

is for the two persons both to use the main one-way road, alternating as to who goes first. In one experimental condition, each person had a gate that he could close, blocking the main road; in another condition, only one person had such a gate; in the third, neither had a gate. The threat that presumably could be implicitly conveyed to the other is "If you don't let me use the main one-way road first, I'll close my gate, forcing us both to take our private [longer, less rewarding] roads." Results showed the possession of a gate to be deleterious. Whereas average earnings were positive when neither had a gate, they were negative when one did, and more negative when both did.

It may appear surprising that the party having the sole gate fared more poorly than the two parties in the condition in which neither had a gate, since the person with the sole gate should be able to force the other to choose between going second on the main road or taking his longer alternate road. (Actually, however, the party lacking a gate also blocks, whenever his truck is on the main road.) It seems unlikely, however, that subjects clearly perceived and unequivocally communicated the full potentiality for the use of threat, and hence this experiment does not provide a test of Schelling's (1960) analysis.

It does seem to imply, however, that subjects were not sufficiently "rational" either to employ appropriately or to disregard a potentially detrimental device; rather they used it with substantial frequency and to their considerable loss. Deutsch and Krauss (1960) suggest the detriment arises from ". . . the cultural interpretation of yielding (to a peer or subordinate) under duress . . . perceived as a negatively valued form of behavior with negative implications for the self-image . . . because the locus of causality is perceived to be outside the person's voluntary control" (p. 188). At the international level, yielding may also be valued negatively, as illustrated earlier by the Kaiser's reaction to the Allied powers. And speaking out of his experience with seventeenth- and eighteenth-century diplomacy, Callieres observed "Menaces always do harm to negotiation and they frequently push one party to extremities to which they would not have resorted without provocation. It is well known that injured vanity frequently drives men into courses which a sober estimate of their own interests would lead them to avoid" (1919, p. 125).

Meeker, Shure, and Moore (1964), in a near-replication of Deutsch and Krauss (1960), similarly found that among pairs of persons both having the capability of threat, those in which neither employed it achieved better outcomes. In exploring further for explanations, they found the achievement of good outcomes in these cases to be associated largely with the initial expectation by both subjects of winning exactly 50 percent of the reward (that is, with cooperative pre-game dispositions on the part of both subjects). Among pairs of subjects who failed to reach a cooperative agreement within the first five trials, however, those using the threat *more* during that time were more likely to reach cooperative agreement eventually. The authors suggest that delay by an initially conciliatory subject "in responding to a threat with a counterthreat displays to the aggressive member a weak intention to resist and encourages him to persist in his original demands. These then become increasingly unacceptable to the conciliatory member" (p. 122). Further, among subjects who seek no more than 50 percent of the earnings, those who respond with a counterthreat within two trials of the other's threat are much more likely to achieve cooperative agreement.

Thus these results are somewhat more consistent with the theory of Schelling (1960) than are those of Deutsch and Krauss (1960); the partial incongruity of the results of these two experiments is indicative of the extent of added experimentation required for more complete and more definitive empirical assessment of the effect of threats and promises.

FAIT ACCOMPLI

Like a successful threat or promise, a *fait accompli* reduces the decision matrix by eliminating as possibilities certain outcomes and alternatives. The result is likewise similar: The party who is the target is left with a situation in which his best outcomes are eliminated and the least undesirable of the remainder are just the ones preferred by the initiating party. If the target party then chooses to his advantage, the initiator benefits. The preemptory nature of the *fait accompli* may to such an extent antagonize its target, however, that punishing the other (even at one's own loss) becomes attractive—if only to discourage repetition.

As an illustration of the *fait accompli*, Lerche (1956) indicates how unilateral action by the United States in establishing SEATO minimized the extent of its compromise in reaching final agreement with Great Britain on the nature of the alliance.

The essential element of the *fait accompli* is the ability of one party to put the choice to the other on a "take it or leave it" basis. This situation has been represented experimentally by Joseph and Willis (1963), who contrasted "simultaneous" choice (where neither person knew the other's choice at the time he made his own) with sequential choice in which the second person could only accept the choice of the first, or reject it and thus cause both to receive nothing. Consistent with the above rationale, sequential choice resulted in greater inequality between the rewards of the two persons.

CREATING NEW ALTERNATIVES

Frequently, two parties to negotiation will be confronted by a decision matrix in which there is no single outcome that both prefer to lack of agreement. Negotiation will then necessarily fail unless higher utilities emerge, either through reassessment of existing outcomes or through development of new outcomes. The first possibility has been considered in connection with communication and persuasion. Often, however, the initial evaluations of outcomes have been made after extensive and public review, and consequently these may be little subject to modification, if only for the reason that otherwise the negotiators might be charged with abandoning their constituency.

Through the modification and addition of alternatives, though, it may be possible to create new outcomes on which agreement can be achieved, as did Churchill, Truman, and Stalin when they solved their problem of precedence in entering the Potsdam negotiating chamber by emerging simultaneously through three doors. New outcomes should, then, in comparison with prior outcomes, increase the utility for one party while, at the least, not decreasing that of the other; thus the utility frontier is extended beyond its previous location.

The process of devising more favorable alternatives and outcomes may be characterized as one of "creative problem-solving" since it involves innovation rather than mere selection among given possibilities. As with creative processes more generally, however, relatively little is understood of its operation. Although the characteristics and the development of creative individuals have been extensively investigated (Stein & Heinze, 1960; Taylor, 1964), only recently has much systematic attention been given to questions concerning the situational conditions and organizational processes that foster creativity (Steiner, 1965). To what extent, for example, is the development of new alternatives promoted by the formality or informality of the proceedings, the size and composition of the negotiating teams, or the degree of time pressure under which the negotiation occurs? May informal or unofficial meetings, like the Pugwash and later Conferences on Science and World Affairs, produce an environment in which a "game of ideas" can result in otherwise unexamined alternatives?

Among the few relevant aspects of group creativity in problem-solving that have been extensively studied is the effect of initial solicitation of a wide range of positions. In surveying several studies, Kelley and Thibaut (1954) concluded,

. . . there is good reason to believe that . . . multiplicity of opinion . . . is a very real basis for the formation of accurate and undistorted judgments within the group. . . . [For this reason] special techniques are sometimes used to maximize expressed heterogeneity in a group, such as that of taking a census of opinions or ideas at the beginning of a group discussion (p. 722).

The way in which such a census contributes is suggested by the work of Lorge, Davitz, Fox, and Herrold (1953); they find that the mode by which training in staff procedures improves group decisions is not through enhancing individual performance but simply through lowering the group's tendency to neglect member suggestions. This finding suggests a need to examine just how tightly the agenda should be set, so as to provide sufficient focus while simultaneously minimizing the loss of good alternatives. If, at the stage of agenda development, the chairman proposes many alternative solutions, greater final consensus is found to develop (Guetzkow & Gyr, 1954). In areas where many alternatives are easily available, this process is facilitated; perhaps the success of the periodic meetings on the General Agreement of Trade and Tariffs stems in part from the multiplicity of items that may be considered.

Given the degree of initial diversity of positions and alternatives, the progressive group interaction and climate further influence the group creativity. Fiedler (1962) examines the nature of interaction within 32 four-person groups seeking to produce three original and different stories for an ambiguous picture from the Thematic Apperception Test. Classifying all interaction into five categories and distinguishing groups as "tense" or "relaxed" on the basis of members' criticality of each other, Fiedler finds ". . . (a) that procedural and irrelevant comments tended to aid the creativity of relaxed groups but hindered tense groups; (b) the more task-oriented 'elaboration of ideas' and higher total activity aided the tense groups but not relaxed groups" (p. 315). This suggests the possible importance, for promoting creative solutions, of tailoring the kind of interaction to the degree of tension inherent in the situation. In this and other studies, Fiedler finds that "leaders who perceive their least preferred co-worker favorably tend to be most effective under pleasant and relaxed group conditions, while leaders who perceive . . . [their least preferred co-worker] unfavorably are more effective under unpleasant stressful group climates" (1962, p. 318). It may be, more generally, that broad acceptance is favorable under relaxed circumstances, sharp differentiation in more tense situations.

* * *

References

Aronson, E., Turner, Judith A., & Carlsmith, J. M. Communicator Credibility and Communication Discrepancy as Determinants of Opinion Change. *J. Abnorm. Soc. Psychol.*, 1963, **67**, 31–36.

Bishop, R. L. Game-Theoretic Analyses of Bargaining. *Quart. J. Econ.*, 1963, **77**, 559–602.

Black, E. R. The Indus: A Moral for Nations. *New York Times Magazine*, December 11, 1960, pp. 24 ff.

Deutsch, M. Trust and Suspicion. *J. Confl. Resol.*, 1958, **2**, 265–279.

————, & Krauss, R. M. The Effect of Threat upon Interpersonal Bargaining. *J. Abnorm. Soc. Psychol.*, 1960, **61**, 181–189.

————, & Krauss, R. M. Studies of Interpersonal Bargaining. *J. Confl. Resol.*, 1962, **6**, 52–76.

Durant, W., & Durant, Ariel. *The Story of Civilization: Part VII. The Age of Reason Begins.* New York: Simon & Schuster, 1961.

Edgeworth, F. Y. *Mathematical Psychics: An Essay on the Application of Mathematics to the Moral Sciences.* London: Kegan Paul, 1881.

Fiedler, F. E. Leader Attitudes, Group Climate, and Group Creativity. *J. Abnorm. Soc. Psychol.*, 1962, **65**, 308–318.

Guetzkow, H., & Gyr, J. An Analysis of Conflict in Decision-making Groups. *Hum. Relat.*, 1954, **7**, 367–382.

Hovland, C. I., Janis, I. L., & Kelley, H. H. *Communication and Persuasion: Psychological Studies of Opinion Change.* New Haven: Yale Univer. Press, 1953.

Iklé, F. C., & Leites, N. Political Negotiation as a Process of Modifying Utilities. *J. Confl. Resol.*, 1962, **6**, 19–28.

Joseph, M. L., & Willis, R. H. An Experimental Analog to Two-Party Bargaining. *Behav. Sci.*, 1963, **8**, 117–127.

Kaplan, M. A. *System and Process in International Politics.* New York: Wiley, 1957.

Kelley, H. H., & Thibaut, J. W. Experimental Studies of Group Problem Solving and Process. In G. Lindzey (Ed.), *Handbook of Social Psychology*, Vol. II. Reading, Mass.: Addison-Wesley, 1954. Pp. 735–785.

Kissinger, H. A. *The Necessity for Choice.* New York: Harper, 1960.

Klineberg, O. *The Human Dimension in International Relations.* New York: Holt, Rinehart and Winston, 1964.

Lerche, C. O. The United States, Great Britain, and SEATO: A Case Study in *Fait Accompli. J. Polit.*, 1956, **18**, 459–478.

Liska, G. *The New Statecraft.* Chicago: Univer. Chicago Press, 1960.

Loomis, J. L. Communication, the Development of Trust, and Cooperative Behavior. *Hum. Relat.,* 1959, **12,** 305–316.

Lorge, I., Davitz, J., Fox, D., & Herrold, K. Evaluation of Instruction in Staff Action and Decision Making. *Air Res. and Devel. Command Tech. Rep. No. 16.* Human Resources Research Institute, Maxwell Air Force Base, Alabama, 1953.

Luce, R. D., & Raiffa, H. *Games and Decisions.* New York: Wiley, 1957.

Meeker, R. J., Shure, G. H., & Moore, W. H., Jr. Real-time Computer Studies of Bargaining Behavior: The Effects of Threat upon Bargaining. *American Federation of Information Processing Societies Conference Proceedings,* 1964, **25,** 115–123.

Messé, L. A., & Sawyer, J. Unexpected Cooperation in a Game Experiment: The Prisoner's Dilemma Resolved? Social Psychology Laboratory, University of Chicago, March 1965.

Minas, J. S., Scodel, A., Marlowe, D., & Rawson, H. Some Descriptive Aspects of Two-Person Non-Zero-Sum Games, II. *J. Confl. Resol.,* 1960, **4,** 193–197.

Morgenthau, H. J. *Politics Among Nations: The Struggle for Power and Peace* (ed. 3). New York: Knopf, 1960.

Nicolson, H. *Diplomacy.* London: Butterworth, 1939.

Pareto, V. *Manuel d'Économie Politique.* Paris: M. Giard, 1909.

Pilisuk, M., & Rapoport, A. A Non-Zero-Sum Game Model of Some Disarmament Problems. *Peace Research Society (International) Papers,* 1964, **1,** 57–78.

Rapoport, A. *Fights, Games, and Debates.* Ann Arbor: Univer. Michigan Press, 1960.

————. Formal Games as Probing Tools for Investigating Behavior Motivated by Trust and Suspicion. *J. Confl. Resol.,* 1963, **7,** 570–579.

Rusk, D. Parliamentary Diplomacy–Debate versus Negotiation. *World Affairs Interpreter,* 1955, **26,** 121–138.

Satow, E. M. *A Guide to Diplomatic Practice* (ed. 4). New York: McKay, 1957.

Sawyer, J., & MacRae, D., Jr. Game Theory and Cumulative Voting in Illinois: 1902–1954. *Amer. Polit. Sci. Rev.,* 1962, **56,** 936–946.

Schattschneider, E. E. Intensity, Visibility, Direction, and Scope. *Amer. Polit. Sci. Rev.,* 1957, **51,** 933–942.

Schelling, T. C. *The Strategy of Conflict.* Cambridge, Mass.: Harvard Univer. Press, 1960.

————, & Halperin, M. H. *Strategy and Arms Control.* New York: Twentieth Century Fund, 1961.

Sharp, W. R. A Checklist of Subjects for Systematic Study of International Conferences. *Intern. Soc. Sci. Bull.,* 1953, **5,** 311–339.

Shubik, M. *Strategy and Market Structure: Competition, Oligopoly, and the Theory of Games.* New York: Wiley, 1959.

Siegel, S., & Fouraker, L. E. *Bargaining and Group Decision Making: Experiments in Bilateral Monopoly.* New York: McGraw-Hill, 1960.

Stein, M. I., & Heinze, Shirley J. *Creativity and the Individual.* New York: Free Press, 1960.

Steiner, G. A. (Ed.) *The Creative Organization.* Chicago: Univer. Chicago Press, 1965.

Taylor, C. W. (Ed.). *Creativity: Progress and Potential.* New York: McGraw-Hill, 1964.

Thibaut, J. W., & Kelley, H. H. *The Social Psychology of Groups.* New York: Wiley, 1959.

Von Neumann, J., & Morgenstern, O. *Theory of Games and Economic Behavior.* Princeton: Princeton Univer. Press, 1944.

Walton, R. E., & McKersie, R. B. *A Behavioral Theory of Labor Negotiation: An Analysis of a Social Interaction System.* New York: McGraw-Hill, 1965.

Zinnes, Dina A., North, R. C., & Koch, H. E., Jr. Capability, Threat, and the Outbreak of War. In J. N. Rosenau (Ed.), *International Politics and Foreign Policy: A Reader in Research and Theory.* New York: Free Press, 1961. Pp. 469–482.

THE EFFECT OF THREAT UPON INTERPERSONAL BARGAINING

Morton Deutsch and Robert M. Krauss

A bargain is defined in *Webster's Unabridged Dictionary* as "an agreement between parties settling what each shall give and receive in a transaction between them"; it is further specified that a bargain is "an agreement or compact viewed as advantageous or the reverse." When the term "agreement" is broadened to include tacit, informal agreements as well as explicit agreements, it is evident that bargains and the processes involved in arriving at bargains ("bargaining") are pervasive characteristics of social life.

The definition of bargain fits under sociological definitions of the term "social norm." In this light, the experimental study of the bargaining process and of bargaining outcomes provides a means for the laboratory study of the development of certain types of social norms. But unlike many other types of social situations, bargaining situations have certain distinctive features that make it relevant to consider the conditions that determine whether or not a social norm will develop as well as those that determine the nature of the social norm if it develops. Bargaining situations highlight the possibility that, even where cooperation would be mutually advantageous, shared purposes may not develop, agreement may not be reached, and interaction may be regulated antagonistically rather than normatively.

The essential features of a bargaining situation exist when:

1. Both parties perceive that there is the possibility of reaching an agreement in which each party would be better off, or no worse off, than if no agreement were reached.

2. Both parties perceive that there is more

Source: M. Deutsch and R. M. Krauss, "The Effect of Threat on Interpersonal Bargaining," *Journal of Abnormal and Social Psychology*, Vol. 61, 1960, pp. 181–189. Copyright 1960 by The American Psychological Association and reprinted by permission.

than one such agreement that could be reached.

3. Both parties perceive each other to have conflicting preferences or opposed interests with regard to the different agreements that might be reached.

Everyday examples of bargaining include such situations as: the buyer-seller relationship when the price is not fixed, the husband and wife who want to spend an evening out together but have conflicting preferences about where to go, union-management negotiations, drivers who meet at an intersection when there is no clear right of way, disarmament negotiations.

In terms of our prior conceptualization of cooperation and competition (Deutsch, 1949) bargaining is thus a situation in which the participants have mixed motives toward one another: on the one hand, each has interest in cooperating so that they reach an agreement; on the other hand, they have competitive interests concerning the nature of the agreement they reach. In effect, to reach agreement the cooperative interest of the bargainers must be strong enough to overcome their competitive interests. However, agreement is not only contingent upon the *motivational* balances of cooperative to competitive interests but also upon the situational and *cognitive* factors which facilitate or hinder the recognition or invention of a bargaining agreement that reduces the opposition of interest and enhances the mutuality of interest.[1]

These considerations lead to the formulation of two general, closely related propositions about the likelihood that a bargaining agreement will be reached.

1. Bargainers are more likely to reach an agreement, the stronger are their cooperative interests in comparison with their competitive interests.
2. Bargainers are more likely to reach an

agreement, the more resources they have available for recognizing or inventing potential bargaining agreements and for communicating to one another once a potential agreement has been recognized or invented.

From these two basic propositions and additional hypotheses concerning conditions that determine the strengths of the cooperative and competitive interests and the amount of available resources, we believe it is possible to explain the ease or difficulty of arriving at a bargaining agreement. We shall not present a full statement of these hypotheses here but turn instead to a description of an experiment that relates to Proposition 1.

The experiment was concerned with the effect of the availability of threat upon bargaining in a two-person experimental bargaining game.[2] Threat is defined as the expression of an intention to do something detrimental to the interests of another. Our experiment was guided by two assumptions about threat:

1. If there is a conflict of interest and one person is able to threaten the other, he will tend to use the threat in an attempt to force the other person to yield. This tendency should be stronger, the more irreconcilable the conflict is perceived to be.
2. If a person uses threat in an attempt to intimidate another, the threatened person (if he considers himself to be of equal or superior status) would feel hostility toward the threatener and tend to respond with counterthreat and/or increased resistance to yielding. We qualify this assumption by stating that the tendency to resist should be greater, the greater the perceived probability and magnitude of detriment to the other and the less the perceived probability and magnitude of detriment to the potential resister from the anticipated resistance to yielding.

---

[1] Schelling in a series of stimulating papers on bargaining (1957, 1958) has also stressed the "mixed motive" character of bargaining situations and has analyzed some of the cognitive factors which determine agreements.

[2] The game was conceived and originated by M. Deutsch; R. M. Krauss designed and constructed the apparatus employed in the experiment.

The second assumption is based upon the view that when resistance is not seen to be suicidal or useless, to allow oneself to be intimidated, particularly by someone who does not have the right to expect deferential behavior, is to suffer a loss of social face and, hence, of self-esteem; and that the culturally defined way of maintaining self-esteem in the face of attempted intimidation is to engage in a contest for supremacy vis-à-vis the power to intimidate or, minimally, to resist intimidation. Thus, in effect, the use of threat (and if it is available to be used, there will be a tendency to use it) should strengthen the competitive interests of the bargainers in relationship to one another by introducing or enhancing the competitive struggle for self-esteem. Hence, from Proposition 1, it follows that the availability of a means of threat should make it more difficult for the bargainers to reach agreement (providing that the threatened person has some means of resisting the threat). The preceding statement is relevant to the comparison of both of our experimental conditions of threat, bilateral and unilateral (described below), with our experimental condition of nonthreat. We hypothesize that a bargaining agreement is more likely to be achieved when neither party can threaten the other, than when one or both parties can threaten the other.

Consider now the situations of bilateral threat and unilateral threat. For several reasons, a situation of bilateral threat is probably less conducive to agreement than is a condition of unilateral threat. First, the sheer likelihood that a threat will be made is greater when two people rather than one have the means of making the threat. Secondly, once a threat is made in the bilateral case it is likely to evoke counterthreat. Withdrawal of threat in the face of counterthreat probably involves more loss of face (for reasons analogous to those discussed in relation to yielding to intimidation) than does withdrawal of threat in the face of resistance to threat. Finally, in the unilateral case, although the person without the threat potential can resist and not yield to the threat, his position vis-à-vis the other is not so strong as the position of the threatened person in the bilateral case. In the unilateral case, the threatened person may have a worse outcome than the other whether he resists or yields; while in the bilateral case, the threatened person is sure to have a worse outcome if he yields but he may insure that he does not have a worse outcome if he does not yield.

METHOD

PROCEDURE

Subjects (Ss) were asked to imagine that they were in charge of a trucking company, carrying merchandise over a road to a destination. For each trip completed they made $.60, minus their operating expenses. Operating expenses were calculated at the rate of one cent per second. So, for example, if it took 37 seconds to complete a particular trip, the player's profit would be $.60 − $.37 or a net profit of $.23 for that particular trip.

Each S was assigned a name, Acme or Bolt. As a "road map" (see Figure 1) indicates, both players start from separate points and go to separate destinations. At one point their paths cross. This is the section of road labeled "one lane road," which is only one lane wide, so that two trucks, heading in opposite directions, could not pass each other. If one backs up the other can go forward, or both can back up, or both can sit there head-on without moving.

There is another way for each S to reach the destination on the map, labeled the "alternate route." The two players' paths do not cross on this route, but the alternate is 56% longer than the main route. Ss were told that they could expect to lose at least $.10 each time they used the alternate route.

At either end of the one-lane section there is a gate that is under the control of the player to whose starting point it is closest. By closing the gate, one player can prevent the other from traveling over that section of the main route. The use of the gate provides the threat potential in this game. In the bilateral threat potential condition (Two Gates) both players had gates under their

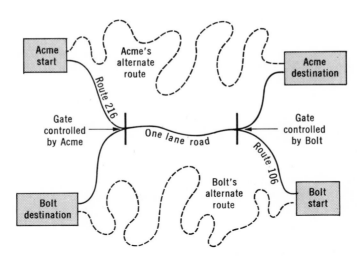

Figure 1.   Subject's road map

control.   In a second condition of unilateral threat (One Gate) Acme had control of a gate but Bolt did not.   In a third condition (No Gates) neither player controlled a gate.

Ss played the game seated in separate booths placed so that they could not see each other but could see the experimenter (E). Each S had a "control panel" mounted on a 12″ × 18″ × 12″ sloping-front cabinet (see Figure 2).   The apparatus consisted essentially of a reversible impulse counter that was pulsed by a recycling timer.   When the S wanted to move her truck forward she threw a key that closed a circuit pulsing the "add" coil of the impulse counter mounted on her control panel.   As the counter cumulated, S was able to determine her "position" by relating the number on her counter to reference numbers that had been written in on her road map.   Similarly, when she wished to reverse, she would throw a switch that activated the "subtract" coil of her counter, thus subtracting from the total on the counter each time the timer cycled.

S's counter was connected in parallel to counters on the other S's panel and on E's panel.   Thus each player had two counters on her panel, one representing her own position and the other representing the other player's. Provision was made in construction of the apparatus to permit cutting the other player's counter out of the circuit, so that each S knew only the position of her own truck. This was done in the present experiment. Experiments now in progress are studying the effects of knowledge of the other person's position and other aspects of interpersonal communication upon the bargaining process.

The only time one player definitely knew the other player's position was when they had met head-on on the one-way section of road. This was indicated by a traffic light mounted on the panel.   When this light was on, neither player could move forward unless the other moved back.   The gates were controlled by toggle switches and panel-mounted indicator lights showed, for both Ss, whether each gate was open or closed.

The following "rules of the game" were stated to the Ss:

1.   A player who started out on one route and wished to switch to the other route could only do so after first reversing and going back to the start position.   Direct transfer from one route to the other was not permitted except at the start position.

2.   In the conditions where Ss had gates, they were permitted to close the gates no matter where they were on the main route, so long as they were on the main route (i.e., they were not permitted to close the gate while on the alternate route or after having reached their destinations).   However, Ss were permitted

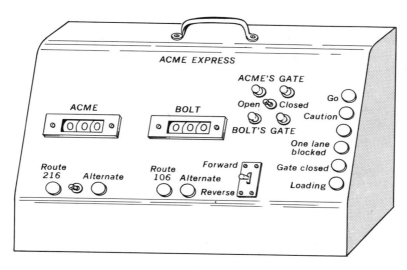

Figure 2.   Subject's control panel

to open their gates at any point in the game.

Ss were taken through a number of practice exercises to familiarize them with the game. In the first trial they were made to meet head-on on the one-lane path; Acme was then told to back up until she was just off the one-lane path and Bolt was told to go forward. After Bolt had gone through the one-lane path, Acme was told to go forward. Each continued going forward until each arrived at her destination. The second practice trial was the same as the first except that Bolt rather than Acme backed up after meeting head-on. In the next practice trial, one of the players was made to wait just before the one-way path while the other traversed it and then was allowed to continue. In the next practice trial, one player was made to take the alternate route and the other was made to take the main route. Finally, in the bilateral and unilateral threat conditions the use of the gate was illustrated (by having the player get on the main route, close the gate, and then go back and take the alternate route). The Ss were told explicitly, with emphasis, that they did *not* have to use the gate. Before each trial in the game the gate or gates were in the open position.

The instructions stressed an individualistic motivational orientation. Ss were told to

try to earn as much money for themselves as possible and to have no interest in whether the other player made money or lost money. They were given $4.00 in poker chips to represent their working capital and told that after each trial they would be given "money" if they made a profit or that "money" would be taken from them if they lost (i.e., took more than 60 seconds to complete their trip). The profit or loss of each S was announced so that both Ss could hear the announcement after each trial. Each pair of Ss played a total of 20 trials; on all trials, they started off together. In other words each trial presented a repetition of the same bargaining problem. In cases where Ss lost their working capital before the 20 trials were completed, additional chips were given them. Ss were aware that their monetary winnings and losses were to be imaginary and that no money would change hands as a result of the experiment.

SUBJECTS

Sixteen pairs of Ss were used in each of the three experimental conditions. The Ss were female clerical and supervisory personnel of the New Jersey Bell Telephone Company who volunteered to participate during their working day. Their ages ranged from 20 to

39, with a mean of 26.2. All were naive to the purpose of the experiment. By staggering the arrival times and choosing girls from different locations, we were able to insure that the Ss did not know with whom they were playing.

DATA RECORDED

Several types of data were collected. We obtained a record of the profit or loss of each S on each trial. We also obtained a detailed recording of the actions taken by each S during the course of a trial. For this purpose, we used an Esterline-Angus model AW Operations Recorder which enabled us to obtain a "log" of each move each S made during the game (e.g., whether and when she took the main or alternate route; when she went forward, backward, or remained still; when she closed and opened the gate; when she arrived at her destination).

RESULTS

The best single measure of the difficulty experienced by the bargainers in reaching an agreement is the sum of each pair's profits (or losses) on a given trial. The higher the sum of the payoffs to the two players on a given trial, the less time it took them to arrive at a procedure for sharing the one-lane path of the main route. (It was, of course, possible for one or both of the players to decide to take the alternate route so as to avoid a protracted stalemate during the process of bargaining. This, however, always resulted in at least a $.20 smaller joint payoff if only one player took the alternate route, than an optimally arrived at agreement concerning the use of the one-way path.) Figure 3 presents the medians of the summed payoffs (i.e., Acme's plus Bolt's) for all pairs in each of the three experimental conditions over the 20 trials.[3] These striking results indicate

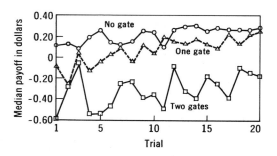

Figure 3. Median joint payoff (Acme + Bolt) over trials

that agreement was least difficult to arrive at in the no threat condition, was more difficult to arrive at in the unilateral threat condition, and exceedingly difficult or impossible to arrive at in the bilateral threat condition (see also Table 1).

Examination of Figure 3 suggests that learning occurred during the 20 trials: the summed payoffs for pairs of Ss tend to improve as the number of trials increases. This suggestion is confirmed by an analysis of variance of the slopes for the summed payoffs[4] over the 20 trials for each of the 16 pairs in each of the 3 experimental treatments. The results of this analysis indicate that the slopes are significantly greater than zero for the unilateral threat ($p < .01$) and the no threat ($p < .02$) conditions; for the bilateral threat condition, the slope does not reach statistical significance ($.10 < p < .20$). The data indicate that the pairs in the no threat condition started off at a fairly high level but, even so, showed some improvement over the 20 trials; the pairs in the unilateral threat condition started off low and, having considerable opportunity for improvement, used their opportunity; the pairs in the bilateral threat condition, on the other hand, did not benefit markedly from repeated trials.

Figure 4 compares Acme's median profit in the three experimental conditions over the 20 trials; while Figure 5 compares Bolt's profit in the three conditions. (In the uni-

---

[3] Medians are used in graphic presentation of our results because the wide variability of means makes inspection cumbersome.

[4] A logarithmic transformation of the summed payoffs on each trial for each pair was made before computing the slopes for a given pair.

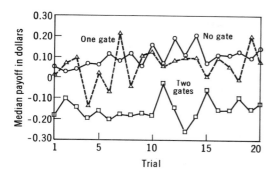

Figure 4.   Acme's median payoff

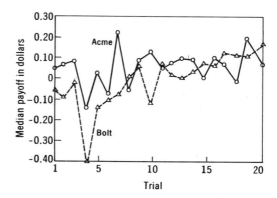

Figure 6.   Acme's and Bolt's median payoffs in unilateral threat condition

lateral threat condition, it was Acme who controlled a gate and Bolt who did not.) Bolt's as well as Acme's outcome is somewhat better in the no threat condition than in the unilateral threat condition; Acme's, as well as Bolt's, outcome is clearly worst in the bilateral threat condition (see Table 1 also). However, Figure 6 reveals that Acme does somewhat better than Bolt in the unilateral condition. Thus, if threat-potential exists within a bargaining relationship it is better to possess it oneself than to have the other party possess it. However, it is even better for neither party to possess it. Moreover, Figure 5 shows that Bolt is better off not having than having a gate even when Acme has a gate: Bolt tends to do better in the unilateral threat condition than in the bilateral threat condition.

The size of the absolute discrepancy between the payoffs of the two players in each pair provides a measure of the confusion or difficulty in predicting what the other player was going to do. Thus, a large absolute discrepancy might indicate that after one player had gone through the one-way path and left it open, the other player continued to wait; or it might indicate that one player continued to wait at a closed gate hoping the other player would open it quickly but the other player did not; etc. Figure 7 indicates that the discrepancy between players in the no threat condition is initially small and remains small for the 20 trials. For the players in both the bilateral and unilateral threat conditions, the discrepancy is initially relatively larger; but it decreases more noticeably in the unilateral threat condition by the tenth trial and, therefore, is consistently smaller than in the bilateral condition.

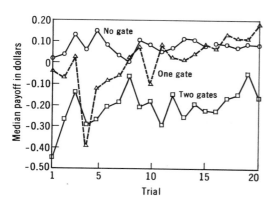

Figure 5.   Bolt's median payoff

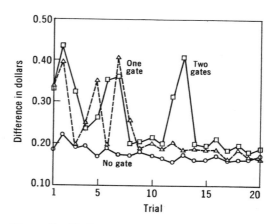

Figure 7.   Median absolute differences in payoff

Table 1.   Mean payoffs summated over the twenty trials

Variable	Means			Statistical Comparisons: p values*			
	(1) No Threat	(2) Unilateral Threat	(3) Bilateral Threat	Overall	(1)vs.(2)	(1)vs.(3)	(2)vs.(3)
Summed Payoffs							
(Acme + Bolt)	203.31	−405.88	−875.12	.01	.01	.01	.05
Acme's Payoff	122.44	−118.56	−406.56	.01	.10	.01	.05
Bolt's Payoff	80.88	−287.31	−468.56	.01	.01	.01	.20
Absolute Differences in							
Payoff (A − B)	125.94	294.75	315.25	.05	.05	.01	ns

* Evaluation of the significance of overall variation between conditions is based on an F test with 2 and 45 df. Comparisons between treatments are based on a two-tailed t test.

By way of concrete illustration, we present a synopsis of the game for one pair in each of three experimental treatments.

NO THREAT CONDITION

Trial 1. The players met in the center of the one-way section. After some back-and-forth movement Bolt reversed to the end of the one-way section, allowing Acme to pass through, and then proceeded forward herself.

Trial 2. They again met at the center of the one-way path. This time, after moving back and forth deadlocked for some time, Bolt reversed to "start" and took the alternate route to her destination, thus leaving Acme free to go through on the main route.

Trial 3. The players again met at the center of the one-way path. This time, however, Acme reversed to the beginning of the path, allowing Bolt to go through to her destination. Then Acme was able to proceed forward on the main route.

Trial 5. Both players elected to take the alternate route to their destinations.

Trial 7. Both players took the main route and met in the center. They waited, deadlocked, for a considerable time. Then Acme reversed to the end of the one-way path allowing Bolt to go through, then proceeded through to her destination.

Trials 10–20. Acme and Bolt fall into a pattern of alternating who is to go first on the one-way section. There is no deviation from this pattern.

The only other pattern that emerges in this condition is one in which one player dominates the other. That is, one player consistently goes first on the one-way section and the other player consistently yields.

UNILATERAL THREAT CONDITION

Trial 1. Both players took the main route and met in the center of it. Acme immediately closed the gate, reversed to "start," and took the alternate route to her destination. Bolt waited for a few seconds, at the closed gate, then reversed and took the alternate route.

Trial 2. Both players took the main route and met in the center. After moving back and forth deadlocked for about 15 seconds, Bolt reversed to the beginning of the one-way path, allowed Acme to pass, and then proceeded forward to her destination.

Trial 3. Both players started out on the main route, meeting in the center. After moving back and forth deadlocked for a while, Acme closed her gate, reversed to "start," and took the alternate route. Bolt, meanwhile, waited at the closed gate. When Acme arrived at her destination she opened the gate, and Bolt went through to complete her trip.

Trial 5. Both players took the main route, meeting at the center of the one-way section. Acme immediately closed her gate, reversed, and took the alternate route. Bolt waited at the gate for about 10 seconds, then reversed and took the alternate route to her destination.

Trial 10. Both players took the main route and met in the center. Acme closed her gate, reversed, and took the alternate route. Bolt remained waiting at the closed gate. After Acme arrived at her destination, she opened the gate and Bolt completed her trip.

Trial 15. Acme took the main route to her destination and Bolt took the alternate route.

Trials 17–20. Both players took the main route and met in the center. Bolt waited a few seconds, then reversed to the end of the one-way section allowing Acme to go through. Then Bolt proceeded forward to her destination.

Other typical patterns that developed in this experimental condition included an alternating pattern similar to that described in the no threat condition, a dominating pattern in which Bolt would select the alternate route leaving Acme free to use the main route unobstructed, and a pattern in which Acme would close her gate and then take the alternate route, also forcing Bolt to take the alternate route.

BILATERAL THREAT CONDITION

Trial 1. Acme took the main route and Bolt took the alternate route.

Trial 2. Both players took the main route and met head-on. Bolt closed her gate. Acme waited a few seconds, then closed her gate, reversed to "start," then went forward again to the closed gate. Acme reversed and took the alternate route. Bolt again reversed, then started on the alternate route. Acme opened her gate and Bolt reversed to "start" and went to her destination on the main route.

Trial 3. Acme took the alternate route to her destination. Bolt took the main route and closed her gate before entering the one-way section.

Trial 5. Both players took the main route and met head-on. After about 10 seconds spent backing up and going forward, Acme closed her gate, reversed, and took the alternate route. After waiting a few seconds, Bolt did the same.

Trials 8–10. Both players started out on the main route, immediately closed their gates, reversed to "start," and took the alternate route to their destinations.

Trial 15. Both players started out on the main route and met head-on. After some jockeying for position, Acme closed her gate, reversed, and took the alternate route to her destination. After waiting at the gate for a few seconds, Bolt reversed to "start" and took the alternate route to her destination.

Trials 19–20. Both players started out on the main route, immediately closed their gates, reversed to "start," and took the alternate routes to their destinations.

Other patterns that emerged in the bilateral threat condition included alternating first use of the one-way section, one player's dominating the other on first use of the one-way section, and another dominating pattern in which one player consistently took the main route while the other consistently took the alternate route.

DISCUSSION

From our view of bargaining as a situation in which both cooperative and competitive tendencies are present and acting upon the individual, it is relevant to inquire as to the conditions under which a stable agreement of any form develops. However, implicit in most economic models of bargaining (Stone, 1958; Zeuthen, 1930) is the assumption that the cooperative interests of the bargainers are sufficiently strong to insure that some form of mutually satisfactory agreement will be reached. For this reason, such models have focused upon the form of the agreement reached by the bargainers. Siegel and Fouraker (1960) report a series of bargaining experiments quite different in structure from ours in which only one of many pairs of *S*s were unable to reach agreement. Siegel and Fouraker explain this rather startling result as follows:

Apparently the disruptive forces which lead to the rupture of some negotiations were at least partially controlled in our sessions. . . .

Some negotiations collapse when one party becomes incensed at the other, and henceforth strives to maximize his opponent's displeasure rather than his own satisfaction. . . . Since it is difficult to transmit insults by means of quantitative bids, such disequilibrating behavior was not induced in the present studies. If subjects were allowed more latitude in their communications and interactions, the possibility of an affront-offense-punitive behavior sequence might be increased (p. 100).

In our experimental bargaining situation, the availability of threat clearly made it more difficult for bargainers to reach a mutually profitable agreement. These results, we believe, reflect psychological tendencies that are not confined to our bargaining situation: the tendency to use threat (if the means for threatening is available) in an attempt to force the other person to yield, when the other is seen as obstructing one's path; the tendency to respond with counterthreat or increased resistance to attempts at intimidation. How general are these tendencies? What conditions are likely to elicit them? Answers to these questions are necessary before our results can be generalized to other situations.

Dollard, Doob, Miller, Mowrer, and Sears (1939) have cited a variety of evidence to support the view that aggression (the use of threat) is a common reaction to a person who is seen as the agent of frustration. There seems to be little reason to doubt that the use of threat is a frequent reaction to interpersonal impasses. However, everyday observation indicates that threat does not inevitably occur when there is an interpersonal impasse. We would speculate that it is most likely to occur: when the threatener has no positive interest in the other person's welfare (he is either egocentrically or competitively related to the other); when the threatener believes that the other has no positive interest in his welfare; and when the threatener anticipates either that his threat will be effective or, if ineffective, will not worsen his situation because he expects the worst to happen if he does not use his threat. We suggest that

these conditions were operative in our experiment; Ss were either egocentrically or competitively oriented to one another[5] and they felt that they would not be worse off by the use of threat.

Everyday observation suggests that the tendency to respond with counterthreat or increased resistance to attempts at intimidation is also a common occurrence. We believe that introducing threat into a bargaining situation affects the meaning of yielding. Although we have no data to support this interpretation directly, we will attempt to justify it on the basis of some additional assumptions.

Goffman (1955) has pointed out the pervasive significance of "face" in the maintenance of the social order. In this view, self-esteem is a socially validated system that grows out of the acceptance by others of the claim for deference, prestige, and recognition that a person presents in his behavior toward others. Since the rejection of such a claim would be perceived (by the recipient) as directed against his self-esteem, he must react against it rather than accept it in order to maintain the integrity of his self-esteem system.

One may view the behavior of our Ss as an attempt to make claims upon the other, an attempt to develop a set of shared expectations as to what each was entitled to. Why then did the Ss' reactions differ so markedly as a function of the availability of threat? The explanation lies, we believe, in the cultural interpretation of yielding (to a peer or subordinate) under duress, as compared to giving in without duress. The former, we believe, is perceived as a negatively valued form of behavior, with negative implications for the self-image of the person who so behaves. At least partly, this is so because the locus of causality is perceived to be outside

---

[5] A post-experimental questionnaire indicated that, in all three experimental conditions, the Ss were most strongly motivated to win money, next most strongly motivated to do better than the other player, next most motivated to "have fun," and were very little or not at all motivated to help the other player.

the person's voluntary control. No such evaluation, however, need be placed on the behavior of one who "gives in" in a situation where no threat or duress is a factor. Rather, we should expect the culturally defined evaluation of such a person's behavior to be one of "reasonableness" or "maturity," because the source of the individual's behavior is perceived to lie within his own control.

Our discussion so far has suggested that the psychological factors which operate in our experimental bargaining situation are to be found in many real-life bargaining situations. However, it is well to recognize some unique features of our experimental game. First, the bargainers had no opportunity to communicate verbally with one another. Prior research on the role of communication in trust (Deutsch, 1958, 1960; Loomis, 1959) suggests that the opportunity for communication would have made reaching an agreement easier for individualistically oriented bargainers. This same research (Deutsch, 1960) indicates, however, that communication may not be effective between competitively oriented bargainers. This possibility was expressed spontaneously by a number of our Ss in a post-game interview.

Another characteristic of our bargaining game is that the passage of time, without coming to an agreement, is costly to the players. There are, of course, bargaining situations in which lack of agreement may simply preserve the *status quo* without any worsening of the bargainers' respective situations. This is the case in the typical bilateral monopoly case, where the buyer and seller are unable to agree upon a price (e.g., see Siegel & Fouraker, 1960). In other sorts of bargaining situations, however, (e.g., labor-management negotiations during a strike, international negotiations during an expensive cold war) the passage of time may play an important role. In our experiment, we received the impression that the meaning of time changed as time passed without the bargainers reaching an agreement. Initially, the passage of time seemed to place the players under pressure to come to an agreement before their costs mounted sufficiently to destroy their profit. With the continued

passage of time, however, their mounting losses strengthened their resolution not to yield to the other player. They comment: "I've lost so much, I'll be damned if I give in now. At least I'll have the satisfaction of doing better than she does." The mounting losses and continued deadlock seemed to change the game from a mixed motive into a predominantly competitive situation.

It is, of course, hazardous to generalize from a laboratory experiment to the complex problems of the real world. But our experiment and the theoretical ideas underlying it can perhaps serve to emphasize some notions which, otherwise, have an intrinsic plausibility. In brief, these are that there is more safety in cooperative than in competitive coexistence, that it is dangerous for bargainers to have weapons, and that it is possibly even more dangerous for a bargainer to have the capacity to retaliate in kind than not to have this capacity when the other bargainer has a weapon. This last statement assumes that the one who yields has more of his values preserved by accepting the agreement preferred by the other than by extended conflict. Of course, in some bargaining situations in the real world, the loss incurred by yielding may exceed the losses due to extended conflict.

SUMMARY

The nature of bargaining situations was discussed. Two general propositions about the conditions affecting the likelihood of a bargaining agreement were presented. The effects of the availability of threat upon interpersonal bargaining were investigated experimentally in a two-person bargaining game. Three experimental conditions were employed: no threat (neither player could threaten the other), unilateral threat (only one of the players had a means of threat available to her), and bilateral threat (both players could threaten each other). The results indicated that the difficulty in reaching an agreement and the amount of (imaginary) money lost, individually as well as collectively, was greatest in the bilateral and next greatest in the unilateral threat condition. Only in the no threat condition did the players make an overall profit. In the unilateral threat condition, the player with the threat capability did better than the player without the threat capability. However, comparing the bilateral and unilateral threat conditions, the results also indicate that when facing a player who had threat capability one was better off *not* having than having the capacity to retaliate in kind.

References

Deutsch, M. A Theory of Cooperation and Competition. *Hum. Relat.*, 1949, **2**, 129–152.

————. Trust and Suspicion. *J. Conflict Resolut.*, 1958, **2**, 265–279.

————. The Effect of Motivational Orientation upon Trust and Suspicion. *Hum. Relat.*, 1960, **13**, 123–140.

Dollard, J., Doob, L. W., Miller, N. E., Mowrer, O. H., and Sears, R. H. *Frustration and Aggression*. New Haven: Yale Univer. Press, 1939.

Goffman, E. On Face-work. *Psychiatry*, 1955, **18**, 213–231.

Loomis, J. L. Communication, the Development of Trust and Cooperative Behavior. *Hum. Relat.*, 1959, **12**, 305–315.

Schelling, T. C. Bargaining, Communication and Limited War. *J. Conflict Resolut.*, 1957, **1**, 19–38.

————. The Strategy of Conflict: Prospectus for the Reorientation of Game Theory. *J. Conflict Resolut.*, 1958, **2**, 203–264.

Siegel, S., and Fouraker, L. E. *Bargaining and Group Decision Making*. New York: McGraw-Hill, 1960.

Stone, J. J. An Experiment in Bargaining Games. *Econometrica*, 1958, **26**, 286–296.

Zeuthen, F. *Problems of Monopoly and Economic Warfare*. London: Routledge, 1930.

INDUCING TRUST: A TEST OF THE OSGOOD PROPOSAL

Marc Pilisuk and Paul Skolnick

ABSTRACT

A partial test was made of the hypothesis that a renewed strategy of small conciliatory moves preceded by honest prior announcements will induce reciprocation from an adversary. The task was a version of the Prisoner's Dilemma extended to permit gradations in cooperative response and cast in the simulated settings of an arms race. 4 false-feedback conditions with 16 Ss in each and 2 groups of natural pairs with 24 in each were compared to test the effects of the conciliatory moves and honest communication of intentions against both matching strategies and natural sequences of play. The results indicated (a) that both matching strategies and conciliatory strategies, with or without prior honest expression of intentions, increase cooperation, (b) that the communication opportunity tends to be used deceptively in the natural condition, reducing cooperation, and (c) that the combination of conciliatory strategy with honest prior announcement of moves presents, by a small margin, the most effective strategy, among those tried, for inducing reciprocal cooperation.

Charles Osgood's "Suggestions for Winning the Real War with Communism" (1959) first contained a proposal later detailed in *An Alternative to War or Surrender* (Osgood, 1962) as "graduated reciprocation in tension reduction." Apart from its intended significance in suggesting a way out of the cold war, "graduated reciprocation in tension reduction" states a theory of the step-by-step evolution of interparty conflict. The theory has particular relevance to the origins of variability—individual or group—which determine conflict outcomes. It is built upon the premise that individual initiative, even in the absence of coercive sanction, can prescribe the behavior of both parties in a conflict situation.

The major contention of the Osgood thesis is that psychological processes working against the possibilities of a complete rapprochement, or a disarmament agreement in the cold-war case, might be overcome by reversing the essentially unilateral steps by which the arms race continues to accelerate. Instead of small graduated increments in armaments, or threatening moves, which tend to be reciprocated ad infinitum, Osgood proposed a set of small, unilateral, conciliatory overtures each preceded by an announcement and carried out without guarantee of reciprocal overtures. After several such moves, none really sacrificing security, reciprocation leading to a reversal of the arms-suspicion deadlock could be anticipated.

Amitai Etzioni in his article on "The Kennedy Experiment" outlines events of the "thaw" period following the Cuban missile crisis which seem to conform, in a general way, to Osgood's thesis (Etzioni, 1967). But the international arena provides too little control for a test of a theory which, in the more general statement, purports to speak to the underlying process of conflict. The laboratory provides opportunity for greater control and has provided the setting for a number of studies dealing with the consequence of unilateral initiatives.

An experimental literature has gradually developed on the effects of unilateral position and/or unilateral moves upon bilateral behavior. Deutsch and Krauss (1960) developed a trucking game in which they found that a unilateral power position was detrimental to cooperation. Raser and Crow,

Source: M. Pilisuk and P. Skolnick, "Inducing Trust: A Test of the Osgood Proposal," *Journal of Personality and Social Psychology*, Vol. 8, 1968, pp. 121–133. Copyright 1968 by The American Psychological Association and reprinted by permission.

using the internation simulation, found that acquisition of a unilateral power advantage (acquisition of an invulnerable weapon) tended to increase the incidence of aggressive actions (Raser & Crow, 1964). Both of these studies were related more to the converse of the Osgood proposition, that is, to the effects of acquiring unilateral power rather than to effects of unilateral conciliation. But another study, using a cleverly devised game of unequal power, tested the effectiveness of a completely pacifist strategy on the part of the player in the weaker position. The strategy proved ineffective in generating mercy from the stronger player (Shure, Mecker, & Hansford, 1965). Again this speaks only obliquely to the proposal in question which called for modest steps toward unilateral disarmament.

While the advantages of manipulation and control are common to these studies, some of the designs are obviously too complex to permit a sequence of controlled experiments systematically varied in detail over a range of circumstances. But the theory under consideration is related to a very simple paradigm. The theory in its general statement applies to all conflict between two contestants in circumstances where mutual distrust prevents finding a mutually satisfactory outcome and where the parties have identifiable moves with payoffs dependent upon these moves. The Prisoner's Dilemma game meets these criteria and provides a most appropriate setting for control.

The basis of interest in the Prisoner's Dilemma situation derives from the significance of the conflicting motivations represented by the two alternatives. The D (defection) choice assures a player of minimal loss (if the other player should also choose D) and maximal gains (should the other player choose C, cooperation). The C choice can be justified only by mutual consideration for the well-being of both players. Such consideration is better served by mutual cooperation which provides small gains to both. As a player controls only his own choices, his selection of the C response reflects his own trust or, in repeated plays, his desire to induce trust in the other's be-

havior. Conversely, suspicion leads to the choice of defection which, when mutual, is detrimental to both players.

A rather extensive literature on the Prisoner's Dilemma game is reviewed by Rapoport and Orwant (1962), by Gallo and McClintock (1965), and by Rapoport and Chammah (1965). Those Prisoner's Dilemma studies using a contrived adversary provide the clearest tests for the consequences of a unilateral patterning of moves upon cooperation. A variety of false-feedback conditions have been used in the Prisoner's Dilemma including the following types:

1. Total unilateral cooperation: The stooge cooperates without regard to the subject's actual moves (Rapoport & Chammah, 1965; Solomon, 1960).
2. Total unilateral defection: The stooge defects without regard to the subject's moves (Solomon, 1960).
3. Random feedback: The stooge cooperates or defects according to a random schedule again without regard to the subject's behavior. The probability of a C or D move is preset and remains the same for every trial (Bixenstine, Potash, & Wilson, 1963b; Marlowe, Gergen, & Doob, 1966).
4. Matching strategies: Here the stooge matches the actual performance of the subject in "tit-for-tat" fashion. The matching may be of the subject's current move or of his previous one. In the latter case a player who defected on one trial would be faced with defection on the subsequent trial. In such strategies the level of cooperation by the stooge is entirely contingent upon the subject's own performance (Komorita, 1965).
5. Partial reinforcement strategy: This lies between the random and matching strategies, for in it the stooge's responses to particular moves are randomly selected but with one probability for a subject's cooperative moves and a different probability for his defecting moves. Hence, one can predetermine the proportion of times cooperation will be rewarded or defection punished, for example, 85% of subject's cooperative moves are met

by the C response while perhaps 60% of subject's D responses are met by defection (Pylyshyn, Agnew, & Illingsworth, 1966; Komorita, 1965).

The matching strategies are categorically distinct from all others in their sensitivity to the play of the real player. This type of contingency is apparently conducive to cooperation (Komorita, 1965). One finding on an entirely noncontingent feedback, that is, on the effectiveness of 100% cooperation, is that the martyr stooge, over a lengthy sequence of trials, evokes two very different responses. About half the subjects take continuous advantage of the stooge while the other half come to a level of complete cooperation themselves (Rapoport & Chammah, 1965). This contrasts with the Shure et al. (1965) study of pacifist strategies, but again is peripheral to the idea of graduated reciprocation. Komorita studied a modified Prisoner's Dilemma adding a third choice for one of the players which permitted the inflicting of a heavy punishment to the other. In this way he demonstrated that unilateral restraint by the party who was alone equipped with a punitive option served to increase the rate of cooperation (Komorita et al., 1967).

The conventional two-choice Prisoner's Dilemma game permits a player to convey to his partner an intention to engage in cooperative behavior. For him to do this, however, he must engage in cooperative behavior himself, and there is an immediate cost associated with the behavior if his partner has not chosen, at the same time, to do likewise.[1]

In the extended form of the Prisoner's Dilemma game (Pilisuk & Rapoport, 1964a, 1964b) the opportunity for conveying a change in one's intentions is made easier by the possibility of engaging in partially cooperative behaviors which would prove less

costly to the initiator at payoff time. On the other hand, these less costly gestures might be viewed more as a "come on" than as a sincere indicator of the desire to achieve mutual cooperation. A way of further increasing the separation between conveying intentions and the cost associated with displaying one's intentions is provided for in the extended form. By virtue of the fact that the decision of how far to cooperate is enacted only gradually, it is possible to permit each player to inspect the performance of the other at some time prior to the terminal payoff. This opportunity for inspection may be used, with varying degrees of honesty, to give an indication of one's intended level of cooperation.

In addition, the entire game can be set in the simulated surrounding of an arms race–disarmament dilemma. The units of cooperation are conversions from missiles to factories, the terminology of weapons' disparity and economic productivity are used to describe the payoff matrix, and one's apparatus is described as a country.[2] This context contains the rudiments needed to test the "graduated reciprocation in tension" proposal, that is, disarming moves of specified sizes, preceded by a demonstration of intentions and repeated over a series of trials. In one study, using the extended Prisoner's Dilemma, it was found that in those pairs where both players had taken a substantial unilateral initiative, at some point early in the course of play, the prognosis for mutual cooperation was very good (Pilisuk, Potter, Rapoport, &

---

[1] The conventional two-choice Prisoner's Dilemma game is played without direct communication between opposing players. This need not be the case and an important methodological contribution for the conduct of controlled communication of basic options and intentions in game experiments is seen in the development of the interaction screen (Sawyer & Friedell, 1965).

[2] Effects resulting from the use of such labels have been reported in Pilisuk, Potter, Rapoport, and Winter, 1965. The use of arms-race terminology adds connotative meanings to the previously described "inspection" procedure. In the arms-control debate, inspection refers to a verification procedure on the reduction of armaments. In the present study the inspection procedure refers only to a peek at an adversary's armament level *before* the time when such a glimpse is useful for verification purposes. Since the word inspection is used in instructions to subjects, it is again used in this report. It must be understood, however, that it functions here as a form of prior announcement of intention and not as a verification procedure.

Winter, 1965). Another study using the extended game permitted an announcement of intentions prior to actual behavior. Where integrity of these announcements occurred, increases in cooperative behavior tended to follow. However, there was a marked tendency to make deceptive use of the communication opportunity which tended to work against cooperation (Pilisuk, Winter, Chapman, & Haas, 1967). Hence, there are limiting conditions under which an earlier finding that communication induces cooperation (Deutsch, 1958) would appear to hold.

These studies still fail to provide a direct test of the Osgood thesis. The limitation is inherent in the use of natural pairs which did not provide cases of a single player consistently making small, conciliatory overtures preceded each time by an indication of intention to do so. Subjects made gestures at odd times of various sizes and with varying degree of integrity of prior announcement. Contrived feedback could correct this. The present study contrasts the conduciveness to cooperation (or disarmament in the particular game) of two types of false feedback and of the presence or absence of an opportunity to communicate intentions via an inspection procedure. The two feedback conditions are a matching strategy and a conciliatory strategy. The latter leads in the direction of cooperation by small steps while remaining entirely contingent upon the subject's behavior. The hypothesis relevant to the Osgood proposal is that the conciliatory strategy when combined with honest communication will produce the greatest amount of cooperation.

METHOD

One hundred and twelve subjects participated in this experiment. The subjects were male student volunteers from the University of Michigan and Purdue University. The actual monetary rewards that the subjects received were dependent upon game outcomes. All subjects were led to believe that they were playing in pairs (some were actually playing against a "simulated other"), and acquaintances were not paired. An experimental session ordinarily contained four simultaneously performing pairs.

Subjects were seated at a table with a partition separating each subject from the others. The experiment was then explained as a simulation of international relations. Each subject had a board in front of him with five levers on it. Each lever exposed a picture of a missile on the left, or a factory on the right. Subjects started every trial with five missiles showing. A move consisted of converting zero, one, or two of the levers from missiles to factories or back again.

There were five moves in every trial but only the state following the last move had a payoff associated with it. Subjects received information of their adversary's performance level by a light signal after the fifth move of every trial. A subject was instructed to refer to his payoff matrix to determine how much money he and the other player had won or lost on that trial. Specific examples of the payoff matrix were illustrated to be certain that the task was understood. Subjects played the game described for 25 repeated trials but were not informed of how many trials they were to play. After the experiment, subjects were asked to fill out a questionnaire.

The principle of payoff is given by the simple rule that a subject is rewarded for his conversion of missiles to factories, punished doubly for the degree that he has disarmed in excess of his opponent's level, and rewarded doubly for his missile superiority.[3] The complete matrix of payoff values, exactly as it is shown to the subjects, is presented in Figure 1.

While there are 6 × 6 contingent outcomes, the basic paradigm of the mixed motive Prisoner's Dilemma game is preserved. On any given trial a subject earns more the more highly he is armed, *regardless* of the armament level of his adversary. Yet, as in

---

[3] The payoff principle is expressed in the following formulae: If players A and B expose F_a and F_b factories, respectively, and receive payoffs P_a and P_b, respectively, then [1] $P_a = 2F_b - F_a$ and [2] $P_b = 2F_a - F_b$.

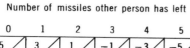

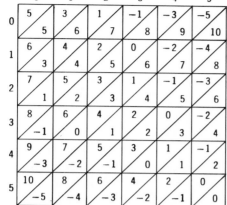

+1 unit for each factory
+2 units for each missile more than other person
−2 units for each missile less than other person

Figure 1. Payoff matrix shown to subjects. (Number to left of diagonal is payoff to subject. Number to right of diagonal is payoff to other player.)

the more conventional two-choice game, mutual defection (armament in this case) reduces substantially the earnings of both parties and disarmament is advantageous to precisely the degree that it is mutual.

While instructions employed the terminology of countries, weapons, and economic units, no preference is expressed for either the armed or the disarmed state. Instructions carefully avoid any reference to goals of the task which might be inferred from such terms as game, competition, cooperation, winning, maximize earnings, etc. Subjects were left to infer from the matrix of outcomes their own purposes of play. Payoffs in actual money were presented after the experiment at the value of 1¢ per unit of the matrix.

The experiment was a factorial design in which three variations of the pattern of other's cooperation were crossed with the presence or absence of an inspection on the third move of each trial (see Figure 2). The natural pair experiment played without inspection has already been described. In the inspection conditions, the experimental procedure was modified to inform each subject, by means of

a lighting device, just how many missiles the other player had after the third move of every trial. It should be noted here that inspection performance, occurring at the third move, is not strictly binding. In the subject's two remaining moves he may still change four of his five units from the state displayed at inspection. In the two false-feedback conditions which used inspections, the artificial subject demonstrated at inspection the precise number of missiles to be shown on his fifth or payoff move, that is, the stooge used his inspection move with absolute integrity.

The two types of contrived feedback used in this experiment will be called matching and conciliatory. In the matching conditions two missiles were always given as the opponent's armament level for the first trial and thereafter the number of missiles the subject himself showed on Trial n was revealed as the number shown by the opponent for Trial $n + 1$. In the conciliatory conditions, feedback (opponent's performance) was also two missiles for the first trial but thereafter the opponent's performance on Trial $n + 1$ was one missile less than the subject had shown on the previous trial. The central prediction was that honest inspection and conciliatory behavior would increase cooperation (disarmament), that is, that the Osgood proposal would work.[4]

The authors further hypothesized (a) that for comparable conditions the conciliatory feedback would produce more cooperation than either the matching feedback or the natural condition, (b) that the matching strategy in turn would be more conducive to cooperation than the natural pair conditions (as in Komorita, 1965), and (c) that when feedback was constant, the conditions providing an opportunity for communication via inspection would produce greater cooperation.

---

[4] The Osgood proposal is richer than this brief description would indicate. While the conciliatory condition meets some aspects of the graduated reciprocation thesis, the matching strategy is also similar to the proposal in its responsiveness to both the belligerent and friendly overtures of the other party. It is on the issue of initiatives that the conciliatory strategy is used here as the closer simulation of the Osgood strategy.

Feedback

	PAIRS with inspection N = 24	MATCHING with inspection N = 16	CONCILIATORY with inspection N = 16
	PAIRS without inspection N = 24	MATCHING without inspection N = 16	CONCILIATORY without inspection N = 16

Inspection (left vertical label)

Figure 2.   Experimental design

In other words, in addition to the success of the Osgood proposal significant main effects were predicted for the presence of contrived feedback and for the presence of inspection in all contrived feedback conditions.

RESULTS

The major findings may be organized under three subheadings: (*a*) indexes of cooperation across conditions, (*b*) change in cooperation over time, and (*c*) utilization of the inspection move.

COOPERATION ACROSS CONDITIONS

The most obvious index of cooperation is the gross number of missiles converted to factories at payoff time. The missile averages, or gross rates of noncooperation taken over all 25 trials, are seen in Figure 3. The results of an analysis of variance performed on these data are presented in Table 1. As predicted, the anova showed a significant feedback main effect ($p < .001$). In comparison with behavior in the natural pairs playing without inspection, the matching condition produced significantly more cooperation ($t = 5.79$; $df = 38$; $p < .001$).[5] The conciliatory condition also produced significantly more cooperation than occurred in the

natural pairs ($t = 4.41$; $df = 38$; $p < .001$), but the differences between matching and conciliatory were not significant.

The difference in cooperation between natural and programmed conditions is even more pronounced in the games which offered opportunity for communication of intention via inspection. Here, total disarming reached an average level of only .8 (out of five possible units) in the natural pairs, which is significantly less cooperative than the 2.6 units average of the matching condition ($t = 5.5$; $df = 38$; $p < .001$). Again the matching condition was not distinguished significantly from the conciliatory condition. Clearly both forms of contrived feedback, matching

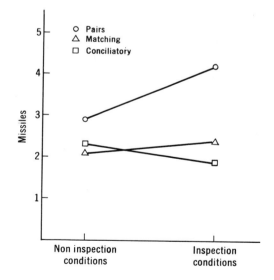

Figure 3.   Mean number of missiles shown at the end of each trial averaged across trials and subjects for each condition

---

[5] All significance levels reported for *t* tests are two-tailed.

Table 1. Overall analysis of variance for effects of variations of feedback and inspection upon missile (noncooperation) ratio

Source	SS	MS	F ratio
Feedback (A)	31651.37500000	15825.687500	10.92***
Inspection (B)	4387.52343750	4387.523438	3.03*
A × B	8263.32031250	4131.660156	2.85**
Error	153683.58593750	1449.345139	

* $p < .10$, $df = 1/106$.
** $p < .056$, $df = 2/106$.
*** $p < .001$, $df = 2/106$.

and conciliatory, induced cooperation beyond what is ordinarily forthcoming in such circumstances, and this major effect is present regardless of the presence or absence of an opportunity for communication via inspection.

The question of whether the presence of inspection itself has discernible effects is not yet answered. The issue is important since inspection provided the only form of opportunity to convey intentions to the other party. Obviously the inspection condition has a somewhat different meaning in the natural and artificial conditions. In both artificial conditions one of the players (the stooge) conveyed his final or payoff move with absolute integrity. In the natural condition the use of inspection was left entirely up to the subjects. In the natural pairs, the presence of an inspection opportunity significantly reduced the amount of cooperation ($t = 3.16$; $df = 46$; $p < .001$).

The artificial conditions suggest an interesting interaction. Contrary to our hypothesis, honest inspection was not uniformly conducive to cooperation. The source of feedback by inspection interaction ($F = 2.85$; $p < .056$) suggests that inspection tends to improve cooperation in the conciliatory condition but weakens it in the matching condition and in the natural pairs. While this only approaches significance, we do report the finding recalling that the Osgood proposal for graduated reciprocation in tension reduction calls for combining an honest prior announcement of intention before each move with a regular progression of small conciliatory moves.

A more subtle index of cooperation takes into account the tendency of pairs of players to polarize or "lock-in" at near total levels of

cooperative or competitive responses. The following measure defines criterion groups on the basis of terminal performance, the state of cooperation to which a pair had evolved toward the culmination of the experimental session. Continuing a practice of previous studies (Pilisuk et al., 1965) every pair of players was classified into one of three discrete categories in accordance with the performance of both players during the last five trials of an experimental session containing 25 trials.[6] The pairs are labeled Dove (cooperators), Hawk (noncooperators) and Mugwumps (intermediate). A pair was labeled Dove if (a) both players showed four or more factories for each of the last five trials, and (b) if none of the subjects had less than 22 factories (more than three missiles) over these same trials. The Hawk criteria are completely symmetrical. A Hawk pair was so designated if (a) neither player had less than four missiles (more than one factory) on any one of the last five trials, and (b) none of the subjects totaled less than 22 missiles (more than three factories) over these same five trials. The third and intermediate group, Mugwumps, contain all the remaining pairs who failed to meet the conditions for classification as either Dove or Hawk. These groupings, while arbitrary, provide for stringent differentiation between cooperators (Doves) and noncooperators (Hawks).

The essential feature of these criteria is that they provide not only for a measure of pair, as opposed to individual, performance

---

[6] Classification for the pair is automatically given by the one real subject in the false-feedback conditions where the stooge copied the subject's behavior.

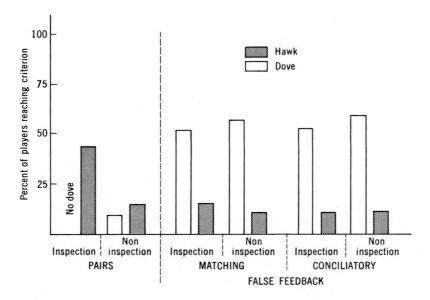

Figure 4. The percentage of subjects who reached the criterion of Dove or Hawk for the six conditions

but also that they reflect a fact about the data on cooperativeness in non-zero-sum games, that is, that it is likely to become increasingly polarized over repeated trials with the two players coming to achieve either the mutually competitive or the mutually cooperative state and to become set in it.

The particular criteria chosen are selected to provide continuity with earlier work (Pilisuk et al., 1965). In actual fact these criteria which were designed to measure *pair* performance could produce artifacts when one of the pair members is a preinstructed stooge. The probability that two players making random choices will fall into one of the two groups is less than 10^{-5}. The probability that a single player making random responses will meet criterion is still quite low but is certainly greater in the false-feedback conditions. Here a subject reaching Dove or Hawk criterion himself assures the selection of the pair into the category. The apparent difference in meanings of Dove and Hawk criterion groups under natural and false-feedback conditions is tempered by the lock-in phenomenon. This lock-in or tendency of members of natural pairs to come to play very much like one another at or near one of the poles of coopera-

tion is repeated in our natural conditions. The percentages of players achieving Dove, Hawk, and Mugwump criteria in each of the six conditions are shown in Figure 4.

It can readily be seen that both false-feedback conditions produce significantly more Doves (at least 50% of players meet the Dove criterion in all false-feedback conditions) than in the comparable conditions using natural pairs. Using both actual number of missiles shown and criterion group, it appears that players receiving false feedback were more cooperative than players receiving real feedback.

TIME COURSE OF COOPERATION

What subjects do on the very first trial may be predictive of their amount of cooperation in later trials.[7] The current experiment finds slight support for this observation by obtaining a correlation of .3 between

---

[7] Terhune (1965), using a two-choice game, found a not quite significant trend between first-trial cooperation and subsequent cooperation.

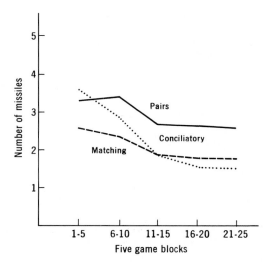

Figure 5. Changes in cooperation or disarmament levels over time in noninspection conditions

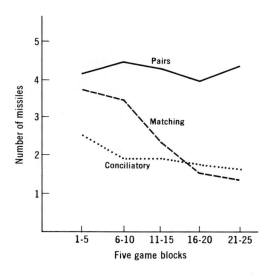

Figure 6. Changes in cooperation or disarmament levels over time in inspection conditions

number of missiles on the first move and total number of missiles for the four false-feedback conditions (correlation is significant at the .01 level). The same correlation for the natural pairs (.18) is not significant. In natural games, randomly matched players tend to arrive at quite close levels of cooperation leaving most of the variance to be accounted for by player interaction and little by predisposing tendencies.

After the first move, a player has a history of experience which becomes a major factor in determining his subsequent decisions (Pilisuk et al., 1965). Changes in cooperative behavior which develop in the course of the experiment are depicted in Figures 5 and 6. The points represent missile levels for nonoverlapping trial blocks of five trials each.

The findings suggest a gradual decline in armament levels in five of the six conditions. Only the natural pairs with inspection were apparently becoming still less cooperative at the end of the experiment. This calls into question exactly how honest were the demonstrations of intention in the natural circumstances which will be discussed shortly. It is obvious here, however, that the mere existence of a channel for communication of intention is not, by itself, conducive to trust. This has been noted in previous findings as

well (Pilisuk et al., 1967b).

Cooperation in the conciliatory condition appears to increase from the start, perhaps with an added boost from the addition of honest inspection, but it appears to level off as the average value approaches one missile. Here an artifact introduced by the conciliatory strategy may be operating. For instance, where a subject takes cognizance of the fixed nature of his adversary's strategy, he (the subject) then gains optimal rewards from a strategy of retaining one missile on every trial. He may, in fact, come upon this one missile strategy inadvertently and stick to it because of the rewarding character without even realizing the nature of the other's strategy. That this is the case is evidenced by another piece of data, namely, that not one subject in the conciliatory condition could state, at the end, the principle of the "one-less" conciliatory strategy used by his adversary. We cannot say, at this point, whether the armament decline would have continued as rapidly if this artifact were removed.

USE OF INSPECTION

The inspection point, where present, was the only opportunity for a player to exchange information with his opposite number prior to the payoff move. In this experiment, inspection occurred only on the third of five moves and a player, permitted up to two conversions per move, could thus demonstrate any level of disarmament (from zero to five) he desired. After this opportunity for demonstration of intentions, the player has two remaining moves in which he might still change as many as four out of his five units from factory to missile or the reverse. Hence, the performance at inspection has necessary implications only for those displaying total armament or total disarmament and even for these cases, the implications for final performance are slight. When the inspection move has such necessary implications for the payoff move, we call the inspection binding. The significance of the performance at inspection was essentially a demonstration or nonbinding promise of intention. It could be matched identically by the player's subsequent performance at the payoff trial (as was done by the stooge in the false-feedback conditions). It could be a promise overfulfilled at payoff time, as happened on occasion, or it could be used to demonstrate a higher level of intention to disarm than actually followed. This latter discrepancy may be taken as an index of deception.

A typical progression of play in conditions without inspections changed markedly when the third move was open as an inspec-

tion. The results of the average performance levels on the first through fifth moves is shown for the three noninspection conditions in Figure 7 and for the three inspection conditions in Figure 8.

The comparison of noninspection with inspection conditions is obvious. In the typical noninspection circumstance a player moves directly from his original state of five missiles to his terminal state. In the typical inspection game a player disarms somewhat to the point of inspection and rearms somewhat in his remaining moves. This difference is found in the conciliatory and matching conditions as well as with the natural pairs.

Using the decreased level in cooperation after inspection as an index of deception, it is possible to plot the amount of deception within five-game trial blocks. The amount of deception is shown as the gray areas in Figure 9, b, d, and f.

The mean discrepancy between displayed level at inspection and at terminal performance again shows a consistent use of the inspection opportunity for deceptive purposes. The natural pairs provide a base against which to measure the effects of the experimental variation in other's strategy upon the integrity of the subject's performance. This contrast suggests that an opponent who uses his inspection opportunity to display his precise

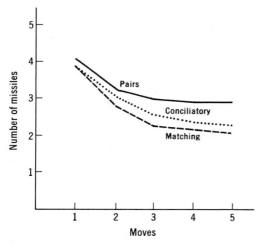

Figure 7. Average number of missiles shown on every move for the noninspection conditions

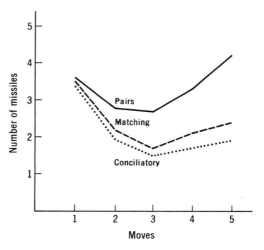

Figure 8. Average number of missiles shown on every move for the inspection conditions (Inspection occurs on the third move.)

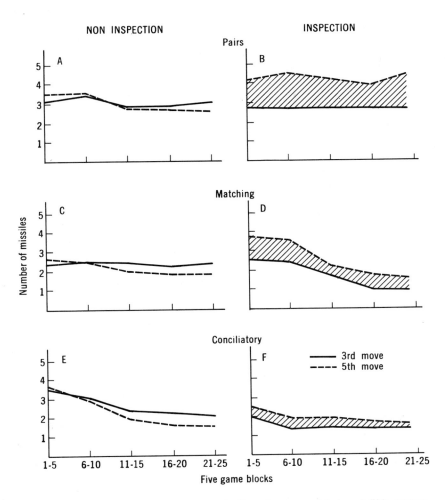

Figure 9.   Differences in number of missiles shown on third and fifth moves
(For inspection conditions the shaded area represents amount of deception.)

intentions with integrity may be having a beneficial effect upon the integrity of the subject himself. Perhaps the clearest way to demonstrate this is with frequency data which indicate the number of times a particular promise was fulfilled, that is, demonstration at inspection was either maintained or over-fulfilled by still greater disarmament at the payoff trial. These data are shown for each inspection condition, broken down by five-game trial blocks in Figure 10.

The results of a trend analysis performed on the data confirm a tendency across conditions to use the inspection opportunity with

increasing integrity $(F = 27.83; p > .001)$.[8] It is instructive to contrast the integrity change in the matching-inspection condition, Figure 10, with the terminal cooperation rate for the same condition over the same trial blocks, Figure 6. Subjects started using the inspection opportunity deceptively 63% of the time during the first trial block of the

---

[8] An unweighted-means analysis of variance to test for linear trend was used for a two-factor (trial blocks versus condition) 5×3 design (see Winer, 1962, p. 377).

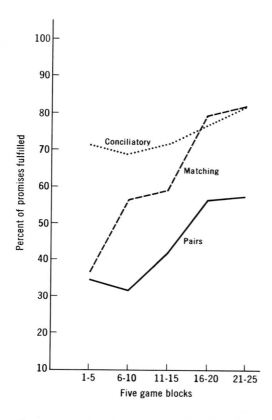

Figure 10. Percentage of promises fulfilled (integrity on inspection move)

matching condition. Here, the matching stooge using absolutely honest demonstrations of intention apparently induced a very sharp reduction in the level of deception as well as an increase in the level of cooperation. Unfortunately, for purposes of comparison, the conciliatory group was essentially honest from the start.

DISCUSSION

The primary results of the study indicate that both matching and conciliatory strategies increase cooperation over the rate naturally found in this experimental game. The Osgood proposal for combining small, consistent, unilateral overtures of good intention with an honest prior announcement of moves

does apparently produce markedly more cooperation than is found in the natural state but only a marginal and contingent increase over the rate found in a comparable matching strategy.

The interaction effect cited, that is, increased cooperation resulting from honest inspection in combination with the conciliatory strategy, was not found where criterion groups were used as the index of cooperation. This may represent an artifact produced by the payoff matrix where a rigid conciliatory strategy is employed. In the conciliatory condition, as previously mentioned, it was possible for a player to secure maximum rewards by less than maximum cooperation. A player consistently converting four missiles to factories would be consistently met by an adversary disarming completely and would stand to win more this way than if he were cooperating at any other level. The discovery of such an optimal state may have served to curtail any tendency to increase cooperation beyond that point. Hence, several players who might otherwise have met the Dove condition detected this peculiar option and fell slightly short of the cooperation level needed for Dove classification. The interpretation is supported by data comparing the rates of cooperation of the matching and conciliatory strategies over time. The conciliatory strategies produce a rapid rise in cooperation which levels at close to the optimum state.

It seems also possible that the conciliatory strategy may have been most useful in inducing movement toward cooperation, but that once the advantages of mutual cooperation have grown apparent that a tit-for-tat strategy will serve to push it all the way. Such combined strategies are certainly worth trying but a third possibility remains, namely that nonpunitive sensitivity to partner's behavior, a variable shared by both conciliatory and matching strategies, is the critical factor which overrides the minor variations found between them.

The results which dealt with the absolute integrity of announcement of intention through inspection suggested that the addition of inspection might be differentially favorable to cooperation, that is, favorable only in the conciliatory condition. Subjects in the conciliatory condition were asked whether they thought the inspection opportunity made a difference in their strategy. Fourteen of 16 felt that the inspection made a difference in their own performance. The same number felt that inspection contributed to cooperation. In the natural condition where cooperation was substantially lower (and the inspection was frequently used deceptively) subjects most frequently felt that the inspection made a difference in the direction of reducing cooperation. There may be some cognitive congruity operation occurring here with the subject's tendency to see consistency between his own final cooperation level and the experimental conditions present at the time.

In the matching strategy the prior announcement of moves appears actually to decrease the amount of cooperation. We did find that the initial reaction to this condition was apparently to be unresponsive to the integrity of the stooge, that is, not to match the stooge in his integrity until later in the time course when the mutual cooperative pattern started to emerge. Without the trusting set (introduced by the conciliatory condition) the presence of an adversary who honestly signals his moves but does not take any cooperative initiatives (only responds to cooperative gestures) may be taken as a temptation for taking advantage of this adversary who has not made known any cooperative intentions of his own. In the conciliatory condition, however, the stooge makes cooperative gestures in addition to responding to the subject's gestures, and the addition of honest communication calls attention to the trustful intentions. This conclusion must be considered as tentative because of the marginal significance of the interaction effect reported above ($p > .056$).

It should be reiterated that the inspection move was not a pure signal of intention. This is important, for communication, once considered the panacea for distrust, is itself a many faceted phenomenon. In this particular study it was possible to make a very modestly binding show of intentions. By showing total disarmament at inspection one could expose himself to loss in that he could only enact an 80% rearmament in the two remaining moves before payoff. This places a very particular significance on the display of total cooperation at inspection. It also leaves ground for suspicion of motives in the display of less than total cooperation. In an analogous study where a total retraction was possible, where the inspection move was purely signal, we found the communication to inhibit lock-in but not to increase total cooperation. But in another condition of that study, a more binding inspection where full disarmament at inspection meant at least 50% disarmament at payoff, the result was first a decrease but then a very sharp increase in mutual cooperation (Pilisuk et al., 1967b). There is obvious need for control on the nature of the communication variable. Osgood's proposal that communication be precise, honest, and placed before each move assists in definition. The degree to which it can be made to appear binding also appears important. The only other evidence bearing upon the hypothesis came when we asked subjects at the end if they would trust the other person. All 16 subjects in the conciliatory group said "yes" in contrast to 62–75% in the other false-feedback conditions and still fewer in the natural groups. Only 7 of 24 subjects in the natural pair inspection condition said they would trust the other party.

In designing the false-feedback situation we were frankly concerned that both matching and conciliatory conditions would be too obvious. We feared not only that the patterns would be discovered but that this would happen sufficiently early in the sequence to arouse suspicions in the subjects regarding the deception. The actual recognition of the pattern proved more difficult than originally anticipated. About half of the subjects saw no formula at all governing the pattern of the preprogrammed other. Of those who did see a plan in the other person's behavior it was often represented by a rather simplified statement like "he stayed armed most of the time to try to win." The dependence of stooge strategy on one's own offered some interesting and perhaps projective insights into the attribution of motives. One subject in the conciliatory condition stated the strategy of the other was to stay mostly armed so he himself reacted by staying armed and "did him one better." Not one of 64 subjects facing either the matching strategy or the conciliatory strategy could satisfactorily state the principle of his adversary's strategy. Whatever effects on the subject's behavior transpired, they were achieved without the mediation of precise awareness of the strategy. In other words, it does not appear to be absolutely necessary to give a public announcement or to let the adversary know the overall plan of strategy, or even for the adversary to perceive the strategy accurately in order for the strategy to be effective.

The Osgood proposal is certainly not tested definitively in a single study. From this study we find support for the effect of honest prior announcement of moves in inter-action with conciliatory steps as productive of cooperative behavior. From the studies reviewed in the introduction, it seems fair to conclude that complete unilateral martyrdom and trust are, at least under some conditions, ineffective in inducing cooperation. The studies also show that unilateral reliance upon power, or threatening moves tends to beget belligerence rather than conciliation. Between the extremes of overt reliance upon belligerent or threatening moves and complete conciliation and trust there lies a strategy of moves which is most effective in the reduction of intergroup hostility. As a first approximation, the Osgood proposals remain a tenable candidate for such a pattern of moves. Why such proposals are not more frequently or more arduously tested in the field is a question which goes beyond the scope of this paper.

References

Bixenstine, V. E., Potash, H. M., and Wilson, K. V. Effects of Level of Cooperative Choice by the Other Player on Choices in a Prisoner's Dilemma Game: Part I. *Journal of Abnormal and Social Psychology*, 1963, **66**, 308–313. (a)

———, ———, and ———. Effects of Level of Cooperative Choice by the Other Player on Choices in a Prisoner's Dilemma Game: Part II. *Journal of Abnormal and Social Psychology*, 1963, **67**, 139–147. (b)

Deutsch, M. Trust and Suspicion. *Journal of Conflict Resolution*, 1958, **2**, 267–279.

———, and Krauss, R. M. The Effect of Threat upon Interpersonal Bargaining. *Journal of Abnormal and Social Psychology*, 1960, **61**, 181–189.

Etzioni, A. The Kennedy Experiment. *Western Political Quarterly*, 1967, **20**, 361–380.

Gallo, P. S., & McClintock, C. Cooperative and Competitive Behavior in Mixed Motive Games. *Journal of Conflict Resolution*, 1965, **9**, 68–78.

Komorita, S. S. Cooperative Choice in a Prisoner's Dilemma Game. *Journal of Personality and Social Psychology*, 1965, **2**, 741–745.

———, Sheposh, J. P., and Braver, S. L. Power, the Use of Power, and Perceived Intentions in a Two-person Game. Unpublished manuscript, Wayne State University, 1967.

Marlowe, D., Gergen, K. J., and Doob, A. N. Opponent's Personality, Expectation of Social Interaction, and Interpersonal Bargaining. *Journal of Personality and Social Psychology*, 1966, **3**, 206–213.

Osgood, C. E.   Suggestions for Winning the Real War with Communism. *Journal of Conflict Resolution*, 1959, **3**, 295–325.

————. *An Alternative to War or Surrender*.   Urbana, Ill.: University of Illinois Press, 1962.

Pilisuk, M., Potter, P., Rapoport, A., and Winter, J. A.   War Hawks and Peace Doves: Alternate Resolutions of Experimental Conflicts.   *Journal of Conflict Resolution*, 1965, **9**, 491–508.

————, and Rapoport, A.   A Non-zero-sum Game Model of Some Disarmament Problems.   In, *Peace Research Society; Papers I*.   Tokyo: International Academic Press, 1964.   (a)

————, and ————.   Stepwise Disarmament and Sudden Destruction in a Two-person Game: A Research Tool.   *Journal of Conflict Resolution*, 1964, **8**, 36–49.   (b)

————, Skolnick, P., Thomas, K., and Chapman, R.   Boredom versus Cognitive Reappraisal in the Development of Cooperative Strategy.   *Journal of Conflict Resolution*, 1967, **11**, 110–116.   (a)

————, Winter, J. A., Chapman, R., and Haas, N.   Honesty, Deceit, and Timing in the Display of Intentions.   *Behavioral Science*, 1967, **12**, 205–215.   (b)

Pylyshyn, Z., Agnew, N., and Illingworth, J.   Comparison of Individuals and Pairs as Participants in a Mixed-motive Game.   *Journal of Conflict Resolution*, 1966, **10**, 211–220.

Rapoport, A., and Chammah, A. M.   *Prisoner's Dilemma*.   Ann Arbor: University of Michigan Press, 1965.

————, and Orwant, C.   Experimental Games: A Review.   *Behavioral Science*, 1962, **7**, 1–37.

Raser, J. R., and Crow, W. J.   Winsafe II: An Internation Simulation Study of Deterrence Postures Embodying Capacity to Delay Response.   La Jolla, Calif.: Western Behavioral Science Institute, 1964.   (mimeo)

Sawyer, J., and Friedell, M. F.   The Interaction Screen: An Operational Model for Experimentation on Interpersonal Behavior.   *Behavioral Science*, 1965, **10**, 446–460.

Shure, G. H., Meeker, R. J., and Hansford, E. A.   The Effectiveness of Pacifist Strategies in Bargaining Games.   *Journal of Conflict Resolution*, 1965, **9**, 106–117.

Solomon, L.   The Influence of Some Types of Power Relations upon the Level of Interpersonal Trust.   *Journal of Abnormal and Social Psychology*, 1960, **61**, 223–230.

Terhune, K. W.   Psychological Studies of Social Interaction and Motives (Siam). Phase 1.   Two-person Gaming Study.   Cornell Aeronautical Laboratory Technical Report #VX-2018-G-1, 1965.

Winer, B. J.   *Statistical Principles in Experimental Design*.   New York: McGraw-Hill, 1962.

Chapter 5

THE EMERGENCE OF STABLE DOMINANCE HIERARCHIES

An important fact about conflict in enduring social relationships is that the domain of conflict does not seem to remain for long an equal contest between equally powerful antagonists. Instead, the struggle tilts to favor one or another of the parties. The game is no longer interesting for the question of who is going to win, for one party usually wins. It is on this point, incidentally, that our attitudes toward "serious" social conflicts and games as play or sport can be distinguished. In serious conflict, we prefer to play an unfair game in which the odds are loaded in our favor, whereas in sports or playful games we prefer a contest with an antagonist who is as near our equal as possible.

The readings in this section all bear on the tendency for areas of uncertainty in conflict relationships to become structured. Warren and Maroney show that as a group of monkeys come to know one another a status hierarchy emerges and the incidence of overt aggression or conflict over desirable goods declines, with the dominant monkeys generally having uncontested priority over the subordinate ones. Hoffman, Festinger, and Lawrence demonstrate that human subjects are less likely to compete against another person who has an advantage over them when they believe that this other is superior to them in ability than when they see him as an equal, that is, that subjects tend to accept a status hierarchy based upon perceived merit. The importance of this point for social class systems is clear. Strodtbeck suggests that conflicts within families are biased in favor of one spouse or the other, and that the nature of this bias is in part determined by the norms of the culture in which the family is located. Finally, Schattschneider documents a similar kind of biasing of participation in our system of political democracy. Those with progressively greater socioeconomic advantages are progressively more likely to be involved in the system of pressure groups that contend for influence in a "pluralist" system, while the least advantaged are least likely to be represented by pressure groups, or even to vote.

COMPETITIVE SOCIAL INTERACTION BETWEEN MONKEYS

J. M. Warren and R. J. Maroney

ABSTRACT

This experiment was designed to determine the effects of several variables upon social interaction between monkeys in a competitive food-getting situation. The following problems were studied: (a) the effect of varying motivation and incentive conditions upon social dominance and submission; (b) the nature of the dominance-submission hierarchy in different groups of monkeys; (c) the relation between aggression and success in competition for food; (d) the relation of dominance status to weight, sex, and level of spontaneous activity.

METHOD

SUBJECTS

The subjects were 18 prepubescent rhesus monkeys, 9 males and 9 females, which ranged in weight from 3¾ to 6½ lbs. at the beginning of the experiment. Six monkeys were assigned to three experimental groups, each consisting of three males and three females that had never been housed in the same cage. The composition of the groups, and the sex and median weights of individual monkeys during the two series of tests are given in Table 1. (One animal, No. 13, died after completing the first series.)

At the time this experiment began, the monkeys had been in the laboratory approximately two months and had been adapted to responding in the Wisconsin General Test Apparatus by 30 days' previous testing of lateral preference and of food preference.

APPARATUS

The Wisconsin General Test Apparatus (Harlow, 1949) was used throughout the experiment; the monkeys occupy a large restraining cage which faces a table upon which is a movable test tray. On each trial, the experimenter placed the incentive upon the tray and, in full view of both monkeys, pushed it within reach.

PROCEDURE—SERIES I

Within each of the groups of six monkeys, every animal was tested in competition with each of the other five monkeys every week for four weeks. Within a group there were 15 pairings of the six monkeys taken two at a time.

The effect of quality and quantity of incentive on social competition was studied by presenting nine incentive conditions: 1, 2, or 4 pieces of raisin, potato, or egg mash pellet. Each of the nine conditions was replicated six times in a test session, so that a total of 54 presentations was made in every test session. The position of the incentive on the test tray was varied from right to left according to a balanced irregular sequence from trial to trial.

The results of the food preference experiment previously mentioned indicated that raisin, potato, and egg mash pellet were high, medium, and low preference foods, respectively, for these monkeys when tested individually.

In the second test period in this series,

Source: J. M. Warren and R. J. Maroney, "Competitive Social Interaction between Monkeys," *Journal of Social Psychology*, Vol. 48, 1958, pp. 223–233. Copyright 1958 by The Journal Press and reprinted by permission of publishers and authors.

Table 1. Characteristics of subjects

Group	Monkey	Sex	Weight I	Weight II	Gain in Weight	Median Activity Score
I	4	F	5½	7	1½	201
	9	F	5⅝	6¾	1⅛	384
	12	F	4½	5½	1	8
	13	M	4¾	Dead		
	14	M	4⅝	6	1⅜	517
	18	M	5⅜	6½	1⅛	421
II	2	F	5⅜	7¼	1⅞	96
	7	F	4⅝	6	1⅜	146
	8	F	4½	5¾	1¼	115
	10	M	6½	7⅜	⅞	327
	15	M	4½	5⅝	1⅛	109
	16	M	4¼	5½	1¼	46
III	1	F	4½	6¾	2½	99
	3	F	5⅛	5⅝	½	97
	5	M	5⅛	5⅜	¼	250
	6	M	5⅛	6⅝	1½	256
	11	F	3¾	5	1¼	39
	17	M	4⅜	5¼	⅞	862

the dominant member of each pair in Groups I and II was fed his daily ration of chim-cracker and fruit immediately before being tested with the subordinate of the first pairing. The subordinate member was tested after 23 hours of food deprivation, the condition which was standard for all monkeys throughout the remainder of the tests.

SERIES II

Approximately six months after the first four tests, all of the groups were retested twice. Two weeks intervened between the first and second of these retest pairings. In this series, 25 presentations of a single raisin were made in each testing session. At the time these tests were made, the monkeys' spontaneous locomotor activity was determined by testing each individual three times in a standard activity cage (French and Harlow, 1956).

Degree of dominance was measured by counting the number of trials on which each of the two competitors obtained the incentive. Occasionally, when several pieces of

food were presented, both animals secured half of the food; each monkey was given credit for one-half success on these trials. In addition, the frequency of hitting, biting, and mounting was recorded for Group A, on Series I, and for all groups on Series II.

RESULTS

QUALITY AND QUANTITY OF INCENTIVE

The percentage frequency with which the subordinated monkey in each pair succeeded in securing food is plotted as a function of the quantity and quality of the incentive in Figure 1. Each of the points on these functions represents 3,240 individual observations. It is apparent that the quantity of the incentive has very little, if any, effect on the outcome of competition for food. The subordinated monkeys, however, obtained the low preference incentive, eggmash pellets, significantly more often than the more

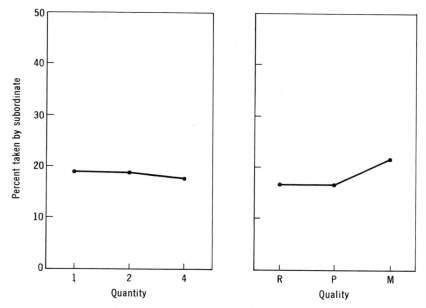

Figure 1. Frequency of success by subordinate monkeys in competing for food, as a function of quantity and quality of reinforcement

highly preferred incentives, potato and raisin ($X^2 = 4.63, P < .05$).

CHARACTERISTICS OF
THE HIERARCHIES

Since every monkey was tested in competition with every other member of his group in all of the testing periods, it was possible to obtain a composite measure of each animal's relative dominance in his group by computing the mean percentage of success in securing food, by the method of paired comparisons. The mean percentage of successful trials is plotted against successive test periods in Figures 2 to 4; the breaks in the abscissae between Test Periods 4 and 5 indicate the interval of six months between these tests. The most obvious similarity among the three groups is that each contained one or two monkeys of very low dominance status; the most striking inter-group differences are in

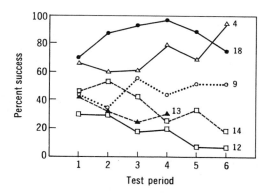

Figure 2. Mean dominance scores for individual monkeys in group *A*

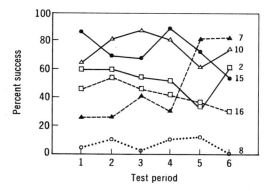

Figure 3. Mean dominance scores for individual monkeys in group *B*

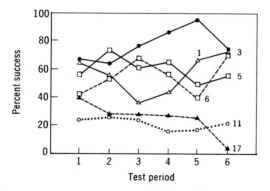

Figure 4. Mean dominance scores for individual monkeys in group C

the degree to which individuals attained consistent high dominance status. Clearly defined status differentiation emerged sooner in Group A than in the other groups.

The consistency of the dominance rankings as measured by rank correlations between successive test periods is presented in Table 2. Twelve of the 15 correlations are significantly greater than zero, and in two of the groups high and significant correlations were obtained between tests after an interval of six months. The consistency of dominance rankings varied somewhat among groups, Group A showing almost perfect correspondence between tests, while Groups B and C's behavior was less constant.

It should be noted that the correlations between Tests 1 and 2, and Tests 2 and 3, for Groups A and B are higher than the corresponding values for Group C, in spite of the fact that the dominant animal in each A and B pair was fed just before being tested in Test Period 2, while the C monkeys were tested under standard conditions.

Table 2. Correlations of ranks on successive tests

tests Periods	A	B	C
1 & 2	1.00**	.94**	.77*
2 & 3	.94**	1.00**	.71
3 & 4	.94**	.94**	.94**
4 & 5	1.00**	.37	.83*
5 & 6	.94**	.71	.77*

* Rho significant at 5 per cent level.
** Rho significant at 1 per cent level.

Table 3. The number of circular triads on successive test periods

		Group		
Test	A	B	C	Sum
1	3	2	1	6
2	2	2	2	6
3	0	1	3	4
4	0	2	1	3
5	0	2	1	3
6	0	0	0	0

Analysis of the outcomes of individual pairings provides additional information regarding the nature of the dominance hierarchy. The linearity of dominance relations may be inferred from the number of circular triads; i.e., relations of the type A > B, B > C, and C > A. Table 3 shows the number of such circular relations within each group on successive test periods; the maximum possible number of circular triads in a group of six is 8. The table shows that no such triads occurred in Group A after the first two periods, but that these departures from a transitive linear hierarchy were persistent in the other groups throughout Test 5.

A second kind of information concerning the nature of dominance relations in young monkeys is derived from the results of individual pairings. The obtained frequency with which individual monkeys dominated competitors in their six encounters is tabulated in Table 4, and is compared with the expected frequency, assuming no significant dominance, from the binomial expansion. The value of X^2 obtained (295.38, with 3 df) permits one to reject the null hypothesis at the 0.1 per cent level of confidence.

Another, and somewhat independent, measure of the stability of dominance-submission relationships is the frequency of reversals in dominance from one testing session to the next meeting of a given pair. One would infer a more stable change in dominance if, after being dominated in two tests, an animal was subsequently dominant in the remaining four tests, than if dominance shifted frequently between two monkeys. The frequency of reversals from one test period to the next is given for each group in Table 5; this table indicates, as do Tables 2 to 4, considerable variability between groups. There

Table 4. Frequency with which monkeys dominated opponents in six testing sessions

				Total	
Proportion	A*	B	C	Observed	Expected
6/6	6	8	6	20	1.25
5/6	3	1	5	9	7.50
4/6	1	5	3	9	18.75
3/6	0	1	1	2	12.50
Total	10	15	15	40	40

* Does not include pairings involving Monkey 13.

were proportionately fewer reversals between individuals in Group A than in Groups B and C. The total frequency of reversals over all groups remains relatively constant; in about 20 per cent of the individual pairings the previous dominance-submission relation is reversed from one test period to the next.

THE INFLUENCE OF WEIGHT, ACTIVITY, AND SEX

In order to determine the effect of weight and level of spontaneous activity upon dominance behavior, the average rank position in the dominance hierarchy for each monkey on Series I and II was correlated with his rank in weight within the group at the time of the two periods. Similarly, average dominance rank on Series II was correlated with median activity level. The results of these computations are presented in Table 6.

There is no indication of a significant relationship between activity level and dominance, nor is there any particularly striking evidence of a significant relationship between weight and dominance, although the correla-

tions are all positive and those for the second series generally higher than for the first set of tests. One consideration, however, suggests that differences in weight are not ineffective in determining dominance: Group A, with the highest consistency in dominance, was the only group with consistent individual differences in weight.

The influence of sex upon social dominance was determined by testing the significance of the difference between the mean ranks for males and females in all groups. The value of t obtained (0.61) was not statistically significant.

AGGRESSION AND MOUNTING

In an attempt to define the behavioral characteristics associated with dominant and submissive social behavior, detailed descriptive protocols were made for Group A on Series I and for all groups on Series II. The frequency of biting, striking, and mounting were recorded.

The records of aggressive behavior in Group A are summarized in Table 7, which gives the frequency with which individual monkeys attacked others and were attacked by others on Series I and II. Note the great decrease in aggressive acts from Series I to

Table 5. Number of reversals in successive pairings

Test Periods Compared	A	B	C	Sum
1 & 2	4/15	3/15	4/15	11/45
2 & 3	3/15	3/15	6/15	12/45
3 & 4	1/15	2/15	2/15	5/45
4 & 5	0/10	6/15	2/15	8/40
5 & 6	1/10	3/15	3/15	7/40
Total	9/65	17/75	17/75	43/215

Table 6. Rank correlations between dominance status and weight and activity

Variables Correlated	A	B	C
Weight I and Dominance I	.48	.39	.89
Weight II and Dominance II	.70	.66	.71
Activity and Dominance II	.10	.54	−.14
Weight I and Weight II	.90	.16	.37

II—the frequency of aggressive behavior was too low to permit any correlational analysis in the second series.

In order to determine the role of aggression in dominance among monkeys, three correlations were computed from the Series I data: (a) rho between rank in dominance and frequency of aggression is +.77 and significant at the 5 per cent level of confidence; (b) rho between the frequency with which a monkey was attacked and the number of his attacks upon others is −.30; (c) rho between position in dominance hierarchy and number of times attacked is −.47. These correlations suggest that, among these monkeys, aggression is an instrumental act to minimize frustration, rather than a response to frustration, since the lower an animal's position in the dominance hierarchy and the

more frequently he is attacked by others, the *less* frequently he is aggressive toward others. This suggestion is compatible with the very low frequency of aggression in Series II. A clear-cut differentiation of status had been attained and little further aggression was required to maintain it; this is supported by similarly low incidence of aggression in Groups B and C.

Mounting of like or opposite sexed subordinates by a dominant male or female is a frequently reported phenomenon in adult monkeys. Mounting was observed in 10 of the 80 pairings of animals in Group A, and only two males (18 and 14) exhibited this behavior; the lowest dominance animals were never mounted. No relation between mounting and social dominance is suggested by these observations.

Table 7.   Incidence of aggression by individual monkeys

Group		Monkey	Bit Others	Struck Others	Was Bitten	Was Struck
AI		4	0	6	2	8
		9	3	7	1	21
		12	0	0	1	9
		13	16	5	1	10
		14	1	1	23	44
		18	9	73	1	0
	Total		29	92	29	92
AII		4	3	0	0	0
		9	3	0	0	1
		12	0	0	1	0
		14	0	0	3	0
		18	1	1	3	0
	Total		7	1	7	1
BII		2	0	0	0	1
		7	5	1	0	0
		8	0	0	1	1
		10	0	0	0	0
		15	1	1	2	0
		16	0	0	3	0
	Total		6	2	6	2
CII		1	0	2	4	0
		3	1	0	0	0
		5	1	7	0	1
		6	3	1	0	0
		11	0	4	1	3
		17	0	0	0	10
	Total		5	14	5	14

DISCUSSION

The results of this study indicate that dominance behavior is not affected by pre-feeding the dominant member of a pair of monkeys competing for food, nor is the competitive behavior influenced by varying the quantity of food incentive; subordinate monkeys obtain more low preference food than middle or high perference foods. These observations are compatible with the view that a separate dominance drive exists, which is essentially social and relatively independent of physiological, homeostatic drives in the primate (Maslow, 1936a).

Insofar as procedures and subjects are comparable, the results of this experiment are in very good agreement with those obtained in similar laboratory investigations with Macaca mulatta (Maslow, 1936b; Miller and Murphy, 1956). Just as Maslow reported, we found that a stable and linear dominance hierarchy was established within relatively few pairings; like Miller and Murphy, we found that the dominance hierarchies were reproducible after several months without testing. The present investigation is of value in confirming in general the results of the previous experiments, and in demonstrating that the dominance-submission behavior of prepuberal monkeys is very similar to that of adult animals.

The most striking difference between the results of this study and those of Maslow and of Miller and Murphy is in the much lower incidence of mounting observed in the present experiment. Such a discrepancy between experiments involving sexually mature and immature subjects is to be expected.

The behavior of cats in the same competitive social situation has been described in a previous publication (Baron, Stewart, and Warren, 1957). The most noteworthy difference between the species was with respect to the relation between aggression and dominance status. In cats, no well-defined relation was found; cats which are most successful in competing for food may be so nonaggressive as not to retaliate when attacked, while cats least successful in food getting may be highly aggressive. In monkeys, only high dominance animals exhibit much aggression, and only during the early tests. This difference suggests that dominance and submission may be more completely defined behaviorally in monkeys than in cats.

SUMMARY

Eighteen rhesus monkeys were divided into three subgroups consisting of three males and three females each. Within each group, every monkey was tested in competition for food with each of the other five members of the group on four occasions over one month (Series I). Two additional repetitions of the 15 paired comparisons within a group were made after an interval of approximately six months. The following results were obtained:

1. Variation in the quantity of incentive had no effect on the degree of dominance observed.
2. Subordinate animals were more successful in obtaining low preference incentives than highly or intermediately preferred foods.
3. Prefeeding the dominant animal did not affect dominant behavior appreciably.
4. A stable and eventually linear dominance hierarchy was obtained in each group.
5. Dominance behavior was not related to weight, sex, or level of spontaneous activity.
6. The correlation between aggression and success in getting food was +.77.

References

Baron, A., Stewart, C. N., and Warren, J. M. Patterns of Social Interaction in Cats (Felis domestica). *Behavior*, 1957, **10**, 56–66.

French, G. M., and Harlow, H. F. Locomotor Reaction Decrement in Normal and Brain-damaged Monkeys. *J. Comp. and Physiol. Psychol.*, 1955, **48**, 496–501.

Harlow, H. F. The Formation of Learning Sets. *Psychol. Rev.*, 1949, **56**, 51–65.

Maslow, A. H. The Role of Dominance in the Social and Sexual Behavior of Infra-human Primates: III. A Theory of Sexual Behavior of Infra-human Primates. *J. Genet. Psychol.*, 1936, **48**, 310–338.

———— (1936b). The Role of Dominance in the Social and Sexual Behavior of Infra-human Primates: IV. The Determination of Hierarchies in Pairs and in a Group. *J. Genet. Psychol.*, 1936, **49**, 161–198.

Miller, R. E., and Murphy, J. V. (1956). Social Interactions of Rhesus Monkeys: I. Food-getting Dominance as a Dependent Variable. *J. Soc. Psychol.*, 1956, **44**, 249–255.

TENDENCIES TOWARD GROUP COMPARABILITY IN COMPETITIVE BARGAINING

Paul J. Hoffman, Leon Festinger, and Douglas H. Lawrence

INTRODUCTION

The present study is concerned with some of the socio-psychological factors that determine behavior in a situation where some ability is being revealed or measured. In such a situation, in order to evaluate their ability, persons frequently tend to compare their own performance with the performance of others whom they accept as comparable to themselves. As a consequence, the individual's behavior is determined more by his performance relative to those others than by the absolute level of his performance. If the situation in which the particular ability is measured is a bargaining situation where coalitions can form, it is possible to predict both the type and strength of the coalitions that form, and the relative stability of these when the composition of the group and the importance of the task for the participants is varied.

A motivational analysis of this type has implications, not only for social psychological theory but also for the theory of games (3). This is seen most clearly when "rational"

Source: P. J. Hoffman, L. Festinger, and D. H. Lawrence, "Tendencies toward Group Comparability in Competitive Bargaining," *Human Relations*, Vol. 7, 1954, pp. 141–159. Copyright 1954 by Plenum Publishing Company Ltd. and used by permission.

bargaining behavior in the typical game situation is analyzed under the assumption that the only motivation present is a tendency on the part of each player to maximize the total number of points he obtains. Imagine a game involving three players where a fixed amount of money, points, or some commodity is to be divided among them. The rules of the game are such that no one individual can obtain the total amount by his own efforts. If any two of them agree to cooperate, they can share the amount on any basis satisfactory to the two of them. In addition the following conditions are assumed: 1. that all individuals are equally and singly motivated to obtain as large a share of the points as possible, and 2. that they are all equal in bargaining skill.

Two things should be noted about this game. First of all, while it is mandatory for two of the three players to form a coalition in order to obtain points, a given player has no rational basis for selecting between the other two members in attempting to form the initial partnership. Hence, in the long run, each of the three possible coalitions in this group will be formed equally often. The second point to note is that there is no logical termination to the bargaining process. Each player can break up any coalition formed in opposition to him by offering one player more points than he is getting from his present coalition. Hence an endless process of bargaining would develop and be maintained.

This result, however, is contrary to everyday experience. It is to be expected that coalitions will form between particular pairs of players more frequently than between others and that these will be of a relatively stable and permanent nature. The difference between the "rational" prediction illustrated above and common psychological expectation centers about the nature and variety of the motivations operating in the bargaining situation.

When the sole motivation present is the desire to obtain a maximum number of points and when the players have equal bargaining skill, all coalitions between members are equivalent and equally likely to occur. Predictable and stable coalitions can form,

however, when there is a variety of motives operating and their strengths are unequally distributed among the players. Then even though two players make identical offers to a third in terms of the absolute number of points involved, these offers are not equivalent in value for that player in terms of the other satisfactions they can provide. This results in the possibility that a particular individual may find himself in an advantageous position relative to the others. His offers may carry both the potentiality of points and the potentiality of other satisfactions. To the extent that a second individual requires both of these types of satisfaction, there is a high probability that he will accept offers from the first player. Moreover, the player left out of such a coalition will be relatively impotent in his attempts to break it up as long as the desire for points is subordinate to the other motivations of the coalition members. From this point of view, it is obvious that coalitions may in fact become predictable and stable.

The hypotheses underlying the present experiment are first, that these additional motivations in a bargaining situation arise in part from each individual's concern about his comparability to other members of the group on the ability that is shown in the bargaining. This results in pressures to achieve uniformity in the group. In our culture, at least, there are also motivations to strive to be better than others which operate simultaneously with the pressures toward uniformity. The contrast between these types of motivation and the motivation to obtain a maximum share of the points is seen most clearly in situations where the points involved are ratings, prestige objects or other symbolic representations of relative status. The individual's concern about them arises not because of their absolute or intrinsic value, but because in this activity they are indicative of his status relative to others. In a competitive society, such concern about the status significance indicated by the symbols tends to operate even where money or other commodities of direct utilitarian value are involved.

The influence of the concern about relative status on the formation of coalitions can be shown by referring to the previously described game. Assume that one of the individuals obtains an early initial advantage of a number of points while the others at this stage have few or none. These points function as symbols indicating to the others that this person is superior to the other two in that activity. The result is an increase in the motivation of the other two individuals of the group to draw close to him. Consequently they will be strongly motivated to form a coalition against him insofar as this aids in overcoming his lead. Furthermore, they will resist any attempt on his part to disrupt this coalition even though by accepting his offers either one of them might gain more points than he is able to obtain by remaining in the coalition. This happens because a conflict has developed between their desire to acquire the maximum number of points possible, and their desire to reduce the discrepancy between themselves and others. The refusal of offers from a person with the large initial advantage in points indicates that the conflict has been resolved in favor of the desire to reduce the discrepancy.

This analysis is based on the hypothesis that a major motivation of each individual is to compare himself with and to draw close to or surpass the others in the group. The reference individuals with whom each compares himself, however, are not selected indiscriminately. The amateur golfer does not compare himself with the professional, nor is the occasional bridge player concerned with his status relative to the expert. The conditions determining which individuals are selected as a reference group are not clearly defined as yet, but in general an individual is concerned about his status relative to others whom he considers of approximately equal ability. He tends to exclude from his comparisons individuals who appear definitely superior or inferior to him in this activity. This is identical to the process of "rejection" when pressures toward uniformity arise concerning opinions. There the individual does not evaluate his opinions by comparison with others who are too divergent. Similarly, individuals do not evaluate their abilities by comparison with those who are too divergent.

Conditions in which all members of a group regard themselves as comparable are known as "peer" conditions. Conditions in which one or more individuals are regarded by the others as non-comparable, as definitely superior or inferior, are known as "non-peer" conditions. In terms of the previous analysis, it is expected that in peer conditions predictable and stable coalitions will form in opposition to the individual who has an initial advantage. In non-peer conditions, however, this tendency will be reduced because the other members of the group are motivated to surpass each other and are less concerned with the status of the non-comparable individual. Even though the tendency to compete with the non-comparable individual is reduced, it does not disappear because the condition of non-comparability is relative and continuous, rather than all or none.

There is a second important determinant of decisions involving the formation of coalitions. It is obvious that the desire to achieve and maintain relative status will vary depending upon whether or not the individual regards his status on that task as important. The golfer or bridge player will be concerned about status differentials which develop in the play of these games but not on a wide variety of other. Similarly, performance on an activity which requires the use of intellectual abilities will result in a motivation to achieve status in direct proportion to the degree to which this type of activity is considered important by the individuals involved. Increasing the importance of a task in effect increases the individual's concern about any status differences that may develop with the result that he becomes even more motivated to equal or surpass the others. Consequently, he becomes even less willing to cooperate with anyone having an initial advantage. Thus under conditions of high task importance the coalitions become highly stable. In contrast, conditions of low task importance may result in a situation in which incidental motivations are as strong as the concern about relative status. In this case the stability of the coalitions is reduced.

In summary, it is postulated that an important motivation in a bargaining situation is the individual's concern about his status in the activity relative to other members of the group and his desire to equal or surpass them. The accumulation of points is significant for him because these represent the degree of comparability among the participating individuals. Consequently, predictable and stable coalitions in opposition to an individual having an initial advantage will occur more frequently when that individual is a peer member of the group than when he is a non-peer member. Similarly, increases in the value placed on the points as a result of making the task important to the individual increases his concern over comparability and indirectly his tendency to form stable coalitions in opposition to an individual who obtains an initial advantage. These predictions are tested by the following experiment.

SUBJECTS AND PROCEDURE

Twenty-eight groups of subjects participated in the original experiment which was performed at Stanford University. The entire experiment was then replicated with twenty-eight groups at the City College of San Francisco. Subjects were undergraduates, drawn from the introductory psychology courses. The two groups were alike with respect to age, but the Stanford subjects were of a higher socio-economic level and probably of higher average intelligence because of the differences in entrance requirements at the two schools. Stanford subjects also appeared to be somewhat more mature and less naive than the San Francisco students, most of whom had had no previous experience as subjects in psychological experiments. Only male students were used.

The twenty-eight groups in each replication were randomly but equally distributed between the four experimental conditions: 1. high task importance and peer relations, 2. high task importance and non-peer relations, 3. low task importance and peer relations, and 4. low task importance and non-peer relations. Of the three individuals in each group, two were subjects and the third was a paid-participant trained beforehand in the role he was to play. Two paid-participants were selected from Stanford for use in the Stanford experiment, and three from San Francisco City College for participation with those groups. These were male seniors who were unknown to the subjects. When the two subjects and the paid-participant arrived for the experiment, a check was made to see that the two subjects had no more than a passing acquaintance with each other and that neither knew the paid-participant. In cases where this was not true, the group was discarded. The three group members were seated around a table with the positions clearly labelled as A, B, and C. The paid-participant invariably was seated at A.

Each group was informed that the purpose of the experiment was to collect standardization and validation data on a new type intelligence test consisting of three parts. Subjects were told that the first part of the test was similar to the usual type of paper and pencil intelligence test, the second measured the ability to interact with others, and the third was designed to measure insight into one's own behavior and the behavior of others. In actuality the first was a paper and pencil intelligence test included to lend credibility to the situation, the second was the bargaining situation or test proper, and the third was a questionnaire to provide independent evidence that the experimental manipulations had changed the individuals' attitudes and perceptions. The low versus high task importance and the peer versus non-peer conditions were established in the following ways:

TASK IMPORTANCE

The importance of the task to the subjects was manipulated in two ways: (i) by the instructions given them concerning the validity of the test purported to be measuring intelligence, and (ii) by the content of the paper and pencil test. In the high importance groups, the instructions given them just prior to beginning the experiment were as follows:

We have asked you to come here today to take a new intelligence test which has recently been devised and which has shown itself to be highly superior to the usual kind of intelligence test. We have scheduled three of you together because, although some parts of the test are taken individually, other parts of the test require interaction among three persons. The test is separated into a number of parts and we will explain each part to you when we come to it.

Let me explain to you why we are asking you to take this test. Recent research in psychology has produced new knowledge about intelligence and intelligent behavior in people which has enabled psychologists to construct this new test. It has been tried out with many different kinds of people and in every case has been shown to be greatly superior and more valid in measuring the intelligence of individuals than the older type test. Needless to say, when such an important development occurs it is extremely valuable to accumulate as much data using the test as possible. As the test has not yet been used with people on the West Coast, we are especially interested in the data we will collect here.

After we measure your I.Q. with this test we will compare it with other records we can get on you and with scores you have made on the older kind of tests. There will be some of you for whom we do not have sufficient records. If that turns out to be the case we may have to ask you to take some other tests sometime within the next month. The results so far with this new test indicate that now, for perhaps the first time, we can really measure how intelligent a person is with an extremely high degree of accuracy. We shall of course be glad to inform each of you about your I.Q. after we have scored the test.

This emphasis on the validity of the test was underscored by the content of the items given the high importance groups during the pencil and paper part of the experiment. The printed booklet given these groups contained 24 synonym-antonym items and 20 verbal analogy items drawn from the Terman Concept Mastery test, a section from the paragraph comprehension section of the Ohio State Psychological Examination, and 10 items from the Minnesota Paper Form Board. A ten minute time limit was imposed on this test.

The instructions for the low importance groups were designed to belittle the validity of the test. After the same introductory paragraph as used for the high importance group, the instructions were as follows:

Let me explain some things to you about why we are asking you to take this test. The psychologist who published the test claimed that it was useful in measuring intelligence. Other people, trying the test out, have disputed this claim and have shown by their results that it has nothing to do with intelligence. In fact their results seem to show that it has nothing to do with anything. We have decided in the department here to do some very careful research to settle once and for all whether or not the test is any good. We have already given the test to large numbers of people, and, comparing their scores on this test with scores on other tests, with grades, and with many other measures, we are quite convinced that the present test which you will take is pretty meaningless. Nevertheless we want more data so that when we publish our results there will be absolutely no question about it.

This lack of validity was underscored by the content of the printed booklet given the low importance groups during the pencil and paper part of the test. The improvised items were of the following types: (a) general information of an extremely low difficulty level, (b) items requiring value judgments on moralistic questions, (c) items requiring judgments of occupation from facial expression, (d) items requiring judgments of emotion from facial expression, and (e) jokes to be rated in terms of their humor.

PEER VERSUS NON-PEER

The peer condition, in which each subject was to regard the other subject and the paid-participant as comparable to himself in intellectual ability, was established in part by instructions and in part by the behavior of the paid-participant. These instructions were given just after the completion of the pencil and paper test and just prior to the bargaining situation. For the peer conditions they were as follows:

Before we start the next part of the test, I would like you to know some of the reasons for scheduling you particular three persons together in the same group. This next part of the test requires that in each of our groups the three persons should be approximately equal in intelligence and mental ability insofar as this can be roughly determined in advance. We consequently have taken the liberty of looking up your grades, your various achievement and aptitude test results, and as much else as we could get about you. We are reasonably certain that you three are very close together in intelligence as measured by those tests.

In this next part of the test you will see why it is necessary to have the three of you matched so closely in intelligence. The next part requires that each of your deal with the other members in the group and consequently it is necessary that all three of you be as equal in intelligence as we could manage.

The paid-participant emphasized his equality with the others by pacing himself during the pencil and paper test at the same rate as the two subjects in the group.

In the non-peer groups, where the two subjects were to regard the paid-participant as definitely superior to themselves in intellectual ability and therefore as non-comparable, the instructions were as follows:

Before we actually start taking the second part of the test, I would like you to know some of the reasons for scheduling you particular three persons together in the same group. We wanted to be sure that in each of our groups that take this test, there was at least one person of very superior intelligence. Now one of you here has taken an intensive battery of tests earlier in the quarter, and we asked specifically that he sign up for this hour. The person in this group who took this intensive battery of tests earlier is the one of extremely superior intelligence.

In this part of the test, part "B," you will see the reason we were so careful to be sure that there was at least one person in the group of extremely high intelligence. The next part of the test involves dealing with others in the group and in the way the test is standardized, it is necessary that such discrepancies in intelligence among you exist.

As neither of the two subjects in the group had taken an intensive battery of tests, it was assumed that each would conclude that either the other subject or the paid-participant must be the one of extremely superior intelligence. This speculation was then directed at the paid-participant as the result of his subsequent behavior. During the paper and pencil test, he worked through the booklet easily and quickly, turning it in well before the expiration of the time limit.

Following these instructions, the next part of the test was the bargaining situation. Each of the three members of a group was given a set of triangular pieces cut out of masonite, the sets differing from each other only in colour. By assembling these pieces correctly it was possible for each member of the group to form an individual square requiring six of the seven pieces provided him. The seventh piece was a large right-angled isosceles triangle. Any combination of two players could form a "group" square by combining their large triangles. This group square had a larger area than did the individual square.

The bargaining was governed by a set of rules read to the subjects in advance of the trials. These rules emphasized that the objective of the players was to earn points, since these points were to be added to the scores on the paper and pencil test to determine the I.Q. There were to be a series of five trials, each of four minute duration, and on each of which it was possible to earn as many as eight points. These could be earned in one of two ways. If a person assembled his individual square and no other squares were formed on that trial, the square was worth eight points. If two persons combined pieces to form a group square, this square was also worth eight points, provided that the two partners agreed on how they would divide these eight points between themselves. It was permissible for either of the two persons in an agreement of this sort to break it at any time during the trial and to enter into a new agreement with the third person in the group. In the event that more than one square was formed in a given trial, only the largest square would win. In case two squares of the same size were formed, no one would get any points. There was one exception to these rules. If any person succeeded in forming the individual square on the first trial, he automatically won that trial and in addition received a bonus of twelve points which he could divide among the three players in any way he wished.

These rules achieved the following results. On the first trial while the situation was still somewhat unstructured for the subjects, each of them attempted to form an individual square because of the bonus of twelve points offered. The problem was so difficult, however, that only the paid-participant was able to do it. He always decided to keep the points for himself, thereby obtaining an initial lead of 20 points over the other two members. Because of his manipulation of the pieces, it was always clear to the other two subjects by the end of the first trial how they should go about constructing their individual squares. But since the assembly of an individual square by either of the remaining group members would result in a tie, with no points awarded, this solution became functionally useless for the remaining four trials. The only possibility remaining was for two players to form a group square from the large isosceles triangles. The paid-participant emphasized this point at the beginning of the second trial by first forming such a square with individual B and then with C as though he were just exploring the possibilities in the situation. As this group square was obviously larger than the individual square, it would always win the points when formed.

The bargaining behavior of the paid-participant during the second through the fifth trial was predetermined. At the beginning of the trial he offered to make the group square with B and to give him four of the eight points. From this point on his behavior was governed by the following rules:

1. If B said "yes," A rested until something else happened. If B said "no," A waited for a moment until some agreement between B and C had been reached.

2. If B and C did not reach an agreement, A offered B five points. If the offer was refused, he offered six. If this was refused, he offered seven. After any acceptance, he rested until something else occurred. If the offer of seven was refused, he began directing offers to C in the same sequence.

3. If the person left out made A an offer, A accepted if it gave him more points. He did not take the initiative as long as he was in a coalition.

4. If the BC coalition formed on an even split, A proceeded as in 2.

5. If the BC coalition formed on an uneven split, A made an offer of four to that player who was getting the least. If the answer was "yes," he rested. If "no," he proceeded as in 2, continuing to direct his offers to the same person until an offer was accepted or until an offer of seven points was refused. In this latter case he began directing his offers to the other coalition member.

The purpose of these rules was in part to make the bargaining behavior of the paid-participant appear natural, but at the same time to ensure that when forced he would always offer up to seven points. In this way the strength of the coalitions against him could be measured. As each offer was made, it was recorded sequentially by the experimenter in such a manner as to indicate the size of the offer, by whom it was made, toward whom it was directed, and whether it was accepted, ignored, or rejected. In the Stanford experiment, the subjects were given a warning 30 seconds before the end of each trial. This was eliminated in the San Francisco replication since its effect was to materially reduce the amount of bidding within the period prior to the warning.

RESULTS

The results of this experiment are described under three headings. First the data from the questionnaire are analyzed to determine the extent to which differences in task importance and in peer relations were actually established between the various groups. Following this, the results bearing on the choice behavior during the last four trials of bargaining are presented under two headings. The first of these covers terminal coalitions, i.e., the agreements which existed at the end of a trial and thereby determined the distribution of points. The second presents the results pertaining to temporary coalitions, i.e., those tentative agreements existing prior to the formation of the terminal coalition.

THE SUCCESS OF THE

EXPERIMENTAL MANIPULATIONS

One item of the questionnaire given as the final part of the test had each subject rate his own I.Q. and that of the paid participant on the assumption that discrepancies in these ratings would be indicative of the extent to which a given subject regarded A, the paid-participant, as comparable to himself. The mean discrepancies in I.Q. ratings (rating of paid-participant minus self-rating) are evaluated in the analysis of *Table 1*. The subjects' rating of A in the peer conditions averages 3.27 I.Q. points more than the subject's rating of himself, but in the non-peer condition it averages 13.00 points more. This difference is significant (P < .001). Discrepancies are not significantly different for comparisons involving task importance, schools, or interactions. The assertion can therefore be made with a high degree of certainty that perceived differences in comparability were in fact established between the peer and the non-peer conditions, such differences being based upon assessment of intellectual status.

A second item in the questionnaire had the subject evaluate the bargaining situation as to the degree of validity they believed it to have as a measure of intelligence. It is possible to infer from these ratings the degree to which subjects considered their performance in the bargaining situation as important, and thus the extent to which they were thereby motivated. The obtained ratings on this item are evaluated in the analysis of *Table 2*. Subjects assigned to conditions of high task importance tend to rate the bargaining procedure as a more valid measure of intelligence than do subjects assigned to conditions of low importance (P < .001). In addition the difference attributable to the replications of the experiment is significant (P < .01), with the San Francisco subjects rating the bargaining situation as more valid than do subjects of the Stanford experiment. Since the San Francisco subjects represented a somewhat less select group in terms of college aptitude, it is reasonable to expect that they would be more concerned over their intellectual status and would consequently ascribe a higher importance to the task.

THE FORMATION OF COALITIONS

Assuming that the groups were differentiated with respect to the importance of the task and the degree of comparability between members of the group, the major question is the influence of these variables on the formation of coalitions. A relatively direct measure of the extent to which coalitions were formed in opposition to the paid-participant is the discrepancy between the number of points he was able to obtain on each trial and the number he would be expected to obtain if the coalitions were formed on the basis of chance.

Table 1. Analysis of discrepancies between subject's rating of paid-participant and rating of self on I.Q.

Source	d.f.	Variance Est.	P
Importance	1	11.16	
Peer vs. Non-Peer	1	5,304.02	<.001
Schools	1	75.45	
Interactions	4	211.66	
Error	48	92.70	

Table 2. Rated validity of bargaining situation as a measure of intelligence

Source	d.f.	Variance Est.	P
Importance	1	46.29	<.001
Peer vs. Non-Peer	1	0.57	
Schools	1	7.00	<.01
Interactions	4	0.14	
Error	104	0.76	

On a chance basis the paid-participant, hereafter referred to as A, would be expected to receive on the average a third of the eight points available for division, or 2.67 points per trial, as would each of the two subjects, B and C. In the event that A receives significantly less than the average of the other members of the group, he is being discriminated against by them as far as their willingness to form coalitions with him is concerned.

The average number of points per trial earned by A in the last four trials under the various conditions of the experiment is shown in *Table 3*, along with the statistical analysis of the sums on which the averages are based.

It is apparent from *Table 3* that A is generally unable to obtain a chance number of points under the various conditions. The one exception is the condition of low importance and non-peer relations at Stanford, in which A receives significantly more points than would be expected. Under each of the two replications of the experiment the pattern of results is essentially the same. A obtains more points under low importance than when task importance is high (P < .02), and more under the non-peer conditions than under peer conditions (P < .01). These differences are in the direction predicted by the theoreti-

cal assumptions underlying the experiment. It should be noted that in each experimental condition A receives fewer points in the San Francisco replication than at Stanford (P < .01). This consistent discrepancy becomes more meaningful when it is recalled that the questionnaire data gave evidence of higher importance being ascribed to the task in the San Francisco groups than at Stanford. The experiment might therefore be interpreted as including three different levels of task importance instead of two. This interpretation would reconcile the differences between the two replications.

The failure of A to secure the number of points expected by chance is due to two factors: 1. he was unable to form a fair share (two-thirds) of terminal coalitions even though he was willing to offer as many as seven points, and 2. even in those coalitions of which he was a member he was unable to obtain a fair division (4 out of 8) of the points. The influence of the first factor is demonstrated in *Table 4* where the average number of terminal coalitions including A during the four trials is tabulated. The pattern of results is the same as that involving point totals for A. For all conditions com-

Table 3a.   Average points per trial earned by A

Impor.	School	Peer	Non-Peer	Avg.
High	S.F.	1.29	1.75	1.52
	Stan.	1.57	2.39	1.98
	(Avg.)	(1.43)	(2.07)	(1.75)
Low	S.F.	1.32	2.54	1.93
	Stan.	2.50	4.36	3.43
	(Avg.)	(1.91)	(3.45)	(2.68)
(S.F. Avg.)		1.30	2.15	1.72
(Stan. Avg.)		2.04	3.37	2.71
(Avg.)		(1.67)	(2.76)	(2.21)

Table 4a.   Average per cent of terminal coalitions having A as a member

Impor.	School	Peer	Non-Peer	Avg.
High	S.F.	36	46	41
	Stan.	57	64	60
	(Avg.)	(46)	(55)	(50)
Low	S.F.	43	64	54
	Stan.	61	86	74
	(Avg.)	(52)	(75)	(64)
(S.F. Avg.)		40	55	48
(Stan. Avg.)		59	75	67
(Avg.)		(50)	(65)	(58)

Table 3b.   Analysis of average points per trial for A

Source	d.f.	Variance	P
Importance	1	200.65	<.02
Peer vs. Non-Peer	1	274.57	<.01
Schools	1	208.28	<.01
Interactions	4	39.25	
Error	48	24.89	

Table 4b.   Analysis of average number of coalitions having A as a member

Source	d.f.	Variance	P
Importance	1	4.57	<.05
Peer Cond.	1	5.78	<.05
Schools	1	5.78	<.05
Interactions	4	0.18	
Error	48	1.01	

Table 5.   Average points per coalition earned by A

Motiv.	School	Peer	Non-Peer	Avg.
High	S.F.	3.60*	3.58**	3.59
	Stan.	3.19	3.77	3.48
	Avg.	(3.36)	(3.68)	(3.53)
Low	S.F.	3.12*	4.00	3.63
	Stan.	4.15**	5.16	4.69
	Avg.	(3.68)	(4.57)	(4.18)
S.F.	Avg.	3.36	3.81	3.61
Stan.	Avg.	3.63	4.46	4.06
		(3.51)	(4.15)	(3.86)

* Mean based on 5 groups.
** Mean based on 6 groups.
Those groups in which A never succeeded in entering a coalition had to be omitted from the analysis.

bined, A is able to form fewer terminal coalitions than would be expected on the basis of chance (P < .01), and therefore fewer than the average of the two subjects. Differences for each of the experimental conditions are significant at the five per cent level and are in the expected direction.

The influence of the second factor is shown in *Table 5* where the average number of points per coalition obtained by A when A is in a coalition is tabulated. This analysis shows whether or not A is able to obtain a fair share of the points when he is one of the partners in a coalition. It is apparent from the table that the differences between means are once more in the anticipated directions. The differences between the peer and non-peer conditions and between the high and low importance conditions are only significant at the ten per cent level of confidence.[1]

The results of these three analyses are consistent in indicating that coalitions tend to form in opposition to the player who obtains an initial advantage. The strength of this tendency is greatest when the task is of high importance to the members of the group and

---

[1] An analysis of co-variance on average points per trial earned by A adjusted for differences in number of coalitions of which A was a member yields the same conclusions.

when they perceive each other as peers or equals. As a result of this tendency, the paid-participant is unable to form his fair share of terminal coalitions and must pay more than a fair share of the points in order to form such coalitions.

One additional analysis of the terminal coalition data was made to check on the validity of a deduction which was made from the theoretical formulation of this experiment. We would expect that in the peer situation B and C would be competing primarily with A and not with each other. We should then find coalitions between B and C took the form of an even division of the points. Conversely, under non-peer conditions, B and C would be competing primarily with each other, since A would be regarded as noncomparable by both of them. As a result, terminal coalitions involving B and C would tend to take the form of an uneven division of the points. An analysis of the types of terminal coalitions involving B and C supports this deduction. Under peer conditions 63 per cent of such coalitions involved an equal split, but under non-peer conditions only 34 per cent of them did so, a difference significant beyond the .05 level. Thus, comparability of A to the other members in the group, induced by the peer conditions, makes a coalition involving an even split a desirable and stable outcome for the two subjects. Conversely, when A is incomparable, the competition between B and C makes the desirable outcome, for either one, an agreement which gives him more than the opposing subject.

Another indication of the opposition to A is shown by an analysis of the temporary coalitions, that is, those coalitions tentatively agreed to during the bargaining process. One measure of these is the number of excess points A must pay in order to break up an existing coalition between B and C. A discrepancy score was computed for all temporary coalitions in which A was not a member. This score is the difference between what the coalition subject was receiving in the coalition and what he accepted from A in breaking up the coalition. If the subject refused all offers from A then the discrepancy

Table 6a. Average discrepancy paid to break B-C coalition

Impor.	School	Peer	Non-Peer	Total
High	S.F.	2.2	2.0	2.1
	Stan.	3.4	2.2	2.8
	(Avg.)	(2.8)	(2.1)	(2.5)
Low	S.F.	2.4	1.8	2.1
	Stan.	1.6	1.2	1.4
	(Avg.)	(2.0)	(1.5)	(1.8)
(S.F. Avg.)		2.3	1.9	2.1
(Stan. Avg.)		2.5	1.7	2.1
(Avg.)		(2.4)	(1.8)	(2.1)

Table 6b. Analysis of discrepancy paid to break B-C coalition

Source	d.f.	Variance	Est. P
Impor.	1	841.1	<.05
Peer Cond.	1	841.1	<.05
Schools	1	1.4	
Impor. schools	1	970.9	<.05
Inter.	3	14.1	
Error	48	164.1	

was calculated as if the subject had accepted an offer of 9 points, one more than the total number available. The average of these for each experimental condition is shown in *Table 6*. The results follow the expected pattern. A must offer more points when the task is of high importance than when it is of low importance, and must offer more under peer conditions than under non-peer. The significant interaction between Importance and Schools is due to the fact that in the San Francisco data there are no differences between the High and Low Importance conditions while in the Stanford data these differences are large.

DISCUSSION

The theory which forms the basis for this experiment hypothesizes that competition arises because individuals, in situations where they are evaluating some ability, are strongly motivated by a concern about their comparability to other members of the group

with respect to the ability which they are evaluating. This concern over comparability leads to attempts to assess the abilities of others in relation to themselves. But an individual is not concerned over the comparability of all individuals. Rather, he tends to exclude those who are perceived as definitely superior or inferior to himself in this activity and to concentrate on those who are perceived as being within the same general range of ability.

To the extent that concern over comparability is present, discrepancies in points or other symbols come to have relative rather than absolute value. They tend to be interpreted primarily as indicators of the individual's status with respect to the other members rather than as something of direct utilitarian value. This is especially true when the points gained represent intellectual, athletic, or social ability, but it is also probably true to a large extent when they represent money or commodities. As a result, whenever the task is made more important to an individual, the value of these points increases. This, in turn, adds to his concern over comparability to others and also to his motivation to surpass them on the task.

It follows from these assumptions that in a bargaining situation where all group members regard one another as comparable, stable coalitions will form in opposition to any member of the group who gains an advantage. The point advantage held by this member of the group is interpreted by the other group members as a loss in status to them, and they are consequently motivated to overcome it. Coalitions between them satisfy the motivations of both to retain comparability with each other while at the same time reducing the discrepancy between them and the individual with the initial advantage. The individual with the advantage in points cannot offer this type of satisfaction. He will be compelled to offer excessive points commensurate with the status differential which exists in order to form a coalition. On the other hand, if this advantage is held by an individual regarded by the other two as noncomparable, coalitions in opposition to him will have less tendency to form, for his point advantage represents a smaller loss of status. Non-peer conditions would therefore be expected to be more favorable for a person with an initial advantage than would peer conditions.

It similarly would be predicted that the formation of stable coalitions will be even more prominent as the importance of the task is increased. This follows from the assumption that any increase in the importance of the symbols involved strengthens the motivation to achieve comparability in the group. Thus, conditions of high task importance will be less favorable to the person with an initial advantage than will conditions of low importance.

The results of the experiment strongly support this general formulation of the motivations involved in bargaining behavior. This is shown clearly in the evidence that a group member receiving an initial advantage in points is generally discriminated against throughout the remaining trials. It is reflected in the inability of the paid-participant to enter into the expected number of terminal coalitions, in the relatively high price he is required to pay in order to enter such coalitions, and in discriminatory bargaining in opposition to him as shown in the within-trials analyses.

The evidence indicates that the strength of this opposition is a direct function of task importance and of the degree of comparability between the group members. Such an interpretation is strengthened by evidence from the questionnaire that the conditions of the experiment were successfully manipulated.

Differences between the two conditions of importance in the experiment are reliable and consistent in the analyses involving terminal coalitions, and in the intra-trial analysis of the excess of points required to break up a coalition between the two subjects. In each of these cases the bargaining was shown to be more favorable to the paid-participant under conditions of low importance than when importance was high.

The effects of the peer and non-peer conditions are similarly in substantial accord with the predictions. Under peer conditions the paid-participant is less able to obtain points, less successful in entering into terminal coalitions, and he is required to pay a higher price in order to do so than under non-peer conditions. This influence of peer relations is shown also by the excess of points which A is forced to pay in order to break up an existing coalition.

It appears then that a large initial advantage in points results in an intensification of competition against the paid-participant when that individual is regarded as comparable in ability. If the individual involved is regarded as non-comparable, the competition persists among the remaining group members, but the discrepant individual gains additional advantage by becoming the medium by which changes in status can be accomplished between the others. Support for this latter statement comes from two sources: 1. examination of the relative frequencies of occurrence of even and uneven point distributions in terminal coalitions involving B and C show that these tend to be formed with equal division of the points under peer conditions, but that under non-peer conditions such coalitions involve mainly inequitable distributions, and 2. an examination of the low importance, non-peer condition indicates that the paid-participant was able to obtain a significantly larger number of points than the average of the two subjects (Table 3).

Insofar as the findings in this experiment have generality, they have implications for two fields of inquiry, that of game theory and that of motivational theory, especially as each applies to social situations. Game theory specifies that the choices between alternative strategies or courses of action should be chosen in such a way as to maximize utility.

The present study suggests that the nature of the utility function for individuals is not necessarily invariant, but is subject to modification from the effects of situational variables which may differ greatly from one context to the next. Consequently, these results indicate that motivational factors such as those suggested in the present experiment need to be included in formulations relating utility to external or behavioral reference points.

The findings are more directly relevant

to theories of social motivation and perception, especially as these pertain to behavior in groups. The suggestion is that an important determinant of behavior in group situations where all members are engaged in a common activity is the concern of each member about his status relative to others on that activity. This is especially true in activities where there is no clear cut criterion available for individuals evaluating the adequacy of their performance. Consequently when a discrepancy between their own standing and that of others is perceived, individuals are motivated to reduce that discrepancy. This motivation will manifest itself in a variety of ways, one of which is to form coalitions in opposition to any other member having a higher status on this task.

Assuming that this formulation has generality, it gives rise to two important theoretical problems. The results of this experiment have shown that the strength of the motivational factors involved depends in part upon the importance of the task to the individuals involved and in part on the degree of comparability between the group members. Consequently, it becomes necessary to formulate the conditions that determine whether or not a given task will be accepted as important by a given individual, and the factors controlling his acceptance or rejection of other individuals as a standard against which to evaluate his own performance. These factors undoubtedly include cultural and social variables as well as those unique to the past history of the given individual.

SUMMARY

The present experiment on competitive bargaining behavior in a group situation utilized 56 groups, each composed of two subjects and a paid-participant. The experimental variables were: 1. the importance of the task for the individuals involved, and 2. the degree of comparability between group members (peer versus non-peer conditions). Subjects were assigned to one of four experimental conditions as follows: 1. high task importance, peer relations, 2. high task importance, non-peer relations, 3. low task importance, peer relations, and 4. low task importance, non-peer relations.

The experiment was designed so that the three group members were competing among themselves for points, but the formation of a coalition between two of them was necessary in order for points to be earned. The procedures used ensured that the paid-participant always obtained a large initial advantage. The rules governing the formation of coalitions specified that any agreements could be broken by either member of the coalition if he desired to enter a coalition with the third member. This made possible a continuous sequence of bargaining between the three members until the conclusion of the trial.

The results of the experiment were as follows:

1. The group member receiving a large initial advantage in points received significantly fewer opportunities to form coalitions than did the other group members, and was required to pay a relatively higher price in order to do so.

2. The reduction in opportunity to form coalitions and the commensurate increase in price demanded of the person receiving a large initial advantage in points were more pronounced under conditions of high task importance than under conditions of low importance.

3. The reduction in opportunity to form coalitions and the corresponding increase in price demanded of the person receiving a large initial advantage in points were more evident under peer conditions than under non-peer conditions.

4. The results summarized in the three preceding paragraphs were reflected not only in the formation of terminal coalitions and the distribution of points therein, but also in the pattern of bargaining which occurred within trials.

References

Festinger, L.   "Informal Social Communication," *Psychological Review*, 1950, 57, 271–282.

————. "A Theory of Social Comparison Processes," *Human Relations*, 1954, 7, 2.

Von Neumann, J., and Morgenstern, O.   *Theory of Games and Economic Behavior.*   Princeton: Princeton University Press, 1944 (2nd ed., 1947).

HUSBAND-WIFE INTERACTION OVER REVEALED DIFFERENCES

Fred L. Strodtbeck

In the course of a series of pilot studies of power, or influence, in small group situations the writer has developed a procedure, called the revealed difference technique, which has shown promise in a first application to husband-wife interaction. In the attempt to validate the results obtained by this technique, use has been made of similar groups in different cultures. The following paper is organized in a form to emphasize how this methodological innovation and the technique itself grew from successive sequences in which pilot findings led to further research operations.

BACKGROUND

During 1948–49 the writer observed a series of groups engaged in decision-making.

Source: F. L. Strodtbeck, "Husband-wife Interaction over Revealed Differences," *American Sociological Review*, Vol. 16, 1951, pp. 468–473. Copyright 1951 by The American Sociological Association and reprinted by permission of publisher and author.

An effort was made to determine some of the correlates of differential ability to persuade others in accordance with the actor's desires. In one instance, four mathematics students were requested to recommend jointly the best of three possible solutions to particular problems. While these students were in the process of developing consensus they were asked to record privately the alternative they personally favored. Thus, the experimenter was provided with a continuous means of relating a type of private opinion to public behavior. The experimentation indicated that the ultimate decision could be most accurately predicted by simply weighting the privately pre-determined opinion of each participant by the total time he had spoken during the experimental interaction. This finding was duplicated in various groups who worked at the task of jointly selecting the best move in a chess problem. This simple answer did little, however, to recapture the subtlety and complexity of social interaction as it is generally understood.

We recognized that we had up to this time worked with *ad hoc* groups which had no group structure at the beginning of the observation period and no expectation of participating with one another at a later time. The problems they had considered were delimited and specific; the nature of their arguments and responses was highly structured. On the basis of this analysis, we were led to consider experimentation with groups whose members approached the opposite extreme of broad common interests, daily contact, and permanence—so-called primary groups.

Among the various types of primary groups that might profitably be studied, husband-wife dyads were selected because of the ease of replication of these units. Each couple was asked to pick three reference families with whom they were well acquainted. The husband and wife were then separated and requested to designate which of the three reference families most satisfactorily fulfilled a series of 26 conditions such as: Which family has the happiest children? Which family is the most religious? Which family is most ambitious? After both husband and wife had individually marked their choices they were requested to reconcile their differences and indicate a final "best" choice from the standpoint of their family. For the first ten couples studied, this pooling took place with the experimenter out of the room and under conditions such that the couple did not know they were being observed or having their voices recorded. Their lack of knowledge of the observation was ascertained after the session, at which time their permission to use the material in a scientific inquiry was obtained.[1] The anticipated experimental difficulties—(a) producing "polite" interaction because of the intrusion of the experimenter, and (b) structuring the task to such a degree that the mode of interaction would be highly determined—were judged to have been satisfactorily avoided.

Omitting, for present purposes, a discussion of the content of the recorded protocols, it was found that women won 47 of the

contested decisions and men, 36. In six of the eight cases in which there was a difference both in number of decisions-won and in talking-time, the spouse who talked most won the majority of the decisions. At this time there was no basis for appraising whether the women had won slightly more decisions because they had known more about the types of information under discussion, or whether the decision winning represented, as we had hoped, the operation of structured power relations in an area in which both participants were equally informed. The observed margin by which the women exceeded the men was not significant—a result which might have been much more valuable if we had predicted it in terms of independent knowledge of the equalitarian characteristics of the married veteran couples used in the sample. In short, further application was necessary to determine whether the technique was a valid method of indicating in any more general sense the balance of power between participants.

A field study was designed to throw further light on this problem. Three communities were selected which presumably differed in terms of the degree to which the wife was favored by the cultural phrasing of power. The communities were at the same time sufficiently small to increase greatly the probability that both spouses would be adequately, if not equally, informed concerning the behavior of the reference couples. The technique as described above was applied to ten couples from each of these cultures. It was proposed that the conformity of the experimental results with the a priori cultural expectations be taken as a crude measure of the validity with which the technique reflected power differences.

DESCRIPTION OF CULTURES

The cultures which were selected for study are geographically adjacent communities in the Arizona-New Mexico area. Briefly described, the groups are Navaho Indians; dry farmers from Texas who have recently

---

[1] Ursula Marsh, Donald Michael, Theodore M. Mills, and Herbert Shepard were joint participants in this phase of the research.

homesteaded in the area; and early settlers who utilize a dam operated under the supervision of the Mormon church. These communities will be described in detail in forthcoming publications of the Comparative Study of Values Project.[2] For present purposes the communities will be designated Navaho, Texan, and Mormon. A brief recapitulation of power attributes of the culturally legitimized role of women in each culture is presented below.

The young Navaho man, who marries a girl from a moderately successful family, typically leaves his own family and resides with the girl's family and works under her father's direction until he has established himself as a responsible person. When this change of residence is made, the man leaves his sheep with his own family of orientation and his work activities result in little immediate increase in his own holdings. The children are considered a part of the wife's consanguine group, and marriages are generally unstable. Both men and women own sheep, but the women do the processing of wool into rugs and blankets. This assures the women a regular income throughout the year. The man has greater earning power when he performs wage work, but the wage work opportunities are scarce and seasonal. The man is considered the head of the household, but the relative economic independence of the wife and her close integration with her own consanguine group effectively limit his exercise of power. All but one of the ten Navaho couples studied maintained Navaho religious practices, the one exception was a recent convert to a fundamentalist church now proselytizing in the area.

The Texan group is composed of migrants who came from Eastern Texas during the drought and depression of the early 1930's. With minor exceptions the households are farms on contiguous sections headed by persons who as young adults made the earlier move, or by their older children who have more recently married. Due to the short growing season and lack of rainfall, the cultivation of pinto beans has developed into the major cash crop. The ten couples who participated in this study were members of the ranking Presbyterian clique in the community.[3]

The ten couples selected for study in the Mormon village were chosen from the most active participants in the affairs of the local church. Religious teachings which exercise a pervasive effect upon local social organization specifically stress the role of the husband as the head of the family. The position of the church is stated in different ways in quotations similar to the following:[4]

There must be a presiding authority in the family. The father is the head, or president, or spokesman of the family. This arrangement is of divine origin. It also conforms to the physical and physiological laws under which humanity lives. A home, as viewed by the Church, is composed of a family group, so organized as to be presided over by the father, under the authority and in the spirit of the priesthood conferred upon him.

This patriarchal order has its divine spirit and purpose, and those who disregard it under one pretext or another are out of harmony with the spirit of God's laws as they are ordained for recognition in the home. It it is not merely a question of who is perhaps best qualified. Neither is it wholly a question of who is living the most worthy life. It is a question largely of law and order, and its importance is seen often from the fact that authority remains and is respected long after a man is really unworthy to exercise it.[5]

[2] Clyde Kluckhohn gives a brief description of the Navaho studies which are now considered a part of this project in the introduction to A. H. and D. C. Leighton, *Gregorio, the Hand Trembler*, Papers to the Peabody Museum, Cambridge, Mass., 1949.

[3] A forthcoming publication by Evon Z. Vogt will describe the social organization of this community in detail.
[4] John A. Widtsoe, *Priesthood and Church Government*, Salt Lake City, 1939, p. 81.
[5] Joseph F. Smith, *Gospel Doctrine*, Salt Lake City, 1929, p. 359.

Corresponding prescriptions for the wife's role emphasize that she should above all else be a mother, for "motherhood is the noblest, most soul-satisfying of all earthly experiences." Mormonism has a this-worldly orientation, divine grace is attained through effort, and the symbol of progress is the advancement the man makes in the priesthood and in extending his flocks and fields. The woman is not eligible for membership in the priesthood and her status is coupled with that of her husband both in her present life and in the next, by the regular Temple marriage. From the incomplete evidence now available, Mormon women of this community do not appear to have important landholdings nor independent sources of income, and accounts of women's participation in church activities confirm the correspondence of women's current attitudes with the church writings quoted above. The historic emphasis by Brigham Young and others on woman's education and political participation was always hedged by the general reservation that motherhood should not be interfered with—the women of the community in question strongly emphasize this reservation.

In Navaho mythology and folklore the actions imputed to women contrast sharply with the emphasis of Mormon theology. For the Navaho the women become major charismatic figures.[6] Marriage customs are also consistent with this conception of the Navaho woman as an active and demanding person. On the morning after a Navaho wedding the groom runs a foot race with his bride. The cultural interpretation is that "the one who wins will become rich."[7] This practice is quite different from the familiar custom in which the bride is passively carried over the threshold, and it is also a commentary on the independence of the economic fortunes of Navaho marriage-mates.

In summary, the favored position of the Navaho woman in contrast to the Mormon woman was judged in terms of economic, religious, and kinship considerations to be quite unequivocal. Between Texan and Mormon women there is less difference, but in terms of holding church office and the present possession of productive land and semi-professional jobs, the women in the Texan community appear to be more favored than the Mormon women. On the basis of this analysis it was predicted that Navaho women would win the highest percentage of the decisions and the Mormon women the smallest.

EXPERIMENTAL PROCEDURE

The area under study had no electrification, and since it was impractical to attempt to bring the subjects to an observation room, the field sessions of the experimental procedure were recorded by portable sound equipment powered from a truck. Although the subjects were separated from the experimenter and other persons, they knew that their voices were being recorded. The task was explained to the Navahos by an interpreter. An appropriate picture was presented for each question and underneath the illustration there were pockets representing the three reference couples. The Navaho would place his marker in the pocket which represented the couple of his choice. In those instances in which there had been a difference between the choice of the man and wife, the illustration was presented again to the two of them with their markers in separate pockets. They were requested to combine their markers in the position which best represented their joint opinion. Some questions were changed somewhat by translation into Navaho; for example, the question, "Which family is the most religious?" became "Which family follows the 'Navaho Way' best?" It was not felt that these changes would significantly modify the results here presented. These recordings

---

[6] These include Changing Woman, Spider Woman and Salt Woman. Blessing Way, the most frequently repeated ceremonial, stresses that each of the four poles of the hogan represent still different female divinities. Kluckhohn and Leighton comment that this practice "speaks volumes for the high place of women in the traditional conceptions." *The Navaho*, Cambridge: Harvard University Press, 1947, p. 56.

[7] Gladys A. Reichard, *Social Life of the Navaho Indians*, New York: Columbia University Press, 1928, p. 141.

were transcribed and, in the case of the Navaho, translated into English.

The written protocols were analyzed to determine the number of acts used by each participant and the distribution of these acts in terms of interaction process categories.[8] This information plus knowledge of the number of decisions won by each participant provides the basis for the analysis presented below.

FINDINGS

We present in Table 1 the sum of the decisions won by the husbands and wives in each of the three cultures. The appropriate null hypothesis is compounded of two elements: (a) the proposition that the Mormon wives win an equal or greater number of decisions than their husbands ($p = .007$); and (b) the proposition that Navaho husbands win an equal or greater number of decisions than their wives ($p = .16$). Since the combined probability associated with these two propositions is less than .01, we reject the null hypothesis and conclude that we were able to predict the balance of decision-winning from our study of the comparative social and cultural organization of the groups from which our sample was drawn.

Having to this limited degree established the validity of the technique, we are encouraged to inquire further into elements of behavior in the small group situation which are linked with decision-winning. Our earlier experience had indicated a very strong relationship between decision-winning, or leadership, and talking-time in *ad hoc* groups of four persons.[9] In the present instance

Table 1. Decisions won, by spouse and culture

Culture	Number of Couples	Decisions Won By:	
		Husband	Wife
Navaho	10	34	46
Texan	10	39	33
Mormon	10	42	29

two-person primary groups are involved. From a broader study of the rank characteristics of participants in groups ranging in size from two to ten persons it is known that differentiation in speaking-time in two-person groups is relatively less than it is in larger groups, hence it is probable that the relation between speaking-time and decision-winning is less clearly defined in two-person than in larger groups.[10] There was no compelling rationale for predicting the effects of the primary relationships upon "speaking and decision-winning." By combining the ten cases observed at Cambridge with the thirty cases from the field and eliminating the six cases in which the decisions were split evenly, we obtain the thirty-four cases compared in Table 2. The null hypothesis of independence between talking most and winning may be rejected at the .05 but not the .01 level.

To approach a more systematic description of the interaction characteristics of the spouse who talks most, we have selected the 24 cases in which there was a significant difference between the number of acts originated by the husband and the wife. We find that the most talking spouse tended more frequently to *ask questions*, carry out *opinion and analysis*, and make *rewarding remarks*. As Simmel suggested, in a dyad there can be no coalitions—the speaker does not have alternative audiences, so the "threat of withdrawal" is generally a more compelling adjustmental device in two-person than in larger groups. While we do not as yet have norms by group size for category usage on a common task, the unexpected finding in the present

---

[8] For a description of the categories used see Robert F. Bales, "The Analysis of Small Group Interaction," *American Sociological Review*, 15 (April 1950), 257–264.

[9] Bass reports a correlation of .93 between the time a participant in an eight-man group spent talking and the votes he received from observers for having demonstrated leadership. See Bernard M. Bass, "An Analysis of Leaderless Group Discussion," *Journal of Applied Psychology*, 33 (1949), 527–533.

---

[10] See Robert F. Bales, Fred L. Strodtbeck, Theodore M. Mills, and Mary E. Roseborough, "Channels of Communication in Small Group Interaction," *American Sociological Review*, 16 (August 1951), 461–468.

Table 2. Decisions won and talking-time for 34 married couples

Spouse Who Talked Most	Spouse Who Won Most	
	Husband	Wife
Husband	14	5
Wife	5	10

study that the most active participant is significantly high in question-asking gives us further insight into how withdrawal is anticipated and prevented. The finding that the frequency of opinion and analysis acts is higher for the most talking person is in agreement with Bales' notion that acts of this type have a central generative function which results in their being heavily represented in the profile of the most talking person in groups of any size.

The categories which discriminate the profile of the least talking participants are, in order of magnitude, the following: simple *acts of agreement, aggressive acts* designed to deflate the other actor's status, and simple *disagreements.* Taken together, these characteristics suggest the passive agreeing person who from time to time becomes frustrated and aggresses.

Concerning cultural differences in category usage, the Navahos gave *opinion, evaluation,* and *analysis* acts during the solution of their differences only one-half as frequently as the Mormon and the Texan group. As a result they required on the average fewer acts per decision (8 in contrast with 30 for the other groups) and the reasoning and persuasion in their protocols seemed extremely sketchy. They did not emphasize the arguments that might bear upon the issue, they tended to reiterate their choices and implore the other person to "go with them"; "go together," or simply consent. This is in marked contrast with the other couples who appeared to feel that they had

to give a reasoned argument to show that they were logically convinced, even when they were giving in to the other person. It is a matter for further research to determine if other "traditional" people show a similar tendency to minimize analysis in social problem solving.

For the Texans it was a rational exercise, sometimes directly commented upon, to see that the decisions came out even, the standard deviation between spouses in decisions won was only 1.3. The Mormons were less concerned with equality, the comparable figure is 2.1, and among the Navaho there were marked differences between spouses, the standard deviation being 5.1. An analysis of the way in which couples tended to go from orientation acts to evaluative acts before making suggestions for a final disposition of the difference, the so-called phases in interaction, will be presented in a later paper.

SUMMARY

The essence of the revealed difference technique here described consists of: (a) requesting subjects who have shared experiences to make individual evaluations of them; and then, (b) requesting the subjects to reconcile any differences in interpretations which may have occurred. It has been shown that the disposition of these reconciled decisions is related both to power elements in the larger social and cultural organization and amount of participation in the small group situation. It is believed that other couples as well as parent-child, foreman-worker, and similar relationships may be profitably studied with the technique, since it appears not only to reveal the balance of power, but also to produce a sample of interaction in which modes and techniques of influence can be studied by methods of content and process analysis.

THE SCOPE AND BIAS OF THE PRESSURE SYSTEM

E. E. Schattschneider

The scope of conflict is an aspect of the scale of political organization and the extent of political competition. The size of the constituencies being mobilized, the inclusiveness or exclusiveness of the conflicts people expect to develop have a bearing on all theories about how politics is or should be organized. In other words, nearly all theories about politics have something to do with the question of who can get into the fight and who is to be excluded.

Every regime is a testing ground for theories of this sort. More than any other system American politics provides the raw materials for testing the organizational assumptions of two contrasting kinds of politics, *pressure politics* and *party politics*.[1] The concepts that underlie these forms of politics constitute the raw stuff of a general theory of political action. The basic issue between the two patterns of organization is one of size and scope of conflict; pressure groups are small-scale organizations while political parties are very large-scale organizations. One need not be surprised, therefore, that the partisans of large-scale and small-scale organizations differ passionately, because the outcome of the political game depends on the scale on which it is played.

To understand the controversy about the scale of political organization it is necessary first to take a look at some theories about

interest-group politics. Pressure groups have played a remarkable role in American politics, but they have played an even more remarkable role in American political theory. Considering the political condition of the country in the first third of the twentieth century, it was probably inevitable that the discussion of special interest pressure groups should lead to development of "group" theories of politics in which an attempt is made to explain everything in terms of group activity, i.e., an attempt to formulate a universal group theory. Since one of the best ways to test an idea is to ride it into the ground, political theory has unquestionably been improved by the heroic attempt to create a political universe revolving about the group. Now that we have a number of drastic statements of the group theory of politics pushed to a great extreme, we ought to be able to see what the limitations of the idea are.

Political conditions in the first third of the present century were extremely hospitable to the idea. The role of business in the strongly sectional Republican system from 1896 to 1932 made the dictatorship of business seem to be a part of the eternal order of things. Moreover, the regime as a whole seemed to be so stable that questions about the survival of the American community did not arise. The general interests of the community were easily overlooked under these circumstances.

Nevertheless, in spite of the excellent and provocative scholarly work done by Beard, Latham, Truman, Leiserson, Dahl, Lindbloom, Laski and others, the group theory of politics is beset with difficulties. The difficulties are theoretical, growing in part out of sheer overstatements of the idea and in part out of some confusion about the nature of modern government.

One difficulty running through the literature of the subject results from the attempt

Source: From *The Semisovereign People: A Realist's View of Democracy in America* by E. E. Schattschneider. Copyright 1960 by E. E. Schattschneider. Reprinted by permission of Holt, Rinehart and Winston, Inc.

[1] Pressure groups have been defined by V. O. Key as "private associations . . . (which) promote their interests by attempting to influence government rather than by nominating candidates and seeking responsibility for the management of government," *Politics, Parties, and Pressure Groups*, 4th ed., New York, 1958, p. 23.

to explain *everything* in terms of the group theory.[2] On general grounds it would be remarkable indeed if a single hypothesis explained everything about so complex a subject as American politics. Other difficulties have grown out of the fact that group concepts have been stated in terms so universal that the subject seems to have no shape or form.

The question is: Are pressure groups the universal basic ingredient of all political situations, and do they explain everything? To answer this question it is necessary to review a bit of rudimentary political theory.

Two modest reservations might be made merely to test the group dogma. We might clarify our ideas if (1) we explore more fully the possibility of making a distinction between public interest groups and special-interest groups and (2) if we distinguished between organized and unorganized groups. These reservations do not disturb the main body of group theory, but they may be useful when we attempt to define general propositions more precisely. If both of these distinctions can be validated, we may get hold of something that has scope and limits and is capable of being defined. The awkwardness of a discussion of political phenomena in terms of universals is that the subject has no beginning or end; it is impossible to distinguish one subject from another or to detect the bias of the forces involved because scope and bias are aspects of the limitations of the subject. It cannot really be said that we have seen a subject until we have seen its outer limits and thus are able to draw a line between one subject and another.

We might begin to break the problem into its component parts by exploring the distinction between public and private in-terests.[3] If we can validate this distinction, we shall have established one of the boundaries of the subject.

As a matter of fact, the distinction between *public* and *private* interests is a thoroughly respectable one; it is one of the oldest known to political theory. In the literature of the subject the public interest refers to general or common interests shared by all or by substantially all members of the community.[4] Presumably no community exists unless there is some kind of community of interests, just as there is no nation without some notion of national interests. If it is really impossible to distinguish between private and public interests the group theorists have produced a revolution in political thought so great that it is impossible to foresee its consequences. For this reason the distinction ought to be explored with great care.

At a time when nationalism is described as one of the most dynamic forces in the world, it should not be difficult to understand that national interests actually do exist.[5] It

---

[2] Earl Latham, *The Group Basis of Politics*, Ithaca, 1952, pp. 35 and 36, says, "The legislature referees the group struggle, ratifies the victories of the successful coalitions, and records the terms of the surrenders, compromises, and conquests in the form of statutes. . . . "the legislative vote which on any issue tends to represent the composition of strength, i.e., the balance of power, among the contending groups at the moment of voting."

[3] The discussion here refers generally to the analysis made by David Truman in his distinguished volume *The Government Process*, New York, 1951. See especially pp. 50–51, 65.

[4] References to the public interest appear under a variety of headings in the literature of political theory.

See G. D. H. Cole's comment on "the will of all" and the "general will," pp. XXX and XXXI of his introduction to Everyman's edition of Rousseau's *Social Contract*, London, 1913.

See Ernst Cassirer, *The Myth of the State*, Garden City, 1955, pp. 88–93, for a discussion of Plato's concept of "justice" as the end of the state in his criticism of the sophists.

See S. D. Lindsay, *The Essentials of Democracy*, Philadelphia, 1929, p. 49 for a statement regarding consensus.

[5] It does not seem necessary to argue that nationalism and national interests are forces in the modern world. E. H. Carr writes about "the catastrophic growth of nationalism" in *Nationalism and After*, New York, 1945, p. 18. D. W. Brogan describes nations as "the only communities that now exist," *The American Character*, New York, 1944, p. 169. "The outstanding and distinctive characteristic of the people of the Western States System is their devotion and allegiance to the 'nations' into which they have got themselves

is necessary only to consider the proportion of the American budget devoted to national defense to realize that the common interest in national survival is a great one. Measured in dollars this interest is one of the biggest things in the world. Moreover, it is difficult to describe this interest as special. The diet on which the American leviathan feeds is something more than a jungle of disparate special interests. In the literature of democratic theory the body of common agreement found in the community is known as the "consensus" without which it is believed that no democratic system can survive.

The reality of the common interest is suggested by demonstrated capacity of the community to survive. There must be something that holds people together.

In contrast with the common interests are the special interests. The implication of this term is that these are interests shared by only a few people or a fraction of the community; they *exclude* others and may be *adverse* to them. A special interest is exclusive in about the same way as private property is exclusive. In a complex society it is not surprising that there are some interests that are shared by all or substantially all members of the community and some interests that are not shared so widely. The distinction is useful precisely because conflicting claims are made by people about the nature of their interests in controversial matters.

Perfect agreement within the community is not always possible, but an interest may

divided," Frederick L. Schumann, *International Politics*, 3rd ed., New York, 1941, p. 300. A. D. Lindsay in *The Essentials of Democracy*, Philadelphia, 1929, p. 49, has stated the doctrine of the democratic consensus as follows: "Nationality, however produced, is a sense of belonging together, involving a readiness on the part of the members of a state to subordinate their differences to it. It involves something more. It has a connection with the notion of a distinctive culture—some sort of rough ideal of the kind of common life for which the community stands, which always exists in people's minds as a rough criticism by which political proposals are to be judged. This at least is clear, that where such common understanding and sense of belonging together either does not exist or is overshadowed by other differences, successful democracy is not really possible."

be said to have become public when it is shared so widely as to be substantially universal. Thus the difference between 99 per cent agreement and perfect agreement is not so great that it becomes necessary to argue that all interests are special, that the interests of the 99 per cent are as special as the interests of the 1 per cent. For example, the law is probably doing an adequate job of defining the public interest in domestic tranquility despite the fact that there is nearly always one dissenter at every hanging. That is, the law defines the public interest in spite of the fact that there may be some outlaws.

Since one function of theory is to explain reality, it is reasonable to add that it is a good deal easier to explain what is going on in politics by making a distinction between public and private interests than it is to attempt to explain *everything* in terms of special interests. The attempt to prove that all interests are special forces us into circumlocutions such as those involved in the argument that people have special interests in the common good. The argument can be made, but it seems a long way around to avoid a useful distinction.

What is to be said about the argument that the distinction between public and special interests is "subjective" and is therefore "unscientific"?

All discussion of interests, special as well as general, refers to the motives, desires and intentions of people. In this sense the whole discussion of interests is subjective. We have made progress in the study of politics because people have observed some kind of relation between the political behavior of people and certain wholly impersonal data concerning their ownership of property, income, economic status, professions and the like. All that we know about interests, private as well as public, is based on inferences of this sort. Whether the distinction in any given case is valid depends on the evidence and on the kinds of inferences drawn from the evidence.

The only meaningful way we can speak of the interests of an association like the National Association of Manufacturers is to draw inferences from the fact that the membership is a select group to which only manufacturers may belong and to try to relate that datum to what the association does. The implications, logic and deductions are persuasive only if they furnish reasonable explanations of the facts. That is all that any theory about interests can do. It has seemed persuasive to students of politics to suppose that manufacturers do not join an association to which only manufacturers may belong merely to promote philanthropic or cultural or religious interests, for example. The basis of selection of the membership creates an inference about the organization's concerns. The conclusions drawn from this datum seem to fit what we know about the policies promoted by the association; that is, the policies seem to reflect the exclusive interests of manufacturers. The method is not foolproof, but it works better than many other kinds of analysis and is useful precisely because special-interest groups often tend to rationalize their special interests as public interests.

Is it possible to distinguish between the "interests" of the members of the National Association of Manufacturers and the members of the American League to Abolish Capital Punishment? The facts in the two cases are not identical. First, *the members of the A.L.A.C.P. obviously do not expect to be hanged.* The membership of the A.L.A.C.P. is not restricted to persons under indictment for murder or in jeopardy of the extreme penalty. *Anybody* can join A.L.A.C.P. Its members oppose capital punishment although they are not personally likely to benefit by the policy they advocate. The inference is therefore that the interest of the A.L.A.C.P. is not adverse, exclusive or special. It is not like the interest of the Petroleum Institute in depletion allowances.

Take some other cases. The members of the National Child Labor Committee are not children in need of legislative protection against exploitation by employers. The members of the World Peace Foundation apparently want peace, but in the nature of things they must want peace for everyone because no group can be at peace while the rest of the community is at war. Similarly,

even if the members of the National Defense League wanted defense only for themselves they would necessarily have to work for defense for the whole country because national security is indivisible. Only a naïve person is likely to imagine that the political involvements of the members of the American Bankers Association and members of the Foreign Policy Association are identical. In other words, we may draw inferences from the exclusive or the nonexclusive nature of benefits sought by organizations as well as we can from the composition of groups. The positions of these groups can be distinguished not on the basis of some subjective process, but by making reasonable inferences from verifiable facts.

On the other hand, because some special-interest groups attempt to identify themselves with the public interest it does not follow that the whole idea of the public interest is a fraud. Mr. Wilson's famous remark that what is good for General Motors is good for the country assumes that people generally do in fact desire the common good. Presumably, Mr. Wilson attempted to explain the special interest of General Motors in terms of the common interest because that was the only way he could talk to people who do not belong to the General Motors organization. *Within* the General Motors organization discussions might be carried on in terms of naked self-interest, but a *public discussion must be carried on in public terms.*

All public discussion is addressed to the general community. To describe the conflict of special-interest groups as a form of politics means that the conflict has become generalized, has become a matter involving the broader public. In the nature of things a *political conflict among special interests is never restricted to the groups most immediately interested.* Instead, it is an appeal (initiated by relatively small numbers of people) for the support of vast numbers of people who are sufficiently remote to have a somewhat different perspective on the controversy. It follows that Mr. Wilson's comment, far from demonstrating that the public interest is a fraud, proves that he thinks that the public interest is so important that even a great private corporation must make obeisance to it.

The distinction between public and special interests is an indispensable tool for the study of politics. To abolish the distinction is to make a shambles of political science by treating things that are different as if they were alike. The kind of distinction made here is a commonplace of all literature dealing with human society, but *if we accept it we have established one of the outer limits of the subject*; we have split the world of interests in half and have taken one step toward defining the scope of this kind of political conflict.

We can now examine the second distinction, the distinction between organized and unorganized groups. The question here is not whether the distinction can be made but whether or not it is worth making. Organization has been described as "merely a stage or degree of interaction" in the development of a group.[6]

The proposition is a good one, but what conclusions do we draw from it? We do not dispose of the matter by calling the distinction between organized and unorganized groups a "mere" difference of degree because some of the greatest differences in the world are differences of degree. As far as special-interest politics is concerned the implication to be avoided is that a few workmen who habitually stop at a corner saloon for a glass of beer are essentially the same as the United States Army because the difference between them is merely one of degree. At this point we have a distinction that makes a difference. The distinction between organized and unorganized groups is worth making because it ought to alert us against an analysis which begins as a general group theory of politics but ends with a defense of pressure politics as inherent, universal, permanent and inevitable. This kind of confusion comes from the loosening of categories involved in the universalization of group concepts.

Since the beginning of intellectual history, scholars have sought to make progress in their work by distinguishing between things that are unlike and by dividing their subject matter into categories to examine them more intelligently. It is something of a novelty, therefore, when group theorists reverse this process by discussing their subject in terms so universal that they wipe out all categories, because this is the dimension in which it is least possible to understand anything.

If we are able, therefore, to distinguish between public and private interests and between organized and unorganized groups we have marked out the major boundaries of the subject; *we have given the subject shape and scope*. We are now in a position to attempt to define the area we want to explore. Having cut the pie into four pieces, we can now appropriate the piece we want and leave the rest to someone else. For a multitude of reasons *the most likely field of study is that of the organized, special-interest groups*. The advantage of concentrating on organized groups is that they are known, identifiable and recognizable. The advantage of concentrating on special-interest groups is that they have one important characteristic in common: they are all exclusive. This piece of the pie (the organized special-interest groups) we shall call the *pressure system*. The pressure system has boundaries we can define; we can fix its scope and make an attempt to estimate its bias.

It may be assumed at the outset that all organized special-interest groups have some kind of impact on politics. A sample survey of organizations made by the Trade Associations Division of the United States Department of Commerce in 1942 concluded that "From 70 to 100 per cent (of these associations) are planning activities in the field of government relations, trade promotion, trade practices, public relations, annual conventions, cooperation with other organizations, and information services."[7]

The subject of our analysis can be reduced to manageable proportions and brought

---

[6] Truman, *op. cit.*, p. 51.

[7] *National Associations of the United States*, p. XI.

under control if we restrict ourselves to the groups whose interests in politics are sufficient to have led them to unite in formal organizations having memberships, bylaws and officers. A further advantage of this kind of definition is, we may assume, that the organized special-interest groups are the most self-conscious, best developed, most intense and active groups. Whatever claims can be made for a group theory of politics ought to be sustained by the evidence concerning these groups, if the claims have any validity at all.

The organized groups listed in the various directories (such as *National Associations of the United States*, published at intervals by the United States Department of Commerce) and specialty yearbooks, registers, etc., and the *Lobby Index*, published by the United States House of Representatives, probably include the bulk of the organizations in the pressure system. All compilations are incomplete, but these are extensive enough to provide us with some basis for estimating the scope of the system.

By the time a group has developed the kind of interest that leads it to organize it may be assumed that it has also developed some kind of political bias because *organization is itself a mobilization of bias in preparation for action*. Since these groups can be identified and since they have memberships (i.e., they include and exclude people), it is possible to think of the *scope* of the system.

When lists of these organizations are examined, the fact that strikes the student most forcibly is that *the system is very small*. The range of organized, identifiable, known groups is amazingly narrow; there is nothing remotely universal about it. There is a tendency on the part of the publishers of directories of associations to place an undue emphasis on business organizations, an emphasis that is almost inevitable because the business community is by a wide margin the most highly organized segment of society. Publishers doubtless tend also to reflect public demand for information. Nevertheless, the dominance of business groups in the pressure system is so marked that it probably cannot be explained away as an accident of the publishing industry.

The business character of the pressure system is shown by almost every list available. *National Associations of the United States*[8] lists 1,860 business associations out of a total of 4,000 in the volume, though it refers without listing (p. VII) to 16,000 organizations of businessmen. One cannot be certain what the total content of the unknown associational universe may be, but, taken with the evidence found in other compilations, it is obvious that business is remarkably well represented. Some evidence of the over-all scope of the system is to be seen in the estimate that fifteen thousand national trade associations have a gross membership of about one million business firms.[9] The data are incomplete, but even if we do not have a detailed map this is the shore dimly seen.

Much more directly related to pressure politics is the *Lobby Index, 1946–1949*, (an index of organizations and individuals registering or filing quarterly reports under the Federal Lobbying Act) published as a report of the House Select Committee on Lobbying Activities. In this compilation, 825 out of a total of 1,247 entries (exclusive of individuals and Indian tribes) represented business.[10] A selected list of the most important of the groups listed in the *Index* (the groups spending the largest sums of money on lobbying) published in the *Congressional Quarterly Log* shows 149 business organizations in a total of 265 listed.[11]

The business or upper-class bias of the pressure system shows up everywhere. Busi-

---

[8] Edited by Jay Judkins, Washington, 1949, p. VIII.

[9] *National Associations of the United States*, p. VIII.

[10] House Report No. 3197, 81st Congress, 2nd Session, December 15, 1950, Washington.

[11] *Congressional Quarterly Log*, week ending February 24, 1950, pp. 217 ff. Another compilation, the list of approximately one thousand associations and societies published in the *World Almanac* for 1953, reflects to a very great extent the economic, professional and leisure interests and activities of the upper economic strata of the community. Scarcely more than a dozen or so of the associations listed in the *World Almanac* can be described as proletarian in their outlook or membership.

nessmen are four or five times as likely to write to their congressmen as manual laborers are. College graduates are far more apt to write to their congressmen than people in the lowest educational category are.[12]

The limited scope of the business pressure system is indicated by all available statistics. Among business organizations, the National Association of Manufacturers (with about 20,000 corporate members) and the Chamber of Commerce of the United States (about as large as the N.A.M.) are giants. Usually business associations are much smaller. Of 421 trade associations in the metal products industry listed in *National Associations of the United States*, 153 have a membership of less than 20.[13] The median membership was somewhere between 24 and 50. Approximately the same scale of memberships is to be found in the lumber, furniture and paper industries where 37.3 per cent of the associations listed had a membership of less than 20 and the median membership was in the 25 to 50 range.[14]

The statistics in these cases are representative of nearly all other classifications of industry.

Data drawn from other sources support this thesis. Broadly, the pressure system has an upper-class bias. There is overwhelming evidence that participation in voluntary organizations is related to upper social and economic status; the rate of participation is much higher in the upper strata than it is elsewhere. The general proposition is well stated by Lazarsfeld:[15]

People on the lower SES levels are less likely to belong to any organizations than the people on high SES (Social and Economic Status) levels. (On an A and B level, we find 72 per cent of these respondents who belong to one or more organizations. The proportion of respondents who are members of formal organizations decreases steadily as SES level descends until, on the D levels only 35 per cent of the respondents belong to any associations).

The bias of the system is shown by the fact that *even nonbusiness organizations reflect an upper-class tendency.*

Lazarsfeld's generalization seems to apply equally well to urban and rural populations. The obverse side of the coin is that large areas of the population appear to be wholly outside of the system of private organization. A study made by Ira Reid of a Philadelphia area showed that in a sample of 963 persons, 85 per cent belonged to no civic or charitable organization and 74 per cent belonged to no occupational, business or professional associations, while another Philadelphia study of 1,154 women showed that 55 per cent belonged to no associations of any kind.[16]

A *Fortune* farm poll taken some years ago found that 70.5 per cent of farmers belonged to no agricultural organizations. A similar conclusion was reached by two Gallup polls showing that perhaps no more than one-third of the farmers of the country belonged to farm organizations[17] while another *Fortune* poll showed that 86.8 per cent of the low-income farmers belonged to no farm organizations.[18] All available data support the generalization that the farmers who do not participate in rural organizations are largely the poorer ones.

A substantial amount of research done by other rural sociologists points to the same conclusion. Mangus and Cottam say, on the basis of a study of 556 heads of Ohio farm families and their wives:[19]

[12] *American Institute of Public Opinion*, May 29, 1946.

[13] Four hundred fifty associations are listed, but figures for membership are given for only 421.

[14] Membership statistics are given for only 177 of the 200 associations listed.

[15] Lazarsfeld and Associates, *The People's Choice*, p. 145.

[16] Reid and Ehle, "Leadership Selection in the Urban Locality Areas," *Public Opinion Quarterly* (1950), Vol. 14, 262–284. See also Powell, *Anatomy of Public Opinion*, New York, 1951, pp. 180–1.

[17] See Carey McWilliams, *Small Farm and Big Farm*, Public Affairs Pamphlet, No. 100.

[18] *Fortune* poll, April 1943.

[19] A. R. Mangus and H. R. Cottam, *Level of Living, Social Participation, and Adjustment of Ohio Farm People*, Ohio Agricultural Experiment

The present study indicates that comparatively few of those who ranked low on the scale of living took any active part in community organizations as members, attendants, contributors, or leaders. On the other hand, those families that ranked high on the scale of living comprised the vast majority of the highly active participants in formal group activities. . . . Fully two-thirds of those in the lower class as defined in this study were non-participants as compared with only one-tenth of those in the upper class and one-fourth of those in the middle class. . . . When families were classified by the general level-of-living index, 16 times as large a proportion of those in the upper classes as of those in the lower class were active participants. . . .

Along the same line Richardson and Bauder observe, "Socio-economic status was directly related to participation."[20] In still another study it was found that "a highly significant relationship existed between income and formal participation."[21] It was found that persons with more than four years of college education held twenty times as many memberships (per one hundred persons) as did those with less than a fourth-grade education and were forty times as likely to hold office in nonchurch organizations, while persons with an income over $5,000 held ninety-four times as many offices as persons with incomes less than $250.[22]

D. E. Lindstrom found that 72 per cent of farm laborers belonged to no organizations whatever.[23]

There is a great wealth of data supporting the proposition that participation in private associations exhibits a class bias.[24]

Station, Wooster, Ohio, Bull. 624, September, 1941, pp. 51, 53.

Another study (of New York farmers) shows that there is a direct relation between organizational activity and the economic status of farmers. The author concludes that "The operators of farms of less than 55 acres in size are represented in only very small proportions in membership in the farm bureau and in the Dairymen's League and other cooperatives."

W. A. Anderson, *The Membership of Farmers in New York Organizations*, Cornell University Agricultural Experiment Station, Ithaca, N.Y., 1937, p. 20.

[20] P. D. Richardson and Ward W. Bauder, *Participation in Organized Activities in a Kentucky Rural Community*. Kentucky Agricultural Experimental Station, University of Kentucky, Bulletin 598, 1953, Lexington, Kentucky, pp. 26, 28. "The number of memberships varied directly with the socio-economic score."

[21] Harold F. Kaufman, *Participation in Organized Activities in Selected Kentucky Localities*, Bulletin 528, Kentucky Agricultural Experiment Station, University of Kentucky, Lexington, 1949, p. 19.

[22] *Ibid.*, pp. 11, 12, 13, 21.

See also Mirra Komoroosky, "The Voluntary Association of Urban Dwellers," *American Sociological Review*, 11:686–98, 1946.

[23] *Forces Affecting Participation of Farm People in Rural Organizations*, University of Illinois Agricultural Experiment Station, Bulletin 423, 1936, p. 103.

[24] "Associational participation is greatest at the top of Jonesville society and decreases on the way down the class hierarchy. The upper class belongs to the greatest number of associations, the upper-middle class next, and so on down to the lower-lower class which belongs to the least." Warner, *Democracy in Jonesville*, New York, 1949, p. 117. See also pp. 138, 140, 141, 143.

"A higher proportion of the members of the upper class belong to more associations than the members of any other class." Warner, *Jonesville*, p. 131.

"The upper and upper-middle classes are highly organized, well integrated social groups. The lower-middle and lower classes are more loosely organized and have fewer devices for maintaining their own distinctiveness in the community." Warner, *Jonesville*, p. 148. See also p. 153.

"Many organized groups touch only a few people in a community. Studies in cities reveal that 40 to 60 per cent of adults are members of these organized groups if church membership is excluded. In rural communities the percentage is smaller. So when we bring in representatives from these organized groups, we should not pretend that we are getting a complete representation of the people of the community. The American practice of 'joining' is not as universal as popularly assumed." G. W. Blackwell, "Community Analysis," *Approaches to the Study of Politics*, Roland Young, ed., Northwestern University Press, 1958, p. 306.

"Aside from church participation, most urban individuals belong to one organization or none. Low socio-economic rank individuals, and middle-rank individuals, usually belong to one organization

The class bias of associational activity gives meaning to the limited scope of the pressure system, because *scope and bias are aspects of the same tendency.* The data raise a serious question about the validity of the proposition that special-interest groups are a universal form of political organization reflecting *all* interests. As a matter of fact, to suppose that everyone participates in pressure-group activity and that all interests get themselves organized in the pressure system is to destroy the meaning of this form of politics. The pressure system makes sense only as the political instrument of a segment of the community. It gets results by being selective and biased; *if everybody got into the act the unique advantages of this form of organization would be destroyed, for it is possible that if all interests could be mobilized the result would be a stalemate.*

Special-interest organizations are most easily formed when they deal with small numbers of individuals who are acutely aware of their exclusive interests. To describe the conditions of pressure-group organization in this way is, however, to say that it is primarily a business phenomenon. Aside from a few very large organizations (the churches, organized labor, farm organizations, and veterans' organizations) the residue is a small segment of the population. *Pressure politics is essentially the politics of small groups.*

The vice of the groupist theory is that it conceals the most significant aspects of the system. The flaw in the pluralist heaven is that the heavenly chorus sings with a strong upper-class accent. Probably about 90 per cent of the people cannot get into the pressure system.

The notion that the pressure system is automatically representative of the whole community is a myth fostered by the universalizing tendency of modern group theories. *Pressure politics is a selective process* ill designed to serve diffuse interests. The system is skewed, loaded and unbalanced in favor of a fraction of a minority.

On the other hand, pressure tactics are not remarkably successful in mobilizing general interests. When pressure-group organizations attempt to represent the interests of large numbers of people, they are usually able to reach only a small segment of their constituencies. Only a chemical trace of the fifteen million Negroes in the United States belong to the National Association for the Advancement of Colored People. Only one five hundredths of 1 per cent of American women belong to the League of Women Voters, only one sixteen hundredths of 1 per cent of the consumers belong to the National Consumers' League, and only 6 per cent of American automobile drivers belong to the American Automobile Association, while about 15 per cent of the veterans belong to the American Legion.

The competing claims of pressure groups and political parties for the loyalty of the American public revolve about the difference between the results likely to be achieved by small-scale and large-scale political organization. Inevitably, the outcome of pressure politics and party politics will be vastly different.

A CRITIQUE OF GROUP THEORIES OF POLITICS

It is extremely unlikely that the vogue of group theories of politics would have attained its present status if its basic assumptions had not been first established by some concept of economic determinism. The economic interpretation of politics has always appealed to those political philosophers who have sought a single prime mover, a sort of philosopher's stone of political science around which to organize their ideas. The search for a single, ultimate cause has something to do with the attempt to explain *everything* about politics in terms of group concepts.

---

at most, and it is usually work-connected for men, child-church connected for women. Only in the upper socio-economic levels is the 'joiner' to be found with any frequency. When attendance at organizations is studied, some twenty per cent of the memberships are usually 'paper' memberships." Scott Greer, "Individual Participation in Mass Society," *Approaches to the Study of Politics,* p. 332.

The logic of economic determinism is to *identify the origins of conflict and to assume the conclusion.* This kind of thought has some of the earmarks of an illusion. The somnambulatory quality of thinking in this field appears also in the tendency of research to deal only with successful pressure campaigns or the willingness of scholars to be satisfied with having placed pressure groups on the scene of the crime without following through to see if the effect can really be attributed to the cause. What makes this kind of thinking remarkable is the fact that in political contests there are as many failures as there are successes. Where in the literature of pressure politics are the failures?

Students of special-interest politics need a more sophisticated set of intellectual tools than they have developed thus far. The theoretical problem involved in the search for a single cause is that all power relations in a democracy are reciprocal. Trying to find the original cause is like trying to find the first wave of the ocean.

Can we really assume that we know all that is to be known about a conflict if we understand its *origins?* Everything we know about politics suggests that a conflict is likely to change profoundly as it becomes political. It is a rare individual who can confront his antagonists without changing his opinions to some degree. Everything changes once a conflict gets into the political arena—*who* is involved, *what* the conflict is about, the resources available, etc. It is extremely difficult to predict the outcome of a fight by watching its beginning because we do not even know who else is going to get into the conflict. The logical consequence of the exclusive emphasis on the determinism of the private origins of conflict is to assign zero value to the political process.

The very expression "pressure politics" invites us to misconceive the role of special-interest groups in politics. The word "pressure" implies the use of some kind of force, a form of intimidation, something other than reason and information, to induce public authorities to act against their own best judgment. In Latham's famous statement already quoted the legislature is described as

a "referee" who "ratifies" and "records" the "balance of power" among the contending groups.[25]

It is hard to imagine a more effective way of saying that Congress has no mind or force of its own or that Congress is unable to invoke new forces that might alter the equation.

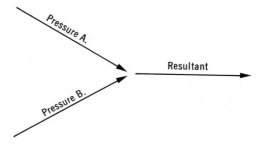

Actually the outcome of political conflict is not like the "resultant" of opposing forces in physics. To assume that the forces in a political situation could be diagrammed as a physicist might diagram the resultant of opposing physical forces is to wipe the slate clean of all remote, general and public considerations for the protection of which civil societies have been instituted.

Moreover, the notion of "pressure" distorts the image of the power relations involved. *Private conflicts are taken into the public arena precisely because someone wants to make certain that the power ratio among the private interests most immediately involved shall not prevail.* To treat a conflict as a mere test of the strength of the private interests is to leave out the most significant factors. This is so true that it might indeed be said that the only way to preserve private power ratios is to keep conflicts out of the public arena.

The assumption that it is only the "interested" who count ought to be re-examined in view of the foregoing discussion. The tendency of the literature of pressure politics has been to neglect the low-tension force of large

---

25 Latham, *op. cit.*, pp. 35–36.

numbers because it *assumes that the equation of forces is fixed at the outset.*

Given the assumptions made by the group theorists, the attack on the idea of the majority is completely logical. The assumption is that conflict is monopolized narrowly by the parties immediately concerned. There is no room for a majority when conflict is defined so narrowly. It is a great deficiency of the group theory that it has found no place in the political system for the majority. The force of the majority is of an entirely different order of magnitude, something not to be measured by pressure-group standards.

Instead of attempting to exterminate all political forms, organizations and alignments that do not qualify as pressure groups, would it not be better to attempt to make a synthesis, covering the whole political system and finding a place for all kinds of political life?

One possible synthesis of pressure politics and party politics might be produced by *describing politics as the socialization of conflict.* That is to say, the political process is a sequence: conflicts are initiated by highly motivated, high-tension groups so directly and immediately involved that it is difficult for them to see the justice of competing claims. As long as the conflicts of these groups remain *private* (carried on in terms of economic competition, reciprocal denial of goods and services, private negotiations and bargaining, struggles for corporate control or competition for membership), no political process is initiated. Conflicts become political only when an attempt is made to involve the wider public. Pressure politics might be described as a stage in the socialization of conflict. This analysis makes pressure politics an integral part of all politics, including party politics.

One of the characteristic points of origin of pressure politics is a breakdown of the discipline of the business community. The flight to government is perpetual. Something like this is likely to happen wherever there is a point of contact between competing power systems. It is the *losers in intrabusiness conflict who seek redress from public authority. The dominant business interests*

resist appeals to the government.* The role of the government as the patron of the defeated private interest sheds light on its function as the critic of private power relations.

Since the contestants in private conflicts are apt to be unequal in strength, it follows that *the most powerful special interests want private settlements* because they are able to dictate the outcome as long as the conflict remains private. If A is a hundred times as strong as B he does not welcome the intervention of a third party because he expects to impose his own terms on B; he wants to isolate B. He is especially opposed to the intervention of public authority, because public authority represents the most overwhelming form of outside intervention. Thus, if

$$\frac{A}{B} = \frac{100}{1}$$

it is obviously not to A's advantage to involve a third party a million times as strong as A and B combined. Therefore, it is the weak, not the strong, who appeal to public authority for relief. It is the weak who want to socialize conflict, i.e., to involve more and more people in the conflict until the balance of forces is changed. In the school yard it is not the bully, but the defenseless smaller boys who "tell the teacher." When the teacher intervenes the balance of power in the school yard is apt to change drastically. It is the function of public authority to *modify private power relations by enlarging the scope of conflict.* Nothing could be more mistaken than to suppose that public authority merely registers the dominance of the strong over the weak. The mere existence of public order has already ruled out a great variety of forms of private pressure. Nothing could be more confusing than to suppose that the refugees from the business community who come to Congress for relief and protection *force* Congress to do their bidding.

Evidence of the truth of this analysis may be seen in the fact that the big private interests do not necessarily win if they are involved in public conflicts with petty interests. The image of the lobbyists as primarily the agents of big business is not easy to support on the face of the record of congressional hearings, for example. The biggest corporations in the country tend to avoid the arena in which pressure groups and lobbyists fight it out before congressional committees. To describe this process exclusively in terms of an effort of business to intimidate congressmen is to misconceive what is actually going on.

It is probably a mistake to assume that pressure politics is the typical or even the most important relation between government and business. The pressure group is by no means the perfect instrument of the business community. What does big business want? The *winners* in intrabusiness strife want (1) to be let alone (they want autonomy) and (2) to preserve the solidarity of the business community. For these purposes pressure politics is not a wholly satisfactory device. The most elementary considerations of strategy call for the business community to develop some kind of common policy more broadly based than any special-interest group is likely to be.

The political influence of business depends on the kind of solidarity that, on the one hand, leads all business to rally to the support of *any* businessman in trouble with the government, and on the other hand, keeps internal business disputes out of the public arena. In this system businessmen resist the impulse to attack each other in public and discourage the efforts of individual members of the business community to take intrabusiness conflicts into politics.

The attempt to mobilize a united front of the whole business community does not resemble the classical concept of pressure politics. The logic of business politics is to keep peace within the business community by supporting as far as possible all claims that business groups make for themselves. The tendency is to support all businessmen who have conflicts with the government and support all businessmen in conflict with labor. In this way *special-interest politics can be converted into party policy.* The search is for a broad base of political mobilization grounded on the strategic need for political organization on a wider scale than is pos-

sible in the case of the historical pressure group. Once the business community begins to think in terms of a larger scale of political organization the Republican party looms large in business politics.

It is a great achievement of American democracy that business has been forced to form a political organization designed to win elections, i.e., has been forced to compete for power in the widest arena in the political system. On the other hand, *the power of the Republican party to make terms with business rests on the fact that business cannot afford to be isolated.*

The Republican party has played a major role in *the political organization of the business community,* a far greater role than many students of politics seem to have realized. The influence of business in the Republican party is great, but it is never absolute because business is remarkably dependent on the party. The business community is too small, it arouses too much antagonism, and its aims are too narrow to win the support of a popular majority. The political education of business is a function of the Republican party that can never be done so well by anyone else.

In the management of the political relations of the business community, the Republican party is much more important than any combination of pressure groups ever could be. The success of special interests in Congress is due less to the "pressure" exerted by these groups than it is due to the fact that Republican members of Congress are committed in advance to a general probusiness attitude. The notion that business groups coerce Republican congressmen into voting for their bills underestimates the whole Republican posture in American politics.[26]

It is not easy to manage the political interests of the business community because there is a perpetual stream of losers in intrabusiness conflicts who go to the government for relief and protection. It has not been

---

[26] See *Reporter,* November 25, 1958, for story of Senator Bricker and the Ohio Right-to-Work referendum.

possible therefore to maintain perfect solidarity, and when solidarity is breached the government is involved almost automatically. The fact that business has not become hopelessly divided and that it has retained great influence in American politics has been due chiefly to the over-all mediating role played by the Republican party. There has never been a pressure group or a combination of pressure groups capable of performing this function.

Chapter 6

PROBLEMS OF COMMUNICATION IN CONFLICT SITUATIONS

In our analytical scheme, established bargaining relationships differ from un-structured ones in that the parties have an enduring relationship, and from normative ones in that conflict is a recognized and legitimated part of that relationship. Both of these facts imply that communication about the conflict will take place. Without by any means adopting the view that misunderstandings or problems of communication are the cause of conflict, we may note that problems of communication seem to accompany conflict and may make the conflict much worse.

White documents the role that a basic set of mutual misperceptions played in the decisions that precipitated the two world wars of the first half of the twentieth century. Kelley and Stahelski then present an impressive body of evidence to indicate that distrustful, hostile persons are especially insensitive to efforts by others to communicate friendly or cooperative intentions. These hostile subjects not only force even cooperatively oriented others to behave competitively in sheer self-defense, but fail to see that their own behavior had anything to do with confirming their belief in a hostile world. The selection by Bach and Wyden moves to the level of family relationships, although the disputes they analyze often seem more like a series of international struggles. These authors make the very important point, central to this whole book, that a sensible adaptation to conflict requires not only the ability to communicate but in particular the ability to communicate about the rules of the conflict itself. Bach and Wyden present a therapeutic model for just such communication, with the avowed goal of making family conflicts fair and productive, rather than unfair and destructive.

MISPERCEPTION AS A CAUSE OF TWO WORLD WARS

Ralph K. White

The fact of continuing war, in a world that desperately wants to avoid it, is a paradox too enormous to be evaded. It is the central problem of the human race in the second half of the twentieth century. Few reflective persons anywhere in the world have not had the thought that, in our nuclear age, only a madman could start a war. Yet wars continue.

Naturally, psychologists and psychiatrists have been especially likely to see the problem in psychological terms. We know something about "madmen," since "madness" in all its forms and degrees, including the madness of normal people like ourselves, is in our bailiwick. Many of us have felt especially that *misperception* or cognitive distortion— a variegated psychological process that is accentuated in the psychotic but that pervades normal living as well—is a clue that may help in resolving the paradox. Perhaps it could help to explain how normally sane human beings can unwittingly, without intending the consequences, involve themselves step by step in actions that lead to war.

The following pages consist largely of an exploration of that idea. Psychological research and psychiatric experience are brought in where they seem relevant, but, since history can be described as "psychology teaching by examples," the main emphasis is on recent and contemporary history, psychologically interpreted. There is first a brief examination of the background of World Wars I and II, with an effort to discover and to clarify the role that misperception played in making possible the actions that were most important in bringing about those two wars. . . . There is no assumption that the amount of misperception is the same or even similar on the two sides. The possibility is left open that one side may be much more realistic than the other in perceiving the "actual facts." But a central hypothesis, which the evidence does seem to justify in both of these conflicts, is that each side is highly unrealistic in perceiving—empathizing with—what is in the minds of those on the other side. As Cantril might put it, they live in different "reality worlds." On each side men assume that what seems real to them seems real also to the enemy. In many ways both are wrong.

To psychologists this approach is, of course, very familiar. Lippmann, when playing the role of a psychologist, talked about "stereotypes" and "pictures in our heads"; Thomas, about varying "definitions of the situation"; Lewin, about "the psychological environment" and "the life space"; Tolman, about "cognitive maps"; Cantril, about "reality worlds." Freud apparently took something of the sort for granted and proceeded to explore the mechanisms, such as projection, that lead to distortion in men's private worlds. Many are now stressing "empathy," defined as an effort to imagine, realistically, how the world looks to another individual or group. The essential proposition running through all of these is the same: that different individuals and groups perceive the world differently, and that we can scarcely begin to understand their behavior until we have begun to understand how reality as they see it differs from reality as we see it.[1]

Source: R. K. White, "Misperception as a Cause of Two World Wars." In R. K. White, "Misperception and the Vietnam War." *Journal of Social Issues*, Vol. 22, 1966, pp. 1–19. Copyright 1966 by The Society for the Psychological Study of Social Issues and reprinted by permission of publisher and author.

[1] The word "perception" has two common uses in psychology: a narrower use in which it means a cognitive response to the immediately presented environment (depth-perception, audio-visual perception, etc.) and a broader use in which it be-

In addition to psychologists many other students of international relations have been concerned with the distorted views that one nation may have of another. They have been studied in detail by historians such as Montgelas (1925), Fay (1928), Gooch (1936, 1938) and Albertini (1953), and by political scientists such as North (Holsti and North, 1965) who have explored the thinking of the "other side," the Austrians and Germans, in the events that led to World War I. Emery Reves, in a brilliant chapter (1963, pp. 1–29), has described the reality worlds of the United States, Great Britain, France, Germany and Russia during the inter-war period that led up to and produced World War II. There is a large literature (especially Heiden, 1944) on Hitler's thinking, including his conception of the political world. The differing worlds of the Russians and the Americans since 1945 have been described by historians such as Kennan (1960) as well as by psychologists (Bronfenbrenner, 1961; Osgood, 1962; White, 1965). Felix Greene has sketched his conception of the international reality world of the Chinese Communists in a jolting chapter that should be read by every American who wants to begin to understand the conflict between that country and ourselves (1961), and others such as Barnett (1961), Fairbank (1958, 1966) and Hinton (1966) have provided much scholarly

background for understanding the same conflict.

Burchett, a pro-Communist Australian journalist, on the basis of first-hand contact, has given us an all too uncritically and one-sidedly empathic picture of how the Vietnamese conflict looks to the Viet Cong (1965), and a French journalist, Chaffard (1965), also with first-hand contact, has given us a less partisan conception of it. Historians such as Buttinger (1958), Devillers (1962), and Hammer (1954), and many first-hand observers of the contemporary scene such as Fall (1964b), Lansdale (1964), Carver (1964, 1966), Malcolm Browne (1965), Robert Browne (1965), Halberstam (1965), Shaplen (1965) and Lacouture (1966) have provided material that is relevant especially to the thinking of anti-Communist Vietnamese and to that of the less articulate inhabitants of Vietnam who may or may not be on one side or the other. In all such concrete efforts to understand the thinking of a group other than our own it is appropriate for the psychologist to play a rather modest role, learning all he can from the historian and the first-hand observer, and applying his "psychological" concepts (derived mainly from a study of other groups in similar conflict situations) only if and when they seem to fit the concrete facts of a particular case.

An enterprise such as this cannot invoke the safeguards and the sanctions of a formal methodology. The value of the discussion depends, to a disconcerting extent, on the writer's efforts to recognize and transcend his own biases. That is too bad, because it goes without saying that every writer does have biases. Though this one has tried to avoid distortion, some of it undoubtedly remains. The reader should therefore be alert to discover—chiefly by comparing this discussion with everything else he knows about the subject—the nature and extent of the distortion.

---

comes synonymous with all forms of cognition, including even the individual's most basic assumptions about the nature of the world and of man. Throughout this study the word will be used in its broader sense. In other words, it will be used with the same meaning as the more technical word "cognition." It is preferred here to the word "cognition" chiefly because the word "misperception," which will recur continually, is somewhat familiar, while "miscognition" would sound barbarous.

The word "misconception" is of course more familiar than "misperception," and would be preferable in that respect, but it refers ordinarily to the end-product of a psychological process rather than to the process itself, while the word "misperception" lends itself to use in both senses. In this study we will consider both the process of misperception (i.e., how a person's beliefs come to differ from the evidence available to him) and the products of that process which are commonly called "misconceptions."

AUSTRIA VS. SERBIA

On the day when Austria-Hungary broke relations with Serbia, setting in motion the escalation that transformed a local dispute into a world war, the perception of the situation in Austrian minds was radically different from the perception of it in the minds of Austria's enemies—a perception which sustained those enemies (ultimately including the United States) through more than four years of one of the bloodiest wars in history. As seen by Austria's enemies, her declaration of war on Serbia was cold-blooded, calculating aggression. In their minds Austria's masters, the militarists who ruled Imperial Germany, had decided to use the essentially unimportant Serbian dispute as a pretext to launch a war that they believed would give them mastery first of Europe and then of the world.

Historical scholarship in the 1920's, however, led to a picture of what happened that apportions war-guilt much more evenly between the two sides, and that includes a more humanly understandable conception of what was in Austrian minds at the time. Historians are now in fair agreement that Austria, not Germany, was the prime mover (Gooch, 1938, p. 445). Germany clearly tried to prevent a major European war. As for the Austrians, from their point of view Serbia was carrying on an intolerable agitation against Austria-Hungary, not stopping even at assassination; it had to be punished, and that was that. Unless Serbia was punished, nationalist agitation throughout the country would get worse, and the very existence of the Austro-Hungarian Empire would be in danger.

To be sure, there were some other thoughts in their minds. One was the terrifying possibility of a bigger war (Gooch, 1938, p. 446). Russia, with her enormous army, might come in. But surely (the Austrians thought) the Czar of Russia, who lived in fear of assassination himself, must realize that the Hapsburg emperor could not tolerate the sort of agitation that had led to the assassination of the Archduke. He must see that Austria-Hungary's very existence as a bastion of civilization and order in Central Europe depended on her taking a firm stand in this new crisis and teaching the conspirators in Belgrade a lesson they could not forget. Also, since the German Kaiser had seen the justice of Austria's position and was standing firmly by her side, the Czar would hardly be so rash as to intervene; he must know that the consequences of a world war would be incalculable. In any case, the risk must be run, because if the Serbian nationalist agitation among the Serbs and Croats who were still under Austrian rule were allowed to continue, it could quickly spread to the other nationalities within the Austro-Hungarian family of nations, and Austria-Hungary herself would disappear as a Great Power—which was, of course, unthinkable.

To the extent that this is a fair picture of what was happening in Austrian minds, it suggests that their reality world was distorted by six forms of misperception:

1. A diabolical enemy-image.
2. A virile self-image.
3. A moral self-image.
4. Selective inattention.
5. Absence of empathy.
6. Military overconfidence.

The Diabolical Enemy-Image. In the central focus of Austrian minds was the "criminal" character of the "assassins" who were violating all standards of human decency and endangering the very survival of the beneficent Austro-Hungarian empire. In their black-and-white picture the black was more fully in focus than the white. To them it seemed that such men, and the conspiracy in Belgrade that was responsible for their actions (though this point remained controversial in the minds of detached observers), were so flagrantly evil that all right-minded people even in Russia must be indignant and must see the need to "punish" them.[2]

The Virile Self-Image. A preoccupation with prestige and a feeling that humiliation would be intolerable were characteristic not only of the Austrians, in 1914, but also of the other

---

[2] For further discussion of the "diabolical enemy image" and of its psychological origins, see below. Here as in the case of other major themes in the discussion, a concept is illustrated concretely in several different contexts before a relatively systematic psychological discussion of it is attempted.

governments involved. In each of the Great Powers there was a fear of "losing our position as a Great Power" and "sinking to the status of a second-class power." In each case, after a "firm stand" had been taken, there was acute consciousness of the danger of backing down, or seeming to back down, and a much less vivid awareness of the pain and death of tens of millions of human beings that might result if one did not compromise. This was true up to the time of the general Russian mobilization, when fear took over as the ruling emotion in Germany, if not in Austria-Hungary, and led directly to a strike-first policy. Up to that time the ruling emotion had been not fear of attack, but fear of humiliation. The chief dimension in which national decision-makers judged themselves, and expected to be judged by others, was not good vs. bad or right vs. wrong but strong vs. weak. The essential goal apparently was to be, and to seem, strong and courageous. The essential thing was to take "a firm stand," a "strong stand," and to do it with such firmness and such obvious lack of fear, on one's own part and on the part of one's allies, that the potential enemy would be sure to back down (Schelling, 1960).

Since this is in the realm of values it is perhaps inappropriate to call it unrealistic in the same sense in which a failure to think about the future is unrealistic. Yet, if at a given time a person or group acts as if prestige-for-its-own-sake were the only goal or the main goal worth striving for, while at other times other goals (such as freedom from pain and death, for oneself or for others) are salient, a question can be raised as to whether there has been selective inattention, not only to certain objective facts but also to certain genuine psychological needs. A compulsive ruling of certain motives out of the field of consciousness, perhaps with a feeling that it would be weak and unmanly to pay attention to them, can be itself a form of unrealism, especially if the main value endangered by the situation is nothing more essential (in the eyes of detached observers) than prestige-for-its-own-sake.

The Moral Self-Image. In the crisis of 1914, the Austrians had a black-and-white picture in which only evil was attributed to the Serbian enemy and only good to the Austro-Hungarian self. While their own moral nobility was perhaps less salient in the Austrians' minds than either the diabolical character of the enemy or their own need to take a "firm stand" in the interest of self-preservation, the self that they assumed to be worth preserving was also noble: peace-loving (they never for a moment sought a bigger war, and always feared it), civilized (they were a bastion of civilization in a Central Europe threatened by the barbarian tide of Pan-Slavism), economically rational (their empire was prospering in unity and would suffer economically if broken up), orderly (the Serbian assassins were violating elementary standards of law and order), democratic (theirs was a limited monarchy, and the subject peoples were advancing toward full autonomy as rapidly as possible), etc.

It is not necessary to deny a large kernel of truth in each of these propositions; it is necessary only to notice that the picture was expurgated at one crucial point. It did not include even a candid consideration of the possibility that this noble nation might now be committing aggression. The ultimatum to Serbia included what the Serbs regarded as a virtual demand for submission by Serbia to Austrian authority, and when this was not clearly accepted by Serbia Austria broke relations and began to mobilize for war. In the eyes of most of the rest of the world, this was aggression. It was aggression also by almost any clear definition of the term; for example, if aggression is defined as the use of force or threat of force on another nation's territory and against the wishes of the majority of the politically conscious people of that nation, Austria's action was aggression, however justified it may have been by the Serbian provocation. But the Austrians did not call it that, or seriously think about what to call it. To them it was not aggression at all, but "a firm stand," or "bringing the criminals to justice." Here again there was selective inattention. The charge of aggression was not answered in their minds; it was ignored.

There was also in their minds a curious sort of automatism in the form of a feeling that they could not do otherwise. The initial steps on the path to war were taken with a feeling of necessity; to do otherwise would be "suicide." And once the initial steps were taken, Austrian minds were gripped by what Anatol Rapoport has called "the blindness of involvement" (1960, pp. 259–272). As the Emperor Francis Joseph put it, "We cannot go back now" (Gooch, 1938, p. 437). All moral guilt was thus shifted from the Austrians themselves to a sort of impersonal Fate or Necessity. This was shown most strikingly at two key points: Austria's refusal to reconsider her course of action on July 25, when the conciliatory Serbian reply to the Austrian ultimatum was seen even by the German Kaiser as "doing away with every reason for war" (Montgelas, 1925, p. 137); and her refusal to draw back even when Germany, on July 29, exerted very strong pressure on her to do so. On that day the German Chancellor, Bethmann Hollweg, wired the Austrians: "we cannot allow Vienna to draw us lightly, and without regard to our advice, into a world-wide conflagration" (Montgelas, 1925, p. 148). Berchtold, the Austrian Foreign Minister, had the bit in his teeth, he had put on his blinders, and with a "courageous" unwillingness to consider any alternative course of action he stepped over the brink of the precipice.

(The strong German pressure on Austria to draw back is interesting also as evidence of how mistaken our own diabolical image of Germany was, throughout the First World War. Germany did not try to precipitate a European war; she tried to prevent it.)

Selective Inattention. Of all the psychological mechanisms involved in misperception of the kinds we have been considering, perhaps the most pervasive is one which in some contexts may be called "resistance" or "repression" (though the Freudians give a more restricted meaning to each of these terms) and which Sullivan, defining it more broadly, has called "selective inattention." It is involved on both sides of the black-and-white picture, when white or grey elements on the enemy side are glossed over and attention is focused only on the black, and also when black or grey elements on one's own side are glossed over and attention is focused only on the white.

In addition, it should be noted that in nations stumbling toward war there are usu-

ally at least three other definable types or aspects of selective inattention: narrow time-perspective, narrow space-perspective, and absence of empathy.

In the minds of the Austrians in 1914 there was vivid and focal awareness of only one aspect of the future as they perceived it: the catastrophic disintegration that they regarded (with much reason) as probable if they could not cope firmly with Serbian nationalism. But this anxiety-filled image was not cognitively well differentiated. It did not distinguish clearly, for example, between what would happen if they merely dealt "firmly" with Serbian and other agitators within their own borders and what would happen if, in the process of "punishing" Serbia, they sent troops beyond their present border into a neighboring country. To most of the rest of the world this distinction seemed the distinction between legitimate maintenance of internal stability and illegitimate aggression that could precipitate world war. But in anxious Austrian minds it was all one thing: a need to punish Serbia, as vigorously as possible, in order to vindicate the image of Austria-Hungary as a virile nation and to stave off destruction.

In addition, there was a failure to pay much attention to any other aspect of the possible future, including what would happen if Russia did intervene, and including the kind of break-up of the Austrian empire that actually did occur as a result of the war that Austria herself had precipitated.

A restriction in their space-perspective was represented by a failure to pay much attention to countries other than the two that were in the main focus of their attention (themselves and Serbia) and the two that were somewhat in the periphery (Russia, whose intervention they feared, and Germany, whose "strong stand" by Austria's side was counted on to deter Russian intervention). Two other countries that were soon to become involved, France and England, were present in their minds but apparently not very seriously considered, and America, which was to join the Allies nearly three years later—partly because of the American impression at the outset that Germany and Austria had committed aggression—was apparently not considered at all.

Still another type of selective inattention, absence of empathy, is of such crucial importance that it deserves a separate section.

Absence of Empathy. Even in the case of a country that was in the bright central focus of Austrian attention, Serbia itself, the Austrians seemed to fail almost completely to realize how the situation looked from their enemy's point of view. They did not see how, for a Serbian patriot, the Austrian demands would appear as naked aggression, calling for a struggle to the last drop of patriotic Serbian blood. They did not see how Russian pride, smarting after a number of setbacks including the high-handed Austrian annexation of Bosnia six years earlier, would respond to a new arbitrary extension of German-Austrian power in an area in which the Russians felt that their honor and their interest were involved. They failed to see that, while the Russian Czar himself was peacefully inclined and would try to avoid a big war, his close advisers were not necessarily so pacific, and Russia might become entangled in a situation in which its pride and prestige were so deeply involved that war might seem the only alternative to intolerable humiliation (Gooch, 1938, p. 369). They failed to anticipate the pendulum swing of the Kaiser's mood from careless overconfidence to panicky fear (Taylor, 1963, pp. 214, 219, 228) once the Russian general mobilization had started and British entry into the war seemed likely. The Kaiser's desperate feeling after July 29 was expressed by his reference to "a war of extermination" waged against Germany, and his exclamation that "if we are to bleed to death, England shall at least lose India!" (Montgelas & Schucking, 1924, p. 350). They failed to see how the British and French would fear a collapse of the balance of power if they left Russia to fight alone against a smaller but far more efficient German army, or how British public opinion would react if the panicky Germans, anxious to capitalize on their one great asset, the superior efficiency and speed of their fighting force, were to strike at France through Belgium. They failed to realize that America would regard their attack on Serbia as a big country bullying a small one, and would regard Germany's march through Belgium in the same light, with the result that America's sympathies would be engaged immediately on the Allied side, and the way would be prepared for America's ultimate involvement against the German-Austrian alliance. In short, they were so wrapped up in their own anxiety and their own righteous indignation that they had little attention left for considering the reality-world of anyone else.

Military Overconfidence. It is paradoxical but true that exaggerated fear can be combined with exaggerated military confidence. The Austrians, for example, had what now seems an exaggerated fear of the spreading disaffection of nationalities within their empire that would result if they failed to take a "firm stand" against Serbia. But at the same time, until the Russian mobilization (which quickly created great anxiety in the Germans if not also the Austrians), they had exaggerated confidence that they could "teach Serbia a lesson" and at the same time, with strong German support, keep Russia from intervening. Like the Germans, they pinned their hopes to the possibility of "localizing" the issue, enjoying mastery and venting righteous indignation within a small sphere while remaining safe from the mastery-impulse and the righteous indignation of others in a larger sphere. They were wrong. They misperceived. And the chief way in which reality differed from their perception of reality lay in their selective inattention to the possibility that strong allies of Serbia (Russia, France, Britain, America) might scorn to be intimidated by the Kaiser's appearing at Austria's side "in shining armour." They did not see that their potential enemies, like themselves, might be trying to live up to an indomitable self-image, afraid of showing fear, and therefore "irrationally" ready to fight.

HITLER VS. POLAND

The essential facts of Hitler's attack on Poland are familiar enough, and the view of historians as to the origins of World War II has not been subject to a general and radical revision, as has their view of World War I. We can proceed immediately, therefore, to check in this context the six forms of perceptual distortion that emerged from our review of Austrian thinking in 1914. All six were present, in the extreme degree that might be expected from the fact that Hitler, though probably not psychotic, was one of the least rational, least evidence-oriented of men, with unmistakable paranoid tendencies.

The Diabolical Enemy-Image. It is now fairly well established that in Hitler's mind the diabolical character of the enemy, especially the Jewish enemy, was extreme and unmitigated. Post-war studies have confirmed the proposition that his anti-Jewish delusions of persecution were no mere propaganda technique; he seems to have actually believed them. What needs further elaboration is the central role played by these delusions of persecution in his justification of his more outrageous aggressive acts.

He had a real task on his hands in his effort to reconcile these actions with the posture of peacefulness that he had consistently maintained since 1930. He had abandoned his earlier, franker, "war propaganda," represented by certain passages in *Mein Kampf,* and adopted a peace line that was far more acceptable to the German people. It was urgently necessary, therefore, in order to keep the full and willing support of the German people, to present his bloodless conquest of the Czech part of Czechoslovakia, his bloody attack on Poland, and his still more bloody attack on Russia in ways that would at least half-convince the German people that he was no war-mad conqueror but a real man of peace, forced into these actions by the provocation of diabolical opponents. His skill in doing so suggests that he was at least half convinced of it himself.

Three quotations will suggest how he attempted to justify these aggressions. According to him, the march into Prague was legitimate and necessary for several reasons, including the need to remove a threat to German security. The role that had been assigned to Czechoslovakia by its Jewish and democratic masters was

none other than to prevent consolidation of Central Europe, to provide a bridge to Europe for bolshevik aggression, and, above all, to act as the mercenary of European democracies against Germany. . . . What was expected from this State is shown most clearly by the observation of the French Air Minister, M. Pierre Cot, who calmly stated that the duty of this State in case of any conflict was to be an airdrome for the landing and taking off of bombers from which it would be possible to destroy the most important German industrial centers in a few hours. (*Speech to the Reichstag, April 28, 1939; translated in De Sales, 1941.*) (Note Hitler's use of the time-honored device of treating arms in the hands of an enemy as equivalent to proof that the enemy has aggressive intentions.)

The attack on Poland was justified, he claimed, not only by the Poles' "increased terror and pressure against our German compatriots" but also by

the sudden Polish general mobilization, followed by more atrocities . . . I have therefore resolved to speak to Poland in the same language that Poland for months has used toward us. (*Speech to the Reichstag, September 1, 1939; 1941, pp. 685, 687*)

The attack on Russia was an attempt to break through a ring of encircling enemies. There was

a new policy of encirclement against Germany, born as it was of hatred. . . . Internally and externally there resulted that plot familiar to us all between Jews and democrats, Bolshevists and reactionaries, with the sole aim of inhibiting the establishment of the new German people's State, and of plunging the Reich anew into impotence and misery. (*Proclamation, June 22, 1941; 1941, pp. 977–8*)

The Virile Self-Image. Readers of *Mein Kampf* are familiar with Hitler's glorious image of himself and his country, with much more emphasis on strength and courage than on any softer qualities such as peacefulness and good will. While it is true that after coming to power he greatly stressed peacefulness, his emphasis on the hard qualities, strength and courage, continued. And, as a study in how aggressive actions can appear to their perpetrators in an acceptable guise, his great emphasis on the courage theme, during the crises of 1938 and 1939, holds special interest. When a hard action has to be given some label, the label "courage" is far more acceptable than the label "aggression."

In his speech on September 1, 1939— the day he precipitated World War II—he showed extreme adroitness in avoiding even the word "war." He was not attacking Poland, committing aggression, or starting a war. He was "speaking to Poland in the language that Poland for months has used toward us," he was recognizing that "no Great Power can with honor long stand by passively and watch such events," he was showing that his patience and love of peace must not be "mistaken for weakness or even cowardice," he was "meeting bombs with bombs," he was showing a "stout heart," he was "seeing to it that a change is made in the relationship between Germany and Poland that shall insure a peaceful coexistence." The final sentence in his peroration was "If our will is so strong that no hardship and suffering can subdue it, then our will and our German might shall prevail" (1941, pp. 686–690). One can almost feel the lump in the throats of German listeners as they contemplated their own indomitable selves.

The Moral Self-Image. A basically mistaken conception of Hitler's propaganda technique is still current in American minds: the assumption that he openly and cynically glorified war, announced his program of world conquest, advocated the "Great Lie" technique, justified oppression of weaker races, etc. This conception can be supported only by selecting extremely atypical quotations and quoting them out of context. Actually, as one might expect of such a thoroughly authoritarian personality, his propaganda after he came to power in 1933 was characterized by an extreme, almost exceptionless adherence (on the verbal level) to conventional standards of morality: peacefulness, respect for the rights of neighbors, truthfulness, etc. (White, 1949). In his words, and perhaps

in some sense in his thoughts also, he and Germany were morally spotless. Three quotations will give the flavor:

I wish to point out first, that I have not conducted any war; second, that for years past I have expressed my abhorrence of war and, it is true, also my abhorrence of warmongers, and third, that I am not aware for what purpose I should wage a war at all. (Speech, April 28, 1939; 1941, p. 661)

We have given guarantees for the States in the West, and to all those States bordering on our frontiers, we have given assurances of the inviolability of their territory as far as Germany is concerned. These are no mere words. That is our sacred determination. (Speech, September 26, 1938, at the height of the Munich crisis; 1941, p. 520)

I will not war against women and children. I have ordered my air force to restrict itself to attacks on military objectives. (Speech, September 1, 1939, declaring war on Poland; 1941, p. 688. This is actually the only point in the speech in which he permits himself to use the word "war," and here it is used only negatively, thoroughly embedded in a moral, humane context.)

Selective Inattention. When he made his fateful decision to attack Poland, what was in the focus of Hitler's conscious mind? What was pushed out of the focus but still dynamically important in determining his decision? And what was not dynamically present at all? We can only speculate, of course, using whatever clues his words and his actions give us, but the speculation may be fruitful.

It should be recognized that we are dealing here with a man who had an exceptional capacity for "double-think"—though double-think may be more widespread in the human race than we usually realize. According to Heiden, "On this day (October 26, 1930) Hitler began his peace propaganda which continued uninterrupted for almost ten years. Inexplicable and incredible, it moved men by this very fact, but also by an undeniable breath of passion. With the same passion

Hitler had said the exact opposite." (1944, p. 414) He apparently had a knack of working up a noble passion that he could "sincerely" feel at the time of making a speech, though it would not necessarily remain salient in his mind at a moment of hard decision-making.

Probably, then, when he decided to attack Poland he took more elements of hard reality into account, and was conscious of more long-range plans of conquest, than he proclaimed in his prepared speech to the German people and to the world. His behavior suggests that in the focus of his conscious mind there were at least these thoughts: elation at the immediate prospect of triumphantly crushing Poland and extending the boundaries of the *Reich*; elation at the thought (somewhat anxiously clung to) that, by the great *coup* of the Nazi-Soviet Pact, he and Ribbentrop had successfully divided his enemies and had made it probable that the British and French would either not dare to fight—they had not fought when he marched into Prague—or succumb quickly to his mighty military machine; real anger at the long-standing injustice of Danzig and the Polish Corridor, now about to be eliminated; intense but consciously somewhat artificial anger at Polish "atrocities" and unwillingness to negotiate about the Corridor; pride in Germany's moral grandeur as contrasted with her vindictive, encircling, Jewish-controlled enemies; pride in his personal courage in facing up to dangers which in his more sober moments he recognized as real, though quite unlikely to materialize; clear plans already forming in his mind for capitalizing on this triumph to extend German hegemony throughout Central Europe and the Balkans, with due regard for the appearance of national autonomy in countries such as Hungary and Rumania; vague and wonderful but very private fantasies, which he probably recognized as fantasies that Fate might or might not permit him to fulfill, of total destruction of the Jewish world-octopus and beneficent German hegemony throughout the world. (When he was preparing or delivering a speech and wearing his peaceful, moral, Dr. Jekyll self, Hitler presumably pushed all these morally dubious thoughts out of his mind as completely as possible, and quite possibly he also refrained from verbalizing them or thinking of them clearly at times of hard decision-making. Yet presumably they were more important in the dynamics of his decision-making than he himself realized.)

On the other hand his behavior suggests that certain other things were not in his mind, or not enough in it: the tough nationalism of the Poles, the Yugoslavs, the Russians, the British, and others who stood in his path; the cumulative fear and anger of those who might be so mean-spirited and so influenced by the Jewish press that they would describe his courageous act as "aggression"; the enormous potential military strength of the United States; his own recent promise and "sacred determination" that the territory of all of Germany's neighbors would be "inviolable," and the effect that his violation of that promise might have on others; the word "aggression" as possibly applicable to what he was doing, the word "imperialism" as possibly applicable to the beneficent control of Central Europe that he was immediately contemplating, the word "dictatorship" as possibly applicable to his totalitarian form of government and the word "paranoia" as possibly applicable to his delusions about a Jewish-plutocratic-bolshevist plot against his country.

Among these blind-spots indicated by both his words and his actions, it is possible to discern the same three overlapping categories that emerged in our study of Austrian thinking in 1914: he tended to ignore major future contingencies, realistically considered (as distinguished from grandiose fantasies about the more distant future, fantasies of catastrophe, and immediate practical matters such as the military campaign against Poland); countries such as America that were geographically far from his immediate focus of attention; and the thoughts and feelings of enemies and neutrals. With certain exceptions his time-perspective appears to have been drastically limited, his space-perspective was drastically limited, and he was almost totally devoid of empathy.

As in the case of the Austrians, this last type of selective inattention was so important that it deserves a section of its own.

Absence of Empathy. Several of the blind-spots that have just been mentioned are at the same time examples of failure of empathy: Hitler's failure to give due weight to the tough, defensive nationalism of peoples such as the Poles, the Yugoslavs and the Russians, who stood in his immediate path; his failure to realize that onlookers such as the French, the British and the Americans would certainly regard his action as naked aggression and as one more violation of his pledged word, with the probable result that they would eventually overcome their extreme distaste for war and that, as his threat grew nearer, their defensive nationalism too would be fully mobilized; his almost total inability to see what was happening in the minds of Jews (instead of seeing their helpless terror he continued to attribute to them a plot to rule the world that must have been, essentially, a projection of his own world-conquering fantasies); an inability to see that others, from their vantage-points, might honestly attribute to him such things as war-making, aggression, imperialism, dictatorship and paranoia.

It may be added that he grossly underestimated, if he perceived it at all, the great change that had occurred in British public opinion and elite opinion after March 1939, when Hitler moved his troops into Prague and took over the purely Czech part of Czechoslovakia. For the British this was the last straw —a final demonstration to all doubters that he was not merely trying to unify Germany (an interpretation they could give to his occupation of the Rhineland, his *Anschluss* with Austria, his taking of the Sudetenland, and even his claim to the Polish Corridor) but that he had embarked upon the conquest of non-German lands, in a career of conquest that could later include Britain itself, and that his word could not be trusted.

Hitler apparently could see none of this. He had his own stereotype of what the British were like: partly proud Nordics like the Germans, and therefore capable of sharing German scorn for the Russians and the inferior peoples of Central Europe; partly calculating imperialists capable of jealousy at Germany's new success, but apparently unwilling to risk war in order to block Germany's ambitions in Central and Eastern Europe— they had not stopped him even when he marched into Prague; partly co-conspirators with the Jews; partly muddle-heads or cowards such as Chamberlain had proved to be at Munich and after Prague.

While there may have been some kernels of truth in this picture, it was probably to a larger extent a projection of his own arrogance and craving for power, and a product of the typical paranoid hypersensitivity to signs of weakness and cowardice in an imagined enemy and potential victim. But, except perhaps for these elements of fear and weakness which Hitler's own basic weakness enabled him to see in others, his picture of the British was external. He did not even try to imagine how their world might look to them, from the inside, on the assumption that they were ordinary peaceloving but proud human beings. He apparently never really asked himself how his own behavior might look from their point of view. As a result, his stereotyped picture was also rigid and static. He could hardly have predicted the great mobilization of pride and of militance that his own behavior evoked in Churchill's Britain, any more than the Japanese militarists could predict the great mobilization of pride and of militance that their attack on Pearl Harbor would evoke in the United States. (In Hitler's speech on September 1 his only reference to Britain, France or the United States was: "When statesmen in the West declare that this affects their interests, I can only regret such a declaration. It cannot for a moment make me hesitate to fulfill my duty.")

Military Overconfidence. Two extreme examples illustrate Hitler's overconfidence: his assumption that, after the Nazi-Soviet Pact, Britain and France would not dare to fight, and his suicidal attack on Russia. Although he was presumably not psychotic, he showed to an extreme degree, within the normal range, not only the typical paranoid delusions of persecution but also the typical paranoid delusions of grandeur.

It should not be assumed, however, that military overconfidence is a rare thing, associated mainly with unusual personalities such as Hitler's. In recent history it has appeared over and over again. Both the Russians and the Austrians were militarily overconfident in 1914. The Allied generals continually prophesied an early victory throughout the First World War. During the period 1917–1924, the Communists grossly overestimated their chances of an early worldwide victory. Stalin apparently thought he could defeat Finland easily and quickly. The Japanese militarists who attacked Pearl Harbor could have had little conception of the anger and the ultimate military strength that their action mobilized in the United States. The French doggedly overestimated the feasibility of holding onto both Indochina and Algeria. In the Suez conflict the British, French and Israelis were overconfident that they could win quickly before worldwide opposition could be mobilized. To be sure, there are in recent history some contrary instances of military *under*confidence. The rule, however, seems to be overconfidence, while underconfidence and strict realism appear to be the exceptions. This is understandable, too, since overconfidence is a form of wishful thinking, and wishful thinking is the rule, not the exception.

Three characteristic forms of military overconfidence can be described. One is common to Austria in 1914 and Hitler in 1939: a failure to take seriously enough the chance that other countries may intervene in support of one's enemy. Austria belittled the chance that Russia, France, Britain or America would intervene in support of Serbia, or be later drawn into the war; Hitler belittled the chance that France, Britain or America would intervene or be later drawn into the war. Similarly the British, French and Israelis were apparently surprised by the speed and strength of opposition to their anti-Egyptian adventure, especially on the part of both the USSR and the United States.

As we have seen, this is related to lack of empathy. It is difficult to realize that one's own behavior, the justification of which seems so obvious to oneself, can appear in the eyes of a neutral or hostile observer as actual aggression. There is also often a failure to realize that, in such a situation, the ally of one's enemy, even if relatively weak, may be too proud to be easily intimidated by one's own or one's allies' threats of intervention. Russia was too proud to be intimidated by the Kaiser's "appearing in shining armour" at the side of Austria; Britain and France were too proud to be intimidated by Hitler's tirades or by the great *coup* of the Nazi-Soviet Pact, even though they felt militarily inferior. This is especially true when the ally of one's enemy feels bound to one's enemy by ties of mutual loyalty or by formal or informal commitments. Russia in 1914 felt in honor bound to protect her Slavic protégé, Serbia; France felt bound by her firm alliance with Russia; Britain felt somewhat bound by her new entente with France. Similarly, though Britain and France had not come to the aid of Czechoslovakia, they became more deeply committed to Poland, and in September, 1939, they felt that if they did not honor their commitments to Poland, Hitler would hardly respect other commitments elsewhere. There is something particularly repulsive to a proud and self-respecting nation in the thought of letting down an ally and violating a commitment because of being intimidated by an enemy even when this seems militarily the rational thing to do. Yet the "enemy" often fails to give enough weight to this factor of obligation-plus-pride, assuming that rational calculations of military advantage and fear of war will be enough to keep "outsiders" from intervening. Sometimes they are right and sometimes they are wrong.

Another form of overconfidence was present to a conspicuous degree only in Hitler's case and not in Austria's: underestimation of the difficulty of coping with an aroused people fighting on its own soil against what it regards as foreign invasion. Hitler encountered this on a vast scale in Russia, as Napoleon had done before him. Others who have encountered it have been Napoleon in Spain, the Allied forces that intervened in Russia in 1918–1920, the Italians in Greece, the Germans in Yugoslavia, the Japanese in China, the French in Indochina, the French in Algeria, the Russians in Poland and Hungary, and the Chinese in Tibet.

Here too, a main reason appears to be lack of empathy. The occupying or invading power usually has a case. Characteristically it focuses on the violent acts, often including atrocities, committed by the activists in the local population, and on its own good intentions. But such black-and-white thinking leads, as always, to selective inattention to the human, non-diabolical characteristics of the local patriots, including their conviction that they are defending their homeland against foreign invasion; and this in turn leads to an underestimate of how difficult the activists may be to handle, helped as they often are by many of the non-activist population.

A third form of overconfidence is the tendency to see another nation or group as disunited, with only the evil rulers hostile to oneself, and the mass of the people either neutral or friendly to one's own side. This has been called the "black-top" enemy-image (White, 1965, p. 249). It is a typical form of the black-and-white picture; as a rule only the leaders at the top of the enemy group are seen as wholly black. The mass of the Serbs and Croats under Austrian rule were not seen by the Austrians as particularly hostile; to them the real enemy consisted of the assassins, the agitators, the nest of conspirators supported by the Serbian government in Belgrade. Similarly, Hitler did not regard the common people of the countries around him as his enemies; it was their Jewish-plutocratic-Bolshevist leaders who were plotting Germany's downfall. The conspiracy theory of history is at the same time a black-top image of the enemy. As such it is similar to many other familiar phenomena: the American public's focus on the Kaiser as the villain of World War I, the complacent employer's conviction that his employees are contented and loyal but misled by union agitators, the Southerner's belief that Negroes in the South would be contented if it were not for "nigger-loving agitators" from the North. It is a wonderfully consoling conception. It simultaneously eliminates the guilt of feeling hostile to a large number of people, creates a positive image of oneself as saving the underdog-masses from their conniving and oppressive leaders, provides a personal, visualizable Devil on whom to concentrate all hostility, and sustains hope that, once the leaders have been firmly dealt with, the battle will be over.

These historical examples of typical, recurrent forms of misperception can sensitize us to possibilities, in our study of perceptions on both sides of the present conflict in Vietnam. Since history seldom comes even close to an exact repetition of itself, all historical analogies should be taken with equal sensitivity to differences between a past situation and a present one. It is always legitimate, however, to formulate them as questions to be asked about the present: Is there now a great absence of empathy on both sides, as there was both in Austrian minds in 1914 and in Hitler's mind in 1939? If so, what thoughts and feelings in the minds of those on one side of the Vietnamese war are typically ignored by most of those on the other side? And so on.

A word is in order also with regard to our own frame of mind as we approach these emotionally explosive questions of fact. The most appropriate frame of mind can perhaps be best described as *tough-minded empathy*.

As the examples we have just cited indicate, the effort to empathize is particularly necessary in the case of one's own worst enemy. For the sake of realism in coping with him, if for no other reason, it is important to try to see the enemy's world as he sees it, from the inside, not assuming that even his worst accusations against oneself are necessarily insincere. But at the same time it is advisable to try to combine empathy with tough-mindedness in several ways. There can be full realization that the enemy's leaders are capable of lying, both to oneself and to their own people, for propaganda purposes, and that therefore no one of their public statements can be taken as necessarily sincere—though all are worth listening to. There can be great skepticism as to the validity of everything the enemy believes, even when his belief is regarded as probably sincere. There can be a similarly tough-minded skepticism about the beliefs of one's own group. And there can be a willingness to act with courage and decisiveness on the basis of much less than a totally black-and-white picture. With no illusions as to the possibility of fully achieving such a synthesis, we can aim at empathy without gullibility, without shirking our responsibility to make an independent appraisal of the facts, and without weakness in action even when action has to be based on much less than a perfect case.

* * *

References

Albertini, Luigi. *The Origins of the War of 1914.* N.Y.: Oxford Univ. Press, 1953.

Barnett, A. Doak. *Communist China and Asia.* N.Y.: Vintage Books, 1961.

Bronfenbrenner, Urie. "The Mirror-image in Soviet-American Relations: A Social Psychologist's Report." *Journal of Social Issues,* 1961, 45–56.

Browne, Malcolm W. *The New Face of War.* N.Y.: Bobbs-Merrill, 1965.

Browne, Robert S. "Vietnam Revisited." *Viet Report,* Aug.–Sept. 1965, 12–14.

Buttinger, Joseph. *The Smaller Dragon.* N.Y.: Praeger, 1958.

Carver, George A., Jr. "The Real Revolution in South Vietnam." *Foreign Affairs,* 1965, **43**, 387–408.

———. "The Faceless Viet Cong." *Foreign Affairs,* Apr., 1966, **44**, 347–372.

Chaffard, Georges. "Talks with the Viet Cong." Paris: *L'Express,* April 19, April 25, 1965. Translated in *Viet Report,* July, 1965.

Devillers, Philippe. "The Struggle for Unification of Vietnam." *China Quarterly,* Jan.–Mar. 1962, pp. 2–23. In Gettleman (ed.), *Vietnam,* 210–235.

Fairbank, John K. *The United States and China.* N.Y.: Viking, 1958.

———. "Why Peking Casts Us as the Villain." *N.Y. Times Magazine,* May 22, 1966, 30–109.

Fall, Bernard B. *The Two Viet-Nams.* N.Y.: Praeger. Rev. ed., 1964b.

Fay, Sidney B. *The Origins of the World War.* N.Y.: Macmillan, 1928.

Gooch, George P. *Before the War: Studies in Diplomacy.* London: Longmans, Green; vol. i, 1936; vol. ii, 1938.

Greene, Felix. *China.* N.Y.: Ballantine Books, 1961.

Halberstam, David. "The Buddhist Crisis in Vietnam." *N.Y. Times,* Sept. 11, 1963. In Gettleman (ed.), *Vietnam,* 262–270.

Hammer, Ellen E. *The Struggle for Indochina.* Stanford: Stanford Univ. Press, 1954.

Heiden, Konrad. *Der Fuehrer.* Boston: Houghton Mifflin, 1944.

Hinton, Harold C. *Communist China in World Politics.* Boston: Houghton Mifflin, 1966.

Hitler, Adolf. *My New Order.* (Speeches, ed. by De Sales). N.Y.: Reynal & Hitchcock, 1941.

Holsti, Ole R., and Robert C. North. "The History of Human Conflict." In McNeil (ed.), *The Nature of Human Conflict,* 155–171.

Kennan, George F.   Testimony to Foreign Relations Committee, Feb. 10, 1966. *New Republic*, Feb. 26, 1966, 19–30.

Lacouture, Jean.   *Viet-Nam Between Two Truces*.   N.Y.: Random House, 1966.

————.   "The Military Situation in Vietnam."   *New Republic*, May 22, 1966, 20.

Montgelas, Max.   *The Case for the Central Powers*.   N.Y.: Knopf, 1925.

————, and Walter Schucking (eds.), *Outbreak of the World War: German Documents Collected by Karl Kautsky*.   N.Y.: Oxford Univ. Press, 1924.

Osgood, Charles E.   *An Alternative to War or Surrender*.   Urbana: U. of Ill. Press, 1962.

Rapoport, Anatol.   *Fights, Games and Debates*.   Ann Arbor, Mich.: Univ. Mich. Press, 1960.

Schelling, Thomas C.   *The Strategy of Conflict*.   Cambridge, Mass.: Harvard Univ. Press, 1960.

Shaplen, Robert.   *The Lost Revolution*.   N.Y.: Harper & Row, 1965.

Taylor, Edmond.   *The Fall of the Dynasties*.   Garden City, N.J.: Doubleday, 1963.

White, Ralph K.   "Hitler, Roosevelt, and the Nature of War Propaganda."   *J. Abnorm. & Soc. Psychol.*, 1949, 157–174.

————.   "Images in the Context of International Conflict: Soviet Perceptions of the U.S. and the U.S.S.R."   In Kelman (ed.), *International Behavior*, 1965, 238–276.

SOCIAL INTERACTION BASIS OF COOPERATORS' AND COMPETITORS' BELIEFS ABOUT OTHERS

Harold H. Kelley and Anthony J. Stahelski

ABSTRACT

In experiments using the Prisoner's Dilemma (PD) game, it is found that when cooperative and competitive persons interact, (a) the cooperative one tends behaviorally to become like the competitive one; (b) because of this behavioral change, the competitor misjudges the cooperator, taking him to be competitive; and (c) the cooperator but not the competitor is aware of the latter's dominant role in their relationship. These results, considered in the light of several plausible assumptions, lead to the deduction that cooperators and competitors will have different beliefs about what other persons are like with respect to cooperativeness and competitiveness. Specifically, it is inferred that cooperators will believe others are heterogeneous as to their cooperativeness versus competitiveness, whereas competitors will

Source: H. H. Kelley and A. J. Stahelski, "Social Interaction Basis of Cooperators' and Competitors' Beliefs about Others," *Journal of Personality and Social Psychology*, Vol. 16, 1970, pp. 66–91. Copyright 1970 by The American Psychological Association and reprinted by permission.

believe other persons are uniformly competitive. Evidence from a variety of experimental situations is found to confirm this inference. . . . These results illustrate what may be a common phenomenon in personality and social psychology, that a personality predisposition acts through its influence upon the person's social behavior to determine the information he gains from his social environment and, thereby, the beliefs he comes to hold about his world. This analysis provides an explanation in terms of social interaction processes for a "projection" phenomenon previously explained almost exclusively in terms of psychodynamic processes.

This article summarizes a series of empirical generalizations drawn from the authors' work conducted with experimental games and from evidence derived from the existing literature. As the various data have been considered and the line of reasoning followed, they indicate the following conclusions:

1. There are two stable types of individuals which may be described approximately as cooperative and competitive personalities. (This could be put more accurately, perhaps, by reference to stable individual differences along a dimension from cooperation to competition, but the terminology of "types" greatly simplifies the exposition of this argument.)
2. These two types have different views of their worlds, specifically of what other people are like with respect to this typology or dimension.
3. These different views can be accounted for most simply in terms of the differential experience of the two types in their social interactions. This experience is itself a function of the personality type (and indeed, of their different views, once these views have developed). Thus, the different views are indirectly caused by their personalities inasfar as the latter have affected their social world and, through this effect, their experience with it.

As the reader will anticipate, these conclusions have important implications. For example, with respect to practical problems

of conflict reduction in interpersonal relations, the present results highlight the self-fulfilling prophecy nature of the competitive person's stereotype of other people. With respect to the theoretical understanding of the bases of different views of the social world, the present results require emphasis on a social interaction analysis rather than a psychodynamic one. In terms of Kurt Lewin's familiar formula that behavior is a function of the person and the environment, the analysis shows an important and probably not atypical instance where a part of the environment, a part of the social environment, is itself a function of the person's behavior (in turn, a function of his personality). Some people, at least, affect their social worlds so that what they are reacting to is, in part, determined by their own behavior and, thus, by their own personal predispositions. Insofar as these people fail to discount their causal role in their social relationships (the authors' data indicate they do), they develop a distorted view of their social environment. In terms of attribution process (Kelley, 1967), this is an important instance in which an attributional error is made by virtue of the person's failure to note the effect on his experiences of his own behavior.

With this preview of where the evidence has led, we now go back and develop the parts of the problem in the sequence in which information was obtained about them. The authors begin with their own research with the Prisoner's Dilemma (PD) game and then pursue its implications in other gaming work and in other types of data, particularly from research on social perception and the "authoritarian personality."

STUDY OF THE PERCEPTION OF GOALS

The authors entered this area by way of research on the perception of intentions in social interaction (Kelley & Stahelski, 1970a). The version of the PD game shown in Figure 1 was chosen as the procedural vehicle for Experiment I. This is a two-person non-

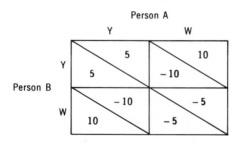

Figure 1.   The Prisoner's Dilemma game

zero-sum game[1] in which on each trial, each of the two players makes choices between his two response alternatives, and then, the consequences for each one are read off from the payoff table (the upper right values in each cell are for Player A and the lower left values, for Player B). The choices are made independently and without communication, so each person makes his decisions under conditions of uncertainty about what the other's choice will be. The relationship poses a number of perplexing questions for the player at each point, these all stemming from the central dilemma, that if they both make the choice that is indicated by their respective individual interests (W), their joint effect is one of mutual harm and of failure to satisfy their collective interest (such as a mutual choice of Y would). This game has been used widely in research and is presumed to pose in an elegant and sharp manner a dilemma that people commonly face in their social relationships. It might be appropriate to note here that this presumption gains credibility from the data assembled here.

For present purposes, since the PD game is played repeatedly over a series of trials, it provides a good setting in which to study the perception of intentions. A person's action at any given point is likely to depend on what he thinks the other person will do, and this in turn is likely to reflect what he thinks the other person is trying to accomplish in the relationship, particularly whether he is trying to satisfy their joint interests or merely his

own interests. Furthermore, the evidence as to the other person's intention is likely to be rather ambiguous for the reason that each response may plausibly be used, depending upon the context, in the pursuit of any goal in the relationship.

The procedure was to let subjects set goals for themselves in the game and then interact in the pursuit of these goals. The authors were interested in what perceptions they would have of one another's goals, what errors of perception would occur, and what would account for these errors. Specifically, subjects were first taught the game and the interaction procedure. They were then asked to decide what they wanted to try to achieve in the relationship. This "goal choice" was made from a list of four specified alternatives which for present purposes can be reduced to two: (a) *cooperative*, which can be paraphrased as "I will try to cooperate with the other player and will be concerned with my own score *and* the other player's score," and (b) *competitive*, paraphrased as "I will work for myself, against the other player, and will be concerned *only* with my own score."[2] Persons were then paired off with different goal choices (e.g., cooperative versus cooperative, cooperative versus competitive, and competitive versus competitive), were instructed to play for a series of trials, and were interrupted to ask for their judgments of each other's goals. At the point where the subjects were permitted to choose what goals they wished to pursue, we left the realm of full experimental control and entered the

---

[1] We actually embedded the PD game relationship in a three-person, zero-sum game, but this is not of material importance for the present discussion.

[2] The reader will note here and elsewhere that our "cooperative" and "competitive" categories are broad and not necessarily unitary. We should, perhaps, make it clear that we recognize that the cooperative and competitive choices are complexly determined. Each category probably covers a number of different motivational components. There are a number of different ways for subjects to specifically interpret the cooperative and competitive choice statements. The authors purposely made them broad and ambiguous for two reasons: (a) We did not want our choice statements to tell the subjects how to *behave*. Each statement was presented as an orientation only. (b) For practical purposes, we did not want to deal with a large number of categories.

domain of personality research. At the time, it was reasoned that this was necessary because there was not enough knowledge to simulate the play of a person pursuing a given goal, and there was little confidence in the ability of the subjects to pursue assigned goals in a realistic manner.   In retrospect, it was this decision which led into the present area of individual differences in orientations to interpersonal relationships.

The results of this procedure, as they bear on the present problem, are simple to summarize. The most common kind of error in perception of goal occurred in the cooperative-competitive pairs and consisted of a judgment by the competitor (the subject who had chosen the competitive goal) that his cooperative partner was also a competitor (i.e., had also chosen the competitive goal). The various data were examined to determine whether this was a case of projection (assumed similarity) or behavior assimilation (the cooperative player having become similar in behavior to the competitive one). The evidence favored the latter explanation.   In a number of respects, the cooperative member of the typical cooperative-competitive pair had become behaviorally like the competitor in the course of the interaction. It was apparently as a consequence of this behavioral shift that the competitive member tended to misjudge the cooperator's intention, inasmuch as these errors tended to occur in those cases where the cooperator's behavior had shifted toward competition. These errors on the part of the competitor suggest that he is not aware of the influence he exerts upon his partner.   Consistent with this point was evidence that the cooperative member was aware of the dominant role played by the competitor in their relationship, but the competitor was not.

At this point the reader is likely to wonder (a) whether the cooperative persons had not changed their goals in the course of the interaction, and (b) how the competitor can be charged with an error if he judges his partner to be competitive when that person is behaving in a competitive manner. With regard to the first question, the data from the present authors' research have not been entirely satisfactory in making a clear case

for mere behavior change without a change in goal. On balance, in view of data from other research and the internal coherence of the present argument, the authors are convinced that the observed effect is a mere shift in behavior, as a temporary means of adapting to a competitive adversary, and not a permanent change in the goal a person has for the relationship. Further discussion on this point appears later. In regard to the second point, the term "error of judgment" is used in a purely descriptive sense. Nothing more or less is meant than that the competitive member of the mixed pair fails to perceive what was the goal or intention his partner had for their relationship at the outset. The subjects were asked to judge, on the basis of their interaction, what the other player's goal choice had been. This question clearly refers to the choice made at the outset of the experiment, and the response is requested in terms of the same set of categories that each subject had used earlier in choosing a goal for himself in the relationship. In response to this question, competitors failed to judge accurately what the cooperator's choice had been, even though they might be said to give an accurate account of how he has been behaving in their recent interaction.

To briefly summarize this first study, the results were that in the cooperative-competitive interactions, (a) the cooperator was behaviorally assimilated to the competitor; (b) apparently because of this assimilation, the competitor misperceived the cooperator, taking him to be competitive; and (c) the cooperator was aware of the influence of the competitor in their relationship, but the competitor was not.   Considered together, these results seem to have a further implication if several additional assumptions (which are explained later) can be made. This implication is that (d) cooperative and competitive persons are likely to develop different views of what "other people" are like with respect to cooperativeness versus competitiveness. Specifically, it seemed probable that competitors would tend to believe that other people are also and uniformly competitive, whereas cooperators would believe other people are heterogeneous in this respect, some being cooperative and others, competitive.

And at this point, some evidence from studies with the F scale was recalled (Scodel & Mussen's, 1953, being the first in the line) that was generally consistent with this implication. The idea and the line of argument from which it stemmed seemed important enough to warrant further investigation and assembly of relevant evidence. The available information on the preceding points is summarized below. Some of it derives from several subsequent studies of the present authors, but much is from previous studies on game behavior. . . .

BEHAVIORAL ASSIMILATION OF COOPERATORS TO COMPETITORS

The results from four separate studies which show behavioral assimilation are summarized in Table 1. Approximately the same format has been used in each case, with the cell entries being the percentage of cooperative moves (the Y move in Figure 1) made by each type of actor (shown on the left) in his interaction with different types of partners (shown across the top). Results are shown separately for successive blocks of trials. The percentage of cooperative moves has been used as the index of behavior because it is the most commonly reported one, and although other indexes also show the assimilation effect (Kelley & Stahelski, 1970a, for data on rate of competitive initiatives and rate of shifts), the rate of cooperative moves seems to be as good an index as any.

The first set of data from the first 10 trials of the Kelley and Stahelski (1970a) study already described shows the assimilation effect (see Kelley & Stahelski, 1970a, for data on rate of competitive initiatives and rate of his rate is fairly uniform regardless of the type of partner with which he is matched. In contrast, although the cooperative actor's rate of cooperation is higher, it varies markedly according to the type of partner. The cooperator clearly makes fewer cooperative moves when paired with the competitive partner than when playing another person like himself. Very much the same pattern of

results appears in each of the two following trial blocks.

The second set of data in Table 1 is from a study by Apfelbaum (1967) who also used the PD game. At the beginning of her experiment, she sorted her sample of students into three categories by means of a series of test items. On each item the subject chose between one option which gave him and the partner equal scores and a second option which, as compared with the first, either yielded himself more, the partner less, or both. From the patterns of their choices, subjects were categorized as *egalitaire* (E, who chose options that equalized the two scores), *personnel* (P, who chose options that maximized the difference between the two, and maximized one's own personal gain), or *donnant-donnant* (D, who chose options that yielded high personal gain, but, taking account of the other's gain, not when it was too harmful to the other). Pairs were formed of all three types of subjects, and each was given a description of the partner which corresponded to the partner's category. For an E partner, the subject was told, "Your comrade appears to want to take account at the same time of his own profit and of your profit"; for a P partner, "Your comrade appears to want to take account of his own profit without concerning himself with yours"; and for a D partner, "Your comrade appears to want to take account of your profit to the degree that you take account of his profit." For present purposes, the E and D types were considered as cooperative players and the P type as competitive. The results, shown in Table 1, reveal an assimilation effect similar to the effect in the Kelley and Stahelski (1970a) study. The difference in rate of cooperation across the top row is greater than that across the bottom row.

Both sets of data just considered reveal an assimilation effect at the end of the first trial block. But both also tend to show an increase in the effect over the successive trial blocks. That is, the difference across the top row tends to become larger, and the difference across the bottom row, smaller. Another aspect of this shift, particularly noticeable in the Kelley and Stahelski (1970a) data, is that in the cooperative-competitive pairs, the co-

Table 1. Percentage of cooperative moves

Kelley & Stahelski (1970a)

Actor			Partner					
	1st 10 trials			2nd 10 trials			3rd 10 trials	
	Coop	Comp		Coop	Comp		Coop	Comp
Coop	85%	64%	Coop	90%	67%	Coop	92%	69%
Comp	34%	32%	Comp	31%	18%	Comp	25%	27%

Apfelbaum (1967)

Actor			Partner		
	1st 25 trials			2nd 25 trials	
	Coop	Comp		Coop	Comp
Coop	62%	42%	Coop	66%	44%
Comp	44%	30%	Comp	43%	34%

Stahelski & Kelley (1969)

Actor			Partner					
	1st 10 trials			2nd 10 trials			3rd 10 trials	
	Coop	Comp		Coop	Comp		Coop	Comp
Coop	✕	64%	Coop	✕	56%	Coop	✕	49%
Comp	41%	✕	Comp	39%	✕	Comp	35%	✕

Sermat & Gregovich (1966)

Actor			Schedule					
	1st 50 trials			2nd 50 trials			3rd 50 trials	
	Tit-for-Tat			Coop	Comp		Coop	Comp
Coop (n = 24)	85%		Coop n = 24	✕	56%	Coop n = 6		81%
						Comp n = 18	80%	
Comp (n = 56)	40%		Comp n = 56	42%	✕	Coop n = 7		69%
						Comp n = 49	39%	

operator's rate of cooperation tends to move closer to the competitor's rate over trial blocks. This latter effect also appears in the third set of data which were derived from a study using only cooperative-competitive pairs.[3] As can be seen in Table 1, both mem- bers of these pairs became less cooperative in their behavior over trials, but the drop is sharper for the cooperative member with the result that the two rates tend to converge (though not to a statistically significant degree).

[3] A. J. Stahelski and H. H. Kelley. Sex and Incentive in the Prisoner's Dilemma Game. Manuscript in preparation, 1969.

The cooperative member had chosen the option, "Cooperation with the other player—I will work to cooperate with the other player. I will be concerned with my own chips *and* the other player's chips." In contrast, the competitive member had chosen, "Work for myself—I will work independently, for myself, against the other player. I will be concerned *only* with my own chips."

The last set of data in Table 1 is from Sermat and Gregovich's (1966) study using the Game of Chicken, the matrix of which is shown in Figure 2. The game derives its name from the game occasionally played by young drivers who, on a dare and in order to prove their bravery, race toward each other on a highway, both straddling the white line, in order to see who will "chicken-out" first and give way to one side. The one who pulls aside (Y response) and lets the other pass on the line (W response) loses the contest, and, of course, if neither pulls off, both suffer poor outcomes. Sermat and Gregovich's results are important first because they show assimilation in a game that is somewhat different from the PD game. Specifically, this game involves a direct conflict for each player. Each person exercises behavioral control over the other (Thibaut & Kelley, 1959), which means that each one's best response depends upon what the other one does. Second, Sermat and Gregovich have evidence relating to what happens if, after his behavioral assimilation to a competitor, the cooperator is subjected to a cooperative mode of play. This bears on the important question raised earlier of whether the cooperator is affected only temporarily in his behavior or whether he changes his basic orientation to the relationship.

In contrast to the preceding three studies where cooperation versus competition was defined by pregame decisions or choices, Sermat and Gregovich's types were defined in terms of their behavior during early trials in interaction with a tit-for-tat strategy. (The tit-for-tat strategy begins with a randomly selected choice and then, on each subsequent trial, gives the subject whatever choice he had made on the immediately preceding trial.) Those who, on the last 20 trials of the first 50 trials, had made four or fewer W choices were classified as "cooperators," and the rest, having made five or more such choices, were classified as "competitors." A second difference between this study and the preceding ones is that subjects played against experimental schedules rather than against each other. However, the subjects thought they were playing against real persons throughout the game, and the programmed schedules correspond approximately to what persons with cooperative or competitive intentions might be expected to do. Thus, for the second 50 trials, cooperators were subjected to a mildly competitive strategy (tit-for-tat, except the subject was given two more W choices than his own choices warranted). During the same period, competitors were treated in a flexible manner by an experimenter, whose intention was to induce them to cooperate. At the end of the second trial block, subjects were reclassified as cooperator or competitor, depending as before upon the number of W responses they had made on the immediately preceding 20 trials. And then, once again, the cooperators and competitors, as identified at this point, were subjected to the two different schedules.

The results are shown in the last row of Table 1. (The percentages are estimated from Sermat & Gregovich's Figure 3.) The rates of cooperation for the first 50 trials provide base rates for the two classes of individuals as they interact against a standard tit-for-tat program. Then, the rates for the second 50 trials show the assimilation effect. The mild competitive schedule has induced the cooperative subjects to drop sharply in their rate of cooperation, but the cooperative schedule (or, more properly, the experimenter's attempt to induce the competitive subjects to be cooperative) has had little effect. Another reflection of assimilation is the fact that at the time of reclassification, only 6 of the 24 original cooperators had persisted in their cooperation and could again be classified as such, but 49 of the 56 original competitors had persisted in their behavior and again met the competitive criterion.

The last block of data is important be-

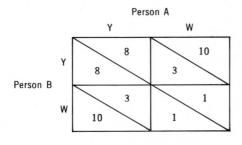

Figure 2.   The Game of Chicken

cause it shows a "rebound" effect among the original cooperators. The 18 who had become competitive behaviorally, when treated with the schedule intended to induce cooperation, *readily returned to their original level of cooperation.* The 49 persistent competitors continued to resist the influence of the cooperative schedule. Interestingly enough, the 7 initially competitive subjects who had become cooperative tended to persist in their cooperation despite being met now with a schedule that was mildly competitive. Perhaps they were encouraged by the cooperative treatment during the second trial block to try to induce its return during the third trial block.

For the present argument, the most important result from Sermat and Gregovich's study is that cooperators are behaviorally assimilated to the competitive schedule, but they readily return to cooperative behavior when the schedule becomes cooperative. The latter fact tells us something about whether cooperators change their goals or simply their behavior. The "rebound" effect suggests that they merely change their behavior in the face of the competitive partner and readily reassert their interest in establishing a cooperative relationship when the partner becomes similarly inclined.

The previously considered results suggest that the behavioral assimilation of the cooperator to his competitive partner is only partial. On the other hand, as has been noted, it appears to become more complete as the interaction continues. Insofar as the behavioral assimilation is rather complete, we would expect the pair relationships to tend to devolve into extreme types.[4] And indeed this implication is generally supported by re-

sults from Rapoport and Chammah (1965), and Pilisuk, Potter, Rapoport, and Winter (1965), who find in the PD game that there are frequent "lockins" of either cooperation or noncooperation. The latter study, which employed an expanded version of the PD game, provides considerable information about the early interactions in pairs that eventually become "doves" or "hawks." Those authors interpreted several of their analyses as suggesting that doves manage to withstand greater discrepancy (akin to the Y-W combination of choices) during early plays. It seems that these results merely reflect the higher rate of cooperative actions in the pairs that eventually become doves, it not being possible for some of these discrepancies to exist with the very low rates of cooperative behavior that characterized the eventual hawk pairs. More significant, we believe, are the authors' other analyses which suggest that the doves were more similar in behavior within the pairs, and that the pairs which eventually became hawks more often had early asymmetric and unilateral behavior. This of course is consistent with the idea of behavioral assimilation, with some of the pairs that eventually lock in on mutual noncooperation including *one* member who began with cooperative intentions for the relationship.

One wonders whether the assimilation may not, in some cases, be an *over*assimilation, with the initially cooperative person behaving even less cooperatively than the competitive partner. This might occur if the cooperator's frustration of having his goals for the relationship thwarted is translated into an extreme aggressiveness. Several sets of data suggest this may occur. Swinth (1967) pitted his subjects against a schedule of play which always made the competitive choice on the first trial. He compared subjects whose own first choice was cooperative versus competitive in terms of their "trust" (willingness to make the cooperative choice) on subsequent test trials. (His procedure was far more complicated than is implied, but these are the essential facts for our present purposes.) The 27 subjects whose first choice was cooperative made cooperative choices on only 30% of the later test trials, but the 72 subjects who also played competitively on the

---

[4] It is tempting to apply a genetic model of "dominant" and "recessive" genotypes to this relation between member dispositions and pair characteristics. Thus, if we knew the frequency of cooperative and competitive genotypes within a given population of persons, the assumption that competition is the dominant characteristic, together perhaps with an assumption about rates of pairing, would enable us to predict the frequency of pairs that would be phenotypically (behaviorally) cooperative or competitive.

first trial made 40% cooperative choices. Apparently, the fact of having trusted the other and then having been exploited on the first encounter made the former set of subjects more negative toward the partner. These data are difficult to compare with the ones already presented, but it is as if, in one of the upper matrices of Table 1, the rate of co-operation in the upper-right cell is lower than that in the lower-right one. This would be an instance of overassimilation, where the co-operator becomes less cooperative in interaction with a competitor than competitors are with each other.

Another set of data suggestive of over-assimilation is provided by Shure, Meeker, Moore, and Kelley (1966). The game, modeled after the Deutsch and Krauss (1960) trucking game, poses a coordination problem for the pair inasmuch as, if each is to gain maximum reward, he is required to share a limited facility which only one can use at a given time. The method of identifying two types of subjects roughly similar to the present authors' cooperators and competitors employed a personality inventory administered to all subjects at a separate session before the game. The scores on this multitest inventory were factor analyzed first, and then subjects were scheduled in a systematic manner, so as to provide equal numbers of all possible pairings of persons high and low on the first two factor scores. The second of these, a measure of conciliation versus belligerence, is of concern here because it was the only factor scores for which pair composition scores bore a relation to the success of the pair, and the high and low scorers seem to correspond, respectively, to the present authors' cooperative and competitive types. (High scorers advocate responding to other people, even the unfriendly and hostile ones, with help and understanding. They urge admission of their own wrongs, refuse to use threats or belligerent means, or to be motivated by revenge, and instead advocate a "diplomatic and constructive response guided by considerations of humanitarianism and cooperation [Shure et al., 1966, p. 25].")

Let us consider the results for high-high, high-low, and low-low pairs. The comparisons were made entirely in terms of indexes for each pair rather than individual behavioral measures, so it is not possible to examine directly how the high scorer is affected by interaction with a low scorer. However, one particular index leaves little doubt on this point. This is an index of mutual interference. Inasmuch as it takes two players to create mutual interference, this index shows what the more cooperative (conciliatory) member of the pair is doing. The results provide striking evidence of an overassimilation effect in degree of mutual interference: the high-highs are lowest, the low-lows are intermediate, and the *high-lows are highest*. Once again, this pattern of results suggests that the more cooperative member in the mixed pairs has become less cooperative than competitive members in the competitive-competitive pairs. Although not as clear in their behavioral implications, other measures of the pairs' success (size of joint payoff and number of trials required to achieve an alternation solution to the coordination problem) show the same pattern. It is clear that the high (conciliatory) member of the mixed pair did not submit to the other's domination. Rather, he appears to have been induced by his low (belligerent) partner to put up more resistance than he shows in high-high pairs and, what is more remarkable, even more resistance than low subjects show each other in their low-low relationship.

COMPETITOR'S MISCONCEPTIONS OF COOPERATORS

The point to be made here is that the competitive members of cooperative-competitive pairs tend to misjudge the goals of their partners, taking them to have competitive rather than cooperative intentions. The results on this point are summarized in Table 2. These are organized in the same way as the data in Table 1. The actor, either cooperative or competitive, is represented by two rows of each subtable. The two columns represent his partner who in this case is acting as the "perceiver," giving his judgments of the

Table 2.   Percentage of accurate judgements of actor's goals

Actor			Perceiver					

Kelley & Stahelski (1970a)

	1st 10 trials			2nd 10 trials			3rd 10 trials	
	Coop	Comp		Coop	Comp		Coop	Comp
Coop	94%	53%	Coop	93%	65%	Coop	97%	65%
Comp	74%	73%	Comp	65%	88%	Comp	82%	85%

Stahelski & Kelley[a]

	1st 10 trials			2nd 10 trials			3rd 10 trials		
	Coop	Comp	Observer	Coop	Comp	Observer	Coop	Comp	Observer
Coop		67%	71%		46%	62%		44%	58%
Comp	65%			67%			75%		

[a] See Footnote 3

goals of the actor. The entries in the table are percentages of accurate judgments for each combination, that is, the percentage of cooperative actors judged to be "cooperative" and the percentage of competitive actors judged to be "competitive."

The first set of results are from the Kelley and Stahelski (1970a) study, which was described earlier in some detail. The reader will note that cooperative actors are judged with high accuracy by cooperative partners. Competitive actors also tend to be judged accurately, and, with the puzzling exception of the second trial block, this is true whether their partners are cooperative or competitive. The least accurate judgments are those made of cooperative actors by competitive partners. (Significance tests show that competitors are judged more accurately than chance by both types of perceivers, whereas cooperators are judged more accurately than chance only by cooperative perceivers.)

The parallel between the behavioral assimilation data in Table 1 and the results on judgmental accuracy suggest the obvious conclusion, that the competitors make their errors because the cooperators have begun to act like competitors. Internal analysis of the results from Kelley and Stahelski (1970a) indicates that this is true. Those cases in which cooperative players are judged to have competitive goals are ones in which they have become behaviorally similar to competitors.

The second set of data in Table 2 is from the Stahelski and Kelley (see Footnote 3) study in which only cooperative-competitive pairs were used. In addition, an observer of the interaction always viewed it from the perspective of the competitive member. That is, the observer knew the competitor's goal choice and, with that knowledge, made judgments of the goal of the other (cooperative) player. The results show that at the end of the first trial block, all judgments are made with modest (and greater than chance) accuracy. Then, as the interaction progresses, the perceivers of the cooperative player decrease in their accuracy (the change from first to third trial block is significant for the competitive perceiver's accuracy), while the cooperative judge becomes increasingly accurate in his judgments of the competitive partner. Thus, paralleling the trend toward increasing behavioral assimilation shown for this study in Table 1, the data in Table 2 show an increasing degree of differential accuracy for judgments of the cooperative and the competitive members of the pair. The competitive member is increasingly seen for what he is, whereas the cooperative member is increasingly taken to be a competitor.

The results from this study indicate that an observer of the interaction also misjudges what the cooperator's goal is, though perhaps to a somewhat lesser degree than the competitive player himself. Similar results were obtained from Kelley and Stahelski (1970a). It is this evidence together with the covariation between errors and behavioral assimilation that allows us to assign a secondary role to projection (assumed similarity) as the process underlying these errors and that indicates instead that they are mediated primarily by the behavioral shift characteristic of cooperators in their interaction with competitors. The competitor is not able to discount his own role in inducing this shift but, by and large, neither are third persons who observe the interaction from the competitor's side. We now turn to evidence bearing more directly on the perceived causal roles of the cooperator and competitor in their interaction.

DIFFERENTIAL AWARENESS OF THE COMPETITOR'S INFLUENCE

It is difficult to see how the competitive member of cooperative-competitive pairs could misjudge the intentions of the partner if he were aware that his own competitive moves dominate the PD game relationship. Thus, his errors of judgment lead us to expect him also to make errors in attributing causal responsibility for the relationship. Specifically, we would expect the competitor to attribute equal responsibility to himself and to his partner. On the other hand, the present analysis suggests that the cooperative member comes to behave competitively because he makes a defensive adjustment to the competitor's actions. If so, the cooperator should be aware of the greater causal role played by his competitive partner.

Results consistent with these expectations are summarized in Table 3. In both experiments, the subjects were asked at the end of the interaction, "Who do you feel was responsible for how the relationship turned out?" They rated the degree of responsibility of self and other player separately on 3-point scales, with 1 meaning "I [he] was slightly responsible"; 2, ". . . somewhat responsible"; and 3, ". . . most responsible."

The results from the Kelley and Stahelski (1970a) study show that the members of the homogeneous pairings (cooperative-cooperative and competitive-competitive) rate each other about equally responsible, at a point between "somewhat" and "most." In

the cooperative-competitive pairs, the competitive member similarly rates the two as equally responsible, but the cooperator rates himself significantly less responsible than the other. Results very similar to the latter were obtained in the mixed pairs from the Stahelski and Kelley study. It is clear that the cooperator but not the competitor is aware of the greater influence the latter's behavior exercised in the development of their relationship.

Very similar results are obtained in these two studies from observers who witnessed the cooperative-competitive interactions from one side or the other. Thus, in the Kelley and Stahelski (1970a) study, observers who knew the cooperative player's goal and made judgments of the other person's (the competitor's) goal rated the responsibility of the two actors as 1.94 and 2.44, respectively. In contrast, observers who witnessed the action knowing the competitor's goal rated him 2.37 and the cooperator, 2.25. In the Stahelski and Kelley study, all observers sat at the side of the competitor, and, like him, they gave rather similar responsibility ratings to the two actors (2.46 for the competitive actor and 2.19 for the cooperative actor). These results correspond closely to those in Table 3. Like the data in the preceding section, they indicate that third perons (who happen to be heterogeneous in the goals they set for themselves in the PD game) are subject to the same judgmental errors and tendencies as are the actors from whose side they view the interaction.

Another type of evidence indicating dif-

Table 3. Degree of responsibility attributed to the actor

Actor	Perceiver			
	Kelley & Stahelski (1970a)			
Coop	Self	2.31	Self	2.47
	Other	2.43	Other	2.30
Comp	Self	1.92	Self	2.31
	Other	2.47	Other	2.19
	Stahelski & Kelley[a]			
Coop			Self	2.33
			Other	2.23
Comp	Self	1.88		
	Other	2.41		

[a] See Footnote 3

ferential awareness of the competitor's role comes from a study by Kelley and Stahelski (1970b) of goal inferences made from short sequences of the interaction. Cooperative and competitive subjects were shown the behavioral choices that Persons A and B had made on a given trial and then, A's choice on the next trial. From this they were asked to infer what intention A had for the relationship. Of particular interest in the present instance are their interpretations of the sequence in which A's initial cooperative choice meets with a competitive choice by B and then, on the next trial, A plays competitively. This event, an elementary example of behavioral assimilation on A's part, can easily be taken as an instance where he has been influenced by B's initial behavior to adopt the same behavior himself. On the assumption that is being argued here, that cooperative subjects are familiar with the experience of being influenced to play competitively by their partners, but competitive subjects are not aware of this effect, we expected cooperative subjects more often to identify A's goal as one of cooperation. Indeed, this proves to be the case. Significantly more cooperative subjects than competitive subjects identified A's goal as cooperative (57 per cent versus 31 per cent). It is important to add that this is not a case of simple projection. There is *no* significant overall tendency for cooperative subjects to attribute a cooperative goal to A regardless of the sequence of behaviors. Cooperative subjects make this attribution 50 per cent of the time, whereas competitive subjects do so on 48.5 per cent of the possible occasions. In fact, it is only for this pattern of "imitative competition" that the cooperative subjects significantly exceed the competitive subjects in frequency of the cooperative attribution.

DIFFERENTIAL VIEWS OF "OTHERS": THE TRIANGLE HYPOTHESIS

The evidence presented thus far shows that the experiences cooperators and competitors have in their interactions with each other are quite different. The cooperator is influenced to behave in a manner similar to the partner, and while he is aware of this fact, the competitive partner is not. And as a consequence, the competitor misjudges the intentions of the cooperator taking him to be a competitor. The evidence also makes clear that the cooperator's experience in these interactions is sharply different from that in his other relationships, for example, with other cooperators. In the latter instances, he behaves cooperatively and is perceived for what he is. In both types of relationships, the cooperator manages to judge accurately the partner's goal, whether it is cooperative or competitive. In contrast, the competitor's experience in interaction with the cooperator is very much the same as it is in interaction with other competitors. In both cases, he finds the partner to behave competitively, and he gains the impression the partner has competitive goals like his own.

If several assumptions are made, these results have important and far-reaching implications regarding the different views of other people that cooperators and competitors are likely to develop. The necessary three assumptions are as follows:

1. The PD game is an analogue of the type of real-life relationship in which people are able to gain information about one another's basic social orientations. This does not imply that the PD game type of relationship is a common one. Rather, the assumption is that the PD game simulates the very important class of social interaction settings in which the situational constraints on behavior are minimal and in which, therefore, the participants can feel they learn something about each other rather than merely about social roles and structure.

2. The goals that subjects set for themselves when they enter the laboratory PD game reflect the orientations they generally adopt for a wide variety of their social relationships. In other words, the cooperative subject tends generally to have a cooperative orientation, and the competitive subject, generally to have a competitive orientation. It is important

to note that this assumption does *not* imply that cooperative and competitive persons always behave in accordance with their orientations. The data which have already been summarized show that cooperatively oriented persons do not necessarily behave according to their orientations. And, of course, even competitors are likely to behave cooperatively in settings where there are strong social pressures to do so.

3. Cooperative and competitive persons encounter and interact with one another in an unsystematic manner. That is, each type of person has experience in social interaction with both his own and the other type of person. There is no marked degree of "selective mating."

These assumptions, together with the results summarized above, imply that cooperators and competitors will develop different views of what other people are like. Specifically, cooperators will be aware of heterogeneity in outlook—that some people are cooperative, but others are competitive. In contrast, competitors will tend to assume that other people are also and uniformly competitive. Translating the types into the underlying dimensions of which they are dichotomized simplifications, this hypothesis can be represented by the triangular plot shown in Figure 3. Hence, the authors term this the "triangle hypothesis." The triangle is simply a way of showing the relationship hypothesized to exist between the person's own orientation to interpersonal relationships and his expectations or beliefs about other persons' orientations. Cooperative persons are

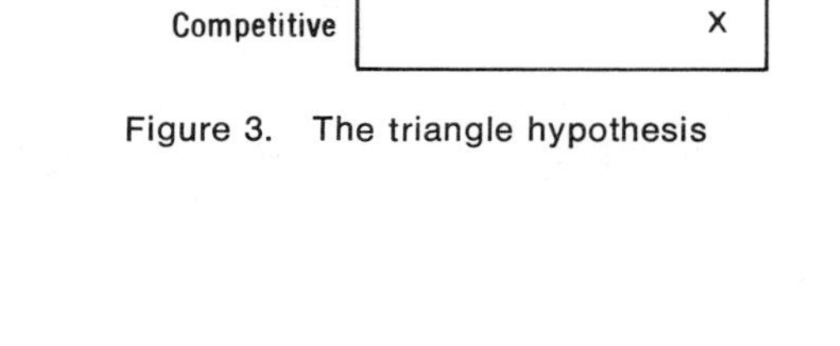

assumed to believe others are heterogeneous as to their cooperativeness versus competitiveness, whereas competitive persons are assumed to believe others are homogeneously competitive.

As to how this hypothesis can be tested, the present assumptions have the further implication that persons who adopt different goals for the experimental game interaction will also have different expectations about the goals other persons will adopt in the same situation. It is the first assumption, that there is a rough isomorphism between the PD game setting for social interaction and certain real-life settings rich in person information, which permits us to generalize from our laboratory results and draw the inference above about the nature of the general relationship between the person's orientation and his expectations about others' orientations. And, it is this same assumption which permits testing of the hypothesized triangular relationship within the laboratory setting.

The remainder of this section is devoted to a summary of evidence from laboratory game research that bears on the triangle hypothesis. . . .

The first two sets of data in Table 4 are from two studies already described which used the PD game. After the subject had been thoroughly instructed in the payoff and procedural rules for the game and after he had chosen his own goal for the interaction, he was asked, "Which goal choice do you think the typical person will choose?" He answered in the same two categories he had just used in making his own goal choice. The relation between the goal choice the subject had chosen for *himself* and the choice he expected the *typical* person to make is shown in each table. The percentages are computed across each row to indicate how subjects of each type distribute their expectations. The expected triangle pattern is seen in the fact that the distribution tends to be even across the top row, but to pile up at the right side in the bottom row.

It is convenient to compute an index of the degree to which each table conforms to the triangle pattern. A triangularity index

Expectations as to Others' Orientations

	Cooperative		Competitive	
Cooperative	X	X	X	X
		X	X	X
			X	X
Competitive				X

Own Orientation

Figure 3.   The triangle hypothesis

Table 4. Expectations of the typical person

		Stahelski & Kelley (PD)					Kelley & Stahelski, 1970b (PD)		
		Expected typical					Expected typical		
		Coop	Comp				Coop	Comp	
Self	Coop	A 60%	B 40%	n = 129		Coop	39%	61%	n = 52
	Comp	C 20%	D 80%	n = 90	Self	Comp	24%	76%	n = 49
		TI = 40					TI = 30		

		Dorris (Bargaining)					Transnational study (Bargaining)			
		Expected typical					Expected typical			
		Coop	Comp				Coop	Neutral	Comp	
Self	Coop	38%	62%	n = 16		Coop	40%	14%	46%	n = 203
	Comp	8%	92%	n = 24		Neutral	16%	31%	53%	n = 90
		TI = 60				Comp	7%	9%	84%	n = 347
							TI = 71			

		Centers & Kelley (Survey data on student protest)							
		Student sample					Nonstudent sample		
		Expected opposition					Expected opposition		
		Coop	Comp				Coop	Comp	
Self	Coop	74%	26%	n = 181		Coop	72%	28%	n = 225
	Comp	9%	91%	n = 57	Self	Comp	14%	86%	n = 64
		TI = 34					TI = 28		

(TI) is computed by a simple formula which combines the four percentages, as designated in the first part of Table 4, in the following manner:

$$TI = (D - C) - |A - B|$$

As the reader will note, this index becomes larger the more D exceeds C and becomes smaller as there is any difference in either direction between A and B. The index is *positive* for a triangular pattern oriented in the expected direction (upside-down, pointing left), *zero* for a symmetrical pattern or a simple positive correlation between the two variables, and *negative* for either a negative correlation or a triangle oriented in any other direction. A perfect triangular pattern of the type expected would yield a TI of 100 (A =.

$B = 50\%$ and $D = 100\%$). The two PD game studies summarized in Table 4 yield indexes of 40 and 30, respectively.

The next two sets of data show that the effect is not limited to experiments using the PD game. In both these instances, complex bargaining games were involved. An additional departure from the procedure used in the PD game studies is that subjects never made an explicit choice of goal for the game, but simply rated how they themselves expected or preferred to behave in the game and how they expected the typical person to behave or prefer to behave. These data had been gathered for other purposes prior to the formulation of the triangle hypothesis and were reanalyzed to provide evidence bearing on it.

In the first of the bargaining studies in

Table 4,[5] two subjects tried to reach agreement on a number falling *between* a high number assigned to one of them and a low number assigned to the other. Each person knew only his own number and was not allowed to agree to a number outside of the boundary set by it. Each one was scored according to how far the final, agreed-upon number deviated from his own. Thus, in an abstract form, the situation resembled the bargaining over price that takes place between a buyer and seller, each of whom is completely in the dark about what the other can afford to agree to. After being instructed in the task, the subjects rated how they themselves preferred to behave in the bargaining situation and how the typical other person would prefer to behave, using a series of 6-point rating scales. The results from the scale anchored with the polar opposites, cooperative and competitive, are shown in Table 4, where it can be seen that they yield a *TI* of 60.

The transnational study[6] employed another simple bargaining game. On each trial, the two subjects received a "joint value" which they could keep if they could agree on how to divide it up between them. At the same time, each subject was given an "individual value" which he received on that trial if they failed to reach agreement of a division of the joint value. These values varied from trial to trial in an unsystematic manner, and each person knew only the joint value and his own individual value, so there was considerable uncertainty in their relationship. Furthermore, it was in their mutual interest to agree on a division of the joint value each time because once they developed an unbroken sequence of agreements at least five in length, all values and, therefore, the amount they could make from the game, increased sharply. Counterposed against this

long-run mutual gain to be made from agreement were short-term individual losses, inasmuch as one or both of their individual values were often larger than the share each could gain from a division of the joint value.

Once again, after subjects were carefully instructed in this game, they used 7-point scales to rate how they expected the typical person to behave and then how they themselves expected to behave on the bargaining problems. This procedure was followed with 40 pairs at each of eight different laboratories; three in Europe, five in the United States. At each laboratory, half of the pairs were run under conditions of low incentive (points) and half under high incentive (money). Because of the large number of cases involved, the data are very useful in answering a number of questions concerning the triangle hypothesis.

The results for all 640 subjects are summarized in Table 4. It can be seen that the triangle pattern is clearly in evidence. The 7-point rating scales include a center position which cannot be assigned to either extreme, so it is described here as "neutral." Omitting these neutral ratings and considering only the four corner values, the *TI* was calculated to be 71.

We may wonder whether the triangle pattern holds under (*a*) high- versus low-incentive conditions and (*b*) in the samples of subjects from the different laboratories. The *TI* value for the low-incentive condition was 59, and for the high, 66. The values for the eight laboratories are as follows: Louvain, 87; Paris, 73; Utrecht, 69; Columbia University, 73; Dartmouth College, 70; System Development Corporation, 37; University of California, Los Angeles, 28; and University of North Carolina, 83. These values seem satisfactorily high and stable, with two exceptions, System Development Corporation and the University of California, Los Angeles. The latter exception is particularly puzzling (and rather embarrassing) inasmuch as the PD game research leading to the development of the triangle hypothesis was conducted in the University of California, Los Angeles, laboratory. These exceptions aside, the triangle hypothesis seems confirmed over a considerable range of conditions and samples.

---

[5] J. W. Dorris. The effects of nonverbal cues on interpersonal judgments in a bargaining situation. Unpublished manuscript, 1969.

[6] H. H. Kelley, G. H. Shure, M. Deutsch, C. Faucheux, J. T. Lanzetta, S. Moscovici, J. M. Nuttin, Jr., J. M. Rabbie, and J. Thibaut. An experimental-comparative study of negotiation behavior. Unpublished manuscript, 1969.

One also wonders whether the triangle pattern may not occur to this same degree for all ratings of *self* and *other*. Perhaps it merely reflects the tendency to rate the self more positively than others (or to rate others more negatively than the self). If the latter is the case, the triangular pattern should appear particularly strongly with ratings that are evaluative in their connotative meaning (Osgood, Suci, & Tannenbaum, 1957). The data from the transnational study bear on these points inasmuch as they include seven other rating scales. The *TI*s for these scales, computed over all 640 subjects and as compared with the *TI* of 71 for the cooperative-competitive scale, are as follows:

Honest–Dishonest, 18
Moral–Immoral, 01
Peaceful–Hostile, 08
Foolish–Wise, 58
Cowardly–Brave, 24
Passive–Active, 53
Weak–Strong, 27

Several things are to be noted: (*a*) All the values are positive, suggesting that there may be a general tendency to rate the self more positively than others. (*b*) The indexes tend not to covary with factor loadings on the evaluative factor. The scales were arranged approximately in order from those with highest evaluative loadings to those with lowest, basing this ordering on information from Osgood, Suci, and Tannenbaum and from a factor analysis made specifically of these data. There does not seem to be any decrease in degree of triangularity as we move down the list. In fact, the opposite seems to be the case, with the lowest *TI*s occurring for those variables high in evaluative connotation. This leaves some doubt as to the importance of a general positive evaluative bias favoring the self. (*c*) All the values are lower than that for the cooperative-competitive scale. Apparently, this last scale incorporates the components of meaning that are especially sensitive to the different world views suggested by the triangle hypothesis. The present authors, of course, believe that this derives from the fact that the cooperative-competitive dimension reflects a salient choice people commonly face in their interpersonal relations

and which they tend to learn to make in fairly consistent ways with the consequences outlined in the present article.

The last set of data shown in Table 4 are derived from survey rather than game research.[7] However, they are most conveniently presented here because they are derived in the same way as the previously considered data. That is, the respondent states the goal he would adopt and also gives his expectation of what goal other persons (in this case, his opponents) would adopt. An interview concerning student protest was conducted with samples of university students and persons from the community around the University of California, Los Angeles. The questions elicited evaluations of the aims and methods of university students and of university administrators in various protest situations and confrontations. At the end of the interview schedule, each person was asked, "If you were the leader of your side, that is the side with which you feel the most sympathy, which of these policies would you follow?" He answered by choosing one of four alternatives ranging from "Be *very* cooperative and *willing* to compromise" to "Be very *un*cooperative and *un*willing to compromise." For present purposes the responses can be collapsed into two categories, cooperative and competitive. The respondent was then asked a similar question with the same response categories as to the policies he would expect the leaders of the other side to follow. The results shown in Table 4 yield patterns with positive *TI*s for both samples of the study. While there is a clear correspondence between the person's preferred orientation to the conflict and what he expects of the opposition, deviant instances of the sort where cooperative persons expect a competitive opposition are more frequent than the other type of deviant cases in which competitive persons expect a cooperative opposition.

The evidence summarized in Table 4 tests the triangle hypothesis by analysis of between-subject variance. Strictly speaking,

---

[7] R. Centers and H. H. Kelley. Some factors affecting attitudes toward student protest. Manuscript in preparation, 1969.

however, the hypothesis refers to differences in within-subject variance, cooperative persons believing others to be heterogeneous in their interpersonal orientations and competitive persons believing them to be homogeneously competitive. More pertinent to this version of the hypothesis is the evidence from Kelley and Stahelski (1970b) derived from subjects' judgments of what percentage of typical persons would choose each of the two goals, cooperation versus competition. The triangle hypothesis leads us to expect cooperative subjects to answer "50:50," that is, 50 per cent cooperative and 50 per cent competitive, and competitive subjects to answer "10:90." The evidence is consistent with this expectation. More competitive subjects gave answers at the 10:90 end of the scale, and more cooperative subjects, answers in the 50:50 zone of the scale. Few subjects of either type gave answers in the region of 90:10, and no more cooperators than competitors appear there. More recent data gathered in an undergraduate class in social psychology at the University of California, Los Angeles, support the evidence presented above. These students made their own goal choices from the same list of two alternatives (cooperation or competition) that was used in the Kelley and Stahelski (1970b) study. The students then made their judgments of what percentage of typical persons would choose each of the two goals. The two distributions are different by the Kolgomorov-Smirnoff test at $p < .01$. Consistent with the hypothesis, the distributions are different mainly in the percentages of subjects stating that few typical persons will choose the cooperative choice. Forty-six percent of the 85 competitors predicted a cooperative-competitive split as extreme as 30:70, but only 17 per cent of the 82 cooperators did so.

In sum, there is evidence of the triangular pattern from a rather wide variety of sources: from pregame ratings made for the PD game and for bargaining games, and from survey data pertaining to student-administration conflict in universities; from samples in laboratories in Europe and in the United States. Cooperative persons show greater variability, both between subjects and within subjects in their beliefs about other persons'

cooperativeness, and competitive persons tend to believe others are homogeneously competitive.

* * *

DISCUSSION

Some of the more far-reaching implications of this analysis may be mentioned briefly. A major social problem concerns the type of persons who fill key roles in the law enforcement and judicial processes. The detrimental consequences of having policemen or judges whose beliefs about people are like those of our competitors are too obvious to require explication. Similar difficulties might be entailed if persons in policy-making positions in competitive organizational or international situations are of the competitive type. There is some evidence that the triangle pattern applies to intergroup conflicts as well as to interpersonal relations (see Footnote 7). And there is considerable evidence that the international views of authoritarians are what we might expect from the triangle hypothesis: that is, high authoritarians tend to be nationalistic, to expect war, and to have unfavorable attitudes toward international cooperation (Faris, 1960; Kirscht & Dillehay, 1967; Levinson, 1957; MacKinnon & Centers, 1956; Smith & Rosen, 1958). It is entirely possible that processes similar to the ones we have identified at the interpersonal level also operate at the international level. The foreign policies of a nation which are based on the assumption that all other nations are competitive and exploitative may be self-justifying through the reactions they dependably instigate from the other nations.

The reader may find it incredible that competitors are not aware of the existence of cooperative persons (or at least, drastically underestimate the number of persons so inclined). After all, are there not many, many social relationships and situations in which cooperation is the rule rather than the exception? And has not the competitive person been a party to such cooperative arrangements? The answer is that of course the competitive person has experienced cooperative relationships and situations. But the real issue is what he has learned from this experience. It is a central tenet of attribution theory that in situations where all persons behave alike, the behavior is attributed to the situation rather than to the persons (Kelley, 1967). This implies that the competitive person who takes part in cooperative relationships learns something about the properties of these situations and nothing about the persons involved. Thus, it is entirely possible for him to know that there are cooperative *situations* but still to believe that most *persons* are competitively predisposed.

If the reader finds our description of the differential behavior of cooperative and competitive persons in interaction easy to accept, and its implications for their different world views to be entirely plausible, he may be less ready to accept our argument if he realizes its central astounding implication. The implication is that two types of persons exist in the world whose dispositions are so stable and their interaction so "programmed" by these dispositions that (*a*) they do not influence each other at the dispositional level, and (*b*) they do not influence each other's world views. Why, if they are in interaction, do not all people evolve into competitors (or less likely, cooperators)? How do these two subpopulations, coexisting in the social world and presumably in interaction, manage to maintain and propagate themselves? How do the two "types" manage to persist in the population, even though the competitive genotype is dominant at the phenotypical level of pair behavior? The answers to these questions are far beyond the reach of the present evidence. One might speculate in psychodynamic terms that the basis of cooperative behavior is laid down deeply and firmly enough in the personality that cooperators are assimilated to competitors only behaviorally and not in their basic orientation.

Alternatively, an explanation for the persistence of cooperative orientations might be sought in social interaction arrangements rather than in personality structure. Cooperation may be a viable disposition because cooperators are able to establish sustaining coalitions and enclaves among themselves, or because they manage to command support from disinterested third parties and social norms.

Perhaps even more significant is the implication that the interaction between the two types is so standardized and programmed that they have not been able to intercommunicate their different views and converge upon a common conception of their social world (of each other—of the fact there are two "types"). Their communication has been so partial and incomplete and their interactions so dependably limited and ambiguous that they have been able to go their separate ways in evolving and maintaining their different world views. If this has been possible, as between the two types of persons *within* a given population, how much easier does it become to believe that the gaps *between* populations, between Eastern and Western world views, or between capitalistic and communistic views, or between the outlooks of old and young—are absolutely unbridgeable? Of course, this is putting the point too strongly. All present evidence implies is that cooperators have little effect on the beliefs of competitors *in the normal course of affairs*. Does this not suggest that an important task for social interaction research is to discover how the conditions of interaction might be changed so that there evolves mutual and accurate understanding—so that all individuals acquire veridical beliefs about the general distribution of intentions and dispositions and develop sensitivity to the specific goals and intentions of their particular interaction partners?

References

Apfelbaum, E.   Représentations du partenaire et interactions a propos d'un dilemme de prisonnier. *Psychologie Française*, 1967, **12**, 287–295.

Deutsch, M., and Krauss, R. M.   The Effect of Threat upon Interpersonal Bargaining. *Journal of Abnormal and Social Psychology*, 1960, **61**, 181–189.

Faris, C. D.   Selected Attitudes on Foreign Affairs as Correlates of Authoritarianism and Political Anomie. *Journal of Politics*, 1960, **22**, 50–67.

Kelley, H. H.   Attribution Theory in Social Psychology. *Nebraska Symposium on Motivation*, 1967, **15**, 192–238.

———, and Stahelski, A. J.   Errors in Perception of Intentions in a Mixed Motive Game. *Journal of Experimental Social Psychology*, 1970, in press.   (a)

———, and Stahelski, A. J.   The Inference of Intentions from Moves in the Prisoner's Dilemma Game. *Journal of Experimental Social Psychology*, 1970, in press.   (b)

Kirscht, J. P., and Dillehay, R. C.   *Dimensions of Authoritarianism: A Review of Research and Theory.*   Lexington: University of Kentucky Press, 1967.

Levinson, D. J.   Authoritarian Personality and Foreign Policy. *Journal of Conflict Resolution*, 1957, **1**, 37–57.

MacKinnon, W. J., and Centers, R.   Authoritarianism and Internationalism. *Public Opinion Quarterly*, 1956, **20**, 621–630.

Osgood, C. E., Suci, G. J., and Tannenbaum, P. H.   *The Measurement of Meaning.*   Urbana: University of Illinois Press, 1957.

Pilisuk, M., Potter, P., Rapoport, A., and Winter, J. A.   War Hawks and Peace Doves: Alternate Resolutions of Experimental Conflicts. *Journal of Conflict Resolution*, 1965, **9**, 491–508.

Rapoport, A., and Chammah, A. M.   *Prisoner's Dilemma.*   Ann Arbor: University of Michigan Press, 1965.

Scodel, A., and Mussen, P.   Social Perceptions of Authoritarians and Nonauthoritarians. *Journal of Abnormal and Social Psychology*, 1953, **48**, 181–184.

Sermat, V., and Gregovich, R. P.   The Effect of Experimental Manipulation on Cooperative Behavior in a Chicken Game. *Psychonomic Science*, 1966, **4**, 435–436.

Shure, G. H., Meeker, R. J., Moore, W. H., Jr., and Kelley, H. H.   *Computer Studies of Bargaining Behavior: The Role of Threat in Bargaining.*   Santa Monica: System Development Corporation, SP2916.   1966.

Smith, H. P., and Rosen, E. W.   Some Psychological Correlates of World Mindedness and Authoritarianism. *Journal of Personality*, 1958, **26**, 170–183.

Swinth, R. L.   The Establishment of the Trust Relationship. *Journal of Conflict Resolution*, 1967, **11**, 335–344.

Thibaut, J. W., and Kelley, H. H.   *The Social Psychology of Groups.*   New York: Wiley, 1959.

HOW TO FIGHT A FAIR FIGHT

G. Bach and P. Wyden

Frank Herman felt frustrated to the point of despair. Year after year, his gunny sack of marital grievances kept filling up. His sex life was highly unsatisfactory and so was his social life. He also felt he had more than his share of trouble in managing his money, his in-laws, and his children. Frank was a hawk at heart, but he had been domesticated by his wife Maureen, a shapely but exceedingly introverted little brunette to whom he had been married for eleven years. Frank loved her dearly, but he could never get her to hold still for a searching discussion of their important differences. While she was outwardly a "charmer," Maureen was a fight-phobic dove, forever wiggling out of "ugly" confrontations.

While the children were awake she was too embarrassed to argue at home. She wouldn't level in front of friends because she was too afraid of gossip. In the car she couldn't "mix it" because she felt it would be dangerous. She wouldn't argue with Frank while they walked the dog because it made the dog nervous, and he started barking like crazy. At bedtime she refused to fight because it would cool her sexually, a form of frigidity that sometimes lasted for two weeks or more.

Finally Frank couldn't stand it any more. His neighbor in the scenic hills above Sherman Oaks, in suburban Los Angeles, was an engineer who was aware of Frank's problem. Together they rigged up a public-address system so anything that was said in Frank's living room could be heard in the neighbor's bedroom. Whenever Frank staged unsuccessful attempts to persuade Maureen to level

Source: G. Bach and P. Wyden, "How to Fight a Fair Fight," in *The Intimate Enemy* by G. Bach and P. Wyden (New York: Morrow, 1968), Chap. 6. Copyright 1968 by William Morrow and Company and reprinted by permission.

with him, he experienced an emotional release of sorts: he knew that his good will and her cowardice were being broadcast before witnesses; and he was so angry at Maureen that he no longer cared how unfairly he fought her fight-evasion tendencies.

Eventually Frank sought help through fight training and confessed his trickery to his self-development group. The therapy group put Frank on the "hot seat" and attacked his undercover methods. Later he and Maureen attended a group together and this group pressured him into confessing to Maureen. At first she refused to believe the story, but the engineer/neighbor confirmed it. Maureen flew into a rage not only because she felt she had been spied upon, but also because she had failed to recognize how desperate Frank had felt. She never quite forgave Frank for having "bugged" her own living room, but his extreme tactics (which we would *not* recommend) did have one result that is salutary for constructive fighting: it lowered Maureen's unfairly high "belt line."

Everyone has such a belt line—a point above which blows can be absorbed, thereby making them tolerable and fair; and below which blows are intolerable and therefore unfair. Some "chickens" like Maureen Herman keep their belt lines tucked around their ears and cry "foul" at every attempted blow. Chickens therefore must be persuaded one way or another to lower their unrealistically high belt lines in order to make themselves accessible to healthy aggressive approaches by their partners. But disparities in belt lines are universal—just like disparities in optimal distance needs or in the ability to make sense while under the influence of liquor or in the case of other inequalities already mentioned. These inequalities must be compensated for, and often that isn't easy.

There are limits of tolerance in every

fight—points beyond which a partner feels he can make no concessions and will no longer negotiate, at least not for the time being. Belt lines are similar limits. They apply to a partner's over-all fighting stance or "weight."

Intimates can live with a partner's belt line only if it is openly and honestly displayed, like the honest weight of a boxer before he steps into the ring. The vagaries of mate selection dictate, however, that lightweight spouses are frequently pitched against middle-weight or heavyweight partners, *i.e.*, a shy husband versus an articulate wife. It's a good thing, therefore, that real intimates realize they fight for better understanding, not for knockouts. If they didn't, the murder statistics would be infinitely more shocking than they are.

Mutual good will is particularly important in the long-term fight for better understanding because the power to inflict major psychological and social or economic damage is always in the hands of intimates. Inevitably, they come to know so much about each other's weaknesses that they can pinpoint quite precisely where to hurt the partner if they care to. We call such a weak spot the Achilles' heel. Just as the belt line is not necessarily located around the waist, so an Achilles' heel need not be part of the foot. The belt line protects the Achilles' heel, and this is no mixed metaphor. Strategic weak spots and their protective shields may be located almost anywhere.

Many people are so concerned about their Achilles' heels that they make elaborate efforts to camouflage their vulnerable spots, especially when they first meet a potential new intimate. A girl may tell her lover she is sensitive about her small breasts. Actually she isn't. In her inner dialogue she is asking herself, "How central is my position in his heart? How far can I trust him?"

Then she replies, "I'll watch what he does with my fake Achilles' heel. If he handles it with tact and support, I'll show him my true vulnerable spots."

Faking an Achilles' heel can produce valuable information on how far intimates can trust each other and to what extent they can count on support for their weaknesses. An attack on an Achilles' heel also indicates that the heel-stabbing partner harbors a high level of resentment. In general, such an attack is provoked either by great concern on the part of the stabber; or because he feels he has been pushed against the wall; or he senses imminent defeat; or because the victim is wearing an armor too thick to be penetrated except at one or two spots.

Fake Achilles' heels and fake belt lines sometimes survive through years of marriage. Marco Polletti and his wife Sylvia already had three small children when this exchange took place between them:

MARCO (*confidentially*): I don't think you can really appreciate how sensitive I am about my Italian background.

SYLVIA (*sympathetically*): Sure I do! I've felt it ever since I met you.

MARCO (*seemingly relieved*): OK, then, just make sure you never call me a "wop," not even as a joke!

SYLVIA: OK, I understand.

More than a year later the Pollettis were at a party, and Marco thought that Sylvia was dancing entirely too much with a friend of his. When they got home, he was terribly angry. Both had had too much to drink. A *Virginia Woolf* free-for-all ensued during which Marco, quite unjustly, called Sylvia a "whore." Sylvia, understandably provoked, hit below the belt, or so she thought. She called him a "stupid wop."

But the belt line had been fake—the last remnant of Marco's premarital reservations about the wisdom of entrusting his future happiness to Sylvia, whom he married after only a few weeks of courtship. Now he realized that when he called his wife a whore he had given her adequate cause to disregard his belt line. He broke up their *Virginia Woolf* stalemate with a loud guffaw and said:

"Hey, I guess that's sort of funny. I know I told you never to call me a 'wop,' but I was only testing you. I don't really mind. I guess it's about time I told you what I'm really sensitive about. What bugs me more than anything is here I am 34 years old and I ought to be getting ahead much faster at the office. I don't think I'll ever make it there and it worries the hell out of me."

Sylvia, greatly relieved, said, "Oh, I don't care! I love you anyway. If things get tough, I can always go back to work."

Many untrained marital fighters think that only suckers give away the location of an Achilles' heel. They believe that a spouse will take advantage of such a weakness whenever possible and that the aggressive partner may yell extra loudly if the sensitive one says, "You know that whenever you yell at me, my stomach acts up!"

In an intimate, leveling relationship, however, the danger of attack on an Achilles' heel is minimized. We encourage trainees to make their area of nonnegotiability and supervulnerability known simply by shouting "Foul!" whenever a partner hits below the belt. This is the surest way to find out how far one can trust the other. One of the most love-inspiring experiences is to watch a partner treat one's sensitivities with care. If he fails to be careful and a below-the-belt blow is struck, this is not likely to do mortal damage. It may even be a good thing; at least the unfairly attacked partner has now established a basis for a legitimate deutero-fight about the choice of weaponry for future fights.

Setting one's belt line too low is masochistic and invites needless injury. Setting it too high is self-pampering and cowardly. Pulling one's belt line way up (like Maureen Herman in the first fight of this chapter) is common because high-belters feel smug and justified when they complain about low blows; they may even feel sufficiently "provoked" to justify resorting to vicious measures in "self-defense." Actually, such high-belters are not being unfairly treated. They are themselves unfair; when even a fair blow lands "below the belt" it is obviously impossible to conduct a constructive fight.

A fair and openly displayed belt line is the one that is most likely to be convincing. As intimates get to know each other better and better, a fake belt line is almost sure to be exposed sooner or later and it will not be respected. When such fakery persists, it isn't likely to do much good to keep shouting "Foul!"—just as it doesn't work to meet nonexistent dangers by crying "Wolf!" too often. Belt-line fakers are helped in their phoniness when Partner A insists he knows the location of "B's" belt line instead of letting "B" tell where it is. People who level about their belt lines, on the other hand, can save themselves a lot of trouble. If a girl knows, for instance, that her lover likes having sex with her, she no longer has to go through the pretense of a fake orgasm; chances are that his masculinity is not as vulnerable as she may have feared.

In a word, it pays to fight fairly, and a fair fight is an open encounter where both partners' "weights" and weapons are equalized as much as possible.

Once a partner's true belt line is known, a heavyweight must generally lower his. He can shout "Ouch!" when the weaker opponent hits him where even a weak blow can hurt; but he shouldn't cry "Foul!" Where great discrepancies exist between partners, it may be wise for them to fight only in front of selected good-willed friends or before a therapy group—at least until the heavyweight has been pressured into some self-disarmament. Again, the motto is "Don't drop the bomb on Luxembourg!" If you do, you can only lose.

Not every heavyweight will allow himself to be handicapped, but usually even a bully can learn to step into the ring with one hand figuratively tied behind his back; or to permit himself to be attacked under conditions when his aggressive drives are inhibited, perhaps just before making love or in front of important company. Above all, he will have to learn to avoid maneuvering his opponent into a corner where the other may become so desperate that he feels he is fighting for his integrity or even his life.

Elegant fighters—and we like to think that *elegance* in fighting is what we teach—never, never drive an opponent against the wall. It's not only unfair; it's also dangerous because it may trigger a needlessly vicious counterattack if the cornered partner panics.

We also recommend that a lightweight fighter be allowed to pick a fight at almost any time and place, but that a heavyweight be restricted to times when the lightweight partner is "loaded" and full of confidence.

This technique isn't hard to master. Dr. Jack Holt, a busy internist, was depressed because his wife, Corinne, no longer wanted to tell him what she did with her time while he was off on his busy daily (and sometimes nightly) routine of caring for his patients. He was earning over $60,000 a year, but neither Jack nor Corinne enjoyed their money. They were living parallel lives and rarely shared their feelings except about inconsequential matters. Jack was beginning to suspect that Corinne was having an affair.

The doctor was the heavyweight in the family. He was more intelligent, more verbal, more logical, and enjoyed more social status than Corinne. When he issued a ruling in his family, his announcement carried the weight of law. Before they entered fight training, Corinne tried to compensate for her "weight" deficiencies by using alienating hit-and-run tactics against Jack. She knew, for instance, that he felt guilty because he treated relatively few nonpaying clinic patients. So she needled him by calling him "money mad." Yet she refused to listen when he tried to level with her. He attempted to find out how she might feel about living on a reduced income, but she would not discuss it.

When Jack found that Corinne could not be engaged on this issue, he got mad and accused his wife of hitting him below the belt and being a sneak fighter. His accusations only made Corinne madder. Before their fight-training group, she explained why she had resorted to her dirty tactics.

CORINNE (*toward Jack*): That's all I could do. Sure I fought dirty! But only when you overwhelmed me and had me in a corner. I got tired of losing practically all the time. Anybody would! So the only way I knew how to slow you down was to get at you with a sort of fifth-column approach.

DR. BACH: In other words, you're telling your husband: "I have to fight dirty when you corner me!" But you shouldn't have to let yourself be cornered. Has there been any improvement?

JACK: Yes, I think so—don't you, sugar?

CORINNE (*toward Jack*): Oh, yes. You're a hundred per cent better.

DR. BACH: What does he do now that he didn't do before?

CORINNE: Well, he gives me a chance to score a point or so now and then and I no longer allow myself to be cornered. I don't wait to fight until my back is against the wall, and so I don't have to fight dirty any more.

JACK (*toward Corinne*): I just follow the fair-fight exercises. I wait until *you* feel really good and *then* I place my beef, and it works. Whenever I see you're "down" and not up to it, I initiate a fight pause.

DR. BACH: Could you both talk about an experience that illustrates your new fight styles?

CORINNE: Well, a while back I was asked to be maid of honor at the wedding of the daughter of the most important family in the little town where I come from. It was a socially important, high-class affair. When I got to my home town I was so thrilled and involved in preparing for the event that I didn't tell Jack for four days.

JACK (*toward Corinne*): Yeah! What really got me good and sore was that I tried to reach you several times by long distance and left messages all over the place for you, and you never returned my calls. Of course I felt rejected and like a goddamn fool.

CORINNE: Well, you were right to tell me off when I got back from Michigan feeling really important and in the swing of things. That's when you made a real good point. I liked that.

DR. BACH: What was that point?

CORINNE (*toward Dr. Bach*): Oh, he was very angry with my excuse that I'd been too involved in the social affairs of the wedding. But he really got fit to be tied when I said that he wouldn't have been interested anyway.

JACK (*smiling at the recollection*): Yeah, I caught you attributing to me what you thought I thought—all that stuff about "spirals" that we've talked about here in the group. Anyway (*turning toward the group now*): I told her to cut it out, that the important point was not my interest or lack of it in the wedding, but that I'm interested in anything involving Corinne; and the way she can be involved with me is to share her other involvements with me.

CORINNE (*toward Jack*): When you said, "You're having your fun; all I ask is that you cut me in on it," that made sense to me. It made me think I can learn to share.

JACK (*toward Corinne*): So why haven't you done anything about that since you got back from Michigan?

CORINNE (*agitated*): Because I'm afraid to share activities with you! I know that you'll belittle them and resent them because I'm not concerning myself every minute with your fate.

JACK (*red-faced and shouting*): Foul! Stop! There you go again, telling me how I think and feel. Stop attributing things to me! Why don't you ask me? I'll tell you how I feel. Actually I'm thrilled when you go into something on your own and that it interests you. I love you for it; but I want you to share it with me. . . .

Jack "scored" a point in this fight because he hit Corinne when she was "Up" and felt strong and important because she had been invited to play a central role in a socially significant occasion. He waited until Corinne felt independent and strong enough to entertain the idea of "sharing," without feeling she might be acting like a child who is reporting to an overwhelming heavyweight. When she felt strong, she was not only able to consider his demand to share her interests with him. She was glad to let him win!

In a constructive fight such as this, there are no losers. Corinne was able to "buy" Jack's point because she gained some fresh information from this fight. She found out that he was not belittling her social interests (which *she*, not he, compared unfavorably with his important medical work); that he really meant it when he said he wanted to be included in her world but did not wish to take it over.

People often underestimate the useful-

ness of constructive fighting as a tool for developing new information about the way an opponent feels. Such fresh intelligence can always be put to good use. Often, as in the above fight between Jack and Corinne, it is the key to the ultimate goal of fighting: to bring about a change for the better.

For real intimates, the process of eliciting information about a partner's feelings never ends because their relationship is forever evolving. One spouse or both may read a stimulating new book; or make new friends; or take an eye-opening adult education course; or undergo psychotherapy; or experience an improvement or deterioration of the sexual relationship. All such events can set off changes in a partner's feelings, and the wise spouse will try to keep up to date on developments.

There is only one area of intimacy where something less than total candor is often indicated, and this applies to partners who probe for information about outside sexual interests as well as partners responding to such probes. When it comes to intelligence about erotic stimulation outside of marriage, whether by fantasies or actual affairs, the sensitivities of most husbands and wives tend to be so great that common-sensical couples are prone to temper the rule of frankness by applying infinite tact. Total honesty is not always a virtue and discretion can still be the better part of valor. In this case, discretion may amount to respect for a partner's previously stated nonnegotiable intolerance for certain topics, *e.g.*, past love affairs. On the other hand, partners who greatly value total, unconditional, and reciprocal transparency, must learn to like or tolerate the other's feelings, fantasies, and actions in response to erotic stimulation away from home. Intimates should remember that the limits of a partner's tolerance are usually reached faster over this issue than any other.

Even when extramarital sex is not at issue, and a fight is scrupulously fair, it can be extremely difficult to retrieve new information from intimate hostilities. Almost everybody becomes blinded in the heat of battle, which is another reason why fighting is best done in a cool state, by appointment, at least during the early stages of training. Fighting in an atmosphere of rationality sheds more light and less heat. It conditions fighters to tolerate conflict better. Like ball players, they benefit from practice and coaching. Ball players, too, get heated up in battle and the ones who have been well coached, are the ones most likely to do the rational thing under pressure. The better trained they are, the better they will be able to blend spontaneous action with tactics that were "programmed" into them in advance.

Marital fighters can train themselves to maximize the information yield from aggressive encounters. They can reduce their anger and become better listeners during a fight by telling themselves a single word: "Tough!" We employ the word here in the sense of "It's tough all over!" It is a reminder for combatants not to become oversensitive even in the heat of battle. It is the same kind of self-warning that overweight people are sometimes urged to adopt; for them the slogan is, "Think slim!"

Other information-retrieving methods for marital combatants are discussed throughout this book. At this point we would merely like to assure beginners that they are not alone if their minds retain little of what a fight was all about.

We discovered this amnesia during the early experimental phase of our training program when we began to ask couples to record their fights on tape and bring them in for scoring by their fight-training group. Typically they made their recording over a weekend and brought them to our Institute on Monday evening. When the couples arrived, we asked them to recall what issues their weekend fights had been about. We then replayed their tape. It developed that even so short a time after a fight the partners had forgotten all but about 10% of what the shouting had been about.

They did remember the inflicted hurts, the insults, the pain, the ego damage of their Sunday punches. They vividly recalled process, style, and form: "we had a terrible fight"; "we were very mean to each other"; "I got terribly upset"; "he hit below the belt." What they could rarely recall was the substance—the point of it all. When a couple reported "We had a good fight," they rarely referred to a change and improvement in their lives. More likely, the "goodness" of their fight reflected just its style: it was fought fairly, above the belt.

What happens is that the intensity of rage itself beclouds mind and memory. In the heat of battle, when intimates are angry, tense, and perhaps fearful, it is impossible for them to think as clearly as they usually do. They should therefore make a special effort to listen to everything that's being said during a fight, not just to the things they want to hear; and they should pause frequently for feedbacks by asking such questions as, "What are you trying to tell me? What do you mean by that?" or by volunteering, "Let me tell you how I heard it." Feedbacks help to sort out any controversial points at issue.

III Conflict in Fully Structured Relationships: Moral Factors in Conflict

Chapter 7
NORMATIVE CONFLICT RELATIONSHIPS

In normative relationships, although conflicts of interest may exist, individuals are not supposed to be engaged in maximizing their own self interests. Instead they are supposed to be doing what is right or moral or normative, even if this is not in their self interest. The fact that one party comes to possess legitimate authority over another party is thus a means by which potential conflicts between them may be resolved (in favor of the legitimate authority) and perhaps even made invisible or unrecognizable as conflicts at all.

In the first selection Elder documents the greater long-term effectiveness of parents who exercise legitimate rather than coercive or arbitrary authority in the family. Milgram then demonstrates in a laboratory experiment that legitimate authority exercised by an experimenter may even cause subjects to do severe harm to others. Some comfort might be taken from the fact that in Milgram's experiments the subjects became more upset at inflicting violence on the victims, and more unwilling to do so, as the victims came nearer and perhaps became more human and real to their antagonists. In the next paper, however, Hughes discusses how society gets around these inhibitions by allowing most people to remain ignorant of and isolated from the victims of official cruelty. Each of these first three papers deals with a paradigmatic situation in which one person is required by a legitimate authority or a general social norm to inflict some damage on a second party (in the Elder study, to give up associating with a friend; in the Milgram study, to shock a learner; and in the Hughes piece, to act as guards in a prison). In the final paper, Stouffer explores the limits of this important paradigm: legitimate power falters when different normative orders clash. If students must choose between reporting or ignoring a cheater who is also a friend, the conflict between an anti-cheating norm and a loyalty-to-friends norm gives them a new freedom (and a moral dilemma) to choose which norm they will follow.

PARENTAL POWER LEGITIMATION AND ITS EFFECT ON THE ADOLESCENT

Glen H. Elder, Jr.

ABSTRACT

Research has shown that the assertion of legitimate power engenders feelings of liking and lowers resistance to conformity with respect to the power agent and his rules. However, the effects of different amounts of power exercised by the influencing agent on the above relationships have been left largely unanswered. The objective of this research was to investigate the relationship between the frequency of parental explanations, employed as an index of the degree of power legitimation, and adolescent (1) desire to model parents, (2) compliance with parental requests, and (3) autonomy in problem solving and decision making, on three levels of parental power in a sample of Ohio and North Carolina adolescents. The effects of the frequency of parental explanations on adolescent behavior were found to vary substantially in relation to levels of power.

When a child requests a reason or explanation concerning a particular restriction, at least two responses are open to the parent. On the one hand, the parent may fulfill the request and demand compliance; on the other, the parent may ignore the child's inquiry. From the child's perspective, this is essentially the difference between the expression of legitimate and coercive power.

The results of small group research suggest the following inferences: adolescents who perceive their parents as asserting coercive rather than legitimate power over them should be less highly attracted to their parents,[1] and less likely to conform to rules of conduct in the absence of parental surveillance,[2] than other adolescents. Research reveals that adolescents have less favorable attitudes toward coercive than legitimate power,[3] and that coercive power expression by mothers promotes the development of hostility and power needs among children of nursery school age.[4] These findings suggest that the legitimation of power by parents leads to a strengthening of affective relations between parents and the adolescent, and tends to encourage behavioral conformity to parental rules.

The effects of legitimate and coercive parental power on adolescents are less clear when the legitimacy of different levels of parental power is considered. Since the effects of different levels of power on adolescent affection for parents vary substantially, it follows that the effects of legitimate and coercive power may also differ by the level of

[1] Bertram H. Raven and John R. P. French, Jr., "Group Support, Legitimate Power and Social Influence," *Journal of Personality*, 26 (December, 1958), pp. 400–409; John R. P. French, Jr., H. William Morrison, and George Levinger, "Coercive Power and Forces Affecting Conformity," *Journal of Abnormal and Social Psychology*, 61 (January, 1960), pp. 93–101.

[2] Bertram H. Raven and John R. P. French, Jr., "Legitimate Power, Coercive Power, and Observability in Social Influence." *Sociometry*, 21 (June, 1958), pp. 83–97.

[3] Anatol Pikas, "Children's Attitudes toward Rational Versus Inhibiting Parental Authority," *Journal of Abnormal and Social Psychology*, 62 (March, 1961), pp. 315–321.

[4] Martin L. Hoffman, "Power Assertion by the Parent and Its Impact upon the Child," *Child Development*, 31 (March, 1960), pp. 129–143.

parental power.[5] For instance, the autocratic parent who, as a rule, does legitimize his demands and restrictions by explaining them, is apt to evoke different kinds of reactions from adolescents than is the permissive parent who offers frequent explanations. Similarly, infrequent explanations at these two levels of power are apt to have different effects on adolescent behavior. Building upon experimental and survey findings regarding the differential effects of legitimate and coercive power, this research is concerned with determining how such effects, as revealed in adolescent behavior and reactions to parents, vary in relation to three levels of parental power.

In an earlier study, seven types of parent-adolescent interdependence in the child rearing relationship were delineated.[6] Five of these structures are condensed in this research to measure high, moderate and low parental power.

Autocratic. The parent does not allow the adolescent to express his views on subjects regarding his behavior nor permit him to regulate his own behavior in any way.

Democratic. The adolescent is encouraged to participate in discussing issues relevant to his behavior although the final decision is always made or approved by the parent.

Permissive. The adolescent has more influence in making decisions which concern him than does his parent. The laissez-faire and ignoring types of interdependence are included in this level of power.

The effects of frequent and infrequent explanations of rules of conduct at the three levels of parental power will be examined on (1) the attractiveness of parents—the desire of adolescents to be like or model their parents; (2) compliance with parental requests—conformity to parental wishes regarding peer associations; and (3) autonomy—adolescent independence in decision making and feelings of self-confidence in personal goals and standards of behavior. First, however, the relationship between parental explanations and level of parental power will be investigated. Let us state some general expectations concerning each of the dependent variables (as well as parental explanation) in the order in which they are considered in the subsequent analysis.

HYPOTHESES

A parent may shrug off a child's inquiry by heatedly exclaiming, "You do it, I don't need to explain," or, in contrast, meet the request with an explanation which seems reasonable.[7] Autocratic parents totally exclude their children from participating in the formulation of decisions which concern them while the children of democratic and permissive parents have much more freedom in self-direction. These differences lead us to predict that *the frequency of explanation is inversely related to parental power.*

Since research indicates that positive sentiment toward a power agent increases as the perceived legitimacy of his power increases, it is likely that modeling is positively related to the frequency of parental explana-

[5] Adolescents with highly dominant parents in contrast to democratic parents were much more likely to feel unwanted by their parents, to be low on affectional orientation toward parents, and to consider their child rearing policy to be unreasonable. See Glen H. Elder, Jr., "Structural Variations in the Child Rearing Relationship," *Sociometry*, 25 (September, 1962), pp. 241–62; and *Family Structure and the Transmission of Values and Norms in the Process of Child Rearing*, unpublished, Ph.D. Dissertation, University of North Carolina, 1961, Chapters IX and X.

[6] Elder, "Structural Variations in the Child Rearing Relationship," *op. cit.*

[7] The legitimation of rules of conduct was consistently a major function of parental explanations in an earlier exploratory study of a number of child rearing variables. In lengthy focused interviews with 60 ninth and twelfth grade adolescents who represented the extremes in social adjustment and in social class status, we found that the control wielded by parents who explained their rules was in practically all cases viewed as right and reasonable.

tions.[8]   However, this relationship is apt to vary by level of parental power, since a recent study shows affection toward parents to be related to parental power in a curvilinear manner.[9]   Adolescents of autocratic and permissive parents tended to be low on affection. From these results we hypothesize that *modeling is most common among adolescents with democratic parents who frequently provide explanations for their rules.*

Miller and Swanson found that parental explanations were strongly associated with resistance to temptation in their sample of adolescent boys.[10]   While explanations may be directly related to obedience, it is apparent that this relationship is likely to vary substantially by level of power.   For instance, we know that autocratic and permissive parents are apt to be less accepting and supportive than the democratic parent[11] and that parental warmth is instrumental in facilitating the adoption of parental standards.[12]   Hence, we predict that *conformity to parental rules is most typical of adolescents with democratic parents who frequently provide explanations.*

The possible effects of non-explaining parents on the autonomy of the child are con-

siderable.   According to Hoffman, the arbitrary, threatening nature of rules and demands left unexplained ("unqualified power assertion," in his terminology) requires from a child the "unconditional surrender of his own interests and involvements," tends to "frustrate his momentary need for task completion," and "constitutes an assault on his autonomy as well."[13]   Miller and Swanson labelled a mother who does not explain requests as *arbitrary.*

If she is arbitrary, he must obey without understanding. His world soon consists of high fences bounding many little spaces from which he can escape only by risking her disapproval. In new situations he cannot afford the risk of arriving at his own judgments. Because he often does not understand the purposes of his mother's regulations, he cannot tell whether she will condemn the actions he takes on his own initiative. He can be sure only that following directions, whether or not they make sense, is the best way to keep out of trouble and win approval.[14]

The non-explaining parent is thus apt to undermine the self-confidence of the adolescent in his ability to make his own decisions as well as weaken his desire for such independence.   While adolescent autonomy may be positively related to the parental practice of explaining rules and requests, it is likely to be inversely related to parental power.   By definition, the autocratic type of parent-child interdependence severely limits opportunities for adolescents to acquire wisdom and confidence in independent decision making.   Assuming that adolescent autonomy is positively related to the frequency of parental explanations and is negatively related to parental power, we hypothesize that *autonomy is most common among adolescents of permissive parents who explain their requests and is least characteristic of autocratically reared adolescents who seldom receive explanations concerning rules of conduct.*

---

[8] For example, see Raven and French, "Group Support, Legitimate Power, and Social Influence," *op. cit.*

[9] Elder, "Structural Variations in the Child Rearing Relationship," *op. cit.*

[10] Miller and Swanson found that boys who received explanations of parental requests were more likely to write stories in which heroes resist temptation than were boys of parents who seldom offered explanations.   Daniel R. Miller and Guy E. Swanson, *Inner Conflict and Defense,* New York: Holt-Dryden & Co., 1960, p. 172.   Reasoning with the child, which is another method of making parental regulations seem reasonable and legitimate, is highly related to the development of conscience.   See Robert Sears, Eleanor Maccoby, and Harry Levin, *Patterns of Child Rearing,* New York: Row Peterson & Co., 1957, p. 393.

[11] Elder, *Family Structure and the Transmission of Values and Norms in the Process of Child Rearing, op. cit.,* Chapter XI.

[12] See, for example, Paul Mussen and Luther Distler, "Masculinity, Identification, and Father-Son Relationships," *Journal of Abnormal and Social Psychology,* 59 (November, 1959), pp. 350–356.

---

[13] Martin L. Hoffman, "Power Assertion by the Parent and Its Impact upon the Child," *op. cit.,* pp. 131–132.

[14] Miller and Swanson, *op. cit.,* p. 80.

METHOD

The data for this investigation were obtained from a larger project on adolescence in the Institute for Research in Social Science at the University of North Carolina. This larger study is concerned with determining the affectional, associational, and value orientations of adolescents in grades seven through twelve. Slightly more than half of these respondents were obtained from public schools in central North Carolina, and the rest from both public and parochial school systems in central Ohio. The data were collected in April and May, 1960, with a structured questionnaire administered by teachers in the classroom. The data for this present study were obtained from a 40 per cent sample of the seventh through ninth grade students and 60 per cent of the tenth through twelfth graders, randomly drawn from the 19,200 white adolescents from unbroken homes.

The frequency of parental explanation is measured by two five-response category items which are similar in wording except for the referent.

When you don't know why your (mother/father) makes a particular decision or has certain rules for you to follow, will (she/he) explain the reason?

Unexplained power expression (low legitimation) (1) Never, (2) Once in a while, (3) Sometimes
Explained power expression (high legitimation) (4) Usually, (5) Yes, always

The seven types of parent-adolescent interdependence are measured by two seven-response category items, one referring to mother and the other to father. The three levels of parental power are measured by response categories (1) autocratic, (3) democratic, and (5, 6, and 7) permissive, to the following question.

In general, how are most decisions made between you and your (mother/father)?

AUTOCRATIC
1. My (mother/father) just tells me what to do.

DEMOCRATIC
3. I have considerable opportunity to make my own decisions, but my (mother/father) has the final word.

PERMISSIVE
5. I can make my own decision but my (mother/father) would like for me to consider (her/his) opinion.
6. I can do what I want regardless of what my (mother/father) thinks.
7. My (mother/father) doesn't care what I do.

PARENTAL POWER AND THE FREQUENCY OF EXPLANATIONS

Differences between autocratic, democratic, and permissive parents are examined with age, sex, and social class of the adolescent controlled (Table 1).[15] The data reveal that democratic and permissive parents are from two to four times as likely to explain their rules and expectations frequently than are autocratic parents.[16] Democratic par-

---

[15] Younger and older adolescents are those in grades seven through nine and ten through twelve, respectively. Adolescents and their families were placed in middle and lower class categories by assigning the youths' fathers' occupations to occupational categories employed by the U.S. Bureau of the Census. "Clerical and kindred workers" and above were classified as middle class. "Farmers, farm managers, and farm laborers" were treated as unclassified. The sample is largely urban.

[16] Nonetheless, the reasonableness of the autocratic parent's child-rearing policy is strongly enhanced when explanations are frequently provided. The evaluations of two groups of autocratically reared adolescents were compared with respect to the fairness of their parents' child rearing policy. One group frequently received explanations when requested and perceived greater freedom in decision making during the past two years, whereas the other group of adolescents was low on both parental explanations and decision-making freedom. The former group of adolescents was more

Table 1. Frequent parental explanations by autocratic, democratic, and permissive parents: age, sex, and social class controlled

Parent	Level of Parental Power	Frequent Parental Explanations: Per Cent of Adolescents							
		Older Males		Older Females		Younger Males		Younger Females	
		Middle Class	Lower Class	Middle Class	Lower Class	Middle Class	Lower Class	Middle Class	Lower Class
Mother	Autocratic	(18) 31.6	(35) 42.7	(10) 16.7	(19) 22.5	(25) 31.2	(62) 43.4	(16) 36.4	(50) 37.9
	Democratic	(232) 75.6	(239) 73.8	(243) 79.2	(250) 76.2	(266) 82.1	(218) 72.9	(276) 87.3	(262) 74.6
	Permissive	(190) 73.1	(208) 70.3	(215) 84.0	(228) 76.0	(121) 74.7	(118) 63.4	(144) 79.1	(144) 76.6
Father	Autocratic	(23) 18.7	(36) 19.5	(32) 23.4	(38) 19.0	(39) 34.2	(78) 36.3	(31) 29.8	(64) 27.2
	Democratic	(224) 74.7	(217) 73.8	(285) 79.2	(187) 73.6	(250) 81.7	(176) 64.7	(253) 83.5	(197) 71.4
	Permissive	(130) 75.6	(139) 63.8	(143) 72.2	(168) 70.6	(85) 65.4	(96) 66.7	(108) 72.0	(109) 63.4

ents are slightly more likely to explain than are permissive mothers and fathers. These differences are most evident among middle class parents. Generally, class differences are greatest among autocratic mothers and democratic and permissive parents; lower class autocratic mothers and middle class democratic or permissive mothers and fathers are more likely to explain their rules and policy. Mothers are more likely to explain frequently to younger than older adolescents and to girls rather than boys. Age and sex differences are inconsistent for fathers.[17]

Within each age, sex, and class subgroup frequent explanations are least common among autocratic parents and are most common among democratic parents. In most categories, more than 70 per cent of democratic and permissive parents frequently

provide reasons for their actions when asked to do so, whereas this is true for generally less than 40 per cent of the autocratic parents. Thus autocratic parents are inclined to resist explaining their rules and thereby impose coercive controls and demands.

THE DESIRE TO MODEL

As a measure of the attractiveness of parents, we asked the following question with respect to each parent: "Would you like to be the kind of person your (mother/father) is?" The five responses to this item ranged from "Yes, completely," to "Not at all." The responses, "Yes, completely," "In most ways," and "In many ways," are considered as indicating the desire to model, i.e., to be like mother and/or father. This item taps the degree to which the adolescent values the attributes and behavior of a parent and is not restricted to sex-appropriate behavior.

In accord with our hypothesis, modeling is most typical of democratically reared adolescents who often receive explanations.[18]

than twice as likely as the latter youths to consider their parents to be usually or more often fair (for older males toward their fathers, 68.7 versus 30.3 per cent). See Elder, *Family Structure and the Transmission of Values and Norms in the Process of Child Rearing*, pp. 637–643.

[17] Tests of significance have not been employed in the evaluation of results due to the nature and size of our sample and to our interest in the general pattern of relationships.

[18] Both the types of parent-adolescent interdependence and the frequency of parental explana-

Table 2. Levels of parental power and frequency of explanations in relation to desire of adolescents to model their parents: age and sex controlled

Parent	Age and Sex	Per Cent of Adolescents Who Would Like to be the Kind of Person Their Mothers/Fathers Are in Many, Most, or All Ways					
		Autocratic		Democratic		Permissive	
		Freq.	Infreq.	Freq.	Infreq.	Freq.	Infreq.
Mother	OM	(41) 77.4	(38) 45.2	(391) 83.4	(100) 62.5	(283) 71.5	(74) 48.1
	YM	(69) 81.1	(66) 48.9	(418) 86.7	(91) 65.5	(136) 57.6	(36) 32.4
	OF	(22) 88.0	(30) 29.7	(499) 93.4	(107) 70.8	(392) 88.2	(68) 59.6
	YF	(57) 85.0	(61) 56.0	(512) 95.0	(90) 69.2	(266) 92.4	(53) 64.6
Father	OM	(42) 71.2	(113) 45.7	(405) 91.8	(119) 76.8	(220) 82.4	(57) 47.5
	YM	(92) 80.0	(123) 58.0	(399) 94.8	(118) 78.7	(164) 90.6	(63) 68.5
	OF	(81) 62.8	(141) 42.0	(243) 78.4	(54) 43.9	(340) 89.9	(58) 64.4
	YF	(43) 45.3	(55) 22.7	(291) 64.1	(50) 39.7	(24) 57.4	(33) 31.1
		Mean Per Cent					
Mother	Boys	79.3	47.0	85.1	63.0	64.6	40.3
	Girls	86.5	42.9	94.2	70.0	90.3	62.1
Father	Boys	75.6	51.9	93.3	77.8	86.5	58.0
	Girls	54.1	32.4	71.3	41.8	73.7	47.8
		Mean Per Cent Difference between Freq. and Infreq. Explanations					
Mother		38.0		23.2		26.3	
Father		22.7		22.5		27.2	

Non-explaining autocratic and permissive parents are least apt to be modeled. Boys are generally more apt to model their fathers and girls their mothers, regardless of level of power and frequency of explanation.

Explaining parents are in all instances more likely to be modeled than are parents who seldom explain. By removing the control on age and sex and computing mean

tions vary in relation to social class. Given a certain level of parental power along with high or low power legitimation, the effects as manifest in adolescent behavior appear similar among middle and lower class youths. The principal variation by social class is in the contrasting distribution of middle and lower class parents by these two variables.

percentage differences between the proportions of youths who desire to model explaining and non-explaining mothers and fathers by each level of power, we find little variation in the differences—five of the six mean percentage differences fall between 22.5 and 27.2 per cent. Thus, adolescent attraction to parents is increased to a similar degree at most levels of parental power by the frequent explanation of rules.

Democratically reared adolescents are more likely to model their mothers and/or fathers than are adolescents of either autocratic or permissive parents who are comparable in frequency of explanation. Since the democratic type of interdependence facilitates greater parent *and* adolescent involvement in decision making concerning the

Table 3. Levels of parental power and frequency of explanations as related to adolescent compliance with parental wishes: sex of adolescent controlled

Sex	Level of Parental Power	Parental Explanations	N	Per Cent of Adolescents Who in Response to Strong Parental Objections to Some of Their Friends Would:		Total Per Cent
				Stop Going with Them or See Them Less	See Them Secretly or Openly	
Boys	Autocratic	Freq.	85	70.6	29.4	100
		Infreq.	123	35.0	65.0	100
	Democratic	Freq.	604	74.2	25.8	100
		Infreq.	110	60.9	39.1	100
	Permissive	Freq.	341	66.0	34.0	100
		Infreq.	100	44.0	66.0	100
Girls	Autocratic	Freq.	54	79.6	20.4	100
		Infreq.	107	43.0	57.0	100
	Democratic	Freq.	626	85.0	15.0	100
		Infreq.	84	77.4	22.6	100
	Permissive	Freq.	385	79.8	21.2	100
		Infreq.	75	53.3	46.7	100

adolescent than the other two types, this result appears to support the Meadian conception of role learning through interaction.[19] The greater the parent-adolescent interaction, the greater the likelihood that the adolescent will desire to be like his parent. This probability of role imitation seems enhanced considerably when the parent, in addition to frequently interacting with the child, frequently explains the reasons for restrictions and demands which may not be understood.

COMPLIANCE WITH PARENTAL RULES

The economic and educational changes in American society have fostered the emergence of what Coleman describes as adolescent subcultures ". . . with values and activities quite distinct from those of the adult society."[20] The significant effects of peers upon an adolescent's values, academic motivation, and achievement is convincingly documented by the findings of Coleman's study. A stringent test of the degree to which an adolescent would comply with parental rules and requests might be represented by a situation in which his parents objected strongly to some of his friends. The way in which these cross-pressures are resolved—in favor of parents or peers—would reflect the salience of each group relative to the youth's behavior and indicate to some extent the nature of the youth's system of values and moral standards. As an occasion of parent-peer conflict, the following question was asked: "If your parents were to object strongly to some of the friends you had, would you: (1) Stop going with them, (2) See them less, (3) See them secretly, (4) Keep going with them openly?" The first two responses indicate a measure of com-

[19] See Orville G. Brim, Jr., "Family Structure and Sex Role Learning by Children: A Further Analysis of Helen Koch's Data," *Sociometry*, 21 (March, 1958), pp. 1–16; and "Personality Development as Role Learning," in I. Iscoe and H. Stevenson (eds.), *Personality Development in Children*, Austin, Texas: University of Texas Press, 1960.

[20] James S. Coleman, "The Adolescent Subculture and Academic Achievement," *American Journal of Sociology*, 65 (January, 1960), p. 337.

pliance with parental wishes; the last two represent resolution in favor of peers.

Similar to the results on the modeling of parents, compliance is most common among adolescents with democratic parents who explain their rules frequently (Table 3).[21] However, variations in the likelihood of compliance by level of power are pronounced only under conditions of infrequent explanations. Hence, the frequency of parental explanations seems to be more crucial in inducing conformity than level of power. This suggests that level of power may be a more significant factor in regulating observable behavior, while the rationalization of rules by explanations is strongly related to the child's adoption of parental rules. Although no meaningful variations in these results were observed by age, girls are in all instances more likely to claim that they would obey their parents than are boys.

Variations in the frequency of parental explanation have relatively little effect on the likelihood of adolescents' conforming in democratically structured relationships. Presumably an authority structure of this kind engenders mutuality of respect, understanding and trust and reduces the necessity for explanatory efforts. It appears that as structural asymmetry increases in parent-child relations toward either autocratic control or permissiveness, obedience to parental rules becomes increasingly contingent on explanatory efforts by parents. In addition to the factor of parental affection and explanations, extreme asymmetry in the structure of the child-rearing relationship may be associated with general communication failures in the transmission of rules and values. Under such conditions parents may simply say little and rigorously control their children or detach themselves completely in child rearing.

---

21 Since compliance to parental wishes and autonomy represent aspects of a child's behavior, it is essential to analyze simultaneously the joint effects of maternal and paternal power and explanations. In order to do this and yet have sufficient cases for analysis, we are forced to limit the analysis to parents who correspond in both level of power and in frequency of explanations.

AUTONOMY

One indication of an adolescent's ability to direct his own behavior is the degree to which he feels confident that his ideas and opinions about what he should do and believe are right and best for him. A youth who expresses confidence in his own values, goals, and awareness of rules is presumably more capable of operating effectively on his own. A second aspect concerns the degree of adolescent self-reliance in problem solving and decision making. When faced with a really important decision about himself and his future, the adolescent who seeks ideas and information from others but makes up his own mind exhibits a high degree of autonomy in problem solving. Two items which measured these two aspects of autonomy were dichotomized and the responses were cross-tabulated to provide four empirical types of dependence-independence; adolescents who have or lack confidence in their own ideas, values, and goals may either be relatively dependent or independent in decision making.

An analysis of the three levels of power and the frequency of parental explanation in relation to these four types of dependence and independence behavior is shown in Table 4. The results partially confirm our hypotheses. As predicted, autonomy (both confident and independent) is most typical of adolescents with parents who are both permissive *and* frequent explainers. On the other hand, we find that youths who seldom receive explanations are least apt to exhibit autonomy, and this result does not vary by level of power.

An examination of variations in the two aspects of autonomy reveals that adolescents with autocratic parents who explain are more apt to feel *self-confident and dependent* in decision making than are children of autocratic parents who seldom explain (a difference of 17.1%), and are more likely to express confidence in their adequacy for self-direction, whether dependent or independent in decision making (a mean difference of 7.5%). There is practically no percentage difference between the proportions of self-

Table 4. Levels of parental power and frequency of explanations in relation to types of adolescent dependence-independence behavior

| Level of Parental Power | Parental Explanations | N | Types of Adolescent Dependence-Independence Behavior[a] | | | | Total Per Cent |
| | | | Lack of Confidence | | Confidence | | |
			Dependent	Independent	Dependent	Independent	
Autocratic	Freq.	139	27.3	6.5	37.4	28.8	100
	Infreq.	231	34.2	14.7	20.3	30.3	100
Democratic	Freq.	1233	10.5	6.7	37.6	45.2	100
	Infreq.	194	22.7	9.8	35.6	31.9	100
Permissive	Freq.	729	13.2	7.2	29.8	49.8	100
	Infreq.	177	28.2	13.6	24.9	33.3	100

[a] The degree of self-confidence in personal ideas and values was measured by the following item: How confident are you that your own ideas and opinions about what you should do and believe are right and best for you? [Lack of confidence] (1) Not at all confident, (2) Not very confident, (3) I'm a little confident. [Confidence] (4) I'm quite confident, (5) I'm completely confident.

Self-reliance in problem-solving and decision making was measured by the following item: When you have a really important decision to make, about yourself and your future, do you make it on your own, or do you like to get help on it? [Dependent] (1) I'd rather let someone else decide for me, (2) I depend a lot upon other people's advice, (3) I like to get some help. [Independent] (4) Get other ideas then make up my own mind, (5) Make up my own mind without any help.

confident and independent youths with explaining and non-explaining parents at this level of power. Thus, among adolescents with autocratic parents, those who receive frequent explanations are most likely to report a dependent type of self-confidence in their ideas and values. As the power of parents decreases, explanations have a different effect on adolescent autonomy; they seem to foster a sense of self-confidence and independence in their children.

About fifteen per cent of the adolescents with parents who are both autocratic and non-explaining report that they lack confidence in their ideas yet prefer to make important decisions on their own. It is plausible that these adolescents feel the need to depend on their parents but find them rejecting and unsympathetic concerning their problems. Hence they function independently in decision making but do so reluctantly. When age and sex were introduced simultaneously as controls, variations by age were observed; younger adolescents were inclined throughout to be less confident and more dependent. However, this age difference did not appreciably alter the above results.

The application of behavior controls which are seldom explained and hence not understood is likely to appear very arbitrary and unpredictable. Under such circumstances,

there is apt to be little security for a child in interaction with a powerful parent.[22] Among adolescents who seldom receive explanations of parental requests, autonomy shows a curvilinear relation to level of power. Youths with democratic parents are more likely than adolescents with autocratic or permissive parents to express confidence in and preference for governing themselves. Infrequent explanation is more negatively related to adolescent autonomy on the autocratic than on the permissive level of power.

The effects of parental explanations on adolescent autonomy vary considerably by level of power. Although frequent explanations of rules tend to make them more meaningful and acceptable, they do not encourage autonomy unless accompanied by moderate or low parental power. Freedom to exper-

---

[22] An adolescent's feeling of security might be expressed in terms of a power ratio in which his perception of the magnitude of his own power *plus* all friendly or supportive power he can count upon from other sources is in the numerator, and with the adolescent's perception of the magnitude of all hostile power that may be used against him in the denominator. See Dorwin Cartwright, "Emotional Dimensions of Group Life," in *Feelings and Emotions,* Martin L. Reynert (ed.), New York: McGraw-Hill Book Co., Inc., 1950, pp. 441–442.

iment in self-direction and to learn by assuming the responsibilities of decision making appear to be necessary experiences for children to desire and feel confident in self-government. Given this allowance of behavioral freedom, frequent parental explanation of requests and regulations seems to increase markedly the likelihood of adolescent self-confidence and independence in decision making.[23] While autonomy is less probable among youths who seldom receive explanations, it is most common under these conditions among adolescents with democratic parents.

The implications of these results seem particularly relevant to academic motivation and aspiration. If the explanation of autocratic control seems to amplify feelings of dependency in decision making, is this type of power assertion related to low adolescent educational goals and to low aspirations regarding the attainment of these goals? Since a restrictive autocratic regime in child rearing does not encourage a strong achievement orientation,[24] it is probable that frequent explanations on this level of power induce acceptance of such power and heighten passivity and indifference toward scholastic achievement. On the other hand, frequent explanations of rules along with some freedom in self-government are likely to augment a youth's desire to achieve scholastically by giving him a sense of emotional security, by providing him with opportunities to operate on his own, and by strengthening his self-confidence with respect to his ability to be independent.

An examination of data bearing on these possibilities revealed that the frequency of explanations was positively related to adoles-cent commitment to completing high school and to a desire to go to college if the opportunity were provided, on each level of power. A comparison of the proportions of college-oriented boys in the "explaining" and "non-explaining" categories by level of power revealed the following percentage differences: 7.1, autocratic; 19.0, democratic; and 15.1, permissive. These differences are similar in each of the four age and sex groups. Thus, it appears that the scholastic impetus provided by autocratic parents, compared to that provided by democratic and permissive parents, is not heightened appreciably by frequent explanations. As in its effects on adolescent autonomy, the level of parental power appears to be the crucial factor.

The relationship between level of power and educational goals and aspirations is curvilinear in form with the frequency of explanations controlled. This relationship is illustrated by the percentage of college-oriented boys who frequently receive explanations from their parents; the respective percentages from autocratic to permissive are 57.1, 78.8 and 69.6. Similar results were obtained for girls. Adolescents with democratic and explaining parents are thus most likely to have high educational goals.

About one-half of the boys and girls in grades seven through nine who have autocratic parents who seldom explain are not sure that they will finish high school. The implications of this result seem relevant to the drop-out problem, particularly in view of findings concerning the character of a group of drop-outs from Chicago schools. In a three year treatment study of 105 drop-outs, Lichter et al. found that, "about two-thirds of the boys and one-half of the girls were dependent children who were unwilling to assume any self-responsibility. The boys generally expressed their dependency in open helplessness and the girls by angry demands for gratification."[25]

These findings suggest that the effects of variations in the legitimacy of parental power

[23] Cf. Lois W. Hoffman, Sidney Rosen and Ronald Lippitt, "Parental Coerciveness, Child Autonomy and Child's Role at School," *Sociometry*, 23 (March, 1960), pp. 15–22, especially p. 20.

[24] See Bernard C. Rosen and R. D'Andrade, "The Psychosocial Origins of Achievement Motivation," *Sociometry*, 22 (September, 1959), pp. 185–218; and Fred L. Strodtbeck, "Family Interaction, Values and Achievement," Chapter V in *Talent and Society*, David McClelland (ed.), New York: D. Van Nostrand, 1958.

[25] Solomon Lichter, Elsie Rapien, Francis Seibert and Morris Sklansky, *The Drop-Outs*, Glencoe, Illinois: The Free Press, 1962, p. 249.

are altered considerably by level of power. We have observed that explanation on the democratic level has an entirely different effect on adolescent autonomy and educational aspirations than it has on the autocratic level. In comparison, the effects of frequent explanations on adolescent desire to model and obey parents vary much less by level of power. Given infrequent explanations of rules and requests, adolescent modeling and compliance tend to decrease sharply as parental power increases.

By assuming that frequent explanations are an indication of a high degree of parental warmth and that level of power is an indication of both parental warmth and the degree of adolescent freedom in decision making, we are able to see why a child's autonomy in decision making and his educational goals are strongly contingent upon the type of parent-adolescent interdependence. Moderate or low parental power appears to be essential in fostering ambitions and effectiveness outside of the family. With opportunities to develop an instrumental orientation, frequent explanations operate as a positive reinforcement.

Since parental attractiveness and obedience to parental rules have been shown to be heavily dependent on the warmth of parents, it is understandable that the effects of explanation are much greater than the effects of level of power on these two variables. Thus, while adolescents who receive frequent explanations from autocratic parents are inclined to model their parents and to obey them, they are most likely to be dependent on them in decision making and to be indifferent concerning school and college. In conclusion, parental explanation is related to a strong parent orientation, while the level of parental power determines whether the child is over-protected and over-controlled.

SUMMARY

The frequency of parental explanations, employed as a measure of the degree of power legitimation, was analyzed in relation to adolescent desire to model parents, obedience to parental rules, and autonomy in decision making on three levels of parental power. Previous research on the effects of legitimate versus coercive power has generally overlooked the significance and potential modifying effects of levels of power. Data for this investigation were obtained from a structured questionnaire administered to white adolescents who lived with both parents in the states of Ohio and North Carolina.

We find that adolescents are more likely to model their parents and to associate with parent-approved peers if their parents explain their rules frequently when asked to do so. The attractiveness of parents as models is less among autocratic and permissive parents than among democratic parents regardless of the frequency of explanations. Variations in compliance by level of power are evident only when explanations are seldom explained—here we find that adolescents with democratic parents are most apt to abide by parental objections to some of their friends.

With the exception of autocratic parents and their adolescents, we find similar results with respect to adolescent autonomy. Generally, adolescents with democratic or permissive parents are much more likely to be confident in their ideas and opinions and to be independent in decision making if their parents explain their rules often than if they do not explain. However, frequent explanations on the autocratic level of power were more related to dependency, which may or may not be of a self-confident type. Infrequent explanations by autocratic parents were related to both low confidence and independence in decision making. Thus, the legitimizing of parental dominance has the effect of making this power more acceptable, and, in doing so, heightens dependency needs as well as self-confidence.

The implications of these results were explored for scholastic motivation and college aspirations. The strongest commitment to high school graduation and to obtaining a college education was evident under conditions of frequent explanations and moderate or low parental power. The effects of level of power appeared to be stronger than the effects of parental explanation.

In summary, the effects of parental explanations on adolescent behavior are generally modified by the level of parental power —whether the parent is autocratic, democratic, or permissive. Thus, any appraisal of the relationship between parental power legitimation and adolescent adjustment and development should include the effects of variations in parental power.

SOME CONDITIONS OF OBEDIENCE AND DISOBEDIENCE TO AUTHORITY

Stanley Milgram

The situation in which one agent commands another to hurt a third turns up time and again as a significant theme in human relations. It is powerfully expressed in the story of Abraham, who is commanded by God to kill his son. It is no accident that Kierkegaard, seeking to orient his thought to the central themes of human experience, chose Abraham's conflict as the springboard to his philosophy.

War too moves forward on the triad of an authority which commands a person to destroy the enemy, and perhaps all organized hostility may be viewed as a theme and variation on the three elements of authority, executant, and victim.[1] We describe an experimental program, recently concluded at Yale University, in which a particular expression of this conflict is studied by experimental means.

In its most general form the problem may be defined thus: if X tells Y to hurt Z, under what conditions will Y carry out the command of X and under what conditions will he refuse. In the more limited form possible in laboratory research, the question becomes: if an experimenter tells a subject to hurt another person, under what conditions will the subject go along with this instruction, and under what conditions will he refuse to obey. The laboratory problem is not so much a dilution of the general statement as one concrete expression of the many particular forms this question may assume.

One aim of the research was to study behavior in a strong situation of deep consequence to the participants, for the psychological forces operative in powerful and lifelike forms of the conflict may not be brought into play under diluted conditions.

Source: S. Milgram, "Some Conditions of Obedience and Disobedience to Authority," *Human Relations*, Vol. 18, 1965, pp. 57–76. Copyright 1965 by Plenum Publishing Company Ltd. and used by permission.

[1] Consider, for example, J. P. Scott's analysis of war in his monograph on aggression:
. . . while the actions of key individuals in a war may be explained in terms of direct stimulation to aggression, vast numbers of other people are involved simply by being part of an organized society.
. . . For example, at the beginning of World War I an Austrian archduke was assassinated in Sarajevo. A few days later soldiers from all over Europe were marching toward each other, not because they were stimulated by the archduke's misfortune, but because they had been trained to obey orders. (Slightly rearranged from Scott (1958), *Aggression*, p. 103.)

This approach meant, first, that we had a special obligation to protect the welfare and dignity of the persons who took part in the study; subjects were, of necessity, placed in a difficult predicament, and steps had to be taken to ensure their well-being before they were discharged from the laboratory. Toward this end, a careful, post-experimental treatment was devised and has been carried through for subjects in all conditions.[2]

TERMINOLOGY

If Y follows the command of X we shall say that he has obeyed X; if he fails to carry out the command of X, we shall say that he has disobeyed X. The terms *to obey* and *to disobey*, as used here, refer to the subject's overt action only, and carry no implication for the motive or experiential states accompanying the action.[3]

To be sure, the everyday use of the word *obedience* is not entirely free from complexities. It refers to action within widely varying situations, and connotes diverse motives within those situations: a child's obedience differs from a soldier's obedience, or the love, honor, and *obey* of the marriage vow. However, a consistent behavioral relationship is indicated in most uses of the term: in the act of obeying, a person does what another person tells him to do. Y obeys X if he carries out the prescription for action which X has addressed to him; the term suggests, more-

[2] It consisted of an extended discussion with the experimenter and, of equal importance, a friendly reconciliation with the victim. It is made clear that the victim did not receive painful electric shocks. After the completion of the experimental series, subjects were sent a detailed report of the results and full purposes of the experimental program. A formal assessment of this procedure points to its overall effectiveness. Of the subjects, 83.7 per cent indicated that they were glad to have taken part in the study; 15.1 per cent reported neutral feelings; and 1.3 per cent stated that they were sorry to have participated. A large number of subjects spontaneously requested that they be used in further experimentation. Four-fifths of the subjects felt that more experiments of this sort should be carried out, and 74 per cent indicated that they had learned something of personal importance as a result of being in the study. Furthermore, a university psychiatrist, experienced in outpatient treatment, interviewed a sample of experimental subjects with the aim of uncovering possible injurious effects resulting from participation. No such effects were in evidence. Indeed, subjects typically felt that their participation was instructive and enriching. A more detailed discussion of this question can be found in Milgram (1964).

[3] *To obey* and *to disobey* are not the only terms one could use in describing the critical action of Y. One could say that Y is cooperating with X, or displays conformity with regard to X's commands.

However, *cooperation* suggests that X agrees with Y's ends, and understands the relationship between his own behavior and the attainment of those ends. (But the experimental procedure, and, in particular, the experimenter's command that the subject shock the victim even in the absence of a response from the victim, preclude such understanding.) Moreover, cooperation implies status parity for the co-acting agents, and neglects the asymmetrical, dominance-subordination element prominent in the laboratory relationship between experimenter and subject. *Conformity* has been used in other important contexts in social psychology, and most frequently refers to imitating the judgements or actions of others when no explicit requirement for imitation has been made. Furthermore, in the present study there are two sources of social pressure: pressure from the experimenter issuing the commands, and pressure from the victim to stop the punishment. It is the pitting of a common man (the victim) against the authority (the experimenter) that is the distinctive feature of the conflict. At a point in the experiment the victim demands that he be let free. The experimenter insists that the subject continue to administer shocks. Which act of the subject can be interpreted as conformity? The subject may conform to the wishes of his peer or to the wishes of the experimenter, and conformity in one direction means the absence of conformity in the other. Thus the word has no useful reference in this setting, for the dual and conflicting social pressures cancel out its meaning.

In the final analysis, the linguistic symbol representing the subject's action must take its meaning from the concrete context in which that action occurs; and there is probably no word in everyday language that covers the experimental situation exactly, without omissions or irrelevant connotations. It is partly for convenience, therefore, that the terms *obey* and *disobey* are used to describe the subject's actions. At the same time, our use of the words is highly congruent with dictionary meaning.

over, that some form of dominance-subordination, or hierarchical element, is part of the situation in which the transaction between X and Y occurs.

A subject who complies with the entire series of experimental commands will be termed an *obedient* subject; one who at any point in the command series defies the experimenter will be called a *disobedient* or *defiant* subject. As used in this report, the terms refer only to the subject's performance in the experiment, and do not necessarily imply a general personality disposition to submit to or reject authority.

SUBJECT POPULATION

The subjects used in all experimental conditions were male adults, residing in the greater New Haven and Bridgeport areas, aged 20 to 50 years, and engaged in a wide variety of occupations. Each experimental condition described in this report employed 40 fresh subjects and was carefully balanced for age and occupational types. The occupational composition for each experiment was: workers, skilled and unskilled: 40 per cent; white collar, sales, business: 40 per cent; professionals: 20 per cent. The occupations were intersected with three age categories (subjects in 20s, 30s, and 40s, assigned to each condition in the proportions of 20, 40, and 40 per cent respectively).

THE GENERAL LABORATORY

PROCEDURE[4]

The focus of the study concerns the amount of electric shock a subject is willing to administer to another person when ordered by an experimenter to give the 'victim' increasingly more severe punishment. The act of administering shock is set in the context of a learning experiment, ostensibly designed to study the effect of punishment on memory. Aside from the experimenter, one naïve sub-

ject and one accomplice perform in each session. On arrival each subject is paid $4.50. After a general talk by the experimenter, telling how little scientists know about the effect of punishment on memory, subjects are informed that one member of the pair will serve as teacher and one as learner. A rigged drawing is held so that the naïve subject is always the teacher, and the accomplice becomes the learner. The learner is taken to an adjacent room and strapped into an 'electric chair.'

The naïve subject is told that it is his task to teach the learner a list of paired associates, to test him on the list, and to administer punishment whenever the learner errs in the test. Punishment takes the form of electric shock, delivered to the learner by means of a shock generator controlled by the naïve subject. The teacher is instructed to increase the intensity of electric shock one step on the generator on each error. The learner, according to plan, provides many wrong answers, so that before long the naïve subject must give him the strongest shock on the generator. Increases in shock level are met by increasingly insistent demands from the learner that the experiment be stopped because of the growing discomfort to him. However, in clear terms the experimenter orders the teacher to continue with the procedure in disregard of the learner's protests. *Thus, the naïve subject must resolve a conflict between two mutually incompatible demands from the social field. He may continue to follow the orders of the experimenter and shock the learner with increasing severity, or he may refuse to follow the orders of the experimenter and heed the learner's pleas. The experimenter's authority operates not in a free field, but against ever-*

---

[4] A more detailed account of the laboratory procedure can be found in Milgram (1963). A similar and independently evolved experimental procedure, employing a shock generator, victim, and learning task, was reported by Buss (1961). Buss used the technique for studying aggression, not obedience, and did not make use of the fundamental measure employed in the present study: break-off points. His investigation promises to be a useful complement to the present research.

mounting countervailing pressures from the person being punished.

A few technical points need to be considered before the findings of the study are described. For the purpose of delivering shock, a simulated shock generator is used, with 30 clearly marked voltage levels that range from 15 to 450 volts (and each activated by one of 30 individual lever switches set in a horizontal line). The naïve subject is given a sample shock of 45 volts to convince him of the authenticity of the instrument. The generator bears verbal designations that range from 'Slight Shock' to 'Danger: Severe Shock.'

The responses of the victim are standized on tape, and each protest is coordinated to a particular voltage level on the shock generator. Starting with 75 volts the learner begins to grunt and moan. At 150 volts he demands to be let out of the experiment. At 180 volts he cries out that he can no longer stand the pain. At 300 volts he refuses to provide any more answers to the memory test, insisting that he is no longer a participant in the experiment and must be freed. In response to this last tactic, the experimenter instructs the naïve subject to treat the absence of an answer as equivalent to a wrong answer, and to follow the usual shock procedure. The experimenter reinforces his demand with the statement: 'You have no other choice, you must go on!' (This imperative is used whenever the naïve subject tries to break off the experiment.) If the subject refuses to give the next higher level of shock, the experiment is considered at an end. A quantitative value is assigned to the subject's performance based on the maximum intensity shock he administered before breaking off. Thus any subject's score may range from zero (for a subject unwilling to administer the first shock level) to 30 (for a subject who proceeds to the highest voltage level on the board). For any particular subject and for any particular experimental condition the degree to which participants have followed the experimenter's orders may be specified with a numerical value, corresponding to the metric on the shock generator.

This laboratory situation gives us a framework in which to study the subject's reactions to the principal conflict of the experiment. Again, this conflict is between the experimenter's demands that he continue to administer the electric shock, and the learner's demands, which become increasingly more insistent, that the experiment be stopped. The crux of the study is to vary systematically the factors believed to alter the degree of obedience to the experimental commands, to learn under what conditions submission to authority is most probable, and under what conditions defiance is brought to the fore.

PILOT STUDIES

Pilot studies for the present research were completed in the winter of 1960; they differed from the regular experiments in a few details: for one, the victim was placed behind a silvered glass, with the light balance on the glass such that the victim could be dimly perceived by the subject (Milgram, 1961).

Though essentially qualitative in treatment, these studies pointed to several significant features of the experimental situation. At first no vocal feedback was used from the victim. It was thought that the verbal and voltage designations on the control panel would create sufficient pressure to curtail the subject's obedience. However, this was not the case. In the absence of protests from the learner, virtually all subjects, once commanded, went blithely to the end of the board, seemingly indifferent to the verbal designations ('Extreme Shock' and 'Danger: Severe Shock'). This deprived us of an adequate basis for scaling obedient tendencies. A force had to be introduced that would strengthen the subject's resistance to the experimenter's commands, and reveal individual differences in terms of a distribution of break-off points.

This force took the form of protests from the victim. Initially, mild protests were used, but proved inadequate. Subsequently, more vehement protests were inserted into the experimental procedure. To our consternation, even the strongest protests from the victim did not prevent all subjects from administering the harshest punishment ordered by the experimenter; but the protests did lower the mean maximum shock somewhat and created some spread in the subject's performance; therefore, the victim's cries were standardized on tape and incorporated into the regular experimental procedure.

The situation did more than highlight the technical difficulties of finding a workable experimental procedure: it indicated that subjects would obey authority to a greater extent than we had supposed. It also pointed to the importance of feedback from the victim in controlling the subject's behavior.

One further aspect of the pilot study was that subjects frequently averted their eyes from the person they were shocking, often turning their heads in an awkward and conspicuous manner. One subject explained: 'I didn't want to see the consequences of what I had done.' Observers wrote:

. . . subjects showed a reluctance to look at the victim, whom they could see through the glass in front of them When this fact was brought to their attention they indicated that it caused them discomfort to see the victim in agony. We note, however, that although the subject refuses to look at the victim, he continues to administer shocks.

This suggested that the salience of the victim may have, in some degree, regulated the subject's performance. If, in obeying the experimenter, the subject found it necessary to avoid scrutiny of the victim, would the converse be true? If the victim were rendered increasingly more salient to the subject, would obedience diminish? The first set of regular experiments was designed to answer this question.

IMMEDIACY OF THE VICTIM

This series consisted of four experimental conditions. In each condition the victim was brought 'psychologically' closer to the subject giving him shocks.

In the first condition (Remote Feed-

back) the victim was placed in another room and could not be heard or seen by the subject, except that, at 300 volts, he pounded on the wall in protest. After 315 volts he no longer answered or was heard from.

The second condition (Voice Feedback) was identical to the first except that voice protests were introduced. As in the first condition the victim was placed in an adjacent room, but his complaints could be heard clearly through a door left slightly ajar, and through the walls of the laboratory.[5]

---

[5] It is difficult to convey on the printed page the full tenor of the victim's responses, for we have no adequate notation for vocal intensity, timing, and general qualities of delivery. Yet these features are crucial to producing the effect of an increasingly severe reaction to mounting voltage levels. (They can be communicated fully only by sending interested parties the recorded tapes.) In general terms, however, the victim indicates no discomfort until the 75-volt shock is administered, at which time there is a light grunt in response to the punishment. Similar reactions follow the 90- and 105-volt shocks, and at 120 volts the victim shouts to the experimenter that the shocks are becoming painful. Painful groans are heard on administration of the 135-volt shock, and at 150 volts the victim cries out, 'Experimenter, get me out of here! I won't be in the experiment any more! I refuse to go on!' Cries of this type continue with generally rising intensity, so that at 180 volts the victim cries out, 'I can't stand the pain,' and by 270 volts his response to the shock is definitely an agonized scream. Throughout, he insists that he be let out of the experiment. At 300 volts the victim shouts in desperation that he will no longer provide answers to the memory test; and at 315 volts, after a violent scream, he reaffirms with vehemence that he is no longer a participant. From this point on, he provides no answers, but shrieks in agony whenever a shock is administered; this continues through 450 volts. Of course, many subjects will have broken off before this point.

A revised and stronger set of protests was used in all experiments outside the Proximity series. Naturally, new baseline measures were established for all comparisons using the new set of protests.

There is overwhelming evidence that the great majority of subjects, both obedient and defiant, accepted the victims' reactions as genuine. The evidence takes the form of: (a) tension created in the subjects (see discussion of tension); (b) scores on 'estimated pain' scales filled out by subjects immediately after the experiment; (c) subjects' accounts of their feelings in post-experi-

The third experimental condition (Proximity) was similar to the second, except that the victim was now placed in the same room as the subject, and 1½ feet from him. Thus he was visible as well as audible, and voice cues were provided.

The fourth, and final, condition of this series (Touch-Proximity) was identical to the third, with this exception: the victim received a shock only when his hand rested on a shockplate. At the 150-volt level the victim again demanded to be let free and, in this condition, refused to place his hand on the shockplate. The experimenter ordered the naïve subject to force the victim's hand onto the plate. Thus obedience in this condition required that the subject have physical contact with the victim in order to give him punishment beyond the 150-volt level.

Forty adult subjects were studied in each condition. The data revealed that obedience was significantly reduced as the victim was rendered more immediate to the subject. The mean maximum shock for the conditions is shown in Figure 1.

Expressed in terms of the proportion of obedient to defiant subjects, the findings are that 34 per cent of the subjects defied the experimenter in the Remote condition, 37.5 per cent in Voice Feedback, 60 per cent in Proximity, and 70 per cent in Touch-Proximity.

How are we to account for this effect? A first conjecture might be that as the victim was brought closer the subject became more aware of the intensity of his suffering and regulated his behavior accordingly. This makes sense, but our evidence does not support the interpretation. There are no consistent differences in the attributed level of

mental interviews; and (d) quantifiable responses to questionnaires distributed to subjects several months after their participation in the experiments. This matter will be treated fully in a forthcoming monograph.

(The procedure in all experimental conditions was to have the naïve subject announce the voltage level before administering each shock, so that—independently of the victim's responses—he was continually reminded of delivering punishment of ever-increasing severity.)

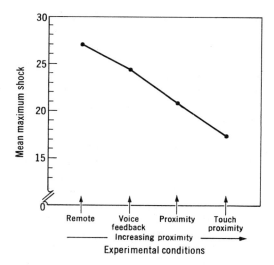

Figure 1.   Mean maxima in proximity series

pain across the four conditions (i.e. the amount of pain experienced by the victim as estimated by the subject and expressed on a 14-point scale). But it is easy to speculate about alternative mechanisms:

Empathic cues   In the Remote and to a lesser extent the Voice Feedback condition, the victim's suffering possesses an abstract, remote quality for the subject. He is aware, but only in a conceptual sense, that his actions cause pain to another person; the fact is apprehended, but not felt. The phenomenon is common enough. The bombardier can reasonably suppose that his weapons will inflict suffering and death, yet this knowledge is divested of affect, and does not move him to a felt, emotional response to the suffering resulting from his actions. Similar observations have been made in wartime. It is possible that the visual cues associated with the victim's suffering trigger empathic responses in the subject and provide him with a more complete grasp of the victim's experience. Or it is possible that the empathic responses are themselves unpleasant, possessing drive properties which cause the subject to terminate the arousal situation. Diminishing obedience, then, would be explained by the enrichment of empathic cues in the successive experimental conditions.

Denial and narrowing of the cognitive field
The Remote condition allows a narrowing of the cognitive field so that the victim is put out of mind. The subject no longer considers the act of depressing a lever relevant to moral judgment, for it is no longer associated with the victim's suffering. When the victim is close it is more difficult to exclude him phenomenologically. He necessarily intrudes on the subject's awareness since he is continuously visible. In the Remote conditions his existence and reactions are made known only after the shock has been administered. The auditory feedback is sporadic and discontinuous. In the Proximity conditions his inclusion in the immediate visual field renders him a continuously salient element for the subject. The mechanism of denial can no longer be brought into play. One subject in the Remote condition said: 'It's funny how you really begin to forget that there's a guy out there, even though you can hear him. For a long time I just concentrated on pressing the switches and reading the words.'

Reciprocal fields If in the Proximity condition the subject is in an improved position to observe the victim, the reverse is also true. The actions of the subject now come under proximal scrutiny by the victim. Possibly, it is easier to harm a person when he is unable to observe our actions than when he can see what we are doing. His surveillance of the action directed against him may give rise to shame, or guilt, which may then serve to curtail the action. Many expressions of language refer to the discomfort or inhibitions that arise in face-to-face confrontation. It is often said that it is easier to criticize a man 'behind his back' than to 'attack him to his face.' If we are in the process of lying to a person it is reputedly difficult to 'stare him in the eye.' We 'turn away from others in shame' or in 'embarrassment' and this action serves to reduce our discomfort. The manifest function of allowing the victim of a firing squad to be blindfolded is to make the occasion less stressful for him, but it may also serve a latent function of reducing the stress of the executioner. In short, in the Proximity conditions, the subject may sense that he has

become more salient in the victim's field of awareness. Possibly he becomes more self-conscious, embarrassed, and inhibited in his punishment of the victim.

Phenomenal unity of act In the Remote conditions it is more difficult for the subject to gain a sense of *relatedness* between his own actions and the consequences of these actions for the victim. There is a physical and spatial separation of the act and its consequences. The subject depresses a lever in one room, and protests and cries are heard from another. The two events are in correlation, yet they lack a compelling phenomenological unity. The structure of a meaningful act—*I am hurting a man*—breaks down because of the spatial arrangements, in a manner somewhat analogous to the disappearance of phi phenomena when the blinking lights are spaced too far apart. The unity is more fully achieved in the Proximity conditions as the victim is brought closer to the action that causes him pain. It is rendered complete in Touch-Proximity.

Incipient group formation Placing the victim in another room not only takes him further from the subject, but the subject and the experimenter are drawn relatively closer. There is incipient group formation between the experimenter and the subject, from which the victim is excluded. The wall between the victim and the others deprives him of an intimacy which the experimenter and subject feel. In the Remote condition, the victim is truly an outsider, who stands alone, physically and psychologically.

When the victim is placed close to the subject, it becomes easier to form an alliance with him against the experimenter. Subjects no longer have to face the experimenter alone. They have an ally who is close at hand and eager to collaborate in a revolt against the experimenter. Thus, the changing set of spatial relations leads to a potentially shifting set of alliances over the several experimental conditions.

Acquired behavior dispositions It is commonly observed that laboratory mice will rarely fight with their litter mates. Scott (1958) explains this in terms of passive inhibition. He writes: 'By doing nothing under . . . circumstances [the animal] learns to do nothing, and this may be spoken of as passive inhibition . . . this principle has great importance in teaching an individual to be peaceful, for it means that he can learn not to fight simply by not fighting.' Similarly, we may learn not to harm others simply by not harming them in everyday life. Yet this learning occurs in a context of proximal relations with others, and may not be generalized to that situation in which the person is physically removed from us. Or possibly, in the past, aggressive actions against others who were physically close resulted in retaliatory punishment which extinguished the original form of response. In contrast, aggression against others at a distance may have only sporadically led to retaliation. Thus the organism learns that it is safer to be aggressive toward others at a distance, and precarious to be so when the parties are within arm's reach. Through a pattern of rewards and punishments, he acquires a disposition to avoid aggression at close quarters, a disposition which does not extend to harming others at a distance. And this may account for experimental findings in the remote and proximal experiments.

Proximity as a variable in psychological research has received far less attention than it deserves. If men were sessile it would be easy to understand this neglect. But we move about; our spatial relations shift from one situation to the next, and the fact that we are near or remote may have a powerful effect on the psychological processes that mediate our behavior toward others. In the present situation, as the victim is brought closer to the man ordered to give him shocks, increasing numbers of subjects break off the experiment, refusing to obey. The concrete, visible, and proximal presence of the victim acts in an important way to counteract the experimenter's power and to generate disobedience.[6]

---

[6] Admittedly, the terms *proximity, immediacy, closeness,* and *salience-of-the-victim* are used in a loose sense, and the experiments themselves represent a very coarse treatment of the variable.

CLOSENESS OF AUTHORITY

If the spatial relationship of the subject and victim is relevant to the degree of obedience, would not the relationship of subject to experimenter also play a part?

There are reasons to feel that, on arrival, the subject is oriented primarily to the experimenter rather than to the victim. He has come to the laboratory to fit into the structure that the experimenter—not the victim—would provide. He has come less to understand his behavior than to *reveal* that behavior to a competent scientist, and he is willing to display himself as the scientist's purposes require. Most subjects seem quite concerned about the appearance they are making before the experimenter, and one could argue that this preoccupation in a relatively new and strange setting makes the subject somewhat insensitive to the triadic nature of the social situation. In other words, the subject is so concerned about the show he is putting on for the experimenter that influences from other parts of the social field do not receive as much weight as they ordinarily would. This overdetermined orientation to the experimenter would account for the relative insensitivity of the subject to the victim, and would also lead us to believe that alterations in the relationship between subject and experimenter would have important consequences for obedience.

In a series of experiments we varied the physical closeness and degree of surveillance of the experimenter. In one condition the experimenter sat just a few feet away from the subject. In a second condition, after giving initial instructions, the experimenter

---

Further experiments are needed to refine the notion and tease out such diverse factors as spatial distance, visibility, audibility, barrier interposition, etc.

The Proximity and Touch-Proximity experiments were the only conditions where we were unable to use taped feedback from the victim. Instead, the victim was trained to respond in these conditions as he had in Experiment 2 (which employed taped feedback). Some improvement is possible here, for it should be technically feasible to do a proximity series using taped feedback.

left the laboratory and gave his orders by telephone; in still a third condition the experimenter was never seen, providing instructions by means of a tape recording activated when the subjects entered the laboratory.

Obedience dropped sharply as the experimenter was physically removed from the laboratory. The number of obedient subjects in the first condition (Experimenter Present) was almost three times as great as in the second, where the experimenter gave his orders by telephone. Twenty-six subjects were fully obedient in the first condition, and only 9 in the second (Chi square obedient *vs.* defiant in the two conditions, 1 d.f. = 14.7; $p < .001$). Subjects seemed able to take a far stronger stand against the experimenter when they did not have to encounter him face to face, and the experimenter's power over the subject was severely curtailed.[7]

Moreover, when the experimenter was absent, subjects displayed an interesting form of behavior that had not occurred under his surveillance. Though continuing with the experiment, several subjects administered lower shocks than were required and never informed the experimenter of their deviation from the correct procedure. (Unknown to the subjects, shock levels were automatically recorded by an Esterline-Angus event recorder wired directly into the shock generator; the instrument provided us with an objective record of the subjects' performance.) Indeed, in telephone conversations some subjects specifically assured the experimenter that they were raising the shock level according to instruction, whereas in fact they were repeatedly using the lowest shock on the board. This form of behavior is particularly interesting: although these subjects acted in a way that clearly undermined the avowed purposes of the experiment, they found it easier to handle the conflict in this manner than to precipitate an open break with authority.

Other conditions were completed in which the experimenter was absent during the first segment of the experiment, but reappeared at the point that the subject definitely refused to give higher shocks when commanded by telephone. Although he had exhausted his power via telephone, the experimenter could frequently force further obedience when he reappeared in the laboratory.

Experiments in this series show that the physical *presence* of an authority is an important force contributing to the subject's obedience or defiance. Taken together with the first experimental series on the proximity of the victim, it would appear that something akin to fields of force, diminishing in effectiveness with increasing psychological distance from their source, have a controlling effect on the subject's performance. As the victim is brought closer, the subject finds it harder to administer shocks to him. When the victim's position is held constant relative to the subject, and the authority is made more remote, the subject finds it easier to break off the experiment. This effect is substantial in both cases, but manipulation of the experimenter's position yielded the more powerful results. Obedience to destructive commands is highly dependent on the proximal relations between authority and subject.

TENSIONS

The description of final scores does not fully convey the character of the subjects' performance, and it would be useful to interrupt our reporting of quantitative relationships to remark on the subjects' general reaction to the situation.

One might suppose that a subject would simply break off or continue as his conscience and temperament dictated. Yet this is very far from what happened. There were powerful reactions of tension and emotional strain in a substantial proportion of the participants. Persons were observed to sweat, tremble, stutter, bite their lips, and groan as they found themselves increasingly implicated in the experimental conflict. Some sense of the subjects' mood can be gotten from a transcript

---

[7] The third condition also led to significantly lower obedience than this first situation, in which the experimenter was present, but it contains technical difficulties that require extensive discussion.

of their remarks at break-off point. Here are the remarks of two defiant subjects:

Is he banging? . . . Is he hurt out there? Well, I don't want to be responsible for anything that happens to him. No, I can't go on with it. I don't know whether he's all right or not. I mean he may have a heart condition or something; I wouldn't feel right doing it. He's banging for help. He's evidently in trouble or he wouldn't bang . . . I don't see any sense to this—to knocking him out or something. I just can't see it.

(*Subject refuses to administer shocks*)
[*Subject 0108*]

The man is banging. He wants to get out . . . I'm sorry. If the man wants to get out I'd just as soon stop . . . I don't want to administer any more [extremely excited] *. . . I will gladly refund the check, but I will not harm this man . . . I'm sorry, I will not give him any more if he obviously wants to get out. There is no money in the world that will make me hurt another individual.*

[*Subject 010X*]

And here is a transcript from an obedient subject. He began the experiment calmly, but became increasingly tense as the experiment proceeded. After administering the 150-volt shock, he began to address the experimenter in agitated tones:

150 volts delivered. *You want me to keep going?*
165 volts delivered. *That guy is hollering in there. There's a lot of them here. He's liable to have heart condition. You want me to go?*
180 volts delivered. *He can't stand it! I'm not going to kill that man in there! You hear him hollering? He's hollering. He can't stand it. What if something happens to him? . . . I'm not going to get that man sick in there. He's hollering in there. You know what I mean? I mean I refuse to take responsibility. He's getting hurt in there. He's in there hollering. Too many left here. Geez, if he gets them wrong. There's too many of them left. I mean who is going to*

take responsibility if anything happens to that gentleman?
[The experimenter accepts responsibility.]
All right.
195 volts delivered. *You see he's hollering. Hear that. Gee, I don't know.* [The experimenter says: 'The experiment requires that you go on.']—*I know it does, sir, but I mean—hugh—he don't know what he's in for. He's up to 195 volts.*
210 volts delivered
225 volts delivered
240 volts delivered. *Aw, no. You mean I've got to keep going up with the scale? No sir. I'm not going to kill that man! I'm not going to give him 450 volts!* [The experimenter says: 'The experiment requires that you go on.']—*I know it does, but that man is hollering in there, sir . . .*

Despite his numerous, agitated objections, which were constant accompaniments to his actions, the subject unfailingly obeyed the experimenter, proceeding to the highest shock level on the generator. He displayed a curious dissociation between word and action. Although at the verbal level he had resolved not to go on, his actions were fully in accord with the experimenter's commands. This subject did not want to shock the victim, and he found it an extremely disagreeable task, but he was unable to invent a response that would free him from E's authority. Many subjects cannot find the specific verbal formula that would enable them to reject the role assigned to them by the experimenter. Perhaps our culture does not provide adequate models for disobedience.

One puzzling sign of tension was the regular occurrence of nervous laughing fits. In the first four conditions 71 of the 160 subjects showed definite signs of nervous laughter and smiling. The laughter seemed entirely out of place, even bizarre. Full-blown, uncontrollable seizures were observed for 15 of these subjects. On one occasion we observed a seizure so violently convulsive that it was necessary to call a halt to the experiment. In the post-experimental interviews subjects took pains to point out that they were not sadistic types and that the

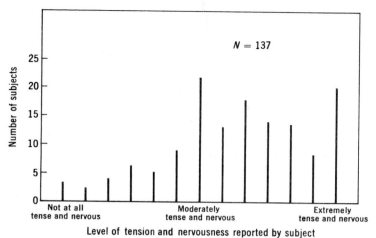

Figure 2.   Level of tension and nervousness*

laughter did not mean they enjoyed shocking the victim.

In the interview following the experiment subjects were asked to indicate on a 14-point scale just how nervous or tense they felt at the point of maximum tension (Figure 2). The scale ranged from 'Not at all tense and nervous' to 'Extremely tense and nervous.' Self-reports of this sort are of limited precision, and at best provide only a rough indication of the subject's emotional response. Still, taking the reports for what they are worth, it can be seen that the distribution of responses spans the entire range of the scale, with the majority of subjects concentrated at the center and upper extreme. A further breakdown showed that obedient subjects reported themselves as having been slightly more tense and nervous than the defiant subjects at the point of maximum tension.

How is the occurrence of tension to be interpreted? First, it points to the presence of conflict. If a tendency to comply with authority were the only psychological force operating in the situation, all subjects would have continued to the end and there would have been no tension. Tension, it is assumed, results from the simultaneous presence of two or more incompatible response tendencies (Miller, 1944). If sympathetic concern for the victim were the exclusive force, all subjects would have calmly defied the experimenter. Instead, there were both obedient and defiant outcomes, frequently accompanied by extreme tension. A conflict develops between the deeply ingrained disposition not to harm others and the equally compelling tendency to obey others who are in authority. The subject is quickly drawn into a dilemma of a deeply dynamic character, and the presence of high tension points to the considerable strength of each of the antagonistic vectors.

Moreover, tension defines the strength of the aversive state from which the subject is unable to escape through disobedience. When a person is uncomfortable, tense, or stressed, he tries to take some action that will allow him to terminate this unpleasant state. Thus tension may serve as a drive that leads to escape behavior. But in the present situation, even where tension is extreme, many subjects are unable to perform the response that will bring about relief. Therefore there must be a competing drive, tendency, or inhibition that precludes activation of the dis-

---

* Figure 2 shows the self-reports on 'tension and nervousness' for 137 subjects in the Proximity experiments. Subjects were given a scale with 14 values ranging from 'Not at all tense and nervous' to 'Extremely tense and nervous.' They were instructed: 'Thinking back to that point in the experiment when you felt the most tense and nervous, indicate just how you felt by placing an X at the appropriate point on the scale.' The results are shown in terms of mid-point values.

obedient response. The strength of this inhibiting factor must be of greater magnitude than the stress experienced, else the terminating act would occur. Every evidence of extreme tension is at the same time an indication of the strength of the forces that keep the subject in the situation.

Finally, tension may be taken as evidence of the reality of the situations for the subjects. Normal subjects do not tremble and sweat unless they are implicated in a deep and genuinely felt predicament.

BACKGROUND AUTHORITY

In psychophysics, animal learning, and other branches of psychology, the fact that measures are obtained at one institution rather than another is irrelevant to the interpretation of the findings, so long as the technical facilities for measurement are adequate and the operations are carried out with competence.

But it cannot be assumed that this holds true for the present study. The effectiveness of the experimenter's commands may depend in an important way on the larger institutional context in which they are issued. The experiments described thus far were conducted at Yale University, an organization which most subjects regarded with respect and sometimes awe. In post-experimental interviews several participants remarked that the locale and sponsorship of the study gave them confidence in the integrity, competence, and benign purposes of the personnel; many indicated that they would not have shocked the learner if the experiments had been done elsewhere.

This issue of background authority seemed to us important for an interpretation of the results that had been obtained thus far; moreover it is highly relevant to any comprehensive theory of human obedience. Consider, for example, how closely our compliance with the imperatives of others is tied to particular institutions and locales in our day-to-day activities. On request, we expose our throats to a man with a razor blade in the barber shop, but would not do so in a shoe store; in the latter setting we willingly follow the clerk's request to stand in our stockinged feet, but resist the command in a bank. In the laboratory of a great university, subjects may comply with a set of commands that would be resisted if given elsewhere. *One must always question the relationship of obedience to a person's sense of the context in which he is operating.*

To explore the problem we moved our apparatus to an office building in industrial Bridgeport and replicated experimental conditions, without any visible tie to the university.

Bridgeport subjects were invited to the experiment through a mail circular similar to the one used in the Yale study, with appropriate changes in letterhead, etc. As in the earlier study, subjects were paid $4.50 for coming to the laboratory. The same age and occupational distributions used at Yale, and the identical personnel, were employed.

The purpose in relocating in Bridgeport was to assure a complete dissociation from Yale, and in this regard we were fully successful. On the surface, the study appeared to be conducted by RESEARCH ASSOCIATES OF BRIDGEPORT, an organization of unknown character (the title had been concocted exclusively for use in this study).

The experiments were conducted in a three-room office suite in a somewhat rundown commercial building located in the downtown shopping area. The laboratory was sparsely furnished, though clean, and marginally respectable in appearance. When subjects inquired about professional affiliations, they were informed only that we were a private firm conducting research for industry.

Some subjects displayed skepticism concerning the motives of the Bridgeport experimenter. One gentleman gave us a written account of the thoughts he experienced at the control board:

. . . Should I quit this damn test? Maybe he passed out? What dopes we were not to check up on this deal. How do we know that these guys are legit? No furniture, bare walls, no telephone. We could of called the Police up or the Better Business Bureau. I learned a lesson tonight. How do I know

that Mr. Williams [the experimenter] is
telling the truth . . . I wish I knew how
many volts a person could take before lapsing
into unconsciousness . . .

[Subject 2414]

Another subject stated:

I questioned on my arrival my own judgment
[about coming]. I had doubts as to the
legitimacy of the operation and the con-
sequences of participation. I felt it was a
heartless way to conduct memory or learning
processes on human beings and certainly
dangerous without the presence of a medical
doctor.

[Subject 2440 V]

There was no noticeable reduction in tension for the Bridgeport subjects. And the subjects' estimation of the amount of pain felt by the victim was slightly, though not significantly, higher than in the Yale study.

A failure to obtain complete obedience in Bridgeport would indicate that the extreme compliance found in New Haven subjects was tied closely to the background authority of Yale University; if a large proportion of the subjects remained fully obedient, very different conclusions would be called for.

As it turned out, the level of obedience in Bridgeport, although somewhat reduced, was not significantly lower than that obtained at Yale. A large proportion of the Bridgeport subjects were fully obedient to the experimenter's commands (48 per cent of the Bridgeport subjects delivered the maximum shock *vs.* 65 per cent in the corresponding condition at Yale).

How are these findings to be interpreted? It is possible that if commands of a potentially harmful or destructive sort are to be perceived as legitimate they must occur within some sort of institutional structure. But it is clear from the study that it need not be a particularly reputable or distinguished institution. The Bridgeport experiments were conducted by an unimpressive firm lacking any credentials; the laboratory was set up in a respectable office building with title listed in the building directory. Beyond that, there was no evidence of benevolence or compe-

tence. It is possible that the *category* of institution, judged according to its professed function, rather than its qualitative position within that category, wins our compliance. Persons deposit money in elegant, but also in seedy-looking banks, without giving much thought to the differences in security they offer. Similarly, our subjects may consider one laboratory to be as competent as another, so long as it *is* a scientific laboratory.

It would be valuable to study the subjects' performance in other contexts which go even further than the Bridgeport study in denying institutional support to the experimenter. It is possible that, beyond a certain point, obedience disappears completely. But that point had not been reached in the Bridgeport office: almost half the subjects obeyed the experimenter fully.

FURTHER EXPERIMENTS

We may mention briefly some additional experiments undertaken in the Yale series. A considerable amount of obedience and defiance in everyday life occurs in connexion with groups. And we had reason to feel in the light of many group studies already done in psychology that group forces would have a profound effect on reactions to authority. A series of experiments was run to examine these effects. In all cases only one naïve subject was studied per hour, but he performed in the midst of actors who, unknown to him, were employed by the experimenter. In one experiment (Groups for Disobedience) two actors broke off in the middle of the experiment. When this happened 90 per cent of the subjects followed suit and defied the experimenter. In another condition the actors followed the orders obediently; this strengthened the experimenter's power only slightly. In still a third experiment the job of pushing the switch to shock the learner was given to one of the actors, while the naïve subject performed a subsidiary act. We wanted to see how the teacher would respond if he were involved in the situation but did not actually give the shocks. In this situation only three subjects out of forty broke off. In a final group experiment the subjects themselves determined the shock level they were going to use. Two actors suggested higher and higher shock levels; some subjects insisted, despite group pressure, that the shock level be kept low; others followed along with the group.

Further experiments were completed using women as subjects, as well as a set dealing with the effects of dual, unsanctioned, and conflicting authority. A final experiment concerned the personal relationship between victim and subject. These will have to be described elsewhere, lest the present report be extended to monographic length.

It goes without saying that future research can proceed in many different directions. What kinds of response from the victim are most effective in causing disobedience in the subject? Perhaps passive resistance is more effective than vehement protest. What conditions of entry into an authority system lead to greater or lesser obedience? What is the effect of anonymity and masking on the subject's behavior? What conditions lead to the subject's perception of responsibility for his own actions? Each of these could be a major research topic in itself, and can readily be incorporated into the general experimental procedure described here.

LEVELS OF OBEDIENCE AND DEFIANCE

One general finding that merits attention is the high level of obedience manifested in the experimental situation. Subjects often expressed deep disapproval of shocking a man in the face of his objections, and others denounced it as senseless and stupid. Yet many subjects complied even while they protested. The proportion of obedient subjects greatly exceeded the expectations of the experimenter and his colleagues. At the outset, we had conjectured that subjects would not, in general, go above the level of 'Strong Shock.' In practice, many subjects were willing to administer the most extreme shocks available when commanded by the experimenter. For some subjects the experiment provides an occasion for aggressive release. And for others it demonstrates the extent to which obedient dispositions are deeply ingrained, and are engaged irrespective of their consequences for others. Yet this is not the whole story. Somehow, the subject becomes implicated in a situation from which he cannot disengage himself.

The departure of the experimental results from intelligent expectation, to some extent, has been formalized. The procedure was to describe the experimental situation in concrete detail to a group of competent persons, and to ask them to predict the performance of 100 hypothetical subjects. For purposes of indicating the distribution of break-off points judges were provided with a diagram of the shock generator, and recorded their predictions before being informed of the actual results. Judges typically underestimated the amount of obedience demonstrated by subjects.

In Figure 3, we compare the predictions of forty psychiatrists at a leading medical school with the actual performance of subjects in the experiment. The psychiatrists predicted that most subjects would not go beyond the tenth shock level (150 volts; at this point the victim makes his first explicit demand to be freed). They further predicted that by the twentieth shock level (300 volts; the victim refuses to answer) 3.73 per cent of the subjects would still be obedient; and that only a little over one-tenth of one per cent of the subjects would administer the highest shock on the board. But, as the graph indicates, the obtained behavior was very different. Sixty-two per cent of the subjects obeyed the experimenter's commands fully. Between expectation and occurrence there is a whopping discrepancy.

Why did the psychiatrists underestimate the level of obedience? Possibly, because their predictions were based on an inadequate conception of the determinants of human action, a conception that focuses on motives *in vacuo*. This orientation may be entirely adequate for the repair of bruised impulses as revealed on the psychiatrist's couch, but as

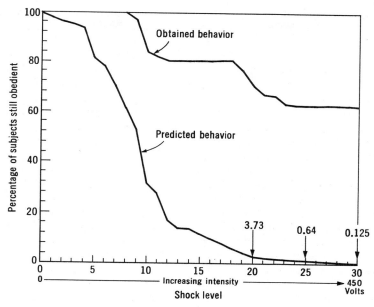

Figure 3.   Predicted and obtained behavior in voice feedback

soon as our interest turns to action in larger settings, attention must be paid to the situations in which motives are expressed. A situation exerts an important press on the individual. It exercises constraints and may provide push. In certain circumstances it is not so much the kind of person a man is, as the kind of situation in which he is placed, that determines his actions.

Many people, not knowing much about the experiment, claim that subjects who go to the end of the board are sadistic. Nothing could be more foolish as an overall characterization of these persons. It is like saying that a person thrown into a swift-flowing stream is necessarily a fast swimmer, or that he has great stamina because he moves so rapidly relative to the bank. The context of action must always be considered. The individual, upon entering the laboratory, becomes integrated into a situation that carries its own momentum. The subject's problem then is how to become disengaged from a situation which is moving in an altogether ugly direction.

The fact that disengagement is so difficult testifies to the potency of the forces that keep the subject at the control board.

Are these forces to be conceptualized as individual motives and expressed in the language of personality dynamics, or are they to be seen as the effects of social structure and pressures arising from the situational field?

A full understanding of the subject's action will, I feel, require that both perspectives be adopted. The person brings to the laboratory enduring dispositions toward authority and aggression, and at the same time he becomes enmeshed in a social structure that is no less an objective fact of the case. From the standpoint of personality theory one may ask: What mechanisms of personality enable a person to transfer responsibility to authority? What are the motives underlying obedient and disobedient performance? Does orientation to authority lead to a short-circuiting of the shame-guilt system? What cognitive and emotional defenses are brought into play in the case of obedient and defiant subjects?

The present experiments are not, however, directed toward an exploration of the motives engaged when the subject obeys the experimenter's commands. Instead, they examine the situational variables responsible for the elicitation of obedience. Elsewhere, we have attempted to spell out some of the structural properties of the experimental situation that account for high obedience, and this analysis need not be repeated here (Milgram, 1963). The experimental variations themselves represent our attempt to probe that structure, by systematically changing it and noting the consequences for behavior. It is clear that some situations produce greater compliance with the experimenter's commands than others. However, this does not necessarily imply an increase or decrease in the strength of any single definable motive. Situations producing the greatest obedience could do so by triggering the most powerful, yet perhaps the most idiosyncratic, of motives in each subject confronted by the setting. Or they may simply recruit a greater number and variety of motives in their service. But whatever the motives involved—and it is far from certain that they can ever be known—action may be studied as a direct function of the situation in which it occurs. This has been the approach of the present study, where we sought to plot behavioral regularities against manipulated properties of the social field. Ultimately, social psychology would like to have a compelling *theory of situations* which will, first, present a language in terms of which situations can be defined; proceed to a typology of situations; and then point to the manner in which definable properties of situations are transformed into psychological forces in the individual.

POSTSCRIPT

Almost a thousand adults were individually studied in the obedience research, and there were many specific conclusions regarding the variables that control obedience and disobedience to authority. Some of these have been discussed briefly in the preceding sections, and more detailed reports will be released subsequently.

There are now some other generalizations I should like to make, which do not derive in any strictly logical fashion from the experiments as carried out, but which, I feel, ought to be made. They are formulations of an intuitive sort that have been forced on me by observation of many subjects responding to the pressures of authority. The assertions represent a painful alteration in my own thinking; and since they were acquired only under the repeated impact of direct observation, I have no illusion that they will be generally accepted by persons who have not had the same experience.

With numbing regularity good people were seen to knuckle under the demands of authority and perform actions that were callous and severe. Men who are in everyday life responsible and decent were seduced by the trappings of authority, by the control of their perceptions, and by the uncritical acceptance of the experimenter's definition of the situation, into performing harsh acts.

What is the limit of such obedience? At many points we attempted to establish a boundary. Cries from the victim were inserted; not good enough. The victim claimed heart trouble; subjects still shocked him on command. The victim pleaded that he be let free, and his answers no longer registered on the signal box; subjects continued to shock him. At the outset we had not conceived that such drastic procedures would be needed to generate disobedience, and each step was added only as the ineffectiveness of the earlier techniques became clear. The final effort to establish a limit was the Touch-Proximity condition. But the very first subject in this condition subdued the victim on command, and proceeded to the highest shock level. A quarter of the subjects in this condition performed similarly.

The results, as seen and felt in the laboratory, are to this author disturbing. They raise the possibility that human nature, or—more specifically—the kind of character produced in American democratic society, cannot be counted on to insulate its citizens from brutality and inhumane treatment at the direction of malevolent authority. A substantial proportion of people do what they are told to do, irrespective of the content of the act and without limitations of conscience, so long as they perceive that the command comes from a legitimate authority. If in this study an anonymous experimenter could successfully command adults to subdue a fifty-year-old man, and force on him painful electric shocks against his protests, one can only wonder what government, with its vastly greater authority and prestige, can command of its subjects. There is, of course, the extremely important question of whether malevolent political institutions could or would arise in American society. The present research contributes nothing to this issue.

In an article titled 'The Dangers of Obedience,' Harold J. Laski wrote:

. . . civilization means, above all, an unwillingness to inflict unnecessary pain. Within the ambit of that definition, those of us who heedlessly accept the commands of authority cannot yet claim to be civilized men.

. . . Our business, if we desire to live a life not utterly devoid of meaning and significance, is to accept nothing which contradicts our basic experience merely because it comes to us from tradition or convention or authority. It may well be that we shall be wrong; but our self-expression is thwarted at the root unless the certainties we are asked to accept coincide with the certainties we experience. That is why the condition of freedom in any state is always a widespread and consistent skeptism of the canons upon which power insists.

References

Buss, Arnold H. *The Psychology of Aggression.* New York and London: John Wiley, 1961.

Kierkegaard, S. *Fear and Trembling.* English Edition, 1843, Princeton: Princeton University Press, 1941.

Laski, Harold J. The Dangers of Obedience. *Harper's Monthly Magazine* **159**, June, 1929. 1–10.

Milgram, S. Dynamics of Obedience: Experiments in Social Psychology. Mimeographed report, *National Science Foundation*, January 25, 1961.

———. Behavioral Study of Obedience. *J. Abnorm. Soc. Psychol.* **67**, 1963. 371–8.

———. Issues in the Study of Obedience: A Reply to Baumrind. *Amer. Psychol.* **19**, 1964. 848–52.

Miller, N. E. Experimental Studies of Conflict. In J. McV. Hunt (Ed.), *Personality and the Behavior Disorders.* New York: Ronald Press, 1944.

Scott, J. P. *Aggression.* Chicago: University of Chicago Press, 1958.

GOOD PEOPLE AND DIRTY WORK

Everett C. Hughes

"... une secte est le noyau et le levain
de toute foule. ... Etudier la foule c'est
juger un drame d'après ce qu'on voit sur la
scène; étudier la secte c'est le juger d'après ce
qu'on voit dans les coulisses."

Sighele, S. Psychologi des sectes. *Paris,
1898. Pp. 62, 63, 65.*[1]

The National Socialist Government of Germany, with the arm of its fanatical inner sect, the S.S., commonly known as the Black Shirts or Elite Guard, perpetrated and boasted of the most colossal and dramatic piece of social dirty work the world has ever known. Perhaps there are other claimants to the title, but they could not match this one's combination of mass, speed and perverse pride in the deed. Nearly all peoples have plenty of cruelty and death to account for. How many Negro Americans have died by the hands of lynching mobs? How many more from unnecessary disease and lack of food or of knowledge of nutrition? How many Russians died

to bring about collectivization of land? And who is to blame if there be starving millions in some parts of the world while wheat molds in the fields of other parts?

I do not revive the case of the Nazi *Endloesung* (final solution) of the Jewish problem in order to condemn the Germans, or make them look worse than other peoples, but to recall to our attention dangers which lurk in our midst always. Most of what follows was written after my first postwar visit to Germany in 1948. The impressions were vivid. The facts have not diminished and disappeared with time, as did the stories of alleged German atrocities in Belgium in the first World War. The fuller the record, the worse it gets.[2]

Several millions of people were delivered to the concentration camps, operated under the leadership of Heinrich Himmler with the help of Adolf Eichmann. A few hundred thousand survived in some fashion. Still fewer came out sound of mind and body. A pair of examples, well attested, will show the extreme of perverse cruelty reached by the

Source: E. C. Hughes, "Good People and Dirty Work," *Social Problems,* Vol. 10, 1964, pp. 3–11. Copyright 1964 by The Society for the Study of Social Problems and reprinted by permission of publisher and author.

[1] "... a sect is the nucleus and the yeast of every crowd. ... To study a crowd is to judge by what one sees on the stage; to study the sect is to judge by what one sees backstage." These are among the many passages underlined by Robert E. Park in his copy, now in my possession, of Sighele's classic work on political sects. There are a number of references to this work in the Park and Burgess *Introduction to the Science of Sociology,* Chicago, 1921. In fact, there is more attention paid to fanatical political and religious behavior in Park and Burgess than in any later sociological work in this country. Sighele's discussion relates chiefly to the anarchist movement of his time. There have been fanatical movements since. The Secret Army Organization in Algeria is but the latest.

[2] The best source easily available at that time was Eugen Kogon's *Der SS-Staat. Das System der Deutschen Konzentrationslager,* Berlin, 1946. Many of my data are from his book. Some years later H. G. Adler, after several years of research, wrote *Theresianstadt, 1941–1945. Das Antlitz einer Zwangsgemeinschaft* (Tuebingen, 1955), and still later published *Die Verheimlichte Wahrheit, Theresienstaedter Dokumente* (Tuebingen, 1958), a book of documents concerning that camp in which Czech and other Jews were concentrated, demoralized and destroyed. Kogon, a Catholic intellectual, and Adler, a Bohemian Jew, both wrote out of personal experience in the Concentration Camps. Both considered it their duty to present the phenomenon objectively to the public. None of their statements has ever been challenged.

S.S. guards in charge of the camps. Prisoners were ordered to climb trees; guards whipped them to make them climb faster. Once they were out of reach, other prisoners, also urged by the whip, were put to shaking the trees. When the victims fell they were kicked to see whether they could rise to their feet. Those too badly injured to get up were shot to death, as useless for work. A not inconsiderable number of prisoners were drowned in pits full of human excrement. These examples are so horrible that your minds will run away from them. You will not, as when you read a slightly salacious novel, imagine the rest. I therefore thrust these examples upon you and insist that the people who thought them up could, and did, improvise others like them, and even worse, from day to day over several years. Many of the victims of the Camps gave up the ghost (this Biblical phrase is the most apt) from a combination of humiliation, starvation, fatigue and physical abuse. In due time, a policy of mass liquidation in the gas chamber was added to individual virtuosity in cruelty.

This program—for it was a program—of cruelty and murder was carried out in the name of racial superiority and racial purity. It was directed mainly, although by no means exclusively, against Jews, Slavs and Gypsies. It was thorough. There are few Jews in the territories which were under the control of the Third German Reich—the two Germanies, Holland, Czechoslovakia, Poland, Austria, Hungary. Many Jewish Frenchmen were destroyed. There were concentration camps even in Tunisia and Algiers under the German occupation.

When, during my 1948 visit to Germany, I became more aware of the reactions of ordinary Germans to the horrors of the concentration camps, I found myself asking not the usual question, "How did racial hatred rise to such a high level?", but this one, "How could such dirty work be done among and, in a sense, *by* the millions of ordinary, civilized German people?" Along with this came related questions. How could these millions of ordinary people live in the midst of such cruelty and murder without a general uprising against it and against the people who did it? How, once freed from the regime that did it, could they be apparently so little concerned about it, so toughly silent about it, not only in talking with outsiders—which is easy to understand—but among themselves? How and where could there be found in a modern civilized country the several hundred thousand men and women capable of such work? How were these people so far released from the inhibitions of civilized life as to be able to imagine, let alone perform, the ferocious, obscene and perverse actions which they did imagine and perform? How could they be kept at such a height of fury through years of having to see daily at close range the human wrecks they made and being often literally spattered with the filth produced and accumulated by their own actions?

You will see that there are here two orders of questions. One set concerns the good people who did not themselves do this work. The other concerns those who did do it. But the two sets are not really separate; for the crucial question concerning the good people is their relation to the people who did the dirty work, with a related one which asks under what circumstances good people let the others get away with such actions.

An easy answer concerning the Germans is that they were not so good after all. We can attribute to them some special inborn or ingrained race consciousness, combined with a penchant for sadistic cruelty and unquestioning acceptance of whatever is done by those who happen to be in authority. Pushed to its extreme, this answer simply makes us, rather than the Germans, the superior race. It is the Nazi tune, put to words of our own.

Now there are deep and stubborn differences between peoples. Their history and culture may make the Germans especially susceptible to the doctrine of their own racial superiority and especially acquiescent to the actions of whoever is in power over them. These are matters deserving of the best study that can be given them. But to say that these things could happen in Germany simply because Germans are different—from us—buttresses their own excuses and lets us off too easily from blame for what happened there and from the question whether it could happen here.

Certainly in their daily practice and

expression before the Hitler regime, the Germans showed no more, if as much, hatred of other racial or cultural groups than we did and do. Residential segregation was not marked. Intermarriage was common, and the families of such marriages had an easier social existence than they generally have in America. The racially exclusive club, school and hotel were much less in evidence than here. And I well remember an evening in 1933 when a Montreal business man—a very nice man, too —said in our living room, "Why don't we admit that Hitler is doing to the Jews just what we ought to be doing?" That was not an uncommon sentiment, although it may be said in defense of the people who expressed it, that they probably did not know and would not have believed the full truth about the Nazi program of destroying Jews. The essential underlying sentiments on racial matters in Germany were not different in kind from those prevailing throughout the western, and especially the Anglo-Saxon, countries. But I do not wish to over-emphasize this point. I only want to close one easy way out of serious consideration of the problem of good people and dirty work, by demonstrating that the Germans were and are about as good and about as bad as the rest of us on this matter of racial sentiments and, let us add, their notions of decent human behaviour.

But what was the reaction of ordinary Germans to the persecution of the Jews and to the concentration camp mass torture and murder? A conversation between a German school-teacher, a German architect and myself gives the essentials in a vivid form. It was in the studio of the architect, and the occasion was a rather casual visit, in Frankfurt am Main in 1948.

The architect: "I am ashamed for my people whenever I think of it. But we didn't know about it. We only learned about all that later. You must remember the pressure we were under; we had to join the party. We had to keep our mouths shut and do as we were told. It was a terrible pressure. Still, I am ashamed. But you see, we had lost our colonies, and our national honour was hurt. And these Nazis exploited that feeling. And the Jews, they were a problem.

They came from the east. You should see them in Poland; the lowest class of people, full of lice, dirty and poor, running about in their Ghettos in filthy caftans. They came here, and got rich by unbelievable methods after the first war. They occupied all the good places. Why, they were in the proportion of ten to one in medicine and law and government posts!"

At this point the architect hesitated and looked confused. He continued: "Where was I? It is the poor food. You see what misery we are in here, Herr Professor. It often happens that I forget what I was talking about. Where was I now? I have completely forgotten."

(His confusion was, I believe, not at all feigned. Many Germans said they suffered losses of memory such as this, and laid it to their lack of food.)

I said firmly: "You were talking about loss of national honour and how the Jews had got hold of everything."

The architect: "Oh, yes! That was it! Well, of course that was no way to settle the Jewish problem. But there was a problem and it had to be settled some way."

The school-teacher: "Of course, they have Palestine now."

I protested that Palestine would hardly hold them.

The architect: "The professor is right. Palestine can't hold all the Jews. And it was a terrible thing to murder people. But we didn't know it at the time. But I am glad I am alive now. It is an interesting time in men's history. You know, when the Americans came it was like a great release. I really want to see a new ideal in Germany. I like the freedom that lets me talk to you like this. But, unfortunately that is not the general opinion. Most of my friends really hang on to the old ideas. They can't see any hope, so they hang on to the old ideas."

This scrap of talk gives, I believe, the essential elements as well as the flavor of the German reaction. It checks well with formal studies which have been made, and it varies only in detail from other conversations which I myself recorded in 1948.

One of the most obvious points in it is

unwillingness to think about the dirty work done. In this case—perhaps by chance, perhaps not—the good man suffered an actual lapse of memory in the middle of this statement. This seems a simple point. But the psychiatrists have shown that it is less simple than it looks. They have done a good deal of work on the complicated mechanisms by which the individual mind keeps unpleasant or intolerable knowledge from consciousness, and have shown how great may, in some cases, be the consequent loss of effectiveness of the personality. But we have taken collective unwillingness to know unpleasant facts more or less for granted. That people can and do keep a silence about things whose open discussion would threaten the group's conception of itself, and hence its solidarity, is common knowledge. It is a mechanism that operates in every family and in every group which has a sense of group reputation. To break such a silence is considered an attack against the group; a sort of treason, if it be a member of the group who breaks the silence. This common silence allows group fictions to grow up; such as, that grandpa was less a scoundrel and more romantic than he really was. And I think it demonstrable that it operates especially against any expression, except in ritual, of collective guilt. The remarkable thing in present-day Germany is not that there is so little reference to something about which people do feel deeply guilty, but that it is talked about at all.

In order to understand this phenomenon we would have to find out who talks about the concentration camp atrocities, in what situations, in what mood, and with what stimulus. On these points I know only my own limited experiences. One of the most moving of these was my first post-war meeting with an elderly professor whom I had known before the Nazi time; he is an heroic soul who did not bow his head during the Nazi time and who keeps it erect now. His first words, spoken with tears in his eyes, were:

How hard it is to believe that men will be as bad as they say they will. Hitler and his people said: "Heads will roll," but how many of us—even of his bitterest opponents—could really believe that they would do it.

This man could and did speak, in 1948, not only to the likes of me, but to his students, his colleagues and to the public which read his articles, in the most natural way about the Nazi atrocities whenever there was occasion to do it in the course of his tireless effort to reorganize and to bring new life into the German universities. He had neither the compulsion to speak, so that he might excuse and defend himself, nor a conscious or unconscious need to keep silent. Such people were rare; how many there were in Germany I do not know.

Occasions of another kind in which the silence was broken were those where, in class, public lecture or in informal meetings with students, I myself had talked frankly of race relations in other parts of the world, including the lynchings which sometimes occur in my own country and the terrible cruelty visited upon natives in South Africa. This took off the lid of defensiveness, so that a few people would talk quite easily of what happened under the Nazi regime. More common were situations like that with the architect, where I threw in some remark about the atrocities in response to Germans' complaint that the world is abusing them. In such cases, there was usually an expression of shame, accompanied by a variety of excuses (including that of having been kept in ignorance), and followed by a quick turning away from the subject.

Somewhere in consideration of this problem of discussion versus silence we must ask what the good (that is, ordinary) people in Germany did know about these things. It is clear that the S.S. kept the more gory details of the concentration camps a close secret. Even high officials of the government, the army and the Nazi party itself were in some measure held in ignorance, although of course they kept the camps supplied with victims. The common people of Germany knew that the camps existed; most knew people who had disappeared into them; some saw the victims, walking skeletons in rags, being transported in trucks or trains, or being herded on the road from station to camp or to work in fields or factories near the camps. Many knew people who had been released from concentration camps; such released persons kept their counsel on pain of death. But secrecy was cultivated and supported by fear and terror. In the absence of a determined and heroic will to know and publish the truth, and in the absence of all the instruments of opposition, the degree of knowledge was undoubtedly low, in spite of the fact that all knew that something both stupendous and horrible was going on; and in spite of the fact that Hitler's *Mein Kampf* and the utterances of his aides said that no fate was too horrible for the Jews and other wrong-headed or inferior people. This must make us ask under what conditions the will to know and to discuss is strong, determined and effective; this, like most of the important questions I have raised, I leave unanswered except as answers may be contained in the statement of the case.

But to return to our moderately good man, the architect. He insisted over and over again that he did not know, and we may suppose that he knew as much and as little as most Germans. But he also made it quite clear that he wanted something done to the Jews. I have similar statements from people of whom I knew that they had had close Jewish friends before the Nazi time. This raises the whole problem of the extent to which those pariahs who do the dirty work of society are really acting as agents for the rest of us. To talk of this question one must note that, in building up his case, the architect pushed the Jews firmly into an out-group: they were dirty, lousy and unscrupulous (an odd statement from a resident of Frankfurt, the home of old Jewish merchants and intellectual families long identified with those aspects of culture of which Germans are most proud). Having dissociated himself clearly from these people, and having declared them a problem, he apparently was willing to let someone else do to them the dirty work which he himself would not do, and for which he expressed shame. The case is perhaps analogous to our attitude toward those convicted of crime. From time to time, we get wind of cruelty practiced upon the prisoners in penitentiaries or jails; or, it may be, merely a report that they are ill-fed or that hygienic conditions are not

good. Perhaps we do not wish that the prisoners should be cruelly treated or badly fed, but our reaction is probably tempered by a notion that they deserve something, because of some dissociation of them from the in-group of good people. If what they get is worse than what we like to think about, it is a little bit too bad. It is a point on which we are ambivalent. Campaigns for reform of prisons are often followed by counter-campaigns against a too high standard of living for prisoners and against having prisons run by softies. Now the people who run prisons are our agents. Just how far they do or could carry out our wishes is hard to say. The minor prison guard, in boastful justification of some of his more questionable practices, says, in effect: "If those reformers and those big shots upstairs had to live with these birds as I do, they would soon change their fool notions about running a prison." He is suggesting that the good people are either naive or hypocritical. Furthermore, he knows quite well that the wishes of his employers, the public, are by no means un-mixed. They are quite as likely to put upon him for being too nice as for being too harsh. And if, as sometimes happens, he is a man disposed to cruelty, there may be some justice in his feeling that he is only doing what others would like to do, if they but dared; and what they would do, if they were in his place.

There are plenty of examples in our own world which I might have picked for comparison with the German attitude toward the concentration camps. For instance, a newspaper in Denver made a great scandal out of the allegation that our Japanese compatriots were too well fed in the camps where they were concentrated during the war. I might have mentioned some feature of the sorry history of the people of Japanese background in Canada. Or it might have been lynching, or some aspect of racial discrimination. But I purposely chose prisoners convicted of crime. For convicts are formally set aside for special handling. They constitute an out-group in all countries. This brings the issue clearly before us, since few people cherish the illusion that the problem of treating criminals can be settled by propaganda designed to prove that there aren't any criminals. Almost everyone agrees that something has to be done about them. The question concerns what is done, who does it, and the nature of the mandate given by the rest of us to those who do it. Perhaps we give them an unconscious mandate to go beyond anything we ourselves would care to do or even to acknowledge. I venture to suggest that the higher and more expert functionaries who act in our behalf represent something of a distillation of what we may consider our public wishes, while some of the others show a sort of concentrate of those impulses of which we are or wish to be less aware.

Now the choice of convicted prisoners brings up another crucial point in inter-group relations. All societies of any great size have in-groups and out-groups; in fact, one of the best ways of describing a society is to consider it a network of smaller and larger in-groups and out-groups. And an in-group is one only because there are out-groups. When I refer to *my* children I obviously imply that they are closer to me than other people's children and that I will make greater efforts to buy oranges and cod-liver oil for them than for others' children. In fact, it may mean that I will give them cod-liver oil if I have to choke them to get it down. We do our own dirty work on those closest to us. The very injunction that I love my neighbor as myself starts with me; if I don't love myself and my nearest, the phrase has a very sour meaning.

Each of us is a center of a network of in- and out-groups. Now the distinctions between *in* and *out* may be drawn in various ways, and nothing is more important for both the student of society and the educator than to discover how these lines are made and how they may be redrawn in more just and sensible ways. But to believe that we can do away with the distinction between *in* and *out*, *us* and *them* in social life is complete nonsense. On the positive side, we generally feel a greater obligation to in-groups; hence less obligation to out-groups; and in the case of such groups as convicted criminals, the out-group is definitely given over to the hands of

our agents for punishment. That is the extreme case. But there are other out-groups toward which we may have aggressive feelings and dislike, although we give no formal mandate to anyone to deal with them on our behalf, and although we profess to believe that they should not suffer restrictions or disadvantages. The greater their social distance from us, the more we leave in the hands of others a sort of mandate by default to deal with them on our behalf. Whatever effort we put on reconstructing the lines which divide in- and out-groups, there remains the eternal problem of our treatment, direct or delegated, of whatever groups are considered somewhat outside. And here it is that the whole matter of our professed and possible deeper unprofessed wishes comes up for consideration; and the related problem of what we know, can know and want to know about it. In Germany, the agents got out of hand and created such terror that it was best not to know. It is also clear that it was and is easier to the conscience of many Germans not to know. It is, finally, not unjust to say that the agents were at least working in the direction of the wishes of many people, although they may have gone beyond the wishes of most. The same questions can be asked about our own society, and with reference not only to prisoners but also to many other groups upon whom there is no legal or moral stigma. Again I have not the answers. I leave you to search for them.

In considering the question of dirty work we have eventually to think about the people who do it. In Germany, these were the members of the S.S. and of that inner group of the S.S. who operated the concentration camps. Many reports have been made on the social backgrounds and the personalities of these cruel fanatics. Those who have studied them say that a large proportion were "gescheiterte Existenzen," men or women with a history of failure, of poor adaptation to the demands of work and of the classes of society in which they had been bred. Germany between wars had large numbers of such people. Their adherence to a movement which proclaimed a doctrine of hatred was natural enough. The movement offered something more. It created an inner group which was to be superior to all others, even Germans, in their emancipation from the usual bourgeois morality; people above and beyond the ordinary morality. I dwell on this, not as a doctrine, but as an organizational device. For, as Eugen Kogon, author of the most penetrating analysis of the S.S. and their camps, has said, the Nazis came to power by creating a state within a state; a body with its own counter-morality, and its own counter-law, its courts and its own execution of sentence upon those who did not live up to its orders and standards. Even as a movement, it had inner circles within inner circles; each sworn to secrecy as against the next outer one. The struggle between these inner circles continued after Hitler came to power; Himmler eventually won the day. His S.S. became a state within the Nazi state, just as the Nazi movement had become a state within the Weimar state. One is reminded of the oft quoted but neglected statement of Sighele: "At the center of a crowd look for the sect." He referred, of course, to the political sect; the fanatical inner group of a movement seeking power by revolutionary methods. Once the Nazis were in power, this inner sect, while becoming now the recognized agent of the state and, hence, of the masses of the people, could at the same time dissociate itself more completely from them in action, because of the very fact of having a mandate. It was now beyond all danger of interference and investigation. For it had the instruments of interference and investigation in its own hands. These are also the instruments of secrecy. So the S.S. could and did build up a powerful system in which they had the resources of the state and of the economy of Germany and the conquered countries from which to steal all that was needed to carry out their orgy of cruelty luxuriously as well as with impunity.

Now let us ask, concerning the dirty workers, questions similar to those concerning the good people. Is there a supply of candidates for such work in other societies? It would be easy to say that only Germany could produce such a crop. The question

is answered by being put. The problem of people who have run aground (gescheiterte Existenzen) is one of the most serious in our modern societies. Any psychiatrist will, I believe, testify that we have a sufficient pool or fund of personalities warped toward perverse punishment and cruelty to do any amount of dirty work that the good people may be inclined to countenance. It would not take a very great turn of events to increase the number of such people, and to bring their discontents to the surface. This is not to suggest that every movement based on discontent with the present state of things will be led by such people. That is obviously untrue; and I emphasize the point lest my remarks give comfort to those who would damn all who express militant discontent. But I think study of militant social movements does show that these warped people seek a place in them. Specifically, they are likely to become the plotting, secret police of the group. It is one of the problems of militant social movements to keep such people out. It is of course easier to do this if the spirit of the movement is positive, its conception of humanity high and inclusive, and its aims sound. This was not the case of the Nazi movement. As Kogon puts it: "The SS were but the arch-type of the Nazis in general."[3] But such people are sometimes attracted for want of something better, to movements whose aims are contrary to the spirit of cruelty and punishment. I would suggest that all of us look well at the leadership and entourage of movements to which we attach ourselves for signs of a negativistic, punishing attitude. For once such a spirit develops in a movement, punishment of the nearest and easiest victim is likely to become more attractive than striving for the essential goals. And, if the Nazi movement teaches us anything at all, it is that if any shadow of a mandate be given to such people, they will —having compromised us—make it larger and larger. The processes by which they do so are the development of the power and inward discipline of their own group, a pro-

---

[3] Op. cit., p. 316.

gressive dissociation of themselves from the rules of human decency prevalent in their culture, and an ever-growing contempt for the welfare of the masses of people.

The power and inward discipline of the S.S. became such that those who once became members could get out only by death; by suicide, murder or mental breakdown. Orders from the central offices of the S.S. were couched in equivocal terms as a hedge against a possible day of judgment. When it became clear that such a day of judgment would come, the hedging and intrigue became greater; the urge to murder also became greater, because every prisoner became a potential witness.

Again we are dealing with a phenomenon common in all societies. Almost every group which has a specialized social function to perform is in some measure a secret society, with a body of rules developed and enforced by the members and with some power to save its members from outside punishment. And here is one of the paradoxes of social order. A society without smaller, rule-making and disciplining powers would be no society at all. There would be nothing but law and police; and this is what the Nazis

strove for, at the expense of family, church, professional groups, parties and other such nuclei of spontaneous control. But apparently the only way to do this, for good as well as for evil ends, is to give power into the hands of some fanatical small group which will have a far greater power of self-discipline and a far greater immunity from outside control than the traditional groups. The problem is, then, not of trying to get rid of all the self-disciplining, protecting groups within society, but one of keeping them integrated with one another and as sensitive as can be to a public opinion which transcends them all. It is a matter of checks and balances, of what we might call the social and moral constitution of society.

Those who are especially devoted to efforts to eradicate from good people, as individuals, all those sentiments which seem to bring about the great and small dirty work of the world, may think that my remarks are something of an attack on their methods. They are right to this extent; that I am insisting that we give a share of our effort to the social mechanisms involved as well as to the individual and those of his sentiments which concern people of other kinds.

AN ANALYSIS OF CONFLICTING SOCIAL NORMS

Samuel A. Stouffer

This paper illustrates an empirical procedure for studying role obligations, with particular reference to simultaneous role obligations which conflict.

The writer became especially interested

Source: S. A. Stouffer, "An Analysis of Conflicting Social Norms," *American Sociological Review*, Vol. 14, 1949, pp. 107–117. Copyright 1949 by The American Sociological Association and reprinted by permission of publisher.

in the problem when considering the strains to which the non-commissioned officer in the Army was subjected. On the one hand, the non-com had the role of agent of the command and in case the orders from above conflicted with what his men thought were right and necessary he was expected by his superiors to carry out the orders. But he also was an enlisted man, sharing enlisted men's attitudes, often hostile attitudes, toward the commissioned ranks. Consequently, the system of informal controls was such as to reward him for siding with the men in a conflict situation and punish him if he did not. There was some evidence that unless his men had confidence that he could see their point of view, he was an ineffective leader; on the other hand, open and flagrant disobedience by him of an order from above could not be tolerated by the command.[1]

The general theoretical viewpoint behind this paper involves several propositions:

1. In any social group there exist norms and a strain for conformity to these norms.
2. Ordinarily, if the norms are clear and unambiguous the individual has no choice but to conform or take the consequences in group resentment.
3. If a person has simultaneous roles in two or more groups such that simultaneous conformity to the norms of each of the groups is incompatible, he can take one of only a limited number of actions, for example:
   (1) He can conform to one set of role expectations and take the consequences of non-conformity to other sets.
   (2) He can seek a compromise position by which he attempts to conform in part, though not wholly, to one or more sets of role expectations, in the hope that the sanctions applied will be minimal.

It need hardly be pointed out that conflicts of role obligations are a common experience of all people, especially in our complex Western society. The foreman in industry, like the non-com in the Army, is an obvious example; the "marginal man," as represented by the second-generation foreign born, for example, has been much studied. But role conflicts are not limited to such situations. Every adolescent is certain to experience situations in which his family and his peer group are in conflict, such that con-

formity to the norms of the one is incompatible with conformity to the norms of the other. Most adults are subject to strains to conformity to norms incompatible from one group to another; although, often enough to make life tolerable, either the conflicts do not arise simultaneously or there is a broad enough range of tolerated behavior to provide some flexibility.

In any authoritarian situation, it is axiomatic that adherence to the rules prescribed by the authority depends to no small extent on the compatibility of the rules with dominant values of those who must obey them. It is likely, in most social situations, that the compatibility is not absolute but a matter of degree. There may be variability among members of the group in the extent to which a given value is held in common. The existence of such variability is a factor which should weaken the sanctions against any particular act and facilitate compromise solutions.

With respect to any social value, there are at least two classes of variability which need to be distinguished:

(1) Each individual may perceive a narrow range of behavior as permissible, but for different individuals the ranges, though small, may constitute different segments of a continuum.
(2) Each individual may perceive a rather wide range of behavior as permissible, even though there is considerable consensus as to the termini of this range.

It is the viewpoint of this paper that the *range* of approved or permissible behavior as perceived by a given individual is an important datum for the analysis of what constitutes a social norm in any group, and especially for the analysis of conflicting norms.

In order to illustrate some of these concepts and to make some preliminary attempts to define them such that statistical operations could be performed with them, an empirical study was made of conflicting role expectations in a sample of 196 Harvard and Radcliffe students, mostly undergraduates. Since the concern was wholly methodological, no effort was made to obtain a random or

---

[1] Stouffer, Suchman, DeVinney, Star, Williams, *The American Soldier*, Vol. I, Chapter 8.

representative sample of the student body, and the data here reported can not necessarily be regarded as typical of how a properly drawn sample would respond. The students were all taking the same course, Social Relations 116. The data were collected on the first day of the course, without any explicit prior discussion of the theoretical problems involved.

Each student filled out a brief questionnaire, anonymously. He was told first:

Imagine that you are proctoring an examination in a middle-group course. About half way through the exam you see a fellow student openly cheating. The student is copying his answers from previously prepared notes. When he sees that you have seen the notes as you walked down the aisle and stopped near his seat, he whispers quietly to you, "O. K., I'm caught. That's all there is to it."

You do not know the student. *What would you as proctor do:*

If you knew that, except for your action, there could be very little chance that either the authorities or your student friends would hear about your part in the incident, which of the following actions (see Table A) *would you as proctor be most likely to take? Next most likely? Least likely? Next least likely?*

After he had finished checking these questions he was presented with a new complication, as follows:

Now, assume that except for your action, there could be very little chance that your student friends would hear about your part in the incident. But assume that, for some reason, there is a good chance, whatever you do, of the authorities finding out about it. Which of the following actions would you as proctor be most likely to take? Next most likely? Least likely? Next least likely?[2]

This was followed by exactly the same check list as before.

Next the respondent was asked to fill out the following check list:

A. Suppose now that a proctor's action would be: *Take away his notes and exam book, dismiss him, and report him for cheating.*

    How would the university authorities feel if they knew you as proctor did this? (check one)

    _____ Would expect one to do something like this

    _____ Would not necessarily expect one to do this, but would not disapprove

    _____ Would disapprove

    _____ Would not tolerate it

    How would your friends in the student body feel if they knew you did this? (check one)

    _____ Would expect one to do something like this

    _____ Would not necessarily expect one to do this, but would not disapprove

    _____ Would disapprove

    _____ Would not tolerate it

B. Suppose that a proctor's action would be: *Take away his notes, let him finish the exam, but report him for cheating.*

C. Suppose now that a proctor's action would be: *If he can be led to withdraw from the exam on some excuse, do not report him for cheating; otherwise report him.*

D. Suppose now that a proctor's action would be: *Take away his notes, but let him finish the exam, and not report him for cheating.*

E. Suppose now that a proctor's action would be: *Act as if nothing had hap-*

---

[2] The questionnaire also contained a parallel set of answer categories for the situation where he was asked:

Now assume that, *except for your action,* there could be very little chance that the authorities would hear about your part in the incident. But also assume that there is a good chance that whatever you do your student friends would hear of it. Which of the following actions would you as proctor be most likely to take? Next most likely? Least likely? Next least likely?

However, only the situations indicated above will be used in the present paper.

Table A.

	Check One in Each Vertical Column			
	My Most Likely Action *(Check One)*	*My Next Most Likely Action (Check One)*	*My Least Likely Action (Check One)*	*My Next Least Likely Action (Check One)*
A. Take away his notes and exam book, dismiss him and report him for cheating.	——	——	——	——
B. Take away his notes, let him finish the exam, but report him for cheating.	——	——	——	——
C. If he can be led to withdraw from the exam on some excuse, do *not* report him for cheating; otherwise report him.	——	——	——	——
D. Take away his notes, but let him finish the exam, and *not* report him for cheating.	——	——	——	——
E. Act as if nothing had happened and *not* report him for cheating.	——	——	——	——

pened and not report him for cheating. (For B, C, D, and E, the same check lists were used as for A, but are here omitted to save space.)

Next the respondent was confronted with what it was hoped, for the methodological purposes of this illustrative study, would be more of a dilemma. He was told:

Now suppose the facts in the case in which you as proctor see a fellow student are exactly the same as in the first case, except for one difference. The student you as proctor see cheating is your own roommate and close friend. You know that your roommate is a hard working, though not a brilliant, student and desperately needs a good grade in this course.

If you knew that, except for your action, there could be very little chance that either the authorities or your student friends would know about your part in the incident, which of the following actions would you as proctor be most likely to take? Next most likely? Least likely? Next least likely?

The check list was the same as in the ordinary case presented first. This was followed by:

Now assume that except for your action, there could be very little chance that your student friends would hear about your part in the incident. But assume that, for some reason, there is a good chance, whatever you do, of the authorities finding out about it. Which of the following actions would you as proctor be most likely to take? Next most likely? Least likely? Next least likely?

Again the check list was the same.

Finally, the identical series of questions about expectations on the part of authorities and students was repeated for this roommate-friend situation.

The five actions described were designed to constitute, from A to E, an ordered sequence along a dimension of *degree of punitiveness.* That they were so perceived generally by the respondents can be shown easily. To illustrate: If a person said that the authorities, for example, would expect or approve more than one act, it is necessary for unidimensionality that the two or more acts be contiguous (for example, A and B, or B and C, or A, B, and C, but not A and C only). Actually, as we shall see, most students reported at least two acts which would be either expected or approved by the authorities; likewise most reported at least two acts which would be either expected or approved by their friends in the student body. In all, there were 4 chances for each respondent to designate such ranges. Of the 744 responses designating ranges of two or more, the acts checked were entirely contiguous in all but 41; in other words, 95 per cent of the responses were consistent with the perception of the sequence of acts as a continuum.[3]

Attention should be called to the likelihood that the responses as to the approval or disapproval of the authorities or of one's friends in the student body to a given act have an intrinsic merit which for our purposes could be superior to the merit of the estimates of one's own probable action in a hypothetical case. In any social situation, we have some kind of awareness of the group expectations as to an act affecting the group. We can verbalize those, and these responses when tabulated are *primary data* as to the agreement among group members concerning such expectations. On the other hand, a guess as to what one would do one's self in a particular hypothetical conflict situation has a more "iffy" quality which, though possibly quite highly correlated with actual behavior, need not necessarily be so correlated. The main stress in the present paper, it will be seen, is on the reported *role expectations*. The hypothetical personal action is introduced mainly to suggest how concepts like role expectations, when adequately measured, can be applied in the study of an individual's behavior in that role. Ideally, in place of the individual's hypothetical behavior we would like to substitute actual behavior, either in a natural or experimental situation, or reported past behavior. Studies may be devised in the future with such improvements, but in any case the basic sorting variables would be the reported role expectations as perceived by different group members.

Figure 1 is a picture of social norms, as perceived and reported by the respondents in this study. At the left, we see (*heavy line*) that almost all of the respondents thought the authorities would approve acts A and B, about a fifth thought the authorities would approve act C, and almost nobody thought the authorities would approve acts D and E.[4] Also at the left we see (dotted line) that the majority of the respondents felt that their friends in the student body would approve the most punitive acts, namely, A and B. But, in addition we see that three-fourths of the respondents thought act C would be approved and a bare majority said the same for act D. Only a few felt E would meet student approval. In other words, if a proctor took action consistent with the authorities' expectations he would not be in conflict with student expectations, although the range of expectations is wider for students than for the authorities.

The left diagram in Figure 1 portrayed the estimate of the situation where the offender was an ordinary student. By contrast, the right-hand diagram shows far less overlap in expectations imputed to authorities and students respectively. The offender in this case was one's roommate and friend. Feelings that the proctor in punishing an ordinary

---

[3] To simplify the subsequent presentation the inconsistencies are here treated as checking errors, although in some cases the respondent may actually have perceived an act as not fitting into an ordered sequence (for example, when he said A and C would be approved, but B would be disapproved, he may really have viewed B in a different way from other respondents). Fortunately, the inconsistencies were so few that it is possible to edit them without appreciable effect one way or another, except to simplify the ensuing presentation materially.

[4] To simplify the presentation, "approval" is here taken to mean that the respondent checked either of the following categories:
—Would expect one to do something like this
—Would not necessarily expect one to do this, but would not disapprove

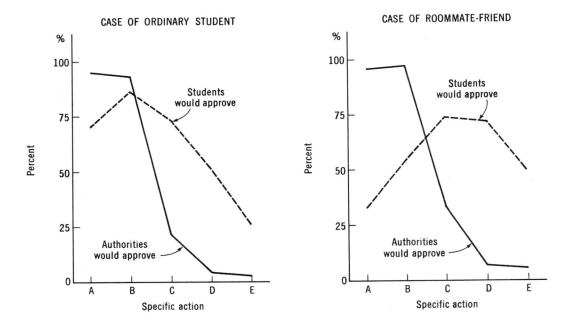

Figure 1. Percentage saying that a specific action as proctor would be approved by authorities and by fellow students, respectively

offender was behaving consistently with the long-range interest of the students are now overshadowed by the obligations involved in codes of personal friendship: "You can't rat on a friend; you can't let a friend down."

In the case of the friend, the respondents perceived the authorities' position to be about the same as in the case of the ordinary student, except that about a third now thought the authorities might let the proctor get away with C in view of the proctor's personal dilemma.   But only a third of the respondents thought the students would approve act A.   The modal acts are C and D. About half believed that the least punitive of all, E, would be approved by most of the students.

In Table 1 each act (separately for the case of the ordinary student and the friend, respectively) is broken down according to the percentage who think it would be approved by (a) the authorities only, (b) both the authorities and students, (c) students only, and (d) by neither the authorities nor students.

Let us now examine the relationship between these role expectations and the respondent's own hypothetical behavior as proctor.   It will be recalled that in both the case of the ordinary student and the roommate-friend, the respondent was asked what he personally would do under two hypothetical conditions: (1) if neither the authorities nor his student friends would hear about his part in the incident; and (2) if there could be very little chance that the authorities would hear about his part in the incident.

In Table 2 we have a percentage distribution of the acts which each student said he would be *most* likely to choose in the given situation.   In the case of the ordinary student, as Table 2 shows, the majority of respondents say they would be most likely to employ acts A or B, the most punitive. There is not a large difference between the hypothetical behavior in private or in public (public only in the restricted sense that the authorities would hear about it in any case, though students need not).   The main differ-

Table 1.   Percentage who attribute given role expectations on the part of authorities and/or students with respect to each specific act

| | Percentage Distribution for Each Specific Action | | | | | |
	A	B	C	D	E	All Actions
Case of Ordinary Student						
Think given action would be approved by:						
Authorities only	28	12	3	—	—	9
Both authorities and students	68	81	19	4	2	35
Students only	1	6	55	48	24	27
Neither authorities nor students	3	1	23	48	74	29
	100	100	100	100	100	100
Case of Roommate-Friend						
Think given action would be approved by:						
Authorities only	63	44	9	1	—	24
Both authorities and students	33	53	25	6	4	24
Students only	—	—	49	66	48	33
Neither authorities nor students	4	3	17	27	48	19
	100	100	100	100	100	100

N = 196

ence is a small increase, from a private 21 per cent to a public 30 per cent, in first choices for the most severe act A. However, the hypothetical behavior in the roommate-friend case shows a very different pattern. As can be seen in Table 2, nearly two-thirds of the respondents elect acts D or E as their first preferences in private action, and only 16 per cent say they would employ as first choice punitive acts A or B. But if the authorities were sure to find out about it, the picture changes. Less than a third would elect D or E as first choice and 40 per cent would prefer A or B. Yet this is still only about half as large as the proportion who would prefer A or B in comparable circumstances in the case of the ordinary student.

Table 2, while of a good deal of interest in itself, is subject to the caveats entered earlier in this paper against taking reports on such hypothetical behavior too literally. But the main purpose for introducing the material in Table 2 is to enable us to see how such hypothetical behavior is related to the reported perceptions of authorities' and students' expectations, respectively, of proper behavior from a proctor. The data in Table 2 are, therefore, next broken down according to the categories used in Table 1. Here we see in Table 3, as we doubtless would expect to see, that most students who chose acts A or B as their first preference if they themselves were proctors, also tended to perceive such acts as one which *both* the authorities and students would approve. But that tended to be true of several of the respondents who would take less punitive action—they had a different perception of expectations and thus thought they were avoiding conflict. In the case of the ordinary student, only 43 of the 196 respondents indicated a private action which was perceived to be acceptable to students only, and only 27 a public action. Contrast this with their hypothetical behavior when the offender was a roommate-friend. Of the 196 respondents, 118 preferred a private action tolerated by the students only. This number was reduced to 74, who would still stick by their friend even if they knew the authorities would find out about their action, or rather, inaction.

Figure 1, it will be recalled, indicated quite a marked range of tolerance in imputed student expectations, especially in the room-

312 NORMATIVE CONFLICT RELATIONSHIPS

Table 2. Percentage distribution of hypothetical actions which the respondents say they would be most likely to take as proctor

Action	In Case of Ordinary Student		In Case of Roommate-Friend	
	Private*	Public†	Private	Public
A	21	30	4	6
B	47	48	12	34
C	16	13	18	31
D	15	7	38	18
E	1	2	28	11
	100	100	100	100
		N = 196		

* "If you knew that, *except for your action* there could be very little chance that either the authorities or your student friends would hear about your part in the incident."

† "If you knew that, *except for your action* there could be very little chance that your student friends would hear about your part in the incident, but that there is a good chance, whatever you do, of the authorities finding out about it."

Table 3. Respondents whose own most likely hypothetical action as proctor is as indicated, broken down by expectations attributed to authorities and/or students

		Would Be Approved by			
		Authorities Only	Both Authorities and Students	Students Only	Neither
Case of Ordinary Student					
(Private Act)	A	6	35	—	—
	B	3	86	3	—
	C	—	13	17	1
	D	—	5	21	4
	E	—	—	2	—
		9	139	43	5
(Public Act)	A	9	50	—	—
	B	5	87	3	—
	C	—	13	13	—
	D	—	4	9	1
	E	—	—	2	—
		14	154	27	1
Case of Roommate-Friend					
(Private Act)	A	1	7	—	—
	B	2	20	—	1
	C	—	14	17	5
	D	—	4	62	9
	E	—	3	39	12
		3	48	118	27
(Public Act)	A	2	10	—	—
	B	14	50	—	2
	C	4	21	30	5
	D	—	4	29	3
	E	—	4	15	3
		20	89	74	13

Table 4. Frequency with which various ranges of acts are perceived as approved by authorities and students, respectively

Range		Case of Ordinary Student Acts Approved by		Case of Roommate-Friend Acts Approved by	
		Authorities	Students	Authorities	Students
1	A	13	4	4	3
	B	5	1	4	3
	C	—	—	—	2
	D	—	3	—	2
	E	—	—	—	4
		18	8	8	14
2	AB	134	37	120	12
	BC	3	10	2	10
	CD	—	7	—	14
	DE	—	5	—	26
		137	59	122	62
3	ABC	33	42	52	20
	BCD	—	14	—	18
	CDE	—	7	1	42
		33	63	53	80
4	ABCD	5	27	8	11
	BCDE	—	14	1	11
		5	41	9	22
5	ABCDE	3	25	4	18
	Total	196	196	196	196

mate-friend situation. But it is not possible to tell directly from Figure 1 the extent to which this is due to (a) different respondents visualizing different role expectations, or to (b) respondents generally agreeing that a wide range of role expectations existed. Let us now look at Table 4, where the frequency with which each range of expectations was indicated is shown. We see here quite clearly the degree of consensus among respondents as to what the authorities would approve. Among the 196 respondents, 134, or two-thirds, checked A, B identically for the case of the ordinary student; 120 checked A, B, for the case of the roommate-friend. The majority of the remainder checked A, B, C, in both cases.

Far different is the picture from Table 4 in the case of imputed student expectations. The majority settled for a range of either two or three acts in both of the situations, but within a given range there were all possi-

ble variations. For example, in the roommate-friend situation there were 80 who indicated a range of student approval covering 3 acts, but of these, 20 perceived the range as A, B, C; 18 perceived it as B, C, D; and 42 as C, D, E. Clearly there is an absence of consensus here, and it is not a mere uniform coverage of the whole range of possibilities by all individuals.

If we take, for illustration, the 120 respondents who perceived the range of acts approved by the authorities in the case of the roommate-friend as A, B, and order the ranges approved by students, according to these same respondents, we see in Table 5 the ways in which these different specific ranges are related to one's personal hypothetical behavior as proctor. Here we show for *each pattern* of role expectation the hypothetical private and public behavior respectively. For convenience, these hypothetical acts A, B, C, D, E have been ranked 1, 2, 3, 4,

Table 5. An illustration of hypothetical actions of respondent as proctor, as related to specific ranges of student approval in case of roommate-friend (These data are for 120 respondents who said the authorities would approve the range AB only)

Range of Student Approval	Private Behavior							Public Behavior						
	A	B	C	D	E	Total Frequency	Average Rank*	A	B	C	D	E	Total Frequency	Average Rank
A	1	—	—	—	—	1	1.0	1	—	—	—	—	1	1.0
AB	2	3	2	2	2	11	2.9	2	6	2	—	1	11	2.3
B	—	—	1	—	1	2	4.0	—	1	—	—	1	2	3.5
ABC	2	5	4	2	2	15	2.7	5	4	4	1	1	15	2.3
BC	—	—	3	2	—	5	3.4	—	3	2	—	—	5	2.4
ABCD	—	1	3	3	1	8	3.5	1	3	4	—	—	8	2.4
C	—	—	2	—	—	2	3.0	—	2	—	—	—	2	2.0
BCD	—	4	1	8	—	13	3.3	—	9	3	1	—	13	2.4
ABCDE	—	3	1	7	3	14	3.7	—	9	2	1	2	14	2.7
CD	1	—	1	4	2	8	3.8	1	—	4	3	—	8	3.1
BCDE	—	1	1	3	1	6	3.7	—	3	1	1	1	6	3.0
CDE	—	1	1	10	9	21	4.3	—	6	9	4	2	21	3.1
DE	—	—	—	6	7	13	4.5	—	2	2	4	5	13	4.0
E	—	—	—	—	1	1	5.0	—	—	—	—	1	1	5.0
Total						120							120	

* A, B, C, D, E ranked 1, 2, 3, 4, 5, respectively.

and 5, respectively, and average ranks computed.

As we move from role expectations A to E we see how the average ranks of the students' hypothetical behavior increase. It is interesting to note that, at least in the present example, this progressive increase seems to depend more on the midpoint of the range than on the termini. For example, if the expectation is BC the average rank of the hypothetical behavior is just about the same as when the expectation is A, B, C, D. In some cases the pattern with the longer range has higher average rank than its counterpart with the same midpoint but shorter range; in other cases the reverse is true. The number of cases available in the present data is, however, exceedingly small for this kind of comparison.

While the average rank of hypothetical acts did not tend to differ consistently when we compared two or more ranges with the same midpoint in Table 5, there is a hint that differences in the *range* of hypothetical acts vary with the *range* of role expectations

which have the same midpoint. It doubtless would be expected that if a respondent perceived the range of approved behavior to be B, C, D, he would be more likely to choose *either* B or D for his own act than if he perceived the range to be only C. Take the following from Table 5:

	A	B	C	D	E	
C	—	—	2	—	—	2
BCD	—	4	1	8	—	13
ABCDE	—	3	1	7	3	14

Most of the other examples in Tables 5 are less neat than this and the number of cases is distressingly few, but if we form other tables like Table 5 for other values of the range of expected approval by the authorities and take all possible matched comparisons thus available (for example, authorities ABC; students BC vs. ABCD) we obtain a rather convincing overall result, in the roommate-friend situation. (see Table 6)

The same tendency is also seen, though somewhat less strikingly, in the case of the ordinary student.

Table 6. Number of respondents whose own hypothetical action falls within minimum range of student expectations in case of roommate-friend

	Student Expectations Which Have Identical Midpoints But Different Ranges	
	Those With Minimum Range	Those With Greater Than Minimum Range
Private Act		
Own behavior more severe than any act within the *minimum* range of student expectation	2	12
Own behavior within *minimum* range	31	20
Own behavior less severe than any act within *minimum* range	8	34
	41	66
Public Act		
Own behavior more severe than any act within the *minimum* range of student expectation	5	29
Own behavior within *minimum* range	32	21
Own behavior less severe than any act within *minimum* range	4	16
	41	66

While interpretation of such a finding should be indulged in only with caution, the results are sufficient to suggest the importance of taking into account not only the midpoints of a given range of role expectations, but the magnitude of the range as well.

We have now completed the analysis of the present data except for one further observation which has implications for further research.

In such a study as this, it would be interesting first to differentiate individuals into types according to the way they perceive conflicting role expectations and then to ask how these different types of persons vary according to other social and psychological characteristics. Information of the latter type was not collected in the present study. However, the foregoing analysis has suggested how typologies could be set up and related to such outside variables. To take a simple illustration from the roommate-friend situation:

One could classify most of our respondents into three main types according as they perceived the role conflict.

Type I—Those who thought the range of approved acts identical from the point of view of authorities and students. (21 cases) For such respondents the problem of conformity in their own hypothetical acts could not have been difficult.

Type II—Those who thought the range of acts approved by the authorities did not overlap in any way with the range of acts approved by the students. (56 cases) For them simultaneous conformity to both was impossible. It is noteworthy, parenthetically, that 51 of the 56 said their own private act would be one conforming to student expectation, though 16 of these 51 shifted their act to a non-student position in the public situation.

Type III—Those who perceived a difference in the range of authorities' and students' expectations but who found at least one act which would be tolerated by both. (119 cases) Privately, only 36 of these individuals would take an action satisfactory to both. Publicly, however, 73 out of the 119 were able to find in an act perceived to be mutually acceptable the basis for their own hypothetical solution.

Why did these three types differ so markedly in their definition of the situation? Why, within these types did different subtypes prefer different solutions? These are the kinds of questions which subsequent research can explore. But first we must have a way of defining and classifying the role expectations relevant to our problem and the purpose of the present study is to illustrate a technique for accomplishing this first step.

From the theoretical standpoint, the most important implication of this paper may stem from its stress on variability. In essay writing in this field it is common and convenient to think of a social norm as a point, or at least as a very narrow band on either side of a point. This probably is quite unrealistic as to most of our social behavior. And it may be precisely the ranges of permissible behavior which most need examination, if we are to make progress in this realm which is so central in social science. For it may be the very existence of some flexibility or social slippage—but not too much—which makes behavior in groups possible.

Chapter 8

INTRODUCTION OF THE RULE OF LAW INTO CONFLICT RELATIONSHIPS

Normative relationships do not always deny the existence of conflicts between parties to these relationships. When they do recognize the existence of conflict, however, these relationships take the conflict out of the hands of the parties involved and submit it to regulation by a higher legitimate authority. The readings in this section explore the all important process whereby such a normatively recognized regulation of conflict is instituted.

In the first reading Lewin describes a piece of "action research" in which a team of social psychologists aided in the resolution of an ongoing conflict in an industrial plant. Special attention should be paid to how the psychologists not only help the parties to communicate but help them to work out a set of rules that will deal with their sources of discontent. Next Thibaut and Faucheux report the results of a laboratory experiment which explored the conditions under which subjects would adopt a set of contractual norms to transform their bargaining relationship into a normative one. In the third paper Redfield discusses how special legal systems function to regulate conflict in primitive societies even in the absence of formal courts, state agents, or written codes. Finally, Larson describes the prospects for the growth of law in the most primitive system of modern times, the "state of nature" known as the international system.

THE SOLUTION OF A CHRONIC CONFLICT IN INDUSTRY

K. Lewin

The purpose of a case study is to describe and analyze an individual incident. Seldom can this analysis be used as proof of a theory. However, it may illustrate the interdependence of some underlying factors and help us to see certain general problems.

The following case study of conflict in a factory is presented as an illustration of certain aspects of group dynamics and theoretical interpretation. The case involves a long-smoldering conflict that has periodically flared out but has always been patched up.

The incident did not take longer than one afternoon—1:30 to 5:00 P.M. The psychologist who handled the matter considers it a routine case and only reluctantly agreed to write an account of it. The author (although feeling that a neat job has been done) does not doubt that similar solutions are brought about by good management in many factories.

The story is part of a larger research project undertaken by Alex Bavelas and will be presented as he has written it, namely, as a sequence of acts, each containing a number of scenes.

The Characters: Paulson, the mechanic; Sulinda, the supervisor; Alanby, the boss; Bavelas, the psychologist and narrator; machine operators (girls).
The Setting: A sewing factory employing about 170 operators, five floor-girls, one supervisor and one mechanic.

Source: K. Lewin, "The Solution of a Chronic Conflict in Industry," *Proceedings of the Second Brief Psychotherapy Council* (Chicago: Institute for Psychoanalysis, 1944), pp. 36–46. Reprinted in K. Lewin, *Resolving Social Conflicts: Selected Papers on Group Dynamics* (New York: Harper, 1948). Copyright 1944 by The Institute for Psychoanalysis and used by permission.

Act I   Scene 1

One afternoon as I was returning to my office, I happened to look into the boss's office as I walked by and saw Paulson and Sulinda standing in front of his desk. All three were obviously painfully ill at ease and I surmised something was wrong.

I was not surprised, therefore, to be summoned by the boss almost immediately. "You're just the man we've been waiting for" were his first words; the other two merely looked more uncomfortable. I made some trifling joking remark and lit a cigarette to gain a little time. I offered cigarettes; only the boss accepted one. I sat on a corner of his desk but this did not noticeably break the rigid atmosphere. "Well, what's going on?" I directed the remark to the boss because although I needed information I saw by now that Paulson and Sulinda had quarreled and I did not want to risk asking either of them.

Act I   Scene 2

The boss explained that Paulson and Sulinda were having some trouble because they did not agree on which machines should be repaired first and that one of the operators was playing them against each other by gossiping with each about the other. At this Sulinda's eyes watered and I was surprised to see Paulson too on the verge of tears. I remarked that such behavior by an operator was quite common and mentioned its occurrence in another factory where I had worked. I pointed out that what was said by whom was not so important as the amount of hurt it could cause people if they took it seriously, and that things got so twisted about after a few repetitions from one person to the other it was hopeless to find out exactly what had been meant by the original remark. I then looked at my watch and remarked that I had made a short appointment with an operator whom I had to meet immediately, but that it would take only a few minutes and I wanted to talk over this thing in detail with each of them and with the girl. I tried to give the impression that I felt the gossiping operator to be the root of the trouble.

ACT I   SCENE 3

Turning to Sulinda I asked her if she would be too busy to see me right after that appointment; if she was, could I see her later that afternoon. I added that I knew she was probably needed upstairs right away. She answered that she could see me any time and we agreed that I would see her right after my interview with the operator. Then turning to Paulson I asked him if I could talk with him in his machine shop. He said it would be O.K.

ACT I   SCENE 4

I walked upstairs to the shop with Sulinda. She started by saying that what got her mad was Paulson telling lies about her and the girl's trying to make a liar of her right to her face. I responded by saying I could understand just how such an incident must make her feel, having been involved once in a similar situation. I could also see how the whole thing might be a misunderstanding. Without allowing further conversation along that line I went on to my "appointment."

ACT I   SCENE 5

In the next few minutes I interviewed the boss who had no more information to offer but who told me that I came in just as Sulinda was getting ready to "walk out" and that Paulson also was saying that he was quitting. The boss hoped that I could smooth things over, saying that although this kind of thing happened every now and then, this time it was worse. In his opinion the trouble was caused because Paulson was too independent and Sulinda lost her temper too easily—the whole thing growing out of a mutual dislike that had always existed.

[The reader may have noticed that the psychologist has quickly succeeded in getting the supervisor and the mechanic out of their overcoats, the one back to his machine shop, the other to her floor.]

ACT II

In the interview with Sulinda, she described the situation as follows: Paulson was not a very good mechanic to start with. Often he didn't know what was wrong with a machine and would tinker around for ages and when he got through it would still not be right. He would blame the operator for mishandling the machine or say that the thread was no good or make other excuses.

According to Sulinda, a girl had come to her that afternoon and said that Paulson refused to fix her machine. She went to Paulson and told him he would have to do it and that the girl had told her he refused to fix it. At this he got very angry and said he had said no such thing. He went to the girl and asked her why she had told Sulinda that he had said he would not fix her machine when he had merely said that he would do it later. The operator answered that she had not told Sulinda that at all and Sulinda was lying. Thereupon, Paulson and the operator went to Sulinda and confronted her with what amounted to proof that she had lied to Paulson. Sulinda at once got her coat and went down to tell the boss she was quitting. The boss heard her story and summoned Paulson.

[The girls who work under Sulinda depend mainly on her but also depend on Paulson for machine repair. It is the problem of Paulson's and Sulinda's authority which has made the lie such an important issue. For Sulinda, acknowledging the lie would mean losing face and might seriously weaken her position with the girls. In addition, Sulinda was particularly hurt because what the girl considered to be a "lie" was an action which Sulinda obviously had done for the sake of this very girl; she wanted the girl not to lose time and money by waiting for the repair. For Paulson the issue involved a threat to his honor, to his position of authority with the girls and to his status of equality with Sulinda.]

ACT III   SCENE 1

I began asking Sulinda factual questions about the frequency of breakdowns and whether they were more frequent in certain types of machines, etc.   After some discussion it became clear that Paulson was kept very busy trying to keep all 170 machines in continuous operation and Sulinda agreed that if he had plenty of time instead of being rushed many sources of irritation would be removed.   I asked whether she thought it would help if those girls were interviewed and their attitude on the problem determined. She was sure that I should talk with them because the girls she had mentioned were always complaining and were causing other girls to take the same attitude.   I told Sulinda that I would do so and asked if she would like to know what the girls said.   She said she would.   I ended the interview by remarking that I thought she was quite correct in attributing a large measure of the irritation between mechanic and girls to the overcrowded time schedule of the mechanic and commended her for so objective an attitude.

ACT III   SCENE 2

Next, I interviewed Paulson.   Paulson started by explaining how hard he had to work and that he had only one pair of hands and could work only on one machine at a time. After easing the situation with a joke or two, I found it easy to arrive with Paulson at the point of attributing the irritation largely to the impatience of the girls and the scarcity of mechanic-time.   He, too, thought that I should talk to the girls and that it would help to know just what they thought.   He was especially interested to know what they thought of him as an individual.

[The interview with the mechanic follows a somewhat similar pattern to the interview with the supervisor.   Like Sulinda, Paulson's perception of the situation had been dominated by the aspect "right or wrong"; he had regarded Sulinda as being in the wrong, himself in the right.   Again the interviewer

is able to lead Paulson to a perception of the objective situation.   The insufficiency of mechanic-time is stressed but this time the natural irritation of the girls is somewhat more emphasized.

This attempt to change perception by an "action interview" (as distinguished from a mere "fact-finding interview") is one of the basic elements of treatment.   By reorienting Sulinda's and Paulson's perception from the field of personal emotional relationship to the same field of "objective" facts, the life-spaces which guide the action of these persons have become more similar although the persons themselves are not yet aware of this similarity.

A few additional points may be mentioned:

(a)   The interviewer does not restructure Paulson's and Sulinda's views by "giving" them the facts although such "induction" of the same cognitive structure would probably have been possible.   Instead, Paulson and Sulinda are themselves encouraged to look at the objective situation and, therefore, "accept" it to a higher degree as "facts." This procedure does not work out fully with Sulinda.

(b)   Being sensitive to power relations, Bavelas is careful to get the consent of Sulinda before approaching the girls under her authority.   Sulinda is glad to give it because the trouble-makers have been a threat to her.   In this way, definite progress is made in several aspects. Bavelas can approach the girls with the full backing of the supervisor's authority.   By asking Sulinda whether she would like him to report back to her he prepares the next action.   The action takes on the character of a co-operative endeavor and establishes a good tie between Bavelas and Sulinda.   Sulinda becomes, thus, actively involved in the planning of the actions and should, therefore, be more ready to identify herself later on with a proposed solution.

(c)   The same procedure is followed with Paulson with slight variations.   Bavelas is careful to give attention to Paulson's special motives. For instance, Bavelas accepts immediately Paulson's wish to learn whether the girls like him. By co-operating closely with the mechanic and the supervisor both become parties of the same plan although, in this stage, only factually and not as the result of a co-operative decision.]

ACT III   SCENE 3

I then called each of the girls in for a short interview. I asked them if they felt that there was insufficient coverage on machine repair. They all agreed that Paulson was O.K. but that he was too busy to do a proper job. I asked each girl if it would be a good idea to get all the girls who were having the most trouble together and see if something couldn't be worked out to reduce the amount of time they had to lose waiting for repairs. They were all eager for some action of this type.

ACT IV   SCENE 1

The girls were called in as a group and I presented the problem. All of them agreed, as did Sulinda and Paulson, that at certain times when more than one machine broke down there was a shortage of mechanic services. Since it was unlikely that another mechanic would be hired in view of the difficulty of deferring even Paulson from military service, the question was how the services of the one mechanic that we had could most efficiently be used. I proceeded to stimulate group discussion as to the fairest action in each of the following situations: when one machine broke down: when two machines broke down at the same time but neither was more critical than the other in terms of throwing more girls out of work; when more than one machine broke down and one was more important in this respect.

The group discussion resulted in the following plan: (1) When machines had no differential in importance, the rule would be "first come, first served." (2) When there was a difference in machine importance, the most critical machine would be serviced first. (3) That this plan would be presented to

Paulson and Sulinda and I would report to the group what they said.

[The accomplishments thus far may be summarized as follows:

1. The mechanic and the supervisor who were ready to leave are back in the plant.
2. The perception of all three fighting parties—the mechanic, the supervisor and the most critical, active group, the operators—who had been preoccupied with the issue of the "lie" and prestige has been turned toward the objective difficulties of production.
3. Without any direct contact between the three parties, it has been established that their views of the production difficulties agree to a reasonable extent.
4. All individuals involved have freely and without pressure expressed their agreement to some future steps.
5. All three parties are in good and friendly rapport with the psychologist.

The procedure of the psychologist is based on the hypothesis that the permanent conflict is at least partly the result of some faulty organization of production. Therefore, before a remedy can be found the production procedure has to be analyzed realistically and sufficiently deeply to lay open the source of the difficulty.

The group lowest in the factory hierarchy is made the foundation for the fact-finding, probably because these operators are most immediately affected and should be most realistically aware of at least some aspects of the problem. Then too, since the operators have a lower position in the factory hierarchy any rule suggested by the authorities, or even a view presented by them as a "fact," is likely to be felt by the operators as something of an imposition. To gain their wholehearted co-operation later on it seems best to start the detailed fact-finding here, and it is also necessary to have the first suggestions for the new rules of production worked out by this group.

Not all the operators but only those who did the most complaining were consulted. This seems strange if one considers that those operators who have less inclination for "trouble-making" are likely to give a more objective picture of the situation. The trouble-makers were made the cornerstone of the investigation since they are particularly important for the group dynamics in the factory. Furthermore, if those operators who usually did not make trouble were to initiate a solution, the trouble-makers would probably resist, feeling that they had been first left out and later pushed into something.

The psychologist as leader of the group discussion presents the problem as an objective question of production procedure. The fact that he has no difficulty in holding the group's attention on this aspect of the situation indicates that the preliminary interviews have set the stage for this perception.

The group discussion discloses that the difficulties are part of the problem of production under war conditions. That these facts emerge through group rather than individual discussion has a number of important advantages. As a rule, group discussion brings out a richer, better balanced, and more detailed picture of the situation. The atmosphere of openness which is possible in group discussion as opposed to the secrecy so characteristic of individual information giving is very important for the readiness to co-operate.

The rules emerging from the discussion were supposed to solve an objective production problem. Impersonal facts rather than power conflicts determine the action in certain situations. These rules are identical with what is required for maximum production output by the factory. The psychologist could have asked the girls what sequence of repair was best for production. The girls would probably have set up the same rules but they would have felt that they were doing something "for the Boss," their motivation being "generosity" or patriotism. The psychologist did not follow this line but asked for a solution on the basis of fairness. This is a matter of relationships between the girls and, since it also involved the question of losing money, it was very close to their self-interest. To have "fairness" the guiding principle for the rules of social conduct in a group is doubtless one of the strongest motives in the American culture.

Since the rules are developed by the girls themselves, their acceptance is implied and strongly entrenched.

Two problems remain: first, acceptance of the rules by the rest of the operators and by the authorities, Sulinda and Paulson; and second, determination of the persons who will be in charge of the execution of the rules.]

Act IV Scene 2

I reported back to Paulson, laying heavy emphasis on the fact that the girls had nothing against him personally; on the contrary they felt that he had more of a job than one mechanic could do. I showed him the girls' plan and his comment was that was exactly what he wanted if only "everybody" would stop trying to order him around. I told him that there was no reason why he should be bothered with making the decisions about which machine was more important at any given time. He was a mechanic and he should be left free of that responsibility. In this he agreed very strongly. I suggested that Sulinda was the one who should take the responsibility of deciding what would have to come first, and the girls could battle it out with her if they didn't like her decisions. In this he also agreed but doubted that Sulinda would like it. I told him that I would see her and that I thought she would be glad to do it if he wouldn't misinterpret her actions as giving orders.

[The psychologist approaches the mechanic first. Paulson's fears are relieved when the psychologist emphasizes at the beginning of the interview that the girls have nothing against him. It makes Paulson feel good and more ready to view the situation objectively. In this atmosphere he finds it easy to agree.

The rest of the interview is dominated by the psychologist's endeavor to solve vital aspects for permanent solution of the conflict. Such a permanent solution requires that a correct set-up be established from the point of view of production, and that the authorities have definite objectives in mind and do not conflict. In our case, the conflict was based on the overlapping authority in the field of repair. Now rules are found and responsibilities assigned.

The psychologist feels that the only sensible and stable procedure would be to have the supervisor in charge of determining the order in which the machines should be repaired since it is her (and not the mechanic's) responsibility to keep up maximum production.

The method by which Bavelas presents the problem to the mechanic follows the same principle which was used in the preceding scene with the operators: The reality is presented correctly, but those aspects are brought into the fore which are linked with the psychological situation of the person in question and are helpful in bringing about favorable permanent motivation. Rather than speak of dividing authority, the psychologist points to the possibility of getting rid of the burden of making decisions and taking responsibility which is actually not the mechanic's job.

That this was a correct and realistic approach is clear if we consider somewhat more closely the situation which the mechanic faced whenever more than one machine needed repair. To Paulson, the shop is an agreeable place, a kind of sanctuary where he is his own boss as long as he has something to do. He has tried to stay in that area as much as possible. When he has to enter the floor for repair work he is on "foreign soil" which is under the authority of the supervisor. If three machines are out of order, the mechanic is in a conflict situation resulting from the forces corresponding to his own wish to repair all three machines. Each of these forces points in a different direction. Parallel forces, induced by the various operators, exist in these different directions, the strength of each force depending somewhat on the clamoring of the operator. In addition, there is the force induced by the supervisor who may either leave the mechanic to guess what she wants or may express a definite preference.

This situation is typical of a decision situation providing the possibility of high emotional tension for two reasons: (a) the restraining forces against the decision must be considerable because any wrong decision is likely to bring about trouble with the operator and supervisor; and (b) cognitively the field is unstructured when the mechanic does not know whether repairing one or the other machine first will lead him into the most trouble.

These factors together made the decision situation most disagreeable to Paulson, so much so that not only did the particular moment of decision have a negative valence but also the fact of being on the floor. Consequently the mechanic is very eager to accept any measure which offers hope of leading him out of this painful situation.

It may be pointed out that the presentation of the problem to Paulson by the psychologist is not designed to "trick" the mechanic into an agreement (and place him under the authority of the supervisor). The presentation by the psychologist is in line with the facts. The new plan sets up definite general rules on an objective basis in regard to what ought to be done. Someone will have to do the fact-finding in each individual situation. Someone has to decide in case of doubt which sequence of repair would waste a minimum of operator hours. But this is all that has to be decided by the supervisor. She is not free to tell the mechanic arbitrarily what he shall do. In fact, she is not supposed to give him orders. All that she can do is pass certain information about the relative importance of machines on to him. On the basis of this information, he will follow the rules readily agreed upon by everyone. The psychologist stresses this point in his final remark to avoid misconception which would hurt the mechanic's pride.

On the whole Scene 2 is short and proceeds smoothly toward a full acceptance of the new plan by the mechanic. His doubt that Sulinda would agree is evidence that the tension between them has not fully disappeared. It indicates, in addition, that the mechanic does not feel that he himself will get the worst of the bargain.]

ACT IV SCENE 3

I showed the girls' plan to Sulinda and she thought that it was exactly what should be done, adding that she had been trying to do it but no one could tell Paulson anything. I told her that Paulson would be ready to accept her decision on priority of repairs to be done. I also indicated that the girls seemed ready to co-operate on such a plan. She was ready to try it, however, although she was skeptical.

The discussion with Sulinda shows a pattern similar to that with Paulson. She accepts the plan readily as something she has always wished for. She can hardly believe that Paulson would be ready to accept her "decision on prerogatives," thereby indicating that she does not feel she is giving up power. On the other hand, it is made clear by the psychologist that her judgment will be limited to decision of the sequence of repairs.

ACT IV   SCENES 4-6

Scene 4. I told Paulson that Sulinda liked the plan and was ready to try it.

Scene 5. Then I called the girls back for a short meeting in which we reviewed the plan and went over the procedure carefully.

Scene 6. After that I reported to Sulinda and Paulson that the arrangements had been concluded and would go into effect and that any ideas would be welcome.

[The last scenes are very short. Each of the parties—the mechanic, the supervisor, and the operators—is informed that all the other parties agree to the arrangement and that the new procedure will go into effect immediately. The psychologist is careful to stress his readiness to welcome new ideas. This is a kind of safety valve for later changes which may seem desirable.]

EPILOGUE

A few weeks later the boss asked me if I had noticed a change in Paulson. I said I had not. He went on to explain that Paulson seemed to have much less work to do and plenty of time to tinker around. His relations with Sulinda were better than they had ever been and there had been no more conflict with the girls. A week or so later, Paulson at his own expense and using his own equipment installed a system of loudspeakers in the factory and played recorded music two periods a day. The whole shop enjoyed this and relations became even more pleasant.

Three months after this incident—during which time no new difficulties arose—a third party had an interview with the mechanic.

This report reads:

Paulson estimates that repairs are a third less now than before; where he now gets an average of 10 calls a day, he previously got 15 or 20. He believes the chief decrease has come in the number of trivial calls; the number of genuine repairs is about the same. He blames the former excessive number of trivial calls on "agitation"—"the girls just wanted to make trouble." Paulson also remarked that there had been a decrease in agitation against Sulinda.

When asked "how come?" Paulson said —"I think the music had a lot to do with it," referring to the loudspeaker system he had installed. This made the girls more friendly. Bavelas' being there had also helped. He talked to some of the girls, showed Sulinda's side of the picture and explained what things were to be expected and accepted.

One change helped to decrease the general agitation. Somehow there was an impression that Sulinda and Paulson were enemies when actually, off the job, they were the best of friends. In the factory, "Well, we bickered back and forth but everybody does it and we thought nothing of it. But they got the impression we hated each other." In consequence, some of the girls attempted to stir up trouble. When it was understood that there was no enmity between Paulson and Sulinda, the girls realized they were no longer vulnerable and a lot of the agitation ceased.

On the whole, then, it seems that the brief treatment has actually solved a chronic conflict. It has established good relations in a previously fighting triangle, the mechanic, the supervisor, and the operators. Finally, it has led to an unexpected diminishing of repairs in the factory.

It seems that the basic principles which guided the action of the psychologist might be summed up as follows: *The realistic demands of production have to be satisfied in a way which conforms with the nature of group dynamics.*

To bring about a permanent solution it does not suffice to create amicable relations. The conflict described arose out of an aspect of production where overlapping authorities existed in a cognitively unclear situation. The procedure is guided to an equal degree by the consideration of production and the problem of social relations.

As to details, one might mention the following points. The factory work can be seen as a process in which the speed is determined by certain driving and restraining forces. The production process runs through certain "channels" as determined by the physical and social setting, particularly by certain "rules" and by the authorities in power (management). To increase production one can try to increase the driving forces by higher incentives or pressure, or try to weaken those forces that keep production down. The procedure described here follows the latter possibility. It tries to eliminate certain conflicts within the group and certain psychological forces acting on a key individual (the mechanic) which deter his efforts.

The attempt for a lasting improvement is based on a study of the present situation in regard to a certain portion (machine repair) of the production channel. By setting up new rules and regulations, the production channels are modified objectively.

Even the best plan of reorganizing production channels is worthless if it does not fit the human beings who have to live and react in that setting. The procedure described is therefore heavily influenced by consideration of group dynamics. Indeed, every step is influenced by this aspect.

It is important that even the first step of fact-finding, which easily might be viewed as a scientific task for an expert rather than a social act itself, is imbedded in a social procedure. It is one of the outstanding characteristics of this case (and seems to be typical of the methods used by this psychologist) that the fact-finding itself is made the cornerstone for the change.

The choice of the operators as a main fact-finding body may have been influenced by the fact that they are nearest to the production problem. If one intends to create a general friendly atmosphere of co-operation rather than a straight authoritarian system, if one wants to gain full co-operation, the lowest group should do the planning for the first step, since they would regard any other action as an attempt to make them agree to a procedure set up by the authorities. On the other hand, the person in position of authority, like the mechanic or the supervisor, will not have the same reaction when asked to agree to a plan first developed by the operators because being in the position of authority they can reject it.

That the fact-finding is based on only part of the operators might be merely the outcome of the factors discussed before. Perhaps it would have been better to include the other operators. At least, for adequacy of fact-finding and co-operation of the machine operators it sufficed to have the most troublesome part of that group involved. Even the definition of a "fact" for this type of treatment has the two aspects of production and of group dynamics. It is correct that a "sufficiently objective" picture of the production channels and problems should arise from the investigation. But it is equally essential to realize that the "subjective" view of the participants counts most.

In addition to establishing the facts, fact-finding has two more important functions in this treatment. Fact-finding is one of the best means of changing the dimensions along which the *perception* of the individual proceeds. It is probably correct to state that *the action of an individual depends directly on the way in which he perceives the situation.* One can propose the theory that whether a change of ideas or values does or does not affect the action of an individual depends upon whether or not his perception is changed. The correctness of this theory seems to be suggested by the experience in rather divergent fields, including those of stuttering and psychopathology. One of the main characteristics of this method is to change action by changing perception.

Fact-finding in this method is consciously used as a first step of action. The psychologist's or expert's knowing the facts does not have any influence unless these data are "accepted as facts" by the group members. Here lies a particular advantage of making the fact-finding a group endeavor. Coming together to discuss the facts and set up a plan is already an endeavor in co-operative action. It goes a long way to establish the atmosphere of co-operation, openness, and confidence toward which this procedure strives. Although the mechanic and the supervisor do not participate directly in the group discussion of the operators, we have seen that the psychologist was very careful to involve them actively in the total scheme of fact-finding and planning.

It has been emphasized already that group meetings are not considered a panacea. They are carefully prepared by steps which take into consideration the psychological situation of the individual, although the individual is considered at every step in his position in the total group. These individual considerations are along two lines. First, the motivation for a change in perception and action is based, as much as possible, on realistic judgment of the person's own situation. Second, much is done to lower the general level of emotionality during each step in the procedure. Wherever possible the individual is praised; his feeling of insecurity or anxiety is eased (Paulson and the girls); everything is done to have the persons appear in a good light to each other without becoming unrealistic. As a rule this lowering of emotionality is attempted by indirect means. One example is the way in which the polarization of the conflict with one operator (lie issue) is depersonalized by bringing up the problems of the group of trouble-makers. It is clear that in this way the issue becomes less personal and at the same time is bent to an objective group question by having this one girl disappear into the group.

It might be worthwhile to note that the original issue—namely, the lie and the resulting threat of quitting by the mechanic and the supervisor—seems to have evaporated into thin air without ever having been treated directly. It seems that with a change in perception of the situation from that of a power problem to that of factory production, the lie issue, in the beginning a hard fact blocking smooth-running factory life, has lost the character of a "fact." This itself can be taken as a symptom of how deep and real the change of the perception and the psychological situation of all parties concerned has been.

THE DEVELOPMENT OF CONTRACTUAL NORMS IN A
BARGAINING SITUATION UNDER TWO TYPES OF STRESS

John Thibaut and Claude Faucheux

The point of view that biological and social systems respond to stress with various adaptive mechanisms, the effects of which often protect the systems from collapse or disruption, has been stated and illustrated by Bertalanffy (1951), Selye (1950), and, with particular reference to psychological systems, by James Miller (1955). Although this conception seems to be an important one for the understanding of group phenomena, its usefulness in predicting social behavior is very limited, and its validity must remain unsupported unless a more detailed theoretical and experimental analysis is made of the processes by which groups respond to various types of stress.

It will be suggested in the following paragraphs that when power differentiation exists in a group whose members have a background of high interdependence and highly convergent interests, the introduction of both external and internal threats to the continued viability of the group creates the conditions for the emergence of norms which to a significant degree reduce the disruptive consequences of the threats.

To present the analysis as simply as possible, let us suppose the existence of a dyad in which the members' interests are highly interdependent and harmonious and in which one member is able potentially to exert more influence on the other than he receives. This situation is strongly favorable to the maintenance of membership. The high degree of interdependence of outcomes means that each member is heavily dependent on the other for positive outcomes and that alternative relationships outside the dyad are relatively unattractive. Motivations to disrupt the dyad by forming mutually exclusive relationships with external alternatives are likely to be minimal. Hence there is little or no need for policing the loyalty of the members or for developing norms that forbid disloyalty.

Furthermore, in this simplified situation the highly convergent interests of the members means that there is no real problem in the sharing of the outcomes produced by the group's efforts. Thibaut and Kelley (1959, Chapter II) show that when members' outcomes are perfectly correspondent (i.e., where there is a positive correlation of unity between member outcomes over the cells of the matrix describing their joint behaviors), the member holding the higher potential power is unable to use that power to advantage himself at the expense of the other. He cannot help himself without also helping the other, nor hurt the other without hurting himself. Hence, in this situation there is no need for the development of norms governing the sharing of outcomes or protecting the weak from exploitation.

The description of such harmony and mutual dependence suggests two types of stress that might threaten the maintenance of such a dyad:[1]

(1) *Conflict of interest.* This "internal" stress will develop when any factors so reduce

---

Source: J. Thibaut and C. Faucheux, "The Development of Contractual Norms in a Bargaining Situation under Two Types of Stress," *Journal of Experimental Social Psychology*, Vol. 1, 1965, pp. 89–102. Copyright 1965 by the Academic Press, Inc. and used by permission.

---

[1] Of course, it is possible for either of these stresses to be sufficiently high so that in fact the group does disrupt. It is assumed in the following that the level of stress, though high, is not overwhelmingly so.

the correspondence of member outcomes that they become negatively correlated. As conflict of interest increases so does the degree of "usable" power of the member whose power is greater. The likelihood that this power will be used against his interests constitutes a real threat to the low-power member. In order to protect himself against serious reductions in his share of the outcomes, he will be expected to appeal to norms of "equity" and "fair sharing."

(2) *Improved alternatives outside the group.* This "external" stress will appear whenever outcomes available outside the dyad become attractive enough to compete with those available inside. This stress threatens the interdependence of the group members. Good external alternatives may, of course, be attractive to both group members. However, if there exists in the dyad a degree of conflict of interest, this will create enough potential advantage to the high-power member so that in evaluating his probable share of the outcomes he is likely to remain loyal to the group. It is the low-power member, then, who will respond to the increasingly attractive external alternative. The potential disloyalty of the low-power member thus constitutes a real threat to the high-power member. In order to preserve the integrity of the group within which he holds the advantage, he will be expected to appeal to norms of "loyalty" and "group spirit."

To make appeals for the invocation of norms is not, of course, a sufficient condition for their realization. The high-power member cannot realistically expect that the low-power one will respond favorably to a contractual restraint on his "disloyalty" unless the eschewing of the temptation to "disloyalty" can be compensated for in some fashion. Nor can the low-power member entertain realistic hopes of a normative approach to "fair sharing" unless he can in some way compensate the high-power member for inhibiting his use of power. How can this compensation be achieved? There is one striking solution which suggests itself.

When *both* external and internal stresses are high, each member is threatened by be-

haviors which the other is tempted to perform, and each member's appeal is to a rule of behavior, a norm, which will forbid such threatening behaviors. Thus a type of "interdependence" appears in which each member's acceptance of the other's appeal is compensated for by a reduction in threat. The low-power member's agreement to inhibit his "disloyalty" is compensated for by the high-power member's willingness to impose restraint on the use of his power. This argument can be put in another way. Only when both types of stress are high are both members motivated to invoke a norm; furthermore, it is only under these conditions that the low-power member is provided with sufficient "counter power," through the presence of an attractive external alternative, to bargain effectively with the high-power member. If this reasoning is correct, two mutually dependent threats may generate norms of behavior which embody the adaptive mechanisms that support the continued integrity of the group.

DESIGN OF THE EXPERIMENT

To explore the foregoing theoretical formulation, an experiment was designed in which two Ss were confronted with a bargaining task. The situation in which the Ss were placed was one which permitted the manipulation of the attractiveness of the external alternative and the degree of conflict of interest. At a standard point of time in the course of the experiment, an opportunity was introduced for the Ss to regulate their bargaining normatively by forming contracts. The frequency and characteristics of the contracts constituted the main dependent variables.

PRELIMINARY PROCEDURE

At the beginning of each experimental session, one member of each dyad was randomly assigned to the high-power position (designated *P*) and the other to the low-power position (designated X). The Ss remained in the same power position throughout the experiment. The Ss in each dyad were seated at a table facing one another, with a cardboard screen rising to eye level placed between them. The Ss in each dyad were instructed not to compete with one another in the bargaining game that was to be played, but rather to compete with the other Ss who were in the same power position, i.e., all P's were in competition, and all X's were in competition. In order to facilitate the instruction of the Ss, to provide practice at the bargaining task, and to create the necessary background of uniformly high interdependence and harmony, all dyads were initially confronted with the same simple task. The task consisted of bargaining for points to be won by playing the game summarized in a matrix (Fig. 1) presented to each S. The procedure for playing the game was as follows. By open discussion, the two Ss arrived at a tentative agreement about their joint behavior. When this tentative agreement was reached, P recorded it on a printed form provided for this purpose. Each S then recorded privately his actual decision about what he would play. In this decision he was not obliged to honor the tentative agreement reached earlier; duplicity was thus possible. When the actual decisions were reached, they were announced publicly and recorded by P. The play was repeated with the same matrix for three trials.

In playing the game, each S had three options among which to decide. He could play either of the two columns (or rows) of the matrix or he could play the external alternative. If both Ss played the external alternative, each received one point. However, if one S played the external alternative, while the other played a column (or row) of the matrix, the first received one point while the latter received zero. The alternative was thus a dependable (though in this instance, a paltry) outcome that each S could attain quite independently of the other's behavior, and it also provided a method for threatening one's partner.

The outcomes to be received from playing the columns and rows of the matrix re-

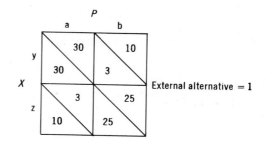

Figure 1.   Matrix summarizing the game played during the preliminary phase of the experiment

flect the interdependence of the Ss. For both players to receive the maximum outcomes (30 points) available in the present matrix, P must play a while X plays y. If P played b while X played z, each would receive 25 points.

However, in the remaining two cells of the matrix, by and az, the outcomes accruing to each player depended on the degree to which P exercised his power. It will be recalled from the discussion in the preceding section that "usable" power depends directly on the degree of conflict of interest (noncorrespondence of outcomes) present in the interdependent situation of the group members. Hence, power can be used only when the outcomes to the members from a given joint action are different. This leads to the experimental definition and manipulation of power in this experiment; P was instructed that in any such cells in which the outcomes to the Ss differed, he was empowered to take for himself any number of points from the smaller of the two values up to the larger, leaving the remaining points to X. Thus, if either by or az were played, P was empowered to take any number of points from 3 to 10. If, for example, P took 8 points, X would receive 5. These rules governing the bargaining procedure, the consequences of playing the external alternative, and the use and meaning of power remained invariant throughout the experiment.

Note in this preliminary matrix that the harmonious solution (ay, leading to 30 points apiece) is the obviously dominant solution, that the conflictual solutions (in which power can be exercised) are relatively unattractive, and that the external alternative (1 point) is extremely low and hence mutual dependence on intradyadic cooperation is strongly reinforced.

EXPERIMENTAL TREATMENTS

After the three trials of the preliminary phase, the experiment proper began and the experimental manipulations were introduced. The treatments consisted of varying both the level of the external alternative and the degree of conflict of interest in the dyadic situation. The essential characteristics of each of the four experimental conditions can be most succinctly described by the matrix governing the play in each of the conditions. Figure 2 shows the matrices representing high and low conflict of interest and the accompanying external alternatives. Pairing the values of the two variables results in the four conditions: high conflict-high alternative (HH), high conflict-low alternative (HL), low conflict-high alternative (LH), and low conflict-low alternative (LL). It should be observed that, in general, the points to be bargained for are higher in the experimental treatments than in the matrix of the preliminary phase, and that the cells containing the largest total number of points are no longer the harmonious solutions. Note too that the single difference between the matrices for high and low conflict consists in the size of discrepancy between the points contained in the cells of the main diagonal: in all other respects, including the total number of points available, the two matrices are identical. The level of the external alternative when high (35) begins to compete effectively with the matrix values; when low (10) this is not so.

It is perhaps apparent that the HH condition is designed to create high stress from both external and internal sources, the HL and LH conditions to produce mixed degrees of stress, and the LL condition little stress of either sort.

The dyads in each treatment used the same assigned matrix and alternative for the remainder of the experiment. The standard sequence which governed the remaining

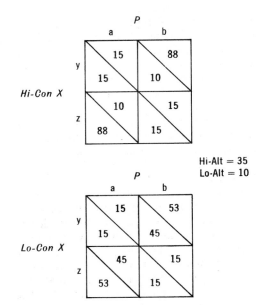

Figure 2. Matrices representing high and low conflict of interest and high and low levels of the external alternative

phases of the experiment was as follows: (1) three trials played with the new matrix and alternative followed by a brief questionnaire; (2) three additional trials with the same matrix and alternative; and finally (3) an opportunity to form contractual agreements which would govern the last three trials on the same matrix and alternative.[2]

DEPENDENT MEASURES

In addition to the tentative agreements, the actual choices in bargaining, and the outcomes received by P and by X on each trial, the dependent measures in the experiment included the interpolated questionnaire and the contractual decisions.

The *questionnaire* which was introduced after the first three trials on the experimental matrices asked each S to indicate on a 100-point scale the degree of his concern or

[2] A final questionnaire, also administered, is discussed elsewhere (Faucheux and Thibaut, in press).

anxiety about the fairness or equity of the division of points and about the likelihood that his partner would play the external alternatives. After each *S* had made his responses in private, the questionnaires were exchanged between partners. This device thus had two aims: to stimulate oral communication between partners about the variables being manipulated in the experiment and to gain data about the degree to which these variables were apprehended by and mattered to the *Ss*.

After the sixth trial on the experimental matrices the procedure for forming *contracts* was introduced. The *E* emphasized that contracts were entirely voluntary and that they need not be formed unless the *Ss* wanted them. On each of the three following trials each *S* recorded privately: (1) whether or not he wanted a contract to be formed, and (2) if in fact he wanted a contract to be formed, the single *rule* (among three presented to him) that he would most prefer to have incorporated in the contract and the type and amount of *sanction* that he would like to have applied to violations of any contractual rules.

The three rules among which each *S* wanting a contract had to choose were as follows:

EA-rule: it is prohibited to play the *external alternative* on this trial if a tentative agreement has been reached to play within the matrix.

D-rule: if on this trial a tentative agreement has been reached concerning the *division and distribution* of points between the partners, it is prohibited in the actual play to change the distribution agreed upon.

RC-rule: if on this trial a tentative agreement has been reached such that each partner is to play a specific *row or column* of the matrix, it is prohibited to shift in the actual play to the other row or column.

It will be apparent that the first two rules are designed to prohibit the kinds of behavior which on theoretical grounds may be expected to threaten differentially the two partners (whose anxiety about specifically these two sources of threat was earlier measured by the brief questionnaire). The third rule, which

involves a type of behavior less central to the present research, was introduced primarily as a plausible third alternative which would permit the formation of types of contracts other than those envisaged by our theoretical formulation.

The two types of *sanction* afforded the *Ss* were indemnities and fines. Indemnities referred to payments (in points) the violator of a rule must make to the injured party. Fines referred to payments (in points) to be made by the violator to *E*. In the private recording of his preference for aspects of a contract, *S* could indicate any number of points between zero and 100 to be applied as an indemnity and/or as a fine.

After recording their individual preferences, the partners discussed the matter and decided whether to form a contract, and if a contract were to be formed, the rules and sanctions to be incorporated. The *Ss* were permitted to include in their contracts as many of the three rules as they liked and either or both types of sanctions. This procedure was repeated for three trials. Adherence to the various provisions of contracts was monitored and enforced by *E*.

SUBJECTS AND ADMINISTRATION

Sixteen young adults of both sexes were formed into 8 dyads for the pretest. The experimental treatment was administered separately to each dyad, and the entire proceeding was tape-recorded. The *Ss* for the experiment proper were 100 14-year-old boys from two public schools in the suburbs of Paris: one at Chatenay and the other at Montrouge. After the elimination from the sample of 2 dyads for failure to adhere to the instructions, there remained 24 dyads from each school. Six dyads at each school were assigned to each of the four treatments, making a total of 48 dyads, 12 for each treatment.

At each of the schools, the six dyads assigned to a given treatment were seated at widely separated tables in one large room, and the administration of the experiment thus proceeded simultaneously for all six dyads.

RESULTS

In presenting the experimental findings, we shall proceed by first showing the objective situation confronting the Ss, then moving to the Ss' perception of this situation, and finally inquiring into the process of contract-formation and the characteristics of the contracts adopted.

The bargaining situation. There are two main aspects to the situation in which the Ss find themselves. These two aspects can be summarized by referring to the difference between the partners in the numbers of points won in the actual bargaining and to the frequencies with which the Ss chose to play the external alternative.

In presenting the data on points won in bargaining, let us consider the six trials that occurred before the opportunity to form contracts was introduced. (Data from the preliminary trials with the training matrix are, of course, omitted, since the experimental variations had not at that point been introduced.) Total points won in bargaining by dyads during these six trials show no mean differences among the four treatments. Dyads in the various treatments, therefore, were equally successful in their total productivity. On the other hand, the various treatments were not alike with respect to the share of the points won by P and X. Table 1 shows the mean differences between P and X in points received over the six trials before contracts were permitted. Although the variances from condition to condition are not homogeneous, it is plain that the sharing of points is much more nearly equal under low conflict of interest than under high. (High and low conflict of interest are different by analysis of variance: $F = 12.24$, $p < .001$.) A closely related finding is that under high conflict of interest there were 8 dyads in which on 19 occasions P failed to respect the agreement about sharing of points, but when conflict of interest was low, there were only 5 such instances in a total of 2 dyads. Hence, under conditions of high conflict of interest, X's share of the points is far exceeded by P's share, and the reduction of this disparity may pose a major problem for X.

The second aspect of the bargaining situation to be summarized here is the incidence of opting for the external alternative. It was frequently observed that an S would threaten to play the alternative without in fact doing so. Since these threats were not recorded (except in the pretests), the present data refer only to actual instances of playing the alternative. Table 2 shows, for all dyads in which either member at any time played the alternative, the number of dyads in which P was the first or only member to play the alternative, X was the first or only one to do so, or both members did so simultaneously. Note first that a total of 14 (58%) of the dyads in the High-Alternative conditions showed at least one instance of playing the alternative, as against only 4 (17%) of those in the Low-Alternative conditions. This difference yields a χ^2 of 7.20, which is significant at the .01 level. Note also that the initiative in playing the alternative rested mainly with

Table 1. Mean differences between P and X in points received during the six trials preceding the contract period

Conflict of interest		Level of external alternative	
		High	Low
High	M[a]	61.62	70.96
	SD	62.40	97.90
Low	M	2.79	3.25
	SD	16.71	48.73

[a] In all four conditions the mean difference signifies the preponderance of P's share over X's.

Table 2. Total numbers of dyads in the various treatments in which one or both members at any time played the alternative, with specification of the order of doing so

Conflict of interest		Level of external alternative	
		High	Low
High	P first	0	0
	X first	5	3
	Simultaneous	4	0
	Total	9	3
Low	P first	1	0
	X first	2	1
	Simultaneous	2	0
	Total	5	1

X: in 11 dyads X was the first or only member to do so, but in only one dyad did *P* show this behavior. Hence, how to prevent X from playing the alternative may pose for *P* a major problem.

THE PARTNERS' PERCEPTION
OF THE SITUATION

Though it may seem clear that the partners theoretically should have and empirically do have the problems just outlined, it may be important to assess the degree to which these problems actually are perceived by the partners and matter to them.

It will be recalled that after the first block of three trials on the experimental matrices, a brief questionnaire was administered, partly to stimulate communication between the partners about "fair sharing" and "loyalty" to the dyad, and partly to gain information about the degree to which at that stage the partners were concerned about these two problems. Our theoretical formulation would lead us to expect that *P* would be more concerned in the High-Alternative than in the Low-Alternative conditions about his partner's playing the alternative, and that X would be more concerned about equitable sharing in the High-Conflict than in the Low-Conflict conditions.

As to the first of these predictions, although *P* does in fact have a greater degree of concern when the alternative is high than when it is low (the means are 37.30 and 26.58, respectively), this difference does not reach an acceptable level of statistical significance. The second prediction, however, is clearly confirmed. X's concern about fair sharing is greater when conflict of interest is high than when it is low. The means are 38.34 and 25.71, respectively, and the variance analysis yields an F of 4.42, which is significant at the .05 level.

An analysis rather similar to that just summarized can be made from the Ss' preference for various types of rules to be incorporated in contracts. It will be recalled that at the beginning of each of the three trials

during which contracts were permitted, each *S* had the opportunity to record privately his preferences for various aspects of a contract which might be negotiated with his partner. From our formulation it might be expected that, in all conditions, *P*'s preference would exceed that of X for a rule prohibiting the use of the external alternative, and that X's preference would exceed that of *P* for a rule prohibiting the violation of any agreement reached about the sharing of points between the partners. Both of these expectations are strongly confirmed. In every one of the four conditions *P* preferred prohibiting the alternative more frequently than did X, the combined probabilities reaching significance at the .01 level. (However, this difference in frequency of preference was not significantly greater under High-Alternative than under Low-Alternative conditions.) Similarly, in every condition X preferred more frequently than did *P* a rule protecting any agreements about sharing, again with combined probabilities reaching the .01 level. (But again, too, this difference in frequency of preference was not significantly greater when conflict of interest was high than when it was low.)

THE CONTRACT

Throughout the following presentation of results, the term contract will be reserved for written agreements specifying at least one rule to be observed and including a sanction for violation in the form of an indemnity. (Fines were so infrequently attached to contracts that we will omit any consideration of them in this discussion.)

Let us now turn to the various measures which reflect the over-all frequency and intensity of contractual activity in the four conditions. Table 3 summarizes these data. The HH condition shows clear superiority on each of the five measures.

Dyads in the HH condition formed on the average 2.75 contracts (the absolute limit being 3.00), as compared with means of less than two contracts in the other three conditions. An analysis of variance yields an F

for interaction of 5.51, which is significant at the .05 level.

Similarly, all 12 of the HH dyads formed at least one contract, while only 64% of the dyads in the remaining conditions did so. This difference between HH and the other conditions combined is significant by χ^2 (4.25) at the .05 level.

The same pattern is revealed by the frequency with which dyads included both rules prohibiting the playing of the external alternative and rules protecting agreements concerning the division of points. In all, 75% of the HH dyads formed such contracts, but only 19% of the remaining dyads did so. This difference yields a χ^2 of 10.13, which is significant at well beyond the .01 level.

The mean size of indemnity for violation of contractual provisions is also atypically high in the HH condition. The F-ratio for interaction resulting from the analysis of variance was 4.93, which is significant at the .05 level.

Finally, an index was constructed to estimate for each dyad the over-all quantity and intensity of its contractual activity by multiplying the number of rules adopted times the magnitude of indemnity to be paid for violations. The shapes of the resulting distributions are markedly different from condition to condition, and hence a variance analysis was not attempted. However, the Mann-Whitney test distinguishes the HH condition from the other conditions combined, yielding a p of exactly .02.

A word about the *effectiveness* of the contracts both from the point of view of the joint profit of the dyads and the division of points between the partners: To make the relevant comparisons, let us consider the joint profit of dyads for the six trials that preceded the contract period. The mean joint profit for these six trials was slightly higher for the 35 dyads that later formed contracts than for the 13 dyads that did not form contracts. Of the dyads forming contracts, 57% achieved the maximum possible joint profit (98 points) on each of the six trials, while only 31% of the "noncontractual" dyads achieved this level of joint profit. In spite of this initially higher level (though it is statistically non-significant), 86% of the dyads forming contracts maintained or increased their joint profit over the three trials of the contract period, while only 78% of the "non-contractual" dyads maintained or increased their initial levels of joint profit.

A more crucial test concerns the efficacy of contracts in reducing disparities in points received by the partners. If one compares the disparity in points received by the partners during the initial six trials with that of the three trials of the contract period, the efficacy of contracts becomes clear. In not a single one of the 13 dyads forming no contracts was there a reduction in this inter-partner disparity from the initial trials to the contract trials. However, 15 of the contractual dyads (including 8 from the HH treatment) showed reduced disparities during the contract phase.

Table 3. Frequency and intensity of contractual activity in the various treatments

Conflict of interest		Level of external alternative	
		High	Low
High	Mean number of contracts	2.75	1.33
	Number of dyads forming one or more contracts	12	6
	Number of dyads adopting both EA- and D-rules[a]	9	2
	Mean indemnity	65.56	26.39
	Index of quantity and intensity	315.83	175.00
Low	Mean number of contracts	1.67	1.92
	Number of dyads forming one or more contracts	9	8
	Number of dyads adopting both EA- and D-rules[a]	2	3
	Mean indemnity	35.83	42.22
	Index of quantity and intensity	194.17	184.17

[a] EA-rules are prohibitions against playing the alternative; D-rules protect agreements about the division of points.

This difference yields a χ^2 of 6.23, which is significant at the .02 level.

DISCUSSION AND CONCLUSIONS

Although the task confronting the Ss in the present research was to bargain for points in the context of a game defined by the given matrix, the focus of the study has been not so much on the microscopic analysis of game-playing behavior as on the game situation as a device for studying the development of contractual agreements. The aim of the study, to relate the genesis of contracts to the joint application of external and internal stresses on groups containing members of unequal power, appears to have been realized.

Nevertheless, there are two aspects of the process of game-playing in the present experiment that require comment. The first has to do with the exercise of power in the bargaining process. The reader will have observed that the matrices employed in this research created an interdependence between the players such that neither partner could attain large outcomes without the cooperation of the other. The manipulation of the external alternative set the limit of outcomes that each player could dependably attain by his own efforts alone. From this point of view, then, the partners were equally dependent on one another for any outcomes superior to those of the external alternative.

Hence it may be difficult to see wherein lies the superior power of P. The answer to this question appears to be that both partners accept the E's definition of P's power and find it plausible that the person endowed with superior power should aim for the larger share of the group's rewards. In any case, if P is to compete successfully with other Ps he is forced to strain the upper limits of his possibilities. It is perhaps this aspiration for affluence, activated by E's definition of the possible prerogatives of power, which holds P to the interdependent solution, while at the same time driving X to abandon it. Moreover, both partners apparently felt it in accord with their experience in other groups, that the powerful member will have greater "usable" power as the conflict of interest increases. The present manipulation of P's power, aimed at insuring this relationship of usable power to conflict of interest, was crystallized during the pretests on the basis of reassuring evidence from the comments of Ss.

The second comment on the game-playing process concerns the intensity of the bargaining activity and the involvement of the Ss. There is no doubt that these were maximal in the HH condition and (though this must be said less confidently) that they were minimal in the LL condition. Though precise timing of the bargaining sessions was not attempted, it is worth noting that, both at Chatenay and Montrouge, the order of time taken to complete the experiment was, from greatest to least: HH, HL, LH, and LL.

A word about the LL condition: From the point of view of global theories of cohesiveness, this is the condition which should produce dyads of the greatest cohesiveness. The minimal external stress on such dyads means that, with minimally attractive external alternatives, the resultant motivation to remain in the group should be high. And minimal internal stress should mean that the attractiveness of the group would not be unnecessarily reduced by intermember conflict. It is entirely possible that such dyads would be maximally effective in enforcing conformity to any norms that existed in the group. But from the present research it seems unlikely that such norms, at least of the sort discussed here (of equity and loyalty), will be generated from within the group in the absence of temptations to violate them.

References

Bertalanffy, L. von.   Theoretical Models in Biology and Psychology.   *J. Pers.*,
1951, **20**, 24–38.

Faucheux, C., and Thibaut, J.   L'approche Clinique et Experimentale de la
Genèse des Normes Contractuelles dans Differentes Conditions de Conflit et
de Menace.   *Bull. C.E.R.P., Paris*, in press.

Miller, J. G.   Toward a General Theory for the Behavioral Sciences.   *Amer.
Psychol.*, 1955, **10**, 513–531.

Selye, H.   The Physiology and Pathology of Exposure to Stress: A Treatise Based
on the Concepts of the General-Adaptation Syndrome and the Diseases of
Adaptation.   Montreal: Acta, 1950.

Thibaut, J., and Kelley, H.   *The social psychology of groups.*   New York: Wiley,
1959.

PRIMITIVE LAW

Robert Redfield

One who sets out to talk about primitive law has a choice of three roads. The road to the right recognizes law to exist only where there are courts and codes supported by the fully politically organized state. This road quickly becomes a blind alley, for only a few preliterate societies have law in this sense, and these few are not characteristically primitive. Making this choice amounts to saying that there is no law in truly primitive society and that therefore there is nothing for one to talk about.

The road to the left has been recently opened with a great flourish by B. Malinowski (1926; 1934) and is apparently preferred by Julius Lips (1938). He who takes this road

Source: R. Redfield, "Primitive Law," *University of Cincinnati Law Review*, Vol. 33, 1964, pp. 1–22. Copyright 1964 by the University of Cincinnati Law Review and used by permission.

does not identify law with courts and codes. To Malinowski law consists of "the rules which curb human inclinations, passions or instinctive drives; rules which protect the rights of one citizen against the concupiscence, cupidity or malice of the other; rules which pertain to sex, property and safety." These rules are of course found everywhere, and in this sense law exists in the most primitive society. Malinowski (1938: lxii) notes that primitive people, like other people, are kept from doing what their neighbors do not want them to do chiefly not because of courts and policemen, but for many other personal and social reasons. In effect he bids us investigate the ways in which social control is brought about in the simpler societies, or at least the mechanisms whereby the individual is induced to do what people expect of him even though through selfish interest he is tempted to do otherwise. This conception requires us to include under "law" any norm of conduct conformity to which is, as Malinowski puts it, "baited with inducements." If we take this road we find ourselves concerned with all the complicated and varying considerations of personal motivation and social advantage or disadvantage which are involved in deciding to do or not to do what people expect of us. Following him down this road, one has not too little to talk about but far too much.

There is no reason why one who wishes to do so should not study the mechanisms of social control. The effects of conventionalized relationships between members of a society in restricting the impulses of human nature and in bringing about established modes of conduct is an important subject. It is indeed highly desirable that we should study the functioning of law in its total social and personal setting, not only in primitive societies but in our own society. But to identify this subject matter with "law" has the great disadvantage of ignoring the special peculiarities of law as it is represented by what we know by that name in civilized societies. To us, who live under a developed system of law, law appears as something very different from the personal and cultural considerations which motivate our day-to-day choices of action. It appears as a system of principles and of restraints of action with accompanying paraphernalia of enforcement. The law is felt to be outside, independent, and coercive of us. Within its labyrinths we find our way as best we can.

This criticism, and others, of Malinowski's viewpoint with regard to primitive law have been effectively made by a lawyer, William Seagle (1937: 285). That writer also points out to students of the subject a middle road to follow. Along it at least one anthropologist, Radcliffe-Brown (1933: 202–6), is already going; it seems to me that this middle road is the wisest choice, so here I set out upon it.

I shall adhere to the idea of law that is derived from our acquaintance with the phenomenon as we know it in civilized societies: the systematic and formal application of force by the state in support of explicit rules of conduct. Like other institutions, law is represented on two sides, as Sumner (1906: 53) said: concept and structure. The concept consists of the principles and the rules restricting or requiring action; it is characteristic of law that these develop an explicitness and internal consistency, and that the maintenance and development of this internal organization becomes to the society, or at least to the lawyers, an objective in itself. The structure of the law is, of course, chiefly, process and court. Law is therefore recognizable in form: in formal statement of the rules, and in forms for securing compliance with the rules or satisfaction or punishment for their breach. The student of primitive law who follows the middle road will not expect to find among the simpler peoples a full development of something which he has first recognized in the complex and literate societies any more than he will expect to find double-entry bookkeeping there, or the outstanding examples of theology. But he may look for the modes of conduct in the simpler societies which in rudimentary form represent or anticipate law. He will not report as "primitive law" all socially or personally induced restraints upon human impulse to do something to the disadvantage of somebody else, but only such rules or procedures which, by their formal or systematic or coercive nature foreshadow our law and seem to illustrate the simpler modes of conduct out of which a law such as ours might develop. Our problem is, in Seagle's words, to determine "whether in the absence of full political organization and of specific juridical institutions such as courts and codes, certain modes of conduct may be segregated from the general body of conduct as at least incipiently legal" (Seagle 1937: 280).

There is, of course, no one "primitive law," any more than there is one primitive society. The preliterate societies vary greatly, and present us with many degrees and kinds of difference with regard to the presence of unwritten codes, of process, and of courts, and with many different forms and combinations of modes of conduct which foreshadow the juridical institutions of our own society. Here I may assemble and compare some of the rudiments of law as they are variously represented in very various societies. Only at the end of this paper shall I say something in general terms about what the rudimentary law found in primitive societies tends typically to be. The paper is chiefly devoted to pointing out that the beginnings of law are diverse, not unified, and to citing some instances of some of the principal elementary juridical, or proto-legal, institutions. The subject might be stated to be "rudimentary law as represented in some of the simpler societies." Rudimentary law might also be studied in such groups within the modern state as clubs, gangs and families. The highly developed state with its powerful law looms so large that perhaps we do not always see that within it are many little societies, each in some ways a little primitive society, enforcing its own special regulations with a little primitive law of its own. But here I stand as an anthropologist, and speak to the subject from what are sometimes called the "savage societies."

As the philosopher has been said to be able to begin any paper with Aristotle and the biologist with the amoeba, so the anthropologist is likely to start off with the Andaman Islanders; in the present instance this very primitive people is at hand to provide an instance of a society without even the most rudimentary elements of law, as I have just defined it. These natives have no means of composing disputes, and no specific sanctions which may be brought to bear on one who commits generally condemned acts. Apparently, quarrels are not infrequent, and may lead to considerable violence: a man may attack his adversary, or he may become so angry that he runs about ragefully destroying property, and not merely that of the immediate object of his anger, but any property that comes in his way. Yet a careful and critical student of the Andamanese (Radcliffe-Brown 1922: 48) tells us that there is no authority to intervene and no procedure to deal with the situation. The conventions of the society include no formal definition of appropriate compensation for the damage such a man may do, nor any specific procedure by which the injured party may secure revenge or damages, nor any way by which the group as a whole may punish the delinquent or secure itself against repetition of the act. A man who feels aggrieved may take whatever measures occur to him, acting for himself. If one man kills another, there are no consequences that are to be called "legal." A murderer will leave the camp and hide until he thinks he will be allowed to re-enter; or else the kinsmen of the dead man will take private vengeance. A man who makes himself generally disliked by violence or bad temper is visited by no specific sanction. Sorcery is recognized and is generally reprehensible, but no measures are taken against the sorcerer. In this particular society, therefore, the diffuse sanctions sometimes loosely lumped as "public opinion" (and the considerations of personal advantage and disadvantage which Malinowski is so interested in) are enough to keep the society running, and the people get along without any law at all.

There are other societies in which law is minimal not because conventional remedies are lacking but simply because controversy is strongly disapproved. This appears to be the case among the Zuni Indians. Here legal process is represented in simple form, for secular officials impose fines (Parsons 1917: 278–79), organizations of religious dancers may punish people who are delinquent in the performance of their ritual duties by ducking them (Parsons 1917), and cases of formal procedure against suspected witches are known (Stevenson 1901–2: 393–98). The Zuni constitute a more highly developed society than do the Andaman Islanders; there is a tribal organization, and certain functionaries are invested with authority on behalf of the tribe and may bring a formalized procedure to bear upon delinquents. Yet such occurrences are apparently rare, and this is so because of the strong dislike of controversy and indeed of any conspicuous behavior. Among the Zuni a man is not supposed to stand up for his rights; he is looked down upon if he gets into any sort of conflict or achieves notoriety. The best that one Zuni may say of another is that he "is a nice polite man. No one ever hears anything from him. He never gets into trouble. He's Badger clan and Muhekwe kiva and he always dances in the summer dances" (Bunzel 1929–30: 480).

The case of the Zuni Indians is probably more exceptional than typical. In a great many primitive societies one is supposed to stand up for one's rights and those of one's kinsmen, even if one makes a great disturbance doing so. There is probably a general human tendency to resent an injury and to strike back at the injurer. If a delict is regarded as an injury or a danger to the entire group, the demand of any specially injured party receives more general support. Yet I think it may be declared that in the primitive societies, on the whole, the specific secular sanctions that are likely to qualify as rudimentary law play a larger role in connection with private delicts, or torts, than they do in connection with public delicts, or crimes. What we so often find in the case of offenses against the entire group is that supernatural or ritual sanctions take care of these. Incest is typically regarded as a crime in primitive society. There are certainly plenty of cases where incest is punished by the society, but on the other hand the sometimes specified, sometimes vague results that are supposed automatically to follow, or to be inflicted by the supernaturals upon one who commits such a delinquency, are apt to be a very large part, or even all, of the sanctions which support the rule as to sex relations.

However this may be, the point to be made is that some of the most rudimentary legal institutions appear in connection with the systematization of the retaliative sanctions. A has done some injury to B; B is disposed to retaliate; the customs of the group say how he is to do it; and we have a very simple anticipation of law. If not curbed by convention a retaliation is likely to lead to a counter-retaliation, and so to public disorder. The Zuni tend to check the tendency at the outset by frowning upon controversy; it is probably commoner to allow the retaliation but to define its terms.

The conventionalization of the retaliative sanctions may involve the way in which the injured party may strike back at the injurer, or it may take the form of a scale of compensation to be paid and accepted in set-tlement of the claim. In the former case the principle involved is that of meeting force with force, but in so restricted a manner as to satisfy the injured person and yet bring the controversy to an end. The duel is an elementary juridical institution of this sort. In the case of payment of compensation the impulse to avenge the wrong is bought off with damages. Primitive societies provide abundant examples of both ways of conventionalizing the retaliative sanctions, and both ways occur in combination. So far as the manner of settlement, including the amounts to be paid, is fixed by custom for classes of cases, a sort of preliterate code results. So far as custom involves the way in which the injured person is to set about getting a settlement, whether by exercise of force in return or by collection of indemnity, there is a primitive anticipation of legal procedure.

The Yurok Indians of Northern California provide an instance of a society with a well-defined code of compensation yet without any formal procedure for punishing delinquents or for righting a wrong done an individual. Kroeber's account (Kroeber 1925) makes it clear that among these very primitive, food-collecting Indians it was well understood that "every possession and privilege, and every injury and offense" could "be exactly valued in terms of property"; and that "every invasion of privilege or property must be exactly compensated." The compensation took the form of handing over certain forms of wealth, including dentalium shells, woodpecker scalps, obsidian blades, and deerskins. The members of the society recognized many well-specified delicts, and the amount of compensation which it was appropriate to demand of one committing the corresponding wrong against another. For killing a man of social standing the indemnity was fifteen strings of dentalium, with perhaps a red obsidian, and a woodpecker scalp headband, besides handing over a daughter. A common man was worth only ten strings of dentalium. A seduction followed by a pregnancy cost five strings of dentalium or twenty woodpecker scalps. To utter the name of a dead man was an injury to his kin demanding a payment of two strings of thirteen shells each. If a couple with children separated, the woman could take them with her only on full repayment of her original purchase price. If a man beat his wife, she might go to her parents, who might keep her until the husband had paid them certain damages; then he might retake her. There were even obligations suggesting our laws of common carriers. A man able to take a traveler over a river had to provide free ferriage; if he refused to do so, the aggrieved traveler could claim three to six short strings of dentalia. A shaman who had declined to visit a patient was liable in the event of the latter's death, even after treatment by another shaman, for the full fee tendered her, or a little more.

In short, these Indians had a strong feeling for the definition of rights and obligations, and recognized certain appropriate damages for any private delicts. Nevertheless, this code was maintained not only without any court, but without any formal procedure at all. In this society there is no tribal organization whatsover. Each little settlement is composed of men related by blood, and their wives. Property and rights pertain to the individual, or to this little hamlet of kinsmen. There are no clans, exogamic groups, or chiefs or governors. The satisfaction of claims is accomplished without any formal process. "Each side to an issue presses and resists vigorously, exacts all he can, yields where he has to, continues the controversy where continuance promises to be profitable or settlement suicidal, and usually ends in compromising more or less" (Kroeber 1925). An even more elaborate unwritten code of indemnity, with a sliding scale of payment depending on the social position of the injured party, is recognized by the Ifugao of Northern Luzon (Barton 1919). These people, like the Yurok, are also without tribal organization, and settlement of claims is effected simply by means of negotiations between the parties. But among the Ifugao the negotiations are carried on not by the parties themselves but by a compromiser, or go-between, selected for the purpose by the parties. The go-between has no authority and no force behind him; there is nothing to support his efforts to secure a settlement by

acting for both parties except the fact that the only alternative to settlement is a long-drawn feud, which is wanted by neither party and nobody else.

It appears, therefore, that in certain societies entirely without legal process the disposition for an injured party to seek redress for a wrong not only is sanctioned, but appropriate compensation is socially recognized, and is, moreover, reduced to system. The rudiments of law may, on the other hand, also be recognized in the systematization of the forms and limits of retaliation by the injured party. In these cases there is a recognized procedure whereby the injured party may do a retaliative injury upon the man who has committed a wrong against him (or them). In many of these cases, the group does not treat the delict as a crime, conceding all interest in retaliation to the parties injured; but general opinion and custom hedge revenge with limitations which assure the termination of the dispute and the restoration of peace and public order. Among the aborigines of Australia there is a widespread pattern of custom whereby differences are composed and social equilibrium is restored by means of a regulated combat in which the blood of the offender is shed. A man charged with an offense meets his adversary, or his representatives, armed and painted in a way highly stylized by custom, and a certain number of weapons are thrown at him, which he attempts to ward off. Among the Gringai tribe individuals fought a personal quarrel with weapons nearest at hand, but in cases of serious offenses, the offender had to stand out, with a shield, while a number of spears, fixed according to the magnitude of his offense, were thrown at him. If he could defend himself, well and good; if he was injured or killed, the result was regarded by the group as concluding the affair. Among the Kurnai the relative of one supposed to have been killed by magic stood up opposite the person accused of the sorcery. The accused, aided by his wife and the women of the tribe, sang certain songs while the slain man's relative and the accused exchanged conventional feints and blows. Whatever was the outcome, the issue was regarded as closed (Howitt

1904: 343–45). In such cases apparently the older men of the tribe act as the agents of public opinion in enforcing these sanctions, requiring the parties to meet and directing the proceedings, although some of the instances reported involve leadership by the medicine man.

The practices just cited from Australia are not so much punishment as feuds shortened in the interests of the public. They are interrupted and restrained killings. In this class of cases as well as in the cases of simple societies with unwritten codes of damages, there is recognition of a sort of principle of equivalent retaliation. The principle is of course perfectly familiar in the law of more complex societies. We know it in one form in the *lex talionis*. The spirit of it is common in primitive societies which do have recognizable juridical institutions. If a man of one clan is killed, that clan may kill an equivalent man of another clan. Among the Bageshu the one killed in retaliation must be exactly equivalent; the wronged clan may wait until the son of the killer is of the age of his father when the murder was done, and then kill him (Roscoe: 1909). Among the Giriama the murderer must be killed in just the same manner as that in which he killed his victim. The principle of equivalence applies also to compensation given in goods or wealth. Among East African Bantu tribes a man pays less compensation for injuries to members of his own clan than he pays to outsiders, because as a clan member he is entitled to share in all compensations. This is certainly a legalistic point of view.

The preceding remarks are made to direct attention to the importance of conventional treatment of the retaliative sanctions in giving rise to proto-legal institutions. Custom restrains an injured party from unlimited revenge. Retaliative force is stylized by custom into a sort of ritualistic revenge, and something like legal process results. The claim is compounded by payment of wealth equivalent to the loss incurred, and a code of damages results. Either or both foreshadowing of full legal institutions may take place without the development of a formal court to try an issue. The few examples

cited suggest that the development of an unwritten code of indemnity is likely to occur in societies where forms of wealth are recognized and much status attaches to its possession. There is something that may be given up, that people hate to give up, and that may be offered as equivalent to vengeance. It is also probably a favorable circumstance for the development of either unwritten codes of indemnity or of procedures for limited revenge that the public resentment of an injury be not too strongly disapproved by general social attitude. The Ifugao, a warlike man and a headhunter, certainly feels differently about contentiousness than does the Zuni Indian. It is expected of the Ifugao that he stand up for his rights. "Did he not do so he would become the prey of his fellows. No one would respect him. . . . he will hear himself accused of cowardice, and called a woman" (Barton 1919). It is notable that it is among some of the societies with the very simplest forms of organization that we encounter wealth and social status dependent thereon, together with the systematization of rules of indemnity.

The foregoing discussion has centered around the development of systems of compensation or of forms of socially approved retaliation in the development of what might be called a rudimentary law of torts. The beginnings of law may also be sought in the extent to which there is formal process in connection with delicts thought to be also, or only, wrongful acts committed against the society. It may be repeated that the commission of such a wrongful act is in many cases attended by several sanctions of different kinds: the diffuse sanctions of public contempt, dislike, withdrawal and the like; a supernatural sanction in the form of an unpleasant consequence to the body or spirit of the one who does the act; and some specific secular sanction imposed by the community or some part of it (Radcliffe-Brown 1933: 203). So far as any of these sanctions has a specific and formal aspect, it at least suggests law to us, although it is only the last of these—the impersonal application of force—that we are likely to think of as criminal law. Among the Chukchee (Hobley 1910: 80) a man who has become notoriously objectionable by bad conduct may be killed by his own clansmen. Such a man one day killed a reindeer by a careless blow. Whereupon his kinsmen stabbed him to death, saying, "Otherwise we shall have a feud on our hands." The other members of the community approved the action. In such a case as this there was no court and no sharply defined form of punishment; the case does not illustrate law at all, in the sense in which the word is used in this paper. Instances of customary punishment that amount to law are generally cases of societies with courts, as among the Akamba of East Africa, where, after a council has deliberated over the case of a notorious bad character, his clansmen will carry out the punishment in a stereotyped manner, by slaying some of his cattle or by dragging him from his hut and beating him.

The punishment of delicts by supernatural agencies plays a great part in the system of controls of primitive societies; insofar as the supposed consequences of committing the act are specific and are thought surely to follow, they might be spoken of as a sort of supernatural law. But to follow this line of thought with reference to the rudimentary legalism of primitive peoples would be to carry the concept of law beyond the point where it is useful. In some cases it is true that the commission of the interdicted act is believed to bring about immediate consequences: to eat of the chief's food is to bring death upon one's self; to profane the sacred object is to cause one's hand to wither. But though there are here rules with sanctions in connection, there is nothing procedural about the matter; there is no society or its representatives to decide an issue or to measure a delict by a scale of punishment or of compensation. Indeed, what is characteristic of these supernatural sanctions is that they are for the most part vague, and for this very reason terrible; they are outside of the realm of orderly process. We have the word "tabu" for those interdicts which are attained by uncertain and perhaps awful consequences. Nemesis is a kind of judgment, but it does not have the qualities of judgment according to law.

A subject more relevant to the consideration of rudimentary law is the conventionalization of the diffuse sanctions of public contempt, criticism, and withdrawal. The systematic and impersonal application of force in the maintenance of individual rights and in the public interest is the central substance of law, but it must be recognized that sanctions other than force may be applied quite as formally and with the same social function. Indeed, to the man upon whom the sanction is applied there may not be much difference between the lash of the whip and the lash of the public's tongue. Moral force, if expressed in defined and open procedures, may fall upon a delinquent much as does physical force. Public ridicule may feel quite as coercive as imprisonment or destruction of property. In not a few primitive societies general disapproval is expressed not merely diffusely and casually, but in a sort of standardized collective gesture of disapproval. These modes of conduct we must recognize as closely related to law in that they are specific secular sanctions that have a public character and that assume a formal nature.

This sort of institution is still at a very low level of the juridical, where the injured party alone carries the sanction into effect. In the case of the Orokaiva of New Guinea, "when a man finds his coconuts stolen he may tie a fragment of husk to a stick and set it up on the track near his palms; then everyone will see that a theft has been committed, and the thief, even though his identity remains unknown, will feel a pang of shame whenever he passes the spot. Similarly, the owner of a ravaged garden will affix a taro leaf to a coconut palm in the midst of the village for all to see and for the special discomfort of the culprit" (Williams 1930: 329–30). But where the victim *is* known, and where the general public participate in application of a specific sanction rendering onerous the general disapproval, the approximation to a legal form is closer. An example of such an institution comes from the Sunda Islands, where a notorious liar receives his punishment in the following manner: Passers-by begin to make a heap of twigs near where the dishonesty occurred; the pile grows, making conspicuous and enduring the name and delinquency of the liar (Kennedy 1937: 363–64). Among the Hottentot an unpopular chief will be publicly lectured by the women (Hahn 1881: 28–29). Examples of the use of publicity in a formal manner without the exercise of force are to be found also in the case of delicts which are regarded chiefly or wholly as violations of the rights of individuals. Malinowski tells us how in the Trobriand Islands parties to a dispute, "assisted by friends and relatives meet, harangue one another and hurl back recriminations" (Malinowski 1926: 60). This conventional name-calling has to some degree the effect of moving toward a solution of the conflict through the aid of publicity, because "such litigation allows people to give vent to their feelings and shows the trend of public opinion," although, Malinowski says, "sometimes it seems, however, only to harden the litigants." The best-reported instance of litigation by regulated abuse, to find a phrase for this class of institution, is the juridical drum songs of the Eskimo. In this case two men (or sometimes two women), having become enemies, encounter each other once a year in what they call a drum fight. Each party has a turn at singing a song, to the accompaniment of drums, in which he heaps abuse and mockery upon his adversary, reciting his version of the dispute, and seeking to bring shame upon the other. The songs are composed in advance, but follow traditional styles, and indeed apparently certain of these styles are belongings or appurtenances of family lines (Thalbitzer 1923: 166–68; 318–21).

These last cases, of the conventionalization of gestures of disapproval, suggest the importance of ceremonial in incipient law. Obligations and rights exist in custom in latency, so to speak, but very commonly there is some overt act which makes the relationship binding; ritual is the seal on the deed; it makes it effective. Two simple examples will stand for a large group of similar cases. In the Trobriand Islands the leader of an expedition, or the promoter of an industrial venture, gives a big ceremonial distribution of food. "Those who participate in it and benefit by the bounty are under an obligation to assist the leader throughout the enterprise" (Malinowski 1926: 61). So among the Maya Indians of present-day Yucatan, the obligation to take charge of the effigy of the patron saint and to assume the leadership of the annual festival is borne by one man, or a small group of men, for a year and is then passed on to a successor or successors. A man will make known his decision to accept the obligation in advance of the festival, but the matter is not irrevocable until at a certain moment in the course of the festivities he accepts certain pieces of ceremonial paraphernalia. This act, trifling as it may appear, is the solemnizing element; thereafter the volunteer may not withdraw. The sanctions that in these cases stand ready to come into operation if the one obligated fails to fulfill his promise may not be legal; the Maya Indian will not be put in jail if he decides not to go through with his obligation, and no one may collect damages for his failure to do so. He merely believes that the saint would punish him with some great misfortune, and he knows that his neighbors would look on him with contempt. We have now shifted the ground of inquiry; we are looking not at the proto-legal sanctions which attend the breach of an obligation or the commission of a wrong against the society, but are mentioning the role of ceremonial as a class of form by which rights and obligations are made less violable in advance of any possible breach. The subject is a very large one, and in a paper of the dimensions of this I can only mention it.

It will be noticed that so far in this discussion very little has been said about courts. The material brought forward has represented the systematization of indemnities so as to produce unwritten codes, and, more especially with rudimentary process in primitive societies. The Andaman Islanders are without either code or process. The Ifugao and the Yurok have explicit and systematic rules of indemnity; the Yurok carry out these rules without any formal procedure, while the Ifugao have only an arbitrator unaided by force. The conventionalized sanctions of retaliation, the exercise of force against a delinquent following the unformalized decisions of public opinion, and the ceremonial expressions of contempt or abuse, are all procedures which do not necessarily depend on courts for their application, and which, in fact, occur, in many of the instances cited, without the existence in the society represented of any court at all. The materials establish that process without courts is common in the simpler societies.

Inquiry as to the elementary forms of courts of law is naturally involved with inquiry as to the origins of the state. The society that is without tribal organization is a society without courts. Conversely, the courts in preliterate societies that do exist are courts maintained not by clans but by a council or a king who represents the entire tribe or local community. The case of the Chukchee, already mentioned, is one in which a conspicuous delinquent is killed by his own clansmen. There is no court to try him; informally expressed opinion results in the execution. In a great many societies the clans or other kinship groups deal with their delinquents directly, without any formal trial of an issue. The simple societies from which examples have been taken more than once in this paper, those of the Andaman Islanders, the Ifugao and the Yurok, are societies in which there is no state, unless we are to call the little settlement of kinsmen and their wives itself a state. Even among the Ifugao, where the settlement consists of a number of such groups of kinsmen, there is no political organization to hold the groups of kinsmen under a single superior authority. In societies that *do* have tribal, political organization, we recognize its existence just in the formal regulation of the conduct of the individual which is here our criterion of law. And the tribal law often has those elements of deliberation and procedure with regard to an issue which, institutionalized, we call a "court."

Some of the Plains Indian tribes provide instances of societies with a very simple tribal organization and a very simple tribal court.

On the whole, the temper of these societies is individualistic. On the whole, the individual and the clan or the band or the soldier-society deals with other equivalent units in matters of dispute, without the exercise of any general tribal authority. On the other hand, a council meets to decide on matters of policy affecting the entire tribe, and legal and police functions are exercised on behalf of the entire tribe by special groups of warriors known in the literature as military societies. Lowie has made a special study of these military societies. They are the police and the law court, acting not simply for one clan but for a tribe made up of familial groups, in a very simple form. "Everywhere the basic idea is that during the hunt a group is vested with the power forcibly to prevent premature attacks on the herd and to punish offenders by corporal punishment, by confiscation of the game illegally secured, by destruction of property generally, and in extreme cases by killing them" (Lowie 1927: 103). On the whole, the authority of these associations lasted only during the emergency of the hunt. Yet a recent writer has shown (Hoebel 1936: 433–38) that they acted as a sort of court and as instruments of execution of judgment even on other occasions. Thus, among the Cheyenne the following incident occurred: An older Indian found his niece struggling through the snow and took her on his horse. They met with the young woman's husband, who became angry at the older Indian (although he was beyond the age of philandering) and wounded him with an arrow. The injury proved serious. The Fox Soldier society was convened by the old Indian's son-in-law. This military society decided to inflict a beating upon the offender. This it did, and also compelled him to remove the arrowhead from the injured man's arm. The delinquent became contrite and presented five horses to the military society in atonement. It should be emphasized that the old Indian, whose injury was made the basis of action both punitive and retributive, was not a member of the military society that acted as a court of law. The society acted on behalf of the total society. In the case of the Omaha, mentioned earlier, the council of chiefs of the tribe deliberated over the case of an evildoer, and if death was decreed, the council designated some trustworthy man to prick the convicted with the poisoned staff kept ready for the purpose (Fletcher and LaFlesche 1905–6: 213).

Among the North American Indians, and also among the aboriginal Australians, the exercise of tribal authority with respect to delicts is maintained with little formal procedure. In both continents power is distributed among the elder men, and councils of these discuss a case and come to a decision, but with little that could be called a rule of procedure or of evidence and without any strong sense of litigation as a contest within rules. The deliberative bodies here are perhaps to be called councils rather than fully developed courts. The case of a serious doer of wrong is considered with solemnity; speeches may be made on his behalf or against him; advice is given and weighed. The assemblies are courts in the sense that a body representative of the entire society deliberatively determines an issue of fact, reaches a decision in accordance with customary rules of justice, and puts into motion some instrument to carry into effect the remedy or punishment agreed upon. But if we demand of a court that it involve formalized procedures and rules by which an issue is to be presented, joined, and determined, then some of the societies in Africa most nearly meet the expectation. Among the Ashanti the procedures include the ordeal, the curse, and swearing on sacred objects. An accused person may demand as of right the procedure of ordeal so as to clear himself of the charge against him. Oaths are important not only in trials but in making obligations binding; everyone entering into any serious undertaking is required to drink a certain liquor accompanied by an imprecation that the supernatural may destroy him if he does not fulfill the obligation (Rattray 1929: 392–95). These African societies are strongly litigious; litigation is like a sport or an art in that it is an end in itself. Lindblom says of the Akamba that "to go into law is one of the most exquisite enjoyments . . . and in what a number of actions every old man has been

a party!" (Lindblom 1920). The knowledge of the law is an important part of the lore of every elder person.

It is worth noting that in Africa the formal court does not everywhere function chiefly to defend the state, or the people, by punishing crimes, although this is very much the fact among the Ashanti, where delinquents are tried before the chief and many delicts are treated as public offenses. But among the natives southeast of Mount Kenya, the delicts of which the court takes cognizance are delicts against individuals. In this part of Africa, therefore, the court operates as a sort of commission of arbitration. When an Akamba court has decided as to the rights of a complaint, the judgment takes the form of a declaration that A has been wronged by B and B should atone or should receive a retaliative sanction at the hands of A's kinsmen. The court leaves the enforcement of the judgment to the kinship groups.

These pages have been devoted to a consideration, in the light of law as we know it in highly developed societies, of some comparable institutions in some primitive societies. The most obvious general conclusion about primitive law is that there is not much of it. Systematic and explicitly formulated rules of conduct and formal procedures for the enforcement of these rules by impersonal authority play a relatively small part in the maintenance of social control, and in some societies they are entirely lacking. On the whole, people do what they are expected to do because that is what they want to do and what (in the light of those inducements and customary advantages and disadvantages which Malinowski sometimes calls "law" and sometimes "effective custom") they find it expedient to do. This is what the old Indian was talking about when, after having been placed on a reservation, he said that in the old times "there was no law; everybody did what was right." On the reservation he found himself surrounded by compulsive regulations exterior to himself and independent of his conscience. It felt different from the good old days. In undisturbed primitive societies, as Durkheim put it, the consciences of individuals are uniform and strong. Human impulses are the same as everywhere else, but there is less need for a state-enforced legal system.

Nevertheless, as we have seen, rudimentary legal institutions are abundantly represented in many of the preliterate societies. The examples considered indicate that the rudiments of law are not to be found so distributed that any society examined will be found to have, in equal degree, the beginnings of code, process, and court. On the contrary, these aspects of the juridical appear singly or in varying combinations. In the case of certain societies that systematize indemnity in settlement of private delicts, a mere give-and-take within the limits set by custom is all that is needed to put these scales of damages into effect. Especially have we noted the frequent occurrences of formal procedure for the composition of disputes without any court to determine the matter at issue. The limited materials examined indicate that primitive law arises out of no single beginning but out of several. Emphasized here has been the formalization of terms of settlement of claims between parties and of procedure for securing satisfaction of claims, but we have also given examples of: the development of procedure for the expression of public condemnation, without force; the development of a formal quality in punitive sanctions imposed on those who commit delicts; the appearance of deliberative and consultive bodies (in at least the African cases with rules of procedure) to decide issues, make awards, and fix punishments; and, most generally, the role of ceremony in solemnizing and rendering more binding customary obligations.

On the whole, the more completely legal institutions are to be found in the most complex of the preliterate societies, while the least complex are without law, or have little of it. Nevertheless a systematization of indemnity may be highly developed in very simple societies. Legal institutions tend to appear, not merely where the society is complex, but also where contentiousness is favored by the mores. So, too, legalism may become a pattern of the culture; we should not hesitate to recognize its presence in the case of the Akamba, and its absence in the case of the Zuni Indians; the importance of law in the one case and its unimportance in the other is not to be explained as a simple function of different levels of social development. Some like litigation, and some don't; and this is true of peoples as of individuals.

In conclusion, two special points may be stated about primitive law, or about the social setting in which it lies, that have fallen through the mesh of the argument as it has been loosely woven here. I have said that, on the whole, primitive peoples get along with little law. One reason why this is so is to be found in the strength of supernatural sanctions in restraining socially disapproved conduct. It is probably not correct to say, as it has been said, that law has developed out of religion. But it is true that in the simple societies the sacred and supernatural sanctions play a large role as compared with the specific secular sanctions. We recognize something of the sort in the self-reproach or perhaps even horror we—or some of us—feel at the thought of committing perjury, but there is nothing in our society which in degree approaches the importance of what Radcliffe-Brown (1933: 203) calls the "ritual sanction." In many of these societies a delinquent brings about by his delinquency a condition of ritual uncleanness which is dangerous to him and to his entire group. This requires lustration or expiation, rather than punishment or compensation to an injured party. Incest, sacrilege, and witchcraft often bring about this result; these are the serious wrongful acts dangerous to the primitive man, above all others. On the other hand, murder and theft are often merely torts with him. The greater dread of the public device behind which stand the sacred sanction may be illustrated by a simple example that comes from the Tlingit Indians (Oberg 1934: 145–46). If murder was committed, it was a matter for the clans to settle. But to prevent a general fight, a chief of high rank might intervene by stepping between the combatants with an important crest, symbolic of the clan status and of the supernaturals. It would be a desecration of the emblem if fighting occurred in these circumstances. In this way the reluctance to incur the supernatural sanction was deliberately utilized as an instrument of control.

The other special characterization of primitive law is the importance of bodies of kindred as parties to controversy and to legal action. The materials cited here have included many instances where the wrongs righted are wrongs against kinship groups, the claims are pressed by kinship groups, and the liability of the individual is to his kinship group. I have said that murder and theft are usually regarded as torts rather than as crimes, but the delict is not so much a wrong done an individual as a wrong done a familial group. Even where a tribal organization is fully developed, and a tribal council acts as a court of law, as among the Akamba, the killing of a member of one clan by a member of another is regarded simply as a wrong done to the clan of the man killed, to be settled by payment of indemnity to the relatives of the victim. Among the Australians, when a life is to be surrendered in payment for a life taken, it is not always the life of the slayer that is given up, but the life of any member of the slayer's group (Howitt 1904: 327–28). We may recognize that in a broad sense Maine was right, when, in considering the early forms of the classic societies, he proposed that primitive society was to be regarded as an aggregation of families rather than of individuals. The prototype of law is to be found in largest part in procedures and standards by which custom regulates disputes between bodies of kin and assures the composition of these disputes in the interest of public peace.

THE ROLE OF LAW IN BUILDING PEACE

Arthur Larson

Most current or recent disputes of major proportions have involved legal questions of a kind which could be handled by judicial and arbitral procedures if the nations of the world, including the United States, would accept these procedures. This is not to say that in today's imperfect world these disputes are in fact going to be settled in court. The point is that by their inherent quality and nature, they are of a kind which could be so handled in whole or in part, if the parties would agree to this method of handling.

The Suez dispute centered around the alleged breach of Egypt's agreement with the Universal Suez Company and the Treaty of Constantinople of 1888. This alleged violation of legal rights was the kind of question that could have been appropriately submitted to the International Court of Justice, just as the nationalization of the Anglo-Iranian Oil Company, an event which also threatened to precipitate war in the Middle East, was submitted.[1]

The present Suez dispute, which takes the form of objections by Israel to Egypt's practice of blocking and searching Israel-bound shipping desiring to transit the Suez

Source: A. Larson, "The Role of Law in Building Peace," in Q. Wright, W. M. Evan, and M. Deutsch (eds.), Preventing World War III: Some Proposals (New York: Simon and Schuster, 1962), pp. 332–341. Copyright 1962 by Quincy Wright, William M. Evan and Morton Deutsch. Reprinted by permission of Simon and Schuster.

[1] See Anglo-Iranian Oil Company Case (United Kingdom v. Iran), ICJ Reports for 1951, p. 89; ICJ Reports for 1952, p. 93.

Canal, consists of a number of questions which are almost all legal in character. All the parties to the dispute, in their presentations to the United Nations, began by invoking their rights under international law. Egypt has accepted the compulsory jurisdiction of the International Court on questions involving the Treaty of Constantinople of 1888, and there seems to be no reason why a country which was a party to that treaty (which would not include Israel) should not in an appropriate case take this question to the International Court.

Another judicable dispute causing tension in the Middle East is the controversy on whether the Gulf of Aqaba and the Straits of Tiran are legally waters open to innocent passage by Israel-bound cargo.

The Berlin crisis involves several specific legal disputes. The principal legal questions concern rights of access under various agreements and under doctrines such as easement of necessity, and the Soviet claim of right to transfer its obligations under the Four-Power Pact to East Germany, as well as the legal effect of any such attempt to transfer on destruction of Western rights of access and of Soviet obligations generally.

Claims of expropriations of private property and of interference with international investment are intrinsically susceptible of judicial or arbitral determination. Boundary disputes are generally amenable to judicial or arbitral settlement. The International Court has already handled several such disputes. The boundary dispute between China and India, which has all the potentialities of a major source of tension, is in this category. Aerial incidents are also amenable to Court treatment, and several attempts to bring them into court have been made by the United States.[2]

It is clear, then, that many of the disputes threatening world peace today are in whole or in part the kind of disputes that judicial and arbitral processes could help settle peaceably. Sometimes, of course, there are mixed questions of law and diplomacy in a controversy. For example, the Berlin question is a mixture of disputes over present rights under existing agreements, which are judicable questions, and disputes over what changes should be made in any new regime that might be set up for Berlin and Germany, which questions are obviously political and diplomatic. But this does not mean that the judicial process would not make an important contribution. In such mixed questions, the judicial process could put to rest questions about existing legal rights, and could forestall arbitrary one-sided action in disregard of present agreements and rights, such as was threatened by Premier Khrushchev in the Berlin situation. While peace and order were thus being kept, any needed changes could be worked out by political means. In addition, and in a more general sense, the gradual strengthening of the judicial process in the world would serve to enhance the "habit of law" and the general atmosphere around the world of resort to peaceful settlement of disputes under law, as against impulsive and highhanded disregard of legal rights and procedures.

What are the building blocks of the law structure of peace? There is no mystery about them; they are the same as the familiar parts of any legal system worthy of the name:

1. A body of law that is accessible, up-to-date, and capable of deciding the disputes that cause tension in the world as it is today.

2. Machinery to apply that law—machinery which also is accessible, up-to-date, and adapted to settling the kind of disputes that today's world produces.

3. Acceptance of that body of law and the machinery by the persons affected—and here we must remind ourselves that most people of the world do not regard the present international law and court as *their* law and *their* court.

4. Compliance with the decisions of international tribunals once they are rendered.

---

[2] See cases Nos. 22, 23, 25, 28, 36, 40, and 44 of the International Court's General List, *ICJ Yearbook for 1958–1959*, pp. 70–84.

THE BODY OF LAW

The task divides itself into two parts: making existing law accessible, and going beyond existing law to create a kind of law that will be usable by, and acceptable to, not just Western Christendom but the more than one hundred nations that now must be reckoned with.

As to accessibility, we face at once a stark axiom. Nonaccessible law is nonexistent law. Philosophers may debate whether there is really a sound when a tree crashes in a wilderness and the sound is not heard by any living creature. But lawyers know that for all practical purposes there is really no law when the law cannot be found and therefore is never heard by any judge. The objective is clear enough: the materials and evidences of international law should be published, annotated, indexed, and cross-referenced to the same extent as domestic materials. But where is the Shepard's Citator of international law? the key-number system? the regional reporter system? the annotated statutes? the Federal Register? the L.R.A. and A.L.R. and C.J. and A.J. and W. & P. and U.S.C.A. and N.C.C.A.? Not to mention the endless list of loose-leaf publications that keep lawyers poor, publishers prosperous, and secretaries frantic.

This relatively unglamorous piece of work, which could keep hundreds of scholars and lawyers busy for years, may seem a far cry from prophetic visions of a world that lives under law—and yet how can a world live under law until it can first find out what the law is?

Here is a task in which universities, bar associations, publishers, and governments can join. Since a task of such magnitude must be spread over years, the best approach may be to begin with areas of law where accessibility of law would now have the most to contribute to relieving of tensions. A good example is the need to compile and annotate all the law bearing on international rivers—so that authoritative guidance will be at hand to aid in the settlement of the many festering disputes on rights in international waters.

But even if all existing international law were accessible, this would only be a beginning. International law must be adapted to today's world, both as to content and as to universality of acceptance.

As to both needs, great promise lies in the "general principles" clause of the Statute of the International Court. This Statute lists as one of the major sources of international law "the general principles of law recognized by civilized nations." Think of the vast treasures of legal principle to which this clause invites us. The clause tells us that if we look at the internal legal principles of the world's various systems and find a common thread of principle, that thread becomes elevated to the status of binding international law.

For an example of how this approach can enrich the content of world law and adapt it to contemporary needs, the first project undertaken at the Duke Law School's World Rule of Law Center may be cited.

The idea of this project had its origin in an interview I had with the late Premier of Iraq, Nuri As-Said. I was no sooner inside the door than Nuri said: "I want some jamming equipment." I muttered something about Americans believing in free communication, but he repeated, "I want jamming equipment. I've got to jam Nasser. Let me tell you why. A few weeks ago Cairo broadcast a news report that I, Nuri, with my own hands, had murdered four Moslem holy men in the holy temple itself. What happened? Rioting, bloodshed, killing all over the place. I need that jamming equipment."

He never got it. But one couldn't help reflecting: if this is to be a world of law, is this kind of thing legal? Isn't international use of words to cause serious harm generally illegal? Isn't incitement to murder in itself an offense under the general principles of civilized nations? Is the offense any less because it is international—or because it is electronic, and therefore superficially novel?

We are hoping, through this project, to find in international law (including "general principles" law) some contributions toward a legal solution of this modern problem. To the extent we find present law deficient, we hope to draw and offer a voluntary code of ethics for international broadcasting.

Another example of how the "general principles" approach can help lay the legal foundations for peace is our newest project at the Center, called "Sovereignty Under the Law."

It is all too easy to assume that in this age of aggressive nationalism, each sovereign of the world's hundred-odd nations is considered by his legal system to be the only source of law and therefore above the law. If this were so, obviously the chance for acceptance of a concept of real supranational law would be slim indeed.

However, if we look at the deepest wellsprings of legal tradition in all parts of the world we find almost universal agreement that the sovereign is not above the law—he is under the law. This is not surprising when it is remembered that most major legal systems have religious origins. In a Moslem country, for example, no temporal sovereign could say, "I am above the Law of Islam."

The most familiar illustration is an Old Testament story which we all know, but whose legal significance we may never have appreciated: the story of King Ahab and Naboth's vineyard, in I King 21.

All King Ahab wanted was to acquire a nearby vineyard belonging to Naboth. Ahab was king of Israel. Naboth was just a plain citizen. Ahab was quite reasonable— he was even willing to pay for the vineyard. But Naboth invoked the Jewish Law of Inheritance, which was above both king and commoner. "The Lord forbid it me, that I should give the inheritance of my fathers unto thee," said Naboth. What did Ahab say? Did he say, "I'm the sovereign around here. I make the laws"? He did not. "He laid him down upon his bed, and turned away his face, and would eat no bread."

At this point entered Jezebel. In one scornful phrase Jezebel summed up the attitude of all those before and since who have thought that the sovereign was above the law: "Dost thou now govern the kingdom of Israel?" Jezebel was what you might call an early type of legal positivist. And we all know what happened to Jezebel. The searing wrath of Jehovah, the appalling punishments visited upon one who would defy the law of Israel, leave no doubt where this particular legal tradition stands on the question of sovereignty under the law.

Our own tradition, of course, is epitomized in the historic colloquy between James I and Lord Coke. The king accused Coke of saying that the king was under the law, "which it were treason to affirm." Coke, in the teeth of this far from subtle threat, stood his ground and said: "The king ought not to be under any man, but under God and the law."

Of course, there is plenty of evidence of a contrary view in some times and places. But the interesting fact is that both the *oldest* traditions and the *newest* legal developments are on the side of placing sovereignty under the law. The progressive abandonment of sovereign immunity is one evidence of this, as is the formation of transnational communities like the European Economic Community. Of great significance also is the appearance in the most modern constitutions, such as those of France, the Netherlands, and West Germany, of provisions expressly stating that international law in the form of treaties takes priority over national laws.

What we hope to discover in our project is whether we can show the nations of the world, including the many newer nations, that on the strength of their own deepest legal traditions they can accept without strain or loss of national pride a legal obligation higher and broader than their own local jurisprudence.

In addition, the body of world law can be enriched and modernized by deliberate jobs of research that do the spadework necessary for treaties and codification in such areas as the interpretation and termination of treaties, harms to persons and property, protection of private international investment, the law of international rivers, disarmament, space law, sea law, and the Law of Antarctica. Exciting projects in such areas as these are already in progress at a number of schools and research centers. One thing is clear: there is plenty of work for everyone.

THE MACHINERY OF LAW

The International Court of Justice at The Hague is, in the words of its Statute, the "principal judicial organ" of the United Nations. In fact, it is the only one. Since the present Court plays such a key role in the future of world rule of law, it has become imperative for everyone to learn more about it. Lawyers agree that, by any familiar objective tests, this is a good court. It numbers among its fifteen judges some of the finest international lawyers in the world.

The Court is hampered by cumbersome procedures and practices—but these are not beyond remedy, and one fertile field of study will be proposals for their revision in the interests of efficiency. The Court's opinions are generally excellent in legal reasoning, scholarship, and judicial integrity. The Rule of Law Center at Duke University has a detailed two-year study of the Court in progress. We have just made an exhaustive check of the opinions and votes of all the judges in the Court's history. There is plenty of evidence, if any were needed, to show that these judges really think and decide as judges—and not as politicians, as some uninformed critics seem to fear they might.

The most direct proof is the fact that judges not infrequently have voted against their own countries when they thought their own country was wrong on the law. Indeed, they have done so in 24 out of 103 votes involving their countries. It might be of passing interest to note that in the recent *Interhandel* case the Soviet judge, Kojevnikov, not only voted in favor of the United States on three of five issues but wrote a separate opinion more strongly in favor of the United States position than that of the majority— while the United States judge voted against the United States on one of these issues.

What is needed, then, is not to displace the present World Court, but to make a thorough study of how it can best be supplemented with a complete world-wide system of regional or lower courts, arbitration tribunals, claims courts for private litigants, and—since there will always be disputes that are political

and nonjudicable in character—mediation and conciliation agencies. As matters now stand, it is as if you had to run to the Supreme Court in Washington to litigate every smashed fender or unpaid alimony claim.

ACCEPTANCE OF THE LAW

Now, say you have a workable body of law and efficient machinery to apply it— what good is all this if it is not accepted by the parties affected? The third component, then, must be acceptance of the system.

At once we encounter the unhappy fact that less than half the members of the United Nations have accepted the obligatory jurisdiction of the World Court, and some of these have interposed reservations so severe as to render their acceptance largely illusory. The problem of our own "self-judging" reservation, under which we reserve the right unilaterally to declare a controversy domestic and hence outside the Court's jurisdiction, is by now becoming quite well known. Its repeal was called for repeatedly by President Eisenhower and other top members of his administration, by President Kennedy and the present administration, by the American Bar Association, and by many state and local bar associations. It is not necessary by this time to elaborate upon the issues. There is one point, however, the matter of reciprocity, that has never been sufficiently stressed, and which is important because it should convince even those who are impatient with arguments based on legal ideals or world leadership toward peace, and who want to get down to cold-blooded national self-interest.

Such people assume that the function of the self-judging clause is to throw up a wall against possible loss to ourselves as defendants. In fact, the principal effect is to throw up a wall against all possible remedies for ourselves as plaintiffs. Let us remember Robert Frost's well-known lines:

Before I built a wall I'd ask to know
What I was walling in or walling out

We are not merely walling the other fellow out of court. We are walling ourselves out, whenever we have a valid claim. France learned this lesson the hard way in the Norwegian loans case. Norway had floated loans payable in gold in France, and later went off the gold standard. France, on behalf of the investors, brought a case against Norway insisting on payment in gold. France had a self-judging clause like ours. Norway did not. The Court held that, as a matter of reciprocity, Norway could exercise France's claimed reservation and call the transaction domestic. Result: financial loss in cold cash to citizens of France. Cause: a supposedly protective clause interposed by France. Sequel: France last year repealed her self-judging clause. Will we similarly have to subject innocent Americans to severe financial loss before we learn our lesson?

After all, we need the protection of law more than any other country. We have billions invested within other countries' boundaries, with the ever-possible danger of damage, confiscation, or discrimination. We have hundreds of thousands of tourists abroad, always in danger of personal injury and property damage. We have foreign bases, communications installations, transportation facilities, and economic and technical aid projects. The chances of our needing, as plaintiffs, the help of the Court are many times as great as the chances of our appearing as defendant. In an oblique commentary on the even-handedness of the law, Anatole France said, "The law forbids both the rich and the poor to sleep in the park." But the poor man most needs the park, just as we most need the Court. In both cases, it is the party with the greatest need that would profit most by repeal of the restrictive law.

The depositing of a new good-faith acceptance of the Court's jurisdiction is an important move in the over-all drive toward international rule of law, since it will show the world we mean business when we talk of rule of law.

Acceptance of a world legal system may come about in various ways in addition to general acceptance of the World Court's jurisdiction. Indeed, in the case of the Communist countries, the best hope for a beginning may be the possibility of entrusting particular matters to the Court, or a panel of it, or some other tribunal. Suppose, for example, we reach the day when a real disarmament treaty is found desirable by the Soviet Union. Obviously such a treaty must contain a procedure for settling disputes as to its interpretation—since otherwise the treaty would collapse in a welter of misunderstandings and recriminations within a matter of months. Only a judicial tribunal can ultimately do the dispute-settling job in the time available. All future treaties should contain a clause submitting disputes on interpretations to an international court, as we have done in our last sixteen commercial treaties. If we insist on this clause as a matter of regular policy, we can go a long way toward bringing important areas of potential conflict within the framework of peaceful legal settlement.

COMPLIANCE WITH THE LAW

The fourth component of the law structure of peace is compliance with the decisions of international tribunals once they are rendered. It is a curious fact that although many people worry more about this item than any other, in practice it may prove to be the least worrisome of all. History demonstrates that with very few exceptions the decisions of international tribunals have always been obeyed. This seems to indicate that, if we can bring nations to the point where they so far accept the body and machinery of the law that they allow a case to go to decision, by that time it becomes unthinkable to flout the judgment after it is rendered. This is a fact of immense significance as we set up our scale of priorities for action. It should help to reassure those people who fear that a world legal system will be ineffectual unless backed by a world army, navy, and air force.

If the record of compliance with international decisions is at least as good as that with domestic decisions, and perhaps better, why is it that some critics go about sneering at international law and saying that it is something no one pays any attention to? I think the answer lies in a failure to distinguish between decisions of tribunals and unilateral assertions of legal rights. We allege that Country X has repeatedly broken treaties. We conclude that Country X is lawless and has no respect for international law. But does Country X admit this? Certainly not. It will give you some formula to show that it did not really break the treaty, but merely "interpreted" it. We may be positive we are right. But as long as matters are in this posture, it is impossible to say with impartiality and finality that Country X has broken international law. But let the case go to Court, let the law be applied to the particular facts—and then, when the rights and wrongs have been authoritatively settled, we shall have an unassailable test of the degree of compliance with law.

The record of compliance judged on this basis, then, is one reason why many feel that we can and should build up the structure of law without waiting for the day to come, if it ever comes, when some kind of global political authority comparable to national governments will stand behind the decisions of international judicial tribunals. Mean-while, of course, we should study every possible means of strengthening measures short of force to ensure compliance, including public opinion, multilateral treaties, and diplomatic and economic sanctions.

The specific job of building the law structure of peace may seem to be a task of almost insuperable difficulty. But, difficult or not, we must try. Rousseau, in his book on education called *Emile*, wrote: "The best way to teach Emile not to lean out of the window is to let him fall out. Unfortunately, the defect of this system is that the pupil may not survive to profit by his experience." The world has been learning about international relations for centuries by a process of periodically falling out the window. The injuries have been severe, but never quite fatal. But we all know that one more fall will be our last. We must profit by our experience, for we will not be given another chance.

There is one factor that was never present before. The shadow of the H-bomb is over us all. Perhaps the mutual realization of capacity for mutual annihilation will telescope history and enable us to achieve a degree of progress in decades that in other times might have taken centuries.

Chapter 9

CONFLICT MANAGEMENT IN NORMATIVE SYSTEMS

When legitimate authorities make decisions that deprive or punish certain parties, steps must be taken to ensure that these parties abide by the unfavorable decisions and do not upset the normative system. These steps are rich and complex and central to the understanding of social systems and socialization processes. In the first selection Gamson offers a general overview of the means system authorities may use to manage potential discontent of those under them. In the second paper Goffman continues this theme with a special emphasis on how an injured person may be brought to accept his injury and to cooperate in putting the best possible face on it. The culmination of this process is reached in the socialization processes discussed by Gold, whereby the individual is taught to direct his frustration and aggression against himself rather than against external agents in the system. As Gold demonstrates, the forces that produce this result are first brought into play in the early childhood training of the person by his parents—the first normative authorities he encounters.

THE MANAGEMENT OF DISCONTENT

W. A. Gamson

In exploring influence, we have taken the perspective of potential partisans affecting the choices of authorities. From the standpoint of authorities, another set of questions emerges. By their very nature, many choices will affect potential partisan groups in different ways. Authorities will inevitably satisfy some groups more than others. Only rarely will their choices be free of some element of conflict, that is, only rarely will there exist an alternative that is the first choice of all groups. This basic fact of conflict confronts authorities with the problem of managing discontent and containing influence.

From their perspective, the basic question is "how does one prevent those potential partisans who are injured or neglected by political decisions from trying to change the nature of the decisions, the authorities, or the political system within which decisions are made?" Authorities, I assume, wish to remain free from the pressure of external limits, free of influence attempts which more or less successfully tie their hands. If this

Source: W. A. Gamson, "The Management of Discontent," in W. A. Gamson, *Power and Discontent* (Homewood, Illinois: Dorsey, 1968), ch. 6, pp. 111–143. Copyright 1968 by W. A. Gamson and reprinted by permission.

sounds cynical, it need not be. For example, Arthur M. Schlesinger, Jr. (1965, p. 120) writes of the interregnum period following Kennedy's election as a test of the President-elect's "executive instincts and, in particular, of his skill in defending his personal authority against people striving, always for the best of motives, to contract his scope for choice."

The authorities in question may be operating to the best of their ability to satisfy the needs of as many potential partisans as possible. They may operate as justly as they possibly can in situations involving conflicts of interest. They may conscientiously seek information from potential partisans so that they can meet these objectives. But, in the end, such authorities no less than self-interested or tyrannical ones, experience attempts to influence them as a limitation on their freedom of action. There are exceptions to this generalization—for example, in situations in which authorities may wish to stimulate pressure from one source to free themselves from some opposing source. But even this exception is governed by the desire to contain influence and thus remain free of its limits.

Perhaps it would be more accurate to say that authorities *qua* authorities desire limitations on the ability of potential partisans to exercise influence. Individuals occupying positions of authority may frequently desire great personal discretion in how they may use this authority because such discretion allows them to use their authority as a resource. Even if such discretion invites influence from others, at the same time it enhances their ability to influence others. Thus, those in authority may welcome freedom from public surveillance and accountability which act as control devices on both potential partisans and themselves. Such desires are an outgrowth of their potential partisan role, not their authority role. From the standpoint of that collectivity for which they serve as agent, the increased opportunity for influence creates control problems; there is less guarantee in such situations that those with authority will function as agents instead of as independent operators. The demands of flexibility and adequate task performance may require that

authorities be given some leeway, but the more that considerations of control are relevant, the more such leeway will be reduced.

RESPONSES TO INFLUENCE PRESSURE

Potential partisans who are discontented with the choices of authorities must be handled in some fashion. The most basic distinction in how such discontent may be handled is between some modification of the content of the decision and some effort to control the potential partisan. The former response deals with the object of discontent by modifying the outcome in some way; the latter deals with the source of the pressure. These responses to discontent have something in common.[1] Both aim at removing the pressure that potential partisans are likely to put on authorities, one by yielding ground and the other by directing counterinfluence.

Why call such counterinfluence social control instead of simply encompassing it under the previous discussion of influence? The answer is that the agents of such counterinfluence are acting *as agents of the social system*. We separate their actions in such a role from their actions in pursuit of personal values and interests in which they may use resources to affect the decisions of others. When they act upon potential partisans in some manner to prevent or lessen the likelihood of influence over an area in which they make binding decisions, they are acting in the role of authorities.

ALTERING THE OUTCOME OF DECISIONS

The distinction has been made between the efficiency of the political system in achiev-

---

[1] This argument is developed in Z. Gamson (1964).

ing collective goals and its bias in handling conflicts of interest. Potential partisans may be unhappy on either account. Those who are dissatisfied with the efficiency of the system feel that more effective leadership or institutions are needed. Government may be criticized as "wasteful" or "inefficient." Such dissatisfaction assumes a basic consensus within which decisions are made.

Discontent about the equity of the political system is more difficult to deal with because conflict is inherent in the nature of some decisions. It is impossible in such cases, even if they have some collective aspects, to meet the desires and interests of all potential partisans. When the problem is one of ineffective leadership on collective goals, then by "wiser" or "better" choices, the discontent of potential partisans can be assuaged. When it involves the handling of conflicts, such notions as "better" invariably raise the question, "better for whom?"

Altering the outcome of decisions is one approach to the problem of discontent. The collective aspects of decisions present few problems for authorities that cannot be met by simply choosing different alternatives. As members of the same collectivity as the partisans, the authorities will presumably be easily susceptible to persuasion or education since the partisans and the authorities will benefit by the same alternative.

Discontent over the handling of conflict can also be treated by outcome modification although this has the effect of redistributing discontent rather than alleviating it. Nevertheless, there may be many reasons why authorities would prefer to see some groups more contented than others. They may share the values and interests of one group and prefer to satisfy them for that reason. Or, some may have more resources or access than others and they may relieve pressure by yielding ground to the most powerful among the potential partisans. *The greater the inverse relation between the amount of resources controlled and the amount of discontent among potential partisans, the freer the authorities are from influence.* In short, they are most free when those with the most discontent have the least ability to influence.

To contain influence, outcome modification will move in this direction.

Finally, outcome modification may be a way of undercutting the mobilization of a partisan group which is in the process of converting dissatisfaction into a force for influence. By giving a little at the right time, authorities may prevent later, more important outcome modifications. "An astute set of authorities," Easton (1965, p. 408) suggests, "in Machiavellian fashion, often meets just enough [demands], at least so as to still any critical accumulation of discontent. In the language of practical politics, this involves offering sops or conciliatory outputs at just the right moment to head off any brewing storm of dissatisfactions." Social movements may falter on partial success, winning small victories which, while leaving basic dissatisfactions untouched, hamper the members in their ability to mobilize resources for further influence.

SOCIAL CONTROL

The alternative to outcome modification is social control. If such control is successful, then there will be little influence and, hence, no need for outcome modification. The authorities will maximize their room for maneuverability and such maneuverability has three virtues.

1. It allows the incumbent authority to exercise his own personal preference. He is free to act as he pleases and to do what he thinks best, within the limits of his role but without the additional limits imposed by influence.

2. If he has no particular preferences, the freedom from influence on a given issue enables him to use his authority as a resource to influence other decisions on which he has a partisan interest. In other words, successful social control increases the resources of authorities by allowing them discretion in the areas in which they exercise authority; such freedom allows them to use their authority as an inducement or constraint on other

authorities whom they would influence. They could not use their authority as a resource if their hands were tied by pressure from partisans just as they would be similarly hampered by structural limitations on their freedom to use their authority.

3. Effective social control increases slack resources. This means that influence is cheaper. "Slack resources provide the political entrepreneur with his dazzling opportunity, . . ." Dahl writes (1961, p. 309). He can influence at bargain rates when the competition has been removed by effective social control.

The tendency for outcome modification and social control to be competing alternatives is nicely illustrated in a study of the impact of students on the operation of an experimental college (Z. Gamson, 1966). Within the college, two faculty subdivisions existed with differing orientations toward students, described by the author as "utilitarian" and "normative." The utilitarian orientation emphasized cognitive effects on students, was less concerned about developing high student commitment to the college and encouraged faculty to maintain some distance from students. The normative orientation emphasized reaching students personally as well as intellectually, encouraged high student commitment and promoted close, egalitarian relationships with students. The author discovered an apparent paradox—those groups within the faculty with the most intense and diffuse concern with students were less responsive to particular student demands than those with a more specific and contractual relationship.

The paradox, of course, was only apparent. While each social control orientation had its own characteristic strains, for a variety of reasons the utilitarian orientation was less successful in forestalling pressures for modification of curriculum decisions. As a result, the pressures for change were greater and the resultant modifications were more frequent and radical in the division with the utilitarian orientation. The normative orientation, while it produced problems of a different sort, proved a stronger fortress against pressures for curriculum change. Thus, student influence was greater where student-faculty relationships were more distant because the closer relationship in one case produced more potent social control and less outcome modification.

TYPES OF SOCIAL CONTROL

There are three general ways in which authorities can contain the influence of potential partisans at its source. They can (1) regulate the access of potential partisans to resources and their ability to bring these resources to bear on decision makers, (2) they can affect the situation of potential partisans by making rewards or punishments contingent on attempts at influence, or (3) they can change the desire of potential partisans to influence by altering their attitudes toward political objects.

INSULATION

An extremely important set of controls operates by giving potential partisans differential access to authorities and to positions which involve the control of resources that can be brought to bear on authorities. Such selectivity operates at two points—entry and exit.

Selective entry. Not all social organizations can control who is let in but many exercise considerable selectivity. A society cannot, of course, control the characteristics of the infants born into it—at least not until the Brave New World arrives. This absence of selectivity makes the control problems more severe than those encountered by an organization that can control entry.

However, most societies do exercise control over entry through immigration. Normally, they do not ask others for their tired and poor and huddled masses yearning to be free. Once the demand for large quantities of unskilled labor has been met, they are more likely to request doctors and engineers and huddled intellectuals yearning to be rich. Those who are presumed to offer particularly acute control problems are not welcomed. This includes both those who are likely to commit a variety of individual acts of deviance and those who are likely to organize themselves or others into groups that threaten the existing social order. Societies, like other forms of social organization, try to simplify their subsequent control problems by refusing entry to those elements most likely to aggravate such problems.

Most complex organizations are able to exercise some degree of selectivity in entry although there is wide variability in this regard. A corporation about to hire an executive is interested in a wide variety of characteristics not directly relevant to job performance. These other characteristics are frequently relevant to control problems. Those who are highly independent or erratic or in other ways seem likely to use the resources of their position in a free wheeling manner are generally regarded with caution. Of course, extraordinary ability or an extraordinary situation may convince an organization that it ought to take risks, but this does involve the assumption of greater problems of subsequent control. In short, I am not asserting that the reduction of control problems alone determines who will be allowed access to important positions, but such considerations are one factor and the problems are minimized by admitting only orthodox people.

Organizations which have little control over whom they let in are confronted with more control problems than those organizations which can select. Prisons, state mental hospitals, public schools and other organizations that have large numbers of their members determined for them by other organizations in their environment have control problems which private mental hospitals and private schools do not have. State universities should, by the same token, have greater control problems than private colleges which exercise high selectivity.

An important aspect of selective entry is *self-selection*. Many voluntary organizations reduce their control problems inadvertently by attracting as members those who will "fit well" and will offer few control problems and by repelling those who are likely to be discontented. In such cases, selective entry occurs not by the organization refusing admittance to potentially difficult individuals but by such individuals removing themselves by not seeking entry.

Self-selection is influenced by the organization's image. *An organization's efforts to project an image which will differentiate it from others can be viewed as a social control device.* The manipulation of organizational image has other purposes as well, the major one of which is to increase the organization's attractiveness, thereby increasing its ability to compete for desirable members, clients, or customers. But the effects of selectivity can be distinguished from the effects of increased attractiveness. In the latter case, we would expect there to be a tendency for members of *all* subgroups in the organization's environment to show approximately the same degree of increase in numbers seeking entry.[2]

However, if the image is serving a function of differentiation rather than increased attraction, this will not be so. Instead, the numbers seeking entry will increase in some groups while decreasing in others, i.e., while the organization is becoming more attractive to some, it is becoming less attractive to others. When an organization's image serves such a process of differentiation we may think of it as serving a social control function; it is increasing selective entry through a process of self-selection among potential members.

Entry is not an all or nothing state. Once in, members may have differential access to resources and communication opportunities. All members of the House of Represen-

---

2 This does not imply that the organization is equally attractive to all subgroups but only that there is a relative increase in attractiveness across the board. For example, Eisenhower received a relatively high Republican voting percentage from *both* businessmen and workers but the absolute percentage of each group that voted for him was quite disparate.

tatives cannot be members of the Rules Committee or of other committees which command large amounts of resources. One may regard most social systems as possessing a series of entry points each of which offers control opportunities by denying further access to certain categories of potential partisans. In fact, if the population arriving at each gate were sufficiently endowed with the "right" kind of individuals and the process of selection were infallible and produced no errors, there would be no need for any other kind of control. Neither of the conditions above is usually met so that other forms of control must come into play.

Besides denying some potential partisans access to positions that control resources, they may also be denied access to resources in other ways. They may be prevented from acquiring sufficient skill and knowledge for access. Daniel Lerner, for example, describes the Ottoman Imperium as "not merely a variety of illiterate populations but an anti-literate elite, who regulated the daily round of public life by maintaining exclusive control over key points of contact between individuals and their larger environment" (1958, p. 113). A communication system which carried the news orally from the Ottoman center to scattered villages served "as an administrative technique of social control, not as an instrument for shaping enlightened public opinion." Preventing the acquisition of communication skills in a population of potential partisans with serious discontent is an aid in controlling such a population. Keeping such a population physically separated so that no sense of common interest or solidarity can easily develop may also be regarded as a way of preventing potential partisans from organizing and mobilizing potential resources for influence.

Subsequently, the lack of requisite skill and training may serve to justify the denial of access should such disadvantaged groups press for it. Members of such a group might be advised that giving them access in the absence of "proper qualifications" constitutes preferential treatment. Thus, the selective entry may be justified on highly legitimate and widely accepted criteria and this control

device may be preserved from becoming the target of pressure *itself*.

Selective exit. Most of the above discussion of selective entry is applicable to selective exit as well. There are some differences worth noting. While some social organizations have small control over whom they let in as members, all have means of removing access. Societies may imprison, exile, or put to death members that prove too troublesome to be handled by other control techniques. Even prisons and state mental hospitals isolate some members from the rest; public schools can expel hard-core control problem students.

There is probably some tendency for selectivity in entry and exit to be inversely correlated. *Those organizations which exercise a great deal of control at entry should be less likely to use expulsion as a control device than those organizations which have little control over who gets in.* If they use care in selection and a "low-risk" policy of entry, they can afford to be more lenient in subsequent actions, and should need to rely less on such drastic measures as expulsion. Those with little control at the point of entry are likely to have a higher frequency of difficult cases that cannot be handled by other control techniques.

Examples of insulation through exit devices are numerous and for the most part obvious. A particularly striking case occurred in the winter following the U.S. military intervention in the Dominican Republic. The provisional government, buffeted by the continuing struggle among powerful partisan groups, attempted to relieve the pressure by requesting the voluntary exile of a number of army officers who were leaders of these groups. The unusual and striking thing in this instance is that the officers were themselves rivals and political enemies; thus, the meaning of the act as an attempt to contain influence is unusually clear. More typically, such actions are aimed at removing influence from a particular source and are not as readily recognizable as an act of social control.

The removal of access as a social control device is not without its own set of problems. Goffman (1964) has helped call attention to the fact that the use of such devices generates its own necessity for control. The removal of access tends to be regarded by the individuals involved as a mark of failure or repression and is consequently resented. This resentment may lead to action on the part of the victim. In the confidence game example from which Goffman draws his terminology, the "mark" may decide to complain to the police or "squawk." In our more drab terminology, the person who has been removed from access may translate his resentment into influence unless it is dealt with in some way. The devices which a social system uses to help a victim accept his failure quietly are now generally called, following Goffman's provocative article, "cooling-out mechanisms." We should expect any organization which makes widespread use of the removal of access as a control device to employ such mechanisms. For example, the device of "kicking upstairs" involves the removal from access to a position which commands significant resources while assuaging the resultant discontent by an accretion in status. Compulsory retirement at a given age is another device which removes access without creating the danger that the victim will squawk. As with discrimination in entry, discrimination in exit is most effective when it can be accomplished using accepted, universalistic criteria.

SANCTIONS

Social organizations maintain systems of sanctions to reward the "responsible" and to punish the "irresponsible" or "deviant." If these words carry with them the connotation of desirability and undesirability, it is because we are accustomed to assuming a social control perspective. Whether being responsible is desirable depends on the nature of the social organization to which one is being responsible. Adolph Eichmann was clearly acting responsibly from the standpoint of Hitler's Germany. There may be a conflict between loyalty to one's friends, constituents, or one's personal values and one's responsibility as agent of the social system. A person's loyalties and convictions may impel him to use the resources of his position in an attempt to bring about decisions that he believes are desirable. But in using his authority as a resource, an individual is acting in the role of potential partisan rather than authority and issues of control are created thereby.

Sanctions will follow what is considered to be the misuse of authority. The limits which these sanctions impose on freedom of action may not be desired by those who exercise authority for it places limits on their ability to influence. Such sanctions act as a control on both potential partisans and authorities who would be potential partisans at other times. Thus, partisans are typically prevented from openly bribing officials and penalties exist both for attempting and for accepting such illicit influence. Specified channels for "proper" influence are frequently provided—for example, petitioning or testifying at open hearings. Such channels contain a double restriction. On the one hand, they restrict the use of resources by potential partisans by subjecting their influence attempts to public surveillance and accountability. On the other hand, they restrict the opportunity of the target of influence to use his authority as a resource which he can exchange in some transaction with potential partisans. From the standpoint of both parties, ex parte presentations may be tempting, allowing as they do for the freer use of reciprocal influence. From a social control perspective, such off-the-record contacts between potential partisans and authorities offer less assurance that the latter are operating as agents of the social system rather than exercising personal influence.

The bestowal and withdrawal of effective authority is an important sanction. Losing effective authority over an area is a double loss: it means that the loser now must spend resources to influence decisions where formerly he could simply exercise authority. Moreover, he has lost an important resource which he previously was able to use in influencing the decisions of other authorities. He is, thus, put in a position in which he has both lost resources and at the same time needs them more. The threat of withdrawing effective authority is, for these reasons, an important form of control on the "abuse" of such authority.

Social structural and normative limits exist on every authority which circumscribe his ability to use his powers as a resource and, hence, operate as a social control. If the limits are sufficiently great and remove from him any discretion in how he may use his authority, then he has no resource at all stemming from his position. Usually, he is left some area of discretion bounded by some set of limits, the violation of which will result in sanctions. If selection mechanisms have failed to prevent an "irresponsible" person from gaining access to resources, sanctions are an additional control that may keep him in line. If he is unmoved by such sanctions, he may be removed from his position. Short of removal, there are a wide variety of sanctions available. One may be passed over for promotion, denied salary increases, given less helpful and prestigeful facilities, and so forth. Daily life can be made exceedingly unpleasant by the noncooperation of associates on whom one is dependent for the performance of one's job. And the threat that one will not be given any benefit of the doubt in the decisions of others can be a powerful deterrent.

Social control is *not* the only consideration in the distribution of inducements and constraints in a social system. Individuals may be rewarded for outstanding performance or for being the son of the company president; they may be punished for their religion or their incompetence. Control is simply one aspect and in many cases may be far from the dominant one. It should be emphasized that this discussion is not intended as a complete explanation of why individuals are given access to resources or are rewarded; rather, it is an attempt to describe the manner in which such things can be and are used for social control, in addition to whatever other uses they may have.

Promotion within an organization has elements of both insulation and sanctions. It is likely to mean some change in access to resources while at the same time it contains certain rewards. The distinction here is an analytic one which is difficult to make in practice. A man who has just been made president of a major corporation now has authority over areas which affect large numbers of people in important ways. Furthermore, he is likely to have wide latitude in the use of this authority. Thus he has gained access to important new resources. On the other hand, there are many things which are personally rewarding to him in the promotion—the greater status, the greater pay, the challenge and difficulty of the job, and the additional resources which he has gained. To the extent that control elements are relevant to his promotion, they operate in a dual fashion. Perhaps he is allowed access to the new resources because he appears more likely than someone else of equal ability and qualifications to act strictly as an agent of the organization. He is given the rewards of the new position because as vice president of the company he has, even at some personal sacrifice, demonstrated his willingness to act as agent of the organization. In this case, access and sanctions amount to essentially the same thing and the distinction is artificial; however, in many other cases, the two processes of control are quite separate and distinguishing them alerts one to different features of the organization.

PERSUASION

Persuasion attempts to control the desire rather than the ability to influence. Potential partisans may be persuaded in a variety of ways either that their interest is well served by political decisions or, if not served on a particular occasion, that the procedures by which decisions are made serve their larger interest. Such persuasion may involve emphasizing the collective aspects of decisions, making those aspects which involve conflict appear less salient or important. Thus, potential partisans may be persuaded that the authorities are operating in the interests of the larger collectivity to which both parties belong even if some *relative* disadvantage is involved for their own subgroup. If potential partisans are convinced that the overall system of decision making is unbiased, they will be more willing to accept temporary setbacks in the belief that "things will even out in the long run."

There is an interesting variety of words used to describe this social control technique—some of them highly pejorative and others complimentary. The approving words include education, persuasion, therapy, rehabilitation, and, perhaps more neutrally, socialization. The disapproving words include indoctrination, manipulation, propaganda, and "brainwashing." The choice of words is merely a reflection of the speaker's attitude toward the social system and its agents. If one believes the authorities are faithful agents of a social system which is accorded legitimacy, then they are "socializing" potential partisans when they exercise social control. If one sides with the potential partisans and identifies with their grievances against the authorities, then this latter group is using "manipulation" as a form of control. The behavioral referent, of course, may be identical in both cases; the choice of word reflects two different perspectives on the same relation.

As in the earlier chapters on influence, the word persuasion is used in the broadest possible sense to include any technique which controls the orientation of the potential partisan *without* altering his situation by adding advantages or disadvantages. Some examples may help to make this breadth clear. The withholding of information from potential partisans about adverse effects of decisions is a use of persuasion as a means of social control. The withholding of information on fallout from atomic tests in Nevada during the period prior to the nuclear test-ban treaty was apparently done to avoid increasing public pressure for the cessation of such tests. Similarly, almost all social systems try to keep knowledge of their failures from circulating lest it generate pressure for change. Potential partisans who acquire such information (perhaps from allies among the authorities) publicize it for exactly the opposite reason—in the hope that it will mobilize their constituency to action. The selective withhold-

ing of information, then, is a technique of social control through persuasion.

Surrounding authorities with trappings of omniscience is another case of this control technique. If the authorities are viewed as distant, awe-inspiring figures possessed of tremendous intelligence and prescience plus access to privileged information that is essential for forming judgments, then the potential partisan may hesitate to challenge a decision even when he feels adversely affected by it.

There is, however, a contrasting technique which *minimizes* social distance between potential partisans and authorities. By personal contact and the "humanization" of authorities, potential partisans may be encouraged to identify with them; this identification, in turn, produces a trust which makes influence appear less necessary. If the people making the decisions are just like me, then I need not bother to influence them; they may be trusted to carry out my wishes in the absence of influence.

Judged strictly as a social control device, awe offers certain protections that the humanization of authority does not. Minimizing the distance between authorities and potential partisans may encourage the development of trust but it also tends to increase access and allow greater opportunities for influence. The control gained by reducing the desire for influence may be offset by the control lost in increasing the capability of influence. Oracular authorities offer no such danger and usually require a minimum of access.

DOING ONE'S DUTY

A particularly important use of persuasion as a source of control involves the activation of commitments or obligations to the social system. Potential partisans can be persuaded to refrain from trying to change or subvert those decisions that have unpleasant consequences for them by convincing them that they have a "duty" to honor such decisions. The importance of legitimacy for a political system comes from its connection with this control technique. If legitimacy is high, then there is a high potential for activating commitments and other, more costly forms of control may be avoided. For example, if "patriotism" and "the duty to serve one's country" are sufficiently strong, then there is no need for conscription; a voluntary army can be counted on. However, if legitimacy is weak and alienation toward the political system is prevalent, then the call to duty may sound hollow.

Not everyone is as committed to duty as the young hero of *The Pirates of Penzance* who insists on fulfilling his obligation to the pirates to whom he was mistakenly bound in childhood in spite of his strenuous disapproval of their profession. Still, a wide variety of unpleasant commitments may be accepted with good grace when there is a surplus of political trust. A good illustration of the dependence on such trust may be found in the relatively sudden increase in opposition to the Selective Service System. Students who were able to reach graduate school were, for many years, given *de facto* exemptions from compulsory service. As long as American foreign policy was generally supported, the unequal sacrifices demanded from different groups in the society did not become an issue. However, with the erosion of confidence stemming from American policy in Vietnam, not only the bases of deferment but conscription itself has been seriously challenged. In World War II, appeals to duty activated many to enlist voluntarily and those who didn't were quiet about it. During the Vietnam War, the threat of severe sanctions has not deterred open and organized opposition to the draft. In fact, some student groups have themselves attempted to activate commitments to "higher" values by urging the duty *not* to serve. The price authorities pay for losing political confidence is a loss in their ability to activate commitments and the necessity of relying on more costly types of social control.

The activation of commitments, then, depends on the existence of political trust but it becomes an even more powerful control when it is mediated by face-to-face interaction. This point is best demonstrated by a series of social psychological experiments going back to the early 1940's. These experiments, particularly the later ones in the series, have shocked and outraged many people and have stimulated a vigorous debate among social psychologists on the proper ethics in experimenting with human subjects. But whether or not such experiments *should* have been conducted, the fact is that they *have* been and their results are both surprising and instructive.

Jerome Frank (1944) designed a series of experiments aimed at exploring the conditions under which subjects would refuse to continue disagreeable or nonsensical tasks. Under some conditions, the experimenter simply told the subject what he was expected to do and this was sufficient to ensure performance. For example, some subjects were asked to perform the task of balancing a marble on a small steel ball; almost all of them continued to pursue this manifestly impossible task for a full hour with no overt resistance in spite of inward annoyance. Frank quotes one subject: "I was griped all the way through . . . [but] I promised a man I'd help him out and I couldn't see any reason for backing down on my word." In another variation, Frank attempted to get subjects to eat unsalted soda crackers. When they were told that the experiment required them to eat 12 crackers, the subjects all ate them without argument or protest.

However, in another condition, the situation was translated from one of social control to one of influence. Subjects were told, "This is an experiment in persuasion. I am going to try to make you eat 12 crackers in the first row on the tray. Whether you eat them or not is entirely up to you and doesn't affect the experiment one way or the other. But if you resist, I shall try to make you eat them anyway." Under such instructions, considerable resistance was produced and while verbal pressure from the experimenter succeeded in making several subjects eat a few more crackers, less than a third ate all 12 crackers. As an influence situation, the eating of crackers became a test of wills; as a social control situation, it simply involved the activation of the commitments involved in agreeing to be an experimental subject and no resistance was encountered.

At the point of refusal in the influence variation, the experimenter attempted to introduce legitimacy, by saying, "The experiment requires that you eat one more cracker and that will be enough," or "If you eat just one more cracker, that will be enough." These instructions were successful in getting two thirds of the recalcitrant subjects to take one more cracker. Eating the final cracker was seen as a way of terminating what had become an embarrassing and extremely awkward situation.[3]

Some other experiments show this form of social control even more dramatically. Pepitone and Wallace (1955) asked subjects to sort the contents of a waste basket which contained cigar butts, soiled paper, dirty rags, broken sticks, pieces of glass, damp kleenex tissue, sodden purina chow, and other disgusting debris. The results were essentially the same in a variety of experimental conditions— the subjects snickered and laughed, and then got down to work and sorted the garbage with no strong protestations.

Martin Orne and his associates (1962; 1965) stumbled onto similar results in pursuing research on hypnosis. Orne sought a task which an unhypnotized subject would break off but not because of pain or exhaustion; that is, the task needed to be so boring and meaningless that a normal subject would simply refuse to do it after awhile. He found it extremely difficult to design such a task because of the powerful social control operating in face-to-face interaction with an experimenter who is accorded legitimacy. In one experiment, Orne gave the subjects a huge stack of 2,000 sheets of simple additions, each sheet containing 224 such additions. The simple instruction of "Continue to work; I will return eventually," was sufficient to get

them to work for many hours with little decrement in performance. It was necessary for the weary experimenter to break off the task for the even wearier subject might have complied indefinitely. Even the addition of instructions to tear each sheet up into 32 pieces and to throw them away upon completion did not lead to significant resistance. When work stoppage occurred, the return of the experimenter to the room with instructions to continue was sufficient to ensure more work for additional hours.

Thwarted in this attempt to produce a breakdown of social control, Orne moved to more extreme tasks. Is the degree of control in hypnosis, Orne asked, actually any greater than the degree of control which an experimenter exercises over a normal waking subject when this subject accepts the legitimacy of the experimental situation? To test this, Orne and Evans (1965) used a series of tasks which were extremely disagreeable, and potentially harmful to either the subject himself or to others. The experiment called for a special apparatus—a box with a glass screen which could be slid into place and removed but which, because of the lighting and the type of glass, was impossible to see. Hypnotized subjects were compared with a group of unhypnotized subjects who were instructed to pretend they were hypnotized and with other control groups of normal waking subjects.

Initially, subjects were asked to pick up a few harmless objects from the box—with the glass screen not in place, of course. Then, a harmless lizard was placed in the box and subjects were told to pick it up, followed by similar instructions for a 14-inch harmless green snake and a 14-inch venomous black snake, capable of inflicting a mortal wound. However, before the last task and unknown to the subject, the invisible glass screen was silently lowered into place so that subjects who attempted to comply would get only bruised knuckles instead of snake bite.

At this point, the box was removed and the subject watched the experimenter pour concentrated nitric acid into a small shallow beaker. The experimenter dropped a coin into the acid and allowed the subject to watch

---

[3] For a discussion of the particular role of embarrassment in such experiments and an ingenious experimental demonstration and theoretical discussion of how it operates in social influence situations, see Modigliani (1966).

it dissolve for approximately a minute. He then asked the subject to remove the coin with his bare hand and to plunge both coin and hand into a nearby basin of soapy, lukewarm water. If the subject complied (or if he did not comply, while he was diverted in some fashion), the beaker with acid was switched with one that appeared identical but contained a harmless solution. The experimenter then instructed the subject to throw the acid in the face of the lab assistant who had been helping with various aspects of the experiment. This completed the experiment proper and was followed by a fairly extensive postexperimental interview.

The results show a good deal of compliance with the experimenter's requests in all conditions. Of the six hypnotized subjects, five complied with all requests; the sixth, a young lady, became hysterical at the sight of the harmless lizard in the beginning and the other tasks were not used. All six of the subjects who were simulating hypnosis complied fully, carrying out all of the experimenter's requests although showing reluctance at a number of points. Of a group of six control subjects who were told that they were normal controls for a hypnosis experiment, five performed the acid tasks and three of the six attempted to pick up the venomous snake.

The latest and most significant work in this genre is that of Stanley Milgram (1963; 1964; 1965). Milgram focused his work on destructive obedience—obedience to demands which injure others. The basic experiment involves a naïve subject who administers what he believes are extremely severe electric shocks to another "subject" who is in fact a confederate of the experimenter. The subject believes that he is participating in an experiment which involves the effect of punishment on learning. He is instructed to raise the shock level administered after each error which the victim makes in a learning task involving the pairing of words. The simulated generator which the subject uses is extremely convincing; it is marked with voltage designations from 15 to 450 which are accompanied by verbal designations of slight shock, moderate shock, strong shock, very strong

shock, intense shock, extreme intensity shock, Danger: severe shock, and two more positions ominously marked XXX. When the naïve subject pulls the generator switch, the generator lights and buzzes but, unknown to him, no shock is actually transmitted.

In Milgram's original experiment, the victim-confederate was in an adjacent room providing answers by pushing buttons. At the 300-volt level and again at the 315-volt level, he was instructed to pound on the wall and, thereafter, provide no more answers. Subjects typically turned to the experimenter at that point who advised them to treat no response as an incorrect response and to proceed with the shock schedule. If the subject asked about injury to the victim, the experimenter replied, "Although the shocks can be extremely painful, they cause no permanent tissue damage."

The results of this experiment are startling. Of the 40 subjects, all proceed past the strong and very strong shock readings and none breaks off before reaching 300 volts. Even more startling, 26 of the 40 reach the maximum level of 450 volts—the XXX category. Such behavior is clearly not sadism. Subjects are under considerable stress and manifest it by sweating, stuttering, uncontrollable laughing fits, trembling, and other manifestations of extreme tension. Milgram quotes one observer:

> I observed a mature and initially poised businessman enter the laboratory smiling and confident. Within 20 minutes, he was reduced to a twitching, stuttering wreck who was rapidly approaching a point of nervous collapse. He constantly pulled on his earlobe and twisted his hands. At one point, he pushed his fist into his forehead and muttered "Oh, God. Let's stop it." And yet he continued to respond to every word of the experimenter and obeyed to the end (Milgram, 1963, p. 377).

Why do subjects continue to honor a presumed obligation to an experimenter whom they do not know, to accomplish goals which are at best vague and obscure to them and which at the same time involve virtually gratuitous injury to another human being whom they have no reason to dislike? Variations of the experiment point to the fact that the strength of the obligation is heavily influenced by the physical presence of the experimenter. In one condition with 40 fresh subjects, the experimenter leaves after presenting the initial instructions and gives subsequent orders over the telephone. Where 26 of 40 were fully obedient when the experimenter was present, only 9 of the 40 subjects were fully obedient when the orders were conveyed over the phone. In a number of cases, the subject lied to the experimenter, saying that he was raising the shock level when he was in fact using the lowest level on the board. If the experimenter appeared in person after the subject refused over the telephone, he was sometimes able to reactivate compliance with the simple assertion, "The experiment requires that you continue."

Similarly, when the victim is brought into the same room with the subject, the number of obedient subjects goes down. The conflict becomes more intense for the subject with the experimenter looking at him and clearly expecting him to continue, while the victim very visibly indicates his pain and his desire to participate no longer. Such results suggest that the blindfolding of a condemned prisoner may have another meaning than the one usually attributed to it. It is not so much to protect the victim's feelings that a blindfold is needed but rather to protect the executioner from his surveillance.

The basic mechanism of control accounting for these results is the activation of commitments. By conveying the definition of the situation that the experimenter is a mere agent, carrying out the sometimes unpleasant demands of "research" or "science," he creates a situation where a refusal is an act of deviance. Well-socialized subjects who have volunteered their services find it difficult to commit such an act under the very eyes of the experimenter, but when they can do it without the embarrassment of a direct confrontation, it is much easier.

Perhaps the most powerful and common means of social control is simply the conveying of expectations with clarity and explicitness coupled with clear and direct accountability for the performance of such expectations. As long as legitimacy is accorded in such situations, individuals will regard their noncompliance as a failure and any interaction which makes such a personal failure salient is embarrassing, unpleasant and something to be avoided.

This point is no less true for complex, modern societies than for small communities. The activation of commitments still depends both on the acceptance of a general obligation and on reminders of what that duty is in specific situations. The connections between the top political leaders in a society and the members of a solidary group may be remote and may pass through many links before they reach a person's boss or neighbor or colleague or whoever else happens to do the reminding. Nevertheless, at the last link in this chain between authorities and potential partisans, the desire to avoid the embarrassment of being derelict under surveillance is a powerful persuader. The possibility of losing such a potent means of control is a strong incentive for any set of authorities to achieve or maintain high trust on the part of potential partisans.

PARTICIPATION AND COOPTATION

One of the most interesting and complicated of control mechanisms is cooptation. Essentially, it involves the manipulation of access, but as a control technique it is double-edged. In his classic study of the Tennessee Valley Authority (TVA), Selznick (1953) defined it as "the process of absorbing new elements into the leadership or policy-determining structure of an organization as a means of averting threats to its stability of existence." Earlier I argued that authorities normally will prefer to limit access to those elements most susceptible to control, but cooptation involves yielding access to the most difficult and threatening potential partisans. Why should any organization wish to deliberately create control problems for itself?

This mechanism arises in situations

where control is already insufficient. It is a response to anticipated or actual pressure from partisans of such magnitude that it threatens the incumbent authorities and perhaps threatens the continuation of the system itself. Bringing such partisans "inside" does not create control problems; it simply transfers the existing ones to a different arena. In particular, while cooptation removes some of the insulation between potential partisans and authorities, it makes the former subject to other control techniques which were previously not available. Representatives of the partisan group, once inside, are subject to the rewards and punishments that the organization bestows. They acquire a stake in the organization, having gained some control over resources whose continuation and expansion is dependent on the organization's maintenance and growth. New rewards lie ahead if they show themselves to be amenable to some degree of control; deprivation of rewards which they now enjoy becomes a new possibility if they remain unruly.

Besides these changes in the situation of the partisans, they are likely to enjoy some changes in orientation as well. First of all, their attitudes and commitment to the system may change. They may come to identify with the collectivity to such a degree that it will mute and subdue their original loyalty to a hostile outside partisan group which is trying to change the organization.

A desire to increase the potentialities for control lies behind the advocacy of admitting Communist China to the United Nations for many who hold such a position. UN membership is regarded less in terms of the access to influence it provides and more in terms of the control opportunities it offers. A hostile China is viewed as a greater threat outside the United Nations than inside. Once inside, it is argued, China would acquire interests which would make it a partner in maintaining the stability of the international system. It lacks such interests as an "outlaw" with relatively little stake in maintaining peaceful and cooperative relations with other countries.

From the perspective of potential partisans, cooptation must be regarded as a risk.

Representatives of coopted groups are likely to be charged with having "sold out" at the least indication that they are pressing the group's demands with less vigor than previously. In fact, there is a tendency for such partisans to regard the entire opportunity for increased access as a form of manipulation. "The more a ruling class is able to assimilate the most prominent men of the dominated classes the more stable and dangerous is its rule," Marx argued. The very act of accepting access by a leader may be taken as evidence of desertion to the enemy either for selfish gain (i.e., as a "fink") or through naïveté (i.e., as a "dupe").

What can a potential partisan group hope to gain by allowing itself and its leaders to be coopted? It can gain increased access to resources which will enhance its influence and bring about outcome modifications. In other words, cooptation does not operate simply as a control device—it is also likely to involve yielding ground. For this reason, there are likely to be parallel fears on the part of authorities. They may worry that the act of cooptation represents the "nose of the camel" and be fearful of their ability to keep the rest of the camel out of the tent. Far from manipulation, some authorities may regard it as an act of undue yielding to pressure and the rewarding of "irresponsible" behavior.

Both the partisan's and the authority's fears about cooptation are valid fears. Cooptation invariably involves some mixture of outcome modification and social control and the exact mix is difficult to determine in advance. The authority who opposes coopting the hostile element fears that outcome modification will dominate the mix; the partisan who opposes accepting it, fears that the social control element will dominate.

The TVA case described by Selznick (1953) is instructive in this regard. The newly founded organization was faced, in 1933, with a powerfully entrenched existing interest bloc in the Tennessee Valley. This bloc consisted of a complex headed by the Land Grant Colleges, the more prosperous farmers represented by the American Farm Bureau Federation, and the Federal Agricultural Extension Service with its county agents. In some fashion, TVA had to confront this bloc whose territory the new organization was invading. Had TVA been firmly established with assured support of its own, it might have considered a strategy which would have challenged this bloc. In trying to become established, an alternative strategy recommended itself—to coopt the Farm Bureau complex into TVA. This policy was justified under the rubric of the "grass roots policy" which emphasized partnership with local groups in the region. The most significant act of cooptation was the appointment of one of the leaders of the Farm Bureau complex to TVA's three-man board.

One of the consequences of the cooptation strategy was a considerable amount of influence by the Farm Bureau complex over TVA's agricultural policies. Decisions on fertilizer programs, on the degree of emphasis on rural cooperatives, on the place of Negro farmers in the TVA program, were apparently all heavily influenced by this partisan group in the valley. On the other hand, TVA was able to carry out successfully its public power program and a number of other important objectives which might have become the target of active opposition if the Farm Bureau complex had not been coopted. It is never easy to assess whether the "price" in outcome modification was worth it or not, especially since one cannot know what would have happened if cooptation had not been used. The lesson to be drawn from the TVA example is not that it acted wisely or foolishly in coopting the Farm Bureau complex. Rather it is that *any* act of cooptation of potential partisans by authorities is likely to be a mixture of modification and social control and the balance of the mix is problematic and of concern to both parties.

Leeds's discussion (1964) of the absorption of nonconforming enclaves again illustrates the double-edged nature of this process. General Chennault and his followers in the period preceding World War II attempted to develop a group of trained fighter pilots (the "Flying Tigers") to furnish air support for Chinese land forces opposing the Japanese. The military had yet to accept, at this time,

the full significance of air warfare and tended to regard it as auxiliary to infantry and artillery. Consequently, the allocation of supplies and personnel to Chennault were limited and a variety of other means were used to control and isolate the Flying Tiger group. However, after the U.S. entry into the war, this conflict proved too costly and a different control technique was used to deal with the rebellious group. In July, 1942, the American Volunteer Group of Flying Tigers was transformed into China Air Task Force and inducted into the U.S. Air Force under General Bissell. Later the group became the 14th Air Force under General Stilwell who was instructed to give Chennault full support. This ended the rebellion and removed the acute pressure from this partisan group. Along with the development of military technology and the experiences of the war, this absorption contributed to a major reorientation in the military toward the importance of air warfare. As in the TVA case, cooptation seems to have involved large amounts of influence for the coopted group.

Closely related to the issue of cooptation and protest-absorption is that of participation in decision making. A long line of social psychological experiments in laboratory and field settings has emphasized the importance of participation as a positive factor in the acceptance of decision outcomes. It is not always clear precisely what is meant by participation.

One may emphasize the influence aspects of participation. To increase the participation of a group of potential partisans may mean to increase its influence over decisions. If there is increased satisfaction in such situations, it is because the modified outcomes are closer to what the partisan group desires. It may have very little or nothing to do with the fact of participation itself. If the significance of participation stems from the attendant influence, then we should expect the same increase in satisfaction and commitment that we would get if outcomes were similarly modified without an increase in participation.

Participation has a social control aspect as well. Here it is claimed that the act of participating in a decision process increases commitment and acceptance of decisions even if outcomes are no more satisfactory. The classic case of such alleged "participation" effects is the Hawthorne Study (Roethlisberger and Dickson, 1939) in which output increased following a variety of decisions made by a group of workers. These particular experiments are a weak reed on which to base any conclusion as Carey (1967) demonstrates in an appropriately harsh review. Carey argues that a "detailed comparison between the Hawthorne conclusions and the Hawthorne evidence shows these conclusions to be almost wholly unsupported" (p. 403). But in a later, more careful study of "participation" effects, Coch and French conclude that resistance to changing work methods can be overcome "by the use of group meetings in which management effectively communicates the need for change and stimulates group participation in planning the changes. Such participation results in higher production, higher morale, and better labor-management relations" (1965, p. 459).

Much of the small group work on "democratic" methods of decision making has a strong social control emphasis. As Verba points out,

> *Participation is in most cases limited to member endorsement of decisions made by the leader who . . . is neither selected by the group nor responsible to the group for his actions. In group discussions, the leader does not present alternatives to the group from which the members choose. Rather, the group leader has a particular goal in mind and uses the group discussion as a means of inducing acceptance of the goal. . . . As used in much of the small group literature, participatory democratic leadership refers not to a technique of decision but to a technique of persuasion (Verba, 1961, p. 220).*

Participation, like cooptation, is most likely to be some mixture of influence and social control. Many of the same issues arise. If the social control emphasis is paramount, partisans are likely to regard the process as pseudo participation and manipulation. But it is not easy to increase participation without

also increasing influence. The increased access may be intended to lead to a greater feeling of participation and increased commitment of members, but those who are so admitted may not be very long satisfied with the trappings of influence. When conflicts arise, the new participants may be in an improved position to pursue their interests effectively.

By the use of *selective* participation, authorities may control some partisans by increasing the ability of others to influence. Hard-pressed authorities may welcome influence attempts by rival partisans for such influence may free rather than confine them. Under such circumstances, authorities may encourage increased participation by selected groups despite, or even because of, the increased influence that it will bring. The new pressures can then be pointed to as justification and defense for failure to take the actions desired by the first group; the second group in turn can be brought to appreciate the constraints which their rival places on the authorities.

The playing off of one partisan group against another as a technique of control is an ancient and familiar one. Machiavelli recommended it to his authorities and Simmel developed it in his discussion of the "tertius gaudens," i.e., the third party who draws advantage from the quarrel of two others. It is captured in the admonition to authorities to "divide and rule." Simmel illustrates it by describing the Inca custom of dividing a "newly conquered tribe in two approximately equal halves and [placing] a supervisor over each of them, but [giving] these two supervisors slightly different ranks. This was indeed the most suitable means for provoking rivalry between the two heads, which prevented any united action against the ruler on the part of the subjected territory" (Simmel, 1950, p. 165).

Such a control technique has certain dangers. First, while it may forestall the necessity of immediate outcome modification and increase the temporary maneuverability of authorities, it does not relieve the pressure in the long run and may even intensify it. For the moment, some of the resources of the partisan groups may be redirected into the conflict with each other but the authorities, by definition, control the choices which these groups are attempting to influence. Second, it is typically the case that rival partisan groups have some degree of common interest. If so, they may find it convenient to pool their resources in a temporary coalition. Thus, increased participation may lead to an enhancement of the influence it was intended to prevent.

Note that in the above discussion we are viewing organizational officials in their role as authorities. As partisans, these same individuals may desire increased influence for members of the same partisan group. The chairman of a state political party may argue for the widest possible citizen participation in the selection of delegates to the nominating convention because he believes that his own preferred candidate has a stronger following among the party rank and file than among the organizational regulars. In encouraging such rank and file participation, he is acting as a partisan attempting to influence the decision on selecting a candidate, not as an authority trying to minimize partisan influence on the decisions over which he personally exercises authority.

SUMMARY

This chapter has emphasized the perspective of authorities on the possible attempts of partisans to influence the outcome of the decisions they make. The central problem from their standpoint is the containment of influence. Pressure from potential partisans can be relieved by yielding ground and modifying the outcome of decisions or by dealing with the source of pressure through some form of social control.

One form of control involves the insulation of decision makers from potential partisans. This can be done at the point of entry by selecting those who will not present problems or at the point of exit by expelling recalcitrant individuals or groups. Once in,

potential partisans are subject to a wide variety of sanctions. Finally, the orientation of potential partisans can be controlled by manipulating information, ideology, image of authorities, friendship ties, norms, and values. If potential partisans are sufficiently socialized and have high political trust they can be controlled by the activation of commitments. Mechanisms like cooptation and participation seem to involve a mixture of outcome modification and social control as a way of dealing with particularly powerful or threatening partisan groups.

There is a major difference in the influence and social control perspectives on the meaning and significance of social conflict. The social control perspective leads to an emphasis on stability. Conflict, under this view, represents a failure of social control—the failure to contain influence.

This is not to suggest that stability, as used here, is a bad thing. The authorities in whose maintenance one is concerned may be a progressive administration, vigorously pursuing land reform and providing effective leadership in a wide variety of ways. Or, they may represent a totalitarian regime relying heavily on terror and repression as social control techniques. In any case, the questions which arise from this perspective focus us on the manner in which authorities are left free to govern.

The influence perspective on the other hand leads to an emphasis on change. Conflict has a different meaning. Rather than a failure of social control, it is likely to be viewed as part of a social movement aimed at changing the content of decisions, the incumbent authorities, or the regime itself. Such potential partisans might be revolutionary or counterrevolutionary, progressive or reactionary. Again, no implication is intended about the desirability of change per se.

Perhaps the emphasis on stability in one perspective and change in the other is avoidable. Yet it seems to flow from the kinds of questions which arise naturally with each perspective. By taking both perspectives, one can avoid the characteristic blind spots of each one taken alone.

ON COOLING THE MARK OUT: SOME ASPECTS OF ADAPTATION TO FAILURE

Erving Goffman

In cases of criminal fraud, victims find they must suddenly adapt themselves to the loss of sources of security and status which they had taken for granted. A consideration of this adaptation to loss can lead us to an understanding of some relations in our society between involvements and the selves that are involved.

In the argot of the criminal world, the term "mark" refers to any individual who is a victim or prospective victim of certain forms of planned illegal exploitation. The mark is the sucker—the person who is taken in. An instance of the operation of any particular racket, taken through the full cycle of its steps or phases, is sometimes called a play. The persons who operate the racket and "take" the mark are occasionally called operators.

The confidence game—the con, as its practitioners call it—is a way of obtaining money under false pretenses by the exercise of fraud and deceit. The con differs from politer forms of financial deceit in important ways. The con is practiced on private persons by talented actors who methodically and regularly build up informal social relationships just for the purpose of abusing them; white-collar crime is practiced on organizations by persons who learn to abuse positions of trust which they once filled faithfully. The one exploits poise; the other, position. Further, a con man is someone who accepts a social role in the underworld community; he

is part of a brotherhood whose members make no pretense to one another of being "legit." A white-collar criminal, on the other hand, has no colleagues, although he may have an associate with whom he plans his crime and a wife to whom he confesses it.

The con is said to be a good racket in the United States only because most Americans are willing, nay eager, to make easy money, and will engage in action that is less than legal in order to do so. The typical play has typical phases. The potential sucker is first spotted, and one member of the working team (called the outside man, steerer, or roper) arranges to make social contact with him. The confidence of the mark is won, and he is given an opportunity to invest his money in a gambling venture which he understands to have been fixed in his favor. The venture, of course, is fixed, but not in his favor. The mark is permitted to win some money and then persuaded to invest more. There is an "accident" or "mistake," and the mark loses his total investment. The operators then depart in a ceremony that is called the blow-off or sting. They leave the mark but take his money. The mark is expected to go on his way, a little wiser and a lot poorer.

Sometimes, however, a mark is not quite prepared to accept his loss as a gain in experience and to say and do nothing about his venture. He may feel moved to complain to the police or to chase after the operators. In the terminology of the trade, the mark may squawk, beef, or come through. From the operators' point of view, this kind of behavior is bad for business. It gives the members of the mob a bad reputation with such police as have not yet been fixed and with marks who have not yet been taken. In order to avoid this adverse publicity, an additional phase is sometimes added at the end

Source: E. Goffman, "On Cooling the Mark Out: Some Aspects of Adaptation to Failure," *Psychiatry*, Vol. 25, 1952, pp. 451–463. Copyright 1952 by The William Alanson White Psychiatric Foundation, Inc. and used by special permission of The William Alanson White Psychiatric Foundation, Inc. and E. Goffman.

of the play. It is called cooling the mark out. After the blowoff has occurred, one of the operators stays with the mark and makes an effort to keep the anger of the mark within manageable and sensible proportions. The operator stays behind his team-mates in the capacity of what might be called a cooler and exercises upon the mark the art of consolation. An attempt is made to define the situation for the mark in a way that makes it easy for him to accept the inevitable and quietly go home. The mark is given instruction in the philosophy of taking a loss.

When we call to mind the image of a mark who has just been separated from his money, we sometimes attempt to account for the greatness of his anger by the greatness of his financial loss. This is a narrow view. In many cases, especially in America, the mark's image of himself is built up on the belief that he is a pretty shrewd person when it comes to making deals and that he is not the sort of person who is taken in by anything. The mark's readiness to participate in a sure thing is based on more than avarice; it is based on a feeling that he will now be able to prove to himself that he is the sort of person who can "turn a fast buck." For many, this capacity for high finance comes near to being a sign of masculinity and a test of fulfilling the male role.

It is well known that persons protect themselves with all kinds of rationalizations when they have a buried image of themselves which the facts of their status do not support. A person may tell himself many things: that he has not been given a fair chance; that he is not really interested in becoming something else; that the time for showing his mettle has not yet come; that the usual means of realizing his desires are personally or morally distasteful, or require too much dull effort. By means of such defenses, a person saves himself from committing a cardinal social sin—the sin of defining oneself in terms of a status while lacking the qualifications which an incumbent of that status is supposed to possess.

A mark's participation in a play, and his investment in it, clearly commit him in his own eyes to the proposition that he is a smart man. The process by which he comes to believe that he cannot lose is also the process by which he drops the defenses and compensations that previously protected him from defeats. When the blowoff comes, the mark finds that he has no defense for not being a shrewd man. He has defined himself as a shrewd man and must face the fact that he he is only another easy mark. He has defined himself as possessing a certain set of qualities and then proven to himself that he is miserably lacking in them. This is a process of self-destruction of the self. It is no wonder that the mark needs to be cooled out and that it is good business policy for one of the operators to stay with the mark in order to talk him into a point of view from which it is possible to accept a loss.

In essence, then, the cooler has the job of handling persons who have been caught out on a limb—persons whose expectations and self-conceptions have been built up and then shattered. The mark is a person who has compromised himself, in his own eyes if not in the eyes of others.

Although the term, mark, is commonly applied to a person who is given short-lived expectations by operators who have intentionally misrepresented the facts, a less restricted definition is desirable in analyzing the larger social scene. An expectation may finally prove false, even though it has been possible to sustain it for a long time and even though the operators acted in good faith. So, too, the disappointment of reasonable expectations, as well as misguided ones, creates a need for consolation. Persons who participate in what is recognized as a confidence game are found in only a few social settings, but persons who have to be cooled out are found in many. Cooling the mark out is one theme in a very basic social story.

For purposes of analysis, one may think of an individual in reference to the values or attributes of a socially recognized character which he possesses. Psychologists speak of a value as a personal involvement. Sociologists speak of a value as a status, role, or relationship. In either case, the character of the value that is possessed is taken in a certain way as the character of the person who possesses it. An alteration in the kinds of attributes possessed brings an alteration to the self-conception of the person who possesses them.

The process by which someone acquires a value is the process by which he surrenders the claim he had to what he was and commits himself to the conception of self which the new value requires or allows him to have. It is the process that persons who fall in love or take dope call getting hooked. After a person is hooked, he must go through another process by which his new involvement finds its proper place, in space and time, relative to the other calls, demands, and commitments that he has upon himself. At this point certain other persons suddenly begin to play an important part in the individual's story; they impinge upon him by virtue of the relationship they happen to have to the value in which he has become involved. This is not the place to consider the general kinds of impingement that are institutionalized in our society and the general social relationships that arise: the personal relationship, the professional relationship, and the business relationship. Here we are concerned only with the end of the story, the way in which a person becomes disengaged from one of his involvements.

In our society, the story of a person's involvement can end in one of three general ways. According to one type of ending, he may withdraw from one of his involvements or roles in order to acquire a sequentially related one that is considered better. This is the case when a youth becomes a man, when a student becomes a practitioner, or when a man from the ranks is given a commission.

Of course, the person who must change his self at any one of these points of promotion may have profound misgivings. He may feel disloyal to the way of life that must be left behind and to the persons who do not leave it with him. His new role may require action that seems insincere, dishonest, or unfriendly. This he may experience as a loss in moral cleanliness. His new role may require him to forgo the kinds of risk-taking and exertion that he previously enjoyed, and yet his new role may not provide the kind of

heroic and exalted action that he expected to find in it.[1] This he may experience as a loss in moral strength.

There is no doubt that certain kinds of role success require certain kinds of moral failure. It may therefore be necessary, in a sense, to cool the dubious neophyte in rather than out. He may have to be convinced that his doubts are a matter of sentimentality. The adult social view will be impressed upon him. He will be required to understand that a promotional change in status is voluntary, desirable, and natural, and that loss of one's role in these circumstances is the ultimate test of having fulfilled it properly.

It has been suggested that a person may leave a role under circumstances that reflect favorably upon the way in which he performed it. In theory, at least, a related possibility must be considered. A person may leave a role and at the same time leave behind him the standards by which such roles are judged. The new thing that he becomes may be so different from the thing he was that criteria such as success or failure cannot be easily applied to the change which has occurred. He becomes lost to others that he may find himself; he is of the twice-born. In our society, perhaps the most obvious example of this kind of termination occurs when a woman voluntarily gives up a prestigeful profession in order to become a wife and a mother. It is to be noted that this illustrates an institutionalized movement; those who make it do not make news. In America most other examples of this kind of termination are more a matter of talk than of occurrence. For example, one of the culture heroes of our dinner-table mythology is the man who walks out on an established calling in order to write or paint or live in the country. In other societies, the kind of abdication being considered here seems to have played a more important role. In medieval China,

---

[1] Mr. Hughes has lectured on this kind of disappointment, and one of his students has undertaken a special study of it. See Miriam Wagenschein, " 'Reality Shock': A Study of Beginning School Teachers," M.A. thesis, Dept. of Sociology, Univ. of Chicago, 1950.

for instance, anchoretic withdrawal apparently gave to persons of quite different station a way of retreating from the occupational struggle while managing the retreat in an orderly, face-saving fashion.[2]

Two basic ways in which a person can lose a role have been considered; he can be promoted out of it or abdicate from it. There is, of course, a third basic ending to the status story. A person may be involuntarily deprived of his position or involvement and made in return something that is considered a lesser thing to be. It is mainly in this third ending to a person's role that occasions arise for cooling him out. It is here that one deals in the full sense with the problem of persons' losing their roles.

Involuntary loss seems itself to be of two kinds. First, a person may lose a status in such a way that the loss is not taken as a reflection upon the loser. The loss of a loved one, either because of an accident that could not have been prevented or because of a disease that could not have been halted, is a case in point. Occupational retirement because of old age is another. Of course, the loss will inevitably alter the conception the loser has of himself and the conception others have of him, but the alteration itself will not be treated as a symbol of the fate he deserves to receive. No insult is added to injury. It may be necessary, none the less, to pacify the loser and resign him to his loss. The loser who is not held responsible for his loss may even find himself taking the mystical view that all involvements are part of a wider con game, for the more one takes pleasure in a particular role the more one must suffer when it is time to leave it. He may find little comfort in the fact that the play has provided him with an illusion that has lasted a lifetime. He may find little comfort in the fact that the operators had not meant to deceive him.

Secondly, a person may be involuntarily deprived of a role under circumstances which reflect unfavorably on his capacity for it. The lost role may be one that he had already acquired or one that he had openly committed himself to preparing for. In either case the loss is more than a matter of ceasing to act in a given capacity; it is ultimate proof of an incapacity. And in many cases it is even more than this. The moment of failure often catches a person acting as one who feels that he is an appropriate sort of person for the role in question. Assumption becomes presumption, and failure becomes fraud. To loss of substance is thereby added loss of face. Of the many themes that can occur in the natural history of an involvement, this seems to be the most melancholy. Here it will be quite essential and quite difficult to cool the mark out. I shall be particularly concerned with this second kind of loss—the kind that involves humiliation.

It should be noted, parenthetically, that one circle of persons may define a particular loss as the kind that casts no reflection on the loser, and that a different circle of persons may treat the same loss as a symbol of what the loser deserves. One must also note that there is a tendency today to shift certain losses of status from the category of those that reflect upon the loser to the category of those that do not. When persons lose their jobs, their courage, or their minds, we tend more and more to take a clinical or naturalistic view of the loss and a nonmoral view of their failure. We want to define a person as something that is not destroyed by the destruction of one of his selves. This benevolent attitude is in line with the effort today to publicize the view that occupational retirement is not the end of all active capacities but the beginning of new and different ones.

A consideration of consolation as a social process leads to four general problems having to do with the self in society. First, where in modern life does one find persons conducting themselves as though they were entitled to the rights of a particular status and then having to face up to the fact that they do not possess the qualification for the status? In other words, at what points in the structures of our social life are persons likely to com-

---

2 See, for example, Max Weber, *The Religion of China* (H. H. Gerth, tr.); Glencoe, Ill., Free Press, 1951; p. 178.

promise themselves or find themselves compromised? When is it likely that a person will have to disengage himself or become disengaged from one of his involvements? Secondly, what are the typical ways in which persons who find themselves in this difficult position can be cooled out; how can they be made to accept the great injury that has been done to their image of themselves, regroup their defenses, and carry on without raising a squawk? Thirdly, what, in general, can happen when a person refuses to be cooled out, that is, when he refuses to be pacified by the cooler? Fourthly, what arrangements are made by operators and marks to avoid entirely the process of consolation?

In all personal-service organizations customers or clients sometimes make complaints. A customer may feel that he has been given service in a way that is unacceptable to him—a way that he interperts as an offense to the conception he has of who and what he is. The management therefore has the problem of cooling the mark out. Frequently this function is allotted to specialists within the organization. In restaurants of some size, for example, one of the crucial functions of the hostess is to pacify customers whose self-conceptions have been injured by waitresses or by the food. In large stores the complaint department and the floorwalker perform a similar function.

One may note that a service organization does not operate in an anonymous world, as does a con mob, and is therefore strongly obliged to make some effort to cool the mark out. An institution, after all, cannot take it on the lam; it must pacify its marks.

One may also note that coolers in service organizations tend to view their own activity in a light that softens the harsher details of the situation. The cooler protects himself from feelings of guilt by arguing that the customer is not really in need of the service he expected to receive, that bad service is not really deprivational, and that beefs and complaints are a sign of bile, not a sign of injury. In a similar way, the con man protects himself from remorseful images of bankrupt marks by arguing that the mark is a fool and not a full-fledged person, possessing an in-

clination towards illegal gain but not the decency to admit it or the capacity to succeed at it.

In organizations patterned after a bureaucratic model, it is customary for personnel to expect rewards of a specified kind upon fulfilling requirements of a specified nature. Personnel come to define their career line in terms of a sequence of legitimate expectations and to base their self-conceptions on the assumption that in due course they will be what the institution allows persons to become. Sometimes, however, a member of an organization may fulfill some of the requirements for a particular status, especially the requirements concerning technical proficiency and seniority, but not other requirements, especially the less codified ones having to do with the proper handling of social relationships at work. It must fall to someone to break the bad news to the victim; someone must tell him that he has been fired, or that he has failed his examinations, or that he has been by-passed in promotion. And after the blowoff, someone has to cool the mark out. The necessity of disappointing the expectations that a person has taken for granted may be infrequent in some organizations, but in others, such as training institutions, it occurs all the time. The process of personnel selection requires that many trainees be called but that few be chosen.

When one turns from places of work to other scenes in our social life, one finds that each has its own occasions for cooling the mark out. During informal social intercourse it is well understood that an effort on the part of one person (ego) to decrease his social distance from another person (alter) must be graciously accepted by alter or, if rejected, rejected tactfully so that the initiator of the move can save his social face. This rule is codified in books on etiquette and is followed in actual behavior. A friendly movement in the direction of alter is a movement outward on a limb; ego communicates his belief that he has defined himself as worthy of alter's society, while at the same time he places alter in the strategic position of being able to discredit this conception.

The problem of cooling persons out in

informal social intercourse is seen most clearly, perhaps, in courting situations and in what might be called de-courting situations. A proposal of marriage in our society tends to be a way in which a man sums up his social attributes and suggests to a woman that hers are not so much better as to preclude a merger or partnership in these matters. Refusal on the part of the woman, or refusal on the part of the man to propose when he is clearly in a position to do so, is a serious reflection on the rejected suitor. Courtship is a way not only of presenting oneself to alter for approval but also of saying that the opinion of alter in this matter is the opinion one is most concerned with. Refusing a proposal, or refusing to propose, is therefore a difficult operation. The mark must be carefully cooled out. The act of breaking a date or of refusing one, and the task of discouraging a "steady" can also be seen in this light, although in these cases great delicacy and tact may not be required, since the mark may not be deeply involved or openly committed. Just as it is harder to refuse a proposal than to refuse a date, so it is more difficult to reject a spouse than to reject a suitor. The process of de-courting by which one person in a marriage maneuvers the other into accepting a divorce without fuss or undue rancor requires extreme finesse in the art of cooling the mark out.

In all of these cases where a person constructs a conception of himself which cannot be sustained, there is a possibility that he has not invested that which is most important to him in the soon-to-be-denied status. In the current idiom, there is a possibility that when he is hit, he will not be hit where he really lives. There is a set of cases, however, where the blowoff cannot help but strike a vital spot; these cases arise, of course, when a person must be dissuaded from life itself. The man with a fatal sickness or fatal injury, the criminal with a death sentence, the soldier with a hopeless objective—these persons must be persuaded to accept quietly the loss of life itself, the loss of all one's earthly involvements. Here, certainly, it will be difficult to cool the mark out. It is a reflection on the

conceptions men have—as cooler and mark—that it is possible to do so.

I have mentioned a few of the areas of social life where it becomes necessary, upon occasion, to cool a mark out. Attention may now be directed to some of the common ways in which individuals are cooled out in all of these areas of life.

For the mark, cooling represents a process of adjustment to an impossible situation—a situation arising from having defined himself in a way which the social facts come to contradict. The mark must therefore be supplied with a new set of apologies for himself, a new framework in which to see himself and judge himself. A process of redefining the self along defensible lines must be instigated and carried along; since the mark himself is frequently in too weakened a condition to do this, the cooler must initially do it for him.

One general way of handling the problem of cooling the mark out is to give the task to someone whose status relative to the mark will serve to ease the situation in some way. In formal organizations, frequently, someone who is two or three levels above the mark in line of command will do the hatchet work, on the assumption that words of consolation and redirection will have a greater power to convince if they come from high places. There also seems to be a feeling that persons of high status are better able to withstand the moral danger of having hate directed at them. Incidentally, persons protected by high office do not like to face this issue, and frequently attempt to define themselves as merely the agents of the deed and not the source of it. In some cases, on the other hand, the task of cooling the mark out is given to a friend and peer of the mark, on the assumption that such a person will know best how to hit upon a suitable rationalization for the mark and will know best how to control the mark should the need for this arise. In some cases, as in those pertaining to death, the role of cooler is given to doctors or priests. Doctors must frequently help a family, and the member who is leaving it, to manage the leave-taking with tact and a minimum of emotional fuss.[3]   A priest must not so much save a soul as create one that is consistent with what is about to become of it.

A second general solution to the problem of cooling the mark out consists of offering him a status which differs from the one he has lost or failed to gain but which provides at least a something or a somebody for him to become.   Usually the alternative presented to the mark is a compromise of some kind, providing him with some of the trappings of his lost status as well as with some of its spirit.   A lover may be asked to become a friend; a student of medicine may be asked to switch to the study of dentistry;[4] a boxer may become a trainer; a dying person may be asked to broaden and empty his worldly loves so as to embrace the All-Father that is about to receive him.   Sometimes the mark is allowed to retain his status but is required to fulfill it in a different environment: the honest policeman is transferred to a lonely beat; the too zealous priest is encouraged to enter a monastery; an unsatisfactory plant manager is shipped off to another branch.   Sometimes the mark is "kicked upstairs" and given a courtesy status such as "Vice President."   In the game for social roles, transfer up, down, or away may all be consolation prizes.

A related way of handling the mark is to offer him another chance to qualify for the role at which he has failed.   After his fall from grace, he is allowed to retrace his steps and try again.   Officer selection programs in the army, for example, often provide for possibilities of this kind.   In general, it seems that third and fourth chances are seldom given to marks, and that second chances, while often given, are seldom taken.   Failure at a role removes a person from the company of those who have succeeded, but it does not bring him back—in spirit, anyway—to the society of those who have not tried or are in the process of trying.   The person who has failed in a role is a constant source of embarrassment, for none of the standard patterns of treatment is quite applicable to him.   Instead of taking a second chance, he usually goes away to another place where his past does not bring confusion to his present.

Another standard method of cooling the mark out—one which is frequently employed in conjunction with other methods—is to allow the mark to explode, to break down, to cause a scene, to give full vent to his reactions and feelings, to "blow his top."   If this release of emotions does not find a target, then it at least serves a cathartic function.   If it does find a target, as in "telling off the boss," it gives the mark a last-minute chance to re-erect his defenses and prove to himself and others that he had not really cared about the status all along.   When a blow-up of this kind occurs, friends of the mark or psychotherapists are frequently brought in.   Friends are willing to take responsibility for the mark because their relationship to him is not limited to the role he has failed in.   This, incidentally, provides one of the less obvious reasons why the cooler in a con mob must cultivate the friendship of the mark; friendship provides the cooler with an acceptable reason for staying around while the mark is cooled out.   Psychotherapists, on the other hand, are willing to take responsibility for the mark because it is their business to offer a relationship to those who have failed in a relationship to others.

It has been suggested that a mark may be cooled out by allowing him, under suitable guidance, to give full vent to his initial shock.   Thus the manager of a commercial organization may listen with patience and understanding to the complaints of a customer, knowing that the full expression of a complaint is likely to weaken it.   This possibility lies behind the role of a whole series of buffers in our society—janitors, restaurant hostesses, grievance committees, floorwalkers, and so on—who listen in silence, with apparent sympathy, until the mark has simmered down.   Similarly, in the case of crimi-

---

[3] This role of the doctor has been stressed by W. L. Warner in his lectures at the University of Chicago on symbolic roles in "Yankee City."

[4] In his seminars, Mr. Hughes has used the term "second-choice" professions to refer to cases of this kind.

nal trials, the defending lawyer may find it profitable to allow the public to simmer down before he brings his client to court.

A related procedure for cooling the mark out is found in what is called stalling. The feelings of the mark are not brought to a head because he is given no target at which to direct them. The operator may manage to avoid the presence of the mark or may convince the mark that there is still a slight chance that the loss has not really occurred. When the mark is stalled, he is given a chance to become familiar with the new conception of self he will have to accept before he is absolutely sure that he will have to accept it.

As another cooling procedure, there is the possibility that the operator and the mark may enter into a tacit understanding according to which the mark agrees to act as if he were leaving of his own accord, and the operator agrees to preserve the illusion that this was the case. It is a form of bribery. In this way the mark may fail in his own eyes but prevent others from discovering the failure. The mark gives up his role but saves his face. This, after all, is one of the reasons why persons who are fleeced by con men are often willing to remain silent about their adventure. The same strategy is at work in the romantic custom of allowing a guilty officer to take his own life in a private way before it is taken from him publicly, and in the less romantic custom of allowing a person to resign for delicate reasons instead of firing him for indelicate ones.

Bribery is, of course, a form of exchange. In this case, the mark guarantees to leave quickly and quietly, and in exchange is allowed to leave under a cloud of his own choosing. A more important variation on the same theme is found in the practice of financial compensation. A man can say to himself and others that he is happy to retire from his job and say this with more conviction if he is able to point to a comfortable pension. In this sense, pensions are automatic devices for providing consolation. So, too, a person who has been injured because of another's criminal or marital neglect can compensate for the loss by means of a court settlement.

I have suggested some general ways in which the mark is cooled out. The question now arises: what happens if the mark refuses to be cooled out? What are the possible lines of action he can take if he refuses to be cooled? Attempts to answer these questions will show more clearly why, in general, the operator is so anxious to pacify the mark.

It has been suggested that a mark may be cooled by allowing him to blow his top. If the blow-up is too drastic or prolonged, however, difficulties may arise. We say that the mark becomes "disturbed mentally" or "personally disorganized." Instead of merely telling his boss off, the mark may go so far as to commit criminal violence against him. Instead of merely blaming himself for failure, the mark may inflict great punishment upon himself by attempting suicide, or by acting so as to make it necessary for him to be cooled out in other areas of his social life.

Sustained personal disorganization is one way in which a mark can refuse to cool out. Another standard way is for the individual to raise a squawk, that is, to make a formal complaint to higher authorities obliged to take notice of such matters. The con mob worries lest the mark appeal to the police. The plant manager must make sure that the disgruntled department head does not carry a formal complaint to the general manager or, worse still, to the Board of Directors. The teacher worries lest the child's parent complain to the principal. Similarly, a woman who communicates her evaluation of self by accepting a proposal of marriage can sometimes protect her exposed position—should the necessity of doing so arise—by threatening her disaffected fiancé with a breach-of-promise suit. So, also, a woman who is de-courting her husband must fear lest he contest the divorce or sue her lover for alienation of affection. In much the same way, a customer who is angered by a salesperson can refuse to be mollified by the floorwalker and demand to see the manager. It is interesting to note that associations dedicated to the rights and the honor of minority groups may sometimes encourage a mark to register a formal squawk; politically it may be more advantageous to provide a test case than to allow the mark to be cooled out.

Another line of action which a mark who refuses to be cooled can pursue is that of turning "sour." The term derives from the argot of industry but the behavior it refers to occurs everywhere. The mark outwardly accepts his loss but withdraws all enthusiasm, good will, and vitality from whatever role he is allowed to maintain. He complies with the formal requirements of the role that is left him, but he withdraws his spirit and identification from it. When an employee turns sour, the interests of the organization suffer; every executive, therefore, has the problem of "sweetening" his workers. They must not come to feel that they are slowly being cooled out. This is one of the functions of granting periodic advancements in salary and status, of schemes such as profit-sharing, or of giving the "employee" at home an anniversary present. A similar view can be taken of the problem that a government faces in times of crisis when it must maintain the enthusiastic support of the nation's disadvantaged minorities, for whole groupings of the population can feel they are being cooled out and react by turning sour.

Finally, there is the possibility that the mark may, in a manner of speaking, go into business for himself. He can try to gather about him the persons and facilities required to establish a status similar to the one he has lost, albeit in relation to a different set of persons. This way of refusing to be cooled is often rehearsed in phantasies of the "I'll show them" kind, but sometimes it is actually realized in practice. The rejected marriage partner may make a better remarriage. A social stratum that has lost its status may decide to create its own social system. A leader who fails in a political party may establish his own splinter group.

All these ways in which a mark can refuse to be cooled out have consequences for other persons. There is, of course, a kind of refusal that has little consequence for others.

Marks of all kinds may develop explanations and excuses to account in a creditable way for their loss. It is, perhaps, in this region of phantasy that the defeated self makes its last stand.

The process of cooling is a difficult one, both for the operator who cools the mark out and for the person who receives this treatment. Safeguards and strategies are therefore employed to ensure that the process itself need not and does not occur. One deals here with strategies of prevention, not strategies of cure.

From the point of view of the operator, there are two chief ways of avoiding the difficulties of cooling the mark out. First, devices are commonly employed to weed out those applicants for a role, office, or relationship who might later prove to be unsuitable and require removal. The applicant is not given a chance to invest his self unwisely. A variation of this technique, that provides, in a way, a built-in mechanism for cooling the mark out, is found in the institution of probationary period and "temporary" staff. These definitions of the situation make it clear to the person that he must maintain his ego in readiness for the loss of his job, or, better still, that he ought not to think of himself as really having the job. If these safety measures fail, however, a second strategy is often employed. Operators of all kinds seem to be ready, to a surprising degree, to put up with or "carry" persons who have failed but who have not yet been treated as failures. This is especially true where the involvement of the mark is deep and where his conception of self had been publicly committed. Business offices, government agencies, spouses, and other kinds of operators are often careful to make a place for the mark, so that dissolution of the bond will not be necessary. Here, perhaps, is the most important source of private charity in our society.

A consideration of these preventive strategies brings to attention an interesting functional relationship among age-grading, recruitment, and the structure of the self. In our society, as in most others, the young in years are defined as not-yet-persons. To a certain degree, they are not subject to success and failure. A child can throw himself completely into a task, and fail at it, and by and large he will not be destroyed by his failure; it is only necessary to play at cooling him out. An adolescent can be bitterly disappointed in love, and yet he will not thereby become, at least for others, a broken person. A youth can spend a certain amount of time shopping around for a congenial job or a congenial training course, because he is still thought to be able to change his mind without changing his self. And, should he fail at something to which he has tried to commit himself, no permanent damage may be done to his self. If many are to be called and few chosen, then it is more convenient for everyone concerned to call individuals who are not fully persons and cannot be destroyed by failing to be chosen. As the individual grows older, he becomes defined as someone who must not be engaged in a role for which he is unsuited. He becomes defined as something that must not fail, while at the same time arrangements are made to decrease the chances of his failing. Of course, when the mark reaches old age, he must remove himself or be removed from each of his roles, one by one, and participate in the problem of later maturity.

The strategies that are employed by operators to avoid the necessity of cooling the mark out have a counterpart in the strategies that are employed by the mark himself for the same purpose.

There is the strategy of hedging, by which a person makes sure that he is not completely committed. There is the strategy of secrecy, by which a person conceals from others and even from himself the facts of his commitment; there is also the practice of keeping two irons in the fire and the more delicate practice of maintaining a joking or unserious relationship to one's involvement. All of these strategies give the mark an out; in case of failure he can act as if the self that has failed is not one that is important to him. Here we must also consider the function of being quick to take offense and of taking hints quickly, for in these ways the mark

can actively cooperate in the task of saving his face. There is also the strategy of playing it safe, as in cases where a calling is chosen because tenure is assured in it, or where a plain woman is married for much the same reason.

It has been suggested that preventive strategies are employed by operator and mark in order to reduce the chance of failing or to minimize the consequences of failure. The less importance one finds it necessary to give to the problem of cooling, the more importance one may have given to the application of preventive strategies.

I have considered some of the situations in our society in which the necessity for cooling the mark out is likely to arise. I have also considered the standard ways in which a mark can be cooled out, the lines of action he can pursue if he refuses to be cooled, and the ways in which the whole problem can be avoided. Attention can now be turned to some very general questions concerning the self in society.

First, an attempt must be made to draw together what has been implied about the structure of persons. From the point of view of this paper, a person is an individual who becomes involved in a value of some kind—a role, a status, a relationship, an ideology—and then makes a public claim that he is to be defined and treated as someone who possesses the value or property in question. The limits to his claims, and hence the limits to his self, are primarily determined by the objective facts of his social life and secondarily determined by the degree to which a sympathetic interpretation of these facts can bend them in his favor. Any event which demonstrates that someone has made a false claim, defining himself as something which he is not, tends to destroy him. If others realize that the person's conception of self has been contradicted and discredited, then the person tends to be destroyed in the eyes of others. If the person can keep the contradiction a secret, he may succeed in keeping everyone but himself from treating him as a failure.

Secondly, one must take note of what is implied by the fact that it is possible for a person to be cooled out. Difficult as this may be, persons regularly define themselves in terms of a set of attributes and then have to accept the fact that they do not possess them —and do this about-face with relatively little fuss or trouble for the operators. This implies that there is a norm in our society persuading persons to keep their chins up and make the best of it—a sort of social sanitation enjoining torn and tattered persons to keep themselves packaged up. More important still, the capacity of a person to sustain these profound embarrassments implies a certain looseness and lack of interpenetration in the organization of his several life-activities. A man may fail in his job, yet go on succeeding with his wife. His wife may ask him for a divorce, or refuse to grant him one, and yet he may push his way onto the same streetcar at the usual time on the way to the same job. He may know that he is shortly going to have to leave the status of the living, but still march with the other prisoners, or eat breakfast with his family at their usual time and from behind his usual paper. He may be conned of his life's savings on an eastbound train but return to his home town and succeed in acting as if nothing of interest had happened.

Lack of rigid integration of a person's social roles allows for compensation; he can seek comfort in one role for injuries incurred in others. There are always cases, of course, in which the mark cannot sustain the injury to his ego and cannot act like a "good scout." On these occasions the shattering experience in one area of social life may spread out to all the sectors of his activity. He may define away the barriers between his several social roles and become a source of difficulty in all of them. In such cases the play is the mark's entire social life, and the operators, really, are the society. In an increasing number of these cases, the mark is given psychological guidance by professionals of some kind. The psychotherapist is, in this sense, the society's cooler. His job is to pacify and reorient the disorganized person; his job is to send the patient back to an old world or a new one, and to send him back in a condition in which he can no longer cause trouble to others or

can no longer make a fuss. In short, if one takes the society, and not the person as the unit, the psychotherapist has the basic task of cooling the mark out.

A third point of interest arises if one views all of social life from the perspective of this paper. It has been argued that a person must not openly or even privately commit himself to a conception of himself which the flow of events is likely to discredit. He must not put himself in a position of having to be cooled out. Conversely, however, he must make sure that none of the persons with whom he has dealings are of the sort who may prove unsuitable and need to be cooled out. He must make doubly sure that should it become necessary to cool his associates out, they will be the sort who allow themselves to be gotten rid of. The con man who wants the mark to go home quietly and absorb a loss, the restaurant hostess who wants a customer to eat quietly and go away without causing trouble, and, if this is not possible, quietly to take his patronage elsewhere—these are the persons and these are the relationships which set the tone of some of our social life. Underlying this tone there is the assumption that persons are institutionally related to each other in such a way that if a mark allows himself to be cooled out, then the cooler need have no further concern with him; but if the mark refuses to be cooled out, he can put institutional machinery into action against the cooler. Underlying this tone there is also the assumption that persons are sentimentally related to each other in such a way that if a person allows himself to be cooled out, however great the loss he has sustained, then the cooler withdraws all emotional identification from him; but if the mark cannot absorb the injury to his self and if he becomes personally disorganized in some way, then the cooler cannot help but feel guilt and concern over the predicament. It is this feeling of guilt—this small measure of involvement in the feelings of others—which helps to make the job of cooling the mark out distasteful, wherever it appears. It is this incapacity to be insensitive to the suffering of another person when he brings his suffering right to your door which tends to make the job of cooling a species of dirty work.

One must not, of course, make too much of the margin of sympathy connecting operator and mark. For one thing, the operator may rid himself of the mark by application or threat of pure force or open insult.[5] In Chicago in the 1920's small businessmen who suffered a loss in profits and in independence because of the "protection" services that racketeers gave to them were cooled out in this way. No doubt it is frivolous to suggest that Freud's notion of castration threat has something to do with the efforts of fathers to cool their sons out of oedipal involvements. Furthermore, there are many occasions when operators of different kinds must act as middlemen, with two marks on their hands; the calculated use of one mark as a sacrifice or fall guy may be the only way of cooling the other mark out. Finally, there are barbarous ceremonies in our society, such as criminal trials and the drumming-out ritual employed in court-martial procedures, that are expressly designed to prevent the mark from saving his face. And even in those cases where the cooler makes an effort to make things easier for the person he is getting rid of, we often find that there are bystanders who have no such scruples.[6] Onlookers who are close enough to observe the blowoff but who are not obliged to assist in the dirty work often enjoy the scene, taking pleasure in the discomfiture of the cooler and in the destruction of the mark. What is trouble for some is Schadenfreude for others.

This paper has dealt chiefly with adaptations to loss; with defenses, strategies, consolations, mitigations, compensations, and the like. The kinds of sugar-coating have been examined, and not the pill. I would like to close this paper by referring briefly to the sort of thing that would be studied if one were interested in loss as such, and not in adaptations to it.

A mark who requires cooling out is a person who can no longer sustain one of his social roles and is about to be removed from it; he is a person who is losing one of his social lives and is about to die one of the deaths that are possible for him. This leads one to consider the ways in which we can go or be sent to our death in each of our social capacities, the ways, in other words, of handling the passage from the role that we had to a state of having it no longer. One might consider the social processes of firing and laying-off; of resigning and being asked to resign; of farewell and departure; of deportation, excommunication, and going to jail; of defeat at games, contests, and wars; of being dropped from a circle of friends or an intimate social relationship; of corporate dissolution; of retirement in old age; and, lastly, of the deaths that heirs are interested in.

And, finally, attention must be directed to the things we become after we have died in one of the many social senses and capacities in which death can come to us. As one might expect, a process of sifting and sorting occurs by which the socially dead come to be effectively hidden from us. This movement of ex-persons throughout the social structure proceeds in more than one direction.

There is, first of all, the dramatic process by which persons who have died in important ways come gradually to be brought together into a common graveyard that is separated ecologically from the living community.[7] For the dead, this is at once a punishment and a defense. Jails and mental institutions are, perhaps, the most familiar examples, but other important ones exist. In America today, there is the interesting tendency to set aside certain regions and towns in California as asylums for those who have died in their capacity as workers and as parents but who are still alive financially.[8] For the old in America

---

[5] Suggested by Saul Mendlovitz in conversation.

[6] Suggested by Howard S. Becker in conversation.

[7] Suggested by lectures of and a personal conversation with Mr. Hughes.

[8] Some early writers on caste report a like situation in India at the turn of the nineteenth century. Hindus who were taken to the Ganges to die, and who then recovered, were apparently denied all legal rights and all social relations with the living. Apparently these excluded persons found it necessary to congregate in a few villages of their own. In California, of course, settlements of the old

who have also died financially, there are old-folks homes and rooming-house areas. And, of course, large cities have their Skid Rows which are, as Park put it, ". . . . full of junk, much of it human, i.e., men and women who, for some reason or other, have fallen out of line in the march of industrial progress and have been scrapped by the industrial organization of which they were once a part."[9] Hobo jungles, located near freight yards on the outskirts of towns, provide another case in point.

Just as a residential area may become a graveyard, so also certain institutions and occupational roles may take on a similar function. The ministry in Britain, for example, has sometimes served as a limbo for the occupational stillborn of better families, as have British universities. Mayhew, writing of London in the mid-nineteenth-century, provides another example: artisans of different kinds, who had failed to maintain a position in the practice of their trade, could be found working as dustmen.[10] In the United States,

the jobs of waitress, cab driver, and night watchman, and the profession of prostitution, tend to be ending places where persons of certain kinds, starting from different places, can come to rest.

But perhaps the most important movement of those who fail is one we never see. Where roles are ranked and somewhat related, persons who have been rejected from the one above may be difficult to distinguish from persons who have risen from the one below. For example, in America, upper-class women who fail to make a marriage in their own circle may follow the recognized route of marrying an upper-middle class professional. Successful lower-middle class women may arrive at the same station in life, coming from the other direction. Similarly, among those who mingle with one another as colleagues in the profession of dentistry, it is possible to find some who have failed to become physicians and others who have succeeded at not becoming pharmacists or optometrists. No doubt there are few positions in life that do not throw together some persons who are there by virtue of failure and other persons who are there by virtue of success. In this sense, the dead are sorted but not segregated, and continue to walk among the living.

---

have a voluntary character, and members maintain ceremonial contact with younger kin by the exchange of periodic visits and letters.

[9] R. E. Park, *Human Communities*; Glencoe, Ill.; Free Press, 1952; p. 60.

[10] Henry Mayhew, *London Labour and the London Poor*; London, Griffin, Bohn, 1881; Vol. II, pp. 177–178.

SUICIDE, HOMICIDE, AND THE SOCIALIZATION OF AGGRESSION

Martin Gold

ABSTRACT

While emphasizing the separation from psychology, Durkheim believed that sociological explanation could be facilitated by a knowledge of psychological variables. This viewpoint is brought to bear on some of the theory and data of Henry and Short's Suicide and Homicide. *After presentation of a theory relating sociological variables to the socialization of aggression, hypotheses are derived similar to those of Henry and Short. These hypotheses are tested, employing an index of preference for suicide or homicide, the Suicide-Murder Ratio (SMR). Consideration of the socialization process as it is related to the American class structure resolves some issues raised by Henry and Short's theory of external restraint and effectively predicts the findings. The results are considered in terms of Durkheim's belief that the choice of suicide or homicide resulting from anomie is purely a psychological problem and from the standpoint of Henry and Short's assertion that the choice is in part determined by sociological variables.*

No one has contributed more significantly to the establishment of sociology as a separate discipline than Émile Durkheim, and nowhere did he make this separation more secure than in *Suicide*. Then will an article frankly "social-psychological" in orientation, which argues from suicide-rate data, seem incongruous in a *Journal* issue dedicated

to Durkheim's memory? Durkheim would not have found it so, for our approach is one he advised.

While Durkheim saw the need to emphasize the separation of sociology from other sciences, especially psychology, we do not think he intended to isolate it. In *The Rules of Sociological Method* he specifically denies that there are no links between sociology and psychology.

We do not mean to say, of course, that the study of psychological facts is not indispensable to the sociologist. If collective life is not derived from individual life, the two are nevertheless closely related; if the latter cannot explain the former, it can at least facilitate its explanation. First, as we have shown, it is indisputable that social facts are produced by action on psychological factors. In addition, this very action is similar to that which takes place in each individual consciousness and by which are transformed the primary elements.[1]

Granting the divisions among levels of generality or abstraction, each with its own reality, laws at any level of abstraction are formulated with proper regard for other levels. Just as psychological laws of perception must be consistent with what is known about neurophysiology or must bear the burden of inconsistency, so sociological laws must face up to current knowledge of psychological processes. For this reason findings at one level are clues at the other.

Our purpose is to explore the relationship between certain psychological and sociological theories and between relevant data

[1] Émile Durkheim, *The Rules of Sociological Method*, trans. S. A. Solvay and J. K. Mueller, ed. G. E. G. Catlin (Glencoe, Ill.: Free Press, 1950), p. 11.

from both disciplines which pertain to the choice of suicide or homicide as an expression of aggression. We will try to show that the choice of suicide or homicide, essentially a psychological problem, is determined in part by the individual's place in a social system. We will focus on socialization as the process by which sociological factors are translated into determinants of a psychological choice between directions of aggression.

Our research gains impetus from the work of the late Andrew F. Henry and James F. Short, reported in their book, *Suicide and Homicide*.[2] A discussion of the sociological and psychological factors leading to these two ultimate forms of aggression is only one of the several problems they discuss, but, it is the one we pursue here. This paper is not intended as a critical review of their book. Rather it is a report of research which attempts to build upon and amplify a portion of the theoretical structure they presented.

We have two specific aims: one, primarily theoretical; the other, methodological.

First, Henry's and Short's theory will be examined from a social-psychological point of view. Where they have dealt separately with psychological and sociological antecedents of suicide and homicide, we will suggest some child-rearing links which mediate between social structural variables and intrapersonal determinants of behavior. Second, we will examine the way in which Henry and Short tested their hypotheses about the choice of suicide or homicide. It seems to us that a more appropriate methodology is needed, and we will suggest a possible alternative. Finally, we will use the suggested methodology to test hypotheses generated by Henry and Short and by the theory of socialization presented here. The findings will be compared.

THEORY OF EXTERNAL RESTRAINT

Henry and Short are interested in suicide and homicide as acts of aggression which

originate in frustration. They theorize that degree of external restraint distinguishes individuals who choose to commit one rather than the other. An individual is externally restrained to the degree that his alternatives of behavior are limited by others. It is postulated that, the more an individual is externally restrained, the more likely it is that he will regard others as legitimate targets for aggression. Hence, the greater the degree of external restraint upon an individual, the more likely that he will commit homicide rather than suicide.

It is assumed that individuals in higher-status categories, as indicated by four of Parsons' criteria, are less externally restrained than those in lower-status categories and are therefore more likely to prefer suicide to homicide. The criteria are achievement, possession, authority, and power. The authors specify the following high- and low-status segments of the American population:

High Status	Low Status
Males	Females
White	Non-white
Aged 25–34	Aged 65 or more
Army officers	Enlisted men

They hypothesize that, given frustration, members of low status are more likely than members of high-status categories to commit homicide rather than suicide. Further, they follow Durkheim in assuming that individuals involved in more intimate social relationships are more externally restrained. Hence, married people and rural dwellers, who are more subject to external restraint, are therefore more likely to prefer homicide to suicide than single or divorced people and urbanites.

A number of Henry and Short's assumptions may be questioned. It is debatable that members of higher-status categories are less restrained externally than their lower-status counterparts. For example, the behavior appropriate for an "officer and gentleman" is in many respects more limited than that allowed an enlisted man. Drunkenness off the base, for example, is apt to earn the enlisted man mild reproof but to invoke strong penalties on an officer. Similarly, eccentricities tolerated in persons over sixty-five may result in institutionalization of a twenty-five-year-old.

---

[2] A. F. Henry and J. F. Short, Jr., *Suicide and Homicide* (Glencoe, Ill.: Free Press, 1954).

External restraints on behavior are exerted not only by persons but also by norms— norms which may apply more stringently to persons in higher-status positions. Rather than arguing directly from status positions, let us consider other sources of behavioral restraints, specifically, limits imposed on expressions of aggression.

What are the interpersonal events through which restraints over aggression are made manifest? What are the processes by which aggression is displaced from the restraining figures to other targets? Why the choice of the *self* as a legitimate target for aggression in the absence of any other legitimate target? In short, what are the social-psychological variables mediating between the sociological conditions and the psychological event?

THE SOCIALIZATION OF AGGRESSION

A body of theory exists which helps to link sociological variables with preferences for self or others as targets for aggression. A brief presentation of the theory and some supporting data will lead us to hypotheses about preferences for suicide or homicide similar to Henry and Short's.

One of the early lessons a child must learn, if he is to continue to live among others, is to control his rages. Sigmund Freud recognized the importance of hate affect as well as love in the developing personality and marked the ego's mastery of these affects as a critical point in personality development.

An individual may control his aggression in many ways. Miller and Swanson order the modes of control in their theory of defenses.[3] An impulse, like the wish to destroy, is taken as an *action-tendency* which has four components: intended act, agent or actor, target object, and affect. Control can be established by manipulation of one or several of these components.

For example, the *intention* to destroy an object may be modulated into tongue-lashing. The aggressive *agent* may be distorted, as in projection: "He wants to destroy me; I don't want to hurt him." The impulse may be displaced to another *object* such as a socially acceptable scapegoat. The *affect* may be shifted, dislike displacing hate, or it may be distorted completely through the working of a reaction formation, hate becoming love. The action-tendency as a whole may be postponed temporarily or frustrated indefinitely.

Which mode or modes of control are selected depends to a great extent on the culture in which the individual participates. Among the Sioux, for example, an infant's tantrums were a matter of pride to his parents, and he was hurt and frustrated as a child to encourage his rage. Rages were later controlled by venting them against extratribal enemies in forays which promised social rewards.[4] Among the Alorese, on the other hand, aggression is suppressed at an early age and later finds expression in intratribal stealing.[5]

There is evidence, too, that modes of control and expression of aggression vary among the social classes in the United States. B. Allinsmith found that the TAT protocols of lower-class adolescent boys were more apt to include direct references to and direct expressions of aggression than those of middle-class boys.[6] While lower-class boys told stories of attacking or fleeing from authority, middle-class boys either told stories devoid of hate or stories in which aggression was turned against themselves.

B. J. Beardslee aroused the anger of lower- and middle-class boys halfway through

---

[3] D. R. Miller and G. E. Swanson, *Inner Conflict and Defense in the Child* (New York: Henry Holt & Co., 1958).

[4] E. H. Erikson, "Observations on Sioux Education," *Journal of Psychology*, VII (1937), 101–56.

[5] A. Kardiner, *Psychological Frontiers of Society* (New York: Columbia University Press, 1945).

[6] B. B. Allinsmith, "Parental Discipline and Children's Aggression in Two Social Classes" (unpublished Ph.D. dissertation, University of Michigan, Ann Arbor, 1954). Summarized in D. R. Miller and G. E. Swanson, "The Study of Conflict," *Nebraska Symposium on Motivation* (Lincoln, Neb.: University of Nebraska Press, 1956).

a set of story-completion projectives.[7] The middle-class boys showed the greater increase in the use of defenses against aggression from the pre- to the post-arousal story endings.

How are these differences in controls of aggression between the social classes established? Allinsmith suggests that one cause is the type of punishment meted out by parents to misbehaving children.[8] Lower-class mothers report that they or their husbands are likely to strike their children or threaten to strike them. Middle-class mothers report that their type of punishment is psychological rather than physical. Middle-class parents are more apt to say to a naughty son, "After all I've done for you . . . ," or, "You ought to be *ashamed. We* don't do that sort of thing."

Allinsmith reports that type of punishment is related to boys' TAT protocols; boys who are punished physically express aggression more directly than those who are punished psychologically. She suggests that type of punishment operates in two ways to generate this relationship. First, physical punishment clearly identifies the punisher. A son can see plainly who controls the flailing arm. The relationship between parent and child is, for the moment, that of attacker and attacked. Psychological punishment creates a more subtle relationship. It is often difficult for the son to tell where his hurt feelings are coming from. Their source is more likely to seem inside him than outside. If there is to be a target for aggression then, the physically punished child, who is more likely to be lower-class, has an external target readily available; the psychologically punished child does not have such a ready target. If he selects one, it is likely to be himself.

Second, the type of punishment a parent administers identifies for the child the approved behavior when one is hurt or angry. The punishing parent serves as a model whom

the child imitates and whose behavior instructs the moral conscience—the superego.

Why is it that lower-class parents are more likely to employ physical punishment and middle-class parents psychological punishment? McNeil has gathered data which suggest that lower-class Americans generally express themselves physically, while members of the middle class express themselves conceptually.[9] He found that lower-class adolescent boys are more spontaneous and expansive in their bodily expression of emotions in a game of statues, while their middle-class peers are more facile at the symbolic task of creating abstract drawings of emotions. He interprets these results as a reflection of the values and skills dominant in the two social classes. Lower-class boys are identifying with fathers who work with their bodies; middle-class boys are identifying with fathers who work with their heads.

Beardslee lends further support to the notion that children's behavior reflects these dominant class values.[10] She finds, as others have, that middle-class boys are apt to do better on tests of verbal intelligence than lower-class boys.

Selective factors are likely to be at work here. Since a great deal of social mobility in modern America is achieved in schools, where verbal ability is a core skill, boys who have such ability have a better chance of becoming middle-class adults. Degree of verbal facility is likely to affect modes of expression, such as the parents' expression of disapproval of the misbehavior of their children.

In an epidemiological study of psychopathology, Faris found a greater incidence of catatonia—a psychosis marked by inhibition of voluntary muscular movement—in the slum sections of cities, where manual workers are more concentrated.[11] But manic-depres-

---

[7] "The Learning of Two Mechanisms of Defense" (unpublished Ph.D. dissertation, University of Michigan, Ann Arbor, 1955). Summarized in Miller and Swanson, "The Study of Conflict," *op. cit.*

[8] Allinsmith, *op. cit.*

[9] E. B. McNeil, "Conceptual and Motoric Expressiveness in Two Social Classes" (unpublished Ph.D. dissertation, University of Michigan, Ann Arbor, 1953). Summarized in Miller and Swanson, "The Study of Conflict," *op. cit.*

[10] Beardslee, *op. cit.*

[11] R. E. L. Faris, "Ecological Factors in Human Behavior," in J. McV. Hunt (ed.), *Personality and the Behavioral Disorders* (New York: Ronald Press Co., 1944), II, 736–57.

sive psychosis is not related to ecological areas. These findings support the statement that expression of and defenses against expression of emotion are more apt to involve the physical apparatuses in the lower class.

Several factors converge in the relationship between social class and modes of aggressive expression. We have already seen how differential skills and occupations may enter into this relationship. It may also be that class ideologies concerning interpersonal relations differ. In the bureaucratic middle class, stress may be laid on "getting along" with others, for economic success rests heavily on the development of harmonious social relations. In this context direct expression of aggression becomes a disruptive force.

But, in the working class, direct aggression is not so dysfunctional. If we assume less interdependency among people and less need for harmony in social relations, the forces against expressing aggression are not so strong.

In this framework, type of punishment becomes an index to the values and skills of a category. As such, it may serve, along with social class, as a predictive variable.

Let us return now to our concern with the preference for suicide or homicide as the mode of aggressive expression. The theory presented above generates predictions similar to Henry and Short's about the kinds of people who are likely to turn aggression outward compared to those who will turn it inward. The predictions are based on the assumption that type of punishment is both an index to and a factor in shaping values concerning expression of aggression. Physical punishment leads to outward expression, while children punished psychologically should turn their aggression against themselves. The derivations below make use of the relationship found between type of punishment and social class.

Of the seven comparisons made by Henry and Short, the theory of socialization of aggression makes predictions in six. There is no prediction here for the married-unmarried comparison.

Since non-whites are heavily concentrated in the working class, the theory of socialization of aggression offers the hypothesis that non-whites should show a greater preference for homicide than whites. If we accept the common assumption that army officers are recruited from the middle class and that enlisted men are more likely to be working class, especially in times of peace, we can hypothesize that army officers are more likely than enlisted men to commit suicide.

Comparing rural to urban populations, it seems safe to assume that the proportion of urban people who work in bureaucratic settings should be greater than the rural proportion. If the previous argument about the source of physical and conceptual values and modes of expression is correct, urbanites should have the greater preference for suicide.

There is evidence that in America boys are more apt to be punished physically than are girls, regardless of race or social class.[12] Therefore, females should have a greater preference for suicide than males.

Were we able to compare the childhood punishments administered to people now over sixty-five with the type borne by people now between twenty-five and thirty-four, we could predict to their preferred expression of aggression. Such data might be obtained by interviewing members of these two age categories or by content-analyzing the child-rearing literature their parents read. Unfortunately, data needed to test this prediction are not available. Similarly, stratified data are not available to test the prediction that middle-class people are more likely than working-class people to destroy themselves.

When we compare the hypotheses based on the socialization theory with those based on external restraint, we find that three of the four to be tested are identical. That is, both theories predict that greater preference for suicide should occur among whites, army officers, and urbanites. On the other hand, Henry and Short expect men to show a

---

[12] E. Douvan and S. Withey, *A Study of Adolescent Boys* (Ann Arbor: Institute for Social Research, 1955); and E. Douvan, C. Kaye, and S. Withey, *A Study of Adolescent Girls* (Ann Arbor: Institute for Social Research, 1956). I am grateful to these authors for making these data available to me.

greater preference for suicide, since they are more externally restrained, while we predict women would. For women's childhood experiences are more apt than men's to be of psychological rather than physical punishment, indicative of an ideology of appropriate behavior expected from and to women.

METHODOLOGY

Before we go about testing our hypotheses, let us examine them a little more closely. We think that careful consideration of what we mean by "choice of" or "preference for" suicide or homicide suggests a more appropriate way of handling the data than Henry and Short employed.

In part I of *Suicide and Homicide* the authors try to establish that the business cycle is a common source of frustration for all segments of the population. But they find that suicide rates do not decrease uniformly in all segments of the population in prosperous times. In addition, they report that homicide rates increase during prosperity. But, if homicidal aggression is an index of frustration, this suggests that prosperity may in part be frustrating. The authors explain that lower-status categories are relatively more deprived and frustrated by prosperity, since they gain less, relative to higher-status categories.

At this point Henry and Short state their crucial hypothesis: People in higher-status categories are more likely to prefer suicide to homicide; people in lower-status categories, homicide to suicide. If this hypothesis is confirmed, then higher homicide rates during prosperity and higher suicide rates during depression are explained. Part I of their work takes this hypothesis as an important assumption.

In part II the authors test this hypothesis. They raise the question: "Why does one person react to frustration by turning the resultant aggression against someone else, while another person reacts to frustration by turning the resultant aggression against himself?[13]

---

[13] Henry and Short, *op. cit.*, p. 65.

They take upon themselves the responsibility of proving that members of higher-status categories are more apt to react to frustration by committing suicide and members of lower-status categories by committing homicide.

To support this, they offer absolute rates of suicide and homicide for specific years or series of years. These data show that the suicide rates presented are higher in most of the higher-status categories and that the homicide rates presented are higher in most of the lower-status categories. But it appears that Henry and Short may not really prove their point with these data.

If Henry and Short wish to demonstrate that members of higher-status categories have a greater preference for suicide than members of lower-status categories, it is not enough to demonstrate a greater suicide rate for higher-status categories. This may only indicate that they are more frustrated and hence more aggressive in general. For example, the authors' work on business cycles indicates that members of higher-status categories may at any one time be more frustrated than those in lower. If this is true, they may commit more homicide as well. Nor is it enough to demonstrate that within the higher-status category the suicide rate is higher than the homicide rate. This does tell us that higher-status citizens prefer suicide to homicide certainly, but it does not show that the preference in this category is any greater than the preference in the lower-status category where the suicide rate may also be higher than the homicide rate.

To illustrate this point, we may consider data in chapters v and vi of *Suicide and Homicide*. The writers first present evidence that the male suicide rate is higher than the female rate and so find support for their hypothesis that the higher-status category prefers aggression against self more than the lower. In chapter vii they show that the male homicide rate is also higher than the female. We might conclude from these data only that men are either more frustrated than women or more given to both these ultimate forms of violence.

In order to demonstrate a preference on the part of a population category, it is neces-

Table 1. Suicide-murder ratios of whites and non-whites, 1930–40*

Year	Suicide Rate		Homicide Rate†		SMR‡	
	White	Non-White	White	Non-White	White	Non-White
1930	18.0	5.9	5.9	39.5	75.3	13.0
1931	19.2	6.0	6.0	41.2	76.2	12.7
1932	19.7	6.8	5.9	40.0	77.0	14.5
1933	18.0	6.1	6.1	44.6	74.7	12.0
1934	16.6	5.9	5.7	46.5	74.4	11.3
1935	15.8	5.6	4.9	40.9	76.3	12.0
1936	15.7	5.2	4.5	41.4	77.7	11.2
1937	16.3	5.5	4.3	38.6	79.1	12.5
1938	16.4	5.5	3.8	34.9	81.1	13.6
1939	15.1	4.7	3.3	35.0	82.1	11.8
1940	15.2	5.1	3.2	34.2	82.6	13.0

* Source: United States Department of Health, Education, and Welfare, *Vital Statistics*, XXX, 467; XXXI, 485.
† Adjusted by age.
‡ All differences within years between white and non-white SMR's are significant beyond .0001 (two-tailed).

sary to take their total amount of suicide and homicide into account. To get an index of preference for suicide over homicide, we can divide the suicide rate by the sum of suicide rate and the comparable homicide rate: (Suicide rate/Suicide rate + Homicide rate). We may call this the Suicide-Murder Ratio, or SMR.[14] Comparing the SMR of one category with the SMR of another, the larger ratio demonstrates the greater preference for suicide.

Whether or not this mode of data analysis yields results different from those obtained by Henry and Short remains to be seen. In any case, it appears to have two advantages. First, it seems a surer way to establish preference for suicide or homicide. Second, it enables us to test whether a difference in preference between categories is statistically significant. For SMR's are proportions, and, assuming an infinite population, tests of significance of differences between proportions may be applied to them.

---

[14] We had originally thought of calling this the Suicide-Homicide Ratio, but "SHR" is immortally Clark Hull's. Another SHR would only cause confusion.

RESULTS

At this point we will apply the suggested methodology to the hypotheses advanced previously. We agree with Henry and Short that whites, urbanites, and army officers will demonstrate a greater preference for suicide—have a higher SMR—than non-whites, rural dwellers, and enlisted men. But, predicting to sex differences, Henry and Short think that males should have the greater preference for suicide, while the present author expects that females should.

In order to compute an SMR for a category, it is necessary to have data on the suicide rate and the homicide rate for the same population and for the same time period. It is not too difficult to get data on the number of suicides and the size of the population, so that a suicide rate can be computed. But data on homicides committed are not so easy to come by.

According to Henry and Short, "Cause of death by homicide statistics provide our most reliable comparison of homicide rates of whites and Negroes [since] the overwhelming majority of murders are committed by members of the same race as the person murdered."[15] The same type of data is used here for the racial comparison. Similarly, on the assumption that most urban murders are committed by urbanites, and most rural murders by rural dwellers, cause of death by homicide statistics are used in the rural-urban comparison also.

Table 1 presents the data comparing the preferences of white and non-whites. Supporting our predictions, it demonstrates that, in every year from 1930 to 1940, whites clearly chose suicide over homicide more often than did non-whites.

Table 2 presents the data on the preferences of the urban compared to the rural population, controlling on race. The predic-

Table 2. Suicide-murder ratios for urban and rural residents, 1930, 1932, and 1933, for whites and non-whites*

	Suicide	Homicide	
	Rate	Rate	SMR†
1930:			
White			
Urban	19.8	6.2	76.2
Rural	14.1	4.9	74.2
Non-white			
Urban	8.0	56.4	12.4
Rural	2.9	23.8	12.2
1932:			
White			
Urban	21.3	6.0	78.0
Rural	16.2	5.4	75.0
Non-white			
Urban	8.6	56.7	13.2
Rural	3.5	24.6	12.4
1933:			
White			
Urban	19.8	6.2	76.2
Rural	15.0	5.7	72.5
Non-white			
Urban	7.4	57.7	11.4
Rural	3.2	26.5	10.8

* Source: United States Bureau of the Census, *Mortality Statistics* for the years 1930, 1932, and 1933.
† Differences between SMR's within the white category are all significant beyond .01 (two-tailed). Differences within the non-white category are not significant (chance probability greater than .10 [two-tailed]).

tion that urbanites have the greater preference for suicide is confirmed. Although the differences in SMR's are not large, they are consistent over the three years we examined and within both race categories. It should be noted that presentation of the homicide rates alone would not have supported the hypothesis. According to the reasoning in *Suicide and Homicide*, the higher absolute homicide rates of the urban population would lead us to conclude that urban residents prefer homicide more than rural residents.

To compare army officers with enlisted men, it was necessary to use number of convictions for homicide as an estimate of the homicide rate. Inasmuch as not all murderers are caught, our data provide us with an approximation. Further, since the figures on convictions for homicide are low in the armed forces (no officers were convicted for this offense in the year for which data were available), data on convictions for assaults against persons are also included. So the homicide rate here is, strictly speaking, an index of "violence against others."

Table 3 reveals that army officers have a greater preference for aggression against the self than do enlisted men. This is as predicted. Note that the data on the suicide rates alone do not reveal the true magnitude of the difference in preferences between these two categories. But, when the suicide and the homicide (assault) rates are combined in the SMR's, a large difference emerges.

To test differences between preferences of males and females for one form of aggression or another, the homicide rate is computed on the basis of convictions for homi-

Table 3. Suicide-murder ratios of army officers and enlisted men, June, 1919—June, 1920*

Category	Suicide Rate	Homicide Rate†	SMR‡
Officers	5.9	7.1	45.4
Enlisted men	5.4	22.7	19.2

* Source: "Reports of the Adjutant General, Judge Advocate General, and the Surgeon General" *Annual Report of the Secretary of War, 1920* (Washington, D.C., 1921).
† Includes assaults on persons.
‡ Significance of difference in SMR's beyond .001 (two-tailed).

[15] Henry and Short, *op. cit.*, p. 82.

cide. Reasoning in terms of external restraint, Henry and Short expect that men will show the greater preference for suicide. The present author, taking socialization processes into account, predicts that women will show the greater preference. Table 4 presents the relevant data.

In every year, for both race categories, women are more likely to choose suicide over homicide than men are. These findings reflect a problem Henry and Short encountered. They found, consistent with their prediction, that males have higher suicide rates, but they also found, contrary to expectations, that males have higher homicide rates. It is just this type of problem which the use of SMR's avoids. Further, these findings suggest that socialization practices loom as important mediating conditions between sociological categories and expressions of aggression.

But Henry and Short have still a point to make. They suggest that the female has a higher status than the male among Negroes; if this is so, they would predict that the male has the higher homicide rate. And, since Negroes are disproportionately represented in the homicide statistics, this reasoning would account for the higher male homicide rate in general. They conclude that "further research should show that the ratio of male to female homicide among Negroes is higher than the male to female homicide among whites."[16]

Table 4 supports this last hypothesis. Among the non-whites, who are predominately Negroes, there are seven male murderers to one female murderer, while the ratio among whites is three to one. Even more important, a comparison of SMR's shows that there is a greater difference between the sexes in the non-white population in the preference for suicide over homicide. So Henry and Short find evidence here for their explanation of the findings.

However, the theory of socialization of aggression also explains why the difference in preference for suicide is greater between sexes among Negroes than among whites. This explanation does not seem co-ordinate

with Henry and Short's. Our findings would be expected if the type of punishment received by boys and girls differs more among Negroes than among whites. Suppose the percentage of Negro boys who receive physical punishment is much greater than the percentage of Negro girls who receive such punishment but that the percentage of white boys who receive physical punishment is only slightly larger than the percentage of white girls who receive such punishment. Then it would follow that Negro boys should have a much lower SMR than Negro girls, while white boys would show an SMR only slightly lower than white girls. Table 5 presents the relevant punishment data on a nation-wide sample of schoolboys and girls. The subjects are aged fourteen to sixteen, and race is controlled.

Table 5 clearly validates the assumption that differences in type of punishment is greater among Negro boys and girls than among white boys and girls. Furthermore, the figures here directly parallel the SMR's in Table 4: the white children are less likely than the Negroes to be punished physically and to show the lower SMR's. There is strong evidence here, then, that the manner in which children are socialized, as indicated by the way in which they are punished, is a factor in determining a later preference for suicide or homicide.

Let us raise one more issue. Henry and Short present us with a contradiction of factors affecting homicide and suicide rates in the "central disorganized sectors of cities": "From the general negative correlation between homicide and status position, we would expect the low status ethnic and Negro inhabitants of these areas to raise the homicide rate. From the suggested relation between homicide and strength of the relational system, we would expect the 'homeless men' and 'anonymous' residents of rooming houses in these areas to lower the homicide rate."[17]

This contradiction of factors becomes unimportant if socialization of aggression is recognized as a crucial mediating process be-

---

16 *Ibid.*, p. 88.

17 *Ibid.*, p. 93.

Table 4. Suicide-murder ratios of males and females, white and non-white 1930, 1932, and 1933* †

Year	Suicide Rate		Homicide Rate		SMR‡	
	Male	Female	Male	Female	Male	Female
1930:						
White	27.7	7.9	2.7	0.1	91.2	98.6
Non-white	9.0	2.6	8.0	1.0	52.8	71.8
1932:						
White	30.9	8.0	3.1	0.1	90.9	98.8
Non-white	10.5	2.8	21.5	2.9	32.8	49.1
1933:						
White	28.0	7.6	3.1	0.2	90.0	97.4
Non-white	9.4	2.6	22.0	2.9	29.9	47.3

* Sources: United States Department of Health, Education, and Welfare, *Vital Statistics* for the years 1930, 1932, and 1933; United States Bureau of the Census, *Prisoners in State and Federal Prisons and Reformatories* for the years 1926–36.
† Data for 1931 were incomplete.
‡ All differences between male and female SMR's each year are significant beyond .001 (two-tailed).

tween sociological categories and determinants of aggressive behavior. For, although there are ethnic and other differences within the central urban population, the overwhelming majority of these people, non-white or homeless, are in the working class. This fact suggests that certain socialization practices concerning aggression are generally present in the hub, which would lead to a choice of homicide rather than suicide. By considering socialization as primary, we can generate this straightforward hypothesis involving comparisons of urban centers with the periphery, which a theory of external restraint could not.

Although the necessary rates were not available to compute the appropriate SMR's, data gathered by Schmid, and cited by Henry and Short,[18] support the hypothesis. They indicate that homicides are more concentrated in the hub than are suicides—quite a different picture from that presented by other areas.

DISCUSSION

Now, Durkheim tentatively regarded the choice of anomic suicide or homicide as a purely psychological matter, unrelated to sociological variables. In *Suicide* he writes:[19]

Anomie, in fact, begets a state of exasperation and irritated weariness which may turn against the person himself or another according to circumstances; in the first case, we have suicide, in the second, homicide. The causes determining the direction of such over-excited forces probably depend on the agent's moral constitution. According to its greater or less resistance, it will incline one way rather than the other.

Henry and Short suggest that the choice of suicide or homicide, prompted by a state of anomie, is not purely a psychological matter. While their *Suicide and Homicide* includes an insightful discussion of psychological determinants of this choice, they assert that sociological variables play an active and separate role as well,[20] that is, external restraint growing directly out of position in the social structure conditions expression of aggression.

Our own position lies somewhere between the two. We assert that, if sociologi-

[18] *Ibid.*, p. 92.

[19] Émile Durkheim, *Suicide*, trans. A. Spaulding and G. Simpson, ed. G. Simpson (Glencoe, Ill.: Free Press, 1951).
[20] *Ibid.*, pp. 106–9.

Table 5. Type of punishment received by fourteen-to-sixteen-year-old males and females, white and negro*

	Per Cent Physical†	Per Cent Other	Per Cent Never Punished	Per Cent Unknown	No.
White:					
Boys	8.9	85.8	3.5	1.4	649
Girls	6.2	90.0	3.2	0.5	769
Negro:					
Boys	50.0	50.0	0.0	0.0	40
Girls	22.0	73.2	4.9	4.9	41

* Source: E. Douvan and S. Withey, *A Study of Adolescent Boys* (Ann Arbor: Institute for Social Research, 1955); E. Douvan, C. Kaye, and S. Withey, *A Study of Adolescent Girls* (Ann Arbor: Institute for Social Research, 1956).
† Significance of differences in percentage of physical punishment given boys and girls: white, > .10; Negro, > .01 (two-tailed).

cal variables condition expression of aggression, it is necessary to search for the manner in which these variables are translated into those psychological determinants which lie closer to the actual individual choice. This position has led us to examine the socialization process, particularly socialization of aggression. We have cited evidence that a pivotal child-rearing variable—type of punishment—is related to position in the social structure. We have tried to show why this relationship exists: outward aggression seems to be more disturbing to the interpersonal relationships inherent to the middle class than to those of the working class; outward aggression is more consistent with the role of men than of women in our society; and verbal ability is closely related to recruitment into social classes in our society and may have a good deal to do with the way parents punish children. It is a short step from these arguments to the choice of suicide or homicide.

We have pointed out that many of the relationships derived by Henry and Short from a theory of external restraint might equally well be derived from the association of particular socialization practices with social classes in America. Further, the problem of suicide and homicide rates in central portions of large cities, unresolved by the former, may be resolved by the latter.

But this does not by any means make the concept of external restraint less useful. On the contrary, if by external restraint we mean the degree to which one's behavior is controlled by an external other, the findings emphasize its value, for the theory of socialization presented and tested here also involves external restraint as a core concept. Physical punishment operates to create a preference for homicide insofar as it represents a pattern of controls which allows expression of aggression and does not build in controls over direct expression. We have assumed that this type of punishment is consistent with a value system which manifests itself in other child-rearing practices as well.

But rather than formulate external restraints in terms of relationships between broad sociological categories, we have availed ourselves of the clues psychology has to offer, particularly, that the relationship between parent and child is the crucial one.

It is possible that our proposal here is not alternative to Henry and Short's. Perhaps it is in addition. Those researchers certainly make it clear that they would not ignore psychological factors. But our feeling is that we are dealing with a unity. We have attempted to bring a social-psychological orientation to bear on the problem in order to show how sociological and psychological factors are related in one process.

IV Conflict over the Rules of Conflict: Revolutionary Conflict

Chapter 10

REVOLUTIONARY CONSCIOUSNESS AND LIBERATION MOVEMENTS

If a party feels that the rules of a competition are themselves unfair or rejects the basis of a normative allocation, this party is defining what we call a revolutionary conflict. Revolutionary movements necessarily seem to involve a heightened consciousness (not necessarily accurate) of how social systems function, if only because attributing bias to a system requires attention to the system and awareness of how system rules and norms affect people's lives.

The first selection, by Portes, provides empirical support for the idea that attributing responsibility to the social structure for one's frustrations (and not merely experiencing the frustrations per se, as some psychological theories would have it) is a crucial element in a radical or revolutionary orientation. The difficulty of achieving an awareness of social system factors is stressed in the next selection by Jones, a passionate analysis of the inequities of marriage. For Jones, one reason that the oppressed may fail to recognize their oppression, or fail to recognize the gulf between their own interests and those of the dominant classes, is that their individual frustrations and failures are made to seem the result of their own psychological inadequacies rather than a product of systematic oppression by a social system. Revolutionary consciousness is thus possible only when a person discovers that her discontent is shared by others who are similarly oppressed.

Fanon in his discussion of the effects of colonialism and Domhoff in his treatment of corporate America are also concerned with revolutionary consciousness among the dispossessed, but these authors further address themselves to the questions of the means and tactics of liberation once oppression has been recognized. Fanon argues that the only way the oppressed can cleanse themselves of their subjection and demonstrate to themselves their equality with their oppressors is through violent action to drive out these oppressors. Domhoff argues that whatever may be the conditions in other parts of the world, there is little hope for violent revolution in America, and that those working for radical change in the United States must innovate new means of raising revolutionary consciousness and commitment.

ON THE LOGIC OF POST-FACTUM EXPLANATIONS: THE HYPOTHESIS OF LOWER-CLASS FRUSTRATION AS THE CAUSE OF LEFTIST RADICALISM

Alejandro Portes

ABSTRACT

The common theme underlying most theories on lower-class leftist extremism views this orientation as dependent on frustration with life situation. Employing data collected in lower-class slums of Santiago, Chile, five theories bearing on this notion are tested. None is supported. Leftist radicalism, however, is associated with imputation of responsibility for frustrations to the social structure. Results support a definition of radicalism as a complex orientation requiring antecedent cognitive variables for its emergence. The popularity of the frustration–radicalism hypothesis is interpreted as a partial result of the post-factum *self-legitimation of successful revolutionary movements.*

The study of working-class politics has been permeated by the idea, expressed in a thousand different forms, that radicalism of the left arises from these sectors as a result of unbearable frustration with their position in the socioeconomic structure. A brief survey of currently available theories for the prediction of leftist radicalism reveals frustration with life conditions as the dominant common theme underlying most hypotheses. Though other variables may be posited as contributory or intervening, the process of working-class radicalization is made ultimately dependent on increasing discontent by its members with their social and economic situation.

In classic Marxist theory, revolutionary activism hinges, in an immediate sense, on the acquisition of "consciousness" by the proletariat. Yet, the crucial process underlying the increasing politicization and increasing intensity of proletarian struggles against the bourgeoisie is the inability of the capalistic order to prevent pauperization of the masses and evermore exploitative arrangements of production, which inevitably generate frustration and discontent (Marx, 1939, 1963, 1967; Marx and Engels, 1955). Intra-bourgeois competition and the process of concentration of capital lead to an ever-widening gap between the economic overabundance of the diminishing few and the abysmal misery among the growing many. The frustration of the latter, the mounting rage among those who have nothing and less to lose constitutes the basic force of revolutionary change in a capitalist order.

At the most general level, this view has been embodied in the hypothesis, unanimously accepted by political sociologists since Marx, of an inverse correlation between reception of socioeconomic rewards from the existing social order and tendencies toward revolutionary extremism. Such notion is certainly present in Max Weber's (1958; 1965) sociology of power, as well as in successive Marxian and neo-Marxian formulations of a theory of classes (Dahrendorf, 1965; Mills, 1970; Moore, 1969).

In contemporary sociology, the notion is usually rephrased as predicting a general negative association between socioeconomic status and leftist radicalism. Status is directly an indicator of differential socioeconomic rewards and indirectly, so the hypothesis assumes, of different levels of satisfaction and, hence, commitment to the existing social order. Lipset (1963:129) presents what is perhaps the best formulation of the hypothesis:

If we look at the supporters of the three major positions in most democratic countries, we find a fairly logical relationship between ideology and social base. The Socialist left derives its strength from manual workers and the poorer rural strata; the conservative right is backed by the rather well-to-do elements. . . . The democratic center is backed by the middle classes. . . . The different extremist groups have ideologies which correspond to those of their democratic counterparts.

Other contemporary theories concerned with political extremism have gone, however, beyond static socioeconomic position in search of causal factors. Despite their relative abundance, most maintain at their core the assumption that it is frustration with one's situation in life which leads to radical orientations.

Thus several theories have concentrated on socioeconomic mobility, rather than static position, as the basic determinant of different political orientations. Downward mobility into the lower classes and its profoundly frustrating consequences have been hypothesized to lead, under certain conditions, toward leftist radicalism (Lopreato and Chafetz, 1970). On the other hand, Germani (1966), Soares (1965), and others have viewed *upward* mobility from very low levels as favorable to leftist extremism. This because upward mobility exposes lower-class individuals to new, unreachable styles of life, thereby increasing relative deprivation and, hence, frustration with existing social arrangements. The objective phenomenon of absolute improvement in socioeconomic position is, thus, transformed into the subjective experience of increased distance between desires, previously kept at a minimum, and the possibilities of their fulfillment. Ensuing anger at a social order which makes these injustices possible is translated into an enhanced receptivity to revolutionary messages.[1]

In the contexts of developing societies, migrants to urban centers have been viewed as sources of political instability because of their greater permeability to leftist radicalism. The rationale of this hypothesis is again based on the concept of frustrated aspirations. The widening gap which the process of migration creates is not, however, between future aspirations and expectations (as for the upwardly mobile) but between past aspirations and present realities. The city, which entices the migrant with the prospects of a better life, does not provide the occupational means for their fulfillment.

Statements linking frustration of aspirations with migrant radicalism in developing societies are usually characterized by a sense of urgency at the imminence of revolutionary explosions. Thus, the often-quoted paragraph by Ward (1964:191–192):

All over the world, often long in advance of effective industrialization, the unskilled poor come streaming away from subsistence agriculture to exchange the squalor of rural poverty for the even deeper miseries of the shantytowns, favelas, and bidonvilles that, year by year, grow inexorably on the fringes of the developing cities. They are the core of local despair and disaffection—filling the Jeunesse movements of the Congo, swelling the urban mobs of Rio, voting communist in the ghastly alleys of Calcutta, everywhere undermining the all too frail structure of public order and, thus, retarding the economic development that alone can help their plight.

---

[1] Similarly, the currently popular hypothesis of status inconsistency, not examined here, envisions radical leftism as the consequence, not of an homogenously low socioeconomic position, but of lack of harmony between different status dimensions (Lenski, 1954, 1967; Rush, 1967; Treiman, 1966). Inconsistency promotes frustration through the social insecurity of the status-holder, his relative isolation, and the constant reminder—via the dimensions where he holds a high position—of his failure to attain or be granted equally high ones in the others (Germani, 1966; Lopreato, 1967; Loy, 1970; Portes, 1970a).

Most statements on the radicalizing consequences of migration implicitly assume, as the one above does, an immediate frustration of migrant aspirations in the city. Thus, receptivity to radical leftism is highest among recent migrants (Cornelius, 1969; Nelson, 1969).

Others, however, have viewed leftist radicalism as positively correlated with length of migrant residence in the city. The hypothesis, as stated by Soares (1965) and Soares and Hamblin (1967), also employs the concept of relative deprivation: no matter how humble their position, recent urban migrants are likely to have gained in comparison with their previous living levels. The satisfaction that they derive from this comparison gives way with time, however, to increasing feelings of frustration as their standards of comparison gradually shift from an abysmal rural past to the levels of living of middle and upper urban sectors. Relative satisfaction is substituted by relative deprivation; it is at this point, not during the first months, when the link between migration and leftist radicalism is established.

The above hypotheses form a non-exhaustive set of the theories advanced for the explanation of lower-class leftist radicalism on the basis of frustration with social situation. It is important at this point to distinguish between two levels of theory: (1) hypotheses linking situations of widespread frustration and discontent with the emergence of radical movements and revolutionary societal change, and (2) hypotheses predicting a causal connection between personal frustration and radical individual attitudes.

Revolutionary processes do not always require a dominant majority of lower-class individuals committed to a radical orientation. Nor does the existence of the latter guarantee the appearance of the former. To impute to individuals political attitudes necessarily congruent with major societal processes is to incur an obvious ecological fallacy. To extrapolate from sums or proportions of individual attitudes to the occurrence of structural transformations, a far more common tendency, is to accept a naive additive image of society and its structure. The phenomena

of societal revolutionary upheavals and of large proportions of radical political attitudes are certainly interrelated. Their relationship, however, is neither automatic nor straightforward. Neither should be taken as a perfect indicator or absolute determinant of the other.

The present paper reports results of testing, on the basis of survey data, several of the above hypotheses concerning leftist extremism. Each is examined, first, for its own value and, second, for its bearing on the general underlying theory: leftist radicalism as a direct function of frustration with social situation.

Implications of the findings are, however, limited to frustration as a predictor of individual political attitudes. The nature of the data, relatively adequate for this purpose, cannot be fitted into a logically appropriate test of macro-societal theories of revolution or revolutionary movements. Thus, the dependent variable to be examined is always limited to an individual outcome—leftist radical attitudes—never a social process.

To anticipate, examination of these hypotheses yields a major finding: frustration with personal situation is, consistently, a very poor predictor of leftist extremism. If this conclusion is correct, two further questions must be answered: (1) What factors are indeed causally linked with the emergence of leftist extremism in the lower classes? (2) What factors account for the diffusion and acceptance of the frustration–radicalism hypothesis despite its empirical weakness?

These questions are examined in turn in the last sections of the paper.

THE DATA

The data on which findings are based were collected in four lower-class urban slums in Santiago, Chile, during 1968–69. Though not randomly drawn, these four areas were deemed to be representative of the major types of slums to be found in Santiago's lower-class periphery. In each area, a 10 percent simple random sample of dwellings was drawn and the family heads interviewed. Sixteen percent of the original sample had to be replaced because of errors in sampling. Refusals, however, amounted to less than *1* percent of the sample. Total sample size was 382.

Detailed comparisons between results of this survey and larger, statistically representative studies conducted by United Nations (ECLA) and the Chilean government on the entire peripheral slum population of Santiago reveal close similarities over a series of social and economic indicators, thus reinforcing the potential generalizability of findings to this universe (Portes, 1970b).

A major difficulty in studies of leftist extremism is the absence or weakness of this ideology in the political culture of some countries and its illegality in those where it exists. In some cases, most commonly developed countries, studies of working-class politics are likely to yield only moderate leftist tendencies; in others, most commonly underdeveloped countries, respondents will not be willing to voice radical leftist opinions for fear of reprisals.

Chile has maintained for more than a century a democratic political system despite wide differences in its political spectrum. The extreme left formed by the FRAP, or alliance of the Communist and Socialist parties, have coexisted with other parties and grown steadily stronger to the point of winning the 1970 presidential election. Radicalism of the left, if not necessarily majoritarian, has certainly become a widespread political orientation among the urban lower classes after several decades of proselytizing by the Marxist left, especially the Communist party (Pike, 1968; Soares and Hamblin, 1967; Zeitlin, 1968). Thus, Chile offers the seldom-found possibility of confronting a population which feels relatively free to voice extreme political opinions and in which radicalism of the left is not an absent tendency.

In connection with this, however, another problem should be noted. Major studies of leftist radicalism have employed voting for or preference for the Communist party as an indicator of this orientation (Kornhauser, 1960; Lipset, 1963; Soares, 1965).

In Chile, as in many other nations, the Communist party played a crucial role in developing radical political consciousness in the working classes; yet, today, new extremist groups, especially those following the Castro-Guevara traditions, regard the Communists as representatives of a traditional, "institutionalized" left incapable of effective revolutionary action. It is, in fact, common among those familiar with the Chilean political situation to place the Communist party to the *right* of its ally, the Socialist party while regarding both, but especially the former, as previously revolutionary parties now oriented to representing lower-class interests within the established democratic framework (Zeitlin, 1968). Thus, equating Communist sympathies with radicalism of the left could be challenged on the grounds that these preferences are really representative of institutionalized leftism and by no means of extreme revolutionary orientations. Overcoming this problem means the need of operationalizing leftist radicalism in terms more general than preferences for the established Marxist parties.

Leftist radicalism was defined in this study as an attitudinal syndrome characterized mainly by an acceptance of revolution and revolutionary violence as legitimate means to overthrow an economic and political order perceived to be exploitative of the poor and its substitution by a socially "just" one.

Twenty closed items were included in the questionnaire as possible operationalizations of this orientation. By inspection, the 13 items most highly intercorrelated were selected and factor analyzed by the principal-components method. Equating the first factor with the theoretical dimension under consideration, those items having low loadings ($<.50$) in the first factor or higher loadings on secondary ones were excluded. The others were combined into a single index by taking the simple sum of their standardized scores. The resulting *leftist radicalism index* (LRI) is composed of 7 items:

1. Attitude toward a popular revolution in Chile. Responses ranged from "very good" to "very bad" for Chile.
2. Attitude toward breaking diplomatic relations with the United States. Responses

were dichotomized into "very important that it be done" versus "should not be done" or "not very important."

3. Attitude toward reestablishing friendly relations with Cuba. Responses were dichotomized as in Item 2.

4. Attitude toward forcibly expropriating the properties of the rich. Responses were dichotomized as in Items 2 and 3.

5. Comparison between these two alternatives:
   (a) Social change must be revolutionary. It is necessary to sweep away the whole past.
   (b) Social change should not be revolutionary. It is necessary to maintain many things from the past.

   Responses were trichotomized into "agrees with *a*," "agrees with neither," "agrees with *b*."

6. Comparison between these two alternatives:
   (a) The best way for a progressive government to attain power is through democratic elections.
   (b) The best way for a progressive government to attain power is through a popular revolution. Responses were trichotomized as in Item 5.

7. Comparison between these two alternatives:
   (a) Force does not lead anywhere. To achieve true social changes it is necessary to seek the cooperation of all.
   (b) To achieve true social changes it is necessary to use force against the powerful.

   Responses were trichotomized as in Items 5 and 6.

Matrix 1 presents the zero-order correlations between these items. Some have been reflected to give the leftist radical extreme in each item the highest score. Further evidence of internal consistency, convergent and predictive validity, omitted here, has been presented in detail elsewhere (Portes, 1970b).

The mean, standard deviation, and range of LRI appear in Table 1, which presents similar figures for all independent variables to be included in the ensuing analysis. Further

Matrix 1. Zero-order correlations between indicators of leftist radicalism

Items	X1	X2	X3	X4	X5	X6	X7
X1	—	.32	.38	.19	.49	.54	.34
X2		—	.24	.27	.41	.32	.30
X3			—	.31	.28	.32	.20
X4				—	.25	.24	.30
X5					—	.50	.43
X6						—	.51
X7							—

X1—attitude toward a popular revolution in Chile
X2—attitude toward U.S.-Chile relations
X3—attitude toward Cuba-Chile relations
X4—attitude toward expropriation of upper-class property
X5—subjective comparison between revolutionary versus reformist alternatives
X6—subjective comparison between popular revolution versus democratic elections
X7—subjective comparison between violent versus peaceful means

specifications concerning measurement and scoring of each variable are presented as they become relevant in the analysis.

A final note concerning hypothesis-testing. With sample size approaching *400*, zero-order correlations of *.10* are statistically significant at the *.05* level. It is obvious, however, that statistical significance is not equivalent in this case with substantive importance. For this reason, an arbitrary criterion requiring coefficients of *.20* ($p < .001$) or larger for non-rejection of a hypothesis was established.

THE SOCIOECONOMIC FACTORS

A.

The notion that differential reception of socioeconomic rewards is causally linked with frustration and, hence, with different tendencies toward leftist radicalism seems appropriately operationalized by the use of socioeconomic status as the independent variable. The hypothesis can then be reformulated as follows:

The higher the socioeconomic status of an individual, the weaker his attraction toward radicalism of the left.

Table 1. Descriptive statistics of variables

Variable	Mean	Standard Deviation	Minima	Maxima
X1—leftist radicalism (LRI)	0.000	4.61	−5.926 (least radical)	10.716 (most radical)
X2—occupational status	2.822	1.328	1.000 (minor services)	6.000 (white collar)
X3—personal income	3.173	1.625	0.000 (no income)	8.000 (E2000 or more)
X4—family income	3.691	1.680	0.000 (no income)	9.000 (E2500 or more)
X5—education	4.458	2.800	0.000 (no education)	12.000 (high school completed or higher)
X6—migration status	0.576	0.495	0.000 (native-born)	1.000 (migrant)
X7—recent migration	0.168	0.374	0.000 (non-recent migrant)	1.000 (recent migrant)
X8—older migration	0.414	0.493	0.000 (non-older migrant)	1.000 (older migrant)
X9—belief in attainment of future aspirations	1.246	0.629	1.000 (will be fulfilled)	3.000 (will not be fulfilled)
X10—expectations of future earnings	6.702	2.543	1.000 (less than E200)	13.000 (E5000 or more)
X11—subjective frustration	0.000	3.455	−8.150 (most satisfied)	6.439 (most frustrated)
X12—focus of blame for personal frustrations	0.000	1.714	−0.996 (least structural blame)	5.171 (most structural blame)
X13—evaluation of opportunities for personal success offered by country	0.539	0.499	0.000 (opportunities offered)	1.000 (opportunities not offered)
X14—perception of concern of Chilean governments in general for poor	0.610	0.488	0.000 (have shown concern)	1.000 (have not shown concern)

Among the dimensions of status, occupational level and income seem most directly relevant to measurement of socioeconomic rewards. Education, though also included in the analysis, can be conceptualized less as a reward in itself than as a means to their attainment.

Occupational level was coded along a 6-point hierarchical scale comprising the following categories: minor services, unskilled blue collar, semiskilled blue collar, skilled blue collar and artisans, intermediate services, and white collar and minor professions.[2]

Income is operationalized with two indicators—individual personal income and total family income. Both are given in

unskilled blue collar: construction and factory workers without training and farm workers. In semiskilled blue collar: construction carpenters, painters, factory machinists, etc. In skilled blue collar: tailors, furniture makers, mechanics, electricians, master plumbers, radio technicians, etc. In intermediate services: barbers, beauticians, bus and cab drivers, and small merchants. In white collar and minor professions: teachers, secretaries, bookkeepers, middle-level merchants, etc. This occupational classification is partially based on the guidelines established by the Chilean National Institute of Occupational Training (INACAP, 1966).

[2] In minor services were included: maids, other house servants, shoe shiners, messengers, etc. In

Matrix 2. Zero-order correlations between leftist radicalism index (LRI) and independent variables

Variables	X1	X2	X3	X4	X5	X6	X7	X8	X9	X10	X11	X12	X13	X14
X1	—	.00	−.05	−.07	−.01	.11	.08	.05	.06	−.01	.11	.27	.30	.35
X2		—	.47	.41	.40	−.14	−.01	−.14	−.03	.31	−.26	.11	−.04	−.07
X3			—	.83	.34	−.14	−.03	−.12	−.05	.41	−.50	.02	−.07	−.09
X4				—	.31	−.10	−.01	−.11	−.03	.38	−.45	.01	−.09	−.07
X5					—	−.16	−.04	−.13	−.04	.31	−.12	.07	−.08	−.12
X6						—	.38	.69	.14	−.19	.09	.02	.10	.05
X7							—	−.38	.05	−.15	.04	.05	.01	.03
X8								—	.12	−.10	.07	−.02	.09	.04
X9									—	−.12	.19	.05	.15	.18
X10										—	−.22	.04	−.12	−.08
X11											—	.18	.25	.24
X12												—	.27	.28
X13													—	.51
X14														—

X1—LRI
X2—occupational status
X3—personal income
X4—family income
X5—education
X6—migration status
X7—recent migration
X8—older migration
X9—belief in attainment of future aspirations
X10—expectations of future earnings
X11—subjective frustration
X12—focus of blame for personal frustrations
X13—evaluation of opportunities for personal success offered by country
X14—perception of concern of Chilean governments in general for the poor

"escudos" of 1968 and range from "no income" to "E2500 or more."[3]

Education is measured in years of formal school completed and ranges from "no education" (0 years) to "high school completed or more" (12 years or more).

Matrix 2 presents the zero-order correlations between indicators of socioeconomic status and leftist radicalism. Correlation of LRI with occupational level (r_{12}) is .00 (n.s.); with personal income (r_{13}) is −.05 (n.s.); with total family income (r_{14}) is −.07 (n.s.); with education (r_{15}) is −.01 (n.s.).

The combined effects of occupation, personal and family income, and education on leftist radicalism are presented in the first row of Table 2. These are the results of regressing leftist radicalism (LRI) on these four variables.

As can be seen, all standardized regression coefficients (*beta* weights) are insignificant. The multiple correlation $(R_{1.2345})$

is .08 (n.s.). Thus, the combined effects of socioeconomic status dimensions succeed in explaining less than 1 percent of the variance in leftist radicalism.

These results clearly lead to the rejection of the hypothesis linking socioeconomic status and leftist radicalism. One point, however, should be noted. Theories predicting a negative association between reception of socioeconomic rewards and radicalism of the left usually refer, implicitly or explicitly, to between-class rather than within-class differences. Limitation of this sample to a lower-class population means that the broader version of the hypothesis remains untested. An appropriate inference would, therefore, be that intra-lower-class differences in socioeconomic rewards are not found to have any effect on radical political attitudes; conclusions concerning the general population cannot be formulated on the basis of these data.

B.

As seen above, the notion that the crucial stratification factor affecting political extremism is not static socioeconomic position but

[3] Equivalence to the dollar in 1968 was U.S. $1.00 = E10.0 approximately. The Chilean government's officially established "subsistence" salary for a worker's family of four was approximately E400.0 in 1968–69.

Table 2. Regressions of leftist radicalism on independent variables

X2	X3	X4	X5	X6	X7	X8	X9	X10	X11	X12	X13	X14	R	R^2
.031 (ns)	.004 (ns)	−.089 (ns)	.002 (ns)										.078 (ns)	.006
				.059 (ns)	.071 (ns)	.038 (ns)							.120 (ns)	.014
							.041 (ns)	.022 (ns)	.105 (p < .04)				.116 (ns)	.014
.037 (ns)	.051 (ns)	−.094 (ns)	.000 (ns)	.089 (ns)	.051 (ns)	.006 (ns)	.030 (ns)	.048 (ns)	.096 (ns)				.174 (ns)	.030
										.172 (p < .002)	.136 (p < .015)	.230 (p < .001)	.410 (p < .0001)	.168
.009 (ns)	.003 (ns)	−.086 (ns)	.032 (ns)	.072 (ns)	.051 (ns)	.009 (ns)	−.019 (ns)	.055 (ns)	−.29 (ns)	.168 (p < .002)	.138 (p < .016)	.237 (p < .0001)	.428 (p < .0001)	.183

X2—occupational status
X3—personal income
X4—family income
X5—education
X6—migration status
X7—recent migration
X8—older migration
X9—belief in attainment of future aspirations
X10—expectations of future earnings
X11—subjective frustration
X12—focus of blame for personal frustrations
X13—evaluation of opportunities for personal success offered by country
X14—perception of concern of Chilean governments In general for the poor

degree and direction of movement in the stratification hierarchy has led to contradictory predictions. Some, following the simpler rationale, have predicted a positive relationship between downward mobility—as a factor promoting frustration—and leftist radicalism. Others, following a more devious theoretical path, have predicted the opposite: a positive association between upward mobility—as a factor producing relative deprivation—and leftist extremism.

Hypotheses involving mobility, in either direction, posit not a main, but an interaction effect. It is not past status level nor present one, nor even the added effects of the two, which are hypothesized to affect political attitudes. Rather it is the *unique* combination of the two indicating *movement* along status dimensions and present neither in the initial nor in the terminal point. This is an interaction effect.

Testing the relationship of mobility to leftist radicalism implies, therefore, the need to establish a basis of additive effects of present and past status levels against which to compare those due to their interaction.

Mobility is operationalized in this sample as difference between respondent's present and past occupation. Only intragenerational mobility is examined since no data were available on father's occupation. Two levels of each independent variable are considered: "high" versus "low." Further subdivisions would yield cells with low or zero frequencies. For both, present and past occupation, the following cutting points were employed:

High—skilled blue collar, artisans, intermediate services, white collar and minor professions

Low—minor services, unskilled and semiskilled blue collar

For purposes of clarity, LRI was also dichotomized[4] into:

---

[4] In theory, use of a dichotomous dependent variable in a regression equation may present statistical difficulties. In the present case, however, results using LRI as a continuous variable were identical

Lefist radicalism—scores equal to or higher than one standard deviation in the leftist radical direction

No-leftist radicalism—scores below one standard deviation in the leftist radical direction.[5]

Additive effects are computed through a dummy-variable regression equation (Boyle, 1970; Suits, 1957; Treiman, 1966). The resulting equation takes the form:

$$\hat{L} = a + b_1 0c_1 + b_2 0c_2 \qquad (1)$$

where $\hat{L}$ is expected proportion of leftist radicalism; $0c_1$ equals "1" if past occupation was high and "0" otherwise; and $0c_2$ equals "1" if present occupation is high and "0" otherwise.

Obtaining the expected proportions of leftist radicalism for upwardly, downwardly, and nonmobile individuals on the basis of the additive effects of the independent variables is a matter of adding to the intercept "a" the regression coefficients (bs) corresponding to the particular intersection of these variables. Thus, the expected proportion of leftist radicalism among the upwardly mobile is, $a + b_2$. That among the nonmobile high group is, $a + b_1 + b_2$. And that corresponding to the nonmobile low group is, a. The least squares solution for Equation 1 yielded the following coefficients:

$$a = .1871$$
$$b_1 = -.0391 \qquad b_2 = .016$$

---

to those obtained with the index dichotomized. Given this situation, it appeared preferable to present the dichotomous version of the variable since results, in the form of proportions, are of much more straightforward and simple interpretation than index means.

[5] The above cutting points are a compromise between two needs. (1) Maximizing the validity of the classifications; that is, insuring that those classified as leftist radicals are really so. This rules out the tendency to use the mean as the cutting point. (2) Providing each category with a sizeable number of cases.

Table 3. Expected proportions of leftist radicalism by present and past occupational status

			Past Occupation	
			Low	High
P	O			
r	c	Low	18.7	14.8
e	c			
s	u			
e	p	High	20.3	16.4
n	a			
t	t			
	i			
	o			
	n			

Table 5. Interaction effects

			Past Occupation	
			Low	High
P	O			
r	c	Low	0.5	−6.1
e	c			
s	u			
e	p	High	−2.1	5.0
n	a			
t	t			
	i			
	o			
	n			

Expected proportions of leftist radicalism on the basis of the added effects of present and past occupations are presented in Table 3. Observed proportions appear in Table 4. Interaction effects (obtained by subtraction) are presented in Table 5.

The hypotheses under consideration lead us to direct attention to interaction effects occurring in the mobile groups. For the downwardly mobile (upper-right cell), the first hypothesis predicts higher-than-expected proportions of leftist radicalism. As can be seen, there is in fact some interaction in the cell, but it is in the opposite direction: Those moving down in the occupational hierarchy are, as a group, even less likely to embrace leftist radicalism than what the simple added effects of their present and past position would predict.

Rejection of this hypothesis suggests support for the prediction of a positive causal

Table 4. Actual proportions of leftist radicalism by present and past occupational status*

			Past Occupation	
			Low	High
P	O			
r	c		19.2	8.7
e	c	Low	(265)	(23)
s	u			
e	p		18.2	21.4
n	a	High	(66)	(28)
t	t			
	i			
	o			
	n			

* Raw cell frequencies are in parentheses.

association between upward mobility in the lower classes and leftist extremism. Examination of the upwardly mobile group (lower-left cell) reveals, however, the opposite result. Departures from additivity are smaller than among the downwardly mobile but again in the opposite direction from that predicted.

The only deviations from additivity in the direction of greater-than-expected leftist radicalism are in fact found among the non-mobile groups, especially the stable high-occupation group. This, however, should not provide grounds for a new theory since neither these interactions nor those found among the mobile categories are statistically significant. This is found by adding an interaction term to Equation 1. The new equation takes the form:

$$\overset{\Lambda}{L} = a + b_1 0c_1 + b_2 0c_2 + b_3 0c_1 0c_2 \quad (2)$$

where the third term is non-zero only when both present and past occupations are high. In a two-by-two situation, addition of an interaction term has the effect of exactly reproducing observed proportions in each cell, as can be easily ascertained. Coefficients associated with Equation 2 are:

$$a = .1924$$
$$b_1 = -.0106 \qquad b_2 = -.1055$$
$$b_3 = .1380$$

The coefficient associated with the interaction term, which both mobility hypotheses would predict to be negative (since it is associated with nonmobile high status), is in fact positive. Yet, because of a large standard error of regression, b_3 yields a t-value of 1.1289 which, for 378 degrees of freedom, is significant only at the .26 level.

In summary, it can be concluded that no mobility effect, either upward or downward, has an effect on radicalism of the left in this sample. Though this finding is again directly applicable only to a lower-class situation, it should be noted that both hypotheses, especially the one predicting frustrating and, hence, radicalizing effects of upward mobility from very low positions to somewhat higher ones are specifically predicated of lower-class populations. Their rejection, therefore, is not greatly attenuated by sample limitations.

MIGRATION

As seen above, a widespread assumption concerning the process of urbanization in Latin America and in other developing countries, is the connection between rural–urban migration and political instability caused by frustration of migrants' aspirations in the city and their subsequently enhanced receptivity to revolutionary ideologies.

Migration is operationalized in this sample through place of birth, dichotomized into "born in Santiago" versus "migrant" (coded highest). The correlation between this variable and LRI (r_{16}) in Matrix 2 is .11 $(p < .04)$. Though larger than previous correlations, this coefficient still falls considerably short of the criterion (.20) established for rejection of the null hypothesis.

It is possible, however, as some writers have speculated, that it is not migration in general, but *recent* migration and its profoundly frustrating impact, which forms the crucial determinant of leftist extremism (Mangin, 1967; Nelson, 1969). This hypothesis is examined by dichotomizing the sample into "recent migrants"—those with less than four years of residence in Santiago (coded highest)—versus all others.

Correlation of this variable with LRI (r_{17}) in Matrix 2 is .08 (n.s.). The hypoth-

esis of a positive association between recent migration to the city and leftist radicalism can, therefore, be rejected.

Opposite to the above prediction is Soares' hypothesis of increasing relative deprivation and, hence, receptivity to leftist radicalism among *older* migrants. The independent variable is operationalized in this case by dichotomizing respondents into "older migrants"—those with ten years or more of residence in Santiago (coded highest)—versus all others. Correlation of this variable with leftist radicalism (r_{18}) is .05 (n.s.). Thus, this hypothesis is also rejected by the data.

The second row of Table 2 presents the combined effects of the three migration variables on leftist radicalism. Corresponding standardized regression coefficients are all nonsignificant. The multiple correlation $(R_{1.678})$ is .12 (n.s.), indicating that less than 2 percent of the variance in LRI is explained by this model.

It can be concluded that no support is found in these data for hypotheses linking migration or different periods of urban residence by migrants with leftist radicalism. Insofar as these hypotheses bear on the general theory of frustration as the main cause of political extremism, the latter is, once more, rejected.

THE SUBJECTIVE FACTORS

A.

Social-psychological approaches to the phenomenon of extremist politics have emphasized the subjective dynamics of frustration, rather than objective factors (Blumer, 1951; Killian, 1964; Toch, 1965). This results in hypotheses which make explicit the rationale underlying theories connecting objective-structural variables with leftist radicalism.

One of the most frequently employed notions is the one which envisions lower-class leftist radicalism as a consequence of a widening gap between aspirations and expectations for their fulfillment. Given the relative nature of this subjective gap, it can vary autonomously and even in the opposite direction of what objective socioeconomic situation would lead us to expect. This forms the rationale of the theory linking lower-class upward mobility and leftist radicalism. Widening gaps between aspirations and expectations lead to increasing feelings of frustration and, hence, to greater receptivity to radical ideologies. The hypothesis, therefore, can be stated as follows:

The greater the subjectively anticipated probabilities of fulfillment of main aspirations, the weaker the tendencies toward leftist radicalism.

A question in the present study asked respondents what their main aspiration for the future was. The following question asked: "Do you really believe you will attain this aspiration?" Closed response categories were "yes," "does not know," and "no." Though crude, this measure appeared to differentiate well between those for whom a gap between goals and expectations existed and those for whom it did not.

Correlation of this variable ("no" responses coded highest) with LRI (r_{19}) in Matrix 2 is .06 (n.s.). The hypothesis, therefore, is not supported by the data.

A second indicator of future expectations was given by the respondent's anticipation of future earnings. The relevant question asked respondents how much money they expected to earn monthly, assuming constant prices and a situation similar to the current one, five years hence. Responses, given in "escudos," ranged from "less than E 200" to "E 5000 or more." It seems reasonable to assume that greater expectations of earnings indicate a more optimistic attitude toward the future and, hence, a narrower gap between aspirations and expectations. Thus, it could be predicted that expectations of future earnings should be negatively correlated with leftist radicalism.

The corresponding zero-order correlation ($r_{1.10}$) in Matrix 2 is −.01 (n.s.).

These results lead to the conclusion that differences in expectations of goal-fulfillment in the future have no effect on the emergence of leftist extremism in the sample.

B.

Theories examined up to this point operationalize frustration with personal situation indirectly. Each posits a factor, objective or subjective, which in turn is assumed to lead to varying levels of frustration. If frustration, in fact, constitutes the crucial determinant of leftist radical attitudes, it would seem that the final and most compelling test of the theory would be to examine the association between frustration and leftist radicalism directly. Rather than assume that objective socioeconomic status, mobility, migration, or future expectations lead to greater or lesser feelings of frustration in the individual, we may ask him directly for his own evaluation of his situation in life and the amount of satisfaction or dissatisfaction that he derives from it. In this general form, the theory predicts that:

The greater the amount of subjective frustration of lower-class individuals with their situation in life, the stronger the tendencies toward leftist radicalism.

Subjective frustration is operationalized in these data as a unit-weighted index of standardized scores in 5 items. Each provides 4 closed response categories:

1. Subjective comparison between present and previous occupation. Answers range from "much better now than before" to "worse now than before."
2. Subjective comparison between present occupation and occupation aspired to when R started working. Responses range from "better now" to "much worse now."
3. Subjective comparison between present income and income aspired to when R started working. Responses range from "earns more now" to "earns much less now."

4. Subjective comparison between present situation in general and situation aspired to at the beginning of adult life. Answers range from "better now" to "much worse now."

.5. Subjective evaluation of present earnings in relation to family needs. Answers range from "earns enough—can save" to "does not earn enough—suffers great deprivations."

These items were selected after a two-step procedure of matrix inspection and factor analysis identical to that employed in constructing LRI. Intercorrelations between these indicators are presented in Matrix 3.[6]

The zero-order correlation between subjective frustration and leftist radicalism ($r_{1.11}$) in Matrix 3 is .11 (p < .04). Though statistically significant, the figure is disappointing in view of the amount of political theorizing asserting the importance of this relationship. The coefficient falls short of the .20 figure established for nonrejection of the hypothesis.

The third row of Table 2 presents the combined effects of the three subjective variables examined: belief in attainment of future aspirations, expectation of future earnings, and frustration with personal situation—on leftist radicalism. Standardized regression coefficients corresponding to the first two variables are nonsignificant. That corresponding to subjective frustration is larger, reaching significance at the .05 level. Nevertheless, the multiple correlation ($R_{1(9.10.11)}$) is .12 (n.s.), indicating that the combined effects of variables measuring discrepancies between aspirations and expectations and a direct measure of subjective frustration explain little more than 1 percent of the variance on leftist radicalism.

The fourth row of Table 2 combines the effects of socioeconomic status

---

[6] Evidence of convergent validity for this index is provided by its zero-order correlations in Matrix 2 with socioeconomic variables, migration status, and expectations of aspiration fulfillment in the future. All are in the predicted direction, and those linking frustration with occupational level ($r_{11.2}$), income ($r_{11.3}$ and $r_{11.4}$), and future expectations ($r_{11.9}$ and $r_{11.10}$) are, as would be expected, sizeable.

Matrix 3. Zero-order correlations between subjective satisfaction indicators

Items	X1	X2	X3	X4	X5
X1	—	.45	.30	.31	.29
X2		—	.30	.44	.31
X3			—	.35	.25
X4				—	.47
X5					—

X1—subjective comparison between present and past occupations
X2—subjective comparison between present occupation and initial occupational aspirations
X3—subjective comparison between present income and initial income aspirations
X4—subjective evaluation of present situation in general in comparison with initial aspirations
X5—subjective evaluation of present income in relation to family needs

indicators, migration factors, subjective expectations for the future, and subjective frustration on LRI. It is found that none of the corresponding regression coefficients is statistically significant. The multiple correlation ($R_{1(2.3.4.5.6.7.8.9.10.11)}$) is .17 (n.s.). The total effect of all the factors examined positing, directly or indirectly, the dependence of lower-class leftist extremism on varying degrees of frustration succeeds in explaining 3 percent of the variance in the dependent variable.

Use of correlation and multiple regression in these data may make results liable to the objection that they are spuriously due to reductions in correlation brought about, first, by the ordinal nature of most variables and, second, by attenuation through restriction of the sample to a lower-class universe. Though effects of ordinality tend in fact to be less marked than those originally assumed (cf. Boyle, 1970) and though considerable variation is apparent in Table 1 for all independent variables, including status indicators, it seems convenient to examine the validity of this objection by checking present results against those obtained from contingency analysis.

Similar tabular results are obtained with the dependent variable, LRI, divided into 2 or 3 categories, with further divisions leading to cells with very low frequencies. For purposes of clarity, results involving the dichotomous version of the dependent variable are presented. Cutting points for the two categories—leftist radicalism versus no-leftist radicalism—are identical to those employed in tests for mobility effects above. The first eight rows of Table 6 summarize these results by presenting the proportions of leftist radicalism for each category of the independent variables employed, *chi*-square and corresponding significance levels, and Cramer's V as a measure of strength of association.[7]

As can be seen, no single contingency association between objective or subjective indicators of frustration and leftist extremism yields statistical significance at the .05 level. No coefficient of association exceeds .15. The relationship between the index of subjective frustration and leftist radicalism, which should be theoretically quite strong, turns out to be one of the weakest encountered. The only association approximating statistical significance is that between occupation and radicalism. This relationship is, however, curvilinear with both the highest and lowest occupational levels exhibiting the lowest proportions of leftist radicalism. Though too weak to merit further discussion at this point, it should be noted that this pattern of association, while interpretable within a different theoretical framework, runs directly contrary to the theory of frustration which would predict a purely linear, negative relationship. Tabular findings, in sum, essentially restate the results encountered in correlational analysis. As in the latter, no significant relationship is detected between direct or indirect indicators of frustration with a lower-class situation and the emergence of radicalism of the left in this sample.

DISCUSSION

The consistent failure of the data to lend support to the causal link between frustration

---

[7] V has the advantage over other contingency measures of association of maintaining stable limits regardless of the number of columns or rows in the table. In all cases its range is: $0 \leq V \leq 1$. It should be noted that in the $2xn$ case V is identical to the more popular, though less general, Φ.

and radicalism of the left brings forth the need to examine the theoretical shortcomings of the frustration–extremism theory. This is especially important in view of the fact that its widespread acceptance among the general public is coupled with its consistent rejection in empirical studies. In the Latin American context, outside the present study, careful surveys and cross-national comparisons by Goldrich (1967–68), Nelson (1969), Cornelius (1969), and Bourricaud (1967), among others, find that frustration, as measured or imputed to the urban lower classes, has little to do with the emergence of leftist extremism. In the case of the peasantry, the study by Petras and Zeitlin (1968) finds the main determinant of peasant leftism to lie in proximity to the radical mining areas, not in differential frustration.

Two main shortcomings can be detected in the rationale of the theory:

1. The link between frustration and radicalism is assumed to be too immediate. Political extremism is implicitly regarded as the direct, automatic consequence of a frustrating situation without mediation of intervening cognitive variables. In this connection, it should be noted that frustration can be channeled through many paths, of which leftist extremism is only one. Here, Lipset's (1963) observation of the role of chiliastic religion, nonpolitical charismatic movements, escapist cultures, and mere withdrawal into apathy, as functional alternatives to leftist extremism deflecting the emotional potential of frustration, should be stressed.

2. More importantly, the assumed immediacy of the effect of frustration on leftist extremism is dependent on a definition of the latter as a simplistic, highly emotional response not requiring prolonged previous exposure or cognitive development. The tenets of a radical leftist ideology are, thus, assumed to be self-evident, at the disposal of anyone, and brought to the fore as a simple emotional reaction to the frustrations of lower-class life.

Formalization in psychology of the frustration-aggression hypothesis (Berkowitz, 1962; Dollard *et al.*, 1939) reinforced the impetus given to the frustration–radicalism

Table 6. Proportions of leftist radicalism for each category of independent variables

Variable	Categories						Totals	X^2	$p <$	V
X2—occupational status	Minor services and unskilled blue collar 14.0 (157)	Semiskilled blue collar 25.6 (117)	Skilled blue collar 21.1 (57)	Intermediate services, white collar, minor professions 13.7 (51)			18.6 (382)	7.00 3df	n.s.	.136
X3—personal income	< E.200 9.8 (41)	< E.600 20.1 (199)	< E.1000 21.4 (98)	≧ E.1000 13.6 (44)			18.6 (382)	3.65 3df	n.s.	.098
X4—family income	< E.200 8.7 (23)	< E.600 19.5 (169)	< E.1000 19.5 (128)	< E.1500 23.7 (38)	≧ E.1500 8.3 (24)		18.6 (382)	3.98 4df	n.s.	.102
X5—education	did not attend 12.5 (40)	1–2 years grade school 16.7 (48)	3–4 years grade school 13.2 (106)	5–6 years grade school 24.4 (119)	1–2 years high school 28.1 (32)	3 years high school or more 16.2 (37)	18.6 (382)	7.81 5df	n.s.	.142
X6, X7, X8—migration	≦ 4 years residence in Santiago 21.7 (23)	5–9 years residence 17.1 (41)	10 or more years residence 22.8 (158)	born in Santiago 14.4 (160)			18.6 (382)	3.93 3df	n.s.	.101

412

Table 6. (Continued)

Variable	Categories				Totals	X^2	$p <$	V
X9—belief in attainment of future aspirations	will not be attained 22.5 (40)	does not know 28.6 (14)		will be attained 17.7 (328)	18.6 (382)	1.50 2df	n.s.	.063
X10—expectations of future earnings	< E.600 10.0 (40)	< E.1500 18.3 (169)	< E.3000 19.2 (120)	< E.4000 20.0 (25)	≧ E.4000 28.6 (28)	18.6 (382)	3.86 4df	n.s.	.101
X11—subjective frustration	high frustration (one SD or above in frustration index) 25.4 (63)	medium (between mean and one SD) 17.5 (120)		low frustration (below mean of index) 17.1 (199)	18.6 (382)	2.32 2df	n.s.	.078
X12—focus of blame for personal frustrations	structural 41.7 (72)	quasi-structural 16.0 (50)		non-structural 12.7 (260)	18.6 (382)	31.54 2df	.001	.287
X13—evaluation of opportunities for success offered by country	country has not offered opportunities 26.2 (206)			country has offered opportunities 9.7 (176)	18.6 (382)	16.11 1df	.001	.205
X14—perception of concern of Chilean govts. for the poor	governments have not concerned themselves with the poor 25.3 (223)			governments have concerned themselves with the poor 8.1 (149)	18.6 (382)	16.79 1df	.001	.210

413

theory by popular versions of Marxism. Extrapolation of the psychological finding of a consistent aggressive response to frustrating stimuli underlies many a modern treatment of political radicalism. Radicalism is often perceived as the political counterpart of aggression. It is only the target that shifts: from individual subjects to the entire social structure.

As an alternative to the above view, it will be proposed that radicalism of the left is in fact a complex attitudinal orientation characterized, not only by intense emotion, but also by a definite *cognitive* approach to social phenomena. The systematic views of society embodied in leftist radical ideologies are neither self-evident nor automatically elicited by the emotional prodding of social and economic deprivation. Frustration ought to be, in fact, a very poor predictor of lower-class leftist radicalism since it provides no guarantee of intellectual exposure or of processes of mediation involved in the cognitive development of this political orientation. The action-potential generated by frustration is, in the absence of these conceptual factors, readily absorbed by the many avenues of release more immediately present in the life space of the individual.

STRUCTURAL BLAME

The revised conception of leftist radicalism proposed above suggests that the emergence of this orientation hinges largely on the presence of cognitive—not emotional—variables. Such a variable is the factor an individual blames for his frustrations in life. The origin of these frustrations in social structural arrangements is not self-evident. Realization by the individual that his situation is largely conditioned by the existing social order, rather than by fate, luck, or his own individual actions, ought to make a difference in his ensuing political orientations. For lower-class individuals, this awareness means that responsibility for continuous deprivations is imputed to the broader social structure rather than to nonstructural and, hence, politically irrelevant factors.

This process, to be labeled *structural blame*, following Morrison and Steeves (1967), lies at the root of the notion of "consciousness" as employed by Marxist writers (Dahrendorf, 1965; Engels, 1964; Lenin, 1929; Marx, 1939, 1963, 1967; Marx and Engels, 1955; Mills, 1956, 1962, 1970). The idea is also present in Max Weber's (1958: 184) treatment of class:

The degree in which "communal action" and possibly "societal action" emerges from the "mass actions" of the members of a class is especially linked to the "transparency" of the connections between the causes and the consequences of the class situation. For however different life chances may be, this fact in itself by no means gives birth to "class action." . . . The fact of being conditioned and the results of the class situation must be distinctly recognizable.

Contemporary formulations have depicted "structural blame" as a crucial factor in the emergence of collective movements (Killian, 1964; Kornhauser, 1960; Lang and Lang, 1961) and as the main characteristic of the mental set of "developing man" (Horowitz, 1966). The notion has already been employed in the study of leftist extremism among Cuban workers (Zeitlin, 1966), NFO members (Morrison and Steeves, 1967), Detroit Negroes (Leggett, 1964) and Chilean and Peruvian slum dwellers (Goldrich et al., 1967–68). The hypothesis can be formulated as follows:

The more lower-class individuals perceive the cause of their frustrations as lying in social structural arrangements rather than in fate, transcendental factors, or themselves, the stronger their tendencies toward leftist radicalism.

Emergence of leftist extremism, therefore, depends more on *who* is blamed for frustrations than on what amount of frustration there is.

Structural blame is operationalized in these data by three indicators:

1. Focus of blame for frustrations. This is a unit-weighted summated index of two closed items. The first asked respondents

who had previously answered that some of their aspirations in life had not been attained, who was to blame for this. The second asked respondents who had previously expressed that they deserved a better situation than their present one, who was to blame for their not having attained it. Response categories in both items were trichotomized into "structural," "quasi-structural," and "non-structural" blame.[8] Zero-order correlation between these items is .47 ($p < .0001$).

2. A closed item asking respondents whether the country had given them the necessary opportunities to succeed in life. Response categories are dichotomous: "yes" (non-structural blame) and "no" (structural blame).

3. A closed item asking respondents whether, in their view, the governments of Chile, in general, had concerned themselves with the situation of the poor. Responses are again dichotomized into "yes" (non-structural blame) and "no" (structural blame).

In all three indicators, the structural blame category is coded highest.

Correlation of focus of blame for personal frustrations and LRI ($r_{1.12}$) in Matrix 2 is .27 ($p < .001$). Correlation of evaluation of structural opportunities for personal success and LRI ($r_{1.13}$) is .30 ($p < .0001$). Correlation of perception of government concern for the poor and LRI ($r_{1.14}$) is .35 ($p < .0001$). All coefficients are significant and in the predicted directions. All three

exceed, being the first to do so, the .20 criterion established for rejection of the null hypothesis.

The fifth row of Table 2 presents the combined effects of the three independent variables on leftist radicalism. All corresponding standardized regression coefficients are highly significant. The multiple correlation ($R_{1(12.13.14)}$) is .41 ($p < .0001$). Thus, the proportion of variance explained by the combined indicators of structural blame on LRI is .17.

Though not high, this figure is by no means negligible. It should in fact be evaluated against the background of the series of independent variables examined before and of the usual results of political research on individual attitudes which tend to yield, in correlational or tabular form, low-level associations.

Contingency analysis of the relationships between structural blame indicators and leftist radicalism yields identical results. These are presented in the three bottom rows of Table 6. Chi-squares associated with these findings considerably exceed, in all cases, values required for significance at the .001 level. Similarly, all coefficients of association are above .20. As in correlational analysis, these are the only significant associations encountered among tabular results.

The last row of Table 2 presents the combined effects on LRI of all the variables examined. As can be seen, addition of 10 variables representing socioeconomic status, migration status, future expectations, and subjective frustration adds less than .02 to the multiple correlation of structural blame indicators and leftist radicalism. Thus, use of these 10 variables improves our predictive ability on LRI by 1 percent.

It can be concluded, therefore, that the data lend support to the hypothesis predicting a positive association between imputation of blame for personal frustrations to the social structure and leftist radicalism.

These data cannot provide a conclusive answer to the objection that structural blame may follow, not precede, adoption of a radical leftist orientation. On purely conceptual grounds it will be argued, however, that the

---

[8] The structural blame category included the following: "society is unjust with the poor," "the rich," "the government," "the upper class," etc. Quasi-structural blame comprised "inflation," "high prices," "lack of work," and other similar responses placing blame on the general social situation, but not on specific agents or centers of power of the social order. The non-structural blame category was composed of such responses as "myself," "bad luck," "fate," "parents," and accounts of purely individual happenings ("sickness," "my husband left me," "started to work too soon"). Individuals declaring themselves to be completely satisfied with their situation were also included in this category.

causal line runs in the direction predicted by Marx, Weber, and other authors. Realization of the general social origins of personal frustration is an event conceptually simpler and logically preceding legitimation of violence as the means to bring about the downfall of the social order. In a conceptual hierarchy, leftist radicalism is both, more complex and more difficult to embrace than structural blame: one must first identify the causes of one's suffering before being willing to destroy them. In this study, many more structure-blamers were non-radicals than vice versa.

Structural blame can, thus, be visualized as an antecedent of leftist extremism mediating whatever relationship exists between the latter and subjective frustration. Initial evidence in support of this view is provided by results of a partial correlation analysis, presented in Table 7. If structural imputation of responsibility in fact intervenes between frustration and leftist extremism, controlling for it should render the already weak correlation between the last two variables entirely insignificant (Blalock, 1964; Hyman, 1967). On the other hand, if leftist radicalism precedes structural blame and mediates the relationship of the latter variable with subjective frustration, the partials of radicalism with frustration controlling for structural blame should not differ significantly from the total correlation, but those of blame indicators with frustration controlling for leftist radicalism should be close to zero.

As results in Table 7 indicate, this latter prediction is not supported by the data. Partial correlations of LRI with the index of subjective frustration controlling for each indicator of structural blame are, without exception, considerably reduced, none differing significantly from zero. On the other hand, correlation of structural blame indicators with subjective frustration are not altered by controlling for leftist radicalism, each total correlation losing only 2 points to its corresponding partial and thus maintaining the same significance level. An identical pattern of results with 3 different indicators of structural blame seems to provide additional support to the present conclusions.

The argument of causal precedence of structural imputation of responsibility over leftist extremism does not rule out, however, the possibility of an intensification or acceleration of the process of structural blame once a leftist radical ideology has been embraced. At this point, a circular model of causation, with each side influencing and intensifying the other, may well be the most theoretically appropriate.

SUMMARY AND CONCLUSIONS

This paper has examined a series of hypotheses based on the general assumption that the main factor determining the emergence of radicalism of the left in the lower classes is

Table 7.   Zero-order and partial correlations between indicators of subjective frustration, structural blame, and leftist radicalism

Zero-Order γ		Partial γ	
$\gamma_{1.11} = .11$ [p < .04]	$\gamma_{(1.11)12} = .06$ [n.s.]	$\gamma_{(1.11)13} = .03$ [n.s.]	$\gamma_{(1.11)14} = .04$ [n.s.]
$\gamma_{12.11} = .18$ [p < .01]	$\gamma_{(12.11)1} = .16$ [p < .01]		
$\gamma_{13.11} = .25$ [p < .001]		$\gamma_{(13.11)1} = .23$ [p < .001]	
$\gamma_{14.11} = .24$ [p < .001]			$\gamma_{(14.11)1} = .22$ [p < .001]

X1—leftist radicalism index (LRI)
X11—subjective satisfaction index
X12—focus of blame for personal frustrations
X13—evaluations of opportunities for personal success offered by country
X14—perception of concern of Chilean governments for the poor

increasing frustration with life situation. Employing data collected in lower-class urban slums of Santiago, Chile, it is found that neither socioeconomic status, nor mobility, rural–urban migration, subjective distance between aspirations and expectations, or a direct measure of subjective frustration have significant effects on leftist radical attitudes.

Theories positing frustration as the main causal factor in the emergence of leftist extremism implicitly define the latter as an elementary emotional reaction to the deprivations of lower-class life. This allows the assumption of an immediate connection between the existence of frustration and the embracing of leftist extremism.

An alternative definition is proposed here which envisions radicalism of the left not only as an emotional reaction but also as a relatively complex cognitive orientation, necessitating previous intellectual exposure and intervening processes for its emergence. The tenets of leftist extremism are not self-evident; therefore, the existence of frustration is no guarantee of acquisition of this political orientation.

This definition leads to positing a cognitive variable, structural blame for personal frustrations, as a crucial antecedent of radicalism. Imputation of responsibility for a frustrating situation to the existing social order and not amount of frustration is hypothesized to lead to increasing levels of leftist extremism. Empirical tests employing three different operationalizations of structural blame consistently support this prediction.

An intriguing byproduct of the present analysis concerns the widespread acceptance of the theory linking frustration to lower-class leftist extremism in spite of consistent empirical findings in the opposite direction. Up to here, the analysis has been limited to the prediction of individual political attitudes. At this point, however, it is necessary to move beyond the data to hypothesize a link between structural processes of revolutionary change and individual radical attitudes as an answer to the above question.

This final hypothesis, for which space does not permit detailed documentation, suggests that the resilience of the frustration–radicalism theory is largely due to the self-legitimating efforts of already successful rev-

olutionary movements. Successful revolutions have sought historical legitimacy through imputation to the previous regime of qualities which made it unbearable for the vast majority of the people. Thus, revolutionary historiography has depicted the origins of the movement as arising from the spontaneous reaction of the masses to intolerable deprivations. Frustration, thus, is assigned the main causal role in the victory of the radical movement. Through this interpretation the revolutionary regime depicts itself as historically "inevitable" and assumes the roles of representative and enforcer of popular, spontaneous "justice."

The impact of successful revolutionary movements on scientific theorizing about political extremism is felt in two ways: first, through accounts by the leaders and staff of the radical movement of the events that brought about its success; second, through post-factum conscienticization of the masses concerning their previous "intolerable" life situation and its structural causes.

The latter point suggests that the casual relationship · between massive presence of leftist radical attitudes in the population and success of revolutionary movements, usually assumed to run from the former to the latter, may well also be in the opposite direction. Successful revolutions tend to generate, post-factum, massive feelings of frustration and structural blame and, hence, create the conditions for widespread acceptance of the new radical ideology.

Detailed studies of the French Revolution (de Tocqueville, 1888; Lefebvre, 1957), the Russian Revolution (Carr, 1953; Malaparte, 1960), and the recent Cuban Revolution (Amaro, 1969; Draper, 1965) indicate that mobilization of the masses occurred after, and with relatively secondary consequences for the takeover of political power by the revolutionary elite. Nevertheless, in each case, official historiography has attributed revolutionary success to the inevitable, invincible action of the people reacting against unbearable conditions. These accounts, impressively legitimated by post-factum conscienticization and radicalization of the masses, cannot fail to have an impact on laymen and scholars. Faced with such a generalized revolutionary militancy, observers have often little choice but to accept the causal sequence of revolutionary origins outlined by movement leaders. The idea eventually filters down to the prediction of individual radical attitudes as a consequence of personal frustrating experiences.

If nothing else, this view points to the need of maintaining a clear conceptual separation between causation of major structural upheavals and the etiology of individual extremism. Blurring of the lines and uncritical extrapolation from one theoretical level to the other account, to a large extent, for the preservation of an empirically weak theory as a reflection, at the individual level, of structural processes and their frequently partial interpretations.

References

Amaro, N., "Class and Mass in the Origins of the Cuban Revolution." *Studies in Comparative International Development*, Vol. 4, No. 10, 1969.

Berkowitz, Leonard, *Aggression*. New York: McGraw-Hill, 1962.

Blalock, Hubert M., Jr. *Causal Inferences in Nonexperimental Research*. Chapel Hill: University of North Carolina Press, 1964.

Blumer, H., "Collective Behavior." Pp. 166–222 in Alfred M. Lee (ed.), *Principles of Sociology*. New York: Barnes & Noble, 1951.

Bourricaud, Francois, *Poder y Sociedad en el Peru Contemporaneo*. Buenos Aires: Sur. 1967.

Boyle, R. P., "Path Analysis and Ordinal Data." *American Journal of Sociology* **75**, January, 1970. Pp. 461–480.

Carr, Edwin H., *The Bolshevik Revolution, 1917–1923*, III. New York: Macmillan, 1953.

Cornelius, W. A., "Urbanization as an Agent in Latin American Political Instability: The Case of Mexico." *American Political Science Review* **63**, September, 1969. Pp. 833–857.

Dahrendorf, Ralf, *Class and Class Conflict in Industrial Society*. Stanford: Stanford University Press, 1965.

de Tocqueville, Alexis, *On the State of Society in France Before the Revolution of 1789*. London: Murray, 1888.

Dollard, John, L. W. Doob, N. E. Miller, O. H. Mowrer, and R. R. Sears, *Frustration and Aggression*. New Haven: Yale University Press, 1939.

Draper, Theodore, *Castroism, Theory and Practice*. New York: Praeger, 1965.

Engels, F., "Ludwig Feuerbach and the End of Classical German Philosophy." Pp. 213–268 in R. Niebuhr (ed.), *Karl Marx and Friedrich Engels on Religion*. New York: Schocken, 1964.

Germani, G., "Social and Political Consequence of Mobility." In Neil J. Smelser and Seymour M. Lipset (eds.), *Social Structure and Mobility in Economic Development*. Chicago: Aldine, 1966.

Goldrich, D., R. B. Pratt, and C. R. Schuller, "The Political Integration of Lower-Class Urban Settlements in Chile and Peru." *Studies in Comparative International Development* **3**: 1–22. 1967–68.

Horowitz, Irving Louis, *Three Worlds of Development*. New York: Oxford University Press, 1966.

Hyman, Herbert, *Survey Design and Analysis*. New York: The Free Press, 1967.

INACAP (Chilean National Institute of Occupational Training), "Necesidades de Mano de Obra, Education y Formacion Profesional: Un Enfoque Global." Santiago (mimeo). 1966.

Killian, L., "Social Movements." Pp. 448–452 in Robert E. Faris (ed.), *Handbook of Modern Sociology*. Chicago: Rand McNally, 1964.

Kornhauser, William, *The Politics of Mass Society*. New York: Free Press, 1960.

Lang, Kurt, and Gladys Lang, *Collective Dynamics*. New York: Crowell, 1961.

Lefebvre, G., *The Coming of the French Revolution, 1789*. New York: Vintage, 1957.

Leggett, J. C., "Economic Insecurity and Working Class Consciousness." *American Sociological Review* 29, April, 1964. Pp. 226–234.

Lenin, Vladimir Ilitch, *What Is to Be Done?* New York: International Publishers, 1929.

Lenski, G., "Status Crystallization: A Non-Vertical Dimension of Social Status." *American Sociological Review* 19, August, 1954. 405–413.

————. "Status Inconsistency and the Vote: A Four-Nation Test." *American Sociological Review* 32, April, 1967. Pp. 288–301.

Lipset, Seymour M., *Political Man*. New York: Anchor Books, 1963.

Lopreato, J., "Upward Social Mobility and Political Orientation." *American Sociological Review* 32, August, 1967. Pp. 586–592.

————, and J. S. Chafetz, "The Political Orientation of Skidders: A Middle-Range Theory." *American Sociological Review* 35, June, 1970. Pp. 440–445.

Loy, N., "Status Inconsistency and Leftist Radicalism." Unpublished M.A. thesis, University of Wisconsin, 1970.

Malaparte, Curzio, *Tecnica del Golpe de Estado*. Buenos Aires: Plaza y Janes, 1960.

Mangin, W. A., "Latin American Squatter Settlements: A Problem and a Solution." *Latin American Research Review* 2, Summer, 1967. Pp. 65–98.

Marx, Karl, *The German Ideology*. New York: International Publishers, 1939.

————. *The Eighteenth Brumaire of Louis Bonaparte*. New York: International Publishers, 1963.

————. *Capital*, I. New York: International Publishers, 1967.

————, and Friedrich Engels, *Manifiesto del Partido Comunista*. Moscow: Ediciones en Lenguas Extranjeras, 1955.

Mills, C. Wright, *The Power Elite*. New York: Oxford University Press, 1956.

————. *The Marxists*. New York: Oxford University Press, 1962.

————. "The Structure of Power in American Society." Pp. 83–91 in S. E. Deutsch and J. Howard (eds.), *Radical Perspectives in Sociology*. New York: Harper & Row, 1970.

Moore, Barrington, *Social Origins of Dictatorship and Democracy*. Boston: Beacon, 1969.

Morrison, D. E., and Steeves, A. D., "Deprivation, Discontent, and Social Movement Participation." *Rural Sociology* **32**, December, 1967. Pp. 414–434.

Nelson, Joan M., *Migrants, Urban Poverty and Instability in Developing Nations.* Cambridge: Harvard University Center for International Affairs, 1969.

Petras, J., and Zeitlin, M., "Miners and Agrarian Radicalism." Pp. 235–248 in James Petras and Maurice Zeitlin, Jr. (eds.), *Latin America, Revolution or Reform?* Greenwich, Connecticut: Fawcett, 1968.

Pike, F. B., "Aspects of Class Relations in Chile, 1850–1960." Pp. 208–218 in James Petras and Maurice Zeitlin, Jr. (eds.), *Latin America, Revolution or Reform?* Greenwich, Connecticut, Fawcett, 1968.

Portes, A., "Leftist Radicalism in Chile: A Test of Three Hypotheses," *Comparative Politics* **2**, January, 1970a. 251–274.

———. "Radicalism in the Slum." Unpublished Ph.D. dissertation, University of Wisconsin, 1970b.

Rush, G. B., "Status Consistency and Right Wing Extremism." *American Sociological Review* **32**, February, 1967. Pp. 86–92.

Soares, G. A., "Desarrollo Economico y Radicalismo Politico." Pp. 516–559 in Joseph A. Kahl (ed.), *La Industrializacion en America Latina.* Mexico, D. F.: Fondo de Cultura Economica, 1965.

Soares, G. A., and R. L. Hamblin, "Socio-Economic Variables and Voting for the Radical Left: Chile, 1952." *American Political Science Review* **61**, December, 1967. Pp. 1055–1966.

Suits, D. B., "Use of Dummy Variables in Regression Equations." *Journal of the American Statistical Association* **52**, December, 1957. Pp. 548–551.

Toch, Hans, *The Social Psychology of Social Movements.* Indianapolis: Bobbs-Merrill, 1965.

Treiman, D. J. "Status Discrepancy and Prejudice." *American Journal of Sociology* **71**, May, 1966. Pp. 651–664.

Ward, B., "The Uses of Prosperity." *Saturday Review*, August, 1964. Pp. 191–192.

Weber, M., "Class, Status, and Party." In Hans H. Gerth and C. Wright Mills (eds.), *From Max Weber: Essays in Sociology.* New York: Oxford University Press, 1958. Pp. 180–195.

———. *The Theory of Social and Economic Organization.* In A. M. Henderson and T. Parsons (trans.). New York: Free Press, 1965.

Zeitlin, M., "Economic Insecurity and the Political Attitudes of Cuban Workers." *American Sociological Review* **31**, February 1966. Pp. 31–51.

———. "The Social Determinants of Political Democracy in Chile." In James Petras and Maurice Zeitlin (eds.), *Latin America, Revolution or Reform?* Greenwich, Connecticut: Fawcett, 1968. Pp. 264–288.

THE DYNAMICS OF MARRIAGE AND MOTHERHOOD

Beverly Jones

No one would think of judging a marriage by its first hundred days. To be sure there are cases of sexual trauma, of sudden and violent misunderstandings, but in general all is happiness; the girl has finally made it; the past is but a bad dream. All good things are about to come to her. And then reality sets in. It can be held off a little as long as they are both students and particularly if they have money, but sooner or later it becomes entrenched. The man moves to ensure his position of power and dominance.

There are several more or less standard pieces of armament used in this assault upon wives, but the biggest gun is generally the threat of divorce or abandonment. With a plucky woman a man may actually feel it necessary to openly and repeatedly toy with this weapon, but usually it is sufficient simply to keep it in the house undercover somewhere. We all know the bit, we have heard it and all the others I am about to mention on television marital comedies and in nightclub jokes; it is supposed to be funny.

The husband says to the wife who is about to go somewhere that doesn't meet with his approval, "If you do, you need never come back." Or later, when the process is more complete and she is reduced to frequent outbreaks of begging, he slams his way out of the house claiming that she is trying to destroy him, that he can no longer take these endless, senseless scenes, that "This isn't a marriage, it's a meat grinder." Or he may simply lay down the law that goddamn it, her first responsibility is to her family and

he will not permit or tolerate something or other. If she wants to maintain the marriage she is simply going to have to accommodate herself.

There are thousands of variations on this theme and it is really very clever the way male society creates for women this premarital hell so that some man can save her from it and control her ever after by the threat of throwing her back. Degrading her further, the final crisis is usually averted or postponed by a tearful reconciliation in which the wife apologizes for her shortcomings, namely the sparks of initiative still left to her.

The other crude and often open weapon that a man uses to control his wife is the threat of force or force itself. Though this weapon is not necessarily used in conjunction with the one described above, it presupposes that a woman is more frightened of returning to an unmarried state than she is of being beaten about one way or another. How can one elaborate on such a threat? At a minimum it begins by a man's paling or flushing, clenching his fists at his sides or gritting his teeth, perhaps making lurching but controlled motions, or wild threatening ones while he states his case. In this circumstance it is difficult for a woman to pursue the argument which is bringing about the reaction, usually an argument for more freedom, respect, or equality in the marital situation. And, of course, the conciliation of this scene, even if he has beaten her, may require his apology, but also hers for provoking him. After a while the conditioning becomes so strong that a slight change of color on his part, or a slight stiffening of stance (nothing observable to an outsider) suffices to quiet her or keep her in line. She turns off or detours mechanically, like a robot, not even herself aware of the change, or only momentarily and almost subliminally.

But these are gross and vulgar techniques.

Source: B. Jones, "The Dynamics of Marriage and Motherhood," in R. Morgan (ed.), *Sisterhood is Powerful: An Anthology of Writings from the Women's Liberation Movement* (New York: Random House, Vintage, 1970), pp. 46–61. Copyright 1970 by B. Jones and reprinted by permission.

There are many more, subtle and intricate, which in the long run are even more devastating. Take, for instance, the ploy of keeping women from recognizing their intelligence by not talking to them in public. After marriage this technique is extended and used on a woman in her own home.

At breakfast a woman speaks to her husband over or through the morning paper, which he clutches firmly in his hands. Incidentally, he reserves the right to see the paper first and to read the sections in order of his preference. The assumption is, of course, that he has a more vested interest in world affairs and a superior intelligence with which to grasp the relevance of daily news. The women's section of the paper is called that, not only because it contains the totality of what men want women to be concerned with, but also because it is the only section permitted to women at certain times of the day.

I can almost hear you demur. Now she has gone too far. What supersensitivity to interpret the morning paper routine as a deliberate put-down. After all, a woman has the whole day to read the paper and a man must get to work. I put it to you that this same situation exists when they both work or when the wife works and the husband is still a student, assuming he gets up for breakfast, and on Sundays. What we are describing here is pure self-indulgence. A minor and common, though none the less enjoyable, exercise in power. A flexing of the male prerogative.

Perhaps the best tip-off to the real meaning of the daily paper act comes when a housewife attempts to solve the problem by subscribing to two papers. This is almost invariably met with resistance on the part of the man as being an unnecessary and frivolous expense, never mind whether they can afford it. And if his resistance doesn't actually forestall the second subscription he attempts to monopolize the front sections of both papers! This is quite a complicated routine but, assuming the papers are not identical, it can be done and justified.

However, we were talking about conversation and noted that it was replaced by the paper in the morning. In the evening men attempt to escape through more papers, returning to work, working at home, reading, watching television, going to meetings, etc. But eventually they have to handle the problem some other way because their wives are desperate for conversation, for verbal interchange.

To understand this desperation you have to remember that women before marriage have on the whole only superficial, competitive, and selfish relationships with one another. Should one of them have a genuine relationship, it is more likely with a male than a female. After marriage a woman stops courting her old unmarried or married female sidekicks. They have served their purpose, to tide her over. And there is the fear, often well founded, that these females will view her marriage less as a sacrament than a challenge, that they will stalk her husband as fair game, that they will outshine her, or in some other way lead to the disruption of her marriage.

Her husband will not tolerate the hanging around of any past male friends, and that leaves the woman isolated. When, as so often happens, after a few years husband and wife move because he has graduated, entered service, or changed jobs, her isolation is complete. Now all ties are broken. Her husband is her only contact with the outside world, aside, of course, from those more or less perfunctory contacts she has at work, if she works.

So she is desperate to talk with her husband because she must talk with *someone* and he is all she has. To tell the truth, a woman doesn't really understand the almost biologic substructure to her desperation. She sees it in psychological terms. She thinks that if her husband doesn't talk to her he doesn't love her or doesn't respect her. She may even feel that this disrespect on his part is causing her to lose her own self-respect (a fair assumption since he is her only referent). She may also feel cheated and trapped because she understood that in return for all she did for him in marriage she was to be allowed to live vicariously, and she cannot do that if he will not share his life.

What she does not understand is that she cannot go on thinking coherently without expressing those thoughts and having them accepted, rejected, or qualified in some manner. This kind of feedback is essential to the healthy functioning of the human mind. That is why solitary confinement is so devastating. It is society's third-rung "legal deterrent," ranking just below capital punishment and forced wakefulness, or other forms of torture that lead to death.

This kind of verbal isolation, this refusal to hear a woman, causes her thought process to turn in upon itself, to deteriorate, degenerate, to become disassociated from reality. Never intellectually or emotionally secure in the first place, she feels herself slipping beyond the pale. She keeps pounding at the door.

And what is her husband's response? He understands in some crude way what is happening to her, what he is doing to her, but he is so power-oriented he cannot stop. Above all, men must remain in control; it's either him or her. The worse she becomes, the more convinced he is that the coin must not be turned. And thence springs anew his fear of women, like the white's fear of blacks. We tend to forget that witches were burned in our own country not too long ago, in those heroic days before the founding fathers. That each day somewhere in our country women are raped and/or killed just for kicks or out of some perverted sense of retribution. And we never even consider the ten thousand innocent women annually murdered by men who refuse to legalize abortion. The fear and hatred must be deep indeed to take such vengeance.

But back to the husband. We all know that marriage is far from solitary confinement for a woman. Of course, the husband talks to her. The questions are, how often, what does he say, and how does he say it? He parries this plea for conversation, which he understands thoroughly, until bedtime or near it and then, exhausted and exasperated, he slaps down his book or papers, or snaps off the TV, or flings his shoe to the floor if he is undressing, and turns to his wife saying, "Oh, for Christ's sake, what is it you want to talk about?"

Now he has just used all of his big guns. He has shown temper which threatens vio-

lence. He has shown an exasperated patience which threatens eventual divorce. He has been insulting and purposely misunderstanding. Since she is not burning with any specific communiqué, since she is now frightened, hurt, angry, and thoroughly miserable, what is she to say? I'll tell you what she does say: "Forget it. Just forget it. If that's the way you are going to respond, I don't want to talk with you anyway."

This may bring on another explosion from him, frightening her still further. He may say something stupid like, "You're crazy, just crazy. All day long you keep telling me you've got to talk to me. OK, you want to talk to me, talk. I'm listening. I'm not reading, I'm not working, I'm not watching TV, I'm listening."

He waits sixty silent seconds while the wife struggles for composure, and then he stands up and announces that he is going to bed. To rub salt in the wound, he falls to sleep blissfully and instantly.

Or, playing the part of both cops in the jailhouse interrogation scene, he may, after the first explosion, switch roles. In this doubletake he becomes the calm and considerate husband, remorseful, apologizing, and imploring her to continue, assuring her he is interested in anything she has to say, knowing full well the limitations of what she can say under the circumstances. Predictably, done in by the tender tone, she falls in with the plot and confesses. She confesses her loneliness, her dependence, her mental agony, and they discuss *her* problem. Her problem, as though it were some genetic defect, some personal shortcoming, some inscrutable psychosis. Now he can comfort her, avowing how he understands how she must feel, he only wishes there were something he could do to help.

This kind of situation, if continued in unrelieved manner, has extreme consequences. Generally the marriage partners sense this and stop short of the brink. The husband, after all, is trying to protect and bolster his frail ego, not drive his wife insane or force her suicide. He wants in the home to be able to hide from his own inner doubts, his own sense of shame, failure, and meaninglessness. He wants to shed the endless humiliation of endless days parading as a man in the male world, pretending a power, control, and understanding he does not have.

All he asks of his wife, aside from hours of menial work, is that she not see him as he sees himself. That she not challenge him, but admire and desire him, soothe and distract him. In short, make him feel like the kind of guy he'd like to be in the kind of world he thinks exists.

And by this time the wife asks little more really than the opportunity to play that role. She probably never aspired to more, to an equalitarian or reality-oriented relationship. It is just that she cannot do her thing if it is laid out so baldly; if she is to be denied all self-respect, all self-development, all help and encouragement from her husband.

So generally the couple stops short of the brink. Sometimes, paradoxically enough, by escalating the conflict so that it ends in divorce, but generally by some accommodation. The husband encourages the wife to make some girlfriends, take night courses, or have children. And sooner or later, if she can, she has children. Assuming the husband has agreed to the event, the wife's pregnancy does abate or deflect the drift of their marriage, for a while anyway.

The pregnancy presents to the world visible proof of the husband's masculinity, his potency. This visible proof shores up the basic substructure of his ego, the floor beyond which he cannot now fall. Pathetically, his stock goes up in society, in his own eyes. He is a man. He is grateful to his wife and treats her, at least during the first pregnancy, with increased tenderness and respect. He pats her tummy and makes noises about mystic occurrences. And since pregnancy is not a male thing and he is a man, since this is cooperation, not competition, he can even make out that he feels her role is pretty special.

The wife is grateful. Her husband loves her. She is suffused with happiness and pride. There is at last something on her side of the division of labor which her husband views with respect, and delight of delights, with perhaps a twinge of jealousy.

Of course, it can't last. After nine months, the child is bound to be born. And there we are back at the starting gate. For many women, giving birth must be like a bad trip with the added feature of prolonged physical exhaustion. Sometimes it takes a year to regain one's full strength after a messy Caesarian. Sometimes women develop post-parturitional psychosis in the hospital. More commonly, after they have been home awhile they develop a transient but recurring state called the "Tired Mother Syndrome." In its severe form it is, or resembles, a psychosis. Women with this syndrome complain of being utterly exhausted, irritable, unable to concentrate. They may wander about somewhat aimlessly, they may have physical pains. They are depressed, anxious, sometimes paranoid, and they cry a lot.

Sound familiar? Despite the name, one doesn't have to be a mother to experience the ailment. Many young wives without children do experience it, particularly those who, without an education themselves, are working their husbands' way through college. That is to say, wives who hold down a dull eight- or nine-hour-a-day job, then come home, straighten, cook, clean, run down to the laundry, dash to the grocery store, iron their own clothes plus their husbands' shirts and jeans, sew for themselves, put up their hair, and more often than not type their husbands' papers, correct the spelling and grammar, pay the bills, screw on command, and write the in-laws. I've even known wives who on top of this load do term papers or laboratory work for their husbands. Of course, it's insanity. What else could such self-denial be called? Love?

Is it any wonder that a woman in these circumstances is tired? Is it any wonder that she responds with irritability when she returns home at night to find her student husband, after a day or half-day at home, drinking beer and shooting the bull with his cronies, the ring still in the bathtub, his dishes undone, his clothes where he dropped them the night before, even his specific little chores like taking out the garbage unaccomplished?

Is it any wonder that she is tempted to scream when at the very moment she has gotten rid of the company, plowed through some of the mess, and is standing in a tiny kitchen over a hot stove her husband begins to make sexual advances? He naively expects that these advances will fill her with passion, melting all anger, and result not only in her forgetting and forgiving, but in gratitude and renewed love. Ever heard the expression, "A woman loves the man who satisfies her?" Some men find that delusion very comforting. A couple of screws and the slate is wiped clean. Who needs to pay for servants or buy his wife a washing machine when he has a cock?

And even the most self-deluded woman begins to feel depressed, anxious, and used when she finds that her husband is embarrassed by her in the company of his educated, intellectual, or Movement friends. When he openly shuts her up; saying she doesn't know what she is talking about, or emphasizes a point by saying it is so clear or so simple even his wife can understand it.

He begins to confuse knowledge with a personal attribute like height or a personal virtue like honesty. He becomes disdainful of and impatient with ignorance, equating it with stupidity, obstinacy, laziness, and in some strange way, immorality. He forgets that his cultivation took place at his wife's expense. He will not admit that in stealing from his wife her time, energy, leisure, and money, he also steals the possibility of her intellectual development, her present, and her future.

But the working wife sending her husband through school has no monopoly on this plight. It also comes to those who only stand and wait—in the home, having kiddy after kiddy while their husbands, if they are able, learn something, grow somewhere.

In any case, we began this diversion by saying that women who are not mothers can also suffer from the "Tired Mother Syndrome." Once a mother, however, it takes on a new dimension. There is a difference of opinion in the medical and sociological literature with regard to the genesis of this ailment. Betty Friedan, in the sociological vein, argues that these symptoms are the natural outgrowth of restricting the mind and body of these women to the narrow confines of the home. She discusses the destructive role of monotonous, repetitive work which never issues in any lasting, let alone important achievement. Dishes which are done only to be dirtied the same day, beds which are made only to be unmade the same day. Her theory also lays great emphasis on the isolation of these women from the large problems of society and even from contact with those concerned with things not domestic, other than their husbands. In other words, the mind no more than the body can function in a strait jacket and the effort to keep it going under these circumstances is indeed tiring and depressing.

Dr. Spock somewhat sides with that theory. The mainline medical approach is better represented by Dr. Lovshin who says that mothers develop the Tired Mother Syndrome because they are tired. They work a sixteen-hour day, seven days a week. Automation and unions have led to a continuously shortened day for men but the work day of housewives with children has remained constant. The literature bears him out. Oh, it is undoubtedly true that women have today many timesaving devices their mothers did not have. This advantage is offset, however, by the fact that fewer members of the family help with housework and the task of child care, as it is organized in our society, is continuous. Now the woman puts the wash in a machine and spends her time reading to the children, breaking up their fights, taking them to the playground, or otherwise looking after them. If, as is often said, women are being automated out of the home, it is only to be shoved into the car chauffeuring children to innumerable lessons and activities, and that dubious advantage holds only for middle and upper-class women who generally can afford not only gadgets but full- or part-time help.

One of the definitions of automation is a human being acting mechanically in a monotonous routine. Now, as always, the most automated appliance in a household is the mother. Because of the speed at which it's played, her routine has not only a nightmarish but farcical quality to it. Some time ago, the *Ladies' Home Journal* conducted and published a forum on the plight of young mothers.

Ashley Montagu and some other professionals plus members of the *Journal* staff interviewed four young mothers. Two of them described their morning breakfast routine.

One woman indicated that she made the breakfast, set it out, left the children to eat it, and then ran to the washing machine. She filled that up and ran back to the kitchen, shoved a little food in the baby's mouth, and tried to keep the others eating. Then she ran back to the machine, put the clothes in a wringer, and started the rinse water.

The other woman stated they had bacon every morning so the first thing she does is put the bacon on and the water for coffee. Then she goes back to her room and makes up the bed. "Generally, I find myself almost running back and forth. I don't usually walk. I run to make the bed." By that time the pan is hot and she runs back to turn the bacon. She finishes making the children's breakfast and if she is lucky she gets to serve it before she is forced to dash off and attend to the baby, changing him, and sitting him up. She rushes back, plops him in a little canvas chair, serves the children if she has not already done so, and makes her husband's breakfast. And so it goes through the day. As the woman who runs from bed to bacon explains, "My problem is that sometimes I feel there aren't enough hours in the day. I don't know whether I can get everything done."

It's like watching an old-time movie in which for technical reasons everyone seems to be moving at three times normal speed. In this case it is not so funny. With the first child it is not as severe.

What hits a new mother the hardest is not so much the increased workload as the lack of sleep. However unhappy she may have been in her childless state, however desperate, she could escape by sleep. She could be refreshed by sleep. And if she wasn't a nurse or airline stewardess she generally slept fairly regular hours in a seven- to nine-hour stretch. But almost all babies returning from the hospital are on something like a four-hour food schedule, and they usually demand some attention in between feedings. Now children differ, some cry more, some cry less, some cry

almost all of the time. If you have never, in some period of your life, been awakened and required to function at one in the morning and again at three, then maybe at seven, or some such schedule, you can't imagine the agony of it.

All of a woman's muscles ache and they respond with further pain when touched. She is generally cold and unable to get warm. Her reflexes are off. She startles easily, ducks moving shadows, and bumps into stationary objects. Her reading rate takes a precipitous drop. She stutters and stammers, groping for words to express her thoughts, sounding barely coherent—somewhat drunk. She can't bring her mind to focus. She is in a fog. In response to all the aforementioned symptoms she is always close to tears.

What I have described here is the severe case. Some mothers aren't hit as hard, but almost all new mothers suffer these symptoms in some degree and what's more, will continue to suffer them a good part of their lives. The woman who has several children in close succession really gets it. One child wakes the other, it's like a merry-go-round, intensified with each new birth, each childhood illness.

This lack of sleep is rarely mentioned in the literature relating to the Tired Mother Syndrome. Doctors recommend to women with newborn children that they attempt to partially compensate for this loss of sleep by napping during the day. With one child that may be possible, with several small ones it's sort of a sick joke. This period of months or years of forced wakefulness and "maternal" responsibility seems to have a long-range if not permanent effect on a woman's sleeping habits. She is so used to listening for the children she is awakened by dogs, cats, garbage men, neighbors' alarm clocks, her husband's snoring. Long after her last child gives up night feedings, she is still waking to check on him. She is worried about his suffocating, choking, falling out of bed, etc. Long after that she wanders about opening and closing windows, adjusting the heat or air conditioning, locking the doors, or going to the bathroom.

If enforced wakefulness is the handmaiden and necessary precursor to serious brainwashing, a mother—after her first child —is ready for her final demise. Too tired to comprehend or fight, she only staggers and eventually submits. She is embarrassed by her halting speech, painfully aware of her lessened ability to cope with things, of her diminished intellectual prowess. She relies more heavily than ever on her husband's support, helping hand, love. And he in turn gently guides her into the further recesses of second-class citizenship.

After an extended tour in that never-never land, most women lose all capacity for independent thought, independent action. If the anxiety and depression grow, if they panic, analysis and solution elude them.

Women who would avoid or extricate themselves from the common plight I've described, who would begin new lives, new movements, and new worlds, must first learn to acknowledge the reality of their present condition. They have got to reject the blind and faulty categories of thought foisted on them by a male order for its own benefit. They must stop thinking in terms of "the grand affair," of the love which overcomes, or substitutes for, everything else, of the perfect moment, the perfect relationship, the perfect marriage. In other words, they must reject romanticism. Romance, like the rabbit at the dog track, is the illusive, fake, and never-attained reward which for the benefit and amusement of our masters keeps us running and thinking in safe circles.

A relationship between a man and a woman is no more or less personal a relationship than is the relationship between a woman and her maid, a master and his slave, a teacher and his student. Of course, there are personal, individual qualities to a particular relationship in any of these categories, but they are so overshadowed by the class nature of the relationship, by the volume of class response, as to be almost insignificant.

There is something horribly repugnant in the picture of women performing the same menial chores all day, having almost interchangeable conversations with their children, engaging in standard television arguments with their husbands, and then in the late hours of the night, each agonizing over what

is considered her personal lot, her personal relationship, her personal problem. If women lack self-confidence, there seems no limit to their egotism. And unmarried women cannot in all honesty say their lives are in much greater measure distinct from another's. We are a class, we are oppressed as a class, and we each respond within the limits allowed us as members of that oppressed class. Purposely divided from each other, each of us is ruled by one or more men for the benefit of all men. There is no personal escape, no personal salvation, no personal solution.

The first step, then, is to accept our plight as a common plight, to see other women as reflections of ourselves, without obscuring, of course, the very real differences intelligence, temperament, age, education, and background create. I'm not saying let's now create new castes or classes among our own. I just don't want women to feel that the movement requires them to identify totally with and moreover love every other woman. For the general relationship, understanding and compassion should suffice.

We who have been raised on pap must develop a passion for honest appraisal. The real differences between women and between men and women are the guideposts within and around which we must dream and work.

Having accepted our common identity, the next thing we must do is get in touch with each other. I mean that absolutely literally. Women see each other all the time, open their mouths, and make noises, but communicate on only the most superficial level. We don't talk to each other about what we consider our real problems because we are afraid to look insecure, because we don't trust or respect each other, and because we are afraid to look or be disloyal to our husbands or benefactors.

Each married woman carries around in her a strange and almost identical little bundle of secrets. To take, as an example, perhaps the most insignificant, she may be tired of and feel insulted by her husband's belching or farting at the table. Can you imagine her husband's fury if it got back to him that she told someone he farted at the table? Because women don't tell these things to each other, the events are considered personal, the woman may fantasize remarriage to mythical men who don't fart, the man feels he has a personal but minor idiosyncrasy, and maledom comes out clean.

And that, my dear, is what this bit of loyalty is all about. If a man made that kind of comment about his wife he might be considered crude or indiscreet; she's considered disloyal—because she's subject, he's king; women are dominated and men are the instruments of their domination. The true objective nature of men must never become common knowledge lest it undermine in the minds of some males but most particularly in the minds of women the male right-to-rule.

And so we daily participate in the process of our own domination. For God's sake, let's stop!

I cannot make it too clear that I am not talking about group therapy or individual catharsis (we aren't sick, we are oppressed). I'm talking about movement. Let's get together to decide in groups of women how to get out of this bind, to discover and fight the techniques of domination in and out of the home. To change our physical and social surroundings to free our time, our energy, and our minds—to start to build for ourselves, for all people, a world without horrors.

CONCERNING VIOLENCE

F. Fanon

National liberation, national renaissance, the restoration of nationhood to the people, commonwealth: whatever may be the headings used or the new formulas introduced, decolonization is always a violent phenomenon. At whatever level we study it—relationships between individuals, new names for sports clubs, the human admixture at cocktail parties, in the police, on the directing boards of national or private banks—decolonization is quite simply the replacing of a certain "species" of men by another "species" of men. Without any period of transition, there is a total, complete, and absolute substitution. It is true that we could equally well stress the rise of a new nation, the setting up

Source: F. Fanon, "Concerning Violence," excerpt of chapter in The Wretched of the Earth (Grove Press, 1965; Presence Africaine, 1963), pp. 35–43. Reprinted by permission of Grove Press, Inc. and MacGibbon & Kee. Copyright 1963 by Presence Africaine.

of a new state, its diplomatic relations, and its economic and political trends. But we have precisely chosen to speak of that kind of tabula rasa which characterizes at the outset all decolonization. Its unusual importance is that it constitutes, from the very first day, the minimum demands of the colonized. To tell the truth, the proof of success lies in a whole social structure being changed from the bottom up. The extraordinary importance of this change is that it is willed, called for, demanded. The need for this change exists in its crude state, impetuous and compelling, in the consciousness and in the lives of the men and women who are colonized. But the possibility of this change is equally experienced in the form of a terrifying future in the consciousness of another "species" of men and women: the colonizers.

Decolonization, which sets out to change the order of the world, is, obviously, a program of complete disorder. But it cannot come as a result of magical practices, nor of a natural shock, nor of a friendly understanding. Decolonization, as we know, is a historical process: that is to say that it cannot be understood, it cannot become intelligible nor clear to itself except in the exact measure that we can discern the movements which give it historical form and content. Decolonization is the meeting of two forces, opposed to each other by their very nature, which in fact owe their originality to that sort of substantification which results from and is nourished by the situation in the colonies. Their first encounter was marked by violence and their existence together—that is to say the exploitation of the native by the settler—was carried on by dint of a great array of bayonets and cannons. The settler and the native are old acquaintances. In fact, the settler is right when he speaks of knowing "them" well. For it is the settler who has brought the native into existence and who perpetuates his existence. The settler owes the fact of his very existence, that is to say, his property, to the colonial system.

Decolonization never takes place unnoticed, for it influences individuals and modifies them fundamentally. It transforms spectators crushed with their inessentiality into privileged actors, with the grandiose glare of history's floodlights upon them. It brings a natural rhythm into existence, introduced by new men, and with it a new language and a new humanity. Decolonization is the veritable creation of new men. But this creation owes nothing of its legitimacy to any supernatural power; the "thing" which has been colonized becomes man during the same process by which it frees itself.

In decolonization, there is therefore the need of a complete calling in question of the colonial situation. If we wish to describe it precisely, we might find it in the well-known words: "The last shall be first and the first last." Decolonization is the putting into practice of this sentence. That is why, if we try to describe it, all decolonization is successful.

The naked truth of decolonization evokes for us the searing bullets and bloodstained knives which emanate from it. For if the last shall be first, this will only come to pass after a murderous and decisive struggle between the two protagonists. That affirmed intention to place the last at the head of things, and to make them climb at a pace (too quickly, some say) the well-known steps which characterize an organized society, can only triumph if we use all means to turn the scale, including, of course, that of violence.

You do not turn any society, however primitive it may be, upside down with such a program if you have not decided from the very beginning, that is to say from the actual formulation of that program, to overcome all the obstacles that you will come across in so doing. The native who decides to put the program into practice, and to become its moving force, is ready for violence at all times. From birth it is clear to him that this narrow world, strewn with prohibitions, can only be called in question by absolute violence.

The colonial world is a world divided into compartments. It is probably unnecessary to recall the existence of native quarters and European quarters, of schools for natives and schools for Europeans; in the same way we need not recall apartheid in South Africa. Yet, if we examine closely this system of compartments, we will at least be able to reveal the lines of force it implies. This approach to the colonial world, its ordering and its geographical layout will allow us to mark out the lines on which a decolonized society will be reorganized.

The colonial world is a world cut in two. The dividing line, the frontiers are shown by barracks and police stations. In the colonies it is the policeman and the soldier who are the official, instituted go-betweens, the spokesmen of the settler and his rule of oppression. In capitalist societies the educational system, whether lay or clerical, the structure of moral reflexes handed down from father to son, the exemplary honesty of workers who are given a medal after fifty years of good and loyal service, and the affection which springs from harmonious relations and good behavior—all these aesthetic expressions of respect for the established order serve to create around the exploited person an atmosphere of submission and of inhibition which lightens the task of policing considerably. In the capitalist countries a multitude of moral teachers, counselors and "bewilderers" separate the exploited from those in power. In the colonial countries, on the contrary, the policeman and the soldier, by their immediate presence and their frequent and direct action maintain contact with the native and advise him by means of rifle butts and napalm not to budge. It is obvious here that the agents of government speak the language of pure force. The intermediary does not lighten the oppression, nor seek to hide the domination; he shows them up and puts them into practice with the clear conscience of an upholder of the peace; yet he is the bringer of violence into the home and into the mind of the native.

The zone where the natives live is not complementary to the zone inhabited by the settlers. The two zones are opposed, but not in the service of a higher unity. Obedient to the rules of pure Aristotelian logic, they both follow the principle of reciprocal exclusivity. No conciliation is possible, for of the two terms, one is superfluous. The settlers' town is a strongly built town, all made of stone and steel. It is a brightly lit town; the streets are covered with asphalt, and the garbage cans swallow all the leavings, unseen, unknown and hardly thought about. The settler's feet are never visible, except perhaps in the sea; but there you're never close enough to see them. His feet are protected by strong shoes although the streets of his town are clean and even, with no holes or stones. The settler's town is a well-fed town, an easygoing town; its belly is always full of good things. The settlers' town is a town of white people, of foreigners.

The town belonging to the colonized people, or at least the native town, the Negro village, the medina, the reservation, is a place of ill fame, peopled by men of evil repute. They are born there, it matters little where or how; they die there, it matters not where, nor how. It is a world without spaciousness; men live there on top of each other, and their huts are built one on top of the other. The native town is a hungry town, starved of bread, of meat, of shoes, of coal, of light. The native town is a crouching village, a town on its knees, a town wallowing in the mire.

It is a town of niggers and dirty Arabs. The look that the native turns on the settler's town is a look of lust, a look of envy; it expresses his dreams of possession—all manner of possession: to sit at the settler's table, to sleep in the settler's bed, with his wife if possible. The colonized man is an envious man. And this the settler knows very well; when their glances meet he ascertains bitterly, always on the defensive, "They want to take our place." It is true, for there is no native who does not dream at least once a day of setting himself up in the settler's place.

This world divided into compartments, this world cut in two is inhabited by two different species. The originality of the colonial context is that economic reality, inequality, and the immense difference of ways of life never come to mask the human realities. When you examine at close quarters the colonial context, it is evident that what parcels out the world is to begin with the fact of belonging to or not belonging to a given race, a given species. In the colonies the economic substructure is also a superstructure. The cause is the consequence; you are rich because you are white, you are white because you are rich. This is why Marxist analysis should always be slightly stretched every time we have to do with the colonial problem.

Everything up to and including the very nature of precapitalist society, so well explained by Marx, must here be thought out again. The serf is in essence different from the knight, but a reference to divine right is necessary to legitimize this statutory difference. In the colonies, the foreigner coming from another country imposed his rule by means of guns and machines. In defiance of his successful transplantation, in spite of his appropriation, the settler still remains a foreigner. It is neither the act of owning factories, nor estates, nor a bank balance which distinguishes the governing classes. The governing race is first and foremost those who come from elsewhere, those who are unlike the original inhabitants, "the others."

The violence which has ruled over the ordering of the colonial world, which has ceaselessly drummed the rhythm for the destruction of native social forms and broken up without reserve the systems of reference of the economy, the customs of dress and external life, that same violence will be claimed and taken over by the native at the moment when, deciding to embody history in his own person, he surges into the forbidden quarters. To wreck the colonial world is henceforward a mental picture of action which is very clear, very easy to understand and which may be assumed by each one of the individuals which constitute the colonized people. To break up the colonial world does not mean that after the frontiers have been abolished lines of communication will be set up between the two zones. The destruction of the colonial world is no more and no less than the abolition of one zone, its burial in the depths of the earth or its expulsion from the country.

The natives' challenge to the colonial world is not a rational confrontation of points of view. It is not a treatise on the universal, but the untidy affirmation of an original idea propounded as an absolute. The colonial world is a Manichean world. It is not enough for the settler to delimit physically, that is to say with the help of the army and the police force, the place of the native. As if to show the totalitarian character of colonial exploitation the settler paints the native as a sort of quintessence of evil.* Native society is not simply described as a society lacking in values. It is not enough for the colonist to affirm that those values have disappeared from, or still better never existed in, the colonial world. The native is declared insensible to ethics; he represents not only the absence of values, but also the negation of values. He is, let us dare to admit, the enemy of values, and in this sense he is the absolute evil. He is the corrosive element, destroying all that comes near him; he is the deforming element, disfiguring all that has to do with beauty or morality; he is the depository of maleficent powers, the unconscious and irretrievable instrument of blind forces. Mon-

---

* We have demonstrated the mechanism of this Manichean world in *Black Skin, White Masks* (New York: Grove Press, 1967).

sieur Meyer could thus state seriously in the French National Assembly that the Republic must not be prostituted by allowing the Algerian people to become part of it. All values, in fact, are irrevocably poisoned and diseased as soon as they are allowed in contact with the colonized race. The customs of the colonized people, their traditions, their myths —above all, their myths—are the very sign of that poverty of spirit and of their constitutional depravity. That is why we must put the DDT which destroys parasites, the bearers of disease, on the same level as the Christian religion which wages war on embryonic heresies and instincts, and on evil as yet unborn. The recession of yellow fever and the advance of evangelization form part of the same balance sheet. But the triumphant *communiqués* from the missions are in fact a source of information concerning the implantation of foreign influences in the core of the colonized people. I speak of the Christian religion, and no one need be astonished. The Church in the colonies is the white people's Church, the foreigner's Church. She does not call the native to God's ways but to the ways of the white man, of the master, of the oppressor. And as we know, in this matter many are called but few chosen.

At times this Manicheism goes to its logical conclusion and dehumanizes the native, or to speak plainly, it turns him into an animal. In fact, the terms the settler uses when he mentions the native are zoological terms. He speaks of the yellow man's reptilian motions, of the stink of the native quarter, of breeding swarms, of foulness, of spawn, of gesticulations. When the settler seeks to describe the native fully in exact terms he constantly refers to the bestiary. The European rarely hits on a picturesque style; but the native, who knows what is in the mind of the settler, guesses at once what he is thinking of. Those hordes of vital statistics, those hysterical masses, those faces bereft of all humanity, those distended bodies which are like nothing on earth, that mob without beginning or end, those children who seem to belong to nobody, that laziness stretched out in the sun, that vegetative rhythm of life—all this forms part of the colonial vocabulary. General de Gaulle speaks of "the yellow multitudes" and François Mauriac of the black, brown, and yellow masses which soon will be unleashed. The native knows all this, and laughs to himself every time he spots an allusion to the animal world in the other's words. For he knows that he is not an animal; and it is precisely at the moment he realizes his humanity that he begins to sharpen the weapons with which he will secure its victory.

* * *

HOW TO COMMIT REVOLUTION IN CORPORATE AMERICA

G. William Domhoff

I appear here today by courtesy of the Legal Staff of the Regents of the University of California. Now I know that they didn't invite me, that the Student Mobilization Committee invited me, but I also know that the Regents put out a ruling that faculty members will be fired for participating in any strike. Thus, being a good and faithful employee, and much enjoying the sunshine and redwoods of Santa Cruz, I thought I'd better get clearance from university experts on the matter of this student strike before I did anything rash and compromising. And, thank goodness, these good and true, legal men assured me that I wouldn't be fired for appearing here today—just as long as I didn't advocate anything illegal.

Since the title of my little talk is "How to Commit Revolution in Corporate Amer-

Source: G. W. Domhoff, "How to Commit Revolution in Corporate America," in W. Lutz and H. Brent (eds.), *On Revolution* (Cambridge, Massachusetts: Winthrop Publisher, 1971), pp. 186–198. Reprinted from *On Revolution* by William Lutz and Harry Brent by permission of Winthrop Publishers, Inc. Copyright © 1971 by Winthrop Publishers, Inc.

ica," and since committing revolution might be construed by some people as being somewhat illegal, I certainly wouldn't want to appear to be advocating it. No, I don't advocate anything. I consider myself as acting in one of the many capacities of a well-rounded professor in the modern multiversity —as a consultant, just a consultant, to some group of citizens within the community that feels a need to call upon its tax-supported knowledge factory to give advice on a particular activity or undertaking. As a consultant, then, I'm not being illegal. In fact, I am doing what every good professor does, although for a tremendously reduced fee, and I expect to get credit for it when I am considered for promotion and tenure.

I am well aware that most of you aren't revolutionaries—that you are mostly upper-middle-class people cutting loose from home by temporarily growing beards or indulging in exotic potions or getting all caught up in doing good things for your less fortunate brethren from the other side of the tracks. I know that most of you think it is just a matter of a little more time, a little more education, and a little more good will before most of this country's social and economic problems are straightened out, and I suspect that many of you who are currently among the earnest and concerned are going to be somewhere else in a few years, as is that idealistic student group of past years, your parents. But maybe someday some of you will be looking around for a revolutionary consulting service. Maybe someday you will wise up to the Square Deals, New Deals, Fair Deals, New Frontiers, and other quasi-liberal gimmicks used to shore up and justify an overdeveloped, inhuman, and wasteful corporate capitalism as it gradually rose to power in the 20th century. Maybe someday some significant number of people, Left and Right, will really learn that courage, integrity, and a casual style aren't enough to bring about meaningful, substantial changes, that moral anguish has to be translated into changes in the social structure to do more than make you feel all warm and good and guilt-free inside. Maybe someday those of you, who are already on the right road, will learn that no matter how militant or violent or critical you may be, you are still not your own person or a revolutionary as long as you merely try to get your leaders to pay attention and better understand, whether it be through letters or sit-ins or time bombs. Maybe you will learn to ignore the leaders you are harassing and decide to replace them and their system—with yourselves and your own system, and on that day you will become revolutionaries instead of militant supplicants appealing to the stuffy Father Figures for a little more welfare and social justice, and a little less war.

At any rate, if and when you give up on these futile attempts at minor social improvements, and turn to the really exhilarating experience of freeing your own self by committing revolution, then perhaps these observations may be of some use. I offer them in a tentative fashion, fully expecting them to be reworked, challenged, developed. Since I am only a consultant, no hard feelings if you reject them. We academics are very philosophical about such matters. It's part of being professional, of being a good consultant.

There are three aspects, I think, to any

good revolutionary program for corporate America. These aspects are closely intertwined, and all three must be developed alongside each other, but there is nontheless a certain logic, a certain order of priorities, in the manner in which I present them. First, you need a comprehensive, overall analysis of the present-day American system. You've got to realize that the corporate capitalism of today is not the 19th-century individual capitalism that conservatives yearn for. Nor is it the pluralistic paradise that liberals rave about and try to patch up. Nor is it the finance capitalism of the American Communists who are frozen in their analyses of another day.

Second, you need relatively-detailed blueprints for a post-industrial America. You've got to show people concrete plans that improve their lot either spiritually or materially. There's no use scaring them with shouts of socialism, which used to be enough of a plan however general, but which today only calls to mind images of Russia, deadening bureaucracy, and 1984. And there's no use boring them with vague slogans about participation and vague abstractions about dehumanization. You've got to get down to where people live, and you've got to get them thinking in terms of a better America without the spectre of Russia, rightly or wrongly, driving any thought of risking social change out of their heads.

Third, and finally, you need a plan of attack, a program for taking power. For make no mistake about it—before most people get involved in revolutionary activity they take a mental look way down the road. Maybe not all the way down the road, but a long way down. They want to know what they are getting into, and what the chances are, and whether there is really anything positive in sight that is worth the gamble. In short, I suspect that most people just don't fit the formula that seems to be prevalent in America: get people involved in anything—rent strikes, anti-nuclear testing demonstrations, rat strikes, draft demonstrations, whatever, and gradually they will develop a revolutionary mentality. According to this theory, apparently, people will realize their power and want more if they win the rat strike, or they will wise up if they are hit on the head by a police officer at the draft demonstration. Well, maybe that works for some people, but I wouldn't count on it, and I wouldn't rely on it to the exclusion of all else. Actually, most people seem to sink back into lethargy when the rats are gone, or nuclear testing in the atmosphere is abandoned. And I know of no convincing evidence that getting people hit on the head or thrown in jail makes them into revolutionaries—certainly many of those who believed this didn't become revolutionaries by this route. So, ponder carefully about this activity for activity's sake. You need a plan of attack, not just some issues like peace or rats. And one thing more on this point: that plan has to come out of your analysis of the present socioeconomic system and out of your own life experience, that is, out of the American experience, and not out of the experiences of Russia, or China, or Cuba, all of which have been different from each other, and are different from the U.S.A. The world moves, even in America, and as it moves new realities arise and old theories become irrelevant. New methods become necessary. If you expect to be listened to, you will have to look around you afresh and build your own plan, abandoning all the sacred texts on "What Is To Be Done."

An analysis of the system, a set of blueprints, and a program for gaining power. That is the general framework. Let me now say something more concrete about each, admitting in advance that some points will be touched on only lightly and that others, which should be read as friendly criticisms of past and present efforts of American revolutionaries, may be too cryptic for those who have not observed these movements or read about their beliefs and strategies.

As to the analysis, here I will be the most cryptic. The name of the system is corporate capitalism. Huge corporations have come to dominate the economy, reaping fabulous, unheard-of profits and avoiding their share of the taxes, and their owners and managers—the corporate rich—are more and more coming to dominate all aspects of American life, including government. Cor-

porate rich foundations like Ford, Rockefeller, and Carnegie finance and direct cultural and intellectual innovations, corporate rich institutes and associations like the Council on Foreign Relations, the Committee for Economic Development and the Rand Corporation do most of the economic, political, and military research and provide most of the necessary government experts and consultants. As for the future, well, Bell Telephone is undertaking a pilot project in which it will run a high school in the Detroit ghetto, and Larry Rockefeller has suggested that every corporation in New York "adopt" a city block and help make sure that its residents are healthy, happy, and nonriotous. Adopt-a-block may never happen, and corporations may not run many high schools any time soon, but such instances are symbolic of where we are probably headed—corporate feudalism, cradle to the grave dependency on some aspect or another of a corporate structure run by a privileged few who use its enormous rewards to finance their own private schools, maintain their own exclusive clubs, and ride to the hounds on their vast farm lands. Even agriculture is being corporatized at an amazing rate. Family farmers are in a state of panic as the corporate rich and their corporations use tax loopholes to gobble up this last remaining bastion of 19th-century America.

Much work on this necessary analysis of corporate capitalism, or feudalism, has been done, but much more needs to be done. It is a scandal, or, rather, a sign of corporate rich dominance of the universities, that so little social stratification research concerns the social upper class of big businessmen; that so little political sociology research concerns the power elite that is the operating arm of the corporate rich, indeed, that so much of the social sciences in general concern themselves with the workers, the poor, and other countries—that is, with things that are of interest to the corporate rich. If you want to know anything interesting about the American power structure you have to piece together the hints of journalists, read the few books by a handful of Leftists who are academic outcasts, follow the research reports of two excellent student groups, and listen to and read Dan Smoot. Dan Smoot? Yes, Dan Smoot. Properly translated, he has a better view of the American power structure than most American political scientists, who of course merely laugh at him. He may not use the same labels I would for the men in charge (he thinks David Rockefeller & Co. are communists or dupes!), but at least he knows who's running the show. It is truly a commentary on American academia that he and one journalist—Establishment journalist Joseph Kraft—have done the only work on the all-important Council on Foreign Relations, one of the most influential policy-forming associations of the corporate rich. While the professors are laughing at Dan Smoot and equating the business community with the National Association of Manufacturers and the U.S. Chamber of Commerce, Smoot is keeping up with the activities of the richest, most powerful, and most internationally oriented of American big businessmen, the vanguard of corporate feudalism.

This really brings you to your first revolutionary act. Research one thing and one thing only—the American power structure. . . . Just turning the spotlight on the power elite is a revolutionary act, although only Act One. Ideas and analyses are powerful, and they shake people up. The problem of would-be American revolutionaries has not been an overemphasis on ideas, but the use of old ones, wrong ones, and transplanted ones. That is why C. Wright Mills grabbed American students and parts of American academia. He had new, relevant ideas and facts about the here and now—he exploded old clichés and slogans. And, I might add without being autobiographical—for Lincoln Steffens and Bertrand Russell had already done the job on me—I think he created more radicals with his work than any hundred Oakland and Los Angeles policemen with their billy clubs.

But analysis is not only important so that you can better criticize the system, it is necessary as well as for developing blueprints and plans of attack. As for the developing of blueprints, to go beyond mere devastating criticism of the system you have to under-stand it so that you can figure out what kind of a better system you can build on it. The most important and obvious point here is that you will be building on a fully industrialized, non-farming system. This means that your post-industrial society can look very different from systems built on pre-industrial, agricultural bases such as was the case in Russia, China, and Cuba.

As to the importance of a good analysis in developing a program for taking power, this is essential because it tells you what you can and cannot expect, what you can and cannot do, and what you should and should not advocate. Let me give four examples:

1. Corporate capitalism, if it can continue to corporatize the "underdeveloped" world and displace small businessmen and realtors in the cities, may have a lot more room for reform. In fact, if creature comfort is enough, it may come to satisfy most of its members. Be that as it may, and I doubt if it can solve its problems in a humanly tolerable way, the important point is that no American revolutionary should feel shocked or irrelevant because the corporate rich agree to nationwide health insurance or guaranteed annual incomes, or agree to pull out of one of their military adventures. And don't get your hopes up for any immediate collapse. Better to be surprised by a sudden turn that hastens your time schedule than to be disappointed once again by the flexibility of the corporate rich. This means that you should rely on your own program, and not on depression or war, to challenge the system and bring about change. It means that you should have a flexible, hang-loose attitude toward the future. Predictions of the inevitability of anything, whether collapse or socialism, fall a little flat and leave us jaded after comparing earlier predictions with the experience of the 20th century. We need a political philosophy that is a little more humble than those which currently entrap most of the world's Leftists.

2. Corporate capitalism seems to be very much dependent on overseas sales and investments, probably much more so than it is on the military spending necessary to defend and extend that Free World empire. And even if some economists would dispute that,

I think it is 100% safe to say that most members of the corporate rich are convinced that this overseas economic empire is essential—and that is what affects their political, economic and military behavior. Thus, the corporate rich fear, nay, more than that, have utter horror of isolationism, and that suggests that you revolutionaries should agree with conservatives about the need for isolationism.

3. The American corporate rich have at their command unprecedented, almost unbelievable firepower and snooping power. This makes it questionable whether or not a violent revolutionary movement has a chance of getting off the ground. It also makes it doubtful whether or not a secret little Leninist-type party can remain secret and unpenetrated for very long. In short, a nonviolent and open party may be dictated to you as your only choice by the given fact of the corporate leaders' military and surveillance capability, just as a violent and closed party was dictated by the Russian situation.

4. The differences between present-day corporate capitalism and 19th-century individual capitalism must be emphasized again and again if you are to reach those currently making up the New Right. Those people protest corporate capitalism and its need for big government and overseas spending in the name of small business, small government, competition, the market place—all those things destroyed or distorted by the corporate system. You must agree with the New Right that these things have happened and then be able to explain to them how and why they have happened, not due to the communists or labor, or liberal professors, but due to the growing corporatization of the society and the needs of these corporations. You can't give up on these New Rightists—they know the Rockefellers, the J. J. McCloys, the Averell Harrimans, the Paul Hoffmans, the Adlai Stevensons, and the John V. Lindsays run American society. (Here I am just naming some of the relatively few multi-millionaire businessmen and corporation lawyers known to the American public.) And, like the New Left, they don't like it. It is your job to teach them that the new corporate system is the problem, not the motives and good

faith of the corporate rich they call communists and dupes of liberal academics.

Now, as to your second general need, blueprints for a post-industrial America. Blueprints are first of all necessary to go beyond mere criticism. Any half-way moral idiot can criticize corporate capitalism, anyone can point to slums, unemployment, waste, phony advertising, inflation, shoddy goods, and so on. To be revolutionary, you have got to go beyond the militantly liberal act of offering some criticism and then asking people to write their congressman or to "sit in" somewhere so that the authorities will do something about the problem. And it is necessary for you to self-consciously begin to develop this plan because it is not going to miraculously appear after a holocaust or emanate mystically from the collective mind of that heterogeneous generalization called "The Movement." Individuals are going to have to develop aspects of these blueprints, wild, yea-saying blueprints that you can present with excitement and glee to Mr. and Mrs. Fed-up America. It is not enough to be for peace and freedom, which is really only to be against war and racism. It is not positive enough. As a smug little man from the Rand Corporation—a consultant for the other side—once reminded me, everyone, even him, is for peace and justice—the differences begin when you get to specifics.

Blueprints are also necessary to break the Russian logjam in everyone's thinking, revolutionary and non-revolutionary alike. Only by talking about concrete plans, thus getting people reacting to them and thereby developing their own plans, will people forget about Russia, a centralized, bureaucratic, industrialized country that is neither here nor there as far as you are concerned, and has no relevance to either your criticisms or your plans. In short, you have got to show people that your concern is America, that you love America, and that your moral concern is based upon what America could be, as compared with what it is. No one should out-Americanize you. You, as revolutionaries, have a right to that flag. And if you don't feel like grabbing the present American flag right at this juncture, then reach back into American revolutionary history, to the unfinished revolution, for your flags. Like that great snake flag, that great phallic message, of the Gadsden Rebellion, with its prideful warning hissing out across the centuries: DON'T TREAD ON ME.

The point is that you are Americans and that you want to build a better, a postindustrial America, that you want to use the base your forefathers gave you to realize the American dream. Forget all this internationalism talk. The foreign revolutions some of you often hope to copy were fought by men who were fervent nationalists, not bigoted ethnocentrics who believed that no other nationalism was as good or moral as theirs, but nationalists who were of their people, who loved their country and its culture, and who really lived and developed their own heritage. They talked internationalism, they read widely, they were appreciative and tolerant of many other cultures, but they were heart and soul products of their land and its traditions. To throw away the potent psychological force of nationalism because it has been identified in this country with an Americanism that is often parochial and ethnocentric, and especially anti-Semitic, is to ignore, ironically enough, one of the few things you can learn from studying other 20th-century revolutions. A feeling for your country and its little nuances is an intimate and potent part of Western man. If that sounds too narrow and unemotional for some of you, I would add that it is probably wrong anyhow to think your internationalism somehow supports foreign revolutionaries. Do you really think the Viet Cong derive any strength from telegrams of support from or demonstrations by little New York-based committees on This and That? That's Dean Rusk's mentality. Don't you think the Cong and the Russians and the Chinese are big enough to take care of themselves? Isn't it perhaps a little bit paternalistic to think you are in any way helping those indigenous movements? Your task is here at home, and the way to get to this task is to develop a set of blueprints to go with your critique.

Now, I don't make these statements, and this distinction between nationalism and ethnocentrism, as one who has not considered the problem long and hard. As a Freudian-oriented psychologist, I believe more than anyone, certainly more than you who subscribe to one or other of the environmentalisms (liberalism and Marxism in their various guises) that predominate in American social science, that people everywhere have the same basic psyche, the same wishes and fears. I believe that the transition rites, myths, and rituals from tribes all over the world show that all men and women suffer from fears of separation from mother and group, that all men come to feel rivalry toward father and brother, that all men must go to the desert or the mountain to struggle for independence from their parents, and that all men have a strange sweet ambivalence toward death. In short, I know that all people have the same problems, but I also know that there are such things as personality and culture, that is, that we all have slightly different ways of handling our wishes and fears. And since I know that these personality and cultural differences are in good part, if not totally, defenses against anxiety and wishes that cause anxiety, I recognize that to attack them, or to ask people to discard them without offering them a new set of defenses, is to invite resistance, is to invite fear and distrust. We are faced with the seeming paradox that men who share the same problems can easily come to mistrust or hate each other if one person's defenses threaten those of the other. So I am saying that you should bypass these resistances, that as theoretical psychologists you should of course recognize the psychic universality of mankind, but that as revolutionaries you should also recognize that such a general truism is of no use to you in your day-to-day dealings with people if you are not sensitive to and sympathetic toward those individual and group defenses called personality and culture. In short, you have got to recognize that we are all nationalists in the sense of our identity, and work with this fact, trying to bring out the best in your own national tradition. If this sounds risky to you somehow, as something that might lead to outcomes you don't advocate, or to a narrow parochialism, then you have underestimated the importance of blueprints in your revolutionary program. For it is the blueprints that are the key to transcending narrow outlooks and ensuring that only the best in the American national character is more fully manifested. It is the explicitly stated blueprints which ensure that some implicit retrogressive program does not come to tacitly guide your actions as a revolutionary movement.

What could this post-industrial society look like? Naturally, as you might suspect of someone trying to be a respectable consultant, I have a few suggestions, all tentative, and I will mention some of them to give you an idea of what I mean, but I want to emphasize that it is on this project that so many more people could become totally involved in the revolutionary process. If it would be by and large intellectuals, academics, and students who would work on the analysis and critique of the growing corporate feudalism, it would be people from all walks of life who would be essential to this second necessity. You need men and women with years of experience in farming, small business, teaching, city planning, recreation, medicine, and so on, to start discussing and writing about ways to organize that part of society they know best for a post-industrial America. You need to provide outlets via forums, discussions, papers, and magazines for the pent-up plans and ideals of literally millions of well-trained, experienced, frustrated Americans who see stupidity and greed all around them but can't do a thing about it. You need to say, for example, "Look Mr. and Mrs. City Planning Expert trapped in this deadly bureaucracy controlled by big businessmen, draw up a sensible plan for street development, or park development, in your town of 30,000 people." "Look, Mr. Blue-Collar Worker, working for this big corporation, how should this particular plant be run in a sensible society?"

And, you need not only to discuss and to develop these programs, you need to make them clear to every American, not only to the ones you might win to your side because the present systems disgusts them morally, or exploits them, or ignores them, or rejects

them. No, even more, you need to reach the many millions more who, once they did not fear you or distrust you, would be willing to live under either the new or old system. And make no mistake about their importance. When people talk about the small percentage of Bolsheviks who took over Russia, they often forget the overwhelming numbers who passively accepted them. They did so out of disgust with war, despair, and the lack of a plan of their own that they really believed in.

Let me repeat to make its importance clear that the neutralization of large masses should be a prime goal for a program to develop and present blueprints for a post-industrial America. To this end it should be personally handed by some revolutionary to every person in America. Each person should receive a short, simple, one-page handbill especially relevant to his situation or occupation. It would begin, for example, "Policeman, standing here protecting us from Evil at this demonstration, Where Will You Be After The Revolution?" And then, in a few short sentences you will tell this bewildered soul, whom you embraced after handing him his message, that there will still be a great need for policemen after the revolution, but that policemen will tend to do more of the things that they like to do—helping, assisting, guiding—rather than the things that get them a bad name, that is, faithfully carrying out the repressive dictates of their power elite masters. You will tell him that you know that some policemen are prejudiced or authoritarian, but that you know that is neither here nor there because orders on whether to shoot ("to do whatever is necessary to keep 'law and order' in this ghetto") or not to shoot come from officials higher up who are intimately intertwined in the corporate system.

Similar handbills should be prepared for every person. Some would hear good things, like more money and better health. Some would hear things that would surprise them or make them wonder, like "You won't be socialized, Mr. Small Businessman producing a novelty or retailing pets on a local level, because the socialized corporations can produce more than enough; and furthermore, keep in mind that government in a post-industrial America couldn't possibly harass you as much as the big bankers who won't lend you money, the big corporations who undercut you, and the corporate-oriented politicians who overtax you." Others, for whom there is no good news, would get such cheery messages as "Stock Broker—we hope you have other skills, like gardening or typing"; "Corporate Manager—we hope you like working for the anonymous public good as much as you liked working for anonymous millionaire coupon clippers"; "CIA man—we hope you are as good at hiding as you are supposed to be at seeking."

Perhaps most of all, there has to be a consideration of the role of Mr. John Bircher, Mr. Physician, Mr. Dentist, and others now on the New Right. Those who are put off or ignored by the increasing corporatization have to be shown that their major values—individuality, freedom, local determination—are also the values of a post-industrial America. This does not mean that they will suddenly become revolutionaries, but it is important to start them wondering as to whether or not they would find things as bad in the new social system as they do in this system which increasingly annoys them, exasperates them, and ignores them. They must be weaned from the handful of large corporations and multi-millionaires who use them for their own ends by talking competition while practicing monopoly, by screaming about taxes while paying very little, and by talking individuality while practicing collectivism.

What would a post-industrial America look like? First of all, it would be certain large American institutions—like the Berkeley food co-op that is locally controlled by consumers, like the Pasadena water and electric systems that are publicly owned, like the Tennessee Valley Authority which has allowed the beginnings of the sane, productive, and beautiful development of at least one river region in our country. In short, the system would start from local controls and work up, like it used to be before all power and taxes were swept to the national level by war and the big corporations. And, as you

can see, it would be a mixed system, sometimes with control by consumers, sometimes with control by local government, sometimes with control by regional authorities, and sometimes, as should be made clear in the handbill to certain small businessmen, with control in private hands. For many retail franchises, for many novelty productions, and, I suspect, for many types of farms and farmers, depending on region, crop and other considerations, private enterprise may be the best method of control.

The question will be raised—is this promise of some private ownership pandering to a voting bloc? Is it like the old Communist trick of the United Front? The answer is a resounding NO. Any post-industrial society that does not maximize chances for freedom, flexibility, and individuality is not worth fighting for. Given the enormous capabilities of corporate production, the economic and cultural insignificance of most small businessmen, and the very small number of family farmers, there is simply no economic or political or cultural reason to socialize everything. . . .

I have left the most obvious for last. Of course the corporations would be socialized. Their profits would go to the people in the form of lower prices (and thus higher real wages) and/or repair to local, state, and national treasuries in the amounts necessary to have a park on every corner (replacing one of the four gas stations), and medical, dental, educational, recreational, or arts facilities on the other corners (replacing the other three gas stations—there being no need for any but a few gas stations due to the ease of introducing electric cars when a few hundred thousand rich people are not in a position to interfere). But how to man this huge corporate enterprise? First, with blue-collar workers, who would be with you all the way in any showdown no matter how nice some members of the corporate rich have been to them lately. Second, with men from lower-level management positions who have long ago given up the rat race, wised up, and tacitly awaited your revolution. Fantasy? Perhaps, but don't underestimate the cynicism at minor levels of the technostructure.

I have spoken with and to these groups, and there is hope. They are not all taken in, any more than most Americans are fooled by the mass media about domestic matters. They are just trapped, with no place to go but out if they think too much or make a wave. Now, "out" is easy enough if you're young and single, but it's a little sticky if you didn't wake up to the whole corporate absurdity until you were long out of college and had a wife and two kids. Cultivate these well-educated men and women whose talents are wasted and ill-used. Remind them that the most revolutionary thing they can do— aside from feeding you information and money so you can further expose the system and aside from helping to plan the post-industrial society—is to be in a key position in the technostructure when the revolution comes. You may not win many of them percentagewise, but then it wouldn't take many to help you through a transition.

Then too, part of the corporate system would disappear—one computerized system of banking and insurance would eliminate the incredible duplication, paperwork, and nonsense now existent in those two "highly profitable" but worthless areas of the corporate economy. Corporate retails would be broken up and given to local consumer co-ops, or integrated into nationalized producer-retailer units in some cases. Corporate transports (air, rails, buses) would be given in different cases to state, local, and national government, as well as to, on occasion, the retailers or producers they primarily serve. The public utilities, as earlier hinted, would finally be given to the public, mostly on the local and regional level, probably on the national level in the case of telephones. The only real problem, I think, is manufacturing, where you have to hold the loyalty of technicians and workers to survive a transition. Blue-collar control—syndicalism—may be the answer in some cases, regional or national government control in others. Here, obviously, is one of those questions that needs much study, with blue-collar and white-collar workers in the various industries being the key informants and idea men.

I have not here presented a final, detailed set of blueprints for a post-industrial America, but I hope I have suggested how important the development of such blueprints is, that I have tossed out a few ideas that might have merit or start you thinking, and that I have made you wonder as to how much energy and enthusiasm might possibly be released by taking such a project to Americans in all walks of life. The "false consciousness" of Americans is not primarily in their misperceptions of the "power structure." Many are already wise to liberal baloney on that score, especially blue-collar workers. The "false consciousness" is in a lack of vision, a resigned cynicism, a hopeless despair. "Struggle" without vision will never achieve success in America.

I come, then, finally to the third necessity, a program for taking the reins of government from the power elite in order to carry out the plan developed by revolutionary visionaries. It is on this point that there is likely to be found the most disagreement, the most confusion, the most uncertainty, and the most fear. But I think you do have something very important to go on—the ideas and experiences and successes of the Civil Rights and New Left and Hippie movements of the past several years. If they have not given you an analysis of corporate capitalism or a set of blueprints, which is their weakness, they have given you the incredibly-precious gift of new forms of struggle and new methods of reaching people, and these gifts must be generalized, articulated, and more fully developed.

I have a general term, borrowed from a radical hippy, that I like to use because I think it so beautifully encompasses what these movements have given to you—psychic guerrilla warfare—the "psychic" part appealing to my psychologist instincts and summarizing all hard-hitting non-violent methods, the "guerrilla warfare" part hopefully giving to those who want to take to the hills enough measure of satisfaction to allow them to stick around and participate in the only type of guerrilla warfare likely to work in corporate America. For make no mistake about it, psychic guerrilla warfare is a powerful weapon in a well-educated, highly-industrialized country that has a tradition of liberal values and democratic political processes. And it is the kind of guerrilla warfare that America's great new acting-out girls can indulge in on an equal basis with any male anywhere. It is the confrontation politics of the New Left— teach-ins, marches, walk-ins, sit-ins, push-ins, love-ins, folk rocks, and be-ins. It is the non-violent, religiously-based, democratically-inspired confrontation morality of Martin Luther King, and it is the unfailing good humor, psychological analysis, and flower power of the Hippie. Together they are dynamite—what politician or labor leader can fault confrontation, what true Christian or Jew can react violently to non-violence, and what disgruntled middle-classer can fail to smile or admit begrudging admiration for the best in American hippiedom?

Before I suggest how and where to lay this psychological dynamite, I know I must force myself to say a few words concerning what you are wondering about the most, the role of violence. The words aren't easy for me to say, a look at history makes the ground shaky under me, and many will secretly or openly assume that this is cowardly rationalization by an academic. Despite all this, I reject the lesson of history by claiming that the situation is different in this over-industrialized country: I don't think violence will work in corporate America, 1968. I don't believe in non-violence as a way of life as some people do, so I don't argue from any philosophic base. . . . No, I'm just afraid violence is not a winning strategy in corporate America, and a winning strategy is the primary concern of the revolutionary consultant. There is first of all the brute fact of this country's incredible military hardware. But there is more than that. This democracy is far from perfect, and the corporate rich have buggered its functioning at a zillion different junctures, but it has never been tested to its limits either. You've got to see just how much there is to the claim that values and political institutions would win out in a showdown. There are even liberals who might be willing to die

for such a cause. In the meantime, the masses you need are deeply committed to the political process.

Is this doubt about the usefulness of violence in corporate America only the opinion of an academic type? I think not. It was also the opinion of one of the greatest violent revolutionaries of all time. I refer to Che, and my reference to him will be my first and only appeal to authority, to sacred text. Indeed, it is almost a tragedy that those who love and admire Che, and at the same time dream of physical guerrilla warfare in the U.S.A., should overlook his very first premise for it—people take to physical guerrilla warfare only when they have lost all hope of non-violent solutions. Che is said to have laughed long and hard when asked about the possibility of guerrilla warfare in this country. In short, he too apparently believed that what works in the maldeveloped, exploited hinterland of the corporate capitalist empire does not necessarily apply in its overdeveloped affluent center.

Americans have not lost their hope. Furthermore, they are not likely to lose it by any of the means currently being used to escalate physical confrontations, for such confrontations do not "expose" the most fundamental aspects of the political system. The only way people would lose their faith in the political system, if they are capable of losing it at all, is in a full and open and honest test of its promise. The political system has got to be tested totally by completely unarmed men and women, and if that doesn't sound courageous enough for you, then you have need for a more hairy-chested proof of masculinity and integrity than I do. And if you argue that people won't listen, that they haven't listened in the past few years, then I say it's because you haven't yet brought to them an analysis that rings true enough, that you haven't yet hit them with a program that is exciting enough, and that you haven't yet provided them with a plan of attack that is believable enough to be worth trying. I say you really haven't turned on with all your intellectual and libidinal resources, that you haven't given them your best shot. What you have done so far is great, but it is only a prelude. You've got to escalate your incredibleness, your audacity, your cleverness, and your playfulness, not your physical encounters, if you are to break through the American malaise.

Enough admonitions, although I fear no one from the Left is any longer listening. Back to the more manic matter of psychic guerrilla warfare. How do you direct this dynamite to its task of destroying the ideological cover of the corporate rich? First, you start a new political party, a wide-open, locally-based political party dedicated to the development of blueprints for a post-industrial America and to the implementation of them through psychic guerrilla warfare. It should be a party with a minimal, low-key ideology which does not find it necessary to have a position on every age-old question in ontology, epistemology, and Russian and Chinese history. It should be a hang-loose outfit open to anyone prepared to abandon all other political affiliations and beliefs—in other words, it would not be an Anti-This-Or-That coalition of liberal Democrats, Communists, Trotskyists, and Maoists. In fact, ignore these groups. The best members will drop out and join yours. For the rest, they have no constituencies and would soon fall to fighting the Old Fights among themselves anyway—Communist and Anti-Communist, Pro-Soviet and Anti-Soviet, and On and On ad tedium. No, you don't need that—it would destroy you like it destroyed them. And like they destroy the organizations they cowbird with their cocksure, know-it-all metaphysics which ignore the various situations from which these theories derived. In fact, they need you, for if you got something going, the party would be big enough for all of them to work in without seeing each other or having to defend the Old Faiths. You've got to patiently show them how to do it here so they can transcend their romantic ties to the ideas and methods of other countries and other ages.

In addition to declining offers of coalition, and instead seeking converts, such a party should reject as inappropriate the Leninist "democratic centralism" for an American

revolutionary party. Not that all the Old Leftists would give it up—some would probably join your party and try to "caucus" or "bore from within," but the open give and take of ideas and the local autonomy of chapters could handle the little organizational games they have become so good at while organizing and reorganizing each other over the past thirty or forty years.

Before I go on, let me pause to make some things clear. For all my despair over certain Old Left ideas, I think many of these people are great and good persons—it's when they start planning that their minds lock into the old patterns. Further, I respect their admiration for their heroes. Lenin was great. So was Trotsky. So were Eugene Debs and Thomas Paine, and so are Mao and Fidel, but they have nothing to teach you except guts and perseverance because your situation is different. Honor them for their courage and their example, but most of all, for their ability to let go of sacred texts and do what was necessary in their given society even when it contradicted received doctrine (as it always did): to take power in a pre-industrial state on a very small base, to march to the countryside instead of waiting for the workers, to rely on peasants. If they could forget the sacred texts of their masters, why can't you go beyond theirs? You need your own Lenins, not theirs, your own Ches, not theirs, and I suspect they will be as different as the first is from the second. Begin this self-reliance by starting your own kind of American revolutionary party, one not open to FBI subversion because an open party depends on ideas, and FBI men, having no ideas, would be unable to maintain their cover.

So what does this party do beside present a constant withering critique of corporate capitalism and build blueprints for a post-industrial America? It practices all forms of psychic guerrilla warfare whenever and wherever there is a possible convert. Eventually, and on the right occasions, it even enters elections, not to win votes, but to win converts. In making its pitch, it doesn't ask men and women to quit their jobs or take to the hills, but rather it asks them to commit their allegiances to new socioeconomic arrangements; to help develop new social and intellectual institutions; to financially support the growth of the party; to read party-oriented newspapers; to convert and neutralize friends and neighbors, and to stand firm if the corporate rich try something funny.

After building chapters in every town or city district in the country by word of mouth and small group contact, you would gradually begin to participate in local elections to gain further attention. Then you would enter legislative elections, both to gain converts and to win seats, for the more legislative seats you hold, state and national, the better for the sudden takeover that will come later. You avoid like the plague winning any executive offices, for to be a mayor or governor when you don't control the whole system is meaningless and a waste of energy. You couldn't do anything liberals won't eventually do until you control the entire system. In other words, I'm not suggesting a gradual takeover, which would wear you down, compromise your program, and perhaps allow you to develop an ameliorist mentality as you got used to a little bit of influence and status. Indeed, the British Labor Party should be as sad a lesson to you as any other recent experience, and you should not repeat their failure to force a total and complete change the minute you have a chance to take power. If they couldn't do it, well, you can, because once you take over the national government in a one-election shot, or general uprising a la France in 1968, there is enough power concentrated there to accomplish drastic changes overnight.

I don't mean to imply that you would only control the Presidency, that you would only move on the national level. Actually, you should move on the whole system at once, for each local chapter would have developed parallel governments that would also go into action for the first time when you decided you had the popular support to take over the system. All members of a given chapter would train themselves to fill some government job at local levels— they would be like the shadow cabinets of

British politics only more so. The transition would be sudden—and it would be total in the sense of taking money, power, and status from the corporate rich.

*   *   *

ADDENDA*

It has been a long four years for American radicalism since "How To Commit Revolution in Corporate America" was written in the early months of 1968. The major organizations of the New Left are dead or shattered, the mood of the students and the country at large has changed considerably, and much of what remains of the New Left has adopted an Old Left mentality.

With all the changes over four years, it is not surprising that there are ways in which "How To Commit Revolution in Corporate America" is out of date. This is most of all apparent in its mood and tone, which reflects the enthusiasm and optimism of the New Left at that time. There was still the chance then that the New Left would continue to challenge the assumptions of past radicals.

In the spring of 1968 I was just beginning to sense what became very apparent to me in the summer and fall of that year, namely, that the New Left was headed the way of the Old. By calling for a continuation of non-violence and of an open, questioning perspective, I had hoped to reinforce those tendencies over orthodox radical analyses and programs. But the New Left was not able to transcend itself, and the result was an acceptance of Old Left viewpoints which soon led to isolation, repression, and confusion for young radicals.

As to the specifics of the speech, I still think it necessary to have a constant withering critique of corporate capitalism combined

---

* February, 1972.

with fairly concrete "blueprints" or alternative visions of how America could be organized. If anything, I have come to put even more emphasis on blueprints. But I see little work in this direction, or little interest in the question on the part of most radicals.

I also continue to believe it is necessary to state quite openly the means by which the alternative vision is to be implemented. In 1968 I opted for non-violent direct action combined with the formation of a third party. Today I hold more strongly than ever to the non-violent approach, and I think the events of 1969–71 bear me out in this emphasis.

However, I am no longer certain that third-party politics are the answer. After a lengthy study of American politics, with emphasis on the Democratic Party, I am not so sure it makes sense to start a third party. It may make more sense to raise all the issues—and present the blueprints—in Democratic Party *primaries!* I am by no means confident of this, but I do think the question needs to be discussed, rather than shouted down, ridiculed, or denounced from one Marxian perspective or another.

My basic plan is to run in Democratic Party primaries on the most radical blueprints that can be developed. Every party election and party primary should be entered, from precinct to President. In fact, it is essential that candidates be running at all levels on every occasion. Top-down is no good. Grass roots alone is not good enough.

The plan differs from other in-the-system attempts of the past. This is not the old, temporary Communist plan of submerging your ideology and supporting moderates against potential fascists. Instead, it stresses presenting your ideology as the most important part of the strategy. (In Marxian terms, the search is for "ideological hegemony.") Nor is this a plan for supporting the "best man" or "good liberals." Nor is it a plan where you seriously expect to win, in which case you are tempted to run only slightly to the "left" of the most liberal candidate.

There are several merits to this plan. For one thing, it allows you to fight ideological battles while not at the same time fighting organizational battles. For another, it allows you to bypass longstanding attachments to party labels so you can quickly get to key issues. Most importantly, it allows you to contend for the working man's sympathy without helping to elect conservative Republicans, which would be the major result of third-party efforts that were very successful. *In other words, it allows you to work for a long-term change in working-class ideology without doing damage to the short-run, bread-and-butter issues so rightfully of concern to the middle American of blue and white collar.*

The major problem with this strategy is that the Democratic Party is "controlled" by wealthy fat cats, conservative Southerners, and urban machine leaders. But these are precisely the problems radicals face in a third party anyhow. That is, most people accept the financial leadership of fat cats, and give very little to political parties. And you would eventually have to defeat Southerners and city bosses even if you were in a third party. You would have to break their hold on Democratic voters who are precisely the people any third party would have to appeal to—the lower levels of American society, whether black, brown, or white. My thought is to do this within the Democratic Party, where the short-run interests of the working classes still lie.

This is not a plan to wreck the Democratic Party. That is, no rule or ruin. No running on a third-party ticket if you lost in the primaries. Two things are required to remain a good Democrat—to register, and to support the candidate selected by the primary. Ideological credentials are not required, and radicals would work to keep it that way. Loyalty to the party would be essential. If anyone is going to bolt, let it be the fat cats.

This plan is not deduced from some grand theory. I arrived at it mostly by a process of elimination. That is, I am clear on what has not worked, and probably will not work. Partly this understanding comes from a reading of history, particularly the disastrous history of third parties in America, and partly from the events of the past four years.

The year 1972 is not the time to launch such a strategy. But if the People's Party and the New American Movement (NAM) do not do well, then 1973 would be an ideal time, with the 1974 and 1976 elections as the first target dates. The idea would be to organize "democratic Democrats," or "real Democrats," into small caucuses that could begin to develop the blueprints on which to run in 1974 and 1976. After the blueprints are developed, then candidates could begin contending for precinct posts, county chairmanships, and government positions.

Until more Americans see the world through new perspectives, and believe in concrete alternatives, there is no hope for any kind of radical action. I think the idea of presenting alternatives to corporate capitalism by running in Democratic Party primaries at all levels might be a reasonable way for radicalism to proceed. The other ways have not worked, radicalism is now at a low ebb, and this particular strategy has not been tried before. Unlikely plans have worked elsewhere—for Chairman Mao and for Fidel and maybe even, let us hope, for Salvador Allende. It is time to re-think everything.

Break the ideological hegemony of the ruling class. Bring the struggle home to the Democratic Party.

Chapter 11
SOURCES OF STRAIN ON THE RULES FOR CONFLICT

What are the conditions that produce radical discontent and a questioning of the existing social order? Although the readings in this section differ greatly in their specific focus, all look at the general phenomenon of social change and the uncertainties, fears, and ambitions that changing conditions generate. Stinchcombe emphasizes the extent to which periods of transition and social change throw up new kinds of social organizations whose ranking in the general scheme of society, of great concern to members, is undefined by previous rules, and also new organizational leaders who have not had much experience with competition under previous rules. Thus conflicts in times of change may easily tend to escalate, provided that strong "neutral" forces of social control are not available to enforce limits on the conflicts of transition.

Next, Coser points out that social conflict is itself an important source of historical change, thus pointing to a possible circular chain of causality whereby change generates conflict which in turn leads to further change and further conflict. (It is interesting to compare this understanding with the arguments by writers like Lorenz that conflict and aggression are the basic sources of order and stability in animal societies.) In the final selection, Gurr pays special attention to gaps between value expectations and value capabilities as the source of discontent, modified in turn by the historical legitimacy of the regime in power, the tradition of strife in the country, and the strength of the social control forces present. Thus Gurr attempts to bring together, refine, and quantify the conditions of transition and order to build a general model for predicting political violence.

STRATIFICATION AMONG ORGANIZATIONS AND THE SOCIOLOGY OF REVOLUTION

A. L. Stinchcombe

What kind of stratification theory is an appropriate theoretical basis for the sociology of revolution? My argument in this section will be that this ought to be a theory of stratification among organizations. Organizations as well as individuals have ranks, and these ranks are defended with substantial resources. For reasons to be developed, rapid structural change in societies introduces uncertainty and dissensus on the principles of ranking of organizations. Whether this dissensus is resolved peacefully seems to depend on characteristics of the military and police apparatus, on the extent of liberty, and on the pattern of socialization of organizational elites. The purpose of this section is to develop a theory of the conditions of stability of stratification among organizations, and to apply this theory to the sociology of revolution.

The first problem is the definition and measurement of the thing to be explained, namely the existence of a "revolutionary situation" in which the means of conflict become unlimited. Second, the phenomena of the ranking of organizations will be discussed. The reasons that rapid structural change tends to produce dissensus on the norms governing this ranking of organizations will be developed. Finally, we turn to the elements in the social structure within which this development occurs, particularly the military forces, legal system, and socialization mechanisms which tend to limit the resulting competition for place among organizations to peaceful means. In each case we try to pro-

Source: A. L. Stinchcombe, "Stratification among Organizations and the Sociology of Revolution," in A. L. Stinchcombe, Social Structure and Organizations, in J. G. March (ed.), *Handbook of Organizations* (Chicago, Illinois: Rand McNally, 1965), pp. 169–180. Copyright © 1965 by Rand McNally & Company and used by permission.

vide indices of the variables (such as the degree of liberty) which could be applied to the systematic comparative study of the revolutionary potential of various societies.

DEFINITION AND MEASUREMENT OF "REVOLUTIONARY SITUATIONS"

Rather than explaining the occurrence of revolution, a sociological theory ought to try to explain the occurrence of a "revolutionary situation." Whether or not a change in the ruling powers of a society takes place by means of violence depends both on the predisposing characteristics of the social structure and on concrete military and political situations at given historical times. The flow of historical events, the disposition of troops at particular times, the political loyalty of strategic groups, the tactical genius of revolutionary or governmental leaders, are all situational variables which a sociological theory ought not explain.

But it is possible to outline the conditions under which the means of political conflict tend to become unlimited. Some governments exercise their monopoly of legitimate violence in keeping with some set of generally understood norms, while some use them so as to maximize the damage done to the internal enemy, regardless of legal or political limitations. In turn, some oppositions to governments restrict their petitions to legal and routine channels, while some use more extreme means to obtain either political leadership more to their liking or governmental policy favorable to themselves. Government terror and violence by revolutionary groups are equally unlimited means of political conflict. If government terror is effective in a particular situation, in bringing about the defeat and destruction of the opposition, no revolution would be said to have taken place, according to ordinary language. If government terror is immobilized by historical accidents, and if the opposing groups use unlimited means to replace the government, a change of the ruling group takes place, and there is a revolution of the garden variety. But what is of primary interest here is the common feature of these two situations, that the use of violence in politics is not limited by rules of the game, that either the Tsar or Lenin imprisons or kills his opponents for being opponents. Whether it happens to be the Tsar or Lenin who imprisons depends on particular circumstances and not on the general social structure.

In other words, a sociological theory of revolution ought not expect to be able to tell who will win in a revolutionary situation, but to tell that there will be a fight with unlimited means, a fight not conducted under defined norms for deciding political battles. Explaining who won, and why, is primarily a problem of military science, not of social science.

The means of competition among political forces may be ranged along a continuum of coerciveness, from speech and press governed by debating norms, to free speech limited by libel laws, to free speech in an absolute sense, to price wars, to strikes, boycotts, and lockouts, to general strikes, to riot and police action with light weapons, to organized conflict with deadly heavy weapons. Ideally, we would want to measure the frequency with which means of conflict with different degrees of coerciveness were used in different societies at different times. The measure should include government terror, which from this point of view is a symptom of lack of limitation of the means of competition.

Perhaps the best single index to substitute for a complete picture of the frequency with which various means are used is the prevalence of serious threats of violence at the time of succession of the head of state, but succession crises do not occur very often in some societies, and even in democracies occur sufficiently seldom as not to be a very reliable measure in the short run. For instance, how much weight should be given to the three or four potentially violent successions to the presidency of the United States during the nineteenth century (including at least 1800, 1860, and 1876), as compared with no serious cases during the first part of this century?

A combination of the following items may be a better short-run indication: the number of political prisoners, the number killed in riots, whether the government deploys the police or the army at election time, the presence or absence of paramilitary forces separate from the government and their sizes, the strike rate, the frequency of accusations that opponents are using illegal tactics or are engaged in treason, the frequency of libelous accusations concerning matters irrelevant to politics (such as accusations of sexual delicts). One could use as a positive indicator of an almost utopian state of normative control of political conflict the proportion of newspapers reporting accurately what was said by politicians who are being opposed on the editorial page of the newspaper itself. This could be judged by a comparison of the reports in supporting and opposing newspapers. Unfortunately, statistics on violence and libel are not reported regularly to the United Nations.

If the number of political prisoners is high, if many are killed in riots, if the army is deployed at elections, if there are paramilitary forces of some significance (either attached to the governing groups, as was the private army of the dictator of Haiti in 1963, which is differentiated from the regular state military forces, or attached to an opposition, as the SA before 1933 in Germany), if opponents are irresponsibly accused, if the communications of one side are not respected by the other side, then one will say that a "revolutionary situation" exists. It is the origin of such situations which a sociological theory of revolution should be expected to explain.

Although the data are not available to construct such a measure, I suspect it would show that the means of political conflict at the present time are more unlimited in the United States than in Britain and Scandinavia, more unlimited in Mexico or France than in the United States, more unlimited in the Soviet Union than in Mexico or France, more unlimited in most pre-civil-war situations than in any of the above countries

(Russia in 1916, the Weimar Republic in Germany before Hitler, pre-Castro Cuba, the United States during the 1850's). The extreme of lack of limitation is a society in civil war or under full-scale governmental terror, in which all the indices above tend to be high. The justification for calling such a measure a measure of the existence of a "revolutionary situation" is an empirical proposition, namely, that violent changes in the personnel of government tend to be preceded by a period in which the political conflict becomes more and more unlimited.

This, then, describes the variable to be explained, the lack of limitation of the means of political conflict. The argument here is that the shift in the character of stratification systems of societies, in which stratification among organizations becomes much more important as compared with stratification among individuals or among families, creates forces in the political system of such a nature as to cause political conflicts to become unlimited. These are not the only kinds of forces which tend to cause unlimited political conflict, but they are among the most important in the modern world.

THE RANKING OF ORGANIZATIONS

In order to verify such a contention, a criterion is needed to decide what the social units of a stratification system are. In traditional stratification theory, the units occupying ranks are either individuals or families, or occasionally descent groups. The justification for this choice has been the nature of the problems at issue. When one is trying to explain an individual's reaction to his rank, or the effects on a man's chances in life of the rank of his relatives, then either families or individuals are the appropriate units. But it is not at all clear that individuals and families make revolutions or use violence in political conflict, particularly in modern times.

The units which are ranked vary among societies and over time within societies. The units in which people cognitively organize the social world in order to distribute ranks vary even within a society. What is needed then, is a general measure of the predominant method of organizing social life into units which are evaluated relative to each other,

and which reap the benefits of high rank or the disadvantages of low rank.

I propose that the social units which have credit ratings are the units of a stratification system. Money and property are some of the main life chances that are distributed by a stratification system, and one of the main places where people in a society make explicit conscious decisions of whether to give money to a person, or family, or organization is the situation of borrowing. Borrowing is the main way of getting money or property which is neither coerced nor a matter of instantaneous exchange, but instead depends on an evaluation of the receiver. A credit rating is a particular kind of "reputational" measure of stratification, which measures prestige at the crucial point where it is turned into the control over resources.

Credit is generally extended to some social unit which guarantees the performance of obligations undertaken. For instance, my wife's credit depends largely on my credit rating, unless I put an announcement to the contrary into the newspaper, and my wife also signs my promissory notes. Thus, it is a social unit, rather than an individual, which has the kind of prestige that can be turned into control over resources on the basis of promised future performance. For the purpose of estimating the credit rating of a social unit, various characteristics of the individuals in it may be used, such as the occupation of a husband, the income of a wife, the amount of personal property of the partners of a firm, or the business acumen shown by the heads of a firm in previous businesses. Also, some aspects of the relations between the individuals are normally used in the estimation of the reliability of the social unit, such as whether the liability of one for the debts contracted by the other is limited or unlimited, or whether the reputation of the father would be hurt by the default of the son.

Societies may be classified according to what kinds of social units provide such guarantees. In feudal societies and in the first stages of commercial development, the unit which has a credit rating is the "house" or lineage, although churches and religious orders also have credit. This emphasis on the lineage as a source of credit may be seen by comparing the establishment of credit in certain of Shakespeare's plays dealing with relations among merchants with the types of questions on an application for a loan at a modern bank. For instance, the way a stranger introduces himself in a new town in the first act of *The Taming of the Shrew* is illuminating. The stranger tells what "house" he belongs to, what wealth his father holds, and so forth, in order to establish his credit for a marriage bargaining situation.

With modernization, and in particular with the growth of limited liability devices in the law, this credit rating of the lineage as both a firm and a family becomes differentiated into a credit rating of nuclear families and a credit rating of special-purpose organizations. Thus, my credit rating depends very little on that of my father, and the credit rating of my university depends very little on my personal wealth or personal performance.

This heuristic device for approaching the problem of what the units of a stratification system are suggests (what is obvious once it is stated) that many of the important stratification phenomena in modern society have to do with the ranking of organizations. Universities are ranked by research productivity and by the wealth of their student bodies, and this rank is an important influence on how much control over resources (in endowments, research grants, faculty recruitment, or students) the organization can gain. Likewise, interest groups rank themselves, and are ranked by politicians, on a scale of capacity to represent important population groups, their capacity to influence their members' votes and contributions, and their coercive power. Detailed knowledge of this ranking in his constituency is one of the main elements of a politician's competence. Firms are ranked every day in the newspaper by their importance in the economic system and are ranked by "reputability" by people who give out contracts. In fact, the ranking of a firm in various reputational systems is explicitly treated in the law as a capital asset, which can be legally defended against certain types of encroachments and can be sold.[1]

One important aspect of the modernization of societies, then, is an increase in the importance in the stratification system as a whole of the rankings of organizations relative to each other. This implies at least a relative decline in the importance of families in the stratification system. If this observation is tentatively accepted, we can proceed to try to show how this is connected to the restriction of the means of conflict in the political system. A convenient method of approaching this problem is to discuss the stratification experience of the leaders of organizations, since the action of an organization as an entity will be importantly determined by the motives and perceptions of its leaders.

Where the system of organizational stratification is well developed, and the bases of rankings of organizations enjoy general consensus, the prestige, power, and wealth of an organizational leader will depend closely on the stratification position of the organization. For instance, Linton Freeman and his colleagues (1962, pp. 15–16) have shown that in Syracuse, a man's reputation for community leadership does not correlate very strongly with his personal degree of participation in community decisions. But if each man's participation in community decisions is attributed not to himself, but to the organization which employs him, then these *organizational* participation rates correlate very highly

---

[1] John R. Commons (1924) explicitly treated this development of property in organizational reputations as crucial for the capitalistic modernization of an economic system. A plant's reputation with the government and press in the Soviet Union is also a crucial asset, as is indicated by the following poetic incident reported by Granick (1954, p. 67). "The director of the largest rubber-fabricating plant in the country was removed in a disciplinary action for fighting against his firm's plan even after it had been confirmed by the highest bodies of the country. Yet as a result of his fight, the head of the glavk which had established the production plan was ordered to assume temporarily the duties of director of the plant. Thus the man who had approved the plan which had been condemned by the director as impossible to fulfill was required to take on the job of carrying it out. In such an environment, the management of a firm may not be able to determine the tasks set for it, but it does have strong weapons with which to combat the imposition of impossible programs." This power of the firm against the glavk would not exist unless the firm and its director had some prestige.

with the reputation for influence of the *leaders* of organizations. That is, an organizational leader's reputation for influence is a good representation of the factual degree of influence of the organization. Likewise, it is known that in industry the income of an organization's top executive is highly correlated with the size of the organization, and a firm's size is probably a good indicator of its stratification position.

This implies that the main type of mobility for an organizational leader is of the "entrepreneurial" kind: that is, the main way for an organizational leader to get ahead is to improve the position of his organization, rather than to move up within it (this was brought to my attention by William Friedland). It is only possible to move up from the top of an organization, while staying within it, by increasing the degree of inequality within the organization. This may be impossible or involve serious inefficiencies for the organization, since it disrupts the internal status system which is closely connected to the performance of organizational functions. Moving up to the top of larger or more prestigious organizations depends to a great extent on a leader's capacity to better the position of the organization he is now in.

The norms governing the means of competition for such mobility and the standards by which it is evaluated usually obtain consensus in a society in which major structural reorganization is not going on. In particular, these standards are fairly likely to be obeyed by the organizational leaders in various fields. Thus, the president of the AFL-CIO understands fairly well, and to a certain extent consents to, the ranking of his organization relative to the American Farm Bureau Federation in the halls of Congress, in the Democratic Party, on the editorial pages of newspapers, and so on. More important, he understands and consents to the norms by which he can legitimately change that relative position. But consider the situation when structural reorganization (or modernization) of a society is taking place, when organizational rankings are being newly instituted. In the first place, any increase in the proportion of wealth, power, and prestige which is claimed on organizational grounds rather than on grounds of lineage is some threat to established stratification principles, resulting in a conflict between aristocracies and new organizational leaders.

In the second place, the norms are being worked out according to which new organizations, created in the process of structural differentiation, are to receive ranks. All three of the major stratification values, power, wealth, and prestige, are in dispute. The distribution of coercive powers such as the right to strike, the franchise, whether or not an organization can be sued in civil courts, the right of eminent domain for organizational purposes, is usually disputed vigorously during modernization. The systems of tariffs, capital and income subsidies, tax privileges, monopolies of markets or of patented technology affect the distribution of wealth among organizations and create conflicts among them. The access of leaders of new organizations to titles and honorary degrees, the language of newspapers in describing organizational leaders, representation on boards of community charities, and other indices of the distribution of prestige and deference among organizations are disputed. When the rules of the game in the distribution of these values are subjects of dispute, as well as the rankings of organizations under the rules, the dispute can become acrimonious.

In the third place, new organizations are generally led by new men, who did not occupy elite positions before. This has been best documented for business organizations (Pirenne, 1953; Schumpeter, 1951), but seems to be true more generally. These new men are, furthermore, often young, so that their own mobility from obscurity to fame, wealth, and influence has been very rapid. Both of these facts mean that they will ordinarily be less committed to the norms of the system of stratification among organizations, because they have not been socialized to them in the old elite and because their own biographies of very rapid movement tend to make them believe that anything is possible. More than that, their biographies have taught them that wealth, power, and prestige come rapidly to those who build new organizations. And they know further that "you can't build a railroad within the law," that new organizations only rise rapidly if they have some disrespect for traditional standards.

Consider, for example, the status of a new university, in the extreme a university in a country which has never before had a university. By looking at the various relations between universities and societies in countries which have had them for some time, and noting the variations in organizational status, we can identify some of the norms which are likely to be in dispute. At least the following questions are likely to come up:

1. Will the university have representation in parliament and in the cabinet?
2. Do students and faculty answer to special courts or are they liable in ordinary criminal and civil proceedings?
3. Is the university to be policed by regular police or by special university police?
4. Are certain jobs—especially in the higher civil service and the higher professions—to be reserved for university graduates? of which universities?
5. Will university professors have different types of tenure than other civil servants, and in particular must they be supporters of the regime? Are students to be permitted special freedom of expression not allowed to ordinary citizens?
6. Is one university to be given a monoply of certain kinds of training, or are other institutions to compete? Or are autonomous professional associations controlled by practitioners rather than university people to be given the right to certify professional training?
7. Are the universities to be under the control of the clergy? Will university graduates monopolize clerical livings?
8. Should men educated abroad be given preferment over those from native universities, or the reverse, or should they be treated equally?
9. Should the state support the arts, and if so, should it leave the control of the arts in a separate oligarchy (e.g., the old French Academy) or in the university?
10. What proportion of the university's budget will come from state subsidy? How much political control over the curriculum and admissions policy does this support entail?
11. Insofar as university professors and students are supported by the state, what should be their income relative to other elites in the society?

A favorable resolution of all of these problems makes the faculty and student body into an aristocracy, and the head of the organization into a political power of substantial magnitude. A large share of these questions were resolved in favor of Oxford and Cambridge during English history, and a number of underdeveloped countries seem to be heading in this direction. Conflicts over such questions now create riots in many poorer countries, because the norms are not yet settled. A man who can settle them in favor of the university is a good bet for a cabinet post and will be mentioned as a possible prime minister.

In sum, because of the decay of older (nonorganizational) stratification principles, because of the lack of consensus on the ranks of organizations and how the ranks may legitimately be improved, and because of the qualities of the biographies of the new leaders, the commitment of the leaders of organizations to the norms which rank organizations tends to be weak during a period of rapid structural differentiation.[2] In the language of sociology, we would say that organizational leaders in such a period tend to be "anomic." But of course this is not necessarily, or even usually, a state of psychological despair, of lonely isolation and disenchantment with the world.[3] Rather, the question

---

[2] The insight that revolutionary and other movements using nonroutine methods have their source more in the failure of a society to incorporate *organizations* than in failure to incorporate individuals I owe to Jerome Kirk, Maurice Pinard, and Donald Von Eschen, who developed the idea systematically in their unpublished study of Freedom Rides.

[3] Perhaps such anomie does have psychological symptoms, such as the alternating despair and elation apparently displayed by Hitler at the time when the decision of whether or not to make him chancellor was being made (Shirer, pp. 247–256). The point that is more crucial for us is Hitler's orientation toward parliamentary norms and its relation to his meteoric career, rather than his

is the degree of commitment to the norms governing the interorganizational distribution of wealth, power, and prestige according to accepted norms.

There is no acceptable sense in which one can say that the organizational leaders in an anomic situation engage in "deviant behavior." What is very generally at stake is the definition of what is deviant. The symptom of this dispute is mutual recrimination among the leaders in the society, who accuse each other of violating the rules of fair play and use this as a justification for not following such rules themselves (see Trotsky, 1942, for one of the most systematic expositions of this justification). There is a degree of incapacity of the society as a whole to limit the means of competition, because powerful people in the society do not believe in such limitation.[4]

Instead of deviant behavior, then, there is a tendency to approach more nearly a war of all against all, in which the hand of every man is turned against his brother. This is not, of course, the Hobbesian war of all with individual participants, but rather its organizational analogue. The life of the main contenders is never solitary, and only rarely poor, nasty, or brutish. It may be short. Rather than engaging in hand-to-hand fights, general strikers compete with fascist militias, and both compete with troops of the regular army.[5]

The argument is, then, that rapid growth of the importance of stratification among organizations, entailed by modernization, tends to produce anomie in the politically crucial elites of the society, for their membership in the elite and their status within it depends on the status of their organizations. Because the norms governing the ranking of organizations are unsettled, and because commitment to what norms there are is weakened by the meteoric careers of organizational leaders, the means of organizational competition tend to become unlimited. Those who control the government on the one hand, and those who control massive resources of loyalty, power, and wealth outside the government on the other, tend to use all means to ensure favorable consideration for their organizations.

MAIN VARIABLES MODIFYING MEANS OF COMPETITION

Obviously, the strength of this connection between the growth of new organizations and the lack of limitation of political conflicts varies among societies, depending on institutions which moderate the conflict. The next problem, then, is to locate the main variables which modify and limit the forces outlined above, to explain those cases in which relatively rapid modernization has gone forward with relatively little violence and only sporadic rather than recurrent civil war and government terror. The main variables may be analyzed under the headings of (a) military control, (b) liberty, and (c) elite socialization.

Military control and liberty function together to stabilize political conflict. If the violent means of conflict are made much more expensive by effective enforcement by the police and army, while nonviolent means are made cheaper by the condition of liberty, then a rational organization leader—even if he is not committed to norms governing organizational competition—will prefer less

---

psychological state. Even if his psychological state were very similar to that, say, of Kennedy on November 8, 1960, his behavior in the face of parliamentary opposition was quite different.

[4] Lenin understood, better than Marx, that the fate of revolutions depended on the commitments of organizational leaders to norms of organizational competition. Lenin spent most of his ideological powers on decreasing the commitment of potential leaders to any norms by which the opposition might claim power superior to the Bolsheviks. Although still clothed in Marxist class terminology, the central elements in the Leninist sociology of revolution are organizational leadership cadres. The Leninist term denoting commitment to norms restricting organizational competition is "petty bourgeois," which only very rarely occurs denoting small businessmen or peasants. On Leninist organizational sociology, see Selznick (1952).

[5] The behavior patterns associated with dissensus on the norms of organizational rankings for a particular case are well described in Bracher's

monograph on the Weimar Republic (1957), especially Ch. 2 of Part 1, pp. 28–63.

violent means. If the police and army are either ineffective, or enter into the conflict as full-fledged participants themselves by denying not only the right to riot but also the right to speak, then the comparative effectiveness of violent means in the competitive struggle increases, while the effectiveness of nonviolent means declines. Under these conditions, a rational organizational leader will choose a higher proportion of violent means.

Institutions such as parliaments, political parties, elite schools, and other devices for socializing prospective elites into acceptance of the rules of the game therefore achieve their effects by two paths. First, they enable new leaders of organizations to estimate much more precisely the costs of various means of competition, by acquainting themselves well with the conditions under which violence is likely to be available in the struggle. And second, they tend to have a direct effect on the norms by which new organizational leaders judge their own competitive activity. They give parvenus a sense of responsibility for the larger system, they validate status already achieved by new leaders and encourage them to accept the rank they can achieve by peaceful means, and they make other elites in the society significant to new organizational leaders, preventing immersion in a purely organizational milieu in which all opposition to the goals of the organization is treated as treason. Both by improving information on the political process, and by making the leaders of new organizations responsive to a common set of norms of competition, the existence of parliaments, of political parties, or of elite schools which are so structured that members of the establishment meet parvenus tends to decrease the anomie of new organizational leaders. With this outline of the role armies, liberties, and elite socialization play in the general process of control of political conflict, we turn to a more detailed analysis of each of these major variables.

From our point of view, the crucial question to ask about the violent organizations of a society is how far their entry into politics is governed by an understood set of limiting norms. For if the army and police enter the conflict unconditionally on one or another side of the conflict, supplying a ruling group or a revolutionary group with unlimited power to dispose of its enemies, then competition for place among organizations tends to become unlimited. Because the opposition to currently ruling powers is equally punished, whether it uses speech or riot, opponents are likely to choose the most effective means. The most effective means of combating government terror are not always peaceful. And a government or revolutionary group supported by the army and police in an unlimited fashion is likely to undertake to root out its opposition, rather than to limit the opposition to approved means of conflict. The armies of all societies are crucial in internal politics, but they may be crucial because they enter politics or only because they prevent the entry of private armies. A measure is needed of the terms on which military violence is available in politics, of the degree to which the army and police are parties to the conflict as opposed to organizations for limiting the means of the conflict.

It seems (this largely follows a suggestion of Janowitz, 1962) that the most fruitful approach to this problem is to classify military participation in politics by the degree of discretion in the application of force. That is, if an army is trying to *win* a political conflict, it is unlikely to discriminate in a detailed way between situations in which different sorts of violence ought to be used, against whom, and to what end. When the object is to restrict competition to legitimate channels, different amounts and kinds of coercion have to be applied for different ends to varied groups of people. What we will be trying to get indices of, then, is the degree to which there are detailed and elaborate norms and procedures for discriminating among the situations in which violence is applied in politics.

Probably, as Janowitz has suggested (1962, p. 378), the fundamental source of greater discretion is a structural differentiation between police and armies. Police, where they are separate from armies, are generally oriented toward discrimination among the ends for which violence is applied, while armies are often professionally committed only to winning. The everyday activity of police involves using violence with such discretion that the routine life of the society can go on, while crime and disorder are suppressed. Sometimes it is difficult to tell whether a violent organization is an army or a police, as in the case of the "Black and Tans" in Ireland, but this in itself is an indication of the state of affairs. In general, we can say that if the army is differentiated from the police, and if most governance of political competition is done by police, then probably the entry of violence into politics is governed by norms which allow the competition to go on in peace.

Within armies and police, the presence or absence of a specialized riot-control tradition, separate from other military tactics or from criminal law enforcement, is also an index of discrimination among types of enemies in a violent encounter.

Once these structural conditions are met, facilitating discretion in the use of violence in politics, the crucial questions revolve around the degree of elaboration of the riot- and insurrection-control ideology. A study of the presence or absence, and the degree of elaboration, of the following traditions in different military and police establishments may serve as a beginning in the study of the problem:

1. Attention to telling the public what behavior will be required, and to giving an opportunity for obedience before any coercion is applied. Reading the riot act before applying violence is an ancient and worthwhile provision of the Anglo-American legal tradition, but it was not always evident in riot-control textbooks in the American Army early in this century. In other societies, it is a less common legal provision than might be supposed that a rioting crowd be given the opportunity to obey before violence is applied.

2. Attention to ways of dispersing an unarmed crowd without injuring them unless they resist, especially a differentiation of appropriate weapons. In general, the greater the attention to weapons that do not injure people seriously (such as the pressure of bodies, clubs, the butts of rifles, tear gas, and bayonets used as prods rather than as stabbing weapons), the more likely it is that the object of riot control is to limit the struggle rather than to win it.

3. Attention to a contingency-reserve strategy in which heavier weapons (such as tanks as opposed to bayonets, or rifles as opposed to clubs, or tear gas as opposed to body pressure) are deployed so that they are available only after lighter weapons have been tried and failed.

4. Attention to the location of leaders of a hostile crowd, or of the most violent members, and to the military problem of arresting a few men from a crowd without arresting them all.

5. A recognition that some of the members, and even leaders, of a rioting crowd may have legitimate grievances, even if their behavior has to be restrained. This is opposed to identification of all crowd leaders as Anarchists (in 1900) or Communists (in 1960).

The argument to this point stands as follows: rapid structural differentiation of societies tends to produce powerful people who are little committed to norms restricting organizational competition to peaceful means. This tends to produce political conflict with unlimited means, *unless* the organs of violence are so structured as to limit the means of conflict. If we assume that the central requirement of such a structuring of violent organs is that they discriminate in detail between the means and ends for which violence is to be applied, then we can construct indices of the degree to which violent organs encourage peace. In particular, entrusting political violence largely to police rather than to armies, and the elaboration of a riot-control tradition which discriminates finely among the ends of governmental violence during a civil dispute, should be good measures of the degree of normative control of the actions of violent organs. Where the violent organization of the state apparatus is prepared to discriminate in detail in a civil dispute, we expect that structural differentiation would be more likely to be peaceful.

So far, the discussion has been concerned only with making the violent means of conflict expensive. If certain means of competition are left at the free disposal of whatever organization or group chooses to use them, for instance, the press, the ballot, the public meeting, the court case, while at the same time other means such as rioting, ownership of arms, or terror are limited, then new organizations have access to the political process through one set of channels but not through another set. The whole significance of the limitation of military violence by norms derives from the fact that if such violence is limited, then peaceful means of competition are more available to potential new elites than are violent means. The condition in which certain means of competition are left open to all comers, including especially openness to new organizations, is traditionally called the condition of liberty.

It seems feasible to choose definite indices of the availability of liberties, and to rank societies on this basis. One could come to a fairly accurate judgment, for instance, of whether 5 per cent of the electorate (or some other specified proportion) can organize a political party or a faction within an existing political party and get representatives into parliament, of what proportion of the economy has monopolistic restrictions on free entry, of whether cultural and religious minorities can organize their own schools or not, of the number and prevalence of restrictions on freedom of assembly or freedom of the press. It seems likely that a series of such items would form a relatively clear scale. At least it is quite clear that the extreme cases exist, that for instance Great Britain and the United States are distinct from the Soviet Union, in 1963, on all the criteria mentioned above. There is also substantial variation among societies at roughly the same level of development, so that India or Mexico or Chile or Japan seem to have substantially more liberties than most other societies at the same levels of economic development and structural differentiation.

Once such a ranking of societies is made, and combined with an examination of the structure of the military apparatus, then a process of structural differentiation such as industrialization could be examined systematically in societies with different degrees of liberty to see whether liberties encourage peaceful development, as argued here.

As suggested, direct socialization of the leadership of new organizations probably has an effect on the limitation of political conflict, independent of the rational effects of making violent means expensive and nonviolent means cheap. The feudalization of the rising bourgeoisie in monarchical Germany, or the ideological socialization of new elites in the Communist parties of the Soviet world and the nationalist parties of India, Mexico, Tunisia, Egypt, or Israel, have effectively regulated interorganizational competition. To the degree that parliament forms a "club" with capacity to make a rising dissident leadership into gentlemen, and to the degree that it is more or less open to new elites, it can function to stabilize the competitive process.

* * *

A number of cases of intraorganizational conflict over whether to use unlimited or legitimate means of conflict can be identified. The split of the Russian Social Democrats into Bolsheviks and Mensheviks, the split of the German Social Democrats into Spartacists and democratic socialists, the division of the monarchists in Germany into supporters and nonsupporters of the Kapp Putsch of 1923, and the similar division over support for Hitler, the division of the North in the United States between supporters of the compromises of the pre-Civil-War period and opponents of the compromises, the advocates of revolution versus parliamentary tactics among the Chartists in England come to mind as obvious cases. Studies of the biographies of a sample of leaders of each faction would show the degree to which the moderate faction had had more parliamentary experience, more education in the schools in which the older elites of the society had been schooled, more experience negotiating concrete grievances through peaceful channels, and so on. The prediction would be, of course, that the moderate leadership would have had much more experience of such a nature as to make other elites in the society into significant others, more experience with channels of peaceful access to organizational advantage, more experience giving them accurate knowledge of the terms on which the military would enter the political process, and the like.

If it is really socialization by these experiences which has the effect of making men moderate, rather than merely lesser commitment to the values of the organization leading to greater opportunism, this should show up in their defense of moderate policies in specific ways. Those with much experience which would tend to socialize them should be more likely, for instance, to trust promises of opposing leaders, to attribute the actions of opposing leaders to constraints upon them instead of to bad will, to refer to small changes in the power situation or concrete advantages obtained as indications of the possibility of peaceful advance, and so on. Arguments involving respect for the opposition, and the perception that one can earn the respect of the opposition, should be more frequent among those with the largest number of socialization experiences with other elites, both among the moderates and among the extremists.

In summary, the argument of this section is that one major source of revolutionary potentiality is instability in the stratification system caused by the rapid growth of the importance of stratification among organizations. This potentiality manifests itself in the lack of restraint with which powerful men pursue the welfare of their organizations at the expense of other organizations and at the expense of lineage-based upper classes. It is indicated either by the growth of uncontrolled violence and other coercion by governments or by the growth of unrestrained opposition to governments.

But lack of restraint in interorganizational competition for place depends not only on the rapidity of structural change and the peculiarities of the careers of the new elites. It also depends on features of the social structure which either shape the conditions of action in the competitive struggle or shape the minds of the men struggling. In particular, restraint is encouraged if the military and police of a society provide violence to the political contenders on normatively controlled terms, and if other means of competition are freely available. Restraint is also encouraged if new elites are socialized, by experience in parliament, in school, around negotiating tables, to expect fair play if they play fairly themselves.

* * *

References

Bracher, K. D. *Die Auflösung der Weimarer Republik.* Stuttgart und Düsseldorf: Ring-Verlag, 1957.

Commons, J. R. *Legal foundations of capitalism.* New York: Macmillan, 1924.

Freeman, L. C., Fararo, T. J., Bloomberg, W., & Sunshine, M. H. *Metropolitan decision-making.* Syracuse, N.Y.: Syracuse Univer., Univer. Coll., 1962.

Granick, D. *Management of the industrial firm in the U.S.S.R.* New York: Columbia Univer. Press, 1954.

Janowitz, M. Review of Samuel Huntington, *Changing patterns of military politics. Amer. J. Sociol.,* 1962, 68, 377–380.

Pirenne, H. Stages in the social history of capitalism. In R. Bendix & S. M. Lipset (Eds.), *Class, status, and power.* Glencoe, Ill.: Free Press, 1953, Pp. 501–517.

Schumpeter, J. A. *Imperialism and social classes.* New York: Kelley, 1951.

Selznick, P. *The organizational weapon.* New York: McGraw-Hill, 1952.

Shirer, W. L. *The rise and fall of the Third Reich.* Greenwich, Conn.: Fawcett Publications, n.d.

Trotsky, L. *Their morals and ours.* New York: Pioneer, 1942.

SOCIAL CONFLICT AND THE THEORY OF SOCIAL CHANGE

Lewis A. Coser

This paper attempts to examine some of the functions of social conflict in the process of social change. I shall first deal with some functions of conflict *within* social systems, more specifically with its relation to institutional rigidities, technical progress and productivity, and will then concern ourselves with the relation between social conflict and the changes *of* social systems.

A central observation of George Sorel in his *Reflections on Violence* which has not as yet been accorded sufficient attention by sociologists may serve us as a convenient springboard. Sorel wrote:[1]

We are today faced with a new and unforeseen fact—a middle class which seeks to weaken its own strength. The race of bold captains who made the greatness of modern industry disappears to make way for an ultracivilized aristocracy which asks to be allowed to live in peace.

The threatening decadence may be avoided if the proletariat hold on with obstinacy to revolutionary ideas. The antagonistic classes influence each other in a partly indirect but decisive manner. *Everything may be saved if the proletariat, by their use of violence, restore to the middle class something of its former energy.*

Sorel's specific doctrine of class struggle is not of immediate concern here. What is important for us is the idea that conflict (which Sorel calls violence, using the word

in a very special sense) prevents the ossification of the social system by exerting pressure for innovation and creativity. Though Sorel's call to action was addressed to the working class and its interests, he conceived it to be of general importance for the total social system; to his mind the gradual disappearance of class conflict might well lead to the decadence of European culture. A social system, he felt, was in need of conflict if only to renew its energies and revitalize its creative forces.

This conception seems to be more generally applicable than to class struggle alone. Conflict within and between groups in a society can prevent accommodations and habitual relations from progressively impoverishing creativity. The clash of values and interests, the tension between what is and what some groups feel ought to be, the conflict between vested interests and new strata and groups demanding their share of power, wealth and status, have been productive of vitality; note for example the contrast between the 'frozen world' of the Middle Ages and the burst of creativity that accompanied the thaw that set in with Renaissance civilization.

This is, in effect, the application of John Dewey's theory of consciousness and thought as arising in the wake of obstacles to the interaction of groups. 'Conflict is the gadfly of thought. It stirs us to observation and memory. It instigates to invention. It shocks us out of sheeplike passivity, and sets us at noting and contriving. . . . Conflict is a *sine qua non* of reflection and ingenuity.'[2]

Conflict not only generates new norms, new institutions, as I have pointed out else-

---

Source: L. A. Coser, "Social Conflict and the Theory of Social Change," *British Journal of Sociology*, Vol. 8, 1957, pp. 197–207. Copyright 1957 by Routledge & Kegan Paul Ltd. and used by permission.
1 George Sorel, *Reflections on Violence*, ch. 2, par. 11.

2 John Dewey, *Human Nature and Conduct*, N.Y., The Modern Library, 1930, p. 300.

where,[3] it may be said to be stimulating directly in the economic and technological realm. Economic historians often have pointed out that much technological improvement has resulted from the conflict activity of trade unions through the raising of wage levels. A rise in wages usually has led to a substitution of capital investment for labour and hence to an increase in the volume of investment. Thus the extreme mechanization of coal-mining in the United States has been partly explained by the existence of militant unionism in the American coalfields.[4] A recent investigation by Sidney C. Sufrin[5] points to the effects of union pressure, 'goading management into technical improvement and increased capital investment'. Very much the same point was made recently by the conservative British *Economist* which reproached British unions for their 'moderation' which it declared in part responsible for the stagnation and low productivity of British capitalism; it compared their policy unfavourably with the more aggressive policies of American unions whose constant pressure for higher wages has kept the American economy dynamic.[6]

This point raises the question of the adequacy and relevancy of the 'human relations' approach in industrial research and management practice. The 'human relations' approach stresses the 'collective purpose of the total organization' of the factory, and either denies or attempts to reduce conflicts of interests in industry.[7] But a successful reduction of industrial conflict may have unanticipated dysfunctional consequences for it may destroy an important stimulus for technological innovation.

It often has been observed that the effects of technological change have weighed most heavily upon the worker.[8] Both informal and formal organization of workers represent in part an attempt to mitigate the insecurities attendant upon the impact of unpredictable introduction of change in the factory.[9] But by organizing in unions workers gain a feeling of security through the effective conduct of institutionalized conflict with management and thus exert pressure on management to increase their returns by the invention of further cost-reducing devices. The search for mutual adjustment, understanding and 'unity' between groups who find themselves in different life situations and have different life chances calls forth the danger that Sorel warns of, namely that the further development of technology would be seriously impaired.

The emergence of invention and of technological change in modern Western society, with its institutionalization of science as an instrument for making and remaking the world, was made possible with the gradual emergence of a pluralistic and hence conflict-charged structure of human relations. In the unitary order of the medieval guild system, 'no one was permitted to harm others by methods which enabled him to produce more quickly and more cheaply than they. Tech-

---

[3] Lewis A. Coser, *The Functions of Social Conflict*, Glencoe, Ill.; London, Routledge and Kegan Paul, 1956.

[4] Cf. McAlister Coleman, *Men and Coal*, N.Y., Farrar and Rinehart, 1943.

[5] *Union Wages and Labor's Earnings*, Syracuse, Syracuse Univ. Press, 1951.

[6] Quoted by Will Herberg, 'When Social Scientists View Labor', *Commentary*, Dec. 1951, XII, 6, pp. 590–6. See also Seymour Melman, *Dynamic Factors in Industrial Productivity*, Oxford, Blackwell, 1956, on the effects of rising wage levels on productivity.

[7] See the criticism of the Mayo approach by Daniel Bell, 'Adjusting Men to Machines', *Commentary*, Jan. 1947, pp. 79–88; C. Wright Mills,

'The Contribution of Sociology to the Study of Industrial Relations', *Proceedings of the Industrial Relations Research Association*, 1948, pp. 199–222.

[8] See R. K. Merton, 'The Machine, The Workers and The Engineer', *Social Theory and Social Structure*, Glencoe, Ill., 1949, pp. 317–28; Georges Friedmann, *Industrial Society*, Glencoe, Ill., 1956.

[9] For informal organization and change, see Roethlisberger & Dickson, *Management and the Worker*, Cambridge, 1939, especially pp. 567–8; for formal organization, see Selig Perlman, *The Theory of the Labor Movement*; on general relations between technology and labour, see Elliot D. Smith and Richard C. Nyman, *Technology and Labor*, New Haven, Yale Univ. Press, 1939.

nical progress took on the appearance of disloyalty. The ideal was stable conditions in a stable industry.'[10]

In the modern Western world, just as in the medieval world, vested interests exert pressure for the maintenance of established routines; yet the modern Western institutional structure allows room for freedom of conflict. The structure no longer being unitary, vested interests find it difficult to resist the continuous stream of change-producing inventions. Invention, as well as its application and utilization, is furthered through the ever-renewed challenge to vested interests, as well as by the conflicts between the vested interests themselves.[11]

Once old forms of traditional and unitary integration broke down, the clash of conflicting interests and values, now no longer constrained by the rigidity of the medieval structure, pressed for new forms of unification and integration. Thus deliberate control and rationalized regulation of 'spontaneous' processes was required in military and political, as well as in economic institutions. Bureaucratic forms of organization with their emphasis on calculable, methodical and disciplined behaviour[12] arose at roughly the same period in which the unitary medieval structure broke down. But with the rise of bureaucratic types of organization peculiar new resistances to change made their appearance. The need for reliance on predictability exercises pressure towards the rejection of innovation which is perceived as interference with routine. Conflicts involving a 'trial through battle' are unpredictable in their outcome, and therefore unwelcome to the bureaucracy which must strive towards an ever-widening extension of the area of predictability and cal-

culability of results. But social arrangements which have become habitual and totally patterned are subject to the blight of ritualism. If attention is focused exclusively on the habitual clues, 'people may be unfitted by being fit in an unfit fitness',[13] so that their habitual training becomes an incapacity to adjust to new conditions. To quote Dewey again: 'The customary is taken for granted; it operates subconsciously. Breach of wont and use is focal; it forms "consciousness".'[14] A group or a system which no longer is challenged is no longer capable of a creative response. It may subsist, wedded to the eternal yesterday of precedent and tradition, but it is no longer capable of renewal.[15]

'Only a hitch in the working of habit occasions emotion and provokes thought.'[16] Conflict within and between bureaucratic structures provides means for avoiding the ossification and ritualism which threatens their form of organization.[17] Conflict, though apparently dysfunctional for highly rationalized systems, may actually have important latent functional consequences. By attacking and overcoming the resistance to innovation and change that seems to be an 'occupational psychosis' always threatening the bureaucratic office holder, it can help to insure that the system does not stifle in the deadening routine of habituation and that in the planning activity itself creativity and invention can be applied.

We have so far discussed change within systems, but changes of systems are of perhaps even more crucial importance for sociological inquiry. Here the sociology of Karl

[10] Henri Pirenne, *Economic and Social History of Medieval Europe*, London, Routledge and Kegan Paul, 1949. P.186.

[11] See W. F. Ogburn, *Social Change*, N.Y.: B. W. Huebsch, 1923, for the theory of 'cultural lag' due to 'vested interests'.

[12] Max Weber, 'Bureaucracy', *From Max Weber*, Gerth and Mills, ed. Pp. 196–244. For the pathology of bureaucracy, see R. K. Merton, 'Bureaucratic Structure and Personality', *Social Theory and Social Structure*, op. cit. Pp. 151–60.

[13] Kenneth Burke, *Permanence and Change*, N.Y., New Republic, 1936, p. 18.

[14] John Dewey, *The Public and Its Problems*, Chicago, Gateway Books, 1946, p. 100.

[15] This is, of course, a central thesis of Arnold Toynbee's monumental A *Study of History*, O.U.P.

[16] John Dewey, *Human Nature and Conduct*, op. cit., p. 178.

[17] See, e.g., Melville Dalton, 'Conflicts Between Staff and Line Managerial Officers', *Am. Soc. R.*, XV (1959), pp. 342–51. The author seems to be unaware of the positive functions of this conflict, yet his data clearly indicate the 'innovating potential' of conflict between staff and line.

Marx serves us well. Writes Marx in a polemic against Proudhon:[18]

Feudal production also had two antagonistic elements, which were equally designated by the names of good side and bad side of feudalism, without regard being had to the fact that it is always the evil side which finishes by overcoming the good side. It is the bad side that produces the movement which makes history, by constituting the struggle. If at the epoch of the reign of feudalism the economists, enthusiastic over the virtues of chivalry, the delightful harmony between rights and duties, the patriarchal life of the towns, the prosperous state of domestic industry in the country, of the development of industry organized in corporations, guilds and fellowships, in fine of all which constitutes the beautiful side of feudalism, had proposed to themselves the problem of eliminating all which cast a shadow upon this lovely picture—serfdom, privilege, anarchy—what would have been the result? All the elements which constituted the struggle would have been annihilated, and the development of the bourgeoisie would have been stifled in the germ. They would have set themselves the absurd problem of eliminating history.

According to Marx, conflict leads not only to ever-changing relations within the existing social structure, but the total social system undergoes transformation through conflict.

During the feudal period, the relations between serf and lord, between burgher and gentry, underwent many changes both in law and in fact. Yet conflict finally led to a breakdown of all feudal relations and hence to the rise of a new social system governed by different patterns of social relations.

It is Marx's contention that the negative element, the opposition, conditions the change when conflict between the sub-groups of a system becomes so sharpened that at a certain point this system breaks down. Each

social system contains elements of strain and of potential conflict; if in the analysis of the social structure of a system these elements are ignored, if the adjustment of patterned relations is the only focus of attention, then it is not possible to anticipate basic social change. Exclusive attention to wont and use, to the customary and habitual bars access to an understanding of possible latent elements of strain which under certain conditions eventuate in overt conflict and possibly in a basic change of the social structure. This attention should be focused, in Marx's view, on what evades and resists the patterned normative structure and on the elements pointing to new and alternative patterns emerging from the existing structure. What is diagnosed as disease from the point of view of the institutionalized pattern may, in fact, says Marx, be the first birth pang of a new one to come; not wont and use but the break of wont and use is focal. The 'matters-of-fact' of a 'given state of affairs' when viewed in the light of Marx's approach, become limited, transitory; they are regarded as containing the germs of a process that leads beyond them.[19]

Yet, not all social systems contain the same degree of conflict and strain. The sources and incidence of conflicting behaviour in each particular system vary according to the type of structure, the patterns of social mobility, of ascribing and achieving status and of allocating scarce power and wealth, as well as the degree to which a specific form of distribution of power, resources and status is accepted by the component actors within the

---

[18] Karl Marx, *The Poverty of Philosophy*, Chicago, Charles H. Kerr & Co., 1910, p. 132.

---

[19] For an understanding of Marx's methodology and its relation to Hegelian philosophy, see Herbert Marcuse, *Reason and Revolution*, N.Y., O.U.P., 1941.

Note the similarity with John Dewey's thought: 'Where there is change, there is of necessity numerical plurality, multiplicity, and from variety comes opposition, strife. Change is alteration, or "othering" and this means diversity. Diversity means division, and division means two sides and their conflict.' *Reconstruction in Philosophy*, N.Y., Mentor Books, 1950, p. 97. See also the able discussion of the deficiencies of Talcott Parsons' sociological theories by David Lockwood, *B.J.S.*, June, 1956.

different sub-systems. But if, within any social structure, there exists an excess of claimants over opportunities for adequate reward, there arises strain and conflict.

The distinction between changes *of* systems and changes *within* systems is, of course, a relative one. There is always some sort of continuity between a past and a present, or a present and a future social system; societies do not die the way biological organisms do, for it is difficult to assign precise points of birth or death to societies as we do with biological organisms. One may claim that all that can be observed is a change of the organization of social relations; but from one perspective such change may be considered re-establishment of equilibrium while from another it may be seen as the formation of a new system.

A natural scientist, describing the function of earthquakes, recently stated admirably what could be considered the function of conflict. 'There is nothing abnormal about an earthquake. An unshakeable earth would be a dead earth. A quake is the earth's way of maintaining its equilibrium, a form of adjustment that enables the crust to yield to stresses that tend to reorganize and redistribute the material of which it is composed. . . . The larger the shift, the more violent the quake, and the more frequent the shifts, the more frequent are the shocks.'[20]

Whether the quake is violent or not, it has served to maintain or re-establish the equilibrium of the earth. Yet the shifts may be small changes of geological formations, or they may be changes in the structural relations between land and water, for example.

At what point the shift is large enough to warrant the conclusion that a change *of* the system has taken place, is hard to determine. Only if one deals with extreme instances are ideal types—such as feudalism, capitalism, etc.—easily applied. A system based on serfdom, for example, may undergo considerable change within—*vide* the effects of the Black Death on the social structure of medieval society; and even an abolition of serfdom may not necessarily be said to mark the end of an old and the emergence of a new system, *vide* nineteenth-century Russia.

If 'it is necessary to distinguish clearly between the processes *within* the system and processes of change *of* the system', as Professor Parsons has pointed out,[21] an attempt should be made to establish a heuristic criterion for this distinction. We propose to talk of a change *of* system when all major structural relations, its basic institutions and its prevailing value system have been drastically altered. (In cases where such a change takes place abruptly, as, for example, the Russian Revolution, there should be no difficulty. It is well to remember, however, that transformations of social systems do not always consist in an abrupt and simultaneous change of all basic institutions. Institutions may change gradually, by mutual adjustment, and it is only over a period of time that the observer will be able to claim that the social system has undergone a basic transformation in its structural relations.) In concrete historical reality, no clear-cut distinctions exist. Change *of* system may be the result (or the sum total) of previous changes *within* the system. This does not however detract from the usefulness of the theoretical distinction.

It is precisely Marx's contention that the change from feudalism to a different type of social system can be understood only through an investigation of the stresses and strains *within* the feudal system. Whether given forms of conflict will lead to changes in the social system or to breakdown and to formation of a new system will depend on the rigidity and resistance to change, or inversely on the elasticity of the control mechanisms of the system.

It is apparent, however, that the rigidity of the system and the intensity of conflict within it are not independent of each other. Rigid systems which suppress the incidence

---

[20] Waldemar Kaemfert, 'Science in Review', *New York Times,* July 27, 1952.

[21] Talcott Parsons, *The Social System,* London, Tavistock Publications: 1951, p. 481.

I owe much to Prof. Parsons' treatment of this distinction despite a number of major disagreements with his theory of social change.

of conflict exert pressure towards the emergence or radical cleavages and violent forms of conflict. More elastic systems, which allow the open and direct expression of conflict within them and which adjust to the shifting balance of power which these conflicts both indicate and bring about, are less likely to be menaced by basic and explosive alignments within their midst.

In what follows the distinction between strains, conflicts and disturbances within a system which lead to a re-establishment of equilibrium, and conflicts which lead to the establishment of new systems and new types of equilibria, will be examined.[22] Such an examination will be most profitably begun by considering what Thorstein Veblen[23] has called 'Vested Interests'.[24]

Any social system implies an allocation of power, as well as wealth and status positions among individual actors and component subgroups. As has been pointed out, there is never complete concordance between what individuals and groups within a system consider their just due and the system of allocation. Conflict ensues in the effort of various frustrated groups and individuals to increase their share of gratification. Their demands will encounter the resistance of those who previously had established a 'vested interest' in a given form of distribution of honour, wealth and power.

To the vested interests, an attack against their position necessarily appears as an attack upon the social order.[25] Those who derive privileges from a given system of allocation of status, wealth and power will perceive an attack upon these prerogatives as an attack against the system itself.

However, mere 'frustration' will not lead to a questioning of the legitimacy of the position of the vested interests, and hence to conflict. Levels of aspiration as well as feelings of deprivation are relative to institutionalized expectations and are established through comparison.[26] When social systems have in-

---

[22] The concept of *equilibrium* is of great value in social science provided it is used, as by Schumpeter, as a point of reference permitting measurement of departures from it. 'The concept of a state of equilibrium, although no such state may ever be realized, is useful and indeed indispensable for purposes of analyses and diagnosis, as a point of reference' (See Joseph A. Schumpeter, *Business Cycle*, N.Y., McGraw-Hill, 1939, p. 69). But certain types of sociological functionalism tend to move from this methodological use of the concept to one which has some clearly ideological features. The ideal type of equilibrium, in this illegitimate use, becomes a normative instead of a methodological concept. Attention is focused on the maintenance of a system which is somehow identified with the ethically desirable (see Merton's discussion of this ideological misuse of functionalism in *Social Theory and Social Structure*, op. cit., pp. 38 ff. and 116–17; see also my review of Parsons' Essays, *American Journal of Sociology*, 55, March 1950, pp. 502–4). Such theorizing tends to look at all behaviour caused by strains and conflict as 'deviancy' from the legitimate pattern, thereby creating the perhaps unintended impression that such behaviour is somehow 'abnormal' in an ethical sense, and obscuring the fact that some 'deviant' behaviour actually serves the creation of new patterns rather than a simple rejection of the old.

[23] See especially *The Vested Interests and the State of the Industrial Arts*, N.Y., 1919.

[24] Max Lerner ('Vested Interests', *Encyclopaedia of the Social Sciences*, XV, p. 240) gives the following definition: 'When an activity has been pursued so long that the individuals concerned in it have a prescriptive claim to its exercise and its profit, they are considered to have a vested interest in it.'

[25] Veblen has described this aptly in 'The code of proprieties, conventionalities, and usages in vogue at any given time and among any given people has more or less of the character of an organic whole; so that any appreciable change in one point of the scheme involves something of a change or readjustment of other points also, if not a reorganization all along the line. . . . When an attempted reform involves the suppression or thoroughgoing remodelling of an institution of first-rate importance in the conventional scheme, it is immediately felt that a serious derangement of the entire scheme would result. . . . Any of these innovations would, we are told, "shake the social structure to its base", "reduce society to chaos", . . . etc. The aversion to change is in large part an aversion to the bother of making the readjustment which any given change will necessitate' (*The Theory of the Leisure Class*, N.Y., The Modern Library. Pp. 201–3).

[26] See Robert K. Merton and Alice S. Kitt, 'Contributions to the Theory of Reference Group Behaviour' for a development of the concept of 'relative deprivation' (originally suggested by Stouffer *et al.* in *The American Soldier*) and its incorporation into the framework of a theory of reference groups.

stitutionalized goals and values to govern the conduct of component actors, but limit access to these goals for certain members of the society, 'departures from institutional requirements' are to be expected.[27] Similarly, if certain groups within a social system compare their share in power, wealth and status honour with that of other groups *and* question the legitimacy of this distribution, discontent is likely to ensue. If there exist no institutionalized provisions for the expression of such discontents, departures from what is required by the norms of the social system may occur. These may be limited to 'innovation' or they may consist in the rejection of the institutionalized goals. Such 'rebellion' 'involves a genuine transvaluation, where the direct or vicarious experience of frustration leads to full denunciation of previously prized values'.[28] Thus it will be well to distinguish between those departures from the norms of a society which consist in mere 'deviation' and those which involve the formation of distinctive patterns and new value systems.

What factors lead groups and individuals to question at a certain point the legitimacy of the system of distribution of rewards, lies largely outside the scope of the present inquiry. The intervening factors can be sought in the ideological, technological, economic or any other realm. It is obvious, moreover, that conflict may be a result just as much as a source of change. A new invention, the introduction of a new cultural trait through diffusion, the development of new methods of production or distribution, etc., will have a differential impact within a social system. Some strata will feel it to be detrimental to their material or ideal interests, while others will feel their position strengthened through its introduction. Such disturbances in the equilibrium of the system lead to conditions in which groups or individual actors no longer do willingly what they have to do and do willingly what they are not supposed to do.

Change, no matter what its source, breeds strain and conflict.

Yet, it may be well to repeat that mere 'frustration' and the ensuing strains and tensions do not necessarily lead to group conflict. Individuals under stress may relieve their tension through 'acting out' in special safety-valve institutions in as far as they are provided for in the social system; or they may 'act out' in a deviant manner, which may have serious dysfunctional consequences for the system, and bring about change in this way. This, however, does not reduce the frustration from which escape has been sought since it does not attack their source.

If, on the other hand, the strain leads to the emergence of specific new patterns of behaviour of whole groups of individuals who pursue 'the optimization of gratification'[29] by choosing what they consider appropriate means for the maximization of rewards, social change which reduces the sources of their frustration may come about. This may happen in two ways: if the social system is flexible enough to adjust to conflict situations we will deal with change *within* the system. If, on the other hand, the social system is not able to readjust itself and allows the accumulation of conflict, the 'aggressive' groups, imbued with a new system of values which threatens to split the general consensus of the society and imbued with an ideology which 'objectifies' their claims, may become powerful enough to overcome the resistance of vested interests and bring about the breakdown of the system and the emergence of a new distribution of social values.[30]

In his *Poverty of Philosophy*, Marx was led to consider the conditions under which economic classes constitute themselves:

> *Economic conditions have first transformed the mass of the population into workers. The domination of capital created for this mass a common situation and common interest. This mass was thus already a class as against capital, but not for itself.*

---

[27] This whole process is exhaustively discussed by Merton in his paper on 'Social Structure and Anomie', *Social Theory*, op. cit.
[28] Ibid., p. 145.

[29] T. Parsons, *The Social System*, op. cit., p. 498.
[30] R. K. Merton, *Social Theory and Social Structure*, op. cit., pp. 42–3 and 116–17.

It is in the struggle . . . that the mass gathers together and constitutes itself as a class for itself. The interests which it defends become class interests.[31]

With this remarkable distinction between class *in itself* and class *for itself* (which unfortunately he didn't elaborate upon in later writings though it informs all of them —if not the writings of most latter-day 'marxists'), Marx illuminates a most important aspect of group formation: group belongingness is established by an objective conflict situation—in this case a conflict of interests;[32] but only by experiencing this antagonism, that is, by becoming aware of it and by acting it out, does the group (or class) establish its identity.

When changes in the equilibrium of a society lead to the formation of new groupings or to the strengthening of existing groupings that set themselves the goal of overcoming resistance of vested interests through conflict, changes in structural relations, as distinct from simple 'maladjustment', can be expected.

What Robert Park said about the rise of nationalist and racial movements is more generally applicable:[33]

[31] Karl Marx, *The Poverty of Philosophy*, op. cit., pp. 188–9.
[32] This makes it necessary to distinguish between realistic and non-realistic conflict: social conflicts that arise from frustration of specific demands and from estimates of gains of the participants, and that are directed at the presumed frustrating object, may be called realistic conflicts. Non-realistic conflicts, on the other hand, are not occasioned by the rival ends of the antagonists, but by the need for tension release of one or both of them. Some groups may be formed with the mere purpose of releasing tension. Such groups 'collectivize' their tensions, so to speak. They can, by definition, only be disruptive rather than creative since they are built on negative rather than positive cathexes. But groups of this kind will remain marginal; their actions cannot bring about social change unless they accompany and strengthen realistic conflict groups. In such cases we deal with an admixture of non-realistic and realistic elements mutually reinforcing each other within the same social movements. Members who join for the mere purpose of tension release are often used for the 'dirty work' by the realistic conflict groups.
[33] Robert E. Park, 'Personality and Cultural Conflict', *Publications of the Am. Soc. Soc.*, 25, 1931, pp. 95–110. See p. 107.

They strike me as natural and wholesome disturbances of the social routine, the effect of which is to arouse in those involved a lively sense of common purpose and to give those who feel themselves oppressed the inspiration of a common cause. . . . The effect of this struggle is to increase the solidarity and improve the morale of the 'oppressed' minority.

It is this sense of common purpose arising in and through conflict that is peculiar to the behaviour of individuals who meet the challenge of new conditions by a group-forming and value-forming response. Strains which result in no such formations of new conflict groups or strengthening of old ones may contribute to bringing about change, but a type of change that fails to reduce the sources of strain since by definition tension-release behaviour does not involve purposive action. Conflict through group action, on the other hand, is likely to result in a 'deviancy' which may be the prelude of new patterns and reward systems apt to reduce the sources of frustration.

If the tensions that need outlets are continually reproduced within the structure, abreaction through tension-release mechanisms may preserve the system but at the risk of ever-renewed further accumulation of tension. Such accumulation eventuates easily in the irruption of destructive unrealistic conflict. If feelings of dissatisfaction, instead of being suppressed or diverted are allowed expression against 'vested interests', and in this way to lead to the formation of new groupings within the society, the emergence of genuine transvaluations is likely to occur. Sumner saw this very well when he said: 'We want to develop symptoms, we don't want to suppress them.'[34]

Whether the emergence of such new groupings or the strengthening of old ones with the attendant increase in self-confidence and self-esteem on the part of the participants will lead to a change *of* or *within* the system will depend on the degree of cohesion that

[34] Wm. G. Sumner, *War and Other Essays*, p. 241.

the system itself has attained. A well-integrated society will tolerate and even welcome group conflict; only a weakly integrated one must fear it. The great English liberal John Morley said it very well:[35]

---

[35] John Morley, *On Compromise*, London, Macmillan & Co., 1917, p. 263.

If [the men who are most attached to the reigning order of things] had a larger faith in the stability for which they profess so great an anxiety, they would be more free alike in understanding and temper to deal generously, honestly and effectively with those whom they count imprudent innovators.

A COMPARATIVE STUDY OF CIVIL STRIFE

Ted Robert Gurr

Group protest and violence are episodic in the history of most organized political communities and chronic in many. No country in the modern world has been free of it for as much as a generation. Sorokin analyzed the histories of 11 European states and empires over a 25-century span and found that they averaged only four peaceful years for each year in which major outbreaks of civil strife were in progress.[1] A comparison of average levels of disturbance, from the 6th to the 19th centuries, indicates that the most violent century, the 13th, had only twice the level of violence of the 18th, the most peaceful century.[2] Between 1900 and 1965, Calvert estimates that 367 revolutions occurred, defining revolution as forcible intervention to replace governments or change their processes. Of these, 135 occurred between 1946 and 1965, an average of 6.75 a year compared with an average of 5.56 a year for the entire 65-year period.[3] The Feierabends found that between 1948 and 1961, collective antigovernmental action occurred in all but one of 82 independent countries.[4] Between 1961 and 1967, some form of civil strife is reported to have occurred in 114 of the world's 121 larger nations and colonies.[5]

Relatively few occurrences of strife are "revolutionary." Most are manifestations of opposition to particular policies of govern-

---

Source: T. R. Gurr, "A Comparative Study of Civil Strife," Chapter 17 in T. R. Gurr and H. D. Graham (eds.), *Violence in America: Historical and Comparative Perceptives*, Washington, D.C.: National Commission on the Causes and Prevention of Violence, 1969 (also published by Bantam Books and Frederick A. Praeger under the title, *The History of Violence in America*), pp. 572–575, 596–618; references on pp. 624–626.

[1] *Social and Cultural Dynamics, Vol. III: Fluctuation of Social Relationships, War, and Revolution* (New York: American, 1937), p. 504.

[2] *Ibid.*, pp. 383–506.

[3] Peter A. R. Calvert, "Revolution: The Politics of Violence," *Political Studies*, vol. XV (No. 1, 1967), p. 1.

[4] See Ivo K. and Rosalind L. Feierabend, "Aggressive Behaviors Within Polities, 1948–1962: A Cross-National Study," *Journal of Conflict Resolution*, vol. X (Sept. 1966), pp. 249–271; and Betty A. Nesvold, "A Scalogram Analysis of Political Violence," *Comparative Political Studies*, vol. II (July 1969).

[5] Data for 1961–63 for 119 polities are reported in Ted Gurr with Charles Ruttenberg, *The Conditions of Civil Violence: First Tests of a Causal Model* (Princeton: Center of International Studies, Princeton University, Research Monograph No. 28, 1967). Data for 1961–65 for 114 polities are summarized in appendices to the present paper.

ments or of hostilities between competing groups. Moreover, certain kinds and levels of civil strife are more likely to occur in some kinds of nations, and under some kinds of socioeconomic conditions, than under others. The kinds of systematic evidence mentioned above have been used not only to determine differences in the types and extent of civil strife among nations but to test various explanations of its causes. This paper summarizes some results of a comprehensive study of civil strife in 114 nations and colonies during the years from 1961 through 1965.

LEVELS AND TYPES OF CIVIL STRIFE AMONG CONTEMPORARY NATIONS

In this study, "civil strife" means all collective nongovernmental attacks on persons or property that occur within a political system, but not individual crimes. We included symbolic attacks on political persons or policies such as political demonstrations and political strikes. Their inclusion does not reflect a normative judgment about their desirability or their legality; demonstrative protests are legal under some conditions in some countries, illegal in many others. Whatever their legal status, they are essentially similar to violent forms of protest: they are collective manifestations of substantial discontent that typically occur outside institutional frameworks for action. The violence used by regimes to maintain social control is not included as an aspect of civil strife because we are concerned with the extent to which ordinary citizens, not officials, resort to force. Regime coercion and violence can be both a cause of and a response to civil strife, and for the purposes of this study is analyzed in those terms, not as an integral part of strife.

Three general kinds of civil strife were distinguished in the study, in addition to more specific kinds:

Turmoil.—Relatively spontaneous, unorganized strife with substantial popular participation, including political demonstrations

and strikes, riots, political and ethnic clashes, and local rebellions.

Conspiracy.—Highly organized strife with limited participation, including organized political assassinations, small-scale terrorism, small-scale guerrilla wars, coups d'état, mutinies, and antigovernment plots.

Internal war.—Highly organized strife with widespread popular participation, accompanied by extensive violence and including large-scale terrorism and guerrilla wars; civil wars; "private" wars among ethnic, political, and religious groups; and large-scale revolts.

Information was collected on all such events reported in general news sources for 114 nations and colonies from 1961 through 1965. More than 1,000 events were identified, counting waves of demonstrations, riots, or terrorism over related issues as single "events." For each reported event or group of related events, we recorded such information as the kinds of socioeconomic groups involved, the approximate number of people who took part, their apparent motives or grievances, whom or what they attacked, how long they persisted, the severity of governmental response, and the costs of the action in terms of damage, casualties, and arrests.

* * *

COMPARATIVE EVIDENCE ON THE CAUSES OF CIVIL STRIFE

SOME PSYCHOLOGICAL PRECONDITIONS OF CIVIL STRIFE

The popular and sociological cliché is that "frustration" or "discontent" or "relative deprivation" is the root cause of rebellion. Cliché or not, the basic relationship is as fundamental to understanding civil strife as the law of gravity is to atmospheric physics: relative deprivation, the phrase used in this research, is a necessary precondition for civil strife of any kind. The greater the deprivation an individual perceives relative to his expectations, the greater his discontent; the more widespread and intense is discontent among members of a society, the more likely and severe is civil strife. Relative deprivation is not whatever the outside observer thinks people ought to be dissatisfied with. It is a state of mind that I have defined as a discrepancy between people's expectations about the goods and conditions of life to which they are justifiably entitled, on the one hand, and, on the other, their value capabilities— the degree to which they think they can attain those goods and conditions.

This is not a complicated way of making the simplistic and probably inaccurate statement that people are deprived and therefore angry if they have less than what they want. Two characteristics of value perceptions are more important than this "want-get ratio": people become most intensely discontented when they cannot get what they think they deserve, not just what they want in an ideal sense; and when they feel they are making inadequate progress toward their goals, not whether they have actually attained them or not.

Underlying the relative deprivation approach to civil strife is the frustration-aggression mechanism, apparently a fundamental part of our psychobiological makeup. When we feel thwarted in an attempt to get something we want, we are likely to become angry, and when we become angry the most satisfying inherent response is to strike out at the source of frustration. Relative deprivation is, in effect, a perception of thwarting circumstances. How angry men become in response to the perception of deprivation is determined partly by the relative importance to them of the expectations to which they are striving; the number of alternatives they have yet to try; and the degree of the discrepancy itself. If angry men believe that collective protest or violence are legitimate responses to anger, and if they think that protest or violence will help alleviate their discontent, the impetus to civil strife is strengthened. If they believe that strife is unjustified and unlikely to succeed, they are more likely to contain their anger or to divert it into other activities.

In brief, the basic psychological factors in the genesis of civil strife are the intensity and extent of deprivation-induced discontent in a group, and people's attitudes about the justifiability and utility of collective protest and of collective violence in response to discontent.[6] To evaluate the relative importance of these psychological variables as causes of civil strife, we devised indirect measures of deprivation and justificatory attitudes about strife for a large number of national populations, and related them statistically to measures of the magnitude of civil strife. Some of the procedures and results are summarized here.

RELATIVE DEPRIVATION AS A CAUSE OF CIVIL STRIFE

The first step toward assessing deprivation-induced discontent among nations was to identify general patterns of social conditions that cause it. Four patterns of conditions likely to cause discontent are shown in Figures 1 through 4. In the first (Fig. 1), group deprivation results when expectations increase without an accompanying increase in the potential for their satisfaction. The pattern has been called the "revolution of rising expectations." To test its importance, we assumed that expectations should be increasing most rapidly in countries in which education has been expanding most rapidly, and that expectations should be highest in countries with the highest educational levels. To take account of differences in capabilities, we hypothesized that discontent would be greatest in countries in which educational levels were expanding more rapidly than the economy.

---

[6] The theoretical argument is made systematically and empirically documented in Ted Robert Gurr, *Why Men Rebel* (Princeton: Princeton University Press, in press), chs. 2, 3, 6, and 7. The relevance of frustration-aggression theory to civil strife is proposed in Gurr, "Psychological Factors in Civil Strife," *World Politics,* vol. XX (Jan. 1968), pp. 245–278.

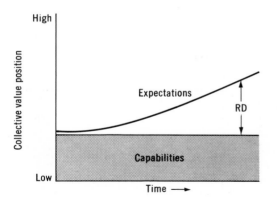

Figure 1.   Aspirational deprivation*

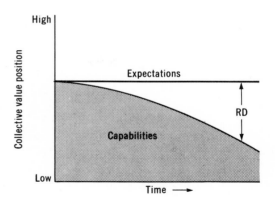

Figure 2.   Decremental deprivation

Measures of educational levels, and of educational levels and changes relative to economic levels and changes, were constructed for 119 nations and correlated with measures of magnitude of civil strife for 1961–63. As predicted, we found that the countries with the most rapidly expanding educational systems experienced the greatest strife, but the correlation for all nations was relatively weak, +0.16. When education was related to economic conditions, however, the results contradicted the assumptions and hypotheses. For example, we found that strife was high in countries with high economic growth but stable or declining education, and lower in countries with relatively little growth but expanding education. We also found that, in the developing nations, the greater the relative increase in higher and technical education compared to the level of development, the less likely was turmoil and the lower the magnitude of strife. These and other findings all point to one general conclusion: In both developed and developing

societies, but not in the least developed, *the expansion of educational opportunities is less likely to raise expectations to an unsatisfiably high level than it is to provide ambitious men with an increased sense of capacity to attain their expectations.*[7] There almost certainly are circumstances in which exposure to new and better ways of life increases men's expectations beyond the possibility of attainment and to the point of violent reaction; expanding education appears to meliorate rather than reinforce them.

The pattern of deprivation-inducing conditions in Figure 2 is one of declining capabilities in the presence of stable expectations. Such "decremental deprivation" is experienced, for example, by people deprived of long-held political liberties; by groups with stable incomes who are hurt by increased taxes or inflation; and by middle-class groups threatened with displacement by the upward mobility of groups below them on the socioeconomic ladder. The pattern tends to lead to defensive protest and violence, sometimes of a revolutionary sort. The American Revolution was preceded by British attempts to increase political and economic control over the colonies; the Civil War by Northern attempts to restrict slavery; the first Ku Klux

---

* "Relative deprivation (RD)" is men's perception of discrepancy between their value expectations and their value capabilities.

"Collective value position" is the average level or amount of goods and conditions of life that members of a collectivity have or expect to attain.

"Value expectations" are the average value positions justifiably sought by members of a collectivity.

"Value capabilities" are the average value positions members of a collectivity perceive themselves capable of attaining or maintaining.

---

[7] The analyses are reported in Gurr with Ruttenberg, *The Conditions of Civil Violence*, pp. 71–76. But also see the paper by the Feierabends and Nesvold, elsewhere in Gurr and Graham, *op. cit.*, which reports contradictory findings.

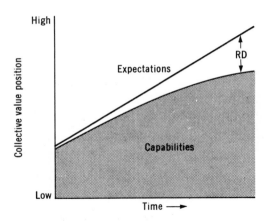

Figure 3. Progressive deprivation

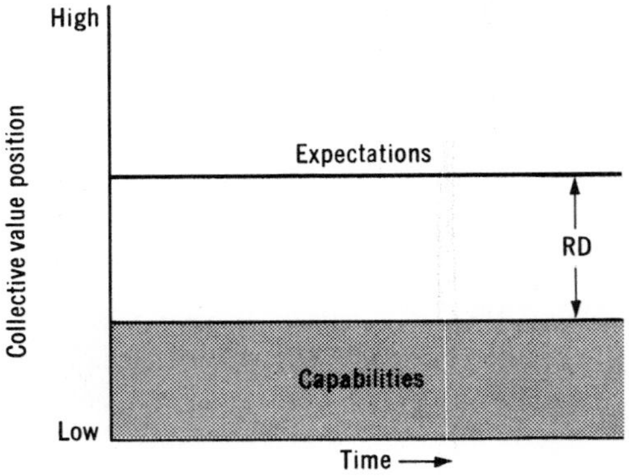

Figure 4. Persisting deprivation

Klan by Northern subjugation and Negro mobility after the Civil War; current vigilante activity in Northern cities by declining law and order and expansion of Negro neighborhoods.

The pattern that seems most often associated with revolutionary movements is shown in Figure 3: a period of substantial increase in capabilities or satisfactions followed by a substantial relative decline. Prolonged experience of increasing well-being generates intense expectations about continued increases; if changing circumstances make those expectations seem unsatisfiable, the likely consequence is intense discontent.[8]

For the purpose of estimating the extent and importance for strife of these two kinds of deprivation, we developed many measures of short-term deterioration in political and economic conditions among nations in the 1950's and early 1960's. The assumption was that any short-term decline in economic conditions, and any governmental policies that restricted political activity or reduced people's socioeconomic status, increased deprivation. Both the relative degree of decline and the proportion of a national population likely to

be affected were estimated. (No attempt was made to distinguish between the two patterns for the purpose of cross-national comparison.) We hypothesized that the greater the degree and scope of all such relative declines in a nation, the greater its magnitude of strife.

The pattern in Figure 4 represents persisting deprivation. In the very long run, men's expectations about the goods and conditions of life to which they are entitled are likely to adjust to what they are capable of attaining. In the medium run, however, some groups may persistently demand and expect such conditions as greater economic opportunity, political autonomy, or freedom of religious expression that their societies will not or cannot provide. Six kinds of persisting deprivation were measured, again taking into account both their relative severity and the proportion of people in each nation who were affected by them: economic and political discrimination, political separatism, dependence on foreign economies, lack of educational opportunity, and religious divisions. A combined measure was devised to facilitate simple comparisons with magnitudes of civil strife.[9]

[8] This pattern was first proposed by James C. Davies, "Toward a Theory of Revolution," *American Sociological Review*, vol. XXVII (1962), pp. 5–19. He provides evidence that the pattern preceded the Russian Revolution, Dorr's rebellion in Rhode Island in 1842, and the Egyptian revolution of 1952.

[9] Evidence for the deprivation measures were obtained from a variety of news, historical, and statistical sources. Procedures and sources are described in Gurr, "A Causal Model of Civil Strife: A Comparative Analysis Using New Indices," *American Political Science Review*, vol. LXII (Dec. 1968).

Some results of the correlation analysis are summarized in Table 1. With few exceptions, both short-term and persisting deprivation are significant causes of the various forms of civil strife among groups of nations. Among highly developed nations, for example, differences in short-term deprivation explain $(0.57)^2$ or 32.5 percent of differences in total magnitude of strife; and differences in persisting deprivation account for $(0.32)^2$ or 10 percent of differences in strife. Two qualifications reinforce the significance of these findings. One is that the relationships are relatively strong, despite the fact that deprivation was measured only partially and indirectly, often on the basis of suspect data. The fact that the correlations between deprivation and strife in the least-developed countries are somewhat weaker than in the developed countries, for example, may reflect the unreliability of economic and other data for these countries. A second qualification is that, generally, deprivation is an apparent cause of all major forms of strife, and of most forms in most groups of countries. This general similarity of results strongly supports the underlying theoretical argument.

Table 1. Correlations between deprivation and magnitudes of civil strife 1961–65, by type of nation

Type of nation*	Correlations[a] between short-term deprivation and magnitudes of—			Correlations[a] between persisting deprivation and magnitudes of—		
	Tur-moil	Conspir-acy	Total strife[b]	Tur-moil	Conspir-acy	Total strife[b]
All nations (114)[c]	32	45	47	27	30	35
Nations grouped according to level of economic development:						
High (37)[c]	50	38	57	30	28	34
Medium (39)	29	55	58	28	46	29
Low (38)	*04	41	23	*19	*07	31
Nations grouped according to type of political system:						
Polyarchic (38)[c]	28	49	46	48	29	46
Centrist (27)[d]	47	63	55	37	*31	52
Elitist (32)	*15	49	58	33	*14	37
Personalist (16)	58	*05	*21	*10	52	*35
Nations grouped according to geocultural region:						
Anglo-Nordic (10)[c]	73	82	80	65	83	80
Western Europe (11)	*16	*08	*30	59	*−31	*41
Eastern Europe (8)	78	*−05	79	*37	*−47	*−05
Latin (24)	43	*28	51	59	43	42
Islamic (21)	37	37	*22	*−06	*26	47
Asian (17)	*25	53	56	*30	*15	*28
African (23)	*15	50	55	*15	*11	*22

* See Appendix at end of article for explanation of procedures used in selecting and grouping countries for cross-national comparison.

[a] The figures shown are product-moment correlation coefficients multiplied by 100. A perfect positive relationship is 100; a perfect negative relationship, −100. The differences among nations in magnitudes of strife that are statistically "explained" by variations in deprivation can be determined by squaring each correlation coefficient. For example, among all nations, variations in extent of short-term deprivation explain $(0.47)^2$ or 22 percent of differences in total magnitude of strife. Asterisked (*) coefficients are statistically significant at less than the 0.10 level.

[b] Total magnitude of civil strife, including internal war. The groups of nations vary so greatly in frequencies of internal war—some groups having none, 1, or 2, others 20 or more—that comparisons of correlations with magnitudes of internal war among groups of nations are misleading. Among all nations the correlations of short-term and persisting deprivation with magnitude of internal war are, respectively, 0.34 and 0.24.

[c] Including data on the United States for 1961–65.   [d] Excluding the colony of Papua-New Guinea, which was included in this group in preceding tables.

Some differences among groups of nations also should be noted. Short-term deprivation is more important as a cause of turmoil than of conspiracy in the most developed nations, whereas it is more important as a cause of conspiracy in the less-developed nations. This difference also is apparent among the geocultural regions: short-term deprivation leads to conspiracy in the least-developed, Asian and African nations; and to turmoil in the more-developed, European and Latin nations. We pointed out above that conspiracy is usually organized by the upper and middle classes. The inference is that in less-developed countries, deprivation of the kinds indexed in this study is more strongly felt by these groups than by the working classes. The deprivations that give rise to turmoil in the less-developed countries may be those caused by the social dislocations of socioeconomic development itself, which are not well represented in these measures.

An unusual pattern is apparent when the "Anglo-Nordic" and the other two groups of European nations are compared. The correlations between deprivation and strife in the Nordic and English-speaking countries are far higher than in any other group of nations. Differences in deprivation account for almost all their differences in strife. The findings reflect partly the close connection between the degree and extent of discriminatory deprivation in countries like South Africa, Rhodesia, and the United States and high levels of ethnic strife in them, and the relative lack of discrimination and negligible strife in the Nordic countries, Australia, and New Zealand. To the same point, we found in an earlier study of the causes of civil violence in 1961–63 that the proportional size of groups subject to discrimination, however intense, correlated 0.30 with magnitude of strife in 119 nations.

In the other Western European nations, persisting deprivation is more closely related to turmoil than short-term deprivation. This is consistent with the findings, discussed above, that persisting deprivation is a source of chronic disorder throughout the Western community, not only in the United States.

On the other hand, the lack of relationship between short-term deprivation and magnitudes of strife has two possible explanations. One is that the immediate causes of strife in Europe are of a specific and idiosyncratic kind not represented in general measures of deprivation. Another is that much European strife is a manifestation of tactical political motives more than of intense discontent. One observation supports the second interpretation: the fact that the political demonstration, riot, and strike are established tactics of both leftwing and rightwing groups in the three European countries with highest magnitudes of strife—Italy, France, and Greece. Both explanations probably apply, and are relevant to other countries as well: the resolution of a nation's most critical problems may lead to heightened awareness of other problems, and in some circumstances to the institutionalization of turmoil as a response to them.

In the Eastern European nations, deprivation is rather closely related to turmoil, the only consequential form of strife that occurred in the Communist countries in the 1961–65 period. This may seem surprising, given the common assumption that collective expressions of opinion are so carefully controlled by the Communist regimes that demonstrative protest occurs only at times and places when control is deliberately or accidentally loosened. Other analyses show, however, that turmoil is substantially lower in these nations than in other European nations. Totalitarian control seems to minimize absolute levels of strife, but in spite of it intense discontents are likely to be given some public expression even in the short run.

LEGITIMACY AND TRADITION OF
STRIFE AS CAUSES OF CIVIL STRIFE

It is all but impossible, without opinion survey evidence, to ascertain men's attitudes about the justifiability and utility of collective protest and violence. Historical and survey evidence suggests that Americans as a whole are more favorably disposed to violence as a solution to problems than many other national groups.[10] For purposes of cross-national comparison, we used two indirect measures to represent these attitudes. A measure of the legitimacy of the political system was devised, on the theoretical assumption that people are less likely to attack their political leaders, or to engage in violence against others, if they have a high positive regard for the political system. Highest legitimacy scores were given to nations whose political system was developed solely by indigenous leaders, rather than borrowed or imposed from abroad, and which had endured for the longest time without substantial structural change.

The second measure is of levels of collective violence in the period from 1946 to 1959. The assumption is that the greater strife has been in a country's past, the more likely some of its citizens are to regard it as justifiable, and the more likely some of them would have found it partially successful in the past, and hence regard it as potentially useful in the future. A history of civil strife should thus facilitate future strife, a relationship that is historically documented in detail for the United States in other contributions to Gurr and Graham, *op. cit.*

The correlations between the measures of legitimacy and past levels of strife are shown in Table 2. Among nations generally, and among most groups of nations, the legitimacy of the political system does inhibit magnitudes of violence, and historical levels of strife do facilitate future strife. But these conditions are not as important, for all nations, as are differences in levels of deprivation, as a comparison with Table 1 indicates. Comparison of groups of nations suggests why: there are striking differences among them in the efficacy of legitimacy in reducing strife, and in the facilitating effects of past strife on future events.

---

[10] Some suggestive survey evidence to this point is summarized in Gurr, *Why Men Rebel*, ch. 6. The historical evidence is amply provided by other papers in Gurr and Graham, *op. cit.*

Legitimacy most strongly inhibits civil strife in the developing nations; in the democratic and the personalist nations; in the non-Communist Western nations; and in Latin, Islamic, and Asian nations. It has relatively weak effects in the most- and least-developed nations; the nations governed by modernizing elites; and in African and Communist nations. In centrist (authoritarian) regimes it tends to inhibit conspiracy but has no effect on turmoil. Historical levels of strife very strongly facilitate subsequent strife in the most-developed, democratic, and Western European nations. Their effects are inconsequential or negative in the developing, personalist, and Eastern European nations.

Many special interpretations could be made of these results. Only some general ones are suggested here. Legitimacy presumably has little inhibiting effect on strife in the new, least-developed nations and in the authoritarian nations because their regimes generally have low legitimacy. Only high degrees of loyalty to leaders and institutions are likely to inhibit strife under conditions of intense deprivation. We know that the dislocations associated with nation-building and socioeconomic development generate intense conflict within nations. The regimes of developing nations, including a number of Latin and Islamic nations, have high apparent legitimacy; Chile, Costa Rica, Morocco, and Iran are examples. The efficacy of legitimacy in minimizing strife in these kinds of countries is manifest in the relatively high correlations for these groups of countries in Table 2.

The close connection between past and future strife in the developed, democratic, and Western nations supports the conclusion of the preceding section that a number of these nations are, in effect, inherently tumultuous. This is partly the result of persisting deprivations, and also of the existence of historical traditions that sanction protest and violence as justifiable responses to a variety of grievances and conflicts. The lack of connection between past and future strife in the developing nations almost certainly reflects the current tensions of socioeconomic change, tensions that in most of them became severe

Table 2. Legitimacy of the political system and historical sanctions for strife as determinants of magnitudes of civil strife, 1961–65, by type of nation

Type of nation*	Correlations[a] between legitimacy and magnitudes of—			Correlations[a] between historical levels of strife and magnitudes of—		
	Tur-moil	Conspir-acy	Total strife[b]	Tur-moil	Conspir-acy	Total strife[b]
All nations (114)[c]	−30	−29	−38	29	23	29
Nations grouped according to level of economic development:						
High (37)[c]	*−10	*−23	*−20	57	48	65
Medium (39)	−44	−34	−52	*−23	*18	*01
Low (38)	*−24	*−11	*−23	38	*14	37
Nations grouped according to type of political system:						
Polyarchic (38)[c]	−46	*−18	−45	51	61	64
Centrist (27)[d]	*10	−32	*−08	*11	*−04	*−07
Elitist (32)	−36	*−05	*−26	29	*13	53
Personalist (16)	−66	−43	−58	*16	*09	*−28
Nations grouped according to geocultural regions:						
Anglo-Nordic (10)[c]	*−45	−72	−61	59	*34	57
Western Europe (11)	−50	*−25	−57	77	57	87
Eastern Europe (8)	*−27	61	*−29	*49	*−49	*07
Latin (24)	−40	*−16	−39	*27	55	37
Islamic (21)	−46	49	−37	46	*09	*29
Asian (17)	*−33	*−19	−63	*−07	56	*39
African (23)	*−25	*−08	*−24	47	36	43

* See footnote in table 1.
[a] See footnote (a), table 1. Asterisked (*) coefficients are statistically significant at less than the 0.10 level.
[b] See footnote (b), table 1. In all nations the correlations of legitimacy and historical levels of strife with magnitudes of internal war are, respectively, −0.26 and +0.15.
[c] Including data on the United States for 1961–65.
[d] See footnote (d), table 1.

only in recent years, when the pace of change increased.

SOCIAL CONTROL AND FACILITATION AS DETERMINANTS OF MAGNITUDES OF CIVIL STRIFE

The extent and intensity of relative deprivation, and justificatory attitudes about protest and violence, are psychological determinants of the potential for civil strife. Whether or not men act on their dispositions to collective action depends partly on some structural characteristics of their societies. Three general kinds of societal characteristics were examined in the cross-national study:

the nature of coercive control; the strength of political and economic institutions; and the availability of physical, organizational, and material support for dissidents.

Coercive control Conventional wisdom and studies of riots and revolutions all emphasize the importance of actual or threatened coercion in minimizing the occurrence and extent of strife. If men are sufficiently afraid of the consequences, the argument goes, they will not riot. Comparative studies of civil strife, and psychological theory, both suggest that the relationship is not so simple: some kinds of coercion are more likely to increase than to deter strife. Several cross-national studies show that strife tends to be greatest in countries that have medium-sized military and security forces, lowest in those with either

Table 3. Coercive control, institutionalization, and facilitation as determinants of the total magnitude of civil strife, 1961–65, by type of nation

| Type of nation* | Correlations* between total magnitude of civil strife and— | | | |
| | Coercive control | | Strength of institutions | Facilitation |
	Relative size of forces	Size weighted by loyalty		
All nations (114)[b]	*—13	—51	—34	66
Nations grouped according to level of economic development:				
High (37)[b]	*—12	—53	—29	59
Medium (39)	*—15	—49	*—02	58
Low (38)	*14	—31	—32	67
Nations grouped according to type of political system:				
Polyarchic (38)[b]	n.d.	—55	—36	65
Centrist (27)[c]	—37	—44	*—26	57
Elitist (32)	*25	—44	—35	76
Personalist (16)	*27	*—29	52	*27
Nations grouped according to geocultural region:				
Anglo-Nordic (10)[b]	*—39	—68	—75	*—44
Western Europe (11)	74	*—18	*—14	58
Eastern Europe (8)	*03	*17	*23	*—12
Latin (24)	*—08	—56	*—03	*33
Islamic (21)	*05	—61	*—29	71
Asian (17)	*—08	—74	*15	80
African (23)	*15	*—19	—45	82

* See footnote in table 1.
n.d. = no data (computations not made).
* See footnote (a), table 1. Asterisked (*) coefficients are statistically significant at less than the 0.10 level.
[b] Including data on the United States for 1961–65.
[c] See footnote (d), table 1.

small or very large forces.[11] Another study suggests that political instability is greatest in countries that exercise intermediate degrees of political control, lowest in those that are either highly democratic or totalitarian.[12] The proposed explanation for these findings is that medium levels of coercive threat and control are more likely to increase men's anger and will to resist than to restrain them from

strife. The consistency with which coercion is used is probably even more important than the degree of control. Coercion is "consistent" to the extent that all the "guilty" are subject to sanctions in proportion to the seriousness of their action, and the "innocent" not sanctioned. The literature of civil strife provides many examples of cases in which random or terroristic coercion by troops or police intensified violence, transforming peaceful demonstrations into riots, riots and conspiracies into revolutionary movements.[13]

Two measures of coercive control were

[11] See Douglas Bwy, "Political Instability in Latin America: The Cross-Cultural Test of a Causal Model," *Latin American Research Review*, vol. III (Spring 1968), pp. 17–66 and Gurr with Ruttenberg, *The Conditions of Civil Violence*, pp. 81–85.
[12] Jennifer G. Walton, "Correlates of Coerciveness and Permissiveness of National Political Systems: A Cross-National Study," M.A. thesis, San Diego State College, June 1965.

[13] Some of this evidence is reviewed in Gurr, *Why Men Rebel*, ch. 8. Also see the comparative study of governmental uses of coercion in Cuba and Venezuela by Gude, in Gurr and Graham, *op. cit.*

used in the cross-national study. One indexed the size of military and internal security forces relative to the adult population. The second weighted the relative size of such forces according to their loyalty to the regime, on the assumption that the greater their historical and contemporary loyalty, the more likely they would be to make consistent use of force and the less likely they would be to use illegal force against the regime.[14] Some correlational results are shown in the first two columns of Table 3. As expected, the size of forces is weakly and inconsistently related to magnitudes of strife. The strongest relationship is found in the Western European nations, in which the larger are coercive forces, the greater is strife. Positive relationships of this sort also are apparent in the elitist and personalist nations, and in the least-developed nations. But when the loyalty of the military establishment, and the implied consistency of coercion, are taken into account, a definite inhibitory effect on strife is apparent in most nations. When coercive forces are both large and loyal, the magnitude of strife tends to be low, with the apparent exceptions of Africa and Eastern and Western Europe.

Evidence regarding the inconclusive effects of reliance on large military and police establishments alone to maintain domestic order is shown in Figures 5 through 8. Figure 5 relates coercive force size to total magnitude of civil strife for all nations. It is evident that total strife is likely to be highest in countries with low-to-medium-sized coercive forces, but not those with very small forces. Moreover, at the very highest levels of coercive force size there is a slight tendency

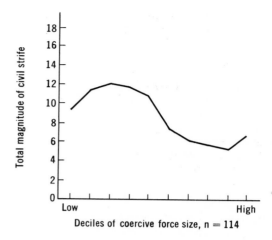

Figure 5. Coercive force, size, and magnitudes of civil strife, 1961–65

for magnitudes of strife to increase. Such an S-shaped curve is considerably more pronounced in the comparison of coercive force size with magnitudes of turmoil; turmoil peaks at both moderate and very high force levels.

Two other factors should be considered in interpreting these results. It is likely that countries with protracted political violence expand their coercive forces to counteract it. It also is plausible that armies in countries facing foreign threats cause less dissatisfaction —by their presence or actions—than armies

[14] Procedures used to construct these measures are described in Gurr, "A Causal Model of Civil Strife." The basic data for size of forces are military personnel per 10,000 adults and internal security forces per 10,000 adults, which were rescaled, weighted equally, and combined; the maximum possible score for a country is 30, the minimum 3. The U.S. score is 22. The "loyalty" scores used to weight these estimates take into account the length of time since the last forceful intervention of the military or police against the regime, and the frequency with which they resorted to illicit force in the 1961–65 period.

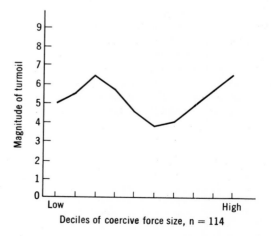

Figure 6. Coercive force, size, and magnitudes of turmoil, 1961–65

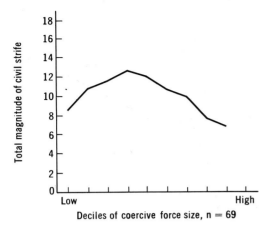

Figure 7. Coercive force, size, and magnitudes of civil strife, 1961–65, 69 low-conflict polities

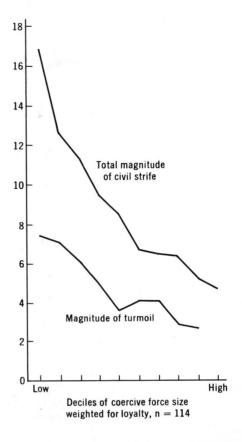

Figure 8. Coercive force, size, weighted for loyalty and magnitudes of civil strife, 1961–65

in states not significantly involved in international conflict. Countries with one or both of these characteristics were removed and the relationship plotted for the remaining 69 countries, with the results shown in Figure 7; the curvilinear relationship is again clearly evident.

The graph in Figure 8 shows the relationships between coercive force loyalty and, respectively, total strife and turmoil. The relationships are essentially linear, though in neither instance does the level of strife approach zero when size and loyalty approach their maximum. For turmoil in particular, the results at the outer end of the "loyalty" scale are inconclusive.

Figure 9 plots measures of coercive force size against total magnitude of strife in the 21 states of the Western community, including the United States. In these nations there is a strong positive relationship between size and magnitude of strife: the larger are armies and police, the greater is internal conflict. The only countries that deviate markedly from the pattern are Rhodesia, whose political and military circumstances are substantially different from the other countries shown, and Finland. The relationship is even more clear when turmoil alone is plotted against force size, as it is in Figure 10.

The correspondence of force size and levels of strife does not necessarily imply a

simple causal connection between the two. The military establishment is relatively large in most Western countries because of cold-war tensions, not because of the threat of internal disorder. Nonetheless, the investment of large portions of national budgets in armaments; military conscription policies; and involvement in foreign conflict have directly generated widespread popular opposition in the United States and France in the past decade, and may have provided a similar though less dramatic impetus to public protest in other Western nations.

Strength of institutions If social institutions beyond the family and community level are broad in scope, command large resources, and are stable and persisting, the disruptive ef-

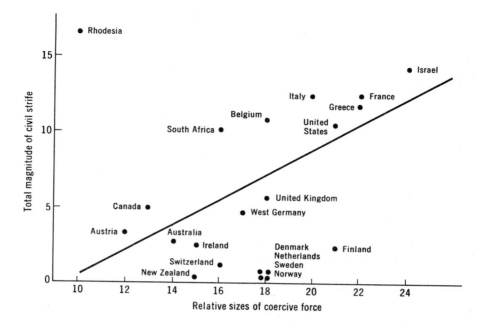

Figure 9. Coercive force, size, and magnitudes of civil strife in the Western community, 1961–65

fects of discontent ought to be minimized. Such institutions are likely to provide additional, peaceful means for the attainment of expectations, and also may provide discontented men with routinized and typically nonviolent means for expressing their grievances. The measure of institutional strength used in this study took into account the proportion of gross national product utilized by the central government; the number and stability of political parties; and the relative size of trades unions.

The results summarized in Table 3 suggest that institutional strength tends to minimize strife in some groups of countries but not in others. Strong institutions have this effect in the most-developed, democratic nations, especially the Anglo-Nordic countries. They also are associated with low levels of strife in the least-developed countries, especially the elitist and African states. They have little effect on strife in the developing or Latin American nations, however, and in the nations with personalistic political systems, strong institutions apparently facilitate strife. The probable cause of these discrepancies is that

the efficacy of strong nongovernmental institutions in minimizing strife depends on their political orientations. If the leaders of political parties and trade unions are strongly opposed to political leaders and their policies, they are likely to direct their organizations into demonstrative and sometimes violent oppositional activity. In Latin America and in some continental European nations, for example, such activity by political parties of the left and right and by unions is quite common. The establishment or reinforcement of strong and stable organizations thus does not necessarily minimize the potential for civil strife; the determining factors are likely to be the discontents and loyalties of the members of those organizations.

Facilitation A great many social and environmental conditions may facilitate the outbreak and persistence of strife. It is easier to organize collective action in organizations of likeminded individuals. Ideologies may provide the discontented with the belief that violent responses to depriving circumstances are justified. Jungle or mountain fastnesses

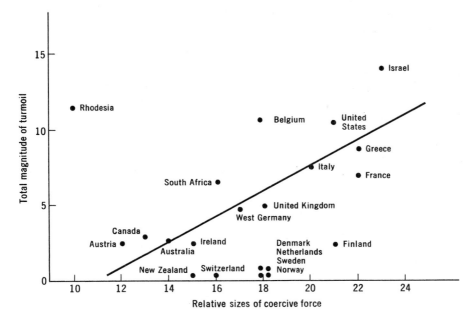

Figure 10. Coercive force, size, and magnitudes of turmoil in the Western community, 1961–65

can provide secure base areas for rebels. Three kinds of facilitation were measured in this study: the size and status of Communist parties (except in countries in which they were in power); the extent of isolated terrain; and the degree of foreign refuge, training, and supplies provided to rebels during the 1961–65 period.[15]

The last of these characteristics was expected to be an especially strong determinant of the magnitude of internal wars. This partly accounts for the high correlations shown in Table 3 between facilitation and magnitudes of strife; the correlations are highest in the elitist, Islamic, Asian, and African nations, those in which internal wars have been most common. The high correlations between facilitation and strife in the polyarchic (democratic) and Western Eu-

ropean nations reflects primarily the oppositional activities of Communist parties in them, only secondarily foreign support for rebels. Generally, extremist political activity by both left and right in the Western nations in the 1960's has led to turmoil of limited objectives, not to the guerrilla or revolutionary activities that attract and require material foreign support. One noteworthy finding was that facilitation, as measured in this study, has a statistically insignificant association with magnitudes of strife in Latin American countries. Despite dramatic cases of Communist instigation of revolutionary movements in Latin America, Communist activity and support apparently had little systematic effect on levels of Latin American strife in the early and mid-1960's.

LEVELS OF EXPLANATION
OF CIVIL STRIFE

Most of the causal variables used in this study have the predicted effects on levels of

---

[15] The facilitation measures are described in Gurr, "A Causal Model of Civil Strife." A better measure of organizational support for civil strife would take account of the size and status of all extremist political organizations; comparative data were available only for Communist parties.

civil strife. To determine their combined explanatory power, the seven major variables discussed above were used in multiple correlation analyses, with the summary results shown in Table 4. On the average, nearly three-quarters of the differences among nations in levels of civil strife are explained, in a statistical sense, by the conditions measured. The Latin nations are the only ones for which the level of explanation seems low. It is low, however, only by comparison with the other results. All the measures used in the study are relatively imprecise and indirect. Differences within nations, and their unique historical and contemporary characteristics, all play significant and largely unspecified parts in the genesis of civil strife. Given these limitations on this kind of study, the levels of explanation shown in Table 4 are surprisingly high. These "explanations" are only statistical. Nonetheless they are persuasive evidence for the essential accuracy of most of the underlying theoretical arguments that dictated the measures to be used, and also

Table 4. Explained variation (R^2) in magnitudes of civil strife, 1961–65, using all causal variables, by type of nation[a]

Type of nation*	Percentages of variation explained in magnitudes of—			
	Turmoil	Conspiracy	Internal war	Total strife
All nations (114)[b]	28	39	47	64
Nations grouped according to level of economic development:				
High (37)[b]	49	41	45	66
Medium (39)	30	58	62	71
Low (38)	45	22	57	82
Nations grouped according to type of political system:				
Polyarchic (38)[b]	45	63	41	64
Centrist (27)[c]	60	67	50	81
Elitist (32)	43	32	71	74
Personalist (16)	70	63	65	71
Nations grouped according to geocultural region:[d]				
Western community (21)[b;d]	66	57	74	74
Latin (24)	62	45	22	49
Islamic (21)	60	73	65	67
Asian (17)	36	61	79	87
African (23)	64	42	76	81
Average variation explained among groups[e]	53	52	59	72

* See footnote in table 1.
[a] Results of multiple correlation analysis using the 7 major explanatory variables discussed previously: short-term and persisting deprivation, legitimacy, historical levels of strife, coercive force size weighted by loyalty, institutionalization, and facilitation. The figures shown as percentages are multiple correlation coefficients squared (R^2), which represent the variation in magnitudes of strife in each group of nations that is statistically explained by the measures taken together. The R^2 statistic is always less than the sum of the separate, squared correlation coefficients because the causal variables themselves are intercorrelated. The correlation matrix for all polities is reported in Gurr, "A Causal Model of Civil Strife."
[b] Including data on the United States for 1961–65.
[c] See footnote (d), table 1.
[d] Multiple correlation coefficients are distorted in the direction of perfect "explanation" when the number of variables used approaches the number of cases (countries). To minimize this effect the Eastern European group (8 nations) is excluded from this table and the Anglo-Nordic and Western Europe groups are combined.
[e] The average of the percentages for the 12 groups of nations.

suggest that the variables used represent many if not all the consequential, general causes of civil strife.

Some forms of strife in some groups of nations are less well explained than others. Turmoil, for example, is best accounted for when nations are grouped on the basis of geocultural similarity, poorly explained when they are grouped by level of economic development. A general interpretation is that the causes of turmoil are more closely linked with cultural differences than with stages of economic development or with type of political system. In other words, the cultural heritage of a nation may tell us more about the conditions to which discontented men are sensitive than information about its economic or political system. Conspiracy is poorly explained in the least-developed nations, and also in the elitist and African nations, most of which are among the least developed. Conspiracy in many of these nations may reflect the largely dispassionate tactics of men seeking political power in situations in which there is little else worth seeking. Discontented they may be, for lack of power, but their discontents are not easily determined by the procedures used in this study, and the likelihood of their expression is probably influenced strongly by many unique rather than a few common circumstances. The minimal explanation provided for internal wars in Latin America, and the relatively weak accounting for all Latin strife, suggests that Latin American strife has causes distinctively different from those of other groups of nations. The common observation that strife in Latin America is "institutionalized" is one approach to the explanation of the difference.

One other pattern in the results worth noting is that the magnitudes of the specific forms of strife are less well explained than total magnitudes of strife in almost all groups of nations. There are partial, technical explanations for this. The most likely substantive explanation is that, despite its widely different manifestations and consequences, all civil strife has fundamentally similar causes, and that distinctions among its general or specific forms are somewhat arbitrary. Our general interpretation, which is largely supported by the results of this study, is that strife is predicated on intense discontents. The precise nature of those discontents, the forms in which they are expressed, their objects, and their immediate consequences are mediated by specific historical and social circumstances. But there seems to be an inescapable social dynamic to collective discontent. Societies in which there are intense and widespread discontents have a potential for disruptive internal conflict that sooner or later will find expression, whatever is done to control or divert it, short only of alleviating its causes.

* * *

Appendix: Procedures Used in Selecting and Grouping Countries for Cross-National Comparison

The universe of analysis includes all distinct national and colonial political entities that had a population of 1 million or more in 1962, excluding four countries for which data were judged unreliable (Albania, Mongolia, North Korea, and North Vietnam) and one (Laos) on grounds that it was a state in name only during the period in question. The remaining 114 polities include more than 98 percent of the world's population.

The 114 countries were grouped in several different ways to permit comparison of the effects of different levels of economic development, types of political system, and geocultural region on characteristics of strife. The bases of the groupings are as follows:

ECONOMIC DEVELOPMENT

Mary Megee[1] identified several factors underlying various measures of economic development for 153 nations and territories. The two major factors found were "industrial development" and "social overhead (infrastructure) and government expenditures." Countries were plotted according to their scores on these two dimensions into four quadrants: those low on both factors (very underdeveloped); those low on one of the factors (developing); and those high on both. A similar set of "regions" (groupings) also identified by Megee included one very underdeveloped set of nations, three sets of developing nations, a number of developed nations, and several dozen "isolate cases." We used the latter set of grouping, with certain modifications: Megee's "very underdeveloped" constitutes our "low economic development" group; her three groups of developing nations were combined into our "medium" group; and the developed nations constitute our "high" group. Megee's "isolate" polities were assigned to one of these three groupings on the basis of their quadrant locations. Six nations that fall just inside the "developed" quadrant we reclassified in the "medium" group: Cuba, Jamaica, Portugal, Greece, Turkey, and Indonesia. China-Taiwan was reclassified to the "high" group because of its very high industrialization score. Some apparent errors in her classifications also were corrected on the basis of her own and other data. Finally, a few polities not included by Megee were assigned to our categories on judgmental grounds. . . .

TYPE OF POLITICAL SYSTEM

The background conditions for civil strife were expected to vary markedly from one type of political system to another, suggesting that polities be grouped on the basis of their political characteristics. The grouping used is based on the results of a Q-factor analysis of 68 specifically political variables for 115 nations.[2] The component variables are measures of such conditions as the degree or nature of ideological orientation, interest articulation, power distribution, role of the military, colonial tutelage (if any), and many others.

The factor analysis distinguished five classes of nations, each characterized by rather distinct patterns of political behavior and rule. We have used the authors' labels for them: *polyarchic*, nations that approximate Western democratic political structures and processes; *centrist*, Communist and other non-Latin American authoritarian regimes; *elitist*, recently independent, predominantly African states with relatively small, modernizing elites: *personalist*, predominantly Latin regimes characterized by unstable personalistic political leadership; and *traditional*, four nations such as Yemen. We reclassified polities from the traditional class to the larger group they most closely resembled. We also judgmentally assigned polities included in our 114 but excluded by Banks and Gregg to the remaining four groups. . . .

GEOCULTURAL REGIONS

Assignment of nations to geocultural region was made on judgmental grounds, with some guidance from a factor analytic study by Bruce M. Russett, "International Regions and International Integration: Homogeneous Regions," Yale University, Department of Political Science, 1965 (mimeo). The groups were distinguished as follows:

Latin (24): All Latin American and Caribbean nations, plus Puerto Rico, Spain and Portugal.

---

[1] "Problems of Regionalizing and Measurement," *Peace Research Society: Papers*, vol. IV (1965), pp. 7–35.

[2] Arthur S. Banks and Phillip M. Gregg, "Grouping Political Systems: Q-Factor Analysis of A Cross-Polity Survey," *American Behavioral Scientist*, vol. IX (Nov. 1965), pp. 3–6.

Islamic (21): Countries whose populations are 50 percent or more Muslim, including the North African and Middle Eastern nations, Lebanon, and Saharan and sub-Saharan African countries of Guinea, Mali, Niger, Senegal, Somalia, and Sudan.

African (23): Non-Islamic African states and colonies. In the analyses of the first two sections of this paper, South Africa and Rhodesia were added to this group; in the correlation analyses in the third section, they are included in the Anglo-Nordic group, below.

Asian (17): Non-Islamic nations and colonies of mainland Asia and its periphery, including Papua-New Guinea but excluding Australia and New Zealand.

European (27): The countries of Eastern and Western Europe (except Spain and Portugal), plus the United States, the English-settled states of the British Commonwealth, and Israel. For the correlational analyses, these countries were divided into three more homogenous groups:

Anglo-Nordic (10): The three Nordic nations, Great Britain, the United States, and the English-settled states of the British Commonwealth, to which were added South Africa and Rhodesia.

Western Europe (11): Other non-Communist European states, plus Israel.

Eastern Europe (8): The European Communist nations.

Chapter 12

THE EXPRESSION AND INTERPRETATION OF DISCONTENT

When will feelings of discontent give rise to actions or movements that will be seen as revolutionary? Expressions of discontent all involve violating, ignoring, or challenging the rule structures of a social system, but not all such violations or challenges are seen as revolutionary. Some are simply classed as criminal, negativistic, or aberrant. The question of how discontent is interpreted, both by participants and by observers, is clearly an important question for the understanding of revolution.

In the first reading of this section, Hobsbawm analyzes a classic form of criminal activity, social banditry, as a primitive form of rebellion against injustice, ultimately unsuccessful for lack of revolutionary consciousness. In the next paper, Paige considers another boundary case in which the expression of discontent may be interpreted in either political or non-political terms, the 1967 Newark riot, and argues, like Hobsbawm, that elements of social protest in this activity deserve serious attention. Riot participants were more likely to be distrustful of the government and well informed (an orientation Paige calls "dissident") rather than distrustful and poorly informed (an orientation Paige calls "alienated"). Finally, Turner presents a systematic overview of the question of when deviant actions will be treated as quasi-legitimate efforts to bargain for change within the system, or what Turner calls "protest," rather than as either criminal efforts to disregard the system's rules or revolutionary efforts to overthrow the system.

THE SOCIAL BANDIT

E. J. Hobsbawm

Bandits and highwaymen preoccupy the police, but they ought also to preoccupy the social historian. For in one sense banditry is a rather primitive form of organized social protest, perhaps the most primitive we know. At any rate in many societies it is regarded as such by the poor, who consequently protect the bandit, regard him as their champion, idealize him, and turn him into a myth: *Robin Hood* in England, *Janošik* in Poland and Slovakia, *Diego Corrientes* in Andalusia, who are probably all real figures thus transmuted. In return, the bandit himself tries to live up to his role even when he is not himself a conscious social rebel. Naturally Robin Hood, the archetype of the social rebel 'who took from the rich to give to the poor and never killed but in self-defence or just revenge', is not the only man of his kind. The tough man, who is unwilling to bear the traditional burdens of the common man in a class society, poverty and meekness, may escape from them by joining or serving the oppressors as well as by revolting against them. In any peasant society there are 'landlords' bandits' as well as 'peasant bandits' not to mention the State's bandits, though only the peasant bandits receive the tribute of ballads and anecdotes. Retainers, policemen, mercenary soldiers are thus often recruited from the same material as social bandits. Moreover, as the experience of Southern Spain between 1850 and 1875 shows, one sort of bandit can easily turn into another—the 'noble' robber and smuggler into the *bandolero*, protected by the local rural boss or *cacique*. Individual rebelliousness is itself a socially neutral phenomenon, and consequently mirrors the divisions and struggles within society. This problem will be further considered in the chapter on *Mafia*.

However, something like an ideal type of social banditry exists, and this is what I propose to discuss, even though few bandits of recorded history, as distinct from legend, correspond completely to it. Still, some—like Angelo Duca (Angiolillo)—do even that.

To describe the 'ideal' bandit is by no means unrealistic. For the most startling characteristic of social banditry is its remarkable uniformity and standardization. The material used in this chapter comes almost wholly from Europe in the 18th to 20th centuries, and indeed mainly from Southern Italy.[1] But the cases one looks at are so similar, though drawn from periods as widely separated as the mid-18th and the mid-20th centuries and places as independent of one another as Sicily and Carpatho-Ukraine, that one generalizes with very great confidence. This uniformity applies both to the bandit myths—that is, to the part for which the bandit is cast by the people—and to his actual behaviour.

A few examples of such parallelism may illustrate the point. The population hardly ever helps the authorities to catch the 'peasants' bandit,' but on the contrary protects him. This is so in the Sicilian villages of the 1940s as in the Muscovite ones of the 17th century.[2] Thus his standard end—for if he makes too much of a nuisance of himself almost every individual bandit will be defeated,

[1] For this area I have used not only the usual printed sources, but the invaluable information of Professor Ambrogio Donini, of Rome, who has had some contact with ex-bandits, and some newspaper material.

[2] J. L. H. Keep, Bandits and the Law in Muscovy, *Slavonic Review*, xxxv. 84, Dec. 1956, 201–23.

though banditry may remain endemic—is by betrayal. Oleksa Dovbush, the Carpathian bandit of the 18th century, was betrayed by his mistress; Nikola Shuhaj, who is supposed to have flourished *c.* 1918–20, by his friends.[3] Angelo Duca (Angiolillo), *c.* 1760–84, perhaps the purest example of social banditry, of whose career Benedetto Croce has given a masterly analysis,[4] suffered the same fate. So, in 1950, did Salvatore Giuliano of Montelepre, Sicily, the most notorious of recent bandits, whose career has lately been described in a moving book.[5] So, if it comes to that, did Robin Hood himself. But the law, in order to hide its impotence, claims credit for the bandit's capture or death: the policemen shoot bullets into Nikola Shuhaj's dead body to claim the kill, as they did, if Gavin Maxwell is to be believed, into Giuliano's. The practice is so common that there is even a Corsican proverb to describe it: 'Killed after death, like a bandit by the police.'[6] And the peasants in turn add invulnerability to the bandit's many other legendary and heroic qualities. Angiolillo was supposed to possess a magic ring which turned away bullets. Shuhaj was invulnerable because—theories diverged—he had a green twig with which he waved aside bullets, or because a witch had made him drink a brew that made him resist them; that is why he had to be killed with an axe. Oleksa Dovbush, the legendary 18th-century Carpathian bandit-hero, could only be killed with a silver bullet that had been kept one year in a dish of spring wheat, blessed by a priest on the day of the twelve great saints and over which twelve priests had read twelve masses. I have no doubt that similar myths are part of the folklore of many other great bandits.[7] Obviously none of these practices or beliefs are derived from one another. They arise in different places and periods, because the societies and situations in which social banditry arises are very similar.

It may be convenient to sketch the standardized picture of the social bandit's career. A man becomes a bandit because he does something which is not regarded as criminal by his local conventions, but is so regarded by the State or the local rulers. Thus Angiolillo took to the hills after a quarrel over cattle-straying with a field-guard of the Duke of Martina. The best-known of the current bandits in the Aspromonte area of Calabria, Vicenzo Romeo of Bova (which is, incidentally, the last Italian village speaking ancient Greek), became an outlaw after abducting a girl he subsequently married, while Angelo Macri of Delianova killed a policeman who had shot his brother.[8] Both blood-feud (the *faida*) and marriage by abduction are common in this part of Calabria.[9] Indeed, of the 160-odd outlaws reported at large in the province of Reggio Calabria in 1955, most of the forty who took to the hills for 'homicide' are locally regarded as 'honourable' homicides. The state mixes in 'legitimate' private quarrels and a man becomes a 'criminal' in its eyes. The State shows an interest in a peasant because of some minor infraction of the law, and the man takes to the hills because how does he know what a system which does not know or understand peasants, and which peasants do not understand, will do to him? Mariani Dionigi, a Sardinian bandit of the 1890s, went because he was about to be arrested for complicity in a 'just' homicide. Goddi Moni Giovanni, another, went for the same reason. Campesi (nicknamed Piscim-

[3] Ivan Olbracht's novel *The Robber Nikola Shuhaj* (*Nikola Šuhaj Loupežnilk*), German edn. Ruetten & Loening (Berlin 1953), is not only, I am told, a modern Czech classic, but far and away the most moving and historically sound picture of social banditry I have come across.

[4] 'Angiolillo, capo di banditti," in *La Rivoluzione Napoletana del 1799* (Bari 1912).

[5] Gavin Maxwell, *God Preserve Me from My Friends* (1956).

[6] P. Bourde, *En Corse* (Paris 1887), 207.

[7] For the actual belief in the efficacy of amulets (in this case a commission from the King), see Appendix 3: A Bourbon brigand examined, in Hobsbawm, *op. cit.*

[8] *Paese Sera* 6.9.1955.

[9] *La Voce di Calabria* 1–2.9.1955; R. Longnone in *Unità* 8.9.1955 observes that, even when the other functions of the local secret society have lapsed, the young men still 'rapiscono la donna que amano e che poi regolarmente sposano.'

pala) was admonished by the police in 1896, arrested a little later for 'contravention of the admonition' and sentenced to ten days and a year under surveillance; also to a fine of 12.50 lire for letting his sheep pasture on the grounds of a certain Salis Giovanni Antonio. He preferred to take to the hills, attempted to shoot the judge and killed his creditor.[10] Giuliano is supposed to have shot a policeman who wanted to beat him up for blackmarketing a couple of bags of wheat while letting off another smuggler who had enough money to bribe him; an act which would certainly be regarded as 'honourable.' In fact, what has been observed of Sardinia almost certainly applies more generally:[11]

The 'career' of a bandit almost always begins with some incident, which is not in itself grave, but drives him into outlawry: a police charge for some offence brought against the man rather than for the crime; false testimony; judicial error or intrigue; an unjust sentence to forced residence (confino), or one felt to be unjust.

It is important that the incipient social bandit should be regarded as 'honourable' or non-criminal by the population, for if he was regarded as a criminal against local convention, he could not enjoy the local protection on which he must rely completely. Admittedly almost anyone who joins issue with the oppressors and the State is likely to be regarded as a victim, a hero or both. Once a man is on the run, therefore, he is naturally protected by the peasants and by the weight of local conventions which stands for 'our' law—custom, blood-feud or whatever it might be—against 'theirs,' and 'our' justice against that of the rich. In Sicily he will, unless very troublesome, enjoy the goodwill of *Mafia*, in Southern Calabria of the so-called *Onorata Società*,[12] everywhere of public opinion. In-

deed, he may—and perhaps mostly will—live near or in his village, whence he is supplied. Romeo, for instance, normally lives in Bova with his wife and children and has built a house there. Giuliano did the same in his town of Montelepre. Indeed, the extent to which the ordinary bandit is tied to his territory—generally that of his birth and 'his' people—is very impressive. Giuliano lived and died in Montelepre territory, as his predecessors among Sicilian bandits, Valvo, Lo Cicero and Di Pasquale had lived and died in Montemaggiore or Capraro in Sciacca.[13] The worst thing that can happen to a bandit is to be cut off from his local sources of supply, for then he is genuinely forced to rob and steal, that is to steal from his people, and may therefore become a criminal who may be denounced. The phrase of the Corsican official who regularly left wheat and wine for bandits in his country cottage, expresses one side of this situation: 'Better to feed them in this way than to oblige them to steal what they need.'[14] The behaviour of the brigands in the Basilicata illustrates the other side. In this area brigandage died out during the winter, some brigands even emigrating to work, because of the difficulty of getting food for outlaws. In spring, as food became available again, the brigandage season began.[15] These Lucanian cut-throats knew why they did not force the poor peasants to feed them, as they would certainly have done had they been an occupying force. The Spanish government in the 1950s ended Republican guerilla activity in the Andalusian mountains by moving against Republican sympathizers and suppliers in the villages, thus obliging the outlaws to steal food and alienate the non-political shepherds,

some village, and takes to the hills, the local secret society feels the duty to help him to escape, to find a refuge and to sustain him and his family, even if he is not a member.'

[10] Velio Spano, *Il banditismo sardo e i problemi della rinascita* (Rome, bibioteca di 'Riforma Agraria' n.d.), 22-4.

[11] Il banditismo sardo e la rinascita dell'isola (*Rinascita*, X, 12, December 1953).

[12] R. Longnone in *Unità* 8.9.1955: 'When, for instance, a man commits an offence of honour in

[13] G. Alongi, *La Maffia* (Turin 1887), 109. In spite of its title this book is much more useful about brigandage than about *Mafia*.

[14] Bourde, *op cit.*, 218-19.

[15] G. Racioppi, *Storia dei Moti di Basilicata . . . nel 1860* (Bari 1909), 304. An eyewitness account by a local liberal revolutionary and official.

who therefore became willing to inform against them.[16]

A few remarks may complete our sketch of the mechanics of the bandit's life. Normally he will be young and single or unattached, if only because it is much harder for a man to revolt against the apparatus of power once he has family responsibilities: two-thirds of the bandits in the Basilicata and Capitanata in the 1860s were under 25 years old.[17] The outlaw may of course remain alone—indeed, in cases where a man commits a traditional 'crime' which may, by custom, allow an eventual return to full legality (as in vendetta or abduction) this may be the usual case. Of the 160 or so existing South Calabrian outlaws most are said to be lone wolves of this sort; that is, individuals living on the margin of their villages, attached to them by threads of kin or support, kept from them by enmities and the police. If he joins or forms a band, and is thus economically committed to a certain amount of robbery, it will rarely be very large, partly for economic reasons, partly for organizational ones; for the band is held together only by the personal prestige of its leader. Some very small bands are known— e.g. the three men who were caught in the Maremma in 1897 (I need hardly say, by treachery).[18] Extremely large bands of up to sixty are reported among the Andalusian *bandoleros* of the 19th century, but they enjoyed the support of local lords (*caciques*) who used them as retainers; for this reason perhaps they do not belong in this chapter at all.[19] In periods of revolution, when bands become virtual guerilla units, even larger groups of some hundreds occurred, but in Southern Italy these also enjoyed financial and other support from the Bourbon authorities. The normal picture of even brigand-guerilla bands is one of a multiplicity of much smaller units, combining for operations. In the Capitanata under Joachim Murat there were something like seventy bands, in the Basilicata of the early sixties thirty-nine, in Apulia some thirty. Their average membership in the Basilicata is given as 'from twenty to thirty,' but can be computed from the statistics as fifteen to sixteen. One may guess that a band of thirty, such as Giuseppe de Furia led for many years in Napoleonic and Restoration times, represents about the limit which can be dominated by an average leader without organization and discipline such as few brigand chieftains were capable of maintaining, larger units leading to secessions. (It may be observed that this is also something like the figure in tiny fissiparous protestant sects, such as the West Country Bible Christians, who averaged thirty-three members per chapel in the 1870s.)[20]

How long a band lasted we do not know exactly. It would depend, one imagines, on how much of a nuisance it made of itself, on how tense the social situation, or how complex the international situation was—in the period from 1799 to 1815 Bourbon and British help to local bandits might make it easy to survive for many years—, and how much protection it had. Giuliano (with heavy protection) lasted six years, but at a guess a Robin Hood of some ambition would be lucky to survive for more than two to four years: Janošik, the prototype bandit of the Carpathians in the early 18th century, and Shuhaj lasted for two years, Sergeant Romano in Apulia after 1860 for thirty months, and five years broke the back of the most tenacious Bourbon brigands in the South. However, an isolated small band without great pretensions, such as that of Domenico Tiburzi on the confines of Latium, could carry on for twenty years (*c.*

[16] J. Pitt-Rivers, *People of the Sierra* (1954), 181–3.

[17] Quoted from Pani-Rossi, *La Basilicata* (1868), in C. Lombroso, *Uomo Delinquente* (1896), I, 612.

[18] E. Rontini: *I Briganti Celebri* (Florence 1898), 529. A sort of superior chap-book.

[19] See the constant complaints of the verbose Don Julián de Zugasti, governor of Cordoba province charged with bandit suppression, in his *El Bandolerismo* (Madrid 1876–80), ten volumes; e.g. Introduction, vol. I, 77–8, 181 and esp. 86 ff.

[20] Lucarelli, *Il Brigantaggio Politico dell Mezzogiorno d'Italia, 1815–1818* (Bari 1942), 73; Lucarelli, *Il Brigantaggio Politico delle Puglie dopo il 1860* (Bari 1946), 102–3, 136–6; Racioppi, *op cit.*, 299. *Blunt's Dictionary of Sects and Heresies* (London 1874), Methodists, Bryanite.

1870–90). If the State let him, the bandit might well survive and retire into ordinary peasant life, for the ex-bandit was easily integrated into society, since it was only the State and the gentry who considered his activities criminal.[21]

It does not greatly matter whether a man began his career for quasi-political reasons like Giuliano, who had a grudge against the police and government, or whether he simply robs because it is a natural thing for an outlaw to do. He will almost certainly try to conform to the Robin Hood stereotype in some respects; that is, he will try to be 'a man who took from the rich to give to the poor and never killed but in self-defence or just revenge.' He is virtually obliged to, for there is more to take from the rich than from the poor, and if he takes from the poor or becomes an 'illegitimate' killer, he forfeits his most powerful asset, public aid and sympathy. If he is free-handed with his gains, it may only be because a man in his position in a society of pre-capitalist values shows his power and status by largesse. And if he himself does not regard his actions as a social protest, the public will, so that even a purely professional criminal may come to pander to its view. *Schinderhannes*, the most famous, though not the most remarkable of the gang-leaders who infested the Rhineland in the late 1790s,[22] was in no sense a social bandit. (As his name shows, he came from a low-caste trade traditionally associated with the underworld.) Yet he found it advantageous for his public relations to advertise the fact that he robbed only Jews, that is, dealers and money-lenders, and in return the anecdotes and chap-books which multiplied around him, gave him many of the attributes of the idealized Robin-Hood hero: the open-handedness, the righting of wrongs, the courtesy, sense of humour, cunning and valour, the ubiquity amounting to invisibility—all bandits in anecdotes go about the countryside in impenetrable disguises—,

and so on. In his case the tributes are totally undeserved, and one's sympathies are entirely with Jeanbon St. André, the old member of the Committee of Public Safety, who laid these gangsters low. Nevertheless, he may well have felt himself at least part of the time as a 'protector of the poor.' Criminals come from the poor and are sentimental about some things. So characteristic a professional crook as Mr. Billy Hill, whose autobiography (1955) deserves more sociological study than it has received, lapses into the usual maudlin self-pity when he explains his continued career as a thief and gangster by the need to distribute money to 'his' people, that is to various families of Irish unskilled workers in Camden Town. Robin-Hoodism, whether they believe in it or not, is useful to bandits.

However, many do not need to have the role thrust upon them. They take to it spontaneously, as did Pasquale Tanteddu of Sardinia whose views (somewhat influenced by communism) are more fully set out in the Appendix. Again, I am told that a leading Calabrian bandit of pre-1914 vintage gave regular donations to the Socialist Party. Systematic Robin Hoods are known. Gaetano Vardarelli of Apulia, who was pardoned by the King and then betrayed and killed by him in 1818, was always distributing part of his booty to the poor, distributing salt free, ordering bailiffs to give bread to estate workers on pain of massacre, and commanding the local landed bourgeoisie to allow the poor to glean their fields. . . . Angiolillo was exceptional in his systematic pursuit of a more general justice than could be achieved by casual gifts and individual interventions. 'When he arrived in any village' it is reported 'he had a tribunal set up, heard the litigants, pronounced sentence and fulfilled all the offices of a magistrate.' He is even supposed to have prosecuted common-law offenders. He ordered grain-prices to be lowered, confiscated the grain-stores held by the rich and distributed them to the poor. In other words, he acted as a parallel government in the peasants' interest. It is hardly surprising that as late as 1884 his village wanted to name the main street after him.

In their more primitive way the South-

---

[21] Pitt-Rivers, *op. cit.*, 183; Count Maffei, *Brigand Life in Italy*, 2 vols. (1865), I, 9–10.

[22] The main source is: B. Becker, *Actenmaessige Geschichte der Raeuberbanden an den beyden Ufern des Rheines* (Cologne 1804).

ern brigands of the 1860s, like those of 1799–1815, saw themselves as the people's champions against the gentry and the 'foreigners.' Perhaps Southern Italy in these periods provides the nearest thing to a mass revolution and war of liberation led by social bandits. (Not for nothing has 'bandit' become a habitual term foreign governments use to describe revolutionary guerillas.) Thanks to a large scholarly literature the nature of these epochs of brigandage is now well understood, and few students now share the incomprehension of middle-class Liberals who saw in them nothing but 'mass delinquency,' and barbarism if not Southern racial inferiority, an incomprehension which is still found in Norman Douglas' *Old Calabria*.[23]   And Carlo Levi, among others, has reminded us in *Christ Stopped at Eboli* how profound the memory of the bandit-heroes is among the Southern peasants, for whom the 'years of the brigands' are among the few parts of history which are alive and real, because, unlike the kings and wars, they belong to them.   In their way the brigands, dressed in torn peasant costume with Bourbon rosettes, or in more gorgeous apparel, were avengers and champions of the people.   If their way was a blind alley, let us not deny them the longing for liberty and justice which moved them.

Consequently also the characteristic victims of the bandit are the quintessential enemies of the poor.   As recorded in tradition, they are always those groups which are particularly hated by them: lawyers (Robin Hood and Dick Turpin), prelates and idle monks (Robin Hood and Angiolillo), money-lenders and dealers (Angiolillo and Schinderhannes), foreigners and others who upset the traditional life of the peasant.   In pre-industrial and pre-political societies they rarely if ever include the sovereign, who is remote and stands for justice.   Indeed, the legend frequently shows the sovereign pursuing the bandit, failing to suppress him, and then asking him to court and making his peace with him, thus recognizing that in a profound sense his and the sovereign's interest, justice, is the same.   Thus with Robin Hood and Oleksa Dovbush.[24]

The fact that the bandit, especially when he was not himself filled with a strong sense of mission, lived well and showed off his wealth did not normally put the public off. Giuliano's solitaire ring, the bunches of chains and decorations with which the anti-French bandits of the 1790s festooned themselves in Southern Italy, would be regarded by the peasants as symbols of triumph over the rich and powerful, as well as, perhaps, evidences of the bandit's power to protect them.   For one of the chief attractions of the bandit was, and is, that he is the poor boy who has made good, a surrogate for the failure of the mass to lift itself out of its own poverty, helplessness and meekness.[25]   Paradoxically therefore the conspicuous expenditure of the bandit, like the gold-plated Cadillacs and diamond-inlaid teeth of the slum boy who has become world boxing champion, serves to link him to his admirers and not to separate him from them; providing always that he does not step too far outside the heroic role into which the people have cast him.

The fundamental pattern of banditry, as

---

23 Lucarelli (who provides copious references) and Racioppi provide a good introduction to the problem.   Walter Pendleton, 'Peasant Struggles in Italy' (*Modern Quarterly*, N.S. VI, 3, 1951), summarizes this research.   Cf. also *Encicl. Italiana*: 'Brigantaggio.'

24 'The Lord Emperor had heard that there was this man whom no power could subdue; so he ordered him to come to Vienna to make his peace with him.   But this was a ruse.   When Dovbush came near, he sent his whole army against him to kill him.   He himself lay in his window to watch.   But the bullets glanced off him and hit the riflemen and killed them.   Then the Emperor ordered the fire to cease and made his peace with Dovbush.   He gave him freedom to fight wherever he wished, only not against his soldiers.   He gave him a letter and seal to prove this.   And for three days and three nights Dovbush was the Emperor's guest at the Emperor's court.'   Olbracht, *op. cit.*, 102.

25 'This is how it was: he was a weakly shepherd, poor, a cripple and a fool.   For as the preachers and the interpreters of scripture say, the Lord wished to prove by his example that all of us, everyone that is frightened, humble and poor, can do great deeds, if God will have it so.'   Olbracht, *op. cit.*, 100.   N.B. that the leaders of legendary bands are rarely the biggest and toughest members of them.

I have tried to sketch it here, is almost universally found in certain conditions. It is rural, not urban. The peasant societies in which it occurs know rich and poor, powerful and weak, rulers and ruled, but remain profoundly and tenaciously traditional, and pre-capitalist in structure. An agricultural society such as that of 19th-century East Anglia or Normandy or Denmark is not the place to look for social banditry. (This is no doubt the reason why England, which has given the world Robin Hood, the archetype of the social bandit, has produced no notable example of the species since the 16th century. Such idealization of criminals as has become part of popular tradition, has seized upon urban figures like Dick Turpin and MacHeath, while the miserable village labourers have risen to little more than the modest admiration for exceptionally daring poachers.) Moreover, even in backward and traditional bandit societies, the social brigand appears only before the poor have reached political consciousness or acquired more effective methods of social agitation. The bandit is a pre-political phenomenon, and his strength is in inverse proportion to that of organized agrarian revolutionism and Socialism or Communism. Brigandage in the Calabrian Sila went out before the First World War, when Socialism and peasant leagues came in. It survived in the Aspromonte, the home of the great Musolino and numerous other popular heroes for whom the women prayed movingly.[26] But there peasant organization is less developed. Montelepre, Giuliano's town, is one of the few places in Palermo province which lacked any peasant league of importance even during the national peasant rising of 1893[27] and where even today people vote much less than elsewhere for the developed political parties and much more for lunatic fringe groups like monarchists or Sicilian separatists.

In such societies banditry is endemic.

But it seems that Robin-Hoodism is most likely to become a major phenomenon when their traditional equilibrium is upset: during and after periods of abnormal hardship, such as famines and wars, or at the moments when the jaws of the dynamic modern world seize the static communities in order to destroy and transform them. Since these moments occurred, in the history of most peasant societies, in the 19th or 20th centuries, our age is in some respects the classical age of the social bandit. We observe his upsurge—at least in the minds of the people—in Southern Italy and the Rhineland during the Revolutionary transformations and wars at the end of the 18th century; in Southern Italy after Unification, fanned by the introduction of capitalist law and economic policy.[28] In Calabria and Sardinia the major epoch of brigandage began in the 1890's, when the modern economy (and agricultural depression and emigration) made their impact. In the remote Carpathian mountains banditry flared up in the aftermath of the First World War, for social reasons which Olbracht has, as usual, described both accurately and sensibly.

But this very fact expressed the tragedy of the social bandit. The peasant society creates him and calls upon him, when it feels the need for a champion and protector—but precisely then he is incapable of helping it. For social banditry, though a protest, is a modest and unrevolutionary protest. It protests not against the fact that peasants are poor and oppressed, but against the fact that they are sometimes excessively poor and oppressed. Bandit-heroes are not expected to make a world of equality. They can only right wrongs and prove that sometimes oppression can be turned upside down. Still less can they understand what is happening to Sardinian villages that makes some men

---

[26] See the special Calabrian issue of *Il Ponte* (1953).

[27] See M. Ganci, 'Il movimento dei Fasci nella provincia di Palermo,' in *Movimento Operaio*, N.S. VI, 6 (Nov.–Dec. 1954).

---

[28] Article: 'Brigantaggio,' in *Encicl. Italiana*. Even the Spanish *bandoleros* were partly the victims of Free Trade. As one of their protectors says (Zugasti, Introduction I, 94): 'Look sir, here we have many poor lads who used to go on the highways to earn a peseta by smuggling; but now there's no more of that, and the poor men don't know where their next meal is to come from.'

have plenty of cattle and others, who used to have a few, have none at all; that drives Calabrian villagers into American coal-mines, or fills the Carpathian mountains with armies, guns and debt. The bandit's practical function is at best to impose certain limits to traditional oppression in a traditional society, on pain of lawlessness, murder and extortion. He does not even fulfil that very well, as a walk through Montelepre will convince the observer. Beyond that, he is merely a dream of how wonderful it would be if times were always good. 'For seven years he fought in our country,' the Carpathian peasants say about Dovbush, 'and while he lived things went well with the people.' It is a powerful dream, and that is why myths form about the great bandits which lend them superhuman power and the sort of immortality enjoyed by the great just kings of the past who have not really died, but are asleep and will return again. Just so Oleksa Dovbush sleeps while his buried axe moves every year nearer to the earth's surface by the breadth of a poppyseed, and when it emerges another hero will arise, a friend to the people, a terror to the lords, a fighter for justice, an avenger of injustice. Just so, even in the U.S.A. of yesterday in which small and independent men fought—if necessary by terror like the IWW—against the victory of big men and corporations, there were some who believed that the bandit Jesse James had not been killed but had gone to California. For what would happen to people if their champions were irrevocably dead?[29]

Thus the bandit is helpless before the forces of the new society which he cannot understand. At most he can fight it and seek to destroy it:[30]

to avenge injustice, to hammer the lords, to take from them the wealth they have robbed and with fire and sword to destroy all that cannot serve the common good: for joy, for vengeance, as a warning for future ages—and perhaps for fear of them.

That is why the bandit is often destructive and savage beyond the range of his myth, which insists mainly on his justice and moderation in killing. Vengeance, which in revolutionary periods ceases to be a private matter and becomes a class matter, requires blood, and the sight of iniquity in ruins can make men drunk.[31] And destruction, as Olbracht has correctly seen, is not simply a nihilistic release, but a futile attempt to eliminate all that would prevent the construction of a simple, stable, peasant community: the products of luxury, the great enemy of justice and fair dealing. For destruction is never indiscriminate. What is useful for poor men is spared.[32] And thus the Southern brigands who conquered Lucanian towns in the 1860s, swept through them, opening jails, burning archives, sacking the houses of the rich and distributing what they did not want to the people: harsh, savage, heroic and helpless.

For banditry as a social movement in such situations was and is inefficient in every way. First, because it is incapable even of effective guerilla organization. Bandits certainly succeeded in launching a Bourbon rising against the Northern conquest—that is,

---

[29] 'According to another version, truly strange and fantastic, it was not Romano who fell at Vallata, but another bandit, who looked like him; for the exalted imagination of the masses considered the Sergeant, as it were, invulnerable and "immortal" owing to the Papal benediction, and Gastaldi reports that he was supposed to have been seen for many years thereafter, roaming the countryside secretly and in solitude.' Lucarelli, *Brigantaggio . . . dopo 1860*, 133 n.

[30] Olbracht, *op. cit.*, 98.

[31] There is a good description of the psychological effect of the burning of the business quarter in a Spanish city in Gamel Woolsey, *Death's Other Kingdom* (1939).

[32] 'Ils ont ravagé les vergers, les cultures scientifiques, coupé les arbres fruitiers. Ce n'est pas seulement par haine irraisonnée contre tout ce qui a appartenu au seigneur, c'est aussi par calcul. Il fallait égaliser le domaine, l'aplanir . . . pour rendre le partage possible et équitable. . . (Voilà) pourquoi ces hommes qui, s'ils ignorent la valeur d'un tableau, d'un meuble ou d'une serre, savent cependant la valeur d'une plantation d'arbres fruitiers ou d'une exploitation perfectionnée, brisent, brulent et saccagent le tout indistinctement.' R. Labry, *Autour du Moujik* (Paris 1923), 76, on the sacking of country-houses in the Chernigov gubernia 1905. The source is the record of interrogations of peasants.

genuine bandits, not simply political partisans so called by their opponents. But when a Spanish Bourbon soldier, Borjes, attempted to form them into an effective guerilla movement, they resisted and threw him out:[33] the very structure of the spontaneous band precluded more ambitious operations, and though the thirty-nine Lucanian bands could continue to make the country unsafe for some years to come, they were doomed. Second, because their ideology debarred them from making revolt effective. Not because bandits were generally traditionalists in politics—for their first loyalty was to the peasants—but because the traditional force whose side they took were either doomed, or because old and new oppression coalesced, leaving them isolated and helpless. The Bourbons might promise to distribute the land of the gentry to the peasants, but they never did; at most they gave a few ex-bandits commissions in the army. More likely than not they betrayed and killed them when they had done with them. Giuliano became the plaything of political forces he did not understand, when he allowed himself to become the military leader of the (*Mafia*-dominated) Sicilian Separatists. The one obvious fact about the men who used him and threw him away is that their conception of an independent Sicily was very different from his, which was certainly closer to that of the organized peasants whose May Day meeting he massacred at the Portella della Ginestra in 1947.

To be effective champions of their people, bandits had to stop being bandits; that is the paradox of the modern Robin Hoods. They could indeed assist peasant risings, for in these mass movements it is generally the smallish band, rather than the vast crowd, which prepares the ground for effective action outside the actual village,[34] and what better nucleus for such shock-troops than the existing bands of the brigands? Thus in 1905 the peasant activities of the Ukrainian village of

Bykhvostova were largely initiated by the cossack Vassili Potapenko (the 'tsar' of his band), the peasant Pyotr Cheremok (his 'minister') and their band, two men who had been formerly expelled from the village community for crimes—we do not know whether voluntarily or under pressure—and later readmitted. As in other villages, these bands who represented poor and landless peasants, and the sense of the community against the individualists and enclosers, were later killed by a village counter-revolution of the *kulaks*.[35] However, the band could not be a lasting form of organization for revolutionary peasants. It could at best be a temporary auxiliary for otherwise unorganized ones.

Thus the romantic poets who idealized the bandit, like Schiller in 'The Robbers,' were mistaken in believing them to be the real 'rebels.' The Bakuninist anarchists, who idealized them more systematically because of their very destructiveness, and who believed that they could harness them to their cause, were wasting their and the peasants' time.[36] They might succeed from time to time. There is at least one case in which a primitive peasant movement in which anarchist doctrine was combined with 'a strong bandit streak' became a major if temporary regional revolutionary force. But who really believes that, with all its chief's genius for irregular warfare, the 'Makhnovshchina' of the Southern Ukraine 1918–21 would have faced any-

---

[33] Racioppi, *op. cit.*, cap. XXI for all this.

[34] This emerges clearly from the study of the English Labourers' Rising of 1830, of which J. L. and B. Hammond, *The Village Labourer*, is still the only real account in print.

[35] Labry, *op. cit.*, reprints 'The Agrarian Troubles in the Gubernia of Chernigov in 1905' from *Istoricheski Vyestnik* (July 1913), 202–26. Nine peasants and six cossacks were killed. Labry correctly notes that this area was on the borders of the zone in which the *mir* was powerful and resistant, and that in which its break-up, and the formation of individualist holdings, was advancing fast (p. 72 ff.).

[36] Cf. Bakunin: 'The bandit is always the hero, the defender, the avenger of the people, the irreconcilable enemy of every State, social or civil régime, the fighter in life and death against the civilization of State, aristocracy, bureaucracy and clergy.' The problem is more fully discussed in F. della Peruta, 'La banda del Matese e il fallimento della teoria anarchica della moderna "Jacquerie" in Italia' (*Movimento Operaio*, N.S. 1954, 337–85).

thing but defeat, whoever won ultimate power in the Russian lands?[37]

---

[37] The most dispassionate account of this movement is in W. H. Chamberlin, *The Russian Revolution*, II, 232 ff., from which the quotation is taken. The standard Makhnovist account is P. Arshinov's. Makhno's own memoirs—from which extracts are quoted in the Appendix—do not appear to go beyond 1918. The 'bandit streak' is strongly denied by anarchist, and over-emphasized by Bolshevik historians, but fits in well with the remarkably pure 'primitivism' of this interesting but sadly neglected movement. It is significant, by the way, that though Makhno's activities ranged over a wide area of the Southern Ukraine, he returned time and again to his home village of Gulai-Polye to which, like any 'primitive' peasant bandleader, he remained anchored. (Chamberlin, *loc. cit.*, 237.) He lived from 1884 to 1934, after 1921 in exile. He became a convert to anarchism in his early '20s.

The future lay with political organization. Bandits who do not take to the new ways of fighting for the peasants' cause, as many of them do as individuals, generally converted in jails or conscript armies, cease to be champions of the poor and become mere criminals or retainers of landlords' and merchants' parties. There is no future for them. Only the ideals for which they fought, and for which men and women made up songs about them, survive, and round the fireside these still maintain the vision of the just society, whose champions are brave and noble as eagles, fleet as stags, the sons of the mountains and the deep forests.

* * *

POLITICAL ORIENTATION AND RIOT PARTICIPATION

Jeffery M. Paige

ABSTRACT

The relationship between political trust, political efficacy and riot participation is analyzed in a survey of 237 black males in Newark, New Jersey. Self-reported riot participants are more likely to be found among the dissident—those high on political efficacy but low on political trust, rather than among the alienated—those who are both distrustful and ignorant of government. When compared to civil rights activists and voters, rioters are similar in their generally higher levels of political information but lower in trust of the government. Rioting appears to be a disorganized form of political protest rather than an act of personal frustration, or social isolation, as has been suggested in some past research.

Source: J. M. Paige, "Political Orientation and Riot Participation," *American Sociological Review*, Vol. 36, 1971, pp. 810–820. Copyright 1971 by The American Sociological Association and used by permission.

The concept of political efficacy has been widely used to explain radical as well as conventional political participation. Indices of political efficacy (Campbell *et al.*, 1954; Milbraith, 1965) usually combine items expressing feelings of political powerlessness and ignorance with items expressing distrust of existing political arrangements and suspicion about government intentions. Individuals with strong subjective feelings of efficacy have been found to be more likely to vote, to take an interest in political campaigns and to participate in party activities (Milbraith, 1965). Alienated or apathetic individuals who lack such feelings of efficacy are less inclined to participate in all forms of conventional politics and are said to be particularly susceptible to radical or revolutionary appeals (Bell, 1964; Kornhauser, 1959; Lipset, 1960; Ransford, 1968). Both Almond and Verba (1965) and Gamson (1968), however, have argued that radical or revolutionary politics cannot be understood as a result of general feelings of alienation or apathy as indicated by a low score on an index of political efficacy. They suggest instead that radical political action depends on a combination of a strong sense of personal political competence combined with a deep distrust of the political system. This distinction between feelings of political competence and distrust is lost in an overall index of political efficacy. The present study is an attempt to examine the value of this distinction in understanding one form of radical political action—participation in the Newark riot of 1967.

The essence of the Almond and Verba and Gamson argument lies in their distinction between trust involving the administrative activities of the government and trust involving the political activities of concerned interest groups. Almond and Verba distinguish between "input" and "output" affect. The political input process refers to the activities of interest groups and individuals presenting demands to government; the output process refers to the decisions made and actions taken by the government and its administrative agencies. Gamson suggests that it might be useful to reserve the term "efficacy" for beliefs about the input process and to use "trust" to refer to beliefs about outputs. Politically efficacious individuals will feel that they can influence government functioning, are well informed about politics and are active politically. Those who are trusting will believe that the government is basically acting in their interests, whether or not they participate in the political input process. These two components of political beliefs may of course be empirically correlated—those who are ill informed or opposed

to government outputs will frequently be apathetic or uninvolved politically. Nevertheless, Almond and Verba, and Gamson, argue that the combination of a sense of political efficacy and distrust of existing government is a critical determinant of radical political action. Almond and Verba use this line of argument in explaining the prominence of revolutionary ideology in the political culture of Mexico. Gamson suggests that the optimum condition for political mobilization is a combination of high efficacy and low trust, "a belief that influence is both possible and necessary" (Gamson 1968:48). This fact poses difficulties for political organizers who must carefully balance the advantages of some small victory which might increase both efficacy and trust, against a small defeat which will have the opposite effect on both trust and efficacy. Particularly in the early stages of a radical movement, it may be useful to convince potential constituents that they cannot put their faith in the authorities by engineering a few small defeats. The organizer can then exploit the distrust to gain support for his movement.

The difference between the views of Almond and Verba and Gamson and more traditional perspectives on political efficacy (Campbell *et al.*, 1954; Campbell *et al.*, 1960; Milbraith, 1965) is a critical one for understanding the meaning of collective violence. If a simple dichotomy is made between the politically efficacious and the politically apathetic and alienated, then extremist tactics can be attributed to withdrawal from political life, or to ignorance of the true intentions of government. Collective violence and other forms of extremist politics can then be attributed to ignorance, despair, authoritarianism or some other personal failing which is not directly related to the behavior of political authorities. Such a theoretical perspective implies an excessively charitable view of authorities since it assumes that the more that is known about the government the more it will be trusted. Such a correlation, of course, depends on the government. The Almond and Verba and Gamson view establishes knowledge and interest in the government as a prerequisite for political participation but ties the exact form of the participation to beliefs about the intentions of the regime. Extremist political tactics, like other forms of politics, require interest in government but, unlike conventional forms, imply that the government is fundamentally untrustworthy.

The relationship between efficacy, trust and political participation depends not only on the characteristics of the group but on the relationship between the group and the political system. A knowledgeable citizenry with an unresponsive regime is likely to turn to radical or violent tactics, while the same level of knowledge in a responsive system would lead to loyalty and conventional political action. The relationships between citizen attitudes and regime behavior are summarized in Figure 1. This diagram shows four possible combinations of trust and efficacy assuming each variable can take simply a high and a low value. Each cell indicates the dominant political orientation of a group with such a combination of trust and efficacy, the behavior of a regime which would most likely be associated with such attitudes,

and the nature of the political system in which such attitudes and behavior would be found. In a situation in which both efficacy and trust are high, the predominant political orientation will be allegiance. Those who feel both that the government will be run in their interests and that they can influence it when necessary will be active supporters of the existing political structure. The high efficacy suggests that this group will be politically active but their actions will not be directed toward radical change. This kind of political orientation depends on a regime which is responsive to the demands of the allegiant groups. Decreased responsiveness to their demands would lower the level of trust. If such responsiveness is maintained, little force will be required to maintain the authority of the regime. Such attitudes and behavior are approximated for some, but certainly not all, interest groups in functioning democratic political systems.

The low efficacy, low trust situation produces an alienated orientation which would lead to withdrawal from any active political participation. Despite the fact that this

Trust

	High	Low
High (Efficacy)	Allegiant Responsive/ non-coercive Democratic	Dissident Unresponsive/ non-coercive Unstable
Low (Efficacy)	Subordinate Unresponsive/ non-coercive Traditional	Alienated Unresponsive/ coercive Totalitarian

Figure 1. Relationship of trust and efficacy to political orientation, behavior of regime, and nature of political system

group regards the existing political structure as unfair, their low levels of political interest and information will prevent them from supporting even radical political movements. The alienated orientation will develop in situations· in which the government is unresponsive and maintains its power largely through coercive force. The result is a resentful population which has learned that political activities are both dangerous and unprofitable. This situation is typical of totalitarian political systems.

The low efficacy, high trust situation also suggests a passive adjustment, although in this case the population believes that the government is basically run in their best interests. Demands are seldom presented by interest groups so that responsiveness is not an important issue in such systems. The ruler maintains an image of beneficient paternalism which, because of the low levels of political interest on the part of his subjects, may or may not be an accurate reflection of his actual behavior. Unless the ruler reveals himself to be unconcerned with the people's welfare through some particularly flagrant act or fails to meet the minimal demands of the population, there will be little need for active coercion to support his authority. Such a situation exists in traditional societies with hereditary rulers. The political orientation associated with paternalism might be called subordinate, since it leads to a loyal, unquestioning faith in the existing political structure.

These three situations share one important property—they are all relatively stable politically. Any of these three situations can and has persisted without apparent change for substantial periods of time. Western democratic societies which remain responsive to most interest groups have managed to retain essentially the same political structure for several generations. The same is true. of totalitarian states when they are supported by sufficiently large and loyal internal security forces. The traditional societies which depend on an implicit faith in the concern of the ruling classes for the welfare of the people are actually the most stable of the three.

The remaining cell in Figure 1, those with low trust in the existing government but high political efficacy is, unlike the other three, inherently unstable. If the government is regarded as untrustworthy and there is a feeling that something can and should be done about it, radical actions aimed at changing the system are likely to result. The more extreme the distrust, the more radical the response. Thus this cell defines a revolutionary situation. Withdrawal of trust is not in itself sufficient to create such a situation since it can lead to withdrawal from politics. What is critical is a combination of high efficacy and low trust. This active dissatisfaction with the political structure might be called a dissident political orientation. It will occur when an essentially unresponsive regime is faced with a politically aware population and for some reason does not or cannot rely on effective military coercion. This situation is unstable since it will usually lead to either repression or increased responsiveness on the part of the government. If the repression is successful, there will be a move to the alienated, totalitarian situation. If the government becomes more responsive to the revolutionary group, the society may move in the direction of greater democracy. There will not, in general, be a return from a dissident to a subordinate situation directly. The myth of the paternalistic ruler will not be readily restored after a revolutionary situation, although extended repression might have this result.

If riot participation can be viewed as a form of revolutionary activity, then it might be expected that riot participants would be overrepresented among the dissident—those high on efficacy and low on trust. The other three groups in Figure 1 would be less likely to participate in a riot but for different reasons. Both the allegiant and the subordinate groups support the existing political arrangements and would be unlikely to join a mass movement aimed at attacking them. The alienated have withdrawn from political life and would be likely to remain uninvolved during a riot. The alienated group is critical for the general line of argument presented here. The conventional view of political efficacy suggests the alienated groups are the base of support for extremist movements and that extremist and conventional politics are at opposite ends of the efficacy dimension. Such a view neglects the political component of extremism in favor of emphasizing its irrational qualities. The alternate view suggested by Almond and Verba and Gamson treats political radicalism as a response to an unresponsive and untrustworthy regime by politically sophisticated activists.

While the high-efficacy, low-trust group should be most likely to participate in revolutionary activities, those high on efficacy but higher on trust will be likely to engage in less extreme forms of political activity. Those low on political efficacy, whether subordinated or alienated, will be unlikely to participate in politics, whatever the form. Within the high efficacy group, then, the exact form of political participation depends on the amount of trust in the government. Gamson (1968) has distinguished three techniques which partisan groups can use to influence authorities: persuasion, inducements, and constraints. Persuasion involves attempts to change the orientations of the authorities by presenting new facts and arguments. The use of inducements is based on some added advantage to the authorities ranging from promised election support to outright bribery. Constraints add some disadvantage to the situation of the authorities and can range from political retaliation to physical violence. Gamson argues that each of these techniques is associated with a particular level of trust in the authorities. Those who are extremely high on trust, who think that even in the absence of influence the authorities will almost always act in their best interests, would be most likely to use persuasion. Those who feel neutral and believe that the chances of the authorities acting in their behalf are about even would be more likely to use inducements. Finally, groups which believe that there is little or no possibility that the authorities will act in their behalf have little to lose and will rely on constraints. This relationship between trust and political tactics should exist for the high efficacy subjects. Not only should it be possible to distinguish low and high efficacy groups on rates of political participation generally, but also to further specify what forms the political participation will take within the high efficacy group.

The success of the predictions based on political trust and efficacy depends on the relationships of rioting to other forms of political behavior. If there is no political component in rioting, then none of these predictions will be supported. In the following sections evidence in support of these hypotheses will be examined in detail.

METHODS AND RESULTS

Riot participation and political attitudes were measured in a sample survey conducted in Newark, New Jersey, approximately six months after the July, 1967 disorders. Although the precipitating incident in the Newark riot was much like those in other cities—an accusation of police brutality—there may have been a closer connection between the initiation of the riot and a peaceful civil rights protest than was the case elsewhere. According to the Kerner Commission (1968) and Hayden (1967), the disorder began with a routine arrest for a traffic violation. Rumors spread that the arrested Negro cab driver had been savagely beaten by police, and pamphlets were circulated urging a protest demonstration at the fourth precinct station house. The station house, in the heart of Newark's Negro central ward, became the focal point for the first two nights of violence. Attempts at negotiation between civil rights leaders and city officials deteriorated into stone throwing, attacks on the police station, running battles with police in the parking lots, courtyards and pathways of a nearby housing project, and finally widespread looting in shops on nearby Belmont Avenue and 17th Street. Rioting rapidly spread over most of the predominantly Negro inner city area, and the disorder was finally put down after considerable indiscriminate gunfire by police and national guardsmen. After the initial attacks on the police station, almost all later riot activity consisted of window breaking, looting, and arson.

The area of the survey probability sample was determined from a map of the riot zone published in the July 15, 1967 issue of the *New York Times,* and included 51% of the 1960 Newark black population. Interviews were conducted with 237 black males between the ages of 15 and 35. Riot participation was determined by asking respondents whether they had been "active" in the disturbance and, somewhat later in the interview, what specifically they had done. If a respondent said that he was active or admitted some specific form of rioting (rock-throwing, window breaking, looting, arson), he was classified as a rioter. Self-reported participation has been used in a number of recent studies of rioting (Meyer, 1967; Sears and McConahay, 1967; Ransford, 1968) without information on external validity. Two criterion variables were used to assess the validity of the self-report measure. First, demographic characteristics of a sample of 10,771 arrestees collected by the Kerner Commission were available for direct comparison with the characteristics of self-reported rioters. Data presented in the Commission's report (1968:172–173) indicate that self-reported rioters, as measured by the survey questions used in Newark and similar questions used in Meyer's Detroit survey, more closely resemble the age and sex characteristics of the arrestees than do self-reported nonparticipants. Secondly, the sample block in the Newark survey with the highest rate of riot participation (86%) was immediately adjacent to the fourth precinct station house where according to both the Kerner Commission (1968) and Hayden (1967) the most intense rioting occurred.

Testing the hypotheses derived from the joint effects of trust and efficacy requires that each of these variables be measured separately. While the two variables may be distinguished conceptually, it is difficult to construct a measure of efficacy which is not contaminated by trust. No matter how interested or active an individual is, he is unlikely to say that he can influence political affairs if he regards the government as essentially unresponsive. Thus a direct question asking about subjective feelings of influence on the government would not only measure the respondent's propensity to attempt influence, but also his estimated chance of success. Similarly questions involving actual participation in various forms of conventional politics would measure both feelings of political competence and belief in the utility of existing political forms. Voting, interest in political campaigns or participation in party activities express both an interest in moderate change and a commitment to working within the political system. Direct measures of radical political action would reduce the analysis to tautology since the relationship between attitudes and radical behavior is the central focus of the study. What is needed is a measure of capability or skill in politics which is not affected by the content or direction of political action. Thus a measure of political information was used to approximate the concept of efficacy. Information is a necessary but not sufficient condition for the exercise of political influence. Knowledge of the political system is necessary if one is to select appropriate targets and tactics for influence, and is therefore a measure of potential political skill. Similarly even the most distrustful potential revolutionary will be interested in knowing his enemy. Thus political information seems to be an efficacy index which is not contaminated by either subjective estimates of the outcomes of political action or the degree of commitment to the existing system.

Political information was measured in Newark by testing knowledge about local and national political figures. Respondents were asked to identify the race of nine Negro and white political figures. These respondents were divided at the median into a high and low group on the basis of the number of names correctly identified. Subjects who identified six or fewer names were placed in the low information group; those who identified seven or more, in the high information group.

Trust in the political system was measured directly by asking, "How much do you think you can trust the government in Newark to do what is right—just about always, most of the time, some of the time, or almost never?" The marginal percentages on this question suggest that this sample was extremely low on trust in the Newark government. Only five subjects (2%) felt that they could trust the government 'just about always," and in the following analysis this group has been combined with the 10% of the sample who felt that the government can be trusted most of the time. A substantial portion of the sample (38%) felt they could almost never trust the government. Although no comparable percentages are available for white samples, these figures suggest an extremely low level of trust. Another index of the low levels of trust in this sample is that there is actually a negative relationship between political information and trust in the Newark government. The correlation between political information (nine-point scale) and trust in the government is −.19. It seems

that the more that is known about the government the less it is trusted. This is, of course, the reverse of the relationship which has been found in white samples (Campbell *et al.*, 1954; Campbell *et al.*, 1960; Milbraith, 1965).

The theoretical analysis of the relationship of trust and efficacy to revolutionary activity suggested first that riot participation and other forms of political activity should be higher among high-information subjects and, second, that there should be an interaction effect between information level and trust. It is not sufficient to demonstrate that information and trust are independently related to riot participation, since the dissident group in Figure 2 was a product of an interaction between distrust and high efficacy. More specifically, we should expect that the

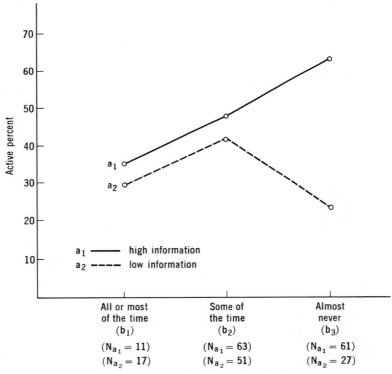

Figure 2.   Riot participation as a function of trust in the Newark government among those high and low on political information

alienated, the subordinate, and the allegiant should all be relatively low on riot participation, and the remaining cell, the dissidents, should be much higher. In statistical terms there should be a main effect for political information and a strong independent contribution of the high-information, low-trust cell. The data to test these hypotheses are presented graphically in Figure 2. Riot participation is shown as a function of trust in the government for both high- and low-information subjects. The solid line (a_1) indicates high information; the dotted line (a_2), low information. Figure 2 demonstrates a striking confirmation of the predicted interaction between information and trust. The high-information, low-trust cell is clearly the highest on riot participation. In fact, there is a 38 percentage-point spread between the low- and high-information cells in the low-trust condition. The alienated, those low on information and low on trust, are actually the lowest cell on riot participation. The subordinate, those high on trust and low on information, are almost as low, and the allegiants (high trust and high information) are at about the same level. The significance of the geometric relationships in Figure 2 was tested by the analysis of variance presented in Table 1. It is clear that there is no significant main effect of trust (B) on riot participation. There is a strong main effect of political information (A) on riot participation, but as the comparison between means indicates, almost all of this effect is attributable to the high-information, low trust; low-information, low-trust difference between means $\overline{(A_1B_3 - A_2B_3)}$. While this difference is significant at the .001 level (one-tailed test),

the other comparisons between high- and low-information means are nonsignificant. In fact, 86% of the sum of squares for the information main effect is contributed by the $\overline{A_1B_3} - \overline{A_2B_3}$ difference. Thus the analysis of variance confirms the strong contribution of the dissident condition to riot participation. The data in Table 2 provide a check on possible sources of spuriousness in this relationship. It is clear that the only relationship approaching significance is the one between political information and education. While it would be surprising to find that political information was not correlated with education, the low correlation between education and riot participation indicates that this cannot be a possible source of spuriousness. The surprisingly low correlation between age and riot participation is an artifact of the restrictive age range of the sample (15–35), although this has no bearing on the strength of the information-trust-participation relationships.

Thus, the hypothesized relationships between trust and information are supported by the survey data. The dissidents are highest on riot activity. The alienated who, despite their mistrust of the government, are likely to withdraw from political activity because of their low information levels are, in fact, the lowest on riot participation. The subordinate and the allegiant are almost equally low.

The second series of predictions derived from the trust-efficacy interaction concerned the choice of political tactics among the high efficacy respondents. The Gamson model predicts that constraints should be used by the most distrustful; persuasion, by the most trusting; and inducements, by those inter-

Table 1. Analysis of variance of riot participation by political information and trust in government

Source	SS	df	MS	F	p	t	p
Pol. Inf. (A)	1.610	1	1.610	6.73	<.01		
Trust (B)	.457	2	.229	.96	—		
A × B	1.230	2	.615	2.57	<.10		
Error	53.582	224	.239				
$\overline{A_1 B_1} - \overline{A_2 B_1}$	.038	1	.038	.16	—	.40	—
$\overline{A_1 B_2} - \overline{A_2 B_2}$	.102	1	.102	.42	—	.65	—
$\overline{A_1 B_3} - \overline{A_2 B_3}$	2.709	1	2.709	11.33	<.001	3.37	<.001

Table 2. Correlations of rioting, information and trust with age, education and income.

	Age	Educ.	Income
Rioting	−.16	.04	−.12
Political Information	.14	.30	.11
Trust in Government	.08	.02	.10

mediate on trust. Riot participation can clearly be used as a measure of the tendency to rely on constraints. Two forms of more conventional political action, civil rights activity and voting, provide two additional points on Gamson's continuum. In general, civil rights groups use the threat of demonstrations or legal action to influence white authorities and, therefore, such activity might be classified as a form of mild constraint. Civil rights activity was measured by asking if the respondent had ever attended a meeting of a civil rights group. Voting seems to be a form of inducement—the exchange of electoral support for favorable decisions—and was measured by asking if the respondent was registered to vote in the 1964 presidential election. There is no clear measure of the tendency to use persuasion in the survey instruments, although this is not as great a disadvantage as it first might seem, since there are few respondents in the high-trust groups who might be expected to use it. It is possible to establish a continuum running from inducements (voting) to mild constraints (civil rights activity) to severe constraints (rioting). The Gamson model predicts that as trust decreases there ought to be a move from voting to civil rights activity to rioting as a preferred political tactic. Since the mean levels of participation differ for the three forms of activity, we should not necessarily expect that one will clearly take precedence over the others at any given trust level. Instead, we should expect the maximum use of each technique to occur at different trust levels. Voting should be highest among those who feel the government can be trusted most of the time; rioting, among those who feel it can almost never be trusted; and civil rights activity should peak among those intermediate on trust. These predictions hold only for the high-information subjects, since those low on information would be unlikely to show any consistent pattern in their reactions to government activities with which they are only peripherally concerned.

The data to test these predictions are presented graphically in Figure 3. In this figure riot participation, civil rights activity, and voter registration are shown as a function of trust in the government for high-information subjects. The shapes of the three curves are precisely those predicted by the Gamson model. Voter registration is highest among those relatively high on trust in the government and declines linearly with decreasing trust. Rioting, on the other hand, is highest among those lowest on trust and *increases* linearly with decreasing trust. Civil rights activity falls between the other two, reaching its highest level among those who are intermediate on trust and declining among those who are both very high and very low on trust.

The significance of these results was tested by the analysis of variance presented in Table 3. Examining first the main effects, it is clear that political information has a significant effect on all three forms of political activity. In each case the higher the level of political information the greater the participation. There are no significant overall trust effects, however. The trends determined by inspection in Figure 3 are in fact statistically reliable. The linear increasing relationship between rioting and trust is significant at the .025 level. The linear decreasing relationship for voting is significant at the .05 level. The civil rights curve approaches significance at the .05 level only for the case of a quadratic trend. The curvilinear contribution is clearly greater than the linear contribution. In general then, the statistical analysis supports the conclusions drawn by inspection of Figure 3.

In conclusion, it has been shown that riot participation can be predicted through the use of variables tied to the political system, at least in the case of the Newark riot. There was strong support in the survey data for predictions drawn from the relationship be-

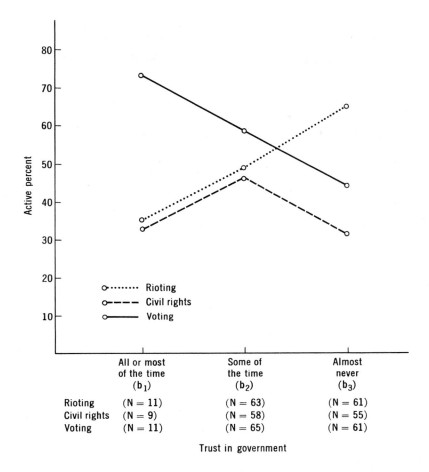

Figure 3. Riot participation, civil rights activity, and voter registration as a function of trust in the government among high-information subjects in Newark

tween trust and efficacy suggested by Almond and Verba, and Gamson. Rioters were most often found among the dissident—those high on political information and low on trust in the government. They were much less likely to be found among the alienated (low information, low trust), the subordinate (low information, high trust), or the allegiant (high information and high trust). Among the high-information subjects there was a clear tendency for respondents to shift from inducements to severe constraints as trust in the government decreased. In general, there is evidence that rioting can profitably be considered a form of disorganized political protest engaged in by those who have become highly distrustful of existing political institutions.

Table 3. Analysis of variance of riot participation, civil rights activity, and voter registration by political information and trust in government

Source	SS	df	MS	F	p	t	p
			Main effects				
Pol. Inf. (A)							
Rioting	1.610	1	1.610	6.73	.01		
Civil rights	1.675	1	1.675	7.98	.01		
Voting	3.503	1	3.503	15.35	.001		
Trust (B)							
Rioting	.457	2	.229	.96	—		
Civil rights	.533	2	.266	1.27	—		
Voting	.092	2	.046	.20	—		
A × B							
Rioting	1.230	2	.615	2.47	.10		
Civil rights	.382	2	.191	.91	—		
Voting	2.003	2	1.002	4.39	.05		
Error							
Rioting	53.582	224	.239				
Civil rights	41.543	201	.210				
Voting	51.594	226	.228				
	Analysis of trends for high-information (a$_l$) condition						
B over a$_l$							
(linear)							
Rioting	1.079	1	1.079	4.51	.05	2.12	.025
Civil rights	.360	1	.360	1.71	—	1.08	—
Voting	.619	1	.619	2.71	—	1.67	.05
B over a$_l$							
(quadratic)							
Rioting	.001	1	.001	—	—	—	—
Civil rights	.538	1	.528	2.52	—	1.59	.10
Voting	.066	1	.066	.03	—	.17	—

References

Almond, G. and Verba S. "National Revolutions and Political Commitment." In H. Eckstein (ed.), Internal War. Glencoe, Illinois: The Free Press, 1964. Pp. 205–232.

——— and ———. The Civic Culture. Boston: Little, Brown, 1965.

Bell, Daniel. The Radical Right. New York: Doubleday, 1964.

Campbell, A., Gurin, G., and Miller, W. E. The Voter Decides. Evanston, Illinois: Row Peterson, 1954.

Campbell, A., Converse, P. E., Miller, W. E., and Stokes, D. E. The American Voter. New York: Wiley, 1960.

Gamson, William A. Power and Discontent. Homewood, Illinois: Dorsey, 1968.

Kerner Commission. See National Advisory Commission on Civil Disorders, 1968.

Kornhauser, William. The Politics of Mass Society. New York: The Free Press, 1959.

Hayden, Thomas, Rebellion in Newark. New York: Vintage, 1967.

Lipset, S. M. Political Man. New York: Anchor, 1960.

Meyer, P. The Detroit Free Press, August 20: 11, 1967.

Milbraith, L. W. Political Participation. Chicago: Rand McNally, 1965.

National Advisory Commission on Civil Disorders, Final Report. New York: Bantam, 1968.

Ransford, H. E. "Isolation, Powerlessness, and Violence: A Study of Attitudes and Participation in the Watts Riot." American Journal of Sociology 73, March, 1968. Pp. 581–591.

Sears, D. and J. McConahay. "The Politics of Discontent." Institute of Government and Public Affairs, University of California, Los Angeles, June, 1967.

THE PUBLIC PERCEPTION OF PROTEST

Ralph H. Turner

ABSTRACT

Collective acts of disruption and violence are sometimes viewed as expressions of social protest, and sometimes as crime or rebellion, leading to different community reactions. Several theoretical perspectives can be used to predict when the protest interpretation will be made: (1) events must be credible as protest; (2) an optimal balance is required between appeal and threat and (3) protest interpretation is often an aspect of conciliation to avoid full-scale conflict. . . .

The year 1965 marked a dramatic turning point in American reactions to racial disorder. Starting with Watts, dominant community sentiment and the verdicts of

Source: R. H. Turner, "The Public Perception of Protest," American Sociological Review, Vol. 32, December 1969, pp. 815–831. Copyright 1969 by The American Sociological Association and used by permission.

politically sensitive commissions have identified mass violence by blacks primarily as acts of social protest. In spite of its well advertized failings, the McCone Commission (Governor's Commission on the Los Angeles Riots, 1965) devoted most of its attention to reporting the justified complaints of Negroes and proposing their amelioration. The Kerner Report (National Advisory Commission on Civil Disorders, 1968) went further in predicating recommendations for action on the assumption that disorders must be understood as acts of social protest, and not merely as crime, anti-social violence, or revolutionary threats to law and order. A few earlier bodies had seen minority protest as a component in racial disorders (Silver, 1968), but in most cases these commissions were far removed from the political process. Even when whites had perpetrated most of the violence, public officials before 1965 typically vented their most intense anger against Negroes, Negro leaders, and their white allies (Lee and Humphrey, 1943; Rudwick, 1964). If comparable data were available from earlier racial disturbances, it is unlikely they would match Morris and Jeffries' (1967:5) finding that 54% in a sample of white Los Angeles residents viewed the disturbance as Negro protest.

The aim of this paper is to suggest several theoretical vantage points from which to predict when a public will and will not view a major disturbance as an act of social protest. Historically, labor strife has sometimes been understood as protest and sometimes not. Apparently the protest meaning in the activities of Cesar Chavez and his farm laborers is discounted by most Americans today. A gang *rumble* is seldom viewed as protest, even when Puerto Ricans and other minorities are prominently involved. Three-fourths of an unspecified sample of Los Angeles residents in May, 1969, are reported to have seen disorders in secondary schools as the work of agitators and not as social protest, (Los Angeles Times, May 19, 1969), even though Mexican-Americans and blacks have played the leading roles. Events of early 1969 hint at a rising movement to redefine all racial and youthful disturbances in other terms than social protest. Hence, it is of both current and continuing sociological interest to advance our understanding of these variable public definitions, in broad terms that might apply to all kinds of disturbances, and eventually to other cultures and eras.

THE MEANING OF PROTEST

Protest has been defined as "an expression or declaration of objection, disapproval, or dissent, often in opposition to something a person is powerless to prevent or avoid." (Random House Dictionary, 1967). An act of protest includes the following elements: the action expresses a grievance, a conviction of wrong or injustice; the protestors are unable to correct the condition directly by their own efforts; the action is intended to draw attention to the grievances; the action is further meant to provoke ameliorative steps by some target group; and the protestors depend upon

some combination of sympathy and fear to move the target group in their behalf. Protest ranges from relatively persuasive to relatively coercive combinations (Bayley, 1962), but always includes both. Many forms of protest involve no violence or disruption, but these will not concern us further in this paper.

The term protest is sometimes applied to trivial and chronic challenges that are more indicative of a reaction style than of deep grievance. For instance, we speak of a child who protests every command from parent or teacher in the hope of gaining occasional small concessions. It is in this sense that the protestations by some groups in society are popularly discounted because "they just protest everything." But the subject of this analysis is *social protest*, by which we mean protest that is serious in the feeling of grievance that moves it and in the intent to provoke ameliorative action.

When violence and disorder are identified as social protest, they constitute a mode of communication more than a form of direct action. Looting is not primarily a means of acquiring property, as it is normally viewed in disaster situations (Dynes and Quarantelli, 1968); breaking store windows and burning buildings is not merely a perverted form of amusement or immoral vengeance like the usual vandalism and arson; threats of violence and injury to persons are not simply criminal actions. All are expressions of outrage against injustice of sufficient magnitude and duration to render the resort to such exceptional means of communication understandable to the observer.

In identifying the principal alternatives to protest we must first differentiate crime and deviance on the one hand and rebellion and revolution on the other. The latter may or may not express a generally understandable grievance, but they constitute direct action rather than communication and their aim is to destroy the authority of the existing system either totally or so far as the rebellious group is concerned. Thus protest and rebellion are distinguished according to their ultimate goal and according to whether the disruptions are meant as communication or direct action. Deviance and crime are actions identified chiefly according to their nonconforming, illegal, or harmful character. Deviance and crime are seen principally in individual terms, and while there may be "social" causes that require attention, the harmful or nonconforming features of the behavior are the primary concern. The distinctions are not absolute. Extortion, "power plays," and similar ideas fall between crime and protest. Nor can the line between protest and rebellion be drawn precisely. Attributing disorders to agitators is another common variation, in which either criminal or rebellious meaning is ascribed to the agitators, but any criminal, protest, or rebellious meaning is blunted for the mass of participants.

In deciding that individuals view a disturbance as social protest, it is helpful but not conclusive to note whether they apply the term protest. Defining a disturbance as protest does not preclude disapproving the violence or disorder by which the protest is expressed, nor does it preclude advocating immediate measures to control and suppress the disturbance. Thus Marvin Olsen's (1968) study of the legitimacy that individuals assign to various types of protest activities is related to the present question, but makes a somewhat different distinction. The principal indicators of a protest definition are concerned with identifying the grievances as the most adequate way of accounting for the disturbance and the belief that the main treatment indicated is to ameliorate the unjust conditions. Fogelson (1968) offers an exceptionally explicit statement of this mode of interpreting racial disorder: ". . . the riots of the 1960's are articulate protests against genuine grievances in the Negro ghettos. The riots are protests because they are attempts to call the attention of white society to the Negroes' widespread dissatisfaction with racial subordination and segregation in urban America. The riots are also articulate because they are restrained, selective, and perhaps even more important, directed at the sources of the Negroes' most immediate and profound grievances."

DEFINITIONS BY PUBLICS

We assume that individuals and groups of individuals assign simplifying meanings to events, and then adjust their perceptions of detail to these comprehensive interpretations. Lemert's (1951) pioneering examination of deviance as a label applied by society's agents serves as a valuable prototype for the analysis of responses to public disturbances. We scrupulously avoid assuming that there are objectifiable phenomena that must be classified as deviance, as protest, or as rebellion. We further assume that participant motivations are complex and diverse, so that a given disturbance is not simply protest, or not protest, according to participant motives. Just as Negroes and whites used different labels for the Watts disturbance (Tomlinson and Sears, 1967), we also assume that publics will often interpret the events quite differently from the participants.

This concern with public definitions contrasts—but is not incompatible—with studies in which protest is defined and examined as an objective phenomenon. For example, Lipsky's (1968) careful statement of the prospects and limitations in the use of protest as a political tool deals with an objectively identified set of tactics rather than a subjective category. Irving Horowitz and Martin Liebowitz (1968) argue that "The line between the social deviant and the political marginal is fading." The political marginal engages in social protest, in our sense, and the authors are pointing out that much of what sociologists heretofore understood as deviance is now taking on the character of social protest, either as objectively defined or according to the motives of the subject individuals.

The question of labelling disturbances has been examined by other investigators from somewhat different points of view. Lang and Lang (1968) have observed that the label "riot" is used to identify quite different kinds of events that are similar only in the kind of official response they evoke. Grimshaw (1968) pointed out the different labels attached to recent disturbances according to whether they are seen as racial clashes, class conflict, or civil disturbances in which the theme of intergroup conflict is de-emphasized.

The nature of the public definition undoubtedly has consequences for the course and recurrence of the disturbance, and for short- and long-term suppression or facilitation of reform. One of the most important consequences is probably that a protest definition spurs efforts to make legitimate and nonviolent methods for promoting reform more available than they had been previously, while other definitions are followed by even more restricted access to legitimate means for promoting change (Turner and Killian, 1957:327–329). Persons to whom the Joseph McCarthy movement was a massive protest against threats to our national integrity were unwilling to oppose the Senator actively even when they acknowledged that his methods were improper. Following the recent student disruption of a Regents meeting at UCLA, a faculty member who perceived the activity as protest against academic injustice advised the Academic Senate to listen more to what the students were saying and less to the tone of voice in which they said it. But the important tasks of specifying and verifying the consequences of protest definition fall beyond the limits of this paper. Any judgment that protest definition is "good" or "bad" must depend upon the findings of such investigation and on such other considerations as one's evaluation of the cause and one's preferred strategy for change.

The rest of this paper will be devoted to suggesting several vantage points from which it is possible to formulate hypotheses regarding the conditions under which one group of people will define events as disturbances and some other group as social protest. First, publics test events for *credibility* in relation to folk-conceptions of social protest and justice. Second, disturbances communicate some combination of *appeal and threat*, and the balance is important in determining whether the disturbances are regarded as social protest. Third, disturbances instigate conflict with a target group, who may define them as social protest in the

course of attempted *conciliation* to avoid full scale conflict. . . .

The paper offers theoretical proposals and not tested findings. The proposals are not a complete catalogue of causes for protest interpretation; notably omitted are such variables as understanding, empathy, and kindness. The proposals generally assume that there is no well-established tradition of disruptive or violent protest (Silver, 1968), that the society is not sharply polarized, and that the disturbances emanate from a clearly subordinated segment of the society.

CREDIBILITY AND COMMUNICATION

If a disturbance is to be viewed as social protest, it must somehow look and sound like social protest to the people witnessing it. If they see that the events are widely at variance from their conception of social protest, they are unlikely to identify the disturbance as social protest in spite of any intergroup process in which they are involved. On the other hand, if events are clearly seen to correspond precisely with people's idea of social protest, intergroup processes will have to operate with exceptional force to bring about a different definition. It is within the limits imposed by these two extreme conditions that the intergroup process variables may assume paramount importance. Hence it is appropriate to begin our analysis by examining these limiting considerations.

Our first two theoretical perspectives concern this preliminary question, whether the events will be recognizable as social protest or not. First, there are the viewer's preconceptions about protest that render believable the claim that what he sees is protest. We look to the predispositions of individuals and groups to ascertain what characteristics a disturbance must exhibit if it is to be *credible* as protest. Second, the ability of the observer to attend to one or another of the melange of potential messages communicated to him will be affected by the specific nature of the disturbance. For example, the balance between *appeal and threat* messages seems especially crucial for whether observers see the disturbance as social protest.

CREDIBILITY: THE FOLK CONCEPT

The main outlines of a *folk concept* (Turner, 1957) of social protest appear to be identifiable in contemporary American culture. The folk concept is only partially explicit, and is best identified by examining the arguments people make for viewing events and treating troublemakers in one way or another. Letters to newspapers and editorial and feature columns supply abundant material in which to conduct such a search. More explicit statements are to be found in essays that present reasoned arguments for viewing disturbances as protest (Boskin, 1968). The folk concept supplies the criteria against which people judge whether what they see looks like social protest or not. Often the process works in reverse: people who are predisposed to interpret a disturbance as protest, or as criminal rioting, perceive events selectively so as to correspond with the respective folk concept. But in so far as there is any testing of the events to see whether they look like protest, crime, or rebellion, the folk concepts are the key. The folk concept will not necessarily correspond with what sociologists would find in a study of objectively defined protest behavior.

Several components of the folk concept of social protest emerge from examination of relevant materials. To be credible as protestors, troublemakers must seem to constitute a major part of a group whose grievances are already well documented, who are believed to be individually or collectively powerless to correct their grievances, and who show some signs of moral virtue that render them "deserving." Any indication that only few participated or felt sympathy with the disturbances predisposes observers to see the activities as deviance or as revolutionary activity by a small cadre of agitators. The claim that a group's conditions explain their resort to unusual means for gaining public attention to their plight is undermined when it appears that many persons in identical situations will not join or support the protest.

Common arguments against protest interpretation take the following form: "Unemployed? Let him go out, walk the streets, and find a job the way I did!" "They have one vote each the same as we do!" Powerlessness and grievance probably cannot be effectively communicated for the first time in a large-scale disturbance. To be credible as protest, a disturbance must follow an extended period in which both the powerlessness and the grievances have already been repeatedly and emphatically advertized.

Any weak individual or group who comes with a plea to more powerful personages is normally required to be more circumspect and more virtuous than those to whom he appeals. The normative principle would not be endorsed in this explicit form by majority groups. But the *de facto* principle operates because the sincerity and justifiability of the pleader's claim is subject to investigation and test while there is no investigation of the other's legitimacy. Since violence and disruption immediately call virtue into question, there must be offsetting indications of goodness in the group's past or current behavior. The group in question must be customarily law-abiding and must have used acceptable means and exercised restraint on other occasions. Nonviolent movements that precede violent disruptions help to establish the credibility of protest. Widespread support and sympathy for the objectives of protest coupled with the group's principled rejection of the violent means employed by a few of their members help to establish the deserving nature of the group without undermining the pervasive character of their grievances.

To be credible as protest, the disturbance itself must be seen either as a spontaneous, unplanned, and naive outburst, or as an openly organized protest of more limited nature that got tragically out of hand. Any evidence of covert planning, conspiracy, or seriously intended threats of violence before the event would weaken the credibility of the protest interpretation. On the other hand, naive expressions of rage, released under the stimulus of rumor and crowd excitement, are consistent with a folk-image of protest. In this connection the protest interpretation is supported by demonstrating that what triggered the disturbances was some incident or act of provocation, and that a succession of recent provocations had prepared the ground for an eruption.

To be credible as protest, indications of the use of riots for self-aggrandisement, the settlement of private feuds, or enjoyment of violence and destruction must be subordinated to naive anger and desperation. Looting for personal gain and the attitude that rioting is "having a ball" are two features of the racial disturbances since 1965 that have repeatedly detracted from the image of social protest. In a widely read article typical of many such statements, Eric Sevareid (1967) challenged the protest definition by describing the carnival atmosphere at certain stages in many of the disturbances.

Finally, some indications of restraint are important cues to interpretation as protest. A belief that only property and not personal injury was the object of attack, that deaths and severe injuries to persons resulted only under special circumstances of confusion and provocation, and that rioters went to exceptional lengths in a few dramatic instances to protect a white person or guarantee a college administrator safe passage is often salient in the imagery of persons defining the activity as protest.

CREDIBILITY: THE ADMISSION

OF INJUSTICE

Interpretations of disruptive activity as protest invoke conceptions of justice and injustice. Homans (1961) and Blau (1964a and 1964b) are among those who interpret the sense of injustice as a feeling of inadequate reciprocation in social exchange. Runciman (1966), applying Merton and Kitt's (1950) conception of relative deprivation, proposes that the selection of reference groups

determines whether there is a sense of injustice with respect to the rewards of position. But these theories do not answer the question: when is it possible and probable that one group will see another group's position as unjust to the point of accepting violence and disruption as the natural expression of that injustice?

If we assume that each group tends to employ its own situation as the point of reference in assessing another group's claims of injustice, we are led to the conclusion that groups who are clearly *advantaged* by comparison with the "protestors" can find the claim of injustice more credible than groups less advantaged. Crucial here is the assumption that objective and detached comparison between the situations of the troublemakers and the target groups is less powerful in shaping the assessment of injustice than the observing group's position vis-a-vis the troublemakers. Consequently, the great middle segment of American population finds it easier to identify black ghetto disturbances as social protest than to interpret college student demonstrations in the same sense. Similarly, black student demonstrations are less amenable to interpretation as protest than ghetto demonstrations.

According to this view, groups who see themselves as even more disadvantaged than the protestors are least likely to grant their claim. Viewed from below, disturbances are most easily comprehended as power plays or as deviance. Groups who see their situation as about the same as that of the protestors likewise do not find it easy to accord the protest interpretation. Leaders in such groups commonly attempt to weld alliances based on mutual appreciation, and these sometimes work as political devices. But they are hindered rather than helped by the spontaneous reaction to disruptive activity by a group whose position is apparently no worse than that of the group passing judgment. Olsen's (1968) finding that persons who score high on measures of political incapability and political disability are least willing to adjudge direct action to correct grievances as legitimate may also be consistent with this reasoning.

CREDIBILITY: CREDITING CRIME, PROTEST, REBELLION

The credibility of a disturbance as protest also reflects the variable strength of resistances against believing that massive crime, protest, or rebellion is taking place. Each person's security system is anchored in some fashion in the assumption that he is part of an integral society. This anchorage poses obstacles to believing that any of these conditions is widespread. But each interpretation of disorder has different implications for societal integrity. Rebellion is difficult to credit by all but those whose disaffection with the social order is such that they delight in the threat of its disintegration. When crime and deviance become extensive and blatant, the assumption of a society integrated on the basis of consensus over major values is shaken. Hence, people whose personal security is rooted in the conviction of a fundamental consensus are resistant to admitting widespread crime and deviance. People who understand society as a sort of jungle accommodation will find it easier to interpret disturbances as criminal outbursts. In contrast, protestors—even when they resort occasionally to desperate means—need not reject the values of those to whom they protest. They may share the same values and seek only their share of what others already have. Therefore, the belief in widespread protest calls into question the mechanics of society's operation, but not necessarily the value consensus.

When judgments by different socioeconomic strata are compared, the middle strata find it more difficult to credit massive deviance and crime and less difficult to acknowledge protest because of their commitment to society as a system of values. The lower strata have more day-to-day experience of crime and the rejection of societal values, and are forced to anchor their security to a less consensual image of society. Hence they do not find massive crime so difficult to believe. If these assumptions about credibility are correct, and if we have characterized the strata accurately, investigators should find middle class populations readier to make protest interpretations than working class groups.

APPEAL AND THREAT MESSAGES

It is a reasonable assumption that most observers could, under appropriate circumstances, see both an *appeal* and a *threat* in a violent disturbance. If this combination of messages is present, reading the disturbance as protest means that the appeal component is more salient to the observer than the threat component. For we can safely assume that when the preoccupation with threat to self and to those objects identified with self is foremost, appeals are no longer heard. Threat so often monopolizes attention to the exclusion of appeals, and acknowledging justice in the appeals weakens the foundation for defensive efforts required to meet the threat. Thus we are led to the proposition that disruptions are interpreted as protest only when the experience of threat is not excessive.

The foregoing observation however is incomplete. Somehow the appeal message must command attention, and resistance to acknowledging the protest message must be overcome. The *credibility* requirements we have just outlined are so restrictive that a positive incentive is required to overlook some of the criteria. An appeal by itself is normally a weak attention-getter; threat is much stronger in this respect. A combination of threat and appeal serves to gain attention and to create the sense of urgency necessary to overcome the resistance to acknowledging protest. When threat is insufficient, the events can be disregarded or written off as deviance, to be contained by the established systems of social control. An optimal combination of threat and appeal is necessary for the probability of seeing disturbance as protest. When the threat component falls below the optimal range, the most likely interpretation is deviance; above the optimal range, preoccupation with threat makes rebellion the probable interpretation.

This approach suggests several hypotheses relating interpretation as protest to the nature and bounds of the disorder and to the position of various population segments reacting to the disorders. Certainly the threat posed by disorders during the last half decade has been sufficient to gain attention and force examination of the message. At the same time, threat has been limited by the localization of disorders in the ghettos and by the minimization of direct personal confrontation between whites and blacks. Without replicable measurements of the magnitude of threat and appeal components, predictions regarding specific situations can only be formed intuitively. Intuition suggests that either pitched battles leading to death and injury of any substantial number of whites, or spread of the disorders outside of the boundaries of black neighborhoods and especially into white residence areas, would substantially reduce the likelihood of disorders being interpreted as a form of protest and would seriously divert attention away from black grievances.

Differential perception of threat by population segments is affected by a combination of personal involvement and proximity to the events and of ability to perceive the limits and patterns of disorder realistically. On this basis it is easiest for groups who live a safe distance from black neighborhoods and who have no stake in ghetto businesses to turn their attention toward the appeal component of the disturbance message. But we must also take note of the principle suggested by Diggory's (1956) findings regarding a rabid fox scare in Pennsylvania. While fear was greater among persons near to the rumored center of rabid fox sightings, the tendency to exaggerate the extent of the menace was less. Persons closest to the events were able to form a more realistic picture. Similarly, whites closest to the disturbances may be better able to discount inflated reports of violence against the persons of whites, and to see a pattern in the properties attacked and protected. Thus persons close enough to fear any spread of disorders but not close enough to correct exaggerated reports from personal experience may find it most difficult to see the activities as protest.

After the 1964 riots, Harper's (1968) Rochester *suburban* subjects were most likely to acknowledge that Negroes had a right to complain; city residents living more than one block from a Negro family were least likely to grant Negroes this right; and subjects living within one block of a Negro family were intermediate in their responses. After the 1965 Watts disorder, Morris and Jeffries (1967) found upper-middle-class Pacific Palisades residents most likely to identify the events as Negro protest and all-white low socioeconomic status Bell residents least likely, among the six white areas of Los Angeles County sampled.

The experience of threat is not entirely an individual matter. The self-conception is made up of group memberships, and the individual is threatened whenever an important membership group seems to be the object of threat. Consequently, we should expect members of such groups as small merchants, police, and firemen, even though they were personally unaffected by the disturbances, to experience much threat because of their identification with these same groups immediately involved in the confrontation. Police and merchants within the ghettos were not generally disposed to view racial disorder as social protest (Rossi, et al., 1968). It would be surprising to discover many people among these groups in the larger community who see the events primarily as protest.

It is possible to overlook what others see as threat because one rejects identification with the group under attack. The phenomenon of a few Jews who supported Hitler and were able to discount his antisemitic policies as threats to themselves suggests such a mechanism. The radical repudiation of Jewish identity, labeled self-hatred by Kurt Lewin (1941), may have been strong enough in these individuals that they were unable to conceive of the attacks as being directed toward themselves. There are many whites who radically reject any identification with American society. For those to whom disidentification with conventional society and conventional people is a strong component of the self-conception, threats directed toward white society, toward *honkies,* or toward *whitey* are unlikely to be perceived as referring to themselves. Hence the personal threat is minimized, and it is easiest for such persons to identify the disturbances as protest.

Finally, according to the assumption of an optimal mixture of threat and appeal, it may be difficult to keep the awareness of protest dominant for an extended period of time. We have noted that escalation of violence is likely to preclude protest definition because of preoccupation with the threat. But repeated threat that is not followed by tangible injury to the threatened loses its impact. The diminishing force of repeated destructive activity confined to ghettos lessens the concern that originally directed attention toward the appeal component. Hence, repeated unescalated disturbances are likely to be accompanied by decreasing degrees of interpretation as protest, replaced by increasing tendencies to see the events as deviance.

Except for understanding protest interpretation as a means to protect the observer from seeing a serious lack of consensus in society, we have thus far treated protest interpretation as a passive matter. But the observation that some of the most unsympathetic interpretations abound among groups far removed from the disorders is difficult to understand with the principles outlined. It is true that small town and rural dwellers often feel somewhat deprived relative to large city dwellers, and therefore may have difficulty seeing justice in the complaints even of ghetto dwellers. They also lack the incentive of the large city dwellers to avoid acknowledging widespread crime by interpreting disturbances as protest. But perhaps the protest interpretation is part of a more active stance, brought about by involvement in a relationship with the troublemaking group. Crime and rebellion are in an important ·sense easier interpretations to make since they can be inferred from the most conspicuous and superficial aspects of behavior, without a search for the motives and grievances behind the violence and disruption.

CONCILIATION OF CONFLICT

A more complex basis for predicting the assignment of meaning to disorders is supplied by viewing the protestors and the interpreters as engaged in a real or potential process of conflict. The aggressive initiative of the moment lies with the protestors. Interpreting the disturbances as protest can then usefully be seen as a *gesture of conciliation,* an action to forestall the incipient conflict or to reduce or conclude the conflict without victory or surrender. We can justify this assertion and use it to suggest conditions leading to protest interpretation only after briefly reviewing the nature of the conflict process.

We shall use the term "conflict," not in the broad sense that includes all disagreements and all efforts by people or groups to pursue incompatible goals, but in the tradition of Simmel (1955), Von Wiese (1932: 246) and Park and Burgess (1921). In Coser's (1968:232) definition of conflict as "a struggle over values or claims to status, power, and scarce resources, in which the claims of the conflicting parties are not only to gain the desired values but also to neutralize, injure, or eliminate their rivals," we underline the latter portion. Conflict has properties that distinguish it from other processes revolving about disagreement because there is an autonomous goal of injuring the antagonist—autonomous in the sense that efforts to injure the antagonist are not fully subjected to the test of effectiveness in promoting the other ostensible goals of the conflicting party. Conflict exists when the relationship between groups is based on the premise that whatever enhances the well-being of one group lessens the well-being of the other, and that impairing the well-being of the antagonist is a favored means for enhancing the well-being of one's own group.

The strategy of conflict centers about injuring the other without simultaneously injuring the self, while inhibiting and defending against retaliatory injury from the opponent. Consequently, conflict tends, particularly as it persists and intensifies, to be volatile and comprehensive with respect to the issues that divide the combatants. Combatants must be able to shift grounds and issues as necessary to fight on terrains that are strategically favorable for them. There has probably never been a war or violent revolution in which the question of what either side was fighting for did not become unclear, nor in which the issue at the close of fighting was defined in the same way as at the start of combat.

When conflict occurs between groups regarded as members of some common social order, the process is circumscribed by a somewhat distinctive set of conflict norms. In certain respects the conflict normative system grants license not available to other relationships. In other respects it imposes stricter obligations, such as those requiring demonstrations of ingroup loyalty. Two consequences of assimilation of conflict to a normative order have bearing on our subsequent discussion of conciliation.

First, because conflict involves inflicting injury on persons who are part of a common social order, a course of action that is not normatively sanctioned except within a recognized conflict relationship, the preoccupation with normative considerations is heightened. There is special attention to painting the antagonist as villainous and to establishing the virtuousness of the protagonist group. An important aspect of conflict strategy is to manipulate the normative aspects of the exchange so as to justify the claim to a reserve of moral credit upon which the combatant can draw when he engages in what might otherwise be considered shocking or reprehensible behavior.

Second, a great deal of conflict is fought symbolically with symbolic injuries in the form of insults and threats and symbolic defenses against such injuries. Much of the symbolic conflict consists of testing the other and jockeying for position. But because the combatants are members of a social order, the effective use of symbols so as to place the other in an unfavorable light is a way of inflicting injury upon him. Thus, what Waller and Hill (1951) called "manipulation of morality" in family conflict is an important part of the repertoire of symbolic tactics available for use in any conflict.

There is frequently confusion between the steps from disagreement toward agreement and the process of conflict resolution. Conflict resolution is more complicated because the combatants must cope with both disagreement and the pattern of reciprocal injury. The past and projected mutual injury is the more fundamental problem since it is possible to resolve conflict without agreement on substantive issues, but agreement on these issues does not erase the injury that each has done to the other in the course of the conflict. The latter supplies independent momentum for the continuation of conflict. Hence the key to all conflict resolution is the repair of previous injury and protection against future injury. When conflict resolution is by surrender, the victor disarms the vanquished and extracts reparations. The vanquished party cannot usually exact compensation in repairing the injury to himself, but he normally surrenders under the assumption that once he no longer offers any threat of injury to the victor, he will be immune from further injury by the victor. When conflict resolution occurs without surrender, both parties must give assurances against doing harm in the future and both must take steps to ameliorate the injury that each has already done to the other. Since surrender is an unlikely response to current disorders, our interest is in conflict resolutions characterized by some degree of mutuality.

We shall refer to any act whose aim is to avert or discontinue conflict without either asking or offering surrender as conciliation. To be effective, a conciliatory act must incorporate both an offer to discontinue attacks and a tender of help to correct the harm already done. To the extent to which the conflict is being fought at the symbolic level, the remedies are partially symbolic.

With respect to the exchange of threats and insults (such as symbolic conflict), conciliation is an offer to discontinue such attacks and to discount the meaning of prior threats and insults. In order to participate in conciliatory exchange, the combatant must be prepared to believe that the other did not fully mean what he said, that his threats were not really meant to be carried out, and that his insults did not express his more enduring feelings and views. Hence an act of conciliation must provide the other with a basis on which such beliefs are credible.

We are now prepared to see reaction to public disturbances as response in a situation of potential conflict. The disturbance involves physical injury and threats of further damage to the property and persons of the dominant white group, the college faculty or administration, management and ownership of industry, or colonial powers. In addition, it conveys insulting characterizations and promises of escalating disrespect. Faced with potential conflict, the dominant group has several alternatives, though not all are viable in any given situation. An effort can be made to ignore or depreciate the conflict significance of the disturbances by interpreting them as deviance. The challenge of conflict can be accepted, in which case the disturbance is defined as rebellion and the appropriate response is retaliatory suppression. This was plainly the dominating white reaction in earlier race riots such as St. Louis in 1919 and Detroit in 1943, when whites not only turned the encounters into massive attacks on Negroes but continued to take punitive action for weeks after the riots were finished and after the evidence of disproportionate injury to Negroes was plain to all (Lee and Humphrey, 1943; Rudwick, 1964). It is also common for some individuals to respond by repudiating their own group identification and joining with the dissidents, at least symbolically. Here too the definition is rebellion, but from the opposite side of the conflict. This position normally includes recognition of the protest orientation, though the identity problems involved in this position often cause the protest theme to become secondary in importance

to the aim of discrediting one's group and disidentifying from it. Some of the difficulties in this response are represented when white students have attempted to participate in black protests, and when the Hell's Angels have offered support to conservative protestors against militant youth.

If we omit the possibility of surrender, the remaining alternative is to extend an offer of conciliation. The prospect of conflict is accepted as real, but the aim is to interrupt the reciprocation of attack that locks the combatants into full-scale conflict. The conciliator offers public acknowledgement that he had done injury to the protestor, promising repentence and corrective actions. By making this acknowledgement he grants that there is some justification for the other's hostility toward him, and he also supplies the basis for believing that the other's antagonism is not unalterable and is not personal to himself or his group. The white man can say that the black's antagonism is not really directed against the white man, but merely against those people who happen to be doing the black an injustice at a particular time. Conciliation is thereby rendered a viable posture, because there is no reason to expect the other to continue his attacks once he is assured of compensation and security from further injury.

Interpreting violent and disruptive action as protest is following exactly this pattern. It means assuming that the intent to do injury is secondary in importance to the effort to secure redress, and it means acknowledging that there is some basis in the behavior of one's own group for the antagonism displayed by the protestor.

If we have correctly identified the process, we must predict the protest interpretation by specifying the conditions that lead to acts of conciliation. Individuals and groups seek to avert conflict for four reasons: to avoid the risk of injury (or further injury) to themselves; to avoid the risk of injury or further injury to the potential opponent; to protect the relationship between the potential combatants from damage or increased damage; and to avoid the diversion of resources and energy into the conduct of conflict at the expense of other activities.

The view of protest interpretation as conciliation and the reasons for conciliation suggest several correlates of protest interpretation.

First, protest interpretation is more likely to occur when there is some apparent danger to the group than when there is none. Second, the stronger the norms, values, or sentiments against doing injury to others, the greater the likelihood of interpreting disorder as protest. Third, the greater the interdependency between groups, the greater the likelihood of protest interpretation. The interdependency may be ecological or social; the solidarity, organic or mechanical in nature. If breaking or weakening the bonds between the groups is threatening, the likelihood of offering the conciliatory protest interpretation will be increased.

Fourth, the greater the commitment to activities and resources that may have to be sacrificed in order to carry on the conflict, the greater the readiness to make a protest interpretation. If there is a greater tolerance for conflict in lower socioeconomic strata and less exploration of conciliatory approaches, it may be because there is less at stake in the disruption of the standard round of life than there is in the higher social strata. Some groups are flexibly organized so that conflict can be sustained alongside of continuing normal activities. Private industry was long able to avoid treating labor unrest as social protest because private police could be hired to isolate the conflict while production continued. Universities are not equipped in this fashion, and must therefore face disruption of their normal functions under even mild conflict. Hence, universities are relatively quick to interpret internal disturbances as social protest.

Fifth, the less the anticipated costs of conciliation, the greater the tendency to see disturbance as protest. College officials who believe that discontinuing an R.O.T.C. program is sufficient to bring an end to campus conflict find it easy to see student activism as social protest, rather than as rebellious confrontation.

Because of the tendency for moralistic perspectives to be an inseparable part of conflict, an offer of conciliation is typically viewed by the conciliator as an act of generosity, going beyond what could be expected or required of him. Under the reciprocity principle (Gouldner, 1960) the act of placing a more generous than necessary interpretation on the other's actions obligates the latter to make generous response. Because the normative system of conflict permits a combatant to place a less favorable interpretation on the other's actions, the sense of self-righteous virtue attached to protest interpretation can be great. Furthermore, the protest interpretation with its clearly implied admission of fault places the conciliator in a precarious position, for his admission of prejudice, militarism, or insensitivity to student needs, for instance, can be used against him later if the other does not respond in kind. The risk he knows he is taking enhances the conciliator's self-righteousness. Hence, there is a strong tendency for conciliatory gestures to be withdrawn and replaced by active promotion of conflict when there is no discontinuance of insults and threats and no retraction of earlier attacks.

Hence we are led again (as under the appeal-threat perspective) to the generalization that interpretation of disorder as protest is a conditional and unstable response. According to the conflict model, it readily gives way to the interpretation of disorder as rebellion when it is not soon followed by subsidance of disorder and threat. On the other hand, without the prospect of involvement in conflict, there is no occasion for conciliation, and crime or deviance is the most natural interpretation.

*   *   *

References

Bayley, David H., "The Pedagogy of Democracy: Coercive Public Protest in India." American Political Science Review 56, September, 1962. Pp. 663–672.

Blau, Peter, "Justice in Social Exchange." Sociological Inquiry 34, Spring, 1964. Pp. 193–206.

————. Exchange and Power in Social Life. New York: John Wiley and Sons, 1964.

Blumer, Herbert, "Collective Behavior." Pp. 221–280 in Robert E. Park (ed.), An Outline of the Principles of Sociology. New York: Barnes and Noble, 1939.

Boskin, Joseph, 1968, "Violence in the Ghettoes: A Consensus of Attitudes." New Mexico Quarterly 37, Winter, 1968. Pp. 317–334.

Coser, Lewis, "Conflict: Social Aspects." International Encyclopedia of the Social Sciences, Vol. 3, 1968. Pp. 232–236.

Diggory, James C., "Some Consequences of Proximity to a Disease Threat." Sociometry 19, March, 1956. Pp. 47–53.

Dynes, Russell and Quarantelli, Enrico L., "What Looting in Civil Disturbances Really Means." Trans-Action 5, May, 1968. Pp. 9–14.

Fogelson, Robert M., "Violence as Protest." Pp. 25–41 in Robert H. Connery (ed.), Urban Riots: Violence and Social Change. New York: Academy of Political Science, 1968.

Gouldner, Alvin W., "The Norm of Reciprocity: A Preliminary Statement." American Sociological Review 25, April, 1960. Pp. 161–178.

Governor's Commission on the Los Angeles Riots, Violence in the City—An End or a Beginning? Los Angeles, 1965.

Grimshaw, Allen D., "Three Views of Urban Violence: Civil Disturbance, Racial Revolt, Class Assault." In Louis H. Masotti and Don R. Bowen (eds.), Riots and Rebellion. Beverly Hills, California: Sage Publications, 1968. Pp. 103–119.

Harper, Dean, "White Reactions to a Riot." In Louis H. Masotti and Don R. Bowen (eds.), Riots and Rebellion. Beverly Hills, California: Sage Publications, 1968. Pp. 307–314.

Homans, George, 1961, Social Behavior: Its Elementary Forms. New York: Harcourt, Brace, and World.

Horowitz, Irving L. and Martin Liebowitz, 1968, "Social Deviance and Political Marginality: Toward a Redefinition of the Relation Between Sociology and Politics." Social Problems 15 (Winter): 280–296.

Kelley, Harold H., "Attribution Theory in Social Psychology." In Nebraska Symposium on Motivation, 1967. Pp. 192–238.

Lang, Kurt and Gladys E. Lang, "Racial Disturbances as Collective Protest." In Louis H. Masotti and Don R. Bowen (eds.), Riots and Rebellion. Beverly Hills, Calif.: Sage Publications, 1968. Pp. 121–130.

Lee, Alfred McClung and Norman D. Humphrey, Race Riot. New York: Dryden Press, 1943.

Lemert, Edwin, Social Pathology. New York: McGraw-Hill, 1951.

Lewin, Kurt, "Self-hatred Among Jews." Contemporary Jewish Record 4:219–232. 1941.

Lipsky, Michael, "Protest as a Political Resource." American Political Science Review 62, December, 1968. Pp. 1144–1158.

Merton, Robert K., "The Self-fulfilling Prophecy." Antioch Review 8, Summer, 1943. Pp. 193–210.

Merton, Robert K. and Alice S. Kitt, "Contributions to the Theory of Reference Group Behavior." In Merton and Paul F. Lazarsfeld (eds.), Studies in the Scope and Method of "The American Soldier." Glencoe, Ill.: Free Press, 1950. Pp. 40–105.

Morris, Richard T. and Jeffries, Vincent, Los Angeles Riot Study: The White Reaction Study. Los Angeles: U.C.L.A. Institute of Government and Public Affairs, 1967.

National Advisory Commission on Civil Disorders, Report of the National Advisory Commission on Civil Disorders (The Kerner Report). Washington: U.S. Government Printing Office, 1968.

Olsen, Marvin E., "Perceived Legitimacy of Social Protest Actions." Social Problems 15, Winter, 1968. Pp. 297–310.

Park, Robert E. and Ernest W. Burgess, Introduction to the Science of Sociology. Chicago: University of Chicago Press, 1921.

Random House, Random House Dictionary of the English Language. New York: Random House, 1967.

Rossi, Peter H., Berk, Richard A., Boesel, David P., Eidson, Bettye K., and Groves, W. Eugene, "Between White and Black: The Faces of American Institutions in the Ghetto." Pp. 69–215 in Supplemental Studies for the National Advisory Commission on Civil Disorders. Washington: U.S. Government Printing Office, 1968. Pp. 69–215.

Rudwick, Elliot M., Race Riot in East St. Louis, July 2, 1917. Carbondale: Southern Illinois University Press, 1964.

Runciman, W. G., Relative Deprivation and Social Justice. Berkeley: University of California Press, 1966.

Sevareid, Eric, "Dissent or Destruction?" Look 31, September 5, 1967. Pp. 21 ff.

Silver, Allan A., "Official Interpretations of Racial Riots." Robert H. Connery (ed.), Urban Riots: Violence and Social Change. New York: Academy of Political Science, 1968.

Simmel, Georg, Conflict and the Web of Group-Affiliations. Translated by Kurt Wolff and Reinhard Bendix. New York: Free Press, 1955.

Smelser, Neil J., Theory of Collective Behavior. New York: Free Press, 1963.

Tomlinson, T. M. and David O. Sears. Los Angeles Riot Study: Negro Attitudes Toward the Riot. Los Angeles: U.C.L.A. Institute of Government and Public Affairs, 1967.

Turner, Ralph H., "The Normative Coherence of Folk Concepts." Research Studies of the State College of Washington 25: 127–136. 1957.

———. "Collective Behavior and Conflict: New Theoretical Frameworks." Sociological Quarterly 5, Spring, 1964. Pp. 122–132.

————. and Killian, Lewis M., Collective Behavior. Englewood Cliffs, N.J.: Prentice-Hall, 1957.

von Wiese, Leopold, Systematic Sociology. Adapted and amplified by Howard Becker. New York: John Wiley and Sons, 1932.

Waller, Willard and Hill, Reuben, The Family: A Dynamic Interpretation. New York: Dryden Press, 1951.

AUTHOR INDEX

SUBJECT INDEX

Accidents in conflict, 229–42, 318–26, 487

Aging, 141–43, 421–28

Aggression, 38–48, 59–63, 70–80, 91–99, 112–23, 123–32, 189–96, 229–42, 261–66, 384–94

Agriculture, 143–45

Alienation, 59–63, 318–26, 371–83, 384–94, 397–445, 446–483, 494–505

Alliances, *see* Coalitions

Altruism, *see* Helping

Ambivalence, 107, 281–316, 327–36, 371–83, 421–28

Animals, 38–48, 63, 70–80, 101–112, 112–123, 189–96

Anomie, 9–10, 38–48, 59–63, 384–94, 451–53

Anonymity, 48–59, 59–63, 281–97, 298–305, 305–316

Arbitration, *see* Mediation

Armies, 64–68, 452–57, 474–79

Aspirations, 153–55, 196–209, 371–83, 458–66, 466–83

Authoritarian personality, *see* Personality

Authority, *see* Legitimacy

Autonomic processes, 70–80, 91–99, 112–23

Balance of power, *see* Coalitions; Power

Bargaining, 10–11, 146–161, 161–72, 196–209, 209–14, 327–36, 511–19

Belief conflict, 6–7, 209–14, 229–42, 242–60, 281–97, 305–16

Blood ties, 101–12, 336–47, 428–32

Bluffing, *see* Credibility; Threats

Brain operations, 113–15

Business, 136–45, 215–27, 318–26

Capitalism, 136–45, 432–45

Catharsis, 59–63, 91–99, 261–66, 377–78, 428–32

Chicken, 248–49

Children, *see* Family conflict

Class, *see* Social Class; Status

Coalitions, 19–21, 196–209, 281–97, 305–16, 318–26, 513–19

Coercion, *see* Power; Threats

Cohesiveness, 81–91, 101–11,

318–26, 327–36, 421–28, 428–32, 488

Colonialism, 428–32

Communication, 153–55, 173–87, 228–66, 318–26, 421–28, 438–39, 508–509

Communism, 65, 173, 398, 433, 436–37, 442

Comparison, 81–91, 196–209, 327–36, 397–432, 466–83

Compliance, *see* Conformity; Legitimacy; Threats

Compromise, *see* Bargaining; Reciprocity

Conciliation, 513–16; *see also* Conflict resolution; Mediation

Conflict resolution, 23–28, 146–61, 173–87, 189–96, 209–14, 215–27, 261–66, 305–16, 317–53, 354–83

Conformity, 48–59, 269–316, 354–94

Conscience, *see* Guilt; Morality

Contagion, *see* Imitation

Contracts, *see* Law

Conspiracy, 466–83; *see also* Coalitions

Cooptation, 327–36, 366–70, 371–83, 421–28, 513–16

Corporations, *see* Capitalism

Corruption, 28

Courts, 336–53

Credibility, 155–57, 173–87, 508–11

Crime, 21, 59–63, 298–305, 336–47, 371–83, 485–94, 505–19

Cross-cultural differences, 209–14, 466–83

Crowding, 38–48, 63, 76

Custom, *see* Law; Morality

De-escalation, *see* Escalation; Conflict resolution

Definitions of conflict, 1–2

Democracy, 270–81, 432–45, 466–83, 505–19

Demonstrations, *see* Protest

Depression (economic), 143

Depression (psychological), 38–48, 384–94, 421–28, 494–505

Deterrence, *see* Threats

Deviance, 38–48, 59–63, 298–305, 305–16, 384–94, 484–519

Disarmament, *see* Weapons

Disciplinary methods, 270–81, 305–16, 318–26, 336–47, 354–70, 384–94

Displacement, *see* Personality

Division of labor, 12, 137–38, 298–305, 318–26, 432–45

Duty, *see* Legitimacy; Morality

Dysfunctions of conflict, *see* Functions of conflict

Electric shock, 70–80, 91–99, 281–97

Elites, 188–227, 298–305, 421–28, 432–45, 447–57, 466–83

Equality, *see* Comparison

Equilibrium, *see* Stability

Equity, *see* Fairness

Escalation, 48–59, 161–87, 229–42, 242–60, 447–57

Ethics, *see* Legitimacy; Morality

Ethnocentrism, *see* Prejudice

Expectations, *see* Aspirations; Legitimacy

Exploitation, 137–39, 242–60, 371–83, 421–45

Evolution, 101–12

Fairness, 261–66, 318–53

Family conflict, 209–14, 261–66, 270–81, 421–28

Fatigue, 73–4, 261–66

Films, 93–98

Freedom, 22–23, 101, 270–81, 454, 456

Frustration-aggression, 69–99, 161–72, 384–94, 398–421, 466–83, 494–505

Fully structured conflict relationships, 11–13, 268–394

Functions of conflict, 22–23, 38–48, 91–99, 101–11, 123–32, 136–45, 189–96, 261–66, 447–57, 458–66

Game theory, 2–7, 146–61; *see also* Prisoner's Dilemma; Simulations

Genetics, *see* Heredity

Government, *see* Legitimacy; State

Guerrilla warfare, 64–68, 261–66, 440–41

Guilt, 107–108, 298–305, 384–94, 421–28

Guns, *see* Weapons